Children's Literature Review

volume 5

Children's Literature Review

Excerpts from Reviews,
Criticism, and Commentary
on Books for Children

Guest Essay, "Heights of Fantasy," by John Rowe Townsend

Gerard J. Senick
Editor

Gale Research Company
Book Tower
Detroit, Michigan 48226

STAFF

Gerard J. Senick, *Editor*

Jeanne A. Gough, Susan Miller Harig, and Melissa Reiff Hug, *Assistant Editors*

Phyllis Carmel Mendelson, *Contributing Editor*

Robert J. Elster, Jr., *Production Supervisor*
Lizbeth A. Purdy, *Production Coordinator*
Denise Michelwicz, *Assistant Production Coordinator*
Eric Berger, Michael S. Corey, Paula J. DiSante, Serita Lanette Lockard, Brenda Marshall,
Janet S. Mullane, Gloria Anne Williams, *Editorial Assistants*

Anne Marie Dadah, Jeannine Schiffman Davidson, Karen Rae Forsyth, Barbara Hammond,
Robert J. Hill, James A. MacEachern, Mary Spirito, Margaret Stewart, Carol Angela Thomas, *Research Assistants*

Linda M. Pugliese, *Manuscript Coordinator*
Donna D. Craft, *Assistant Manuscript Coordinator*
Colleen M. Crane, Maureen A. Puhl, Rosetta Irene Simms, *Manuscript Assistants*

L. Elizabeth Hardin, *Permissions Supervisor*
Filomena Sgambati, *Permissions Coordinator, Text*
Janice M. Mach, *Assistant Permissions Coordinator*
Margaret Chamberlain, Mary P. McGrane, Anna Maria Pertner, Joan B. Weber, *Permissions Assistants*
Elizabeth Babini, *Permissions Clerk*

Patricia A. Seefelt, *Assistant Permissions Coordinator, Photos and Illustrations*
Margaret Mary Missar, *Photo Research*

Cover design by Arthur Chartow

Copyright © 1983 by Gale Research Company

Library of Congress Catalog Card Number 75-34953
ISBN 0-8103-0330-2
ISSN 0362-4145

CONTENTS

Preface   1

Authors Forthcoming in *CLR*   3

Acknowledgments   5

Guest Essay, "Heights of Fantasy" by John Rowe Townsend   7

Appendix   251

Cumulative Index to Authors   259

Cumulative Index to Titles   261

Cumulative Index to Critics   275

Authors Included in Volume 5

Lloyd Alexander   1924- 13

Jose Aruego   1932- 27

Jeanne Bendick   1919- 33

Lucille Clifton   1936- 51

Joanna Cole   1944- 61

Carlo Collodi   1826-1890 69

Barbara Emberley   1932-
   see Ed and Barbara Emberley

Ed and Barbara Emberley 88

Ed Emberley   1931-
   see Ed and Barbara Emberley

Muriel Feelings   1938-
   see Muriel and Tom Feelings

Muriel and Tom Feelings 104

Tom Feelings   1933-
   see Muriel and Tom Feelings

Kenneth Grahame   1859-1932 109

Maria Gripe   1923- 137

Jill Krementz   1940- 150

Arnold Lobel   1933- 157

Joan Phipson   1912- 177

H(ans) A(ugusto) Rey   1898-1977
   see H(ans) A(ugusto) Rey and
   Margret Rey

H(ans) A(ugusto) Rey and
   Margret Rey 188

Margret Rey   1906-
   see H(ans) A(ugusto) Rey and
   Margret Rey

Uri Shulevitz   1935- 201

Shel Silverstein   1932- 208

Peter Spier   1927- 214

Patti Stren   1949- 230

Chris Van Allsburg   1949- 237

Nancy Willard   1936- 243

PREFACE

Walter de la Mare has said that "only the rarest kind of best of anything can be good enough for the young." The editors of *Children's Literature Review* enthusiastically endorse this belief. Accordingly, *CLR* has been designed and published to assist those who select reading materials for children in making wise choices.

Each biannual volume contains selected excerpts from published criticism on the literary works of approximately twenty-five authors and author/illustrators who create books for children from preschool to junior high age. The author list for each volume of *CLR* is compiled to represent a variety of genres—including picture books, fiction, nonfiction, poetry, and drama—and is international in scope. Since the majority of authors covered by *CLR* are living and continue to write, it is necessary to update their entries periodically. Future volumes of *CLR* will include criticism on the works of authors covered in earlier volumes and the entire careers of authors new to the series.

Organization of the Book

An author section consists of the following elements: author heading, bio-critical introduction, author's commentary and general commentary (when available), title entries, and bibliographical citations.

- The *author heading* consists of the name under which the author is most frequently published and his or her birth and death dates. If an author writes consistently under a pseudonym, the pseudonym will be listed in the author heading and the real name given in parentheses on the first line of the bio-critical introduction.

- The *bio-critical introduction* contains background information designed to introduce the reader to an author. The introduction begins with a phrase describing the author's nationality and the genres in which he or she writes. The text of the introduction presents an overview in two to four paragraphs of the author's themes and styles, biographical facts, a summary of the critical response to the author's works, and major awards and prizes. Where applicable, the introduction includes references to other biographical and critical reference books published by Gale Research Company. These books include *Contemporary Authors, Contemporary Literary Criticism, Something about the Author, Yesterday's Authors of Books for Children,* and past volumes of *CLR.* When available, a photograph of the author accompanies the introduction.

- The *author's commentary* presents background material written by the author being profiled. This commentary may cover a specific work or several works, or discuss the reasons why an author writes.

- *General commentary* consists of critical excerpts from articles that consider more than one work by the author being profiled.

- *Title entries* consist of critical excerpts on the author's individual works, arranged chronologically. They generally include two to six reviews per title, depending on the stature of the book and the amount of criticism it has generated. In some cases not every title published by the author is represented. The editors select titles which reflect the author's variety of genres and subjects as well as his or her most important books. Thus, the reader is provided with a record of the author's literary development. An effort is made to reprint criticism from sources which represent the full scope of each title's publication history—from the year of its initial publication to current references. Titles by authors being profiled in *CLR* are highlighted in boldface within the text for easier access by researchers.

Where available, two to six illustrations are featured within the title entries of authors who illustrate their own works. An effort has been made to select illustrations which are mentioned in the criticism and to place each one as close as possible to its critical reference. Each illustration is accompanied by a caption identifying the work in which it originally appeared. An acknowledgments section giving credit to copyright holders of illustrations follows the preface.

• A complete *bibliographical citation* designed to facilitate the location of the original article or book follows each piece of criticism. An asterisk following a citation indicates that the essay or book contains information on more than one author.

Each volume of *CLR* contains cumulative indexes to authors, titles, and critics. An appendix is also included in volume 5 which lists the sources from which material has been reprinted in this volume. It does not, however, list every book or periodical consulted during the preparation of the volume.

New Features

Each volume of *CLR* will include a guest essay following the acknowledgments section. Guest essays are original pieces written specifically for *CLR* by prominent critics on subjects of their choice. The subject of each essay will incorporate one or more of the authors being profiled in the current volume. *CLR,* volume 5, contains John Rowe Townsend's "Heights of Fantasy" as its guest essay. The editors are honored to have Mr. Townsend introduce this feature.

All title entry headings include publication information on the work being reviewed. Previous volumes of *CLR* listed the title of each work as it appeared in the United States, followed by its first U.S. publication date. Starting with volume 5, the title heading will list the work's title as it appeared in its country of origin, followed by its U.S. title in brackets. The work's first publication date is listed in parentheses following the brackets. When the work has been published in Great Britain under an alternate title, this information follows the publication date.

Acknowledgments

The editors wish to thank the copyright holders of the excerpts included in this volume, as well as the permissions managers of many book and magazine publishing companies, Michael F. Wiedl III, and Jeri Yaryan for their assistance in locating copyright holders, and Henrietta Epstein for her editorial assistance. We are also grateful to the staffs of the Kresge Library at Wayne State University, the libraries of the University of Michigan, and the Detroit Public Library.

Suggestions Are Welcome

If readers wish to suggest authors they are particularly anxious to have covered in upcoming volumes, or if they have other suggestions, they are cordially invited to write the editors.

Authors Forthcoming in *CLR*

Hans Christian Andersen (Danish author of fairy tales, novels, poetry, and nonfiction)—*The Ugly Duckling, The Little Mermaid, The Nightingale,* and *The Little Match Girl* are a small representation of the many internationally acclaimed stories written by Andersen, who rose from poverty to fame by creating original fairy tales which are enjoyed by all ages.

Isaac Asimov (American author of fiction and nonfiction)—One of the most notable science writers for children and adults, he recently added *How Did We Find Out about the Universe?* to the list of more than 100 books he has written for children.

Ludwig Bemelmans (Austrian-born American author/illustrator)—Creator of the popular *Madeline* series, he has a strong sense of design and humor that continue to appeal to readers.

Arna Bontemps (Black American author of fiction and nonfiction)—He remedied the need for a body of objective black literature for children.

Vera and Bill Cleaver (American authors of fiction)—Best known for the acclaimed *Where the Lilies Bloom,* they have created realistic fiction on sensitive topics.

Nikki Giovanni (Black American poet, short story writer, and essayist)—Giovanni's poetry is noted for presenting the black perspective while successfully representing the world of the child.

Kate Greenaway (British author/illustrator)—A picture book pioneer known for her innocent mob-capped children and her intricate flower borders, she is credited with preserving the countryside of preindustrial England through her beautiful outdoor settings.

Leo Lionni (Dutch-born American author/illustrator)—Winner of numerous international awards for his illustrations, he has written such animal fables as *Inch by Inch* and *Frederick.*

Lois Lowry (American author of fiction)—Her well-crafted fiction includes such novels as the topical *A Summer to Die* and the humorous *Anastasia* series.

L.M. Montgomery (Canadian author of fiction)—Several decades after their initial publication, her *Anne of Green Gables* and its sequels remain best-sellers.

Evaline Ness (American author/illustrator)—Winner of the Caldecott Medal in 1967 for *Sam, Bangs, and Moonshine,* she continues to delight children with such works as *Fierce the Lion.*

Mary Norton (British author of fiction)—Her *Borrowers* series and *Bedknob and Broomstick* are considered classic fantasy and continue to captivate readers. *The Borrowers Avenged* is a recent addition to the series which began in 1952.

Jay Williams (American author of fiction and nonfiction)—A prolific writer of science fiction and historical novels who is best known for his Danny Dunn adventures, he is also the creator of such popular turn-about fairy tales as *The Practical Princess,* in which the princess and the prince reverse roles.

ACKNOWLEDGMENTS

are made to the following publishers, authors, and artists for their kind permission to reproduce copyrighted material.

Doubleday & Company, Inc. Illustration by Peter Spier from *The Fox Went Out on a Chilly Night: An Old Song* by Peter Spier. Copyright © 1961 by Peter Spier./ Illustration by Peter Spier from *Noah's Ark* by Peter Spier. Copyright © 1977 by Peter Spier./ Illustration by Peter Spier from *The Star-Spangled Banner* by Peter Spier. Copyright © 1978 by Peter Spier./ Illustration by Peter Spier from *People* by Peter Spier. Copyright © 1980 by Peter Spier. All reprinted by permission of Doubleday & Company, Inc.

Elsevier-Dutton Publishing Co., Inc. Illustration by Tom Feelings from *Moja Means One: Swahili Counting Book* by Muriel Feelings. Text copyright © 1971 by Muriel Feelings. Illustration copyright © 1971 by Tom Feelings./ Illustration by Tom Feelings from *Jambo Means Hello: Swahili Alphabet Book* by Muriel Feelings. Text copyright © 1974 by Muriel Feelings. Illustration copyright © 1974 by Tom Feelings. Both reprinted by permission of the publisher, Dial Books for Young Readers, a Division of E.P. Dutton, Inc./ Illustration by Patti Stren from *Mountain Rose* by Patti Stren. Copyright © 1982 by Patti Stren. Reprinted by permission of the publisher, E.P. Dutton, Inc.

Farrar, Straus and Giroux, Inc. Illustration by Uri Shulevitz from *Rain Rain Rivers* by Uri Shulevitz. Copyright © 1969 by Uri Shulevitz./ Illustration by Uri Shulevitz from *Soldier and Tsar in the Forest: A Russian Tale,* translated by Richard Lourie. Pictures copyright © 1972 by Uri Shulevitz. Text copyright © 1972 by Farrar, Straus and Giroux, Inc./ Illustration by Uri Shulevitz from *Dawn* by Uri Shulevitz. Copyright © 1974 by Uri Shulevitz./ Illustration by Uri Shulevitz from *The Treasure* by Uri Shulevitz. Copyright © 1978 by Uri Shulevitz. All reprinted by permission of Farrar, Straus and Giroux, Inc.

Harper & Row, Publishers, Inc. Illustration by H.A. Rey from *Pretzel* by Margret Rey. Copyright 1944 by Margret Rey./ Illustration by H.A. Rey from *Billy's Picture* by Margret and H.A. Rey. Copyright 1948, 1976 by Margret and H.A. Rey./ Illustration by Arnold Lobel from *Frog and Toad Are Friends* by Arnold Lobel. Copyright © 1970 by Arnold Lobel./ Illustration by Arnold Lobel from *On the Day Peter Stuyvesant Sailed into Town* by Arnold Lobel. Copyright © 1971 by Arnold Lobel./ Illustration by Arnold Lobel from *The Man Who Took the Indoors Out* by Arnold Lobel. Copyright © 1974 by Arnold Lobel./ Illustration by Arnold Lobel from *Owl at Home* by Arnold Lobel. Copyright © 1975 by Arnold Lobel./ Illustration by Patti Stren from *Hug Me* by Patti Stren. Copyright © 1977 by Patti Stren./ Illustration by Arnold Lobel from *Fables* by Arnold Lobel. Copyright © 1980 by Arnold Lobel. All reprinted by permission of Harper & Row, Publishers, Inc.

Houghton Mifflin Company. Illustration by H.A. Rey from *Curious George* by H.A. Rey. Copyright 1941, and © renewed 1969 by H.A. Rey./ Illustration by H.A. Rey from *Cecily G. and the Nine Monkeys* by H.A. Rey. Copyright 1942, and © renewed 1969 by H.A. Rey./ Illustration by H.A. Rey from *Find the Constellations* by H.A. Rey. Copyright 1954, © 1962, 1966, 1976 by H.A. Rey./ Illustration by H.A. Rey from *Curious George Gets a Medal* by H.A. Rey. Copyright © 1957 by H.A. Rey./ Illustration by Chris Van Allsburg from *The Garden of Abdul Gasazi* by Chris Van Allsburg. Copyright © 1979 by Chris Van Allsburg./ Illustration by Chris Van Allsburg from *Jumanji* by Chris Van Allsburg. Copyright © 1981 by Chris Van Allsburg./ Illustration by Chris Van Allsburg from *Ben's Dream* by Chris Van Allsburg. Copyright © 1982 by Chris Van Allsburg. All reprinted by permission of Houghton Mifflin Company.

Alfred A. Knopf, Inc. Illustration by Jill Krementz from *A Very Young Dancer* by Jill Krementz. Copyright © 1976 by Jill Krementz./ Illustration by Jill Krementz from *How It Feels When a Parent Dies* by Jill Krementz. Copyright © 1981 by Jill Krementz. Both reproduced by permission of the author.

Little, Brown and Company. Illustration by Ed Emberley from *The Wing on a Flea: A Book about Shapes* by Ed Emberley. Copyright © 1961 by Edward R. Emberley./ Illustration by Ed Emberley from *Ed Emberley's Drawing Book of Animals* by Ed Emberley. Copyright © 1970 by Edward R. Emberley./ Illustration by Ed Emberley from *The Wizard of Op* by Ed Emberley. Copyright © 1975 by Ed Emberley./ Illustration by Ed Emberley from *Ed Emberley's ABC* by Ed Emberley. Copyright © 1978 by Edward R. Emberley. All reprinted by permission of Little, Brown and Company.

Macmillan Publishing Company. Illustration by Uri Shulevitz from *The Magician: An Adaptation from the Yiddish of I.L. Peretz* by Uri Shulevitz. Copyright © 1973 Uri Shulevitz. Reprinted with permission of Macmillan Publishing Company.

GUEST ESSAY

Heights of Fantasy
by John Rowe Townsend

Epic, saga, and romance are ancient literary forms, compared with which the modern novel is an upstart. Folklore, passed down by word of mouth, is older still by far. "To ask what is the origin of stories (however qualified)," wrote J.R.R. Tolkien in a famous essay, "is to ask what is the origin of language and of the mind."[1]

Tolkien, who was not much interested in contemporary fiction, himself wrote what he called fairy-story. By this he meant stories of "Faerie, the Perilous Realm," which "contains many things besides elves and fays, and besides dwarfs, witches, trolls, giants or dragons: it holds the seas, the sun, the moon, the sky; and the earth and all things that are in it: tree and bird, water and stone, wine and bread, and ourselves, mortal men, when we are enchanted."[2]

In *The Lord of the Rings,* in fact, Tolkien bypassed many centuries of English-language literary development. True, he was deeply aware of Spenser's *Faerie Queene;* true, his Sauron has unmistakable resemblances to Milton's Satan; true, he was interested by the work of William Morris and George MacDonald. But, to put it simplistically, *The Lord of the Rings* goes back to *Beowulf.* As one critic, Charles Moorman, said, it is "essentially a Nordic myth"; it embodies "the great Nordic theme of courage," and "the monsters, the landscapes, the battles all have a Nordic feel to them."[3]

And when the story of Frodo's great endeavor to thwart the Dark Lord and cast the fatal Ring into the Cracks of Doom appeared in the mid-1950s, it had the air of being at the same time something immensely old and something startlingly new. It was of its own kind; it established a genre. It appealed (as any book must do which is to achieve great sales and widespread fame) to the non-bookish as well as to the bookish. And it inspired much work by other writers: often worthless but sometimes of genuine value and interest.

Like many of the books it inspired, *The Lord of the Rings* raises the question of where the border is to be drawn between children's literature and general fiction. This question has always seemed to me to be more organisational than literary. The distinction between children's and "adult" fiction is itself a recent one, accompanying the rise of the novel. For long ages nobody troubled to draw such a line; a tale was a tale, and was for everyone.

Tolkien himself however gave some thought to this distinction, and devoted several pages to it in the essay already quoted. His conclusion was that if fairy-story (as defined by him) was worth reading at all it was worthy to be written for and read by adults; then, "as a branch of a genuine art, children may hope to get fairy-stories fit for them to read and yet within their measure"—though, he added, it might be better for them to read some things, especially fairy-stories, that were beyond their measure rather than short of it.[4]

The Hobbit was written as a children's story and is always regarded as one; *The Lord of the Rings* was clearly intended by its author for adults, though Edmund Wilson concluded that adults who liked it must have "a lifelong appetite for juvenile trash."[5] His judgment was not the general one. But in fact all adult devotees of Tolkien read and enjoy *The Hobbit,* and great numbers of children have the enthusiasm and stamina to make their way through *The Lord of the Rings.* The borderline remains elusive.

It is not my aim to consider at length why the genre which Tolkien established—I would rather call it high fantasy than fairy-story—appeals so widely both to adults and children. But one may hazard a few guesses. In spite of the conventional wisdom, reinforced by the harsh economics of present-day publishing, that novels and above all novels for children should be kept short, there is clearly an attraction in the book or sequence which is long enough to lose oneself in and live with. And the staple plot-ingredient of high fantasy is the Quest, which is surely a profound analogy for the pattern of human life. Life is a long journey, in the course of which one will assuredly have one's adventures, one's sorrows and joys, one's setbacks and triumphs, and perhaps, with luck and effort, the fulfillment of some major purpose. Children, it can confidently be supposed, look forward to the journey at least as much as those who have advanced farther along the way.

It should be said that the genre as established or re-established by Tolkien had limitations. In *The Lord of the Rings,* the struggle between good and evil, light and dark, is expressed in action. There is never any doubt what *is* good or evil, light or dark. "Our" side is in the right; and although there are interesting resonances between some of the good and bad characters—Gandalf and Saruman, Frodo and Gollum—the proper course of action is always clear.

It can be pointed out of course that the epic mode is not concerned with moral or psychological subtleties; those are the realm of the novel. Nonetheless, in the real world, the assumption that one side in a conflict is by definition totally good and the other side totally bad can be seen to be dangerous and usually mistaken; one need not look hard to find examples. As a way of thinking about the world, a division into goodies and baddies is inadequate for our times, and one might well hope that modern writers, especially with the young in mind, would move away from it.

My intention in the present essay is to look at some of the successors to *The Lord of the Rings:* specifically, at four sequences which have all been published on the children's lists, could all be described as high fantasy, and are more than mere imitations of Tolkien. They are Lloyd Alexander's five books of *Prydain,* Susan Cooper's *Dark Is Rising* quintet, Ursula Le Guin's *Earthsea* trilogy, and Patricia Wrightson's Australian trio which began with *The Ice Is Coming.*

Obviously, this choice is arbitrary. One could, for instance, among much else, have discussed *Watership Down* or some of the books of Alan Garner. But *Watership Down* has been much discussed already, and Garner's development as a writer has led him in a different direction from that of his early work. And although there is no special virtue in mere length, the size and substance of the sequences I have chosen have been recommendations in themselves.

I have not the space, or the wish, to make a detailed examination of the writers' sources. Such an investigation would reach far into matters of archaeology, anthropology, and psychological theory, as well as into legend, myth, and folktale. The results would be of scholarly interest, but would not necessarily help one to make a concise critical evaluation. It is what the author does with his or her sources that counts, rather than the sources themselves. Support for this view can be found in Tolkien, for he quotes with approval Sir George Dasent's words in the introduction to *Popular Tales from the Norse:* "We must be satisfied with the soup that is set before us, and not desire to see the bones of the ox out of which it has been boiled." Tolkien adds: "By 'the soup' I mean the story as it is served up by its author or teller, and by 'the bones' its sources or material—even when (by rare luck) those can be with certainty discovered. But I do not, of course, forbid criticism of the soup as soup."[6] It is with the soup as soup that I shall be concerned.

Of the sequences named, Lloyd Alexander's *Prydain* came first in point of time. *The Book of Three* appeared in 1964 and was followed in successive years by *The Black Cauldron, The Castle of Llyr, Taran Wanderer,* and *The High King.* The time is long ago; the inspiration comes from Wales and its legends, but the land of Prydain is imaginary. The books tell of successive battles against the forces of evil commanded by Arawn, Lord of Annuvin (originally Hades), culminating in final victory for the "good" side and in the destruction of Arawn by the hero Taran with the aid of the magic sword Dyrnwyn. In the course of the series, Taran and the young Princess Eilonwy "of the red-gold hair" grow to manhood and womanhood, and at the end Taran, once an assistant pig-keeper, becomes High King of Prydain and Eilonwy his queen.

This is the most straightforward of the four sequences, and is fairly evidently "for" children. The storyline is simple and somewhat repetitive. Four of the five books begin with a renewed threat from the evil forces, followed by journeyings, fights, ambushes, bewitchments, imprisonments, and releases, and in the end success for the side of right.

Some of the inhabitants of Prydain are drawn from legend, but the little band who most often fill the foreground —Taran and Eilonwy and their companions—are Lloyd Alexander's own creations. Taran is a satisfactory hero. From being young, thoughtless, and hotheaded he matures into wisdom and responsibility. Interestingly, *Taran Wanderer,* which is an outrider to the other four books, leaves the main storyline to follow Taran in a subsidiary quest to find himself. Taran is searching for knowledge of his parentage, hoping he will prove to be of noble blood in order to ask for the hand of Eilonwy. He does not learn of his birth, but he learns the crafts of the smith and the weaver, and he also learns about failure, for he cannot master the potter's art. And in the end he finds out *who* he is: "myself and none other. I am Taran." There are elements here not only of the self-discovery of a man but the education of a prince.

The other main characters, however, are two-dimensional. Eilonwy is an attractive, independent heroine with a distinctive tone of voice which however becomes predictable and in the end a little tiresome. Their companions announce themselves by perpetually-repeated actions and phrases. The bard Fflewddur Flam, for instance, boastfully stretches the truth but is invariably called to order by the snapping of a string of his magic harp. The timid, self-pitying, hairy creature Gurgi hopes for crunchings and munchings, while trying to avoid slashings and gashings and anything that might hurt his poor tender head.

The landscape of Prydain is so sketchily presented as to be little more than a backdrop, and at times an adult reader may well get the feeling that cardboard figures are being pushed around against a cardboard setting. And the dialogue, sometimes stilted, is just as often jarringly colloquial. Here for instance is King Eidilegg of the Fair Folk:

> "The Lake Sprites have been quarreling all day; now they're sulking. Their hair's a mess. And who does that reflect on? Who has to jolly them along, coax them, plead with them? The answer is obvious.

> "What thanks do I get for it?" King Eidilegg ranted on. "None at all. Has any of you long-legged gawks ever taken the trouble—even once, mind you—to offer the simplest expression of gratitude . . . Just a few words of honest appreciation?"

Presumably there is satire here on the self-pitying, self-important small-time boss; perhaps also the humor of deliberate anachronism and a poking of fun at fairies and the fairytale tradition. But after King Eidilegg's remarks (from which the quotation is only an excerpt) it is impossible to take seriously a scene in which the hero and his companions have in fact been captured and are at the king's mercy.

Whatever their flaws, the Prydain books have given pleasure to a great many children. Part of the explanation may lie in the dedication of the final volume: "For the boys who might have been Taran and the girls who will always be Eilonwy." There is ample scope for self-identification in this sequence. There is kindliness and wisdom too, and a reminder at the end, directed at Taran, that the conquest of evil enchantments is "only a beginning, not an ending. Do you believe evil itself to be so quickly overcome? Not so long as men still hate and slay each other, when greed and anger goad them . . ." If Tolkien was right in hoping that children might get "fairy-stories fit for them to read and yet within their measure," then Lloyd Alexander has provided a likeable example of what was needed. I do not think he has done more than that.

Susan Cooper's *Dark Is Rising* sequence is also, I think, clearly "for" children. Unlike the worlds of Tolkien, Alexander, and Le Guin, Cooper's setting is an actual country, namely Britain; and apart from a few flashbacks it is the Britain of today, lovingly and perhaps yearningly realized. (Susan Cooper is a British writer, long resident in the United States.) There is an obvious advantage in using an accurately-portrayed, actual landscape as one's setting; its solidity will tend to lend credibility to the story, in contrast to the loss of credibility that comes from flimsiness of background.

On the other hand, Susan Cooper has set herself a problem by employing two sets of central child characters, none of them fully equal to their roles in the sequence. It is not easy to keep them all occupied; still less is it easy to make believable an ordinary-sounding eleven-year-old boy who wields awesome powers in a cosmic conflict of Light and Dark. The surplus of characters, very evident in the last book, may have arisen from the lapse of time between the first book, *Over Sea, Under Stone* (1965), and the rest of the sequence *The Dark Is Rising* (1973), *Greenwitch* (1974), *The Grey King* (1975), and *Silver on the Tree* (1977).

To be frank, *Over Sea, Under Stone* did not look as if it were the start of anything special. It was a rather ordinary holiday adventure story, featuring three standard fictional children, whose parents, though not actually absent, played no significant part in the proceedings. The children—Simon, Jane, and Barney—found a map which set them off on a quest for a treasure, duly found and retrieved after clashes with sinister opponents. All this was reinforced by Arthurian elements: the treasure was a grail, and there was much emphasis on the children's Great Uncle Merry, "old as the hills," whose name of Merriman Lyon was derived from Merlin. And the villains turned out to be instruments of the Dark. The Arthurian touches did not seem appropriate to the story, which in fact would have been better without them. And although the author left "hooks" onto which later books could be attached, there was no immediate indication that a successor was to come.

Eight years then went by before the appearance of *The Dark Is Rising,* which was immeasurably more powerful and gave its name to the whole sequence. Merriman Lyon is the only character this book has in common with the earlier one. The protagonist now is Will Stanton, seventh son of a seventh son, who finds on Midwinter Day, his eleventh birthday, that he is the last of the Old Ones who have fought the Dark for centuries past. And now, with its power at its height, the Dark is active again, and must be defeated.

For sheer energy, for the potency of its material and the chill of its winter landscape, this book is tremendous. Susan Cooper has an unmatched power to send spurts of adrenalin into the bloodstream; to read *The Dark Is Rising* is a shaking experience. Yet in the end, as the action grows ever more wild and whirling, the book seems to get out of hand and the clash of supernatural forces to become mere noise.

The third book, *Greenwitch*, slighter and quieter than *The Dark Is Rising*, links the earlier two. The three children from *Over Sea, Under Stone* are joined in a Cornish fishing village by Will Stanton, the young Old One. There is competition with an emissary of the Dark to retrieve a crucial manuscript. But this manuscript, rolled up in a lead cylinder and lying on the seabed, is the cherished possession of the Greenwitch, a thing of boughs and blossoms thrown into the sea to secure good harvests of crops and fish. And the Greenwitch, a primitive and rather appealing creature, releases the powers of the Wild Magic, indifferent alike to Light and Dark. It's the Light that wins the manuscript, none the less.

With the fourth book, *The Grey King*, the struggle moves to Wales, and the unravelling of a puzzling verse prophecy leads on to the ultimate triumph of the Light in the fifth book, *Silver on the Tree*. There are more audacities: a Welsh farm boy called Bran turns out to be the Pendragon, son of King Arthur, projected forward in time; and Arthur himself appears at the end of the last book. Tension is maintained; yet by the time it is all over the reader may be beginning to wonder whether the Dark actually *does* much, other than taunt and threaten, interfere with the weather, and create astonishing spectacles in the sky.

Indeed, it is hard to work out just what the Dark *is*, and what its victory would imply. We learn that the Dark Ages were a time of triumph for the Dark. A corresponding triumph now would imply successful invasion of Britain, if not the destruction of much of its civilisation, but there is nothing to indicate that this would occur, or *how* it would occur. Success for the Dark through mass occupation of people's minds might be more plausible, but again it is not clear that this is an imminent danger, or, if it were, that the Light has any convincing means of fighting it. And we are told there is a Law to which both Light and Dark are subject, but we are not told who formulated this Law and how it is enforced. My own understanding may of course be deficient, but after reading twice through the entire *Dark Is Rising* sequence I have to confess to a good deal of bafflement.

One must however look for what books have, rather than for what they appear not to have, and possibly logical coherence can be overvalued. Susan Cooper's writing has a high emotional charge, derived in part I think from a passionate nostalgia and an eye and ear for the legendary and historical associations of the Welsh and English landscapes. We can be grateful for these, and for her rare, electric ability to convey excitement.

To turn from Cooper to Ursula Le Guin is to turn to a contrasting world of cool, controlled precision. Earthsea is an imagined archipelago comprising scores of islands, each with its name on the map. There are no machines, but magic is everywhere, much of it being small-time stuff like weatherwork:

> In a land where sorcerers come thick, like Gont or the Enlades, you may see a raincloud
> blundering slowly from side to side and place to place as one spell shunts it on to the next,
> till at last it is buffeted out over the sea where it can rain in peace.

The higher levels of magic, more subtle, complex, and dangerous, are studied and taught at a central school of wizardry, to which, in the first book, *A Wizard of Earthsea* (1968), the hero Ged, a lad more than commonly handy with a spell, is sent. There is nothing facetious about this. The author treats magic with total seriousness, and as the story goes on it becomes clear that wizardry and wisdom are hardly distinguishable:

> All power is one in source and end, I think [says Ged in his maturity]. Years and
> distances, stars and candles, water and wind and wizardry, the craft in a man's hand and
> the wisdom in a tree's root; they all arise together.

It is a responsibility of those who practise the high arts of magic to preserve the great Equilibrium, for any tampering with the balance of things can be disastrous. Balance is a characteristic of the writer's own approach; indeed, the trilogy can be said to be carefully balanced within itself. The first and third books tell principally of two quests of Ged: in the first as a young man; in the second as a much older one, now Archmage. They range widely over Earthsea. Between them comes the second book, *The Tombs of Atuan*, whose setting is closed and claustrophobic.

The first quest of Ged arises when, arrogant in his youthful prowess, he looses into the world a great evil, a sinister Shadow which he must pursue and face. The climax is an unforgettable confrontation at the world's end, when Ged reaches out and takes hold of the Shadow, his own black self: "Light and darkness met, and joined, and were one." It is not hard to grasp the meaning of this; one does not even need to be versed in the psychology of Carl Gustav Jung; but anyone who seeks full enlightenment should read Mrs. Le Guin's magnificent Library of Congress lecture on *The Child and the Shadow*. This is reprinted in *The Openhearted Audience*, edited by Virginia Haviland and published by the Library of Congress (1980).

In *The Tombs of Atuan* (1971), the High Priestess Tenar finds Ged trapped in the sacred labyrinth at the Place of the Tombs. He should be killed or left to die; but Tenar, reluctantly at first, keeps him alive, talks to him, comes to know him, and eventually escapes with him—thereby gaining freedom from her own sterile imprisonment. Here again is a meaning which can be grasped imaginatively without needing to be spelled out. The last book of the trilogy, *The Farthest Shore* (1973), sees Ged arriving in the land of the dead to confront a great mage who has contrived to open the door to immortality. Immortality has been often and deeply desired; but of all disturbances of the Equilibrium its achievement would be the most dreadful, since "death is the price we pay for our life, and for all life." The theme is a profound one.

The Earthsea trilogy has many brilliancies, many ingenuities and intricacies, and great felicity of style. And though Earthsea is an imaginary world, the concerns of the trilogy are directly and sharply relevant to our concerns in this world today.

Patricia Wrightson's threesome, which began with *The Ice Is Coming* in 1977, was the culmination of a quarter-century's steady development of her writing talent. During this time she had built up a reputation extending far beyond her native Australia. *The Ice Is Coming* is prefaced by a declaration:

> This is a story of today and of Australia. It is my own story, grown out of my thinking. Its human characters are my invention, but its spirit characters are not. They are the folk-spirits of the Australian Aborigines—not the ritual figures of the creative myths but the gnomes and heroes and monsters of Australia.
>
> I might have written a story about more familiar spirits, the elves and fairies and dragons and monsters of Europe . . . But for that story I would have had to invent a foreign setting, an Earthsea or a Middle Earth; and powerfully magical as those countries are I know one as powerful and as magic. It is the only one I know and the one I want to write about. . .

This note appears to invite comparison with Tolkien and Le Guin; and Mrs. Wrightson can sustain the comparison. Her work has weight, substance, and imaginative power.

Wirrun, a young Aborigine, wins the reputation of a hero of the People in the first book, and as a result is called upon to play a hero's role in each of the other two, *The Dark Bright Water* (1979) and *Behind the Wind* (1981). In each book Wirrun, helped and sometimes hindered by the native spirits of the land, must defeat a great threat to the People; and finally, at the end of *Behind the Wind,* he must go among the dead and himself face death in order to deal with an evil thing of man's making: a thing that kills and that can call men's spirits from their graves. Wirrun's body dies, yet the ending is a curiously happy one. In life he has fallen in love with a water-spirit; as human and spirit respectively they cannot stay together; but now that he is dead his spirit can be reunited with the water-girl, while his memory as hero remains in the stories of the People.

Brief summary can give little idea of the strange and challenging nature of this trilogy. At its heart is the land—the old south land that "lies across the world like an open hand"—with its People and their stories and spirits. The newcomers, the Happy Folk who live in Australia's cities and play on its beaches, know little of it: "Along its green margins, clustered in towns here and there, they live with their faces to the sea. . . They have no time to look over their shoulders at the old land behind them." The Happy Folk figure a little in the first book; in the other two hardly at all.

The trilogy is not, I think, a total success. It does not grip continuously; there is a lot of to-ing and fro-ing; there are many encounters both with men and spirits that seem not to contribute a great deal. But there is also much that is powerful and finely imagined, and the love story of young man and water spirit—a perilous subject for any writer—is sensitively and touchingly handled. With a setting that will be more foreign to many readers than a purely fictional one, it would be surprising to me (though I should be glad to be proved wrong) if the Wrightson trilogy became as well known and successful as the other sequences discussed in this essay. Yet it may well be the most impressive achievement of Australian children's literature so far.

My own opinion, which in the circumstances I can hardly avoid offering, is that of these four post-Tolkien sequences the Earthsea trilogy has the highest literary merit. Indeed, I believe it is fully equal to *The Lord of the Rings,* although the latter came first and for that reason can still claim precedence

In a sense the authors are *all* heroes, for the writing of a sequence of epic length is itself a heroic undertaking. Few of us have the strength and courage to embark on so daunting a quest, and those who complete it have surely earned respect and admiration.

---

[1] J.R.R. Tolkien, *On Fairy Stories,* in *Tree and Leaf,* London, Allen & Unwin paperbacks, p. 23.

[2] ibid., p. 16.

[3] Charles Moorman, from *The Precincts of Felicity*, University of Florida Press (1966), pp. 86-100; reprinted in *Tolkien and the Critics*, ed. Isaacs and Zimbardo, University of Notre Dame Press (1968).

[4] Tolkien, op.cit., p. 48.

[5] E. Wilson, *Oo, Those Awful Orcs!* The Nation, April 14, 1956, pp. 312-314.

[6] Tolkien, op.cit., pp. 25-26.

John Rowe Townsend is an English author, critic, editor, journalist, and lecturer. He has written such novels for children and young people as the Jungle Trilogy (Gumble's Yard, *1961* [U.S. edition, Trouble in the Jungle, *1969*], Hell's Edge, *1963,* Widdershins Crescent, *1965* [U.S. edition, Good-bye to the Jungle, *1967*]), The Intruder *(1970), and* A Foreign Affair *(1982). He is also the author of a historical survey of children's literature,* Written for Children *(1965; revised edition, 1974), and a set of essays on contemporary children's writers,* A Sense of Story *(1971; revised edition,* A Sounding of Storytellers, *1979).*

Lloyd Alexander

1924-

American author of fiction and nonfiction.

Alexander is among the most successful post-Tolkien fantasists for children. He writes in contemporary language about classic themes such as the battle between good and evil and combines them with more modern concerns like the search for self. His first venture into fantasy came with *Time Cat,* the story of a feline adventurer who can travel backward in time to various eras when cats were held in high esteem. He followed it with a five book series, the Prydain Chronicles, which includes *The Book of Three, The Black Cauldron, The Castle of Llyr, Taran Wanderer,* and *The High King.* Loosely based on the *Mabinogion,* a document of Welsh myths and tales, the Prydain Chronicles relate the adventures of Taran, a young hero who becomes enmeshed in the battle between the forces of good and evil. Throughout the five books, Taran and his companions skillfully thwart the intentions of various evil princes, enchantresses, and lords. Underscoring each story is Taran's search for his identity and his struggle for maturity; through Taran's decision making, both wrong-headed and heroic, he rises from Assistant Pig-Keeper to King of Prydain. Three other books, *Coll and His White Pig, The Truthful Harp,* and *The Foundling and Other Tales of Prydain,* are stories written for younger readers about some of the Chronicles's minor characters. While most of Alexander's works are fantasies, he has also written biographies of lesser-known Jewish historical figures. Two recent works, *Westmark* and *The Kestrel,* mark the beginnings of another fantasy series which is set in the eighteenth century and considers political and philosophical questions.

Reviewers are not always in agreement on the success of the Prydain series. Alexander is criticized for not developing the potential of his promising ideas and themes, and for failing to complete plot details. However, most critics agree he presents imaginative, tightly-woven conclusions in the later volumes of the series. Alexander is also acclaimed for the originality and excitement of the series, his plot and character development, the poignancy of the lessons learned, and his clear understanding of the sad necessity of the battles of good and evil. *The Black Cauldron* was a Newbery Honor Book in 1966. Alexander won the Newbery Award in 1969 for *The High King,* which was a finalist for the National Book Award the same year and the American Book Award in 1981. Alexander was given the National Book Award in 1971 for *The Marvelous Misadventures of Sebastian* and was a finalist in 1979 for *The First Two Lives of Lukas-Kasha.* He also won the American Book Award in 1982 for *Westmark.*

(See also *Children's Literature Review,* Vol. 1; *Contemporary Authors,* New Revision, Vol. 1; and *Something about the Author,* Vol. 3.)

AUTHOR'S COMMENTARY

The muse in charge of fantasy wears good, sensible shoes. . . . She does not carry a soothing lyre for inspiration, but is more likely to shake you roughly awake at four in the morning and rattle a sheaf of subtle, sneaky questions under your nose. And you had better answer them. The Muse will stand for no non-

Photograph by Alexander Limont; courtesy of Lloyd Alexander

sense (that is, non-sense). Her geometries are no more Euclidean than Einstein's, but they are equally rigorous.

I was aware of the problems and disciplines of fantasy, but in a left-handed sort of way; because there is a difference between knowing and doing. Until I met the Muse in Charge of Fantasy personally, I had no hint of what a virago she could be.

Our first encounter was relatively cordial and came in the course of working on a book called *Time Cat.* I suspect I learn more from writing books than readers very likely learn from reading them, and I realize now that *Time Cat* is an example of a fantasy perhaps more realistic than otherwise. Basically, only one fantastic premise moved the story: that Gareth, a black cat, could take the young boy Jason into nine historical periods. The premise included some built-in and plausible hedges. Boy and cat could talk together during their journeys—but only when no one else was around to overhear them; after their return home they could no longer speak to each other, at least not in words. They enjoyed no supernatural protection or privilege; what happened to them, happened—indeed, if Gareth met with a fatal accident, Jason would be forever marooned in the past. They weren't allowed to interfere with or change the course of history, or do anything contrary to laws of the physical world and their personal capacities. Jason was a boy and Gareth was a cat.

Within those boundaries, the problem became one of straight-forward historical research, with some investigation into how cats were regarded in various eras. Ichigo, the boy emperor in the Japanese adventure, really existed. His wanting to dress kittens in kimonos was valid; there was an extravagant preciousness in the Japanese court of that epoch, and historical records state that such things happened. In other adventures, only slight accommodations made it acceptable for Jason and Gareth to be where they were, doing what they were doing.

The creation of a fantasy that starts from the ground up is something else again. Melancholy men, they say, are the most incisive humorists; by the same token, writers of fantasy must be, within their own frame of work, hardheaded realists. What appears gossamer is, underneath, solid as prestressed concrete. What seems so free in fantasy is often inventiveness of detail rather than complicated substructure. Elaboration—not improvisation.

And the closer a self-contained imaginary world draws to a recognizably real one (Tolkien's Middle Earth instead of Carroll's Wonderland) the more likely its pleasant meadows are to conceal unsuspected deadfalls and man-traps. The writer is wise if he explores it thoroughly and eliminates them. His world must be all of a piece, with careful and consistent handling of background, implements, and characters.

I began discovering the importance of consistency as a result of some of the research for *Time Cat,* originally planned to include an adventure in ancient Wales. Surely everyone cherishes a secret, private world from the days of childhood. Mine was Camelot, and Arthur's Round Table, Malory, and the *Mabinogion.* The Welsh research brought it all back to me. Feeling like a man who has by accident stumbled into an enchanted cavern lost since boyhood, both terrified and awestruck, I realized I would have to explore further. Perhaps I had been waiting to do so all these years, and some kind of moment had come. In any case, I replaced the Welsh episode with an Irish one and later turned all my attention not to the beautiful land of Wales I knew in reality, but an older, darker one.

My first intention was to base a fantasy on some of the tales in the *Mabinogion,* and I started research accordingly. However, I soon found myself delving deeper and deeper into the legends' origins and significance: searching for what exactly I didn't know. . . . A historical-realistic approach did not work. Unlike the Irish and Norse, the Welsh mythology has been irreparably tampered with, like so many pictures, old and new, cut apart and pasted every which way.

Sifting the material, hoping to find whatever I was groping for, I accumulated box after box of file cards covered with notes, names, relationships, and I learned them cold. With great pains I began constructing a kind of family tree or genealogical chart of mythical heroes. (Eventually I found one in a book, already done for me. Not the first book, but the fifteenth!) Nothing suited my purposes.

At that point, the Muse in Charge of Fantasy, seductive in extremely filmy garments, sidled into my work room. "Not making much headway, are you? How would it be," she murmured huskily, "if you invented your own mythology? Isn't that what you *really* want to do?"

She vanished. I was not to see her again in her aspect as temptress, but only as taskmistress. For she was right.

Abandoning all I had collected, I began once more, planning what eventually became *The Book of Three.* My previous labor had not been entirely in vain; it had given me roots, suggestions, possibilities. In addition, I was now free to do as I pleased. Or so I thought.

True enough, the writer of fantasy can start with whatever premises he chooses (actually, the uncomplicated ones work best). In the algebra of fantasy, A times B doesn't have to equal B times A. But, once established, the equation must hold throughout the story. You may set your own ground rules and, in the beginning, decree as many laws as you like—though in practice the fewer departures from the "real" world the better. A not-very-serious breach and the fantasy world explodes just as surely as if a very real hydrogen bomb had been dropped on it. With inconsistency (so usual in the real world), the machinery moving the tale grinds and screeches; the characters cease to be imaginary and become simply unreal. Truth drains out of them. Admittedly, certain questions have to be begged, such as "How did all these people get here in the first place?" But they are like the axioms of geometry, questioned only by metaphysicians.

Once committed to his imaginary kingdom, the writer is not a monarch but a subject. Characters must appear plausible in their own setting, and the writer must go along with their inner logic. Happenings should have logical implications. Details should be tested for consistency. Shall animals speak? If so, do *all* animals speak? If not, then which—and how? Above all, why? Is it essential to the story, or lamely cute? Are there enchantments? How powerful? If an enchanter can perform such-and-such, can he not also do so-and-so? These were a few of the more obvious questions raised by the Muse, now disguised behind steel-rimmed spectacles. Others were less straightforward.

"This person, Prince Gwydion," she said, "I presume, is meant to be a heroic figure. But what I should like to know is this," she added in an irritating, pedantic voice. "How is he different from an ordinary human being?"

I replied that I was prepared to establish that Gwydion, though not invincible, had a somewhat longer life span, greater strength and physical endurance. If he had powers of enchantment, these were to be limited in logical ways. I admitted, too, that he would nonetheless get hungry, thirsty, and tired.

"All very well," she said. "But is that the essential? Is he a human being with only a little more capacity? You must tell me how he is truly and rationally different."

I had begun to sweat. "He—he knows more? Experience?" I choked. "He sees the meaning of things. Wisdom."

"I shall accept that,"she said. "See that you keep it in mind."

On another occasion, I had planned to include a mysterious and menacing portent in the shape of a dark cloud. The Muse, an early riser, prodded me awake sometime well before dawn.

"I've been meaning to speak with you about that cloud," she said. "You like it, don't you? You think it's dramatic. But I was wondering if this had occurred to you: you only want a few of your people to see the cloud, is that not correct? Yet you have already established a number of other characters in the vicinity who will see it, too. An event like that? They'll do nothing but talk about it for most of the story. Or," she purred, as she always does before she pounces, "did you have something like closed-circuit television in mind?"

She clumped off in her sensible brogans while I flung myself from bed and ripped up all my work of the night before. The cloud was cut out.

Her subsequent interrogations were no gentler. Perhaps I should have foreseen all her questions and spared myself much revision. In defense, I can only say that I must often put something on paper and test the idea in practice. I did, gradually, grow more aware of pitfalls and learned to distinguish the telltale signs of mare's-nests.

The less fantastic it is, the stronger fantasy becomes. The writer can painfully bark his shins on too many pieces of magical furniture. Enchanted swords, wielded incautiously, cut both ways. But the limits imposed on characters and implements must be more than simply arbitrary. What does not happen should be as valid as what does. (pp. 141-45)

Insistence on plausibility and rationality can work for the writer, not against him. In developing his characters, he is obliged to go deeper instead of wider. And, as in all literature, characters are what ultimately count. The writer of fantasy may have a slight edge on the realistic novelist, who must present his characters within the confines of actuality. Fantasy, too, uses homely detail, but at the same time goes right to the core of a character, to extract the essence, the very taste of an individual personality. This may be one of the things that makes good fantasy so convincing. The essence is poetic truth.

The distillation process, unfortunately, is unknown and must be classed as a Great Art or a Major Enchantment. If a recipe existed, it could be reproduced; and it is not reproducible. We can only see the results. Or hear them. Of Kenneth Grahame—and the same applies to all great fantasists—A. A. Milne writes: "When characters have been created as solidly . . . they speak ever after in their own voices."

These voices speak directly to us. Like music, poetry, or dreams, fantasy goes straight to the heart of the matter. The experience of a realistic work seldom approaches the experience of fantasy. We may sail on the *Hispaniola* and perform deeds of derring-do. But only in fantasy can we journey through Middle Earth, where the fate of an entire world lies in the hands of a hobbit.

Fantasy presents the world as it should be. But "should be" does not mean that the realms of fantasy are Lands of Cockaigne where roasted chickens fly into mouths effortlessly opened. Sometimes heartbreaking, but never hopeless, the fantasy world as it "should be" is one in which good is ultimately stronger than evil, where courage, justice, love, and mercy actually function. Thus, it may often appear quite different from our own. In the long run, perhaps not. Fantasy does not promise Utopia. But if we listen carefully, it may tell us what we someday may be capable of achieving. (pp. 145-46)

Lloyd Alexander, "The Flat-Heeled Muse" (reprinted by permission of the author), in The Horn Book Magazine, Vol. XLI, No. 2, April, 1965, pp. 141-46.

GENERAL COMMENTARY

Lloyd Alexander is a perfect example of one who, before he could come into his own as a writer, had to discover that place which was, for him, the spiritual symbol or expression of something hidden. Geographical place most certainly exerted a power over it, and the experience of childhood was related. (p. 185)

Alexander's Welsh research brought back his secret, private world of Camelot, Arthur's Round Table, Malory, and the Mabinogion. He realized he would have to explore further and that some kind of moment had come. . . .

If one is to judge by public reaction to **The Book of Three, The Black Cauldron, The Castle of Llyr** and **Taran Wanderer**, possibly it had. His first children's book, **Time Cat,** for which he had been doing the Welsh research, had been undistinguished, but **The Book of Three** was an ALA Notable Book and its sequel, **The Black Cauldron,** was runner-up for the 1965 Newbery Award. These books, as **Time Cat** did not, take place in a region of Alexander's own creation in the Welsh past of Arthur's time. Here at last he entered the enchanted cavern and thus could be wholly happy and released because he was writing about what was intimately related to childhood, to what he had loved as a child. The cavern returned him to a private country of the mind which was, in a way, a geographical place but, even more potently, the habitation of Arthur, the landscape and atmosphere of Arthur, which so possessed him that out of it he could write four books in five years, the Prydain cycle, which children, apparently, have taken to with delight despite the strangeness and difficulty of the y-fraught names. (p. 186)

Here are children's books which offer in abundance their creators' translations of their own dimensions of amazement into fictions in which the critical can discover excellence of style, construction, and characterization, as well as depth of meaning, the vivid communication of atmosphere, of place, and in many cases a true sense of poetic overtone. (p. 241)

Eleanor Cameron, "Writing Itself" and "The Child and the Book," in her The Green and Burning Tree: On the Writing and Enjoyment of Children's Books (copyright © 1962, 1964, 1966, 1969 by Eleanor Cameron; reprinted by permission of Little, Brown and Company in association with The Atlantic Monthly Press), Atlantic-Little, Brown, 1969, pp. 137-230, 231-76.*

May Hill Arbuthnot in *Children and Books* states that the most convincing modern fantasies have come chiefly from England but that American writers are working with increasing success.

America arrived, so to speak, with Lloyd Alexander and his five books about Prydain. While Tolkien remains the master at the art of sub-creation, Alexander rivals him on an only slightly smaller scale—a scale intended for younger readers. . . .

The mythical world of Prydain is carefully created; Alexander establishes a strong sense of time and place although there is not the historical and philological detail of Middle-earth. By his own admission, the author has drawn upon the ancient Welsh legends known as the *Mabinogion*. He weaves occasional characters and legends, indeed the land of Wales itself in and out of Prydain—creating, most successfully, a legend of his own. (p. 940)

If one could venture a hope for the Land of Prydain it would be this: that Prydain, Taran and Eilonwy would be available for all children to read about and dream about in these perilous years of the space age and for many years to come. Lloyd Alexander has truly created a story, a myth, that children can claim as their own—untouched by adult tampering or changing—unshared with adults unless the grown-up reader himself chooses to go adventuring. (pp. 942-43)

[The] Chronicles of Prydain are not stories of unrelieved battle. Humor does exist by the side of gallantry and sheer exuberance of living is exhibited by Taran and his companions. The Princess Eilonwy, first met in *The Book of Three,* shares the adventures of growing-up. As Taran learns, so does she and readers will recognize and delight in Eilonwy's struggles with the problems of becoming a lady.

In a most un-didactic way, young readers (and for that matter, older readers as well) of the Chronicles of Prydain learn about the dreams of youth and the realities of growing up. They learn that dreams and dreamers can be honored and encouraged but that much is expected of those who would fulfill the dreams. (p. 943)

> *Mary Lou Colbath, ''Worlds As They Should Be: Middle-earth, Narnia and Prydain,'' in* Elementary English *(copyright © 1971 by the National Council of Teachers of English; reprinted by permission of the publisher and the author), Vol. XLVIII, No. 8, December, 1971, pp. 937-45.*

In the Prydain chronicles Good and Evil are exemplified in different ways through different characters, some of them conceived in contemporary terms and others (like Achren) more markedly traditional. Lloyd Alexander's use of different kinds of characters lightens the difficulty that faces any writer of chivalric fantasy, of expressing moral truths dramatically. Achren conveys through her deeds and words the actuality of wickedness which is less directly described in the almost wholly unseen character of Arawn, the very fount and symbol of Evil. (p. 9)

Eilonwy is in many ways the most human and likable character in the cycle; with Taran, she promotes the contemporary flavour of speech and outlook which contrasts with the traditional aspect of the books and contributes to their particular elusive atmosphere. (p. 101)

Like many of the minor characters in the Prydain chronicles, Ellidyr is recognized by certain fixed traits—envy, jealous pride, arrogance, in his case—which are seen as coming from some deep flaw or lack in his life; the cause of the 'black beast' which rides Ellidyr in fact remains a mystery. It is the function of this young warrior to show up by contrast the genuine humility of Taran . . . , central figure of the whole saga. . . .

Ellidyr is an interesting example of a dual character. His threadbare attire and 'pale, arrogant face', his nervous, bad-tempered steed, his lofty manner, fit the derivative, chivalric element in *The Black Cauldron* and at the same time his character is seen in psychological terms, so that the human aspect, the universal lesson, of the Prydain chronicles is once more enforced. (p. 290)

The character of Taran has less obvious individuality than many of the minor, part-comic characters. This is because he has to be a representative, of Good against Evil, of Man seeking his own identity, of Youth growing up. His inner growth is sometimes demonstrated in sharp particularized remarks; for example, as he prepares for the last great march against Arawn, Coll remarks 'I remember a day when an Assistant Pig-Keeper would have been all flash and fire to ride with Lord Gwydion. Now you look as glum as a frost-bitten turnip.' We do not know Taran as a person any better for such comments. We only know what other people think about him, and their thoughts always stress his steady progress towards maturity.

The underlying irony of Lloyd Alexander's story, indicated in Taran's role of Assistant Pig-Keeper and his humility as a result

of it, successfully carries out his aim of writing a fantasy full of traditional overtones which will yet be a story of human beings, their frailties and their glory. Taran has to be at once a man and the anonymous, unidentified, cryptic prince of fairy tale. In the first of these roles he has some of the flexibility of human nature: in the second he is to some extent a ceremonial figure, and perhaps the latter role masks the former except in *Taran Wanderer,* where he most definitely shoulders the responsibility for himself. (p. 340)

> *Margery Fisher, ''Who's Who in Children's Books,'' in her* Who's Who in Children's Books: A Treasury of the Familiar Characters of Childhood *(copyright © 1975 by Margery Fisher; reprinted by permission), Holt, Rinehart and Winston, 1975, Weidenfeld & Nicholson, 1975, pp. 9-388.**

Lloyd Alexander ranks as one of the best writers of high fantasy to emerge since Tolkien, and his five novels comprising the Chronicles of Prydain are true classics of the genre. *The Book of Three* introduces the series and, like the books that follow, draws much of its material from the Welsh *Mabinogion,* thus relating Alexander to Evangeline Walton and Kenneth Morris. Alexander, however, unlike Walton or Morris, alters his source considerably. In fact, Alexander uses his ancient source as a guide or a jumping-off point for his own invention, though much of the original still shows through concretely in places and imbues the spirit of Alexander's work throughout. . . . Interesting as [Taran's] adventures are, Alexander's memorable characters are by far his greatest achievement: Princess Eilonwy, garrulous and engaging; Fflewddur Fflam, a comically inept minstrel; Gurgi, perhaps best described as an apelike creature who speaks in rhymes and is generally so covered with leaves and twigs that he looks like ''a walking beaver dam.'' These characters all reappear in the next books, which like *The Book of Three,* are characterized by magic, humor, and warmth. (p. 40)

In his introduction to [*The Black Cauldron,* the] second of the Chronicles of Prydain, Alexander comments that his intention is to add to the series and to deepen it. He accomplishes this in several ways. In *The Book of Three* there was hardship, but the conflict was resolved with the side of good and its protagonist Taran emerging relatively unscathed. There is more at stake in *The Black Cauldron.* The quest here is to destroy the Cauldron, through which Arawn, prince of the underworld, enslaves men after their death, depriving them of their final rest of both body and, presumably, soul. In accomplishing this objective, two of Taran's company knowingly sacrifice their lives and their dreams. These are Adaon, the bard and son of Taliesen, and Prince Ellidyr, a basically noble warrior, but one torn and tormented by a distorted vision of heroism. Also, Taran's own desire for heroic achievement and recognition comes to the fore, paralleled somewhat by Ellidyr's. Taran must also sacrifice his dream and he does so before it corrupts him. . . . Alexander creates in *The Black Cauldron* a successful blend of tragedy and comedy with a resultant wisdom. Taran and the readers come to recognize that one can never come to terms with evil without being corrupted. (pp. 40-1)

It is certainly clear by [*The Castle of Llyr*], the third chronicle, how consciously Alexander has substantively integrated the series through the theme that the desire for greatness, if not controlled, can lead one astray. . . . The significant difference in [*Taran Wanderer*] is that Taran is entering manhood, and the book takes on a more serious tone. Indeed, it becomes a classic quest tale, a rite of passage into manhood; like all serious quests it is, or at least includes, the journey of self-discovery. Significantly, Taran gives up even his title of Assistant Pig-Keeper for the less specific one of Wanderer. *Taran Wanderer* continues the progressive deepening of the chronicles, but without sacrificing the warm humor and excitement of the earlier books. . . . Alexander's humor ripples through the book and is even more refreshing than in the earlier works, flowing as it now does through a more serious Prydain. (p. 42)

If writing a good ending to a single book is a challenge, then doing so for a closely integrated series such as the Chronicles of Prydain is doubly challenging. No one succeeds better at this than Lloyd Alexander in *The High King*, fifth and last of the chronicles. . . . It is clear by now to readers familiar with Tolkien's *The Lord of the Rings* how much Alexander's conclusion resembles Tolkien's—the last all-out battle and the departure for a mystical realm. In one major respect, at least, Alexander improves on Tolkien. Whereas Tolkien rarely describes conflicts between large forces in any great length or detail, Alexander does and does it well, thereby more closely involving the reader in so important an action as the decisive last battle. And he does so with finesse, avoiding the gruesome butchery detailed in many works of sword and sinew. Indeed, the conclusion points out that winning the battle is the easy part; ruling the people will be considerably more demanding. This theme is a variation on the idea that integrates the five chronicles—that greatness is not a matter of birth or even of bold deeds, but of wisdom and humility and responsible choice. (p. 43)

Although Alexander's works, including those in [*The Foundling and Other Tales of Prydain*], are often classified as juvenile fantasy, it will not take the open-minded and discerning adult reader long to find that his fantasy works appeal to readers of all ages. Like Lewis's Narnian tales, the Prydain stories are both entertaining and substantive. A case in point is **"The Smith, the Weaver, and the Harper,"** which not only effectively satirizes human greed, but also subtly articulates the profound importance of integrity and pride in one's craft. All the stories in this fine collection display the lucid style, instructive satire, and sly wit for which Alexander is noted. (p. 44)

Marshall B. Tymn, Kenneth J. Zahorski and Robert H. Boyer, "Core Collection," in their Fantasy Literature: A Core Collection and Reference Guide *(reprinted with permission of the R. R. Bowker Company; copyright © 1979 by Xerox Corporation), Bowker, 1979, pp. 39-198.**

A step below [T. H.] White, certainly, but genuinely interesting are the children's fantasies by Lloyd Alexander known as the Chronicles of Prydain.

The Chronicles take place, not in an Arthurian setting, but in the mythological Wales that preceded Arthur, altered a bit to make it conform to the Tolkienian pattern. . . . The first story, *The Book of Three*, is no more than a clever imitation of Tolkien, lighter in tone than its model and based primarily on Welsh myth, rather than on a combination of Northern motifs. By the last two books, however, Taran has grown up, the land of Prydain has taken on a degree of solidity, and the author has found in his story an outlet for some real philosophical exploration.

Interestingly enough, the Chronicles of Prydain become most engaging when Taran reveals himself to be a hero in the American grain. In the fourth book, *Taran Wanderer*, he becomes,

as the title indicates, a wanderer, an experimenter, a seeker after an identity that always seems to lie over the next hill. In his metamorphoses and in his restlessness he resemble Hawthorne's Holgrave, Cooper's Leatherstocking, and that other orphan, Twain's Huckleberry Finn. And in the final volume, *The High King*, . . . Taran finds his identity, as Americans have throughout our literary tradition, in the future rather than the past. Without ties or ancestry, and with a wife who renounces her own heritage, he becomes King of Prydain and leads it into a new, unmagical age. Like the nameless couple in Hawthorne's short story, "The Maypole of Merrymount," Taran and Eilonwy stand together at the end of the story, shorn of the trappings and enchantments of a lost age, ready to move together into a soberer world. It is a moving ending and an appropriate one, an ending which is the natural flowering of the cross between alien motifs and the author's own culture. (pp. 156-57)

Brian Attebery, "After Tolkien," in his The Fantasy Tradition in American Literature: From Irving to Le Guin *(copyright © 1980 by Brian Attebery), Indiana University Press, 1980, pp. 154-86.**

Alexander's fantasy is based firmly upon legend, with a multitude of natural and supernatural characters, and some halfway between. Indeed, we learn at the end that all of the major characters except Taran himself are from the Summer Land, where they live forever. Alexander creates distinctive characters, and he is a true master of the light, sophisticated style, preferring discussion to action, although there are great goings and comings in these books. There is much humor as well, but it is the wry shrug of the adult and not the slapstick antic of the child.

Alexander uses many elements of folk literature in his tales—the magic bauble or light that Eilonwy carries, the ability of the pig to prophesy, the magic cauldron and sword, the inexhaustible knapsack of food. Throughout the books runs the muted theme of the hero, the champion of good against the forces of evil—not just the external manifestations of it, but the evil within oneself—the hero who emerges triumphant at the end. (p. 219)

Zena Sutherland, Dianne L. Monson, and May Hill Arbuthnot, in their review of the "Prydain" Books and "The Marvelous Misadventures of Sebastian," in their Children and Books *(copyright © 1981, 1977, 1972, 1964, 1957, 1947 by Scott, Foresman and Company; reprinted by permission), sixth edition, Scott, Foresman, 1981, pp. 219-20.*

BORDER HAWK: AUGUST BONDI (1958)

Much has been written about John Brown, the famous Abolitionist, but little is known about the men who rode with him. One of them was a Jewish pioneer from Kansas, named August Bondi. How Bondi met John Brown and was fascinated by his personality; how Bondi risked his life for freedom and eventually settled down to become a distinguished citizen make up the material of Lloyd Alexander's book. There is a great deal of warfare and bloodshed in **"Border Hawk."** Nevertheless, the author manages to inject—painlessly and usefully—thoughts about liberty, Americanism and the values of Judaism.

Harold V. Ribalow, "New Books for the Younger Readers' Library," in The New York Times Book Review *(© 1958 by The New York Times Company; reprinted by permission), March 23, 1958, p. 36.**

This is a fast-paced biography of August Bondi, whose Jewish heritage was the key to his lifetime devotion to freedom's cause, first in Austria and later in the United States. Kansas' struggle to enter as a free state and the political and ideological ferment which precipitated civil war serve as the major canvas for this intimate glimpse of Bondi and other dedicated members of John Brown's rugged band.

> *Julia Jussim, in her review of ''Border Hawk: August Bondi,'' in* Junior Libraries, *an appendix to* Library Journal *(reprinted from the May, 1958 issue of* Junior Libraries, *published by R. R. Bowker Co./A Xerox Corporation; copyright © 1958), Vol. 4, No. 9, May, 1958, p. 39.*

TIME CAT: THE REMARKABLE JOURNEY OF JASON AND GARETH   (1963; British edition as *Nine Lives*)

Lloyd Alexander is [a] felicitous writer who knows about boys and pets. His **"Time Cat"** . . . is a provocative fantasy about Jason and his cat Gareth. Gareth takes Jason back into nine periods of time, with stops in ancient Egypt, medieval Japan, seventeenth-century Germany in the days of witch-hunters and New England in April, 1775. Filled with excitement and humor the book also leaves the receptive reader with some interesting reflections on human conduct.

> *Ellen Lewis Buell, ''Young Reader's Shelf: A Selection from Recent Titles,'' in* The New York Times Book Review *(© 1963 by The New York Times Company; reprinted by permission), April 14, 1963, p. 56.**

The strong point of the book is its good delineation of the character of the peoples living in the various historical periods. However, the episodic treatment fails to sustain excitement throughout, but this will appeal to good readers who enjoy an occasional fresh, humorous insight into history.

> *Miriam S. Mathes, in her review of ''Time Cat: The Remarkable Journey of Jason and Gareth,'' in* Library Journal *(reprinted from* Library Journal, *June 15, 1963; published by R. R. Bowker Co. (a Xerox company); copyright © 1963 by Xerox Corporation), Vol. 18, No. 12, June 15, 1963, p. 2548.*

[*Nine Lives* has] the true-blue classic touch of Success. The little boy hero goes back in history (Leonardo, the ancient Britons, and a grim German witchcraft episode) with his sage cat Gareth. Clear-cut style. No nonsense.

> *Stevie Smith, in her review of ''Nine Lives,'' in* New Statesman *(© 1963 The Statesman & Nation Publishing Co. Ltd.), Vol. LXVI, No. 1704, November 8, 1963, p. 668.*

THE BOOK OF THREE   (1964)

Following the tradition of the great writers of fantasy, Mr. Alexander introduces his readers to a new and complete world. Time will tell how satisfying boys and girls will find the chance to live for a while in Prydain. I believe that the book will wear well, and that the children will be eager for other stories in which Taran may yet learn the meaning of heroism.

> *Ruth Hill Viguers, in her review of ''The Book of Three,'' in* The Horn Book Magazine *(copyright © 1964, by The Horn Book, Inc., Boston), Vol. XL, No. 5, October, 1964, p. 496.**

The Alexander books have been highly praised by some American reviewers but this sample fails to come up to expectations. There is a duffer-hero of unspecified age who completes a dangerous mission against the forces of evil in a land half imaginary, half legendary Wales. He encounters many hazards, some distinctly nasty in a horror-comic way, but is accompanied by such trivial characters the menace is rendered ineffectual by their reactions. His comrades are a Golem-like creature who reforms, a petty king turned funny bard and a most irritatingly girlish girl whom the author evidently finds charmingly feminine. The book has its moments, but the lessons it incorporates are rather heavily tacked-on instead of coming as a revelation. The jokes, especially those about the hero's status as Assistant Pig Keeper and the similes with which his girl-friend ends practically *every* sentence, are too contrived and the mixture of comic-book elements—of both horror and comedy—with legendary elements gives the impression that the author's intentions were probably good but his equipment was feeble.

> *A review of ''The Book of Three,'' in* The Junior Bookshelf, *Vol. 30, No. 5, October, 1966, p. 310.*

Lloyd Alexander has attempted a great deal in **The Book of Three.** To start with, he has combined comedy with fairy-tale poetry in a way which demands greater literary originality than he shows here. . . . The book is full of echoes—of Tolkien and Garner, of Masefield and T. H. White; perhaps with only one of these models, or influences, it would be better.

> *Margery Fisher, in her review of ''The Book of Three,'' in her* Growing Point, *Vol. 5, No. 5, November, 1966, p. 792.*

A very fine fantasy-adventure with its roots in the Mabinogion. Not in the same class as Tolkien perhaps, but with a quite compelling magic of its own.

> *A review of ''The Book of Three,'' in* The Times Literary Supplement *(© Times Newspapers Ltd. (London) 1966; reproduced from* The Times Literary Supplement *by permission), No. 3378, November 24, 1966, p. 1089.*

THE BLACK CAULDRON   (1965)

The chronicles of Prydain, begun in **The Book of Three,** are continued here, but each book is complete in itself. . . . The same kind of engagingly fantastic nonsense lightens this story as it did the first one; but the overtones here are more truly heroic. The reader's involvement is intense as the excitement leads up to the climactic meeting of tragedy and triumph. An exalting experience for the fortunate children whose imaginations are ready for great fantasy.

> *Ruth Hill Viguers, in her review of ''The Black Cauldron,'' in* The Horn Book Magazine *(copyright © 1965, by The Horn Book, Inc., Boston), Vol. XLI, No. 3, June, 1965, p. 274.*

[**The Black Cauldron**] is the second book of a trilogy based on old Welsh legends. This involves the use of old Welsh names, which in large numbers can daunt the reader considerably. However, once you have sorted out Eilonwy from Ellidyr, and realized that Fflewddur Fflam is a person and Drynwyn is not, you can enjoy the story, which is exciting and well-constructed. The sharp rivalry between the main characters is effective, and there are three really spine-chilling witches, and nearly every chapter ends on a cliff-edge of suspense. Unfortunately the author tries too hard to be funny as well as dramatic, and the result is a forced flippancy out of keeping with the main theme of noble warriors and self-sacrificing heroes.

> *"Over the Dream Wall," in* The Times Literary Supplement *(© Times Newspapers Ltd. (London) 1967; reproduced from* The Times Literary Supplement *by permission), No. 3404, May 25, 1967, p. 451.**

This second book, following **The Book of Three,** has no outstanding qualities. The story-telling is fairly fluent, but in every way the two volumes fall well below the works of Lewis, Tolkien, Garner and others who work in the tradition Mr. Alexander evidently tries to follow. A fundamental difficulty which Taran and his rather tiresome associates set out to wrest from the Lord of the Underworld, produces living dead—dead men, obtained by murder or robbing graves, emerge from it as unkillable dehumanised warriors in the service of whoever put them in. This is not a subject to introduce lightly into a child's book, though familiar enough in horror-comics, and once introduced it should be honestly and seriously considered, but Mr. Alexander has simply played around the edges in both books. There are two sacrifices, not counting Taran's continual forbearance, one made by a good and noble knight, one by a bog-knight's son who destroys the cauldron along with himself after behaving so dishonourably. The solution is obvious long before the end. Set against English legends and original fantasy it seems a thin, strained tale with no music in it at all.

> *A review of "The Black Cauldron," in* The Junior Bookshelf, *Vol. 31, No. 3, June, 1967, p. 175.*

The second instalment of the adventures of Taran . . . is distinctly better than the first, **The Book of Three.** The self-conscious humour is kept within bounds and the plot is tighter and better organised. . . . The author adds no real note of individuality to his echoes of Tolkien and the Mabinogion except perhaps in one or two of the non-knightly characters (like the melancholy dwarf Gwystyl or the three witches of the marsh); but there is always room for this kind of magical-heroic tale even if this one does not reach the literary heights which have occasionally been claimed for it.

> *Margery Fisher, in her review of "The Black Cauldron," in her* Growing Point, *Vol. 6, No. 2, July, 1967, p. 941.*

COLL AND HIS WHITE PIG (1965)

In **The Book of Three** reference is made to the time Hen Wen the pig was kidnaped, because of her oracular powers, by the Lord of the Land of Death. This is the tale of how Coll, with the help of Ash-Wing the owl, Oak-Horn the stag, and Star-Nose the mole, found Hen Wen and brought her back to Prydain. The skillfully told story, combined with paintings in glorious colors [by Evaline Ness]—some of the artist's best work—makes an exciting picture-story book that will give young children a glimpse into the mythical land they will know when they are a bit older and read **The Book of Three** and **The Black Cauldron.**

> *Ruth Hill Viguers, in her review of "Coll and His White Pig," in* The Horn Book Magazine *(copyright © 1965, by The Horn Book, Inc., Boston), Vol. XLI, No. 6, December, 1965, p. 619.*

The [Prydain] tales are rather lush, bristling with incidents, descriptions and a great variety of characters that are difficult for all but avid readers to follow. It was a happy thought, therefore, to take an incident from the first of these tales—the loss of the pig, Hen Wen, belonging to Coll, the farmer—and make it into a short story for younger children. It is a good short story on the time-honored theme: "What truly counts is not a strong arm but a kind heart; not a fist that smites, but a hand that helps."

> *Margaret Sherwood Libby, "Helping Hands, and Feet," in* Book Week—New York Herald Tribune *(© 1966, The Washington Post), January 30, 1966, p. 16.**

THE CASTLE OF LLYR (1966)

In a new story about the mythical land of Prydain, the Princess Eilonwy is captured and bewitched by the wicked enchantress Achren. . . . The story reaches dramatic heights with the struggle against the magical powers of Achren to restore Eilonwy to reality. Although this third book showing the growth of Taran, the young Assistant Pig-Keeper, toward noble manhood may not reach the powerful heights of **The Black Cauldron,** it has its own strong identity. Children can enjoy it without having read the other books, but they will most certainly want the others once they have entered Prydain (a helpful map of the country is included) and met the brave but strangely assorted companions. And they will look forward to further adventures, for Taran and Eilonwy still have room to grow. (pp. 304-05)

> *Ruth Hill Viguers, in her review of "The Castle of Llyr," in* The Horn Book Magazine *(copyright © 1966, by The Horn Book, Inc., Boston), Vol. XLII, No. 3, June, 1966, pp. 304-05.*

The story has plenty of action, and there is much in it to enjoy, but **"The Black Cauldron"** is still my favourite of the trilogy. **"The Castle of Llyr"** has neither the simplicity of **"The Book of Three"** nor the tremendous dramatic power of **"The Black Cauldron"**; the author did not intend that it would have; he states in his introductory note that the mood is "bitter-sweet rather than grandly heroic". Perhaps it is unfair to criticize the book for not being something that it was never intended to be. But the best of **"The Castle of Llyr"** is the parts that *are* almost "grandly heroic"; it is only in these later chapters that the characters re-emerge fully as the memorable "companions" of the previous two books—just in time to make the reader question whether the chronicles of Prydain can really be contained in a trilogy. And to hope that they cannot. (p. 259)

> *N. Danischewsky, in her review of "The Castle of Llyr," in* Children's Book News *(copyright © 1968 by Baker Book Services Ltd.), Vol. 3, No. 5, September-October, 1968, pp. 257, 259.*

[**The Castle of Llyr**] is an adventure which, in spite of one or two exciting moments, is in the main padded and inflated but basically pedestrian. This is a far cry from the Mabinogion from which it is said to derive.

> *Margery Fisher, in her review of "The Castle of Llyr," in her* Growing Point, *Vol. 7, No. 4, October, 1968, p. 1193.*

TARAN WANDERER (1967)

Lloyd Alexander has fashioned, in the series of which this is the fourth, one of the enduring realms of fantasy. Taran, now grown to manhood, leaves Caer Dallben and travels through the land of Prydain searching for a clue to his identity. He feels ne must know whether or not he is of noble enough birth to wed the princess he loves. . . . The story has a nice balance of humor and poignant sadness.

> *Zena Sutherland, in her review of "Taran Wanderer," in* Saturday Review *(© 1967 Saturday Review Magazine Co.; reprinted by permission), Vol. L, No. 11, March 18, 1967, p. 36.*

Taran, the assistant pig keeper for the wizard Dallben, has been growing steadily since **The Book of Three.** Now a teenager in pre-Medieval Prydain, Taran still smarts with ambition, still aches to know who his parents were, who he is and what he dares become. Taran follows the oracular hints of a bilious witch, and the comic and adventurous interludes of the surface story close around a core of eternal realities. By telescoping the time required, the author shows Taran learning to weave his own cloak and forge his own sword and failing to achieve a personal vision of beauty while learning how to throw clay. Here is an introduction to the ideals of craftsmanship and its demands, ideals difficult to present without preachiness in our mass production-mass culture society. They are perfectly natural and most persuasive in this setting, rich with figures and events drawn from Welsh legends. Taran's search for identity brings him closer to self-discovery and self-discipline than it does to his genealogy. Therefore, and happily, there will be another book. This is an independent title in the strongest fantasy series being created for children in our time.

> *Lillian N. Gerhardt, in her review of "Taran Wanderer," in* School Library Journal, *an appendix to* Library Journal *(reprinted from the May, 1967 issue of* School Library Journal, *published by R. R. Bowker Co./A Xerox Corporation; copyright © 1967), Vol. 13, No. 9, May, 1967, p. 61.*

This is a wise and noble book, learned with the same humor that the other three boasted. The Taran of this book is a far cry from the Assistant Pig-Keeper who was so disappointed when his hero, Prince Gwydion, looked so little like Taran's dream of him. There is nothing childish or silly about Taran now. The great adventures he had in the previous three books and his love for Princess Eilonwy have given him a measure of strength and wisdom, but in this book he matures enough to accept failure and disappointment and gains much in insight and understanding.

There are as many exciting and frightening adventures in this book as there are in the others, and many of the characters reappear. . . . On the level of excitement and adventure it is tops, the more serious level, it is even better. This series ranks with the Narnia books and comes close to Tolkien's Hobbit books. They need readers who can bring imagination, perception, and a degree of maturity to them, and they offer a full measure of entertainment and involvement.

> *Phyllis Cohen, in her review of "Taran Wanderer," in* Young Reader's Review *(copyright © 1967 Young Readers Review), Vol. III, No. 10, June, 1967, p. 12.*

Out of the succession of fairy tales Lloyd Alexander has been writing, the Prydain cycle, I like best **Taran Wanderer,** the story of Taran's search for his parents. Each episode of Taran's quest is absorbingly told and freshly seen (not an easy task considering that the tale of quest has such a long and distinguished tradition), and the truth of each episode brought out in such a way as to build strongly toward the moment of Taran's final illumination. (p. 240)

> *Eleanor Cameron, "The Child and the Book," in her* The Green and Burning Tree: On the Writing and Enjoyment of Children's Books *(copyright © 1962, 1964, 1966, 1969 by Eleanor Cameron; reprinted by permission of Little, Brown and Company in association with The Atlantic Monthly Press), Atlantic-Little, Brown, 1969, pp. 231-76.**

THE TRUTHFUL HARP (1967)

It had better be said right out loud—your reviewer is not one whom Lloyd Alexander had enthralled—until **"The Truthful Harp."** But he captured me with this one: its light-hearted quality, its Baron Munchausen hero and its happy ending captured me. I can even overlook the cuteness of those f's in the hero's name, Fflewddur, because he isn't a cute hero, but an endearing one.

> *A review of "The Truthful Harp," in* Publishers Weekly *(reprinted from the November 20, 1967 issue of* Publishers Weekly, *published by R. R. Bowker Company; copyright © 1967 by R. R. Bowker Company), Vol. 197, No. 21, November 20, 1967, p. 56.*

The Truthful Harp is outstanding for originality both in story and [Evaline Ness's] illustrations. . . .

[The] reader closes the book reluctantly, longing for the next adventure.

> *Martha Bennett King, in her review of "The Truthful Harp," in* Book World—Chicago Tribune *(© 1967 Postrib Corp.; reprinted by permission of Chicago Tribune and The Washington Post), November 26, 1967, p. 16.*

As he did in **Coll and His White Pig,** the author tells a short story through a picture book about one of the characters in his continuing chronicles of pre-medieval Prydain. . . . Fflewddur Fflam, rustic king of a one-horse country and unsuccessful bard, has served multiple functions in the Prydain series. Whenever the pages darken with battle passages or close escapes from entrapments conjured by evil magicians, Fflam, who always fights or behaves bravely, can be counted on to give immediate, grandiloquently reorganized and enlarged recollections of the event. Each time he stretches the truth, a string on his beloved harp breaks. Children, who know all about instant punishment for clumsily self-serving distortions of fact, can find the necessary comic relief in Fflam. Adult book selectors can recognize a gentle satire on oral history's unreliability and the celebrators' irresistible urge to make good tales taller. This account of Fflam's acquisition of his conscience-striking harp belongs with Alexander's longer books, although it can stand alone as one of the very few amusing stories for younger children about growth in self-discipline.

> *Lillian Gerhardt, in her review of "The Truthful Harp," in* School Library Journal, *an appendix to* Library Journal *(reprinted from the December, 1967 issue of* School Library Journal, *published by R. R. Bowker Co./A Xerox Corporation; copyright © 1967), Vol. 14, No. 4, December, 1967, p. 66.*

THE HIGH KING   (1968)

This is a tremendously satisfying finish to what was so well begun in *The Book of Three* four years ago. . . . The long-standing questions of orphaned Taran's heritage and the difference between royalty and nobility are adroitly handled. The author dedicates this book to ''. . . the boys who might have been Taran and the girls who will always be Eilonwy'' and that takes in just about all the confirmed romantic readers today between the ages of 10 and 14 and all the readers to come for the strongest high fantasy written for children in our times.

> *Lillian N. Gerhardt, in her review of ''The High King,'' in* School Library Journal, *an appendix to* Library Journal *(reprinted from the February, 1968 issue of* School Library Journal, *published by R. R. Bowker Co./A Xerox Corporation; copyright © 1968), Vol. 14, No. 6, February, 1968, p. 86.*

For the admirers of Lloyd Alexander, and their name is legion, it will be news both glad and sad that he has written the finale to his chronicles of Prydain. . . . In the tradition of Tolkien's fantasies, it will appeal to the same dedicated readers.

> *A review of ''The High King,'' in* Publishers Weekly *(reprinted from the March 11, 1968 issue of* Publishers Weekly, *published by R. R. Bowker Company, a Xerox company; copyright © 1968 by Xerox Corporation), Vol. 193, No. 11, March 11, 1968, p. 49.*

With the publication of this fifth volume in the saga of Taran, the assistant Pig-keeper, and the story of the fate of the kingdom of Prydain, Lloyd Alexander brings to a close one of the best fantasy tales of the last ten years. There is action a-plenty and wondrous events enough to charm not only the younger readers it is obviously intended for, but also the more mature who find fascination in a well-plotted, well-written tale. . . . It may not be as complicated and erudite as J.R.R. Tolkien's ''Fellowship of the Ring'' trilogy, but in its own special province it has much of the same enchantment.

> *A review of ''The High King,'' in* Best Sellers *(copyright 1968, by the University of Scranton), Vol. 28, No. 3, May 1, 1968, p. 62.*

The squeals of delight from the children who have already become acquainted with the Land of Prydain through the earlier books of Lloyd Alexander's series will rend the air when they encounter the concluding volume, ''**The High King**''. . . . This is imaginative literature at its finest. Adventure, mystery, suspense, humor, the supernatural, the struggle between good and evil are blended into a story rich with overtones and undertones. . . . The heroic qualities developed by the overcoming of fears propel events to a startling conclusion. While this volume can be read independently, it will be most meaningful to those who have followed Taran through ''**The Book of Three**,'' ''**The Black Cauldron**,'' ''**The Castle of Llyr**,'' and ''**Taran Wanderer**.''

> *Marjorie D. Hamlin, ''Far Back and Far Out,'' in* The Christian Science Monitor *(reprinted by permission from* The Christian Science Monitor; *© 1968 The Christian Science Publishing Society; all rights reserved), May 2, 1968, p. B8.**

Considering the high level of excitement which characterized the first four volumes, it is something of a wonder that the author has managed to summon the requisite surge of energy and dramatic power to provide so fitting a grand finale. The many and devious threads of mystery are all adroitly knitted together and there is a gratifying sense of resolution and fulfillment, especially in the melancholy awareness that the time of heroes and magic is at an end, as the Sons of Don depart for the land of everlasting youth while Taran and his princess elect to remain and shoulder the burdens of a new age.

In retrospect, the author's total creation is a remarkable achievement, a rich and varied tapestry of brooding evil, heroic action and great natural beauty, vividly conceived, romantic in mood yet curiously contemporary in its immediacy and fast action. Perhaps less winning has been his weakness for opéra-bouffe comic relief in the form of the subsidiary characters, a number of whom are little more than tiresome running jokes. The bald appeal to juvenile risibilities is, in the end, rather too calculated, and inconsistent with the eloquence and grandeur of the best episodes. A shame if this element should limit the story to a young audience, when there are riches here for every age.

> *Houston L. Maples, in his review of ''The High King,'' in* Book World—The Washington Post *(© 1968 Postrib Corp.; reprinted by permission of* Chicago Tribune *and* The Washington Post*), May 5, 1968, p. 22.*

High adventure and emotional richness support the magical in the epic stories of Lloyd Alexander, who in *The High King,* completes the splendid chronicles of the land of Prydain. . . .

Mr. Alexander's gift is perhaps the greatest of all [compared to Joan Aiken and Jack Sendak]; his kingdom and annals of Prydain are so complete, so compelling, that the reader leaves them for the last time with genuine regret.

> *Robert Ostermann, ''Three Authors Soar on Flights of Fancy to Never-Never Land,'' in* The National Observer *(reprinted by permission of* The National Observer; *© Dow Jones & Company, Inc. 1968; all rights reserved), September 23, 1968, p. 21.**

THE MARVELOUS MISADVENTURES OF SEBASTIAN   (1970)

A solid adventure story, with likable protagonists. . . . Sebastian is a young fiddler, not overly dedicated but enjoying his relatively easy life in a country baron's household. But the kingdom is growing uneasy under politically and financially repressive rule of the Regent Grinssorg, as Sebastian discovers when he loses his place with the baron and must seek his future elsewhere. When he meets the runaway Princess Isabel, his wanderings take on a new purpose: to help the orphaned girl escape forced marriage to the Regent. Sebastian and Isabel are befriended by mild-mannered Nicholas, who turns out to be the chief organizer of popular resistance to the Regent; they join a circus, and Sebastian acquires a strange fiddle which produces music of unearthly beauty and power and which eventually helps him to decide on his future course. The action—both physical (a multitude of narrow escapes) and psychological (the gradual humanization of haughty Isabel)—will hold young readers' attention; and the characters, whether sympathetic, like Nicholas, or villainous, like the bloodthirsty barber who dogs Sebastian's steps, are similarly involving. When he's not trying to be profound and epic, as in the Prydain books, Mr. Alexander writes a jolly good story and still manages to provide his readers with plenty of food for thought.

Margaret A. Dorsey, in her review of "The Marvelous Misadventures of Sebastian," in School Library Journal, *an appendix to* Library Journal *(reprinted from the November, 1970 issue of* School Library Journal, *published by R. R. Bowker Co./A Xerox Corporation; copyright © 1970), Vol. 17, No. 3, November, 1970, p. 104.*

Lloyd Alexander's untrammeled imagination has produced a swift, vivacious tale, set in a vaguely eighteenth-century, middle-European, rococo world. . . .

The characters speak in the extravagant accents of the opera buffa, and, while not profoundly conceived, are consistently engaging in their energy and panache. This is effortless entertainment from an author who knows how to please and obviously enjoys himself at the same time.

Houston L. Maples, in his review of "The Marvelous Misadventures of Sebastian," in Book World—The Washington Post *(© 1970 Postrib Corp.; reprinted by permission of* Chicago Tribune *and* The Washington Post*), November 8, 1970, p. 10.*

A colorful, romantic tale about a naive but plucky fiddle player. . . . The story has an intriguing cast of characters and exhibits the author's flair for wit and irony.

A review of "The Marvelous Misadventures of Sebastian," in The Booklist *(reprinted by permission of the American Library Association; copyright © 1970 by the American Library Association), Vol. 67, No. 6, November 15, 1970, p. 266.*

Had this book been created by anyone but Lloyd Alexander, the reader could dismiss it as being too conventional: an adventure story of mean tyrants, princesses in distress and daring heroes. But Mr. Alexander . . . is not an ordinary writer. . . . It is all very eloquent, action-packed and ridiculous; but hybrids are the author's special talent. His prose is a disarming mixture of Regency grandeur and Medieval robustness. His plot uses and discards a dozen clichés of children's books without batting an eye. Most important, he knows how to write character in a way that can touch the heart.

Barbara Wersba, in her review of "The Marvelous Misadventures of Sebastian," in The New York Times Book Review *(© 1970 by The New York Times Company; reprinted by permission), November 15, 1970, p. 42.*

THE KING'S FOUNTAIN (1971)

Here is a beautiful book, a moving parable of a modest man who saves his city because he cares about the people who live there. It is a beautiful book to read (out loud if possible). . . . Lloyd Alexander has never written with a cleaner pen. . . .

A review of "The King's Fountain," in Publishers Weekly *(reprinted from the May 24, 1971 issue of* Publishers Weekly, *published by R. R. Bowker Company, a Xerox company; copyright © 1971 by Xerox Corporation), Vol. 199, No. 21, May 24, 1971, p. 69.*

Once upon a time a king planned a fountain for his palace garden that would have cut off the water supply for those who lived in the town below. Neither the strong man, the sage, nor the silver-tongued tradesman would intercede, so the poor man who had asked their help went to the king himself. While the

humorous gibes may not be clear to children ("The scholar wrote a long account of the matter in one of his books, and misplaced it.") the message that you cannot expect others to act for you will. Beautiful.

Zena Sutherland, in her review of "The King's Fountain," in Saturday Review *(© 1971 Saturday Review Magazine Co.; reprinted by permission), Vol. LIV, No. 25, June 19, 1971, p. 26.*

THE CAT WHO WISHED TO BE A MAN (1973)

Lionel, a wizard's cat, persuades his master to turn him into a man so that he may go to Brightford and learn what humans are like. The wizard warns him that he will find only greed and corruption, and he does. . . . However, Lionel also finds courage and determination in Gillian, who is resisting Mayor Pursewig's attempts to take over her inn, and kindness and loyalty in the Latin-spouting Dr. Tudbelly. . . . Infused with humor, high spirits and compassion, Lionel's story is a parable of the human condition that recognizes mankind's many frailties without despairing and offers hope that love and justice may sometimes prevail.

Linda R. Silver, in her review of "The Cat Who Wished to Be a Man," in School Library Journal, *an appendix to* Library Journal *(reprinted from the September 15, 1973 issue of* School Library Journal, *published by R. R. Bowker Co./A Xerox Corporation; copyright © 1973), Vol. 20, No. 1, September 15, 1973, p. 2647.*

And now for the book not to get—**"The Cat Who Wished to be a Man"**. . . . Lloyd Alexander, who in 1971 won the National Book Award in Children's Books, didn't write a prize winner this time. . . . [It] is slightly pretentious—trying too hard to be a fantasy—and fails to hold the reader's interest.

The story is adequate, but fairy tales must be more than that to rate a niche on the discriminating bookshelf and be read happily ever after.

June Goodwin, "Once and Twice Upon a Time," in The Christian Science Monitor *(reprinted by permission from* The Christian Science Monitor; *© 1973 The Christian Science Publishing Society; all rights reserved), November 7, 1973, p. B5.*

Theme in fine fantasy can be simple if the story itself is simple in tone and mood. . . . The brilliant, light-hearted story of *The Cat Who Wished to Be a Man* . . . says that people can be corrupt and mean but that it's wonderful to be a person after all. Alexander has the good grace to leave it at that. He doesn't break the mood to try to explain that this theme is profound. (p. 194)

Sam Leaton Sebesta and William J. Iverson, in their review of "The Cat Who Wished to Be a Man," in their Literature for Thursday's Child *(© 1975, Science Research Associates, Inc.; reprinted by permission of the publisher), Science Research Associates, 1975, p. 194.**

THE FOUNDLING AND OTHER TALES OF PRYDAIN (1973)

To read before or after the chronicles of Prydain, these six tales enlarge upon and explain "certain threads left unraveled in the longer weaving." (Even Gurgi would give up his "rumblings and grumblings" to read these!)

Lillian N. Gerhardt, in her review of "The Foundling and Other Tales of Prydain," in School Library Journal, *an appendix to* Library Journal *(reprinted from the December, 1973 issue of* School Library Journal, *published by R. R. Bowker Co./A Xerox Corporation; copyright © 1973), Vol. 20, No. 4, December, 1973, p. 30.*

Lovers of the five books about Prydain which feature Taran the Assistant Pig-Keeper will doubtless greet this book with joy. . . . Some readers will feel a certain disappointment with this book—it's awfully slight—but others will be delighted to add it to their other books by Alexander.

A review of "The Foundling and Other Tales of Prydain," in Publishers Weekly *(reprinted from the January 7, 1974 issue of* Publishers Weekly, *published by R. R. Bowker Company, a Xerox company; copyright © 1974 by Xerox Corporation), Vol. 205, No. 1, January 7, 1974, p. 54.*

THE WIZARD IN THE TREE (1975)

Deft storytelling weaves together the fate of a dauntless orphan girl Mallory and an ancient enchanter Arbican. . . . Trying to leave for Vale Innis involves the reluctant Arbican in rescuing Mallory from a life of drudgery and in saving an old-fashioned English village almost doomed, by the villain's exploitive plan, to a black future in coalmining. The enchanter's loss of control over his powers during his long entrapment provides some funny as well as tense moments, while the handful of Dickensian characters—a murderous squire, cookshop shrew, kind-but-weak husband, fair-minded notary, and miscellany of country folk—plays out a script graced with quotable bits of wisdom about the real nature of magic.

A review of "The Wizard in the Tree," in The Booklist *(reprinted by permission of the American Library Association; copyright © 1975 by the American Library Association) Vol. 71, No. 15, April 1, 1975, p. 813.*

Long years spent stuck inside an old oak tree haven't petrified the wizard Arbican's tongue. On the contrary, he is glad to escape the boredom ("It's the same slow, vegetable sort of business over and over again. One tends to lose interest") and he is positively scathing when Mallory, the girl who rescues him, demands her three wishes. . . . However it seems his wizard powers have gone rusty and he soon needs Mallory's help to escape the persecution of Squire Scrupnor, the villain who has already murdered her employer, saddled Mallory's guardians with a ruinous "hypothecation" (mortgage) and plotted to turn the whole village into a coal field. Arbican survives a number of aborted spells, including one that turns him into a talking pig. . . . But of course in the end we have our cake and eat it too; after being warned against reliance on wishful thinking, we are given a wonderfully efficient magical solution. The period is the beginning of the industrial revolution, but the tempo is reminiscent of the **Marvelous Misadventures of Sebastian**—quick-witted melodrama and nimble-tongued romanticism.

A review of "The Wizard in the Tree," in Kirkus Reviews *(copyright © 1975 The Kirkus Service, Inc.), Vol. XLIII, No. 8, April 15, 1975, p. 451.*

The combination of magic gone awry and earthly danger has all the elements that kids love—broad humor, cliff-hanging suspense, villains to hiss, and a heroine to cheer. Independent readers will love it, and **Wizard** . . . will make a fine read-aloud as well.

Marjorie Lewis, in her review of "The Wizard in the Tree," in School Library Journal *(reprinted from the May, 1975 issue of* School Library Journal, *published by R. R. Bowker Co./A Xerox Corporation; copyright © 1975), Vol. 21, No. 9, May, 1975, p. 45.*

THE TOWN CATS AND OTHER TALES (1977)

Eight fanciful, sparkling fairy tales, all demonstrating, in Alexander's words, that cats are "more sensible than the rest of us." They're certainly cleverer here: cat Pescato, masquerading as the mayor, saves the remote town of Valdoro, in Mondragone, from official harrassment; another, Margot, fools a tyrannical king into allowing his daughter's love-match; a wise, feline "Master of Revels" rewards a young musician's kindness and fidelity; and the rest variously one-up their human acquaintances by playing to their greed, pride, or vanity. In the last story a cat who has failed at a number of apprenticeships proves himself a "master at being a cat"; those who appreciate that talent—and consider it sufficiently various—will find Alexander too a light-footed master of graceful entertainment.

A review of "The Town Cats and Other Tales," in Kirkus Reviews *(copyright © 1977 The Kirkus Service, Inc.), Vol. XLV, No. 20, October 15, 1977, p. 1096.*

Though some of the pieces definitely outshine others, this is an enjoyable grouping, slyly humorous and treated lightly.

Sara Miller, in her review of "The Town Cats and Other Tales," in School Library Journal *(reprinted from the November, 1977 issue of* School Library Journal, *published by R. R. Bowker Co./A Xerox Corporation; copyright © 1977), Vol. 24, No. 3, November, 1977, p. 52.*

There is no question about Lloyd Alexander's heroes. They are welcome additions—all eight of them—obviously equal to more formidable dangers and more baffling problems than you or I could dream of. They have the advantage, of course, of being cats, especially of being Lloyd Alexander's cats. So it should not be surprising that they display such creative genius, such feline style, as they go about setting the world to rights. . . .

The language is delicious and the moral is clear. We should pay more attention to cats, especially to Lloyd Alexander's cats. (p. 63)

Jean Fritz, "Six by Winners," in The New York Times Book Review *(© 1977 by The New York Times Company; reprinted by permission), November 13, 1977, pp. 37, 63.**

The stories appear to be set in various countries and resemble European folk tales; each one shows a cat as a devoted, loyal, but independent creature—and wiser than human beings. . . . The author is well known for his esteem and affection for cats, and there are few writers better qualified to give them their due. An excellent collection for reading or storytelling. . . .

Ann A. Flowers, in her review of "The Town Cats and Other Tales," in The Horn Book Magazine *(copyright © 1978 by the Horn Book, Inc., Boston), Vol. LIV, No. 1, February, 1978, p. 42.*

THE FIRST TWO LIVES OF LUKAS-KASHA (1978)

Emerging from a river to find himself king of an exotic and dangerous world, former ne'er-do-well Lukas rises grandly to the occasion, placing more demands upon himself than are imposed by the situation, while occasionally berating the shabby traveling conjurer who seems to have transported him there— though Lukas doesn't know if the man has power to snatch him back or even if he can hear Lukas calling him. Costume existentialism? Not so you'd notice. For Lukas ends up securely back in his old familiar town, and though his maturing adventure in Shirazan takes only a few seconds from his "real life," it fills the book with escapades, battles, colorful encounters, loyal friendships, and clever schemes—all part of pacifist Lukas' campaign to wrest power from a palace strongman and bring peace and autonomy to the people. Felicitously spun, ingeniously framed adventure.

> *A review of "The First Two Lives of Lukas-Kasha," in* Kirkus Reviews *(copyright © 1978 The Kirkus Service, Inc.), Vol. XLVI, No. 16, August 15, 1978, p. 878.*

Having won singular honors for his many books, Alexander is now represented by a fantasy so original, told in such imaginative English, that it may be considered his peak performance.

> *A review of "The First Two Lives of Lukas-Kasha," in* Publishers Weekly *(reprinted from the October 30, 1978 issue of* Publishers Weekly, *published by R. R. Bowker Company, a Xerox company; copyright © 1978 by Xerox Corporation), Vol. 214, No. 18, October 30, 1978, p. 50.*

Occasionally an author gets an idea for a book that suits his or her individual talents so perfectly that the end result is not another book but a work of art. [Lloyd Alexander has had that fortunate experience and, happily, has had it again.] . . .

Lloyd Alexander's **The First Two Lives of Lukas-Kasha** is an exceptional book, filled with lively dialogue, fun and high adventure. . . .

[It] is Lukas-Kasha who makes the book outstanding. As he changes from a superficial rogue to a young man who cares deeply about the lives of his fellow men, he becomes one of the most appealing characters in recent children's literature. Yet, all the while he remains himself. . . .

The author's skill in making the kingdom of Abadan and its inhabitants real is so great that when Lukas-Kasha falls into the sea and is abruptly transported back to the magician's wagon, the reader shares his shock and disbelief. Lukas (as well as the reader) recovers, however, and in the end Lukas goes out into the world to become a storyteller. His first effort, told to a group of travelers in a courtyard, begins "'Once, in the kingdom of Abadan. . . .'"

This book is great fun to read and is never sober. Moreover, any book which makes non-violence attractive and enforces the value of human life has to be taken seriously.

> *Betsy Byars, "King Kasha and Kim Chu," in* Book World—The Washington Post *(© 1978, The Washington Post), November 12, 1978, p. E4.* *

Lloyd Alexander is one of the most respected names in children's literature. For years he has continued to produce books that are high in literary quality and rich in entertainment, and this is such a large thing to achieve that one has been grateful to have Mr. Alexander in the field. His contribution has been enormous, his books have won prizes. But his newest effort, at least to this reviewer, is less than satisfying.

Perhaps we have gone beyond the days when children's stories could deal over and over again with courts and kings, escaped slave girls and rascals who become virtuous under stress. Or perhaps Mr. Alexander has simply failed to dust off these materials and make them shine. At any rate, **"The First Two Lives of Lukas-Kasha"** made me feel that I had just seen an old movie on television: one starring Tony Curtis and Virginia Mayo and set in Hollywood's idea of ancient Persia. . . .

[We soon meet] a number of people who are distressingly familiar: Nur-Jehan, the slave girl with a mysterious past; Shugdad, the wicked Grand Vizier; and Kayim, a merry and irreverent versifier. And as the plot thickens so does our tedium, for it all seems to have happened before. One does not enjoy criticizing a writer as good as Lloyd Alexander—but at this point in his career, it might be wise to leave the swashbuckling behind.

> *Barbara Wersba, "Six Novels," in* The New York Times Book Review *(© 1978 by The New York Times Company; reprinted by permission), December 10, 1978, p. 85.* *

Alexander is in top form in this sparkling fantasy. Characterization is marvelous, structure convoluted, and dialogue brilliant. Word games abound as in an extended, tension-building, good news/bad news report. The intrinsic venality and inevitable corruption that mark the grasp for power are the subject of numerous sly observations. The dependence on astrological interpretations and the ability to bend predictions to support whatever one wishes to believe are the object of much hilarity. Delightful wit, a good sense of pacing, and a fine sense of place and language characterize this enchanting tale. (p. 81)

> *Barbara H. Baskin and Karen H. Harris, "A Selected Guide to Intellectually Demanding Books," in their* Books for the Gifted Child *(reprinted with permission of the R. R. Bowker; copyright © 1980 by Xerox Corporation), Bowker, 1980, pp. 75-250.* *

WESTMARK (1981)

A multi-layered picaresque novel that raises questions with no pat answers, yet manages to satisfy readers. . . . Rich language, excellent characterization, detailed descriptions and a dovetailed plot equal superb craftsmanship. Alexander has done it again.

> *Patricia Manning, in her review of "Westmark," in* School Library Journal *(reprinted from the May, 1981 issue of* School Library Journal, *published by R. R. Bowker Co./A Xerox Corporation; copyright © 1981), Vol. 27, No. 9, May, 1981, p. 62.*

Lloyd Alexander is obviously a bard who has traveled the roads of many kingdoms, perfecting the art of storytelling and becoming ever more wise in the ways of humankind. Like a juggler, he keeps four stories going at once in this book: tossing them lightly apart, calling them together, crisscrossing their paths until at last he has described a complete circle. Of course there is always the danger that power-hungry Cabbarus, chief minister to a grieving, ineffective king, will bring the other stories crashing down to an evil end. He comes close to it many times. He tries to drown a princess, cage a so-called magician and to run down an idealistic young printer's apprentice.

The wisdom of the book lies in its difficult solution: good does not triumph over evil simply because it *is* good. Theo, the printer's apprentice, may think so at first when he wants to face his accusers and confront injustice head-on. Yet is he himself completely innocent? He had always believed in his own good nature, but he finds himself lying, swindling, even trying to kill. He may be acting in the cause of justice, but still—"What kind of person does that make me?" he asks.

"No different from anyone else," he is told.

Lloyd Alexander does not answer questions; he raises them. Who can be certain what he'll do in any given situation? Can right even exist in a pure form? As grave as these considerations are, Mr. Alexander keeps his adventures spinning and in the end we are happy at how it all turns out. Moreover, we have a better understanding of his dedication: "For those who regret their many imperfections, but know it would be worse having none at all."

> *Jean Fritz, in her review of "Westmark," in* The New York Times Book Review *(© 1981 by The New York Times Company; reprinted by permission), May 10, 1981, p. 38.*

A superb craftsman, Alexander has concocted a marvelous tale of high adventure, replete with a lost princess, an engaging scoundrel, a modest orphan-hero, and an enjoyably hateful villain, and he makes them and their adventures wholly credible. . . . [There's] a smash ending, the way for which has been artfully paved, in a story that includes some amusing incidents with a con man and his troupe, a love story, some good chase scenes, and some militant action by those who rebel against the regime. Indeed, the political situation in Westmark gives the author scope for some pithy comments on oppressive governance. Lloyd Alexander is a master of writing dialogue, of blending many facets and plot threads into a smooth whole, and above all of conceiving characters with depth and conviction. (pp. 185-86)

> *Zena Sutherland, in her review of "Westmark," in* Bulletin of the Center for Children's Books *(reprinted by permission of The University of Chicago Press; © 1981 by The University of Chicago), Vol. 34, No. 10, June, 1981, pp. 185-86.*

The author's most inventive book in many years is both a picaresque novel and an energetic cloak-and-dagger tale with a climax as breathtaking as that of a Douglas Fairbanks film. . . . Adroitly the author maneuvers the crisscrossing threads of his complex, but brilliantly controlled, plot, which is filled with bloodshed, intrigue, ghostly apparitions, disguises, and trickery. Lacing the storytelling with incisive epigrammatic wit, he presents the reader with the age-old perplexities of right and wrong, human weakness and decency, the temptation of power, and the often unclear call of conscience. (pp. 428-29)

> *Ethel L. Heins, in her review of "Westmark," in* The Horn Book Magazine *(copyright © 1981 by The Horn Book, Inc., Boston), Vol. LVII, No. 4, August, 1981, pp. 428-29.*

[*Westmark* is] among Alexander's finest. . . . The author writes that *Westmark* "let me explore ideas that have concerned me for some while, and work with a fascinating range of characters; Mickle, the street girl; Theo, the young fugitive haunted by a

crime he wanted to commit; kings, queens, conniving courtiers, revolutionaries, spiritualists. *Westmark* isn't a fantasy but it is, I hope, no less fantastic." No less fantastic than the creator of a *tour de force* whose theme lies in its dedication: "For those who regret their many imperfections, but know it would be worse having none at all." A book to hug to one's heart.

> *Ruth M. Stein, in her review of "Westmark" (copyright © 1981 by the National Council of Teachers of English; reprinted by permission of the publisher and the author), in* Language Arts, *Vol. 58, No. 7, October, 1981, p. 847.*

Lloyd Alexander is back with a rousing tale that gives promise of becoming at least a trilogy. . . . Though the ending is foreshadowed, the strength of the story is in the explorations of the characters into the meaning of good and evil. This is accomplished in an exciting and adventurous story replete with the marvelous facility for language play that Alexander always exhibits.

> *M. Jean Greenlaw, in her review of "Westmark" (copyright 1981 by the International Reading Association, Inc.; reprinted with permission of the International Reading Association and M. Jean Greenlaw), in* Journal of Reading, *Vol. 25, No. 3, December, 1981, p. 288.*

THE KESTREL (1982)

The high adventure and picaresque comedy of *Westmark* . . . moves, in this fine sequel, into a more realistic and complex narrative form as the struggle for power in the kingdom erupts into betrayal, war and foreign invasion. The fast-paced plot, subtleties of character, ironic wit, quiet understatement and pervasive animal imagery—all work with superb concentration to undercut the heroics of war, its slogans, uniforms and myths of comradeship and glory. The main focus is on Theo, who becomes a soldier for a mixture of reasons, including a vague idealism and the need to prove himself to Mickle (his love, once a beggar-thief, now Queen), to Justin (the charismatic leader, in love with war) and to himself. We see Theo slowly corrupted and brutalized by the "necessities" of war, until, at the sight of the butchered body of his friend, he loses control and becomes a ferocious beast, mad to kill. . . . In a terrible irony he unwittingly wounds his love, the disguised Queen; this shocks him from his monstrous hatred and begins the slow process of healing. Not all of the novel is as grim in tone. Alexander's range is wide, and he moves easily from the brutality to the absurdity of war.

> *Hazel Rochman, in her review of "The Kestrel," in* School Library Journal *(reprinted from the April, 1982 issue of* School Library Journal, *published by R. R. Bowker Co./A Xerox Corporation; copyright © 1982), Vol. 28, No. 8, April, 1982, pp. 64-5.*

There are not many political novels for young people, so we should probably be glad when a new one comes along. In "Westmark," the book to which "The Kestrel" is the sequel, the ragamuffin Mickle was discovered to be the lost Princess Augusta of Westmark, an imaginary kingdom with a post-Napoleonic cast. The revelation came as a great surprise to Mickle's friends (the mountebank Count Las Bombas, the revolutionary Florian, the satirical journalist Keller, and Theo, a former printer's devil) and as a rude shock to the Rasputin-like chief minister, Cabbarus, who had engineered the little princess's disappearance in the first place.

All these characters reappear in "**The Kestrel,**" and readers would be well advised to read the earlier book first to avoid confusion. . . .

The story brings its characters face to face with a number of ethical and political dilemmas. Is unenlightened monarchy any better than enlightened despotism? Should the press be free to criticize the good as well as the bad? How can there be peace unless one is ready to kill for it?

There is a lot going on in "**The Kestrel,**" some of it quite exciting as adventure literature, but the story loses vitality because Lloyd Alexander seems determined to make issues come before character, language, atmosphere or even emotion. Poor Theo, in his journey from printer's devil to bloodthirsty tyrant, is a tool for instruction rather than a character we can care about. Even his constant self-questioning seems less a trait of character than a means of discussing issues. The big scene in which he shoots at and wounds Mickle seems patently contrived.

No one can fault Mr. Alexander for his commitment to ideas, but the hand of the puppeteer is a little too much in evidence here.

> *Georgess McHargue, "A Political Education," in* The New York Times Book Review *(© 1982 by The New York Times Company; reprinted by permission), April 25, 1982, p. 47.*

In a sequel to *Westmark* . . . Alexander moves, as he did in the Prydain cycle, to deeper issues and subtler levels. This is no less appealing as an adventure tale with a strong story line and rounded, consistent characterizations, but it also considers the ambivalence its protagonist feels when having to choose between love and loyalty or duty, the compassion one may feel for a foe, the decision between battle and conciliation, and the assuming and sharing of responsibility. The book has the added appeal of familiar characters. . . . Another smasher. (pp. 181-82)

> *Zena Sutherland, in her review of "The Kestrel," in* Bulletin of the Center for Children's Books *(reprinted by permission of The University of Chicago Press; © 1982 by The University of Chicago), Vol. 35, No. 10, June, 1982, pp. 181-82.*

Again the author has skillfully used the overt devices of a story of war and adventure but, as before, he reveals the weaknesses and strengths of his characters, endowing his imagined kingdom with a psychological and a moral reality. Theo and Mickle take on new dimensions; and Constantine, the sixteen-year-old king of Regia—at first somewhat petulant—contributes an engaging touch of ingenuous verve to the narrative. (p. 411)

> *Paul Heins, in his review of "The Kestrel," in* The Horn Book Magazine *(copyright © 1982 by The Horn Book, Inc., Boston), Vol. LVIII, No. 4, August, 1982, pp. 410-11.*

Jose Aruego

1932-

Filipino author/illustrator and illustrator of fiction.

Aruego's fascination with comic books and a talent for doodling cartoon animals led him to abandon a career in law for one in illustration. After the publication of his first book, *The King & His Friends,* Aruego began illustrating for other authors as well. The chief concern of his work is its appeal to children. He looks for humor in a manuscript and attempts to establish cheerful moods with his illustrations. He believes that funny animal characters are easy for children to identify with positively and to love.

Critics laud Aruego's blending of colors, from brilliant and bold splashes to pale pastels and subtle tones. Reviewers also notice his simple yet detailed line drawings and comment that his illustrations expand and develop the descriptions they represent. It has been said that Aruego's works often do not need text and, indeed, *Look What I Can Do* contains less than twenty words. Not all the books Aruego has illustrated, including his own, have been enthusiastically received for their subject matter. However, critics are quick to note that Aruego's illustrations often exceed the quality of the text and stand alone on their own merit.

The awards for Aruego's illustrations are numerous. Among them are the *New York Times* Choice of Best Illustrated Children's Books of the Year, 1971, for *Look What I Can Do,* the 1971-72 American Institute of Graphic Arts Children's Book Show award for *A Crocodile's Tale* (with his wife, Ariane Dewey) and *Pilyo the Piranha,* and The Children's Book Showcase in 1972 for *Look What I Can Do.*

(See also *Contemporary Authors,* Vols. 37-40, first rev. and *Something about the Author,* Vol. 6.)

GENERAL COMMENTARY

Cinderella's godmother had her magic wand; Aladdin had his magic lamp; Aruego has his pen and ink. Using this medium, Jose Aruego creates unusual animals which have endeared themselves to children as well as adults. With a touch of magic and genius, he manages to change a commonplace theme into an object of irresistible charm. (p. 585)

Each [of Aruego's books] is unique. Varied subject matter and form indicate his versatility. Aruego has touched ecology, maturational problems, daily living, friendships, folktales, and poetry. (p. 587)

Aruego has made a substantial contribution to the field of children's literature. His books are sought by children, teachers, librarians, and parents. His appeal lies in the universality of his themes, his deep understanding of human nature, and his positive outlook on life. With each succeeding book, Aruego's magic grows, enchanting and delighting both young and old. (p. 590)

> *Dr. Ida J. Appel and Dr. Marion P. Turkish, "Profile: The Magic World of Jose Aruego" (copyright © 1977 by the National Council of Teachers of English; reprinted by permission of the publisher and*

> *the author), in* Language Arts, *Vol. 54, No. 5, May, 1977, pp. 585-90.*

THE KING AND HIS FRIENDS (1969)

A non-story that serves only to showcase the artistic dexterity of Mr. Aruego. King Doowah's three friends—a griffin and a couple of dragons—delight in amusing him by decorating various objects in the palace—with themselves. The artist's delicate, stylized, cartoon-like drawings in red, pink, gray and tan cleverly depict the dragons forming a bed with the griffin serving as the canopy; the dragons forming the throne on which the king sits and reads, with the griffin positioned as a book stand; etc. . . . The text includes a few words, such as canopy and chamber likely to puzzle young readers and listeners; the pictures are imaginatively conceived and skillfully executed but this dragon fantasy doesn't unfold as naturally or magically as Nash's *Custard the Dragon* (Little, 1959) or Stockton's and Sendak's *The Griffin and the Minor Canon* (Holt, 1963).

> *Elma Fesler, in her review of "The King and His Friends," in* School Library Journal, *an appendix to* Library Journal *(reprinted from the May, 1970 issue of* School Library Journal, *published by R. R. Bowker Co./A Xerox Corporation; copyright © 1970), Vol. 16, No. 9, May, 1970, p. 57.*

SYMBIOSIS: A BOOK OF UNUSUAL FRIENDSHIPS (1970)

It takes an unusually strong stomach to look at this exposé of unusual friendships which that dimpled darling of the grotesque, Mother Nature, has arranged and which José Aruego has described in text and pictures. A dedicated naturalist may find it rewarding to discover that "the crocodile has clean sparkling teeth" because his pal, the plover, walks in and out of his mouth as he "eats leeches and whatever else it finds to pick from the crocodile's teeth." But for the rest of us effete weaklings, it will reinforce our determination to limit our knowledge of nature to what we can see and read in Belloc's "Bad Child's Book of Beasts."

> *A review of "Symbiosis: A Book of Unusual Friendships," in* Publishers Weekly *(reprinted from the February 9, 1970 issue of* Publishers Weekly, *published by R. R. Bowker Company, a Xerox company; copyright © 1970 by Xerox Corporation), Vol. 197, No. 6, February 9, 1970, p. 83.*

The incongruous camaraderie of nine animal pairs is custom-made for the clever Mr. Aruego. . . . Hardly everyday animals these, but they have a comic presence. . . . The introductory definition of symbiosis suggests that the animals "become close friends in order to help one another," which is putting reciprocity on the basis of personal relations—but to question it may be pedantic, and that's just what this isn't. In the hands of an imaginative teacher **Symbiosis** could be great fun, on the shelves of the library goodness knows what will become of it. (pp. 384-85)

> *A review of "Symbiosis: A Book of Unusual Friendships," in* Kirkus Reviews *(copyright © 1970 The Kirkus Service, Inc.), Vol. XXXVIII, No. 7, April 1, 1970, pp. 384-85.*

What's going on here? A bird is perched in a crocodile's mouth, and getting away with it. Crazy. . . .

In nature's chain of life it's usually a matter of the quick and the dead, the predator and the prey. But not always, as Jose Aruego shows here in an eye-catching exhibit of nine "odd couples.". . . [They're] all delightfully exotic in a Ripleyesque way. Always inventive, always in control, the author-artist simplifies without condescension. (He leaves you to field a few questions though, like what is a tuatara? A ratel?) His illustrations extend and expand the descriptions in marvelously endless ways. Fresh, animated, abounding in good humor, this book proves that even though animals do some of the strangest things, they also do some of the smartest.

> *Margaret F. O'Connell, in her review of "Symbiosis: A Book of Unusual Friendships," in* The New York Times Book Review *(© 1970 by The New York Times Company; reprinted by permission), April 26, 1970, p. 30.*

Nine unusual animal associations are represented in this picture book unfortunately designed to enchant rather than to instruct. It misses excellent opportunities to introduce words such as mutualism and commensalism, which are really no more difficult than symbiosis. And, although the examples cited are well chosen—the crocodile and plover, goatfish and wrasse, the sooty shearwater and tuatara—the cartoon-style illustrations grossly misrepresent nature: i.e., insects are depicted with human-type eyes and mouths, some even pictured with eight legs. This book is a classic example of pictorial accuracy needlessly

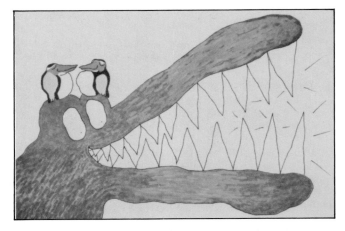

From Symbiosis: A Book of Unusual Friendships, *written and illustrated by Jose Aruego.*

sacrificed to an idea of reader entertainment. A superior treatment of the same material is Earle's *Strange Companions in Nature* (Morrow, 1966).

> *A. C. Haman, in a review of "Symbiosis: A Book of Unusual Friendships," in* School Library Journal, *an appendix to* Library Journal *(reprinted from the May, 1970 issue of* School Library Journal, *published by R. R. Bowker Co./A Xerox Corporation; copyright © 1970), Vol. 16, No. 9, May, 1970, p. 57.*

[Aruego illustrates nine unusual animal associations or symbiotic relationships] in an imaginative manner that will delight children. . . . The book will do best in an adult-child sharing situation. Adults should be prepared to reveal the identity of the tuatara (a lizard, *Sphenodon*), and to describe more in detail the morphology of the Portuguese man-of-war and the sea anemone, and to answer other questions. Despite the anthropomorphisms which seem to be inevitable in books for the very young, the book should be both entertaining and educationally useful.

> *A review of "Symbiosis: A Book of Unusual Friendships," in* Science Books *(copyright © 1970 by the American Association for the Advancement of Science), Vol. 6, No. 3, December, 1970, p. 236.*

JUAN AND THE ASUANGS (1970)

Essence of picture book, tincture of jungle, ephemeral texture of dream . . . a rainbow, multi-color-controlled, of watch-closely pages as Juan on his caribao hunts the *Manananggal*. . . . The tactile foliage, the bustling *barrio*, and cheerily fearable parade of *Asuangs* tell the story better than the clumsy text does, to friends of **The King's Friends** . . . and a new host of lookers-again. And again. (pp. 375-76)

> *A review of "Juan and the Asuangs," in* Kirkus Reviews *(copyright © 1970 The Kirkus Service, Inc.), Vol. XXXVIII, No. 7, April 1, 1970, pp. 375-76.*

Where have all the dogs and chickens gone? Juan rides into the jungle on his *carabao* to find them and there isn't a child anywhere who won't want to go along. This picture book is a genuine treasure—a simple success story, told in rather sober prose and rich in benevolently menacing spirits, each of which can be outwitted if you're as cool as Juan and can remember the proper tricks. The pictures, full of delicious melted-sherbert colors, are knee-deep in creatures that have a certain lunatic complacence happily reminiscent of a sort of tropical Thurber.

Jose Aruego has used the real Philippine words for each spirit, and for a few of the everyday things, too. But they are not difficult—and he has wisely put them into italics so that you know when one is coming. Children will like them—they have a pleasing sound to them that makes you think of bananas. From the jacket right through to the very last page, this book is an endearing and very special piece of work.

> *Natalie Babbitt, in her review of "Juan and the As-uangs," in* The New York Times Book Review *(© 1970 by The New York Times Company; reprinted by permission), September 13, 1970, p. 42.*

PILYO THE PIRANHA (1971)

Will predatory Pilyo get the somnolent sloth? Will the boa constrictor, the jaguar or the eagle? "Hey, that's my sloth, and no one else is going to get him," says Pilyo, outwitting each of them one funny way or another. But the sloth, playing possum, is slyer still: as long as he fails to awaken, Pilyo, a fish with scruples, will go on protecting him. You have to see the smile on the face of the sloth, and catch his last wink, to appreciate the joke, but if you know Mr. Aruego's work, you know it's cleverly carried off.

> *A review of "Pilyo the Piranha," in* Kirkus Reviews *(copyright © 1971 The Kirkus Service, Inc.), Vol. XXXIX, No. 4, February 15, 1971, p. 167.*

The story makes no sense, especially in its misrepresentation of piranhas (known to strip most victims to the bone in seconds): e.g., "He [Pilyo] had bitten the sloth many times, but the sloth hadn't felt a thing through his tough hide." The use of piranhas in this story, uncharacteristic as they are here, is merely a gimmick. And the result is not even amusing, despite the support the text gets from Aruego's typically humorous illustrations.

> *Rosemary S. Martin, in her review of "Pilyo the Piranha," in* School Library Journal, *an appendix to* Library Journal *(reprinted from the May, 1971 issue of* School Library Journal, *published by R. R. Bowker Co./A Xerox Corporation; copyright © 1971), Vol. 17, No. 9, May, 1971, p. 57.*

Can a picture book that stars a greedy piranha and has a supporting cast that includes a sloth, a boa constrictor, a jaguar and a harpy eagle be all bad? The answer is no. But it's not all good, either. . . . [For] all the expressive line drawings—they are delightful and amusing—the tale itself is curiously inept. It has a Perils of Pauline flavor without a resolution. Pilyo saves the sleeping sloth from one would-be gormand after another, saves it for his own supper, that is. But the sloth is neither eaten nor saved, but merely stored away, still sleeping. For the next Pilyo book?

> *Jane Yolen, in her review of "Pilyo the Piranha," in* The New York Times Book Review *(© 1971 by The New York Times Company; reprinted by permission), May 2, 1971, p. 44.*

Whilst the author/artist, born in the Philippines, may have had some success with this title in the Americas, it is unlikely that it will have much appeal in this country. The thin story with an unconvincing ending does not have the saving merit of distinguished illustration to help it. There is a continuing and regrettable tendency for some English publishers of excellent children's books to publish more and more mediocre imported titles from abroad and this is one of them.

> *Edward Hudson, in his review of "Pilyo the Piranha," in* Children's Book Review *(© 1972 by Five Owls Press Ltd.; all rights reserved), Vol. II, No. 2, April, 1972, p. 37.*

Pilyo the Piranha is a very funny book. . . . "Even when he was not hungry Pilyo enjoyed frightening the animals who lived along the banks of the river"—not an exemplary hobby for the central character of a children's book, but Pilyo's optimism and weird kind of integrity make him an endearing creature in spite of his nasty propensities.

> *"O! What Transports of Delight," in* The Times Literary Supplement *(© Times Newspapers Ltd. (London) 1972; reproduced from The Times Literary Supplement by permission), No. 3661, April 28, 1972, p. 483.**

LOOK WHAT I CAN DO (1971)

This is a book of rare good humor, this almost wordless story of two *carabaos.* Who needs words when it's Jose Aruego who has illustrated this spirited ballet of the absurd adventures of the two as they attempt the impossible?

> *A review of "Look What I Can Do," in* Publishers Weekly *(reprinted from the August 30, 1971 issue of* Publishers Weekly, *published by R. R. Bowker Company, a Xerox company; copyright © 1971 by Xerox Corporation), Vol. 200, No. 9, August 30, 1971, p. 274.*

A game of follow the leader gets out of hand in this humorous, virtually textless picture book illustrating the old Philippine proverb: "A carabao who herds with a fence jumper becomes a fence jumper too." The protagonists are two young carabao (water buffalo): one hops up on one foot, executes a somersault, and brags ("Look what I can do!"); the other imitates what the first one does ("I can do it too!"). From this first mild trick, the two progress to ever wilder stunts involving a profusion of very expressive jungle animals. . . . The illustrations—black-and-white cartoon outlines filled with washes of grey, beige, and on some pages brown, yellow, and orange-red—become more detailed, colorful and lively as the story reaches its dry-high-to-wet-low point, and then fade away again to beige and grey with the calm, perfectly logical ending.

> *Janet Strothman, in her review of "Look What I Can Do," in* School Library Journal, *an appendix to* Library Journal *(reprinted from the December, 1971 issue of* School Library Journal, *published by R. R. Bowker Co./A Xerox Corporation; copyright © 1971), Vol. 18, No. 4, December, 1971, p. 51.*

In Jose Aruego's picture-book world carabaos dance whimsically with tails held like the trains of ladies' gowns, while turtles balance on their horns. Aruego's jungles are inhabited by purple elephants and brown-nosed lions, prancing with snakes, butterflies, owls and alligators in fields of yellow and orange flowers.

This zoological ecumenicism is limned with chromatic and linear delicacies which, in the best tradition of illustration,

From Look What I Can Do, *written and illustrated by Jose Aruego.*

establish mood through gesture, stance and facial expression. . . . Aruego's style sets a consistent mood of lightness. The white page provides a kind of buoyancy in which his creatures cavort.

["**Look What I Can Do**"] is a really superb book of pictures, subtly toned in brown and gray, with deft accents of red and yellow. A brilliant example of illustrative mime showing two carabaos competing in aerial acrobatics, it is filled with incident—and hardly a word is spoken. The action is so well carried by the pictures that words would be an intrusion.

> Barbara Novak, "Aruego's Art," in The New York Times Book Review (© 1972 by The New York Times Company; reprinted by permission), January 16, 1972, p. 8.

There's very little text in this amusing story, and words are hardly needed. . . . The details of the illustrations are both handsome and amusing, especially the faces of other creatures [than the two carabaos] watching the exhibition.

> Zena Sutherland, in her review of "Look What I Can Do," in Bulletin of the Center for Children's Books (reprinted by permission of The University of Chicago Press; © 1972 by The University of Chicago), Vol. 25, No. 9, May, 1972, p. 134.

This kind of book has universal visual appeal. . . . The illustrations show enchanting economy of line and colour, the buffs and greys contrasting delicately with oranges and yellows in the backgrounds. Children will love the funny expressions and the wealth of unexpected detail. (pp. 299-300)

> A review of "Look What I Can Do," in The Junior Bookshelf, Vol. 36, No. 5, October, 1972, pp. 299-300.

A CROCODILE'S TALE: A PHILIPPINE FOLK TALE　(with Ariane Aruego, 1972)

What is gratitude? If you happen to be the greedy crocodile in this story it means taking advantage of the person who saved your life. As in most folktales, there is an obvious moral: with the help of a clever monkey, Juan manages to escape the crocodile's menacing jaws, but not before he and the reader have learned a valuable lesson about being grateful. An original interpretation with lively illustrations.

> A review of "A Crocodile's Tale: A Philippine Folk Story," in Publishers Weekly (reprinted from the March 13, 1972 issue of Publishers Weekly, published by R. R. Bowker Company, a Xerox company; copyright © 1972 by Xerox Corporation), Vol. 201, No. 11, March 13, 1972, p. 66.

This folktale, aimed at pre-schoolers, frequently uses the word "gratitude," but the idea of being grateful doesn't come across. Rather, "I'll do something for you if you do something for me" seems to dominate the story: a form of bribery, not gratitude. The Aruegos' illustrations are amusing and colorful. . . .

> Mary Ann Fish, in her review of "A Crocodile's Tale: A Philippine Folk Story," in School Library Journal, an appendix to Library Journal (reprinted from the September, 1972 issue of School Library Journal, published by R. R. Bowker Co./ A Xerox Corporation; copyright © 1972), Vol. 19, No. 1, September, 1972, p. 112.

The illustrations are decorative, done simply. The trees and flowers bloom in jungly profusion. The animals and people are amusing, and each scene is composed to contribute to the rhythm of the story and the design of the page. The colors are not quite up to the rest of the art, neither really soft nor really sparkling, and the ending may be a little too understated to be absolutely clear on first reading. However, it is ungrateful to quibble, and I am grateful that there are books like these.

> Karla Kuskin, in her review of "A Crocodile's Tale," in Saturday Review (© 1972 Saturday Review Magazine Co.; reprinted by permission), Vol. LV, No. 34, August 19, 1972, p. 61.

A tale from Philippine folklore, illustrated with humorous flair. . . . No moral is pointed, but the lesson is clear despite the fact that there is no retribution. Some creatures are grateful, others are not. The tale has a modicum of suspense and is adequately told, but it is slight and the ending is anticlimactic.

> Zena Sutherland, in her review of "A Crocodile's Tale: A Philippine Folk Story," in Bulletin of the Center for Children's Books (reprinted by permission of The University of Chicago Press; © 1972 by The University of Chicago), Vol. 26, No. 1, September, 1972, p. 1.

WE HIDE, YOU SEEK　(with Ariane Dewey, 1979)

An oafishly good-natured rhino, invited into a jungle-wide game of hide and seek, bumbles from one scene to the next, accidentally exposing would-be hiders (leopards, crocodiles, lions) at every stop; then, turning the tables on his playmates, cleverly hides himself. Readers are served up a wealth of information in 27 words (plus end-papers that give a page-by-page identification of the species pictured) and droll scenes drenched in the vibrant tones of an East African palette. Here are lessons in camouflage, in animals' ecological niches, in topographics, and in East African wildlife. And if the game seems to go on a shade too long, one has only to think of the number of times a child will hide behind cupped hands, peek out, and laugh; hide, and laugh again. A generous helping of information, entertainment, and visual excitement.

> Kristi L. Thomas, in her review of "We Hide, You Seek," in School Library Journal *(reprinted from the September, 1979 issue of* School Library Journal, *published by R. R. Bowker Co./ A Xerox Corporation; copyright © 1979), Vol. 26, No. 1, September, 1979, p. 102.*

Aruego and Dewey are no strangers to honors earned during their careers in children's literature. But the husband-and-wife team cap their previous performances in this bountiful picture book in wonderful color. It combines an invitation to develop one's powers of observation with the entertainment evolving from antic play.

> A review of "We Hide, You Seek," in Publishers Weekly *(reprinted from the September 17, 1979 issue of* Publishers Weekly, *published by R. R. Bowker Company, a Xerox company; copyright © 1979 by Xerox Corporation), Vol. 216, No. 12, September 17, 1979, p. 145.*

Jose Aruego is no slouch at producing children's picture books. . . . ["**We Hide, You Seek**"] is a brightly colored tale of a red rhino (a bit odd, that) stumbling through the forests and plains of East Africa playing hide-and-seek with the other creatures. He's such a bumbler, tripping over things and sneezing, that he flushes the others from their natural hiding places. This is done in a series of double-page spreads—first spread a scene full of animals blending with their habitation, second spread with clumsy rhino barging in and sending them fleeing. Ingenious, but I think that a less cartoony illustrator could have made more of it.

> William Cole, in his review of "We Hide, You Seek," in The New York Times Book Review *(© 1979 by The New York Times Company; reprinted by permission), October 21, 1979, p. 52.*

The pictures have humor and vitality as well as a game element; most of the animals are well-camouflaged by their protective coloration, so that the rhino barges about surrounded by dozens of friends but can't see them. . . . Last page, a nice visual gag: the rhino is in full sight, but he's in the midst of a herd of rhinos, and the other animals look on, baffled; they know he's there, but which one is he? Aruego and Dewey have outdone themselves visually. . . .

> Zena Sutherland, in her review of "We Hide, You Seek," in Bulletin of the Center for Children's Books *(reprinted by permission of The University of Chicago Press; © 1980 by The University of Chicago), Vol. 33, No. 5, January, 1980, p. 87.*

From We Hide, You Seek, *written and illustrated by Jose Aruego and Ariane Dewey.*

The ending, when rhino asserts ''Now I want my turn to hide,'' is a surprise and a delight. The clear, colorful, humorous pictures are as enjoyable as the task of finding the camouflaged animals. The endpapers provide an informative catalog of the animals found in the East African bush, desert, swamp, plains, river and forest. Large print and few words make it a good choice for beginning readers.

A review of ''We Hide, You Seek'' (copyright 1980 by the International Reading Association, Inc.; reprinted with permission of the International Reading Association), in The Reading Teacher, *Vol. 33, No. 6, March, 1980, p. 732.*

Jeanne Bendick

1919-

American author/illustrator and illustrator of fiction and nonfiction.

Bendick is one of the most prominent contemporary science writers for children. Her inability to locate a simple how-to book led her to write and illustrate *Electronics for Boys and Girls*, the first of more than one hundred books. Despite having no background in science before she became an author, Bendick's science books are successful because of the thorough research she completes before beginning her writing and illustrating. She approaches her work with the concept that the children using her books know absolutely nothing about her subjects. Thus she begins with the very simplest ideas, using equally simple drawings and diagrams for illustrations.

Bendick deals with such diverse areas of science as TV, movies, time, shapes, numbers, ecology, astronomy, and heredity. She also writes basic information books to introduce young readers to the history and inner workings of ships and airplanes and the rules of etiquette. *The Emergency Book* is one of the most fascinating and well-received works of this type as it calmly explains immediate procedures and keeps in mind the natural hesitancy of children. She has also written two works of fiction, *The Good Knight Ghost* and *The Blonk from Beneath the Sea*. Although most critics react favorably, some complain that Bendick introduces subjects with vague generalities that may produce more confusion than inquisitiveness in children. However, many consider her works to be excellent stepping stones to more complex explanations, and several of Bendick's books have been revised and updated many times over.

Besides her own works, Bendick has illustrated for other authors and has written and coauthored several textbooks. She was the recipient of the 1975 Eva L. Gordon Award from the American Nature Society.

(See also *Contemporary Authors*, Vol. 5, rev. ed. and *Something about the Author*, Vol. 2.)

AUTHOR'S COMMENTARY

About a thousand years ago when I first started to read, I was fired with ambition to be an illustrator. I even knew what kinds of books I wanted to illustrate—the ones that were called, "Information Books." Nobody called them science books then. Science was a majestic subject, certainly too complicated for children.

Maybe I made up my mind because I was so frustrated by the pictures in those books. And I made up my mind that when *I* reached the exalted state of being a book artist I was going to do things differently. I hope I have.

Resolution One was that in the books I illustrated, nobody would *ever* have to flip through pages looking for the picture that matched the text. Maybe "matched" isn't the right word. I think that the text and pictures should complement, not duplicate each other. Of course words give information in one way, pictures in another. But I think an illustration should add new information. Maybe it shows scale, in relation to the child: Maybe it locates and labels parts. Maybe it simply shows some-

thing or somebody as part of the world—growing or being alive, enjoying and being enjoyed.

I have always been allowed to lay out the books I illustrate, so I can put pictures where I want them. It is certainly more work to do this. It means counting type, and figuring and "dressmaking." Maybe it's easier to have someone else do all this and just give me a description of the picture and a size, but, "I'd rather do it myself," and I think most illustrators would. Drawings in a science book aren't an extra, added attraction. They are part of the book itself and should be right from the beginning.

Generally, these days, I am illustrating books that I have written myself, and I find that I write the book and draw pictures in my head at the same time. I almost write the book in spreads, writing a paragraph or two where I know the picture will be big or detailed, writing more words where they can do the job better.

Even before I was writing it seemed to me to be the artist's obligation to find out what pictures the writer had in his head and to get those on paper. Of course this means direct communication between author and artist, a contact which for some reason many editors and agents feel would be fatal to both. But I have never seen a documented case of such a fatality. I have only seen books come together with a wholeness when there is a real exchange of ideas.

Another resolution I made as a future science illustrator had to do with the somewhat amorphous, wholly idealized character of the pictures. Everything was soft, pretty, and rather picturesque. All children were beautiful, which I grant they are in their own ways, but have you ever seen a picturesque vacuum-cleaner motor? I wasn't cynical but I *was* lazy and I had an immediate jolt of recognition for those artists who took the easy way of drawing from photographs, or from another artist's illustrations, instead of looking at real things for themselves.

One of the best things any illustrator can give to a picture is his own viewpoint—the special way he sees things. That's hard to do, once removed. Someone else's viewpoint gets in the way. So I made up my mind to look at things myself, in my own way. I've looked at the insides of wasps nests, the insides of flowers, and the insides of toilet tanks; I've watched spiders make webs, people make cars, and chameleons shed skins. I learn a lot that way!

Along the same lines, it used to disappoint me—and it seems as if I became an illustrator out of sheer frustration—when I tried to build something from pictures, or make an investigation, and found that the thing I was building couldn't be built or that the investigation wouldn't work. So whether I am drawing a milk-carton elevator or a sundial that *really* works as a clock, I always build it myself and try it out before I draw the picture. The placement of a tack or a paperclip, the position of a light bulb or the thickness of a piece of string can make the difference between a working model and a disappointment, or a successful investigation and a confusion.

Sure it takes longer, but it's worth it. If I were "into" needle-work I would embroider a sampler to hang over the drawing board: THERE ARE NO SHORT CUTS.

I am certainly not the best artist in the world. (Once an art editor told me that my people looked as if they were made of spaghetti.) But I get a lot of letters from children saying that they like my pictures because that's the way *they* would draw things. Children do see things in a different way from adults. Maybe that's because they look for different things. I like the way they look and what they see. I've tried to keep looking at the world their way, adding a little of what I see to that and coming up with a picture that is theirs and mine—*our* way of looking at science and the world we live in. (pp. 20-1)

> *Jeanne Bendick, "Illustrating Science Books for Children," in* Science and Children *(reproduced with permission from* Science and Children, *April, 1973; 1742 Connecticut Avenue, N.W., Washington, D.C. 20009; copyright © 1973 by the National Science Teachers Association), Vol. 10, No. 7, April, 1973, pp. 20-1.*

GENERAL COMMENTARY

The early books [designed to present mathematical concepts], whose purpose appeared to be instructional in mathematical content, lacked consistency and a clear focus in both conceptual and literary development. Two such books by Jeanne Bendick written in the early 1960's, *Take Shapes, Lines and Letters* and *Take a Number,* dealt largely with abstract mathematical ideas and relationships. She introduced an extraordinarily large number of complex terms and concepts (horizontal, vertical, intersect, revolution, obtuse, equilateral, axis, dimension, rep-

resentation, etc.) often with the assumption that young readers had a high level of intuitive conceptual understanding.

Bendick confused her points of emphasis on occasion (e.g., she explained that a drawing of a *straight line* is only a representation of the idea of a line—and used the equator, an obvious *curve,* to illustrate this concept), and often asked almost insultingly obvious questions while conveying complex information. The picturebook format and Bendick's oscillation between simple and complex treatments of the material causes confusion in determining the reading level of these books. Her books are useful only as a review or overview of the general field of mathematics by older children who have already had considerable experience in concrete manipulation of materials. (p. 100)

> *Pamela C. Farr, "Trends in Math Books for Children," in* School Library Journal *(reprinted from the October, 1979 issue of* School Library Journal, *published by R. R. Bowker Co./ A Xerox Corporation; copyright © 1979), Vol. 26, No. 2, October, 1979, pp. 99-104.**

Jeanne Bendick is probably best known for her lively, humorous illustrations. Her easily recognizable style, which she describes as "relaxed representational" is echoed in the brisk and vigorous writing that skillfully clarifies difficult concepts. . . . [She presents complex subjects] in simple terms and in a light, often breezy manner. (p. 447)

> *Zena Sutherland, Dianne L. Monson and May Hill Arbuthnot, "Information Books," in their* Children and Books *(copyright © 1981, 1977, 1972, 1964, 1957, 1947, by Scott, Foresman and Company; reprinted by permission), sixth edition, Scott, Foresman, 1981, pp. 442-501.**

ELECTRONICS FOR BOYS AND GIRLS   (1944)

This is an excellent primer of electronics, of interest to any scientific minded youngster today (and how many there are!) There is some historical and factual background from the discovery to the harnessing of electrons to work for us. There is a sense of adventure and of limitless future in the whole science of electronics—and this, in understandable and yet not too simplified terms—serves as an introduction.

> *A review of "Electronics for Boys and Girls," in* Virginia Kirkus' Bookshop Service, *Vol. XII, No. 18, September 15, 1944, p. 433.*

An introduction to electronics written in terms easily understandable to children. . . . Its history, relationship to electricity and importance in science and industry are well described.

> *Dorotha Dawson, in her review of "Electronics for Boys and Girls," in* Library Journal *(reprinted from* Library Journal, *December 15, 1944; published by R. R. Bowker Co. (a Xerox company); copyright © 1944 by Xerox Corporation), Vol. 69, No. 22, December 15, 1944, p. 1104.*

MAKING THE MOVIES   (1945)

Lucid, simple, interesting to any child who goes to the movies, this book is so arranged that it tells how movies are made without roughly jarring the illusion that is one of their great gifts. . . . The margins are wide; on every one is at least one lively drawing, really illustrating something said on that page. You read it and see a picture of it almost together.

The first chapter runs through the experts in three hundred trades and crafts making the movies, describing what the producer does, director, readers and writers, technical advisers and the research department [as well as the roles of designers, property men, builders, artists, wardrobe people, sound men, make-up men, film and sound editors, and actors, among others]. This is done rapidly, but thoroughly enough to make it real.

Sketching the history of the movie, the story then follows a copy of the script through the various departments, describing the sets. When the shooting starts various lights, cameras and sound effects are shown. Toward the end the account becomes a little more technical, but not too much so for a young person who has read the first part. . . .

> *May Lamberton Becker, in her review of "Making the Movies," in* New York Herald Tribune Weekly Book Review *(© I.H.T. Corporation; reprinted by permission), October 28, 1945, p. 6.*

Here is a really first-rate book about how movies are made, from story conference clear through to preview, with a vast amount of fascinating information on the way. This is no press agent's blurb about his colossal industry, but a direct, precise account of how writers, directors, designers and technicians do their job. Although Mrs. Bendick is writing for young people, she neither leaves out nor skips over [technical matters]. . . . In fact, she makes the camera man and technicians seem more interesting and exciting than the actors. . . . Her drawings, most of which are spotted in the margins, are amusing and expert in clarifying details.

> *Creighton Peet, in his review of "Making the Movies," in* The New York Times Book Review *(© 1945 by The New York Times Company; reprinted by permission), November 11, 1945, p. 20.*

For all its compact simplicity, this is an amazingly well-organized and informative explanation of the professions, crafts, techniques and processes which make the movies. . . . Excellent bibliography, glossary of movie terms and an index. Recommended for both children's and young people's collections.

> *Margaret C. Scoggin, in her review of "Making the Movies," in* Library Journal *(reprinted from* Library Journal, *December 1, 1945; published by R. R. Bowker Co. (a Xerox company); copyright © 1945 by Xerox Corporation), Vol. 70, No. 21, December 1, 1945, p. 1139.*

HOW MUCH AND HOW MANY: THE STORY OF WEIGHTS AND MEASURES (1947)

I don't know a book of general information more likely to be read more eagerly by children than this one about weighing, measuring and counting. Miss Bendick's art in lending vivacity to facts will keep them fascinated from the first weight—that a man could hold or carry—and the earliest measures such as those involving the hand, to calibre, light-years and hectoliters over in the science section. Open to any page and something seizes attention, usually heightened by a picture that is funny without being flippant. I don't know how to measure the amount of time it will save parents who won't have to answer questions

of the sizes of shoes, hats or printing types, whether troy weight started in Troy, or why a real sailor never speaks of "twenty knots an hour."

> *May Lamberton Becker, in her review of "How Much and How Many: The Story of Weights and Measures," in* New York Herald Tribune Weekly Book Review *(© I.H.T. Corporation; reprinted by permission), November 23, 1947, p. 8.*

A good book for fifth- and sixth-graders. It's fun and it's interesting, and should prove a blessing in disguise to unmathematically-minded youngsters.

> *Jane Cobb and Helen Dore Boylston, in their review of "How Much and How Many: The Story of Weights and Measures," in* The Atlantic Monthly *(copyright © 1947, by The Atlantic Monthly Company, Boston, Mass.; reprinted with permission), Vol. 180, No. 6, December, 1947, p. 150.*

A subject that could be dry comes alive in the author's clever drawings and bits of historical background. . . . In spite of small-child silhouettes in dedication and words spelled out for pronunciation, should be useful for general science for ages 10-14.

> *Frances L. Morrison, in her review of "How Much and How Many: The Story of Weights and Measures," in* Library Journal *(reprinted from* Library Journal, *December, 1947; published by R. R. Bowker Co. (a Xerox company); copyright © 1947 by Xerox Corporation), Vol. 72, No. 1, December 1, 1947, p. 1693.*

[This] book has been thoroughly revised and reset to give due prominence to metrication. . . . The changeover in major in-

From How Much and How Many: The Story of Weights and Measures, *written and illustrated by Jeanne Bendick.*

dustries like building and textiles and the use of the international system of units in science are explained alongside the more obvious changes in currency and linear measurement. The historical origins of our terminology for weights and measures makes fascinating reading; the style throughout is informative and entertaining, supported by amusing black and white drawings. . . . Highly recommended as a reference book in junior school libraries.

Audrey J. Kelly, in her review of "How Much and How Many," in Children's Book Review *(© 1971 by Five Owls Press Ltd.; all rights reserved), Vol. I, No. 1, February, 1971, p. 25.*

TELEVISION WORKS LIKE THIS (with Robert Bendick, 1949)

Jeanne Bendick, . . . whose many books give evidence that she knows all about everything, is now explaining television. . . . It's a brave and on the whole very successful attempt. . . .

Miss Bendick's bold, cartoonlike drawings of studios, electron tubes, etc., are simple and easy to follow. Often they splash all over double-page spreads in the manner of the illustrations in a fiction magazine. The brief, non-technical text is fitted into what space remains. . . .

"Television Works Like This" covers everything from the production of shows in studios to the operations in the master control room through which they are broadcast. Plenty of adults will find this book interesting, too.

Creighton Peet, "Explaining Television," in The New York Times Book Review *(© 1949 by The New York Times Company; reprinted by permission), September 4, 1949, p. 13.*

Technical knowledge and illustrative skill combined in the preparation of this attractive book with its clever, lively drawings on every page and its accurate but very informal text. Although it looks young, almost a picture book, it contains plenty of nontechnical information for anyone interested in learning what television is and how a station operates in sending out all kinds of programs.

Frances L. Morrison, in her review of "Television Works Like This," in Library Journal *(reprinted from* Library Journal, *November 1, 1949; published by R. R. Bowker Co. (a Xerox company); copyright © 1949 by Xerox Corporation), Vol. 74, No. 19, November 1, 1949, p. 1682.*

It might be supposed from the title that this book is mainly technical, yet it is more concerned with the technique of television. In good clear prose we are given the story of what happens from the birth of an idea for a television programme to its transmission. Every page has good clear diagrams and drawings.

A review of "Television Works Like This," in The Junior Bookshelf, *Vol. 15, No. 6, December, 1951, p. 270.*

The authors are generally expert and accurate; occasional oversimplifications lead to minor technical inaccuracies, but in the amount of detail and clearness of explanations the text is admirable. The style is terse and somewhat telegraphic, with a few lapses into redundancy or jargon: "A treatment is a fuller treatment. . ." (p. 46) and ". . . mikes are hot (which means

open)" (p. 52). In general, however, this is one of the best television books available, with considerable new material and most of the illustrations up to date.

Norwood Long, in his review of "Television Works Like This," in School Library Journal, *an appendix to* Library Journal *(reprinted from the February, 1966 issue of* School Library Journal, *published by R. R. Bowker Co./A Xerox Corporation; copyright © 1966), Vol. 12, No. 6, February, 1966, p. 79.*

ALL AROUND YOU (1951)

The first "why, what and how" questions are bound to be big ones—about the sun, the moon, wind, clouds, animals, and other natural phenomena—and Jeanne Bendick anticipates these questions and answers them in unaffected, simple prose. This is indeed an exciting "first look at the world." . . . On each page the illustrations by the author keep pace with the text:— a crocodile writhes across the page; a giraffe thoughtfully peers over the top; leaves flutter down the margins; and throughout drawings and diagrams dramatize the text. As exhilarating as Saturday mornings in spring with an invitation to experience, observe and investigate the wonderful world in which we live. An important addition to the home and elementary school natural science library. . . .

A review of "All Around You," in Virginia Kirkus' Bookshop Service, *Vol. 19, No. 8, April 15, 1951, p. 208.*

It is amazing how much elementary information [Mrs. Bendick] has packed into these few pages. The material is carefully organized, simply phrased, well-illustrated and presented with an understanding of a child's interests and queries. It should make youngsters realize that the universe is exciting and so, like all good informational books, lead them on to further investigation of these matters.

Ellen Lewis Buell, "Everyday Wonders," in The New York Times Book Review *(© 1951 by The New York Times Company; reprinted by permission), May 27, 1951, p. 22.*

Little wonder . . . that [Bendick] produced the first omnium gatherum of basic science, that hardy perennial *All Around You.*

How it happens that this unassuming—one could even say, unprepossessing—book, with none of the structural logic of a Webber or the factual exactitude of a Zim, has survived a revolution in science teaching and remains both popular and reputable does not so much defy understanding as analysis. Just taking note, then, there is in *All Around You* a sort of cozy clutter and, with it, a casual intermix of the sciences . . . ; there are pictures that look as if your favorite aunt drew them on the spur of the moment and the answers to lots and lots of questions. . . . Herein, perhaps, lies an explanation, in that children, before they want to know anything in particular, want to know about everything—so we tell them that Washington won the Revolution, Eskimos live in igloos and giraffes eat the leaves of tall trees: we tell them *something*, knowing it is only a partial truth but one that will, for the moment, adequately fill their needs. On that basis *All Around You* can be considered a constructive ramble, a sort of *Farmer's Almanac* on home grounds. (pp. 389-90)

Barbara Bader, "More Information," in her American Picture Books from Noah's Ark to the Beast Within (reprinted with permission of Macmillan Publishing Co., Inc.; copyright © 1976 by Barbara Bader), Macmillan, 1976, pp. 383-415.*

THE FIRST BOOK OF AIRPLANES (1952)

This little book gives more information about aviation than many a larger volume. Starting with the rudiments of flying, it goes on to tell about the various uses of airplanes and the different types that are made for these various purposes. There is a brief history of aviation, and the book ends with many pages devoted to fighting planes of the world. Suitable for any age from eight up.

> *Elsie T. Dobbins, in her review of "The First Book of Airplanes," in* Library Journal *(reprinted from* Library Journal, *July, 1952; published by R. R. Bowker Co. (a Xerox company); copyright © 1952 by Xerox Corporation), Vol. 77, No. 13, July, 1952, p. 1212.*

The text deals simply in a basic vocabulary with many aspects of flight. Some attempt has been made to introduce simple experimental activities to illustrate the many scientific aspects of the subject.

There are some photographs but most of the illustrations are sketches which vary from the adequate to the utterly inadequate. As a useful book on flight, this one never gets off the ground.

> *Alan Bowker, in his review of "The First Book of Flight," in* The School Librarian and School Library Review, *Vol. 14, No. 3, December, 1966, p. 364.*

THE FIRST BOOK OF SPACE TRAVEL (1953)

"So your're going to be a spaceman. Some of you surely will be, because many scientists say that in about twenty years people will be traveling through space." So . . . we might as well know the what, where, how of space, "who has gotten to space," (answer: nobody), and then what rockets are and how it probably will feel to travel in one. "Where to?" brings some thrilling suggestions. It is all in the familiar, excellent Bendick style, "easy" but never patronizing, and with as much space for her clever pictures as for words, all fine for ages 8 to 12, and not too bad either to prepare us who are nervously adding up that twenty years, for what's to come.

> *Louise S. Bechtel, in her review of "The First Book of Space Travel," in* New York Herald Tribune Book Review *(©I.H.T. Corporation; reprinted by permission), May 17, 1953, p. 7.*

Essential facts and some of the conjectures of authorities are the meat of this accurate introduction to space travel. . . . The animated pictures make an idea like Og (weightlessness, no gravity), clear, understandable and as convincingly real as gravity.

> *Iris Vinton, in her review of "The First Book of Space Travel," in* The New York Times Book Review *(© 1953 by The New York Times Company; reprinted by permission), July 26, 1953, p. 16.*

The author of this book is clearly one who understands how to keep the interest of young children, for she writes in their idiom, does not dwell too much on any one topic, and has

From The First Book of Space Travel, *written and illustrated by Jeanne Bendick.*

included a host of relevant and exciting illustrations. It is difficult, in fact, to think of any important aspect of the subject that has been omitted in these few pages, for, from basic ideas of what conditions in space are like, the reader is asked to consider the difficulties to be faced in putting either satellites or living beings in orbit, and the principles of the propulsion unit required to do so.

An illustrated account is given of the design and function of a variety of orbiting devices already in use, of those contemplated for human space-travel, and of the regions waiting to be explored. Biological problems posed by the existence of harmful radiation, weightlessness and excessive acceleration are dealt with in a way which every child will understand: a way which lays sound foundations for his further study. (pp. 247-48)

> *B. J. Hopper, in a review of "The First Book of Space Travel," in* The School Librarian and School Library Review, *Vol. 13, No. 2, July, 1965, pp. 247-48.*

THE FIRST BOOK OF SUPERMARKETS (1954)

Children ask endless questions; here are many of the answers, far more than most adults could answer for themselves. A modern way of marketing, geared to the customers' convenience, is given its due. Modern style illustrations seem appropriate to the topic. . . .

> *A review of "The First Book of Supermarkets," in* Virginia Kirkus' Bookshop Service, *Vol. 22, No. 20, October 15, 1954, p. 710.*

With her usual flair for interesting detail, Mrs. Bendick briskly presents many amazing facts about the business—how items are bought in great quantities, how they are stored, displayed and marketed, with a quick glance at some of the fascinating gadgets used and at some of the possible devices and methods of the future. It's a highly entertaining introduction to one of the distinctive features of this age.

> *Ellen Lewis Buell, "To Market, To Market," in* The New York Times Book Review *(© 1955 by The New York Times Company; reprinted by permission), February 27, 1955, p. 32.*

[*The First Book of Supermarkets*] alerts the young shopper to the fact that the "owners want to sell as many things as possible, so they try to design the supermarket to make a person buy even more than he went in for!" She describes an experimental design where, to make the buyer add more things to his cart than he really wants, "one row leads you into another, and you can't skip any." The necessity for making choices is also explicitly stated in the Bendick book, where she tells the young shoppers to get all the necessities first, such as green and yellow vegetables, milk, etc., and *then* such extras as candy and gum. (One suspects that the impact of such exhortations is relatively slight). (p. 127)

> *Katherine M. Heylman, "No Bargains for Frances: Children's Trade Books and Consumer Education," in* Issues in Children's Book Selection: A School Library Journal/Library Journal Anthology *(reprinted with permission of the R. R. Bowker, Company; copyright © 1973 by Xerox Corporation),* Bowker, *1973, pp. 125-35.**

THE GOOD KNIGHT GHOST (1956)

[Museums] will never seem the same after you read Jeanne Bendick's jolly **"The Good Knight Ghost."** . . . You'll watch lumpiness about the dragons woven in old tapestries or parts of armor that don't seem to fit together properly, for you'll be sure they are haunted. In her first work of fiction this gifted author and illustrator has written a hilarious tale of a curator, Mr. Modderbod, and two children who encountered the ghost of Sir Robert Lancaster Arthur Galahad McBen and his enemy, the dragon Kensington. In words and in lively pictures in bold black and purples she convinces any one over nine that "there's always something going on in a museum."

> *Magaret Sherwood Libby, "Ghosts and Witches," in* New York Herald Tribune Book Review *(© I.H.T. Corporation; reprinted by permission), October 21, 1956, p. 9.*

Although Jeanne Bendick's **"Good Knight Ghost"** takes place in the spring it's a lighthearted tale for any season. . . . The story slopes off a bit at the climax but still it's a fine frolic—especially for the army of youngsters who are fascinated by armor.

From The Good Knight Ghost, *written and illustrated by Jeanne Bendick.*

> *Ellen Lewis Buell, "Ghoulies and Ghosties," in* The New York Times Book Review *(© 1956 by The New York Times Company; reprinted by permission), October 28, 1956, p. 42.**

HAVE A HAPPY MEASLE, A MERRY MUMPS AND A CHEERY CHICKENPOX (with Candy Bendick and Robert Bendick, Jr., 1958)

The mumpy or measly sick-a-bed can console himself with this book of do's and don'ts for a speedy recovery. His itching chum with chicken pox can also find this an infectious tonic. Jeanne Bendick's pictures of spotted and lumpy little patients and the accompanying stories and verses about a mermaid who caught cold when her tail dried out, and the knight who couldn't raise his visor when he had mumps, should coax a smile from the most dispirited convalescent. A wonderful gift item too for the child with a fracture, for it counsels . . . "bones are not like glass or dishes. They can't be fixed with glue and wishes." A real cure-all.

> *A review of "Have a Happy Measle, a Merry Mumps, and a Cheery Chickenpox," in* Virginia Kirkus' Service, *Vol. XXVI, No. 5, March 1, 1958, p. 182.*

We can practically guarantee that many a measly, mumpsy, chicken-poxy household this spring will receive this book with delight and that they will find it mightily cheering under the circumstances. . . . The pictures are big, bright and splashy in the vein of Mrs. Bendick's for **"Good Knight Ghost."** Very sensible foolishness.

> *Margaret Sherwood Libby, "Much Merriment in Gay Stories and Pictures for the Young," in* New York Herald Tribune Book Review *(© I.H.T. Corporation; reprinted by permission), May 11, 1958, p. 58.*

THE BLONK FROM BENEATH THE SEA (1958)

Described as a "tongue-in-cheek story," this is not as good as others by this author nor as amusing as the publishers seem to think it is.

> *Sonja Wennerblad, in her review of "The Blonk from Beneath the Sea," in* Junior Libraries, *an appendix to* Library Journal *(reprinted from the September, 1958 issue of* Junior Libraries, *published by R. R. Bowker Co./A Xerox Corporation; copyright © 1958), Vol. 5, No. 1, September, 1958, p. 68.*

This happy nonsense spoofing the collecting of specimens for marine exhibition and study will serve the need for humorous stories. . . . How, because [the Blonk] can think and Peter is ingenious on its behalf, it escapes from the oceanarium tank and then generously returns will seem enjoyably, if crazily, funny to children.

> *Virginia Haviland, in her review of "The Blonk from Beneath the Sea," in* The Horn Book Magazine *(copyright, 1958, by the Horn Book, Inc., Boston), Vol. XXXIV, No. 4, August, 1958, p. 265.*

THE FIRST BOOK OF SHIPS (1959)

[*The First Book of Ships* is] an unpretentious, clearly presented history of ships and shipping, with plenty of simple line-drawings, and isn't the sort of book that would catch the eye before a lot of flashier offerings in a bookshop. I like its brisk tone, its appeal to the imagination: 'The big sailing ships were the most beautiful ships ever built, They flew over the water like fast-moving clouds.' There's also a wonderfully apt list of qualities needed to be a good sailor that I wish I'd seen in 1940, including 'Are you friendly? But can you mind your own business? Does your heart lift at the sight of the sea?' The book was an instantaneous success with a group of eight- and nine-year-olds. One boy wrote firmly, 'I think this book is great for an eight-year-old boy'. At all events, to enjoy it I don't think one needs to have a special interest in ships.

> *Charles Causley, in his review of "The First Book of Ships," in* New Statesman *(© 1970 The Statesman & Nation Publishing Co. Ltd.), Vol. 80, No. 2068, November 6, 1970, p. 614.*

LIGHTNING (1961)

A hearty welcome once again to Jeanne Bendick for this new addition to her collection of environmental guides for the 8 to 11 year old. This time Miss Bendick ventures into the scientific world of lightning and its components, bringing with her a talent for reducing the complicated and technical to the simple and lucid; she emerges victorious. Amusing descriptions of ancient and traditional beliefs about thunder and lightning start us off. . . . Later in a discussion of electricity including definitions of protons, electrons and atoms, the author builds a solid background of her final explanation of the creation of that great spark of current we call lightning. Both the dangers and advantages of lightning are set forth along with the original experiment by Ben Franklin. Throughout, an awareness of the young reader pervades, as she asks him questions and relates her subject to his life. Informative material, perceptively rendered.

> *A review of "Lightning," in* Virginia Kirkus' Service, *Vol. XXIX, No. 1, January 1, 1961, p. 12.*

Uneven treatment of lightning: what it is, its benefits, superstitions about it, and types. Much emphasis placed on positive and negative charges, with some explanation of protons and electrons. Neutrons are not mentioned by name, although so labeled in illustrations. Two-page discussion of Franklin's experiment interrupts section on conductors and safety measures during storms. Illustrations seem accurate.

> *Susan Bush, in her review of "Lightning," in* School Library Journal, *an appendix to* Library Journal *(reprinted from the September, 1961 issue of* School Library Journal, *published by R. R. Bowker Co./A Xerox Corporation; copyright © 1961), Vol. 8, No. 1, September, 1961, p. 119.*

THE FIRST BOOK OF HOW TO FIX IT (with Barbara Berk, 1961)

"Every house needs a handy man (or a handy girl) who can take up a hammer or a screw driver, a paint brush or a can of glue and get things back in shape." And on this sensible premise the authors launch their exuberant fact-filled guide for Mr. or Miss Fixit! The first part of the book is wisely devoted to limits beyond which the young handy man cannot go, preventive check lists, and descriptions of tools. A partial list of the actual "how to's" include changing a fuse, minor plumbing repairs, furniture finishing, painting, and curing sticky drawers. Cheerful yet instructive illustrations, diagrams and charts support this excellent deciphering of some complicated activ-

ities and rules. Unfortunately, few parents will permit their children to practise what the authors "preach", but no age barrier to appreciation exists here. Even non-mechanical adults can profit.

> *A review of "The First Book of How to Fix It," in* Virginia Kirkus' Service, *Vol. XXIX, No. 2, January 15, 1961, p. 60.*

This earns a place on a selected list because it really is a *first* book in its field. If widely purchased and its precepts applied, it could have a revolutionary impact on family life. Its underlying assumption is that children can be useful while happily employed. Clear, illustrated instructions (except those on page 27, for fixing an electric plug) are given for many simple but common home repair jobs, usually left inconveniently for fathers, who are never at home when things break or go wrong. . . . The book is inspiring evidence of a belief that children may enjoy a knowledge of how their homes operate and a share in making them function. It offers real work instead of "busy" work. The mother whose child adopts this book with enthusiasm will enjoy more leisure; if not, she will find it easy to make repairs herself.

> *Margaret Warren Brown, in her review of "The First Book of How to Fix It," in* The Horn Book Magazine *(copyright, 1961, by the Horn Book, Inc., Boston), Vol. XXXVII, No. 2, April, 1961, p. 172.*

TAKE A NUMBER (with Marcia Levin, 1961)

Dedicated to the notion that numbers can be fun, this book undertakes to explain what numbers are and how our systems of counting and figuring came about and to teach simple arithmetic through a series of short sentences and simple drawings. The book probably attempts too much, and it tends to fly off in all directions. It seems likely that the children who need it most are those who are unenthusiastic about numbers and need to be convinced that the fun is there, may be confused.

> *A review of "Take a Number," in* Publishers Weekly *(reprinted from the May 29, 1961 issue of* Publishers Weekly, *published by R. R. Bowker Company; copyright © 1961 by R. R. Bowker Company), Vol. 179, No. 22, May 29, 1961, p. 62.*

Despite its unpromising beginning ("How did we get the idea of 7? Could we say that a set of 7 children is like a set of clouds?"), Jeanne Bendick and Marcia Levin help even the reluctant figures to find countless fascinating details behind our everyday numerals. Tricks and games and discussions lend a refreshing variety . . . . [Its] tidbits of information are agelessly appealing.

> *Pamela Marsh, "Widening Horizons for Children," in* The Christian Science Monitor *(reprinted by permission from* The Christian Science Monitor; *(© 1961 The Christian Science Publishing Society; all rights reserved), June 22, 1961, p. C7.**

Will not help slow students to solve problems but will definitely stimulate intelligent students. Miss Bendick's illustrations are simple and easy to follow. Excellent stepping-stone. . . .

> *Thomas Goonan, in his review of "Take a Number," in* School Library Journal, *an appendix to* Library Journal *(reprinted from the July, 1961 issue of* School Library Journal, *published by R. R. Bowker Co./A*

Xerox Corporation; copyright © 1961), Vol. 8, No. 1, September, 1961, p. 119.

"Take a Number" presents useful material [on the history and possible future uses of mathematics] and includes a history of counting discussions on various number systems, a simple but satisfactory explanation of computers and a look at some of the amazing and amusing qualities that mathematicians have discovered in their never-ending investigation of numbers. Through its informal, breezy manner **"Take a Number"** should attract even the determined opponent of arithmetic.

> *Fritz Kain, "Fun with Figures," in The New York Times Book Review (© 1961 by The New York Times Company; reprinted by permission), August 13, 1961, p. 20.**

ARCHIMEDES AND THE DOOR OF SCIENCE   (1962)

In many of her books, Jeanne Bendick makes science and mathematics intelligible to the average interested child. In choosing to define the theories and discoveries of Archimedes, she is now writing for an audience whose proficiency in math and science has led to the interest in the history of these subjects—namely—an audience who might seek out a less simplified, more intense approach than the one Miss Bendick traditionally offers. This is the only problem that arises in a book which sketches in the biography of Archimedes and goes on to describe his various achievements. . . . The book is well organized and well written, though not as exciting as earlier titles by this author.

> *A review of "Archimedes and the Door of Science," in Virginia Kirkus' Service, Vol. XXX, No. 1, January 1, 1962, p. 12.*

Offers what is known about Archimedes' life, some general background about the times, and a clear, interesting presentation of his contributions to science. Miss Bendick is capable of really good simple explanation of relatively complex ideas. The book never lags in these sections, but some of her fictionizing is written down and irritating. She's too good to need to do this. . . .

> *Theodore C. Hines, in his review of "Archimedes and the Door of Science," in School Library Journal an appendix to Library Journal (reprinted from the September, 1962 issue of School Library Journal, published by R. R. Bowker Co./A Xerox Corporation; copyright © 1962), Vol. 9, No. 1, September, 1962, p. 150.*

THE DAY THE NUMBERS DISAPPEARED   (with Leonard Simon, 1963)

"Numbers, who needs them?" Mr. Dibbs lets his class abolish them, but when they find life too hard without numbers, they must earn them back by working through the Egyptian, Greek and Roman systems. Interesting and important information in amusing pictures, examples, and a minimum of text.

> *A review of "The Day the Numbers Disappeared," in Publishers Weekly (reprinted from the February 4, 1963 issue of Publishers Weekly, published by R. R. Bowker Company; copyright © 1963 by R. R. Bowker Company), Vol. 183, No. 5, February 4, 1963, p. 78.*

Leonard Simon and Jeanne Bendick approach the subject [of arithmetic] in a felicitous manner, telling a story of an arithmetic class that tried to get along without numbers, with surprising complications. The material has been presented before in non-fiction, but the story technique used here is well designed to catch and hold attention. The characters, though lightly sketched are warm and real and a gentle humor leavens the whole. Make room for this one.

> *Fritz Kain, in his review of "The Day the Numbers Disappeared," in The New York Times Book Review (© 1963 by The New York Times Company; reprinted by permission), May 5, 1963, p. 22.*

SEA SO BIG, SHIP SO SMALL   (1963)

[This book] will have a natural appeal for the younger members of the family. All the important points are illustrated with gay, two-color drawings as well as explained in a short, direct text. An amazing amount of information is packed into this attractive book, including what to do in different emergencies, and what rules to follow in connection with skin-diving and water skiing.

> *A review of "Sea So Big, Ship So Small," in Publishers Weekly (reprinted from the March 11, 1963 issue of Publishers Weekly, published by R. R. Bowker Company; copyright © 1963 by R. R. Bowker Company), Vol. 183, No. 10, March 11, 1963, p. 55.*

A handbook of rules of the sea for young and old, whether they set out on a mill pond or the ocean. . . . [It has] interesting and clear illustrations by the author. Anyone stepping into a boat should know all its contents. This [is an] exceptionally good quiz book for parents to give young yachtsmen. . . .

> *Robert C. Bergenheim, "Off on the Right Tack," in The Christian Science Monitor (reprinted by permission from The Christian Science Monitor; © 1963 The Christian Science Publishing Society; all rights reserved), May 9, 1963, p. B5.**

"Sea So Big, Ship So Small" by the capable Jeanne Bendick, who can, with brisk text and funny drawings, make almost any subject clear and palatable to those under 11, begins as though the reader had no knowledge of boats whatever and carefully builds up his body of essential information.

Anyone who has not grown up by the sea or lake shore and served an apprenticeship with adult sailors or knowledgeable young people could benefit by reading it.

The basic rules of safety, the simpler principles of navigation, weather signs you should note in order not to be caught in a dangerous situation, how to dock a boat and much more, are all here. With boats crowding the waterways as cars crowd the roads, it behooves us to see that everyone knows enough for safety in a sport that has hazards of nature in addition to man-made ones.

> *Margaret Sherwood Libby, "On Ships, From Sailing to Nuclear," in Books (© I.H.T. Corporation: reprinted by permission), July 14, 1963, p. 9.**

THE FIRST BOOK OF TIME   (1963)

In bright, orderly prose and with unfailing instincts, the author presents to readers of fifth grade through junior high school the many faces of time, and shows how very basic the tool is to our existence.

Henry W. Hubbard, in his review of "The First Book of Time," in The New York Times Book Review (© 1963 by The New York Times Company; reprinted by permission), July 21, 1963, p. 24.

Throughout the text is illuminated by some amusing drawings and diagrams, and with a good but simple index, the book stands out as an essential for the junior school library, and for the basic mathematics work in the classroom. Jeanne Bendick possesses the essential knowledge of an authority but she shows that one can present the most difficult topics to juniors in a stimulating way by relating one area of knowledge to another; in this book, biology, history, mathematics, and geology.

Eric Linfield, in his review of "The First Book of Time," in The School Librarian and School Library Review, Vol. 12, No. 2, July, 1964, p. 216.

Jeanne Bendick uses the written word with direct personal force as a teaching instrument. *The First Book of Time* . . . , intended for readers from eight or so, offers not only knowledge, clear thinking and logical planning but also a lively humour and, in her illustrations, something almost amounting to wit. (p. 179)

One of Jeanne Bendick's assets is her highly professional planning of factual subjects; the structural virtue of her book on time has more than clarity to commend it. Her sixty-eight pages are divided into clearly marked sections which develop her thesis point by point. . . . The assumption behind this book is that children can be trusted to think for themselves. It is not intended to be an exhaustive account of man's manipulation of time. Jeanne Bendick selects examples to support ideas and does not multiply them to show off her knowledge or her superior conscientiousness as a teacher. She recognises that the best way to learn is to recognise that facts are a step towards reasoning, and her book ends with an invitation to the reader to take over from her. . . . Jeanne Bendick has chosen a prose style which will put no strain on a reader trying to understand the points she makes; a child of above-average intelligence would hardly find her book daunting in his earliest reading years. (pp. 179-81)

Margery Fisher, "Foundations," in her Matters of Fact: Aspects of Non-Fiction for Children (copyright ©1972 by Margery Fisher; reprinted by permission of Harper & Row, Publishers, Inc.), Thomas Y. Crowell Co., Inc.), 1972, pp. 9-200.*

THE FIRST BOOK OF FISHES   (1965)

A professional ichthyologist probably could not have prepared as as skillful and adequate an introduction to the study of fishes for young readers as this admirable work of Miss Bendick. It is a dynamic treatment in logical sequence of essential elements of environment, general morphology, evolution, major taxonomic groups, taxonomic characters and identification, age determination from scales, physiology, reproduction, and other features, concluding in a good index. The only lack is a list of suggested additional books to read.

A review of "The First Book of Fishes," in Science Books (copyright © 1965 by the American Association for the Advancement of Science), Vol. 1, No. 3, December, 1965, p. 160.

WHAT TO DO: EVERYDAY GUIDES FOR EVERYONE   (with Marian Warren, 1967)

The basic premise is tried-and-still true: consideration is the essence of good manners, so do unto others, etc. A concise outline of correct behavior not according to Post but according to kindness and common sense, this clear-cut presentation of dos and don'ts covers most family, community, and social situations. A child well brought up in the middle-class tradition will find the advice completely familiar; the unguided youngster will benefit from a simple code of up-to-date, informal politeness.

A review of "What to Do: Everyday Guides for Everyone," in Kirkus Service (copyright © 1967 Virginia Kirkus' Service, Inc.), Vol. XXXV, No. 7, April 1, 1967, p. 425.

Although marred by too many "don'ts" and by unattractive cartoon drawings, the book is a sensible guide to basic etiquette and personal management. . . . Its greatest value will be to young people needing simply stated guidelines to acceptable, rather than highly refined, behavior.

Ruth P. Bull and Mary Simons, in their review of "What to Do: Everyday Guides for Everyone," in The Booklist and Subscription Books Bulletin (reprinted by permission of the American Library Association; copyright © 1968 by the American Library Association), Vol. 64, No. 14, March 15, 1968, p. 866.

THE EMERGENCY BOOK   (1967)

A compendium of common sense that is not necessarily common knowledge, this should be on every family's reference shelf. With her usual acumen—and what is also a justification for library purchase—Jeanne Bendick advises reading the book through at least once because "the facts you need . . . can come popping out at you" in an emergency. After general advice (including the reminder that "people are more important than things") and a suggested list of emergency telephone numbers, she approaches first aid by establishing priorities in each of four common serious emergencies—severe bleeding, cessation of breathing, swallowing poison, bad burns. (Typical of her understanding of kids is this amplification of mouth-to-mouth resuscitation: "if you'd rather, you can open a handkerchief between the victim's mouth and yours.") However, most of the first aid instructions are included in the sections on emergencies of various sorts—in the household, in public places, on roadways, in bad weather, in the woods, during water or winter sports. Fire emergencies are treated in detail (with equal attention to apartments) and one of the best sections is advice to the sitter (including the handling of predatory papas—"If you have to be rude, be rude"). Both the ounce of prevention and the pound of cure—each adjusted to the circumstances and capabilities of youngsters.

A review of "The Emergency Book," in Kirkus Service (copyright © 1967 Virginia Kirkus' Service, Inc.), Vol. XXXV, No. 19, October 1, 1967, p. 1221.

A book of advice and caution that is utterly sensible, quite comprehensive, and often entertaining; the material is neatly compartmentalized and cross-referenced for easy accessibility. . . . The illustrations are in cartoon style, some simply amusing and others in amplification of the text. . . . (pp. 33-4)

Zena Sutherland, in her review of "The Emergency Book," in The Best in Children's Books: The University of Chicago Guide to Children's Literature, 1966-1972, edited by Zena Sutherland (reprinted by permission of The University of Chicago Press; ©1973 by The University of Chicago), University of Chicago Press, 1973, pp. 33-4.

SHAPES (1967)

[This] is quite up-to-date in terms of what is currently considered "good" in young children's science if not entirely successful in presentation. The attempt to cover everything about shapes from the standard fare (squares, circles, numbers) to more interesting notions (rhythm, emotion, symmetry) would seem to be a tall order for such a brief book. (Often, what is left out of a book for children is as important as what is left in.) But the approach is useful although . . . it may have to be read to the children who will benefit most. (pp. 7-8)

A review of "Shapes," in Kirkus Service (copyright ©1968 Virginia Kirkus' Service, Inc.), Vol. XXXVI, No. 1, January 1, 1968, pp. 7-8.

Although cluttered with an overabundance of cartoonish drawings and instructional diagrams that are not always clear, this book . . . may prove valuable especially in school libraries. Using the process or discovery method of presentation which encourages the child to draw appropriate conclusions from demonstrated or observed data, the author supplements her explanations of shapes, line, plane, and three-dimensional figures and symmetry with stimulating questions and problems. Because of the wide scope and complexity of some of the concepts discussed, the book will probably be of most benefit when used in connection with classroom science units.

A review of "Shapes," in The Booklist and Subscription Books Bulletin (reprinted by permission of the American Library Association; copyright © 1968 by the American Library Association), Vol. 64, No. 17, May 1, 1968, p. 1039.

SPACE AND TIME (1967)

The simple, useful illustrations and the crowded text are characteristic of Jeanne Bendick and this is best considered in connection to her *First Book of Time*: whereas that treated time only in terms of a relationship to space, this focuses on space with some concern for time; it is also a little more elementary in presentation. Notions of space—in the fundamental sense of position or location rather than in its astronomical context—are presented and found to be inextricably bound to time. (Can you think of a question that asks *where* without asking *when*?) Many of the simple experiences suggested (such as water and air occupy space) are the perennial favorites of collections of science experiments but this at least concentrates on a single important area and stays with it.

A review of "Space and Time," in Kirkus Service (copyright © 1968 Virginia Kirkus' Service, Inc.), Vol. XXXVI, No. 1, January 1, 1968, p. 8.

The concept of space and time is a difficult one for young children to grasp, but it should be made much easier with the aid of this useful book. . . . The bold Americanised pictures do make the book attractive, lively and will induce even the slowest child to use the very simple and clear text to find out what it is all about. Many ideas are given for further experiment and the imaginative child will find that there is plenty there for him too.

A review of "Space and Time," in The Junior Bookshelf, Vol. 35, No. 1, February, 1971, p. 31.

[*Space and Time*] makes a notable attempt to relate concepts to actions.

All through this exceptionally lucid exposition the author has taken the unusual course of putting concept first and method afterwards, so that a child could become aware, just by the pattern of argument, that the idea of time preceded and overshadows objects like clocks and sundials. The relation of fact and concept has been . . . carefully thought out in this very junior book. . . . (p. 177)

Margery Fisher, "Foundations," in her Matters of Fact: Aspects of Non-Fiction for Children (copyright ©1972 by Margery Fisher; reprinted by permission of Harper & Row, Publishers, Inc.), Thomas Y. Crowell Co., Inc., 1972, pp. 9-200.*

LIVING THINGS (1969)

In this one small book [the student] learns some of the characteristics of all living things, the environmental conditions necessary for life, the great diversity in plant and animal habitats, the interaction and interdependence of plants and animals, and the salient characteristics of the major groups of plants and animals. Whether or not a child is receiving science instruction in school by the process of approach he can use and enjoy [the Science Experience] books, for they make everything in his total experience and environment scientifically meaningful.

A review of "Living Things," in Science Books (copyright © 1969 by the American Association for the Advancement of Science), Vol. 5, No. 1, May, 1969, p. 13.

As are all the Bendick books, this introduction to biology is written in crisp, straightforward style and illustrated with lively drawings that are moderately useful. Although the text covers so much ground that it only skims the subject, it gives a good overview of what distinguishes living things from non-living, how plants and animals are grouped, ecological balance, adaptation, etc. The writing is in harmony with the process approach, suggesting observation and some home experiments.

A review of "Living Things," in Saturday Review (© 1969 Saturday Review Magazine Co.; reprinted by permission), Vol. LII, No. 29, July 19, 1969, p. 43.

The author's illustrations are racially integrated and depict both urban and country living. She continually questions the reader or asks him to search out illustrations and examples of the lessons for himself.

A review of "Living Things," in The Christian Science Monitor (reprinted by permission from The Christian Science Monitor; © 1969 The Christian Science Publishing Society; all rights reserved), July 31, 1969, p. 11.

Ecology is an exact science and the plan of this book is not entirely exact. The author makes the proper points about ecosystems and our part in a wide band of life but she confuses the issue by using far too many drawings. They lose emphasis because they are crowded together so that a real effort is required to relate each to its appropriate piece of text. The restless effect of the illustrations interrupts the sense and authority of the text.

> *Margery Fisher, in her review of "Living Things,"*
> *in her* Growing Point, *Vol. 9, No. 6, December,*
> *1970, p. 1646.*

WHY CAN'T I? (1969)

A bird can fly. Why can't you? You are too heavy and you don't have wings. But you have hands, and think of all that you are able to do with them. . . . This is the pattern: an explanation of why certain creatures can do things a human can't and a note of consolation that follows. Although this is mildly interesting as an introduction to comparative physiology, it is really only a random assembling of biological facts. Not as substantial as Bendick's usual work.

> *Zena Sutherland, in her review of "Why Can't I?"*
> *in* Bulletin of the Center for Children's Books (re-
> *printed by permission of The University of Chicago*
> *Press; © 1969 by The University of Chicago), Vol.*
> *23, No. 2, October, 1969, p. 22.*

Although Jeanne Bendick does not use a continuous narrative to hold together her book *Why Can't I?* she does use children to wonder about the things they see. From a series of comparisons, we discover why we can't do several things such as breathe under water like a fish, or walk on the ceiling like a fly. . . . The relating of the facts to the reader, the "I" of the title and the "you" of the text, makes these facts personal, interesting, and remarkable. Comparisons make the facts understandable, and each comparison has some narrative quality. The young reader is involved in this explanatory situation by the simplest of narrative elements.

> *Rebecca J. Lukens, in her review of "Why Can't I?"*
> *in her* A Critical Handbook of Children's Literature
> *(copyright © 1976 by Scott, Foresman and Company;*
> *reprinted by permission), Scott, Foresman, 1976,*
> *p. 187.*

A PLACE TO LIVE (1970)

Conservation and environmental quality are introduced to the young reader who will have weighty decisions to make influencing the livability of the earth. Since the author is also illustrator, the story unfolds pictorially and with suitable words. . . . The young ecologist will feel informed at his level of understanding about the subject his parents are discussing and viewing on the television screen. An index is helpful to locate and retrieve facts which were read in the text.

> *A review of "A Place to Live," in* Science Books
> *(copyright © 1970 by the American Association for*
> *the Advancement of Science), Vol. 6, No. 2, Septem-*
> *ber, 1970, p. 134.*

This attractive primer-style book, apparently designed to be a supplementary reader, is directed to a younger age group than are most nature books. . . . Bendick's book has a more immediate application to the child's world, both rural and urban. Whereas the emphasis in, for example, such titles as *Small Pond* by Marguerite Walters (Dutton, 1966) or Augusta Goldin's *The Sunlit Sea* (Crowell, 1968) has been limited to a

microcosm or a natural region, the approach here is always in terms of human experience and of the neighborhood or community. An earthworm, for example, is shown to have an effect on plant life, and therefore on our food supply. As usual, this author's simple but expressive pictures of active children keep readers' attention and help them to better appreciate the ideas in the text.

> *Della Thomas, in her review of "A Place to Live,"*
> *in* School Library Journal, *an appendix to* Library
> Journal *(reprinted from the November, 1970 issue of*
> School Library Journal, *published by R. R. Bowker*
> *Co./A Xerox Corporation; copyright © 1970), Vol.*
> *17, No. 3, November, 1970, p. 96.*

Right now everyone is concerned with environment and ecology, and this is a simple explanation of the former which offers reasons for the latter. The text is simple and in good, clear type. The illustrations are adequate—cartoony and one or two are a little indistinct—and the conclusion is sound. The author sprinkles questions throughout (which are answered in the text) and invites the reader to apply what he is learning to his own environment. The purpose of the book is to show the importance of each member of a living community and the importance of providing proper living conditions for each community, i.e., clean air, clean water, and sunshine. The point is made without undue emotion and the book is a useful one, but not, I feel, inspired. It has been produced to fill a need.

> *Nancy Bond, in her review of "A Place to Live," in*
> Appraisal: Science Books for Young People *(copy-*
> *right ©1971 by the Children's Science Book Review*
> *Committee), Vol. 4, No. 2, Spring, 1971, p. 5.*

NAMES, SETS, AND NUMBERS (1971)

The crisp, to-the-point approach found in other Bendick books is lacking in this slim volume which concentrates heavily on sets (some 38 pages) while the other two topics, names and numbers, share 17 pages. The author writes in a rambling style, and the age level of the intended audience is questionable: the main text aims at the low-to-middle elementary grades: digressions, under special headings, would appeal to upper elementary students.

> *Josette A. Boisse, in her review of "Names, Sets,*
> *and Numbers," in* School Library Journal, *an ap-*
> *pendix to* Library Journal *(reprinted from the May,*
> *1971 issue of* School Library Journal, *published by*
> *R. R. Bowker Co./A Xerox Corporation; copyright*
> *© 1971), Vol. 17, No. 9, May, 1971, p. 88.*

Here is the simplest, clearest, and most attractive introduction to the process of logical thinking one could hope to find. Every activity and fact in the book is illustrated in two-color line drawings, cartoon-like with an immediacy and humor children love. The reader will see why we need names and numbers; he can appreciate how his own understanding and memory develop once he is totally involved observing similarities and differences, and he will be able to group everything that bombards his senses accordingly. Abundant pertinent questions are found throughout the text. Those that are not answered on the page or are not self-evident are answered on the last page to which the child is told to turn. This rather detracts from the fun of this learning experience. The future success of a child's education could be more easily insured if at an early stage in his learning he had the good fortune to find and like this book.

From A Place to Live, *written and illustrated by Jeanne Bendick.*

Sister Mary E. Rock, in her review of "Names, Sets, and Numbers," in Appraisal: Science Books for Young People *(copyright © 1972 by the Children's Science Book Review Committee), Vol. 5, No. 2, Spring, 1972, p. 3.*

HOW TO MAKE A CLOUD   (1971)

On the whole this is a good, easy-to-understand scientific presentation of weather concepts, including cloud formations, the water cycle and even smog. Terms are clearly defined; illustrations accompany the text with captions that summarize and ask thought-provoking questions. Easy experiments which emphasize safety, simple weather poems and recipes for different weather forms add interest and reinforce the concepts presented. . . . It is more complete and more attractive than similar books on the same level. . . . (pp. 100-01)

Judith Sima, in her review of "How to Make a Cloud," in School Library Journal, *an appendix to* Library Journal *(reprinted from the October, 1971 issue of* School Library Journal, *published by R. R. Bowker Co./A Xerox Corporation; copyright © 1971), Vol. 18, No. 2, October, 1971, pp. 100-01.*

In general this is a well written simplified account of the dynamics of cloud formation and as a most welcome adjunct what the different types of clouds mean in terms of forecasting the weather. A few gaffes are present, however, and should be pointed out. On page fifteen the statement "The sun does not heat the air directly" just isn't so. Most of the heating of the air does take place indirectly via the heating of the ground, as the author correctly describes, but some heating is direct. On page sixteen, "lighter things float on heavier ones". . . . again, not so. Clouds are heavier than air but cloud droplets being small fall very slowly through the air—so slowly that a very slight rising motion of the air will keep them aloft, seemingly, but not actually floating. Other than these two difficulties the book can be well recommended.

John D. Stackpole, in his review of "How to Make a Cloud," in Appraisal: Science Books for Young People *(copyright © 1972 by the Children's Science*

Book Review Committee), Vol. 5, No. 1, Winter, 1972, p. 8.

WHAT MADE YOU YOU?   (1971)

How do you explain genetic coding without getting into the intricacies of the double helix, of transfer RNA, nucleotides, or even chromosomes? Jeanne Bendick does it very nicely by simply describing for the young reader how genes carry hereditary traits and by emphasizing the continuity in families and the love that is part of human conception. In discussing copulation, conception, gestation, and birth, the text is direct in tone and restrained in coverage, always stressing the unique quality of each human being.

A review of "What Made You You?" in Saturday Review *(© 1972 Saturday Review Magazine Co.; reprinted by permission), Vol. LV, No. 13, March 25, 1972, p. 110.*

Inherited traits and family continuity are the focus for the relentless jollity of **"What Made You You?"**. . . . Amplifying the central theme are breezy summaries of love and reproduction (naked couples leering at each other in arch surmise, or embracing while standing up, apparently asleep), pregnancy, fetal life and childbirth, with special attention to the genes—"the recipe for you."

These are not quite the biologist's genes; they are the "smile genes and nose genes / fingers and toes genes / and elbows and knees genes / and maybe some sneeze genes." All of which add up to "you genes"—a rhymed conceit, perhaps requiring some elaboration on mummy's part if the boy next door happens to be named Eugene.

It is typical of the book's playful ambiguities. These may amuse a young child. They may also suggest that sometimes when you ask adults serious questions you get silly answers.

Paul Showers, "Sex of One and Half a Dozen of Another," in The New York Times Book Review, *Part II (© 1972 by The New York Times Company; reprinted by permission), May 7, 1972, p. 32.**

A superficial, sentimental text and generally uninformative pictures combine to confuse readers about sexuality and reproduction. Inadequately described are such subjects as sexual intercourse . . . , the appearance and union of the sperm and egg; the role of genes . . . , the baby's growth and nourishment inside the womb; and the birth process. . . . Neither definitions nor pronunciations are given for penis, vagina, or womb. Bendick misleadingly refers to "smile genes" and "sneeze genes" and explains genes in general only as constituting "the recipe for you." Coy descriptions abound as do abstract you-isms. . . . One picture confusingly shows ancestors—including some children—of an adult labelled "You." Nothing in the book explains why a child differs from his or her siblings when they all share the same genetic background, and Bendick doesn't tell *why* "Right from the beginning you were a boy or a girl." Even very young children can handle more substantial information than is offered here. . . .

> *Diane Gersoni-Edelman, in her review of "What Made You You?" in* School Library Journal, *an appendix to* Library Journal *(reprinted from the September, 1972 issue of* School Library Journal, *published by R. R. Bowker Co./A Xerox Corporation; copyright © 1972), Vol. 19, No. 1, September, 1972, p. 112.*

Jeanne Bendick adds tenderness to her usual breezy, informal style and blithe illustrations. . . . The emphasis is on love, and this is carried throughout the text and the subsequent discussion of hereditary traits carried by genes. . . . Nicely done.

> *Zena Sutherland, in her review of "What Made You You?" in* The Best in Children's Books: The University of Chicago Guide to Children's Literature, 1966-1972, *edited by Zena Sutherland (reprinted by permission of The University of Chicago Press; © 1973 by The University of Chicago),* University of Chicago Press, *1973, p. 34.*

MEASURING (1971)

An exciting book that introduces the reader to what measurement is, how measurements are made, and how measurements can be used. . . . The format of the book presents a logical development of measuring skills. Each new concept is reinforced by activities and well-directed questions. Points of potential confusion are carefully treated to insure a positive learning experience.

> *Harry O. Haakonsen, in his review of "Measuring," in* Appraisal: Science Books for Young People *(copyright © 1972 by the Children's Science Book Review Committee), Vol. 5, No. 3, Fall, 1972, p. 8.*

This is a carefully organized, neatly developed explanation of measurement—what it is, how we do it, and why. The "Think for yourself" and "Try it yourself" sections scattered liberally throughout the book suggest amusing but valid and thought-provoking experiments for the reader to do himself. The metric system is explained and discussed, and compared with the English system of measuring. Using the process approach to science teaching, the author has produced a book invaluable to the teacher, attractive and stimulating to the student. The two-color illustrations are essential to the text, as is the page of answers to questions incorporated in the text. (p. 8)

> *Martita U. Stitt, in her review of "Measuring," in* Appraisal: Science Books for Young People *(copyright © 1972 by the Children's Science Book Review Committee), Vol. 5, No. 3, Fall, 1972, pp. 7-8.*

OBSERVATION (1972)

A cohesive, interesting, and appealingly illustrated book on observation. The use of questions and activities on almost every page involves readers, and their attention is drawn to such characteristics as shape, color, speed, size, temperature, weight, and sound. Briefly covered are inference, record keeping, and observation tools. This title is more challenging than the author's **All Around You** . . . and it constitutes an important addition to general science collections.

> *Shirley A. Smith, in her review of "Observation," in* School Library Journal, *an appendix to* Library Journal *(reprinted from the March, 1973 issue of* School Library Journal, *published by R. R. Bowker Co./A Xerox Corporation; copyright © 1973), Vol. 19, No. 7, March, 1973, p. 104.*

Skills in observing are a fundamental prerequisite for experimental scientists; indeed, observation is a necessary art in our daily lives. Careful observation would help us all to interpret better the many bits of information that stimulate our senses, and there is a definite need for introducing children to proper methods of observation. Thus, the idea behind this book is a good one, although the implementation has not been totally successful. The reader is first introduced to observation as a concept, then shown how to apply it in various situations, using a group of different but related objects. The reader is shown how to analyze the objects, how to think for himself in making comparisons and then how to try it in another situation. The sequence is very useful in teaching the art of observation. Nevertheless, the child may become bored with a monotonous repetition of look-at-this and look-at-that. Recording observations and useful tools in observing are treated very briefly, as are techniques of developing relations between observations and on differences in observation by different observers. An excellent index is included. (pp. 156-57)

> *A review of "Observation," in* Science Books *(copyright © 1973 by the American Association for the Advancement of Science), Vol. IX, No. 2, September, 1973, pp. 156-57.*

The reader becomes a detective looking for the answers to posed questions. The illustrations are well drawn and aid the written material. Because it is a question and answer book with no set answers, a child can read it over and over and still find it an enjoyable experience. **Observation** is one of the better books printed in recent years.

> *Howard W. Wong, in his review of "Observation," in* Appraisal: Science Books for Young People *(copyright © 1973 by the Children's Science Book Review Committee), Vol. 6, No. 3, Fall, 1973, p. 8.*

MOTION AND GRAVITY (1972)

Those who know this author's previous simple outlines of natural phenomena . . . will know what to expect and will welcome this addition with its humorous illustrations which are calculated to take the sting out of learning. Her books are good because they ask questions without giving all the answers, thus forcing the eight-year-old to think for himself, perhaps doing simple experiments in order to reason out the solution. For once there is an index which is really superfluous in this kind of book.

Sometimes an observer uses his experience to guess, from what he is observing, that something is *going* to change.

Try It Yourself

Look at the pictures. What is going to happen? Why do you think so?

From Observation, *written and illustrated by Jeanne Bendick.*

A review of "Motion and Gravity," in The Junior Bookshelf, *Vol. 37, No. 4, August, 1973, p. 247.*

The somewhat difficult concepts of motion and gravity are carefully and sequentially developed in this book. Simple, clear illustrations aid the reader's understanding. . . . Throughout the book, many thought-provoking questions are posed to the reader. While some of these questions are answered on the page overleaf, many are left unanswered. This lack could be rather frustrating to some young readers trying to cope with the book by themselves.

A review of "Motion and Gravity," in Science Books *(copyright © 1973 by the American Association for the Advancement of Science), Vol. IX, No. 2, September, 1973, p. 159.*

_____

WHY THINGS CHANGE: THE STORY OF EVOLUTION (1973)

From the time when "there were no living things at all" to the emergence "out of one of the primates" of that mammal with the "wonderful brain"—in 59 pages of which the drab, easily overlooked pictures take up more space than the words. As for the text, Bendick makes it all extremely simple . . . but simple isn't quite the same as clear. An easy word might bear an unfamiliar meaning (some kinds of living things can survive without change "because they are not too special"), the early definition of evolution (as "the slow changing of living things so they can keep on going in the changing world around them") never points out that it's not the individual living thing that changes, Bendick's few generalizations are

oddly ambiguous ("the amphibians themselves were never very important animals"—not famous?), and unexplained words (such as cell) are used loosely: the first plants and animals "had one cell" but later "some cells joined together to make bigger, more complex plants and animals" (with some sort of forward-looking Bergsonian purpose?). In all, what this childishly written introduction chiefly explains is why young readers yawn.

A review of "Why Things Change: The Story of Evolution," in Kirkus Reviews *(copyright © 1973 The Kirkus Service, Inc.), Vol. XLI, No. 23, December 1, 1973, p. 1311.*

The story of evolution is adequately told in this book, there are no obvious errors of fact, but there is the usual error of presenting the theory of evolution as if it were a fact instead of a hypothesis. Such a presentation does harm to science, since it misleads young readers and does not help them learn to distinguish between observable *facts* (which do not change) and *interpretations* of facts (which may change). In the elementary school years, children should be learning scientific scepticism and how to carry out the activities essential to accurate inductive/deductive thinking. There is one activity suggested in the book (making a time line). If carried through consistently, it may clarify the concept of evolutionary development and assist the reader to develop his or her own sense of the immensity of time elapsed since earth's beginning. Ms. Bendick writes well and the text and illustrations are clear and appealing. If only she had represented the study of evolutionary development as it truly is: an exciting, open-ended attempt to solve a fabulously interesting and important puzzle. Then the book would have been highly recommended.

A review of "Why Things Change: The Story of Evolution," in Science Books *(copyright © 1974 by the American Association for the Advancement of Science), Vol. IX, No. 9, March, 1974, p. 329.*

In the simplest possible terms, Jeanne Bendick's book explains the process of evolution for children possibly as young as eight. Not only are the terms very simple, but the whole concept is arranged so carefully and clearly that it is not above the grasp of primary school. . . . The illustrations are a bit crude and not very attractive, but they serve; and the examples chosen for illustration are the perfect ones to help make this a very good book for a school library. (pp. 11-12)

Heddie Kent, in her review of "Why Things Change: The Story of Evolution," in Appraisal: Science Books for Young People *(copyright © 1974 by the Children's Science Book Review Committee), Vol. 7, No. 2, Spring, 1974, pp. 11-12.*

Perhaps the author might have been more modern through explaining carefully that the "higher" forms of life, by our standards, are "better" only because they fit more precisely in our current environment. But, after all, scientists have been a bit lax about clarifying such background. In all, it's a very good book, reflecting the restless change that all who survive must keep themselves tuned to.

Wayne Hanley, in his review of "Why Things Change: The Story of Evolution," in Appraisal: Science Books for Young People *(copyright © 1974 by the Children's Science Book Review Committee), Vol. 7, No. 2, Spring, 1974, p. 12.*

_____

SOLIDS, LIQUIDS, AND GASES (1974)

Solids, liquids, and gases all take up space and can be measured and weighed but only solids have shape and only solids and liquids can be seen. . . . Interspersed with questions ("What do you think") and simple experiments ("Now try this") and definitions (of things and sets and size and weight), this is strictly for classroom use and only semisolid.

> *A review of "Solids, Liquids, and Gases," in* Kirkus Reviews *(copyright © 1974 The Kirkus Service, Inc.), Vol. XLII, No. 7, April 1, 1974, p. 365.*

This is more of a workbook than a textbook. The author's method is to ask a number of questions, make some helpful or leading statements, with suggestions for simple experiments, and then give the answers. She asks the reader to separate all things in the world into three sets. To do this one has to decide on the definition of a thing. I found her constant question method extremely distracting. Sometimes she is confusing. . . . Occasionally, the illustrations are irrelevant. . . . It is a very busy, unsatisfactory book. . . .

> *Ethanne Smith, in her review of "Solids, Liquids, and Gases," in* Appraisal: Science Books for Young People *(copyright © 1974 by the Children's Science Book Review Committee), Vol. 7, No. 3, Fall, 1974, p. 6.*

Some people think that it's important that young children develop sophisticated understanding of fairly abstract notions like density and the impenetrability of matter. This book will appeal to such people. I'm still not convinced that we should aim at producing "junior scientists" in the elementary school, so I think this book deals essentially with uninteresting, irrelevant, and overly abstract scientific concepts. The complexity of the author's approach to such a simple topic as "states of matter" would be laughable except that it is likely to destroy so many youngsters natural interest in the simple beauty of nature. When the book limits itself to some straightforward experiments and observations on solids, liquids, and gases, and the conclusions derived from them, it does a very nice job, with many good exercises and problems suggested. Too bad we couldn't have just *that* part of the book! (pp. 6-7)

> *David E. Newton, in his review of "Solids, Liquids, and Gases," in* Appraisal: Science Books for Young People *(copyright © 1974 by the Children's Science Book Review Committee), Vol. 7, No. 3, Fall, 1974, pp. 6-7.*

HEAT AND TEMPERATURE (1974)

Here is a well-written, nicely printed and amusingly illustrated book with well-known and repeatedly written about information on heat. . . . Both pictures and text are sometimes confusing, but the book could be used in second and third grades, provided the activities are supervised. The mathematics of converting from Celsius scale to Fahrenheit and vice versa is too difficult for this level, but perhaps the picture showing that it can be done by computation is useful.

> *A review of "Heat and Temperature," in* Science Books *(copyright © 1975 by the American Association for the Advancement of Science), Vol. X, No. 4, March, 1975, p. 334.*

Mrs. Bendick has used some effective gimmicks in her book on heat and temperature. . . . At first glance, the book may appear cartoonish. Subjects like radiation, conduction, and convection are not easy concepts, but Mrs. Bendick's approach really makes them clear. The experiments are easy, fun, and revealing; and the explanations of, for instance, the Fahrenheit and Celsius thermometers can be readily absorbed by this age.

> *Heddie Kent, in her review of "Heat and Temperature," in* Appraisal: Science Books for Young People *(copyright © 1975 by the Children's Science Book Review Committee), Vol. 8, No. 2, Spring, 1975, p. 7.*

Any author who decides to take on a conceptually difficult subject like heat (especially beyond the most obvious points) is a brave soul indeed. Bendick does so with great success. She treats such abstract ideas as "energy" and the differences between "heat" and "temperature" in a manner that most students should be able to understand. The book makes use of lots of experiments and many questions for students to "think about." This is an encouraging approach—many more authors and publishers should attack science in the same way! I regret, however, that there is still far too much use of the obvious, "self-answering" question that doesn't allow students freedom really to think about possible solutions. All in all, a very nice treatment. If students could understand everything that is in this book, they would know all the "heat and temperature" they would ever need.

> *David E. Newton, in his review of "Heat and Temperature" in* Appraisal: Science Books for Young People *(copyright © 1975 by the Children's Science Book Review Committee), Vol. 8, No. 2, Spring, 1975, p. 7.*

HOW HEREDITY WORKS: WHY LIVING THINGS ARE AS THEY ARE (1975)

"Elephants make elephants. Ladybugs make ladybugs. Owls make owls, and eels make eels. People make people. Ferns make ferns and grass makes new grass . . . " and so on reiterated until readers can't escape learning that like produces like. . . . There are also a few words on cells and genes, sperm and eggs, generations (a trait might skip one), differences within a family, and, at the end, the influence of "outside things." (This last helps clarify what might have been an occasional misleading sentence earlier on, but the heading "Can outside things change heredity?" introduces communication problems of its own.) This is probably the sort of general and simple introduction that primary school teachers want—though of course it has nothing like the style and subtlety and potential for turning kids on of Charlotte Pomerantz's *Why You Look Like You*. . . .

> *A review of "How Heredity Works: Why Living Things Are As They Are," in* Kirkus Reviews *(copyright ©1975 The Kirkus Service, Inc.), Vol. XLIII, No. 6, March 15, 1975, p. 310.*

Simplistic and confusing, Bendick's *How Heredity Works* never gets beyond cats resembling cats and dogs looking like dogs. The lack of specific information on Mendel's experiments, dominant traits, and other basic principles will be frustrating to most young readers.

> *Virginia Reese, in her review of "How Heredity Works: Why Living Things Are As They Are," in* School Library Journal *(reprinted from the September, 1975 issue of* School Library Journal, *published by R. R.*

Bowker Co./A Xerox Corporation; copyright © 1975), Vol. 22, No. 1, September, 1975, p. 76.

The basic concepts of genetics are handled well, and the author does a good job of explaining the effects of environmental influences on genetic traits. In general, the vocabulary is suitable for elementary readers, although new terms are frequently introduced without adequate definition. The numerous illustrations compliment the text nicely. Throughout the text there are a small number of questions which are designed to explore and expand topics further, and several good teaching units could be developed around the subject matter.

> *Donald J. Nash, in his review of "How Heredity Works: Why Living Things Are As They Are," in* Science Books & Films *(copyright © 1975 by the American Association for the Advancement of Science), Vol. XI, No. 2, Spetember, 1975, p. 94.*

In trying to reduce a complicated, difficult subject to the level of a young child, the author has given us a dull book of little interest to the small child and of little use to the young student. . . . The only redeeming section is one on cells, parents, and genes. The black, white, and orange illustrations add little to the subject matter.

> *Sallie Hope Erhard, in her review of "How Heredity Works: Why Living Things Are As They Are," in* Appraisal: Science Books for Young People *(copyright © 1976 by the Children's Science Book Review Committee), Vol. 9, No. 1, Winter, 1976, p. 9.*

[This] profusely illustrated book for children in the elementary grades gives a lot of facts and asks a lot of questions of the reader. It covers a good deal of ground; and, with help, the reader can learn from it. It is so weak in pointing out principles, however, that the reader may have enough trouble with the questions to not bother with them. It is difficult to develop a true understanding of heredity from the text, for not much attention is paid to developing concepts.

> *Esther H. Read, in her review of "How Heredity Works: Why Living Things Are As They Are," in* Appraisal: Science Books for Young People *(copyright © 1976 by the Children's Science Book Review Committee), Vol. 9, No. 1, Winter, 1976, p. 9.*

ECOLOGY   (1975)

Strictly for the classroom, with pauses and questions for thought and discussion, this is essentially a string of definitions—of food chain, cycle, niche, species, etc.—tied together with a few ecological home truths. . . . Ending up with a definition of *consequences* might be a neat trick, but the trivializing example—"If people throw a lot of litter around a park, it stops being a place where anybody wants to go. That's a consequence"—is likely to stifle any larger thoughts or discussion.

> *A review of "Ecology," in* Kirkus Review *(copyright © 1975 The Kirkus Service, Inc.), Vol. XLIII, No. 22, November 15, 1975, p. 1290.*

I wish that the author had defined "ecology" as the *study* of the interaction of all living things with each other and their environment. The young reader may well fall into the trap, as so many of his elders have so repeatedly done, of saying "good (or bad) ecology" while meaning "good (or bad) treatment of the environment and/or its inhabitants." In spite of this slight

defect I find this book an extremely well-developed and stimulating introduction to ecology on an interest-arousing level, well suited to eight-to-twelve-year-olds. The frequently introduced questions are indeed excellent activities.

> *R. Gregory Belcher, in his review of "Ecology," in* Appraisal: Science Books for Young People *(copyright © 1976 by the Children's Science Book Review Committee), Vol. 9, No. 2, Spring, 1976, p. 8.*

FINDING OUT ABOUT JOBS: TV REPORTING   (with Robert Bendick, 1976)

After warming up with some grand statements ("Work is what people do to keep the world going") and a four-page glossary of terms (cue card, network, story board . . .), Bendick asks children to consider their qualifications for various specialties: "Could you be a foreign correspondent? Maybe you could, if you like having friends of different nationalities. . . . Try eating some food that is very different from what you eat at home." Any class that can't think up better material on its own has no future in reporting.

> *A review of "Finding Out about Jobs: TV Reporting," in* Kirkus Reviews *(copyright © 1976 The Kirkus Service, Inc.), Vol. XLIV, No. 6, March 15, 1976, p. 325.*

In simple and clear language, the Bendicks discuss the different kinds of news reporting done at a television station—investigative, feature, etc. Most helpful are the "Try This" sections after each chapter which give exercises to help develop skills needed in the various types of TV news work. A good choice because there's little else on this glamour field for the age level.

> *Marsha E. Huddleston, in her review of "Finding Out about Jobs: TV Reporting," in* School Library Journal *(reprinted from the September, 1976 issue of* School Library Journal, *published by R. R. Bowker Co./A Xerox Corporation; copyright © 1976), Vol. 23, No. 1, September, 1976, p. 109.*

HOW ANIMALS BEHAVE   (1976)

Although Bendick purports to discuss animal behavior, stressing the importance of species diversity for survival, it is an unsettling blend of contrasts. On the pro side, individual and species differences are surveyed in exemplary fashion, and I applaud considerations of stimuli and responses, learning and the concept that animals live each in their own kind of world. The example that all puppies in a litter do not behave the same, accompanied by an appealing illustration of quiet, fearful, bouncy and bossy puppies, was an excellent treatment of individual differences. On the con side, circular explanations begin and end the book: "When birds start singing in the morning it doesn't mean that they are happy. They are behaving like birds"; and "People behave in many different ways. They behave like people." This reasoning is inappropriate for any age level. A correct statement is "Birds sing to defend their home and to communicate with other birds." The book's strengths are destroyed by referring to adaptive behavior patterns as "instinct" and saying "animals just do them." Geese do not have an instinct that makes them migrate! Instead, using terms already introduced: "Geese respond to stimuli like day length and temperature by migrating." There are some inaccuracies: a barnacle extends its "gills" or lungs, not legs, and insects can learn. Statements that some animals are "more intelligent" than others obscures the point of the book, which is that behavior is influenced by various biological constraints. I would hesitate to read this book to my children because of conceptual confusion and crowded, uninteresting illustrations.

> Wayne P. Aspey, in his review of "How Animals Behave," in Science Books & Films (copyright © 1976 by the American Association for the Advancement of Science), Vol. XII, No. 3, December, 1976, p. 160.

Jeanne Bendick is a born teacher for she knows how to stimulate interest and make a book both interesting and attractive without boring the reader. . . . [She] introduces children to the subject of animal behavior and instinct. Each topic is explained clearly, using repetition to reinforce what concepts she wants understood. . . . [Each point is] briefly but clearly presented and each page has many illustrations which, with their captions, do make the text very easy to follow. Naturally this is not in any way profound although it does cover much, but it is a most interesting and well-presented introduction to animal behavior.

> Beryl B. Beatley, in her review of "How Animals Behave," in Appraisal: Science Books for Young People (copyright © 1977 by the Children's Science Book Review Committee), Vol. 10, No. 2, Spring, 1977, p. 12.

Terms such as instinct, response, imprinting, etc. are presented as facts; man as superior. The process behind the tentative conclusions in science or the struggles of thinking about animal behavior by such greats as Tingberger are not presented. Children will form many misconceptions as difficult concepts are simply presented without background of their context in scientific thought. (p. 13)

> Anne E Matthews, in her review of "How Animals Behave," in Appraisal: Science Books for Young People (copyright © 1977 by the Children's Science Book Review Committee), Vol. 10, No. 2, Spring, 1977, pp. 12-13.

THE MYSTERY OF THE LOCH NESS MONSTER (1976)

If a monster exists in Loch Ness, it is reasonable to assume that it must live in accordance with the same natural laws that govern the life of any similar animal. Acting on this assumption, the author carefully examines the available evidence for the possible existence of the legendary creature that has excited popular interest for many years and should capture the imagination of the young reader. There are no outright mistakes in the book, but the explanations given for earth plates and the ice age might have been more precisely stated.

> Elliot H. Blaustein, in his review of "The Mystery of the Loch Ness Monster," in Children's Book Review Service (copyright © 1977 Children's Book Review Service Inc.), Vol. 5, No. 7, February, 1977, p. 67.

Bendick's book is an excellent, comprehensive review of what is really known about the Loch inhabitants. . . . Throughout the narrative, Bendick acts as a friendly, inquisitive skeptic. Continual questioning heightens the aura of mystery and leads the reader eagerly on to each succeeding section, only to be left dangling to await final proof from ongoing investigations. There are interesting drawings and/or photographs on every page. . . . [Adults] will find it difficult not to be caught up in this fascinating investigation.

> Theodore Munch, in his review of "The Mystery of the Loch Ness Monster," in Science Books & Films (copyright © 1977 by the American Association for the Advancement of Science), Vol. XIII, No. 2, September, 1977, p. 92.

This book offers a fascinating historical account of reports concerning the "Loch Ness Monster" and related "sea monster" phenomena. More importantly, perhaps, the author has produced an extraordinary case study which shows how a very broad range of evidence (some scientific, some highly suspect, and some contradictory) can be synthesized into a limited number of alternative working hypotheses. It is unfortunate that some of the illustrations (particularly the author's original drawings) fall short of the book's overall level of quality, while some other illustrations are inadequately captioned; but this does not seriously detract from the value of the text. (pp. 7-8)

> Ronald J. Kley, in his review of "The Mystery of the Loch Ness Monster," in Appraisal: Science Books for Young People (copyright © 1977 by the Children's Science Book Review Committee), Vol. 10, No. 3, Fall, 1977, pp. 7-8.

PUTTING THE SUN TO WORK (1979)

This book covers solar energy principles concisely and accurately. The large type and simple prose style make it extremely easy to read. Even better than the text are clear and simple illustrations that provide a ready index to the subjects discussed. Students of all ages can gain a great deal from studying the illustrations. Of particular interest to younger readers are five simple and instructive solar energy experiments. This book is highly recommended as a primer on solar energy.

> Robert McWilliams, in his review of "Putting the Sun to Work," in Science Books & Films (copyright © 1980 by the American Association for the Advancement of Science), Vol. XV, No. 4, March, 1980, p. 231.

Even after a ninety-three-million-mile space trip from the sun, "More energy falls on the earth in a few minutes than people everywhere use in a year." Ms. Bendick presents the marvelous subject of solar energy so clearly that a second- or third-grader can take off from that sentence and study, experiment, and enjoy the whole thing. Familiar situations are used—a day at the beach, for instance—to demonstrate many of the things the sun does. The book goes on into what solar heat is and how it has been used in ages past, is being used now, and what we may be able to develop in the future. All along the way, friendly and most helpful drawings either show exactly what the text says, or illustrate the workings of the various machines that use the sun's energy, or invite one to do an experiment. There is only one weak spot on page forty-eight where the author sails over an important statement without any elucidation: "And since the turning earth makes day and night, there is no night." A child is going to need help here, but any good teacher will realize that. This book should make a most rewarding class study for early grades. (pp. 11-12)

> Heddie Kent, in her review of "Putting the Sun to Work," in Appraisal: Science Books for Young People (copyright © 1980 by the Children's Science Book

Review Committee), Vol. 13, No. 2, Spring, 1980, pp. 11-12.

Most persons over twenty-one know as little, or less than, the children about solar energy, so many parents and even a few teachers probably could benefit from this fascinating small volume. One of the strong features of the volume are the how-to-do-it, all well-illustrated in step-by-step detail, on making one's own tests or experiments with solar energy. The volume makes it clear that sunshine keeps the world rolling along and thus assures young readers that the sun is worthwhile whether its rays can be captured for profit or not. Unfortunately, not all solar energy volumes contain that broader message.

> *Wayne Hanley, in his review of "Putting the Sun to Work," in* Appraisal: Science Books for Young People *(copyright © 1980 by the Children's Science Book Review Committee), Vol. 13, No. 2, Spring, 1980, p. 12.*

SUPER PEOPLE: WHO WILL THEY BE? (1980)

This covers many aspects of the subject but treats none of them in depth; the tone of the writing, like that of the illustrations, is breezy, the chapters broken into short topics; a double-page spread headed "New Designs" consists of drawings and two questions, "Would extra parts be useful? How about some of these?" and the pages tend to have less than a paragraph of print each. The book is not strengthened by the "quoted" remarks of people (real or fictional) of the past. "I am Dr. Victor Frankenstein, created by . . ." or "I am the Greek god Hephaestus . . . I created many super people, but my most famous creation was . . ." or "Perhaps you've heard of me—Denis Diderot . . .". The tone may attract readers who wouldn't tackle a more substantial treatment in a book like John Langone's *Genetic Engineering*, but it is superficial albeit accurate in the facts it gives. (p. 207)

> *Zena Sutherland, in her review of "Super People: Who Will They Be?" in* Bulletin of the Center for Children's Books *(reprinted by permission of The University of Chicago Press; © 1980 by The University of Chicago), Vol. 33, No. 11, July-August, 1980, pp. 206-07.*

Who are the super people Bendick writes about?—clones, bionic people, androids, robots and humans. Each of the groups is described with tongue-in-cheek instructions on how to make one. Bendick has recalled clever examples of robots and clones from mythology. She poses some serious philosophical questions for a young reader to contemplate. Are human beings creating their own successors? Is it smart to invent machines or super people that could perhaps destroy your own species? Should humans be allowed to control their evolution? The author has illustrated her book with whimsical drawings, turn-of-the-century engravings and recent photographs. With illustrations popping up all over the page, the reader's eye is always roving and the text is greatly enlivened. A delightful book, both in its synthesis of ideas and in its physical format.

> *Theodore Munch, in his review of "Super People: Who Will They Be?" in* Science Books & Films *(copyright © 1981 by the American Association for the Advancement of Science), Vol. 16, No. 4, March-April, 1981, p. 212.*

Super People is not a super book. I found it to be sketchy and diffuse. Though there are no major errors in content, certain terms are not properly defined (i.e. evolution), and descriptions of mythological and folklore recipes for robots, clones, and androids might lead some young readers to conclude that such tales are true.

> *Bertrand Gary Hoyle, in his review of "Super People: Who Will They Be?" in* Appraisal: Science Books for Young People *(copyright © 1981 by the Children's Science Book Review Committee), Vol. 14, No. 1, Winter, 1981, p. 14.*

Lucille Clifton

1936-

Black American author of poetry, fiction, and nonfiction.

Clifton's books focus on themes and settings which are especially relevant to black and urban children; these works are noted for their positive view of black heritage and their natural inclusion of city backgrounds—apartment living, single parents, working mothers, and busy streets—as a normal part of life. Critics compliment Clifton's skillful writing style and her ability to produce the popular *Everett Anderson* series as poetry in black dialect. Although her works direct themselves to a specific audience, she is praised for her ability to recreate the thoughts and emotions of all children.

Clifton draws from her childhood and the experiences of her children for ideas and inspiration. She grew up in a family atmosphere which facilitated pride through ancestry. She heard African folktales and stories about family heritage daily from her father, just as he had been told the same stories by his African-born mother. Her familiarity with the past is evident in such books as *The Lucky Stone*, which follows the passage of four generations. In this book critics approve of Clifton's optimistic, accepting focus on life's highs and lows. They also note that her technique of presenting history through an object (the lucky stone) brings the concept of past within the grasp of the younger child. Critics say that *The Times They Used to Be*, a rendition of society as it was during Clifton's childhood, accurately captures the spirit of black rural life in the 40s. Many of her contemporary settings developed from observations of her children and their needs; *My Brother Fine with Me*, for example is based on her son's attempt to run away from home. "They keep you aware of life," she has said of her children, "and you have to stay aware of life, keep growing to write."

Critics approve of Clifton's realistic characters and her development of strong, positive relationships between them. Whether these interactions are between friends, parent and child, or brother and sister, she has the ability to depict supporting bonds between her characters. Many reviewers praise Clifton's realistic, sensitive portrayal of the friendship between a young black boy and an emotionally handicapped teenager in *My Friend Jacob*. Although Clifton has been faulted for Johnetta's unlikely irresponsibility and quick change of heart in *My Brother Fine with Me*, most of her works are consistently praised for their ability to establish characters and their relationships accurately and positively.

The *Everett Anderson* series about a young boy who is known for his warmth and candor is perhaps the best example of Clifton's poetic style. Critics say that Clifton's verse occasionally sounds forced, but most reviewers praise her skill in creating a story within a rhyming text and state that her poetry is primarily free from the stilted sound which often occurs when writers tell a story through verse. Clifton receives positive reviews for her lyrical use of language in both her poetry and prose. While some critics who consider black dialect improper English do not approve of her use of it, most say that Clifton's affectionate relationships portrayed in this style soften their negative views. Others praise its moderate, accurate use

and state that it promotes the realism of Clifton's children's books. This realism, coupled with honest relationships and settings, allows her works to have universal appeal despite their concentration on black and urban subjects. Clifton was named Poet Laureate of Maryland in 1979.

(See also *Contemporary Authors*, Vol. 49 and *Something about the Author*, Vol. 20.)

AUTHOR'S COMMENTARY

[*Rudine Sims:*] How do you go about writing? Do you have a daily routine? (p. 160)

Clifton: I write in spurts; that is, when I'm writing, I write pretty much all day, and [my] kids are quite used to that. When they were little, I did stop when they needed me, and if I lost some idea, I'd just hope I'd get it again.

I'm very lucky, too, in that I write two different kinds of things—poetry and stories—so if one isn't flowing, I can go to the other, and that helps both. But, when I'm writing, I write a lot; and when I'm not writing I'm doing it in my head. Writing is a good thing in that you don't have to be writing to be writing. Things are going on in my head, so that by the time I get to the typewriter, I'm not starting at "A" and going to "Z," I'm starting at, for instance, "L," or "M," which is helpful. (pp. 160-61)

Sims: Are there differences between writing poetry and prose? It seems, for instance, that the idea for a poem might come whole—all at once—or does it?

Clifton: No. Poetry to me is much harder than prose. It doesn't come whole, though you do have a fair idea of where you're going but the way to get there is something you have to figure out. In prose, you have so much room, but in poetry you don't really have *any* room. The bare bones are all you're allowed. In prose, you can say what you meant, explain your explanation, even give diagrams. So I think prose is easier. Poetry takes much more out of me than prose.

Sims: Do you think of yourself primarily as a poet? When someone asks "What you do professionally," do you say "I'm a poet," or "I write children's books"?

Clifton: I never say "I'm a poet." I have a faint distrust of people who say that. It's a *faint* distrust, and I'm sure it's my own problem. I think I say "I make poems" or "I write things." Somebody else says you're a poet. But I think the poetry is my heart.

Sims: Besides the *Everett Anderson* books, have you ever done any poetry—a book of poetry—for children? Do you contemplate doing anything like that?

Clifton: Interestingly enough, I don't think of "Everett Anderson" as poetry, because it doesn't take as much out of me. I think it's very good verse, and I think it's useful. It's a way to get kids into poetry, to head them towards poetry. But I don't think it's poetry. It sounds as if I'm saying that something that is easy isn't valuable. I'm not. I *do* think "Everett Anderson" is valuable, but I don't think of it as poetry. When I'm doing poetry, I'm probably not doing "Everett Anderson."

Sims: I see. The question is, then, will you or have you done children's poetry?

Clifton: I have not. But I have written poetry that I think children can relate to. I'm wondering if really good poetry isn't just poetry. Some children can deal with, some they can't. It seems to me that if you write poetry for children, you have to keep too many things in mind other than the poem. So I'm just writing a poem. I'm not writing for people who are forty-five either (though maybe I am!). But some people can get something from some of my poems, and other people get something from some other of my poems. Nobody gets everything, including me.

Sims: Let's move on to talk about some of your books. Some of them, like *The Boy Who Didn't Believe in Spring,* and *My Friend Jacob* have both black and white characters. Was that always *your* decision?

Clifton: Oh, definitely! Tony Polito [the white boy in *The Boy Who Didn't Believe in Spring*] is he because I wanted him to be. Recently someone who had seen those two books asked if this means I won't be writing about black children anymore. I can't imagine why anybody would think that; why they would think that *I* wouldn't write about black children since that is something I know quite well. My whole *thing* is geared to black children.

But I *wanted* Tony Polito. I wanted a book with two boys, and I wanted the black boy to be clearly the leader. There is a world in which black and white children play together, and they ought to see themselves in books. In the Spanish version, the editor wanted to make Tony Polito Spanish and change his name, but I said no. Tony is definitely Italian, and that's not casual to me.

Jacob, I wanted to be white, too. He's a big, rich-hearted boy, and though the black boy is clearly the leader here, they have a friendly loving relationship, which is something I'm about, also. (pp. 161-63)

[*Sonora Beautiful*] has only white characters. . . . In this book, I *heard* the characters as white. I have a tendency to *hear* the language of the characters, and then I know something about who the people are. When I heard this girl talking I knew this was not a black kid, not a black urban kid at any rate. This was a white girl, so I saw no reason why I should not make her white.

Sims: Speaking of hearing language, one of the things you do very well is to reflect the language of your characters. How do you respond to people who object to the black vernacular you often use?

Clifton: . . . I do not write out of weakness. That is to say, I do not write the lnaguage I write because I don't know any other. I often say I write **"Everett Anderson"** to prove I know about iambic pentameter and standard written speech.

But I have a certain integrity about my art, and in *my* art you have to be honest and you have to have people talking the way they really talk. So all of my books are not in the same language. (p. 163)

Sims: . . . [You've] talked about *Jacob* being based on the boy next door, and elsewhere about your son Baggy's running away being the inspiration for *My Brother Fine With Me.* Where else do you get ideas for stories?

Clifton: Well, I had six kids in seven years, and when you have a lot of children, you tend to attract children, and you see so many kids, you get ideas from that. And I have such a good memory from my own childhood, my own time. I have great respect for young people; I like them enormously. (p. 164)

Sims: . . . Do you feel any special pressures or special opportunities as a black author?

Clifton: I do feel a responsibility. . . . First, I'm going to write books that tend to celebrate life. I'm about that. And I wish to have children see people like themselves in books. That's why I use names the way I do. Ujamaa [*All Us Come Cross the Water*], for example, is a Muslim kid, and there's no reason in the world why he shouldn't be in a book.

I also take seriously the responsibility of not lying. There's a poem by A. B. Spelman that says "Sometimes we lie and steal. These are things we sometimes do." I'm not going to say those are things we do all the time. I'm not going to say that life is wretched if circumstance is wretched, because that's not true. So I take that responsibility, but it's a responsibility to the truth, and to my art as much as anything. I owe everybody that. So when I talk about black families loving each other in spite of poverty, for instance, I'm talking about something I *know.* It's the truth as I see it, and that's what my responsibility is.

Now, it isn't a responsibility not to say bad things, because that's not what I know, either. I grew up absolutely on the streets of Buffalo, so I know what that is like. I may be the only black writer with two siblings who were narcotics addicts and are now alcoholics. I know that milieu, and I know that even *it* is not as extreme as it has been portrayed. So I try to depict it as I know it to be. It is terrible, there's no question; but even in the middle of that, love and hope are possible, and that's what I want to write. That's my responsiblity to the truth. (pp. 164-65)

Rudine Sims, "Profile: Lucille Clifton" (copyright © 1982 by the National Council of Teachers of English; reprinted by permission of the publisher and the author), in Language Arts, *Vol. 59, No. 2, February, 1982, pp. 160-7.*

SOME OF THE DAYS OF EVERETT ANDERSON (1970)

As ticked off by a young black poet . . . , *some of the days* are all the days in what might be any wigwag week. . . . [Everett Anderson is distinctly] a boy to contend with, as again in **"Wednesday Noon Adventure":** "Who's black / and was lost for / hours and hours? / Everett Anderson / Hid!" . . . The rhythm impels, the off-beat arrests, the meaning *pounces* on the reader. . . .

A review of "Some of the Days of Everett Anderson," in Kirkus Reviews *(copyright © 1970 The Kirkus Service, Inc.), Vol. XXXVIII, No. 8, April 15, 1970, p. 44.*

Some of the days of six-year-old "ebony Everett Anderson" are happy; some lonely—but all of them are special, reflecting the author's own pride in being black; also, her knowledge of the triumphs and tragedies of childhood make this book of nine gracefully simple poems a particularly perceptive one. Without coyness or militancy she says in rhyme much about being black that writers have said for older children in less deft manner. . . . Reading or listening to these poems will bring the gifts of pride and pleasure to Everett Andersons everywhere! Truly, this is a lovely book. . . . A must for black children, but fun for all.

Marjorie Lewis, in her review of "Some of the Days of Everett Anderson," in School Library Journal, *an appendix to* Library Journal *(reprinted from the May, 1970 issue of* School Library Journal, *published by R. R. Bowker Co./A Xerox Corporation; copyright © 1970), Vol. 16, No. 9, May, 1970, p. 58.*

Everett is a black six-year-old, affectionate, bold, and sometimes (although no one says so) frightened when the sirens wail in the city streets at night. But regardless of color and race, Everett is a real boy in a real, loving family.

Lucille Clifton is a black poet, and **"Some of the Days of Everett Anderson"** is a real poem for preschoolers to Grade 3. The overtones may stir adults as well. . . .

It's not long, but it's good.

Neil Millar, "Things That Rhyme," in The Christian Science Monitor *(reprinted by permission from* The Christian Science Monitor; *© 1970 The Christian Science Publishing Society; all rights reserved), May 7, 1970, p. B4.**

For those on the American racial firing line, there are times of creeping despair when there is fear that all has been sound and fire and no movement, that perhaps the elusive moment came and was lost. Then along comes a Lucille Clifton with a profoundly simple way of saying all that is important to say, and we know that the struggle is worth it, that the all-important battle of image is being won, and that the future of all those

beautiful black children out there need not be twisted and broken.

In **"Some of the Days of Everett Anderson"** . . . Mrs. Clifton has written a deceptively uncomplicated story. . . . The story has "universality": like most little boys, Everett enjoys playing in the rain, likes candy and adores his father. The story has humor, pathos and the suggestion of serious drama, and Mrs. Clifton tells it in verse that is sprightly and without self-consciousness. But little Everett is also black, and there are certain particular perceptions which flow from that fact ("Daddy's space / is a black empty place / and Everett Anderson misses it").

Hoyt W. Fuller, in his review of "Some of the Days of Everett Anderson," in The New York Times Book Review *(©1970 by The New York Times Company; reprinted by permission), September 6, 1970, p. 16.*

THE BLACK BC'S (1970)

What begins as a good idea—a relevant alphabet for black children—is in fact an uneven effort: some of the choices are poor, much of the development is banal, and many of the rhymes share a flat, singsong rhythm. Although Malcolm may be a more meaningful selection than the inevitable xylophone or X-ray, he is poorly served. . . . Africa, Douglass, Freedom, King, Slavery, (Sojourner) Truth, Underground Railroad, and Vesey are fitting choices but their value is sometimes offset by a sugar-coated treatment. . . . A few are highly questionable: "G is for Ghetto / a place where we / can be at home / loved and free." The bonds that make Harlem a community ("poverty, housing problems, and unemployment") are hardly the ties of a "free" people. Kids can surely do better than this on their own.

A review of "The Black BC's," in Kirkus Reviews *(copyright © 1970 The Kirkus Service, Inc.), Vol. XXXVIII, No. 19, October 1, 1970, p. 1091.*

Utilizing the alphabet as a unifying theme, the author has effectively combined prose and poetry to describe some achievements of black men and women (in the area of books, inventions; as cowboys, etc.); to point up some important events and people in their history; to highlight some meaningful expressions ("natural," "underground"). . . . The text is concisely written and the facts, though not presented in chronological sequence, are selected judiciously and related in an easy-to-read, entertaining manner. . . . A good browsing attraction for most anyone, this should be even better for reluctant readers.

Barbara S. Miller, in her review of "The Black BC's," in School Library Journal, *an appendix to* Library Journal *(reprinted from the December, 1970 issue of* School Library Journal, *published by R. R. Bowker Co./A Xerox Corporation; copyright © 1970), Vol. 17, No. 4, December, 1970, p. 44.*

["**The Black BC's**"] starts out with "A is for Africa . . ." and ends with "Z is for Zenith / the highest, the top / the place for us / and there we'll stop." . . . A paragraph of historical or biographical text accompanies each topic, determinedly one-sided to redress the cultural imbalance, but mainly lucid and sensible. The purpose is therapeutic—to boost the black child's self-respect—and we leave it to parents, teachers, and librarians better informed than ourselves about the quantity and quality of books already on the market which are designed to accomplish the same thing to decide whether this one fills a need.

> *Harve Zemach and Margot Zemach, "Running through the ABC's," in* The New York Times Book Review *(© 1970 by The New York Times Company; reprinted by permission), December 6, 1970, p. 62.*

This is the book's pattern: A brief poem, an illustration, a paragraph or two of bland prose. While the book may give information, it is scant in treatment of subjects included; the rhyme is often faulty ("together" and "better"; "activist" and "persists") and the book's most positive aspect is its theme: black people have always played contributing roles in American history.

> *Zena Sutherland, in her review of "The Black BC's," in* Bulletin of the Center for Children's Books *(reprinted by permission of The University of Chicago Press; © 1971 by The University of Chicago), Vol. 24, No. 7, March, 1971, p. 104.*

EVERETT ANDERSON'S CHRISTMAS COMING (1971)

Yes, Virginia, Christmas is celebrated in the cities too. In Lucille Clifton's *Everett Anderson's Christmas Coming* . . . , short, natural-sounding, childlike verses (nine in all) relate young, black, middle-class Everett Anderson's feelings as Christmas approaches. . . . Covering a wide range of Christmas phenomena and activities—cold, snowy weather, gifts, parties, setting up a tree—this is also one of the few new books to offer any insightful or original comment about the meaning of the holiday . . . [The] book overall comes closest among what's available to capturing Christmas as it is today for that large number of American children whose ambience is slushy sidewalks rather than rolling hills.

> *Diane Gersoni-Edelman, in her review of "Everett Anderson's Christmas Coming," in* School Library Journal, *an appendix to* Library Journal *(reprinted from the October, 1971 issue of* School Library Journal, *published by R. R. Bowker Co./A Xerox Corporation; copyright © 1971), Vol. 18, No. 2, October, 1971, p. 129.*

Each of the five days before Everett's Christmas is described by a verse . . . , and December twenty-third and twenty-fourth are presented in two verses . . .—thereby nicely capturing the child's increased anticipation of the arrival of the holiday. . . . Although poignant touches such as an absent father and "downer lives" are mentioned, the overall richness of Everett's experiences dominates the text: Ringing bells, misty snowfalls, window shopping, and grownup parties crowd his days and nights. Freer in form than the poetry in the previous volume, the verse still sparkles. . . . The book closes with a Christmas greeting as moving as Tiny Tim's classic blessing in *A Christmas Carol.* . . . (p. 598)

> *Anita Silvey, in her review of "Everett Anderson's Christmas Coming," in* The Horn Book Magazine *(copyright © 1971 by The Horn Book, Inc., Boston), Vol. XLVII, No. 6, December, 1971, pp. 598-99.*

Everett Anderson, black and boyish, is glimpsed, rather than explained through poems about him, written by Lucille Clifton. White middle-class parents will want answers to certain questions. For example, on Dec. 22 Everett thinks about "If Daddy was here," but where Daddy is, is never explained. It doesn't

really have to be and city children know that. The joys of living in Apt. 14A are perfectly clear. . . .

> *Jane O'Reilly, in her review of "Everett Anderson's Christmas Coming," in* The New York Times Book Review *(©1971 by The New York Times Company; reprinted by permission), December 5, 1971, p. 90.*

THE BOY WHO DIDN'T BELIEVE IN SPRING (1973)

For small children, words must refer to observable phenomena if they are to be unquestioningly accepted. Children particularize; adults generalize. This dichotomy is captured in a simple but imaginative account of one young Black child's determination to "'get me some of this Spring.'" . . . How King Shabazz and his faithful but equally skeptical companion, Tony Polito, searched for and found spring is an original reworking of the traditional quest theme, scaled to primary school comprehension and set in a contemporary urban environment. The first journey of the two boys alone beyond the corner streetlight, past the stores, churches, and restaurants of a city neighborhood subtly underscores the notion that the line between the real and the fantastic shifts imperceptibly with age and experience. (pp. 371-72)

> *Mary M. Burns, in her review of "The Boy Who Didn't Believe in Spring," in* The Horn Book Magazine *(copyright © 1973 by The Horn Book, Inc., Boston), Vol. XLIX, No. 4, August, 1973, pp. 371-72.*

It's fun. It's believable. It makes you smile awhile. The idea—about two boys who disbelieve in the season until they find flowers bursting and birds nesting—is interesting and clear and simple and strong enough to keep you going with real pleasure. . . . Besides which, both the story and the pictures place the boys, King Shabazz and Tony Polito, in a recognizable, big-as-life environment through which they walk or, actually, *bop*, in a beautiful way. Thank you, Sister Lucille.

> *June Jordan, in her review of "The Boy Who Didn't Believe in Spring," in* The New York Times Book Review *(© 1973 by The New York Times Company; reprinted by permission), November 4, 1973, p. 27.*

ALL US COME CROSS THE WATER (1973)

Lucille Clifton's latest tells how a young black boy learns the meaning of nationhood. Ujamaa ("Unity"), still called "Jim" by his Negro teacher, gets upset when she asks the kids in the class to tell what country they came from. Ujamaa only knows the continent—Africa—and so asks all around to find out his place of origin. . . . At the Panther Book Store, an older man he's friendly with (who like Big Mama knows about spirits and magic) also tells him the answer's in his name: "All us crossed the water. We one people, Ujamaa. Boy got that name oughta know that." That night, Ujamaa reflects that even though his black friends in class didn't know why he balked at the teacher's question, they ". . . went right along with me on the not standing up cause we brothers." This exemplifies unity to him, and the next day he proudly tells the teacher: ". . . my name is Ujamaa and that mean Unity and that's where I'm from." Clifton's attention-holding story, told in black English, is better than [John Steptoe's pictures]. However, her lesson of unity rests on a very flimsy premise: mindlessly supporting somebody because you share his or her race (or whatever) is admirable. Sacrificing individual judgment and freedom of thought never is.

> *Diane Gersoni-Edelman, in her review of "All Us Come Cross the Water," in* Library Journal *(reprinted from* Library Journal, *July, 1973; published by R. R. Bowker Co. (a Xerox Company); copyright © 1973 by Xerox Corporation), Vol. 98, No. 13, July, 1973, p. 2185.*

The story builds, wobbling and weak, to not much of an ending. But it is written well, in convincing, good, black English, except for the title, which strikes my ear as awkwardly missing a preposition.

> *June Jordan, in her review of "All Us Come Cross the Water," in* The New York Times Book Review *(© 1973 by The New York Times Company; reprinted by permission), November 4, 1973, p. 27.*

All Us Come Cross the Water, [is] . . . one of the best picture books yet. In a very straight-forward way, Ms. Clifton easily shows the relationship of Africa to Blacks in the U.S. without getting into a heavy rap about "Pan-Africanism" which most adults, and certainly most children, neither understand nor particularly care about. . . . [Ms. Clifton] seems able to get inside a little boy's head, and knows how to represent that on paper. . . . This is a very special book. (pp. 396-97)

> *Judy Richardson, in her review of "All Us Come Cross the Water," in* The Journal of Negro Education, *Vol. XLIII, No. 3 (Summer, 1974), pp. 396-97.*

DON'T YOU REMEMBER? (1973)

The story is all right, but forced. It reads like an off-Monday for this author, who is capable of so much breathing charm. . . .

> *June Jordan, in her review of "Don't You Remember?" in* The New York Times Book Review *(© 1973 by The New York Times Company; reprinted by permission), November 4, 1973, p. 27.*

Tate, a four-year-old person, enthusiastically remembers everything her parents would rather not—especially things like her father's promise to take her to work with him one day, or her mother's pledge to make a black cake with "Tate" written on it. . . . Nothing unusual in this easy close-up of a familiar childhood situation, but Clifton's warmth is refreshing. . . .

> *Betsy Hearne, in her review of "Don't You Remember?" in* The Booklist *(reprinted by permission of the American Library Association; copyright © 1973 by the American Library Association), Vol. 70, No. 7, December 1, 1973, p. 385.*

This child's experiences with promises that are never kept provide a good illustration of a four-year-old's limited concept of time. The story demonstrates how easily what adults say can be misinterpreted by children.

> *Sharon Spredemann Dreyer, in her review of "Don't You Remember?" in her* The Bookfinder: A Guide to Children's Literature about the Needs and Problems of Youth Aged 2-15, Vol. 1 *(© 1977 American Guidance Service, Inc.),* American Guidance Service, Inc., *1977, No. 209.*

GOOD, SAYS JEROME (1973)

"I don't want to move . . . What's black? . . . She (the new teacher)'ll hate me . . . Are we lost? . . . I saw a monster . . . Who dies? . . . Are girls smarter than boys?" Attempting to still the fears expressed in all these questions in short, illustrated rhymes is quite an undertaking, but Clifton at least manages a temporary deflection of anxiety with the warm, simple exchanges that constitute her text. . . .

> *A review of "Good, Says Jerome," in* Kirkus Reviews *(copyright © 1973 The Kirkus Service, Inc.), Vol. XVI, No. 22, November 15, 1973, p. 1257.*

Run-of-the-security blanket responses to standard childhood fears. Janice Marie's replies to sibling Jerome's queries . . . are usually pat but palatable reassurances couched in pleasant verse. However, the deceptive explanation that dying is what happens to people "who are lonely" and afterlife is a family reunion makes death the cause and cure for loneliness—a copout that could shock and scare kids who don't comprehend death but have certainly experienced lonely separations from parents. . . . On balance, Clifton's "I'm O.K., You're O.K." bibliotherapy is just O.K. for libraries.

> *Pamela D. Pollack, in her review of "Good, Says Jerome," in* School Library Journal, *an appendix to* Library Journal *(reprinted from the January, 1974 issue of* School Library Journal, *published by R. R. Bowker Co./A Xerox Corporation; copyright © 1974), Vol. 20, No. 5, January, 1974, p. 38.*

The author's brief verses convey a deep understanding and mutual respect between a young black boy and his older sister. Jerome has many questions, but no matter what he asks, Janice Marie gives him just the right answer. . . . [She] always has a reassuring reply. . . . This realistic book should hit a familiar note. . . .

> *Barbara Dill, in her review of "Good, Says Jerome," in* Wilson Library Bulletin *(copyright © 1974 by the H. W. Wilson Company), Vol. 48, No. 8, April, 1974, p. 633.*

The questions [in **Good, Says Jerome**] should appeal because of their universality, the answers because they are encouraging; the repetition of pattern is an asset. . . . Not quite convincing: Janice Marie's sagacity.

> *Zena Sutherland, in her review of "Good, Says Jerome," in* Bulletin of the Center for Children's Books *(reprinted by permission of The University of Chicago Press; © 1974 by The University of Chicago), Vol. 27, No. 10, June, 1974, p. 155.*

EVERETT ANDERSON'S YEAR (1974)

Yes, Everett still has his shining moments, but one small verse per month makes a rather skimpy year. . . . A more doleful Everett . . . still there are fond associations for those who remember some of his happier days.

> *A review of "Everett Anderson's Year," in* Kirkus Reviews *(copyright © 1974 The Kirkus Service, Inc.), Vol. XLII, No. 24, December 15, 1974, p. 1298.*

A year in the life of a city child is celebrated in appealing verses. . . . This third book about Everett Anderson contains a dozen sensitive, child-like poems. . . . Everett Anderson is a secure and happy child, although wistful references are made about Daddy—"where-ever he is." Mischief, fun, gaiety, and poignancy are a part of his days as the year progresses. The portrayals of child and mother are lively and solid, executed with both strength and tenderness.

> *Beryl Robinson, in her review of "Everett Anderson's Year," in* The Horn Book Magazine *(copyright ©1975 by the Horn Book, Inc., Boston), Vol. LI, No. 1, February, 1975, p. 62.*

If your response to this title is, "Oh, we already have something like that"—we don't. There isn't anything like this. Lucille Clifton is a gifted poet with the greater gift of being able to write poetry for children. . . . Everett Anderson [is] a very special seven-year-old Black boy.

> *Barbara Walker, in her review of "Everett Anderson's Year," in* Interracial Books for Children Bulletin *(reprinted by permission of* Interracial Books for Children Bulletin, *1841 Broadway, New York, N.Y. 10023), Vol. 5, Nos. 7 and 8, 1975, p. 18.*

THE TIMES THEY USED TO BE (1974)

In short, uneven lines set down to look like verse (and, not incidentally, to move by fast for reluctant readers) Mama reminisces about 1948. . . . Lucille Clifton brings back the times they used to be—Jim Crow in the Army, The Hit Parade and Amos and Andy on the radio, and a first glimpse of TV in the hardware store window ("We ain't going to look too long," Daddy whispers: "a fellow was telling me the tubes is poison")—with warmth and humor far beyond *Everett Anderson's* range.

> *A review of "The Times They Used to Be," in* Kirkus Reviews *(copyright © 1974 The Kirkus Service, Inc.), Vol. XLII, No. 11, June 1, 1974, p. 580.*

[This] short and impeccable vignette—laced with the idiom and humor of rural Black folk—recalls when a young girl's best friend grapples with the "unexplained 'sinnin' in her body"—menstruation. . . . [The] story which captures the spirit of the girls' family, the times, etc. is sure to appeal to a junior high audience.

> *Rosalind K. Goddard, in her review of "The Times They Used to Be," in* School Library Journal, *an appendix to* Library Journal *(reprinted from the September, 1974 issue of* School Library Journal, *published by R. R. Bowker Co./A Xerox Corporation; copyright © 1974), Vol. 21, No. 1, September, 1974, p. 76.*

Most books that awaken adult nostalgia are not quite as appealing to young readers, but this brief story has enough warmth and vitality and humor for any reader. . . . Woven through the story are bits about Amos and Andy, the end of segregation in the army, Satchel Paige getting up to the major league, all a fluid collage of the period and of a black family's life. (pp. 39-40)

> *Zena Sutherland, in her review of "The Times They Used to Be," in* Bulletin of the Center for Children's Books *(reprinted by permission of The University of Chicago Press; © 1974 by The University of Chicago), Vol. 28, No. 3, November, 1974, pp. 39-40.*

In Lucille Clifton's book, a mother, with very little prodding from her children, recalls an unforgettable summer from her

childhood. . . . [This] passage conveys a sense of the sensitivity and craftsmanship of this . . . story in which a young girl catches her first glimpse of the new technological era in a hardware store window, and learns of death and life. It is a story adults as well as children will enjoy.

> *Lee A. Daniels, "Girlchild in the Promised Land," in* Book World—The Washington Post *(© 1974, The Washington Post), November 10, 1974, p. 5.**

MY BROTHER FINE WITH ME (1975)

In a contemporary, urban picture book, Johnetta's brother Baggy has decided to run away for "[h]e say he a Black man, a warrior. And he can make it by hisself." Of course, Johnetta isn't exactly crying about his departure. An only child until Baggy was born, she's quite willing to help him pack his possessions, and when he leaves, she exlaims, "I feel just like Dr. King say, free at last." But Johnetta goes through the traditional change of heart about her brother and decides that a warrior's place is with his family. . . . [Despite] the use of Black English [the text has a gentle, old-fashioned quality]. And it is the traditional elements in the book—the childlike, humorous story and the soft, wispy pencil drawings [by Moneta Barnett]—that give it a particular charm.

> *Anita Silvey, in her review of "My Brother Fine with Me," in* The Horn Book Magazine *(copyright © 1975 by the Horn Book, Inc., Boston), Vol. LI, No. 6, December, 1975, p. 584.*

[Before] Baggy departs [Johnetta] says, "Somebody have to stay here, see after the house while mama and daddy at work." Throughout the summer, Johnetta is responsible for taking care of herself and Baggy during the day. While this is an accurate representation of the role of an older child in a family of working parents, sexist roles are being reinforced—particularly when the characterizations of Johnetta and Baggy are compared. Baggy sees himself as a Black warrior. Rationalizing his fear of running away, he says, "Seem to me, a warrior better stay at home and take care of his family." Johnetta is pleased with this statement. Once more children will conclude that the male is the protector and the female, the one to be protected.

Also disturbing is the lack of family unity (the mother seems insensitive and the father only gives orders), as well as Johnetta's competitive spirit and preoccupation with her own needs. Johnetta's desire for Baggy to leave is a selfish one, and her subsequent acceptance of him stems mainly from her inability to cope with loneliness.

The beauty of the book lies in Clifton's keen sense of reality and her talent for capturing the flavor of children's speech.

> *Emily R. Moore, in her review of "My Brother Fine with Me," in* Interracial Books for Children Bulletin *(reprinted by permission of* Interracial Books for Children Bulletin, *1841 Broadway, New York, N.Y. 10023), Vol. 7, No. 1, 1976, p. 18.*

The mood is tender, the psychology sound, and the writing style . . . [is] casual but firm. Yet the change of heart is a bit too quick, especially since Johnny's decision that she can't see her friend Peaches because Peaches' little sister won't have Johnny's little brother to play with (one can't take a child to a playground alone?) seems irrational and because it just doesn't seem quite believable that an eight-year-old deemed responsible enough by working parents to be left in charge of house and brother would encourage his departure and not worry about parental reaction.

> *Zena Sutherland, in her review of "My Brother Fine with Me," in* Bulletin of the Center for Children's Book *(reprinted by permission of The University of Chicago Press; © 1976 by The University of Chicago), Vol. 29, No. 7, March, 1976, p. 107.*

My Brother Fine with Me is a story easily and deliciously told. The brief plot unfolds rapidly.

Johnny is an intensely human little girl. Much of the plot and even the person of her younger brother, Baggy, are revealed through her reflections. . . . The author depicts these children with color and warmth. The use of Black vernacular English with Black characters is credible; Johnny's monologue is entertaining, alive. . . . I am not sure what kind of audience Clifton had in mind, and her style may not be to everyone's taste, but it is important to note that children clearly relish this book.

> *A review of "My Brother Fine with Me," (copyright 1977 by the International Reading Association, Inc.; reprinted with permission of the International Reading Association), in* Journal of Reading, *Vol. 20, No. 5, February, 1977, p. 533.*

[While *My Brother Fine with Me*] has charm and moments of humor, [it] expresses some nationalist and sexist notions that, I think, detract from its value to young readers. The story is . . . a simple tale of sibling rivalry, this time as felt by the eight year old narrator for her five year old brother. Johnetta, named, as she tells us, after her father, relates her story in Black English. (p. 110)

While Johnetta's narration of her story in Black English feels appropriate, some of her phrasing seems too arch or poetical to be the speech of an eight year old girl. One appreciates expressions like ''I was the first-born child'' . . . , or the metaphor ''Mama come spreading out like a pancake'' as the phrasing of a poetic adult, which Lucille Clifton is, rather than the natural speech of a small girl.

A side issue appearing at the beginning and end of the book also seems a flaw and is, perhaps, of a piece with the inappropriateness of some of the language. . . . Baggy distorts the true nature of his and Johnetta's relationship which is dependent on her taking care of him by saying, when he ''returns'' home, '''Seem to me, a warrior better stay home and take care of his family'''. . . . This little vignette mimes the stereotypical relations of some black women and men. The women are, because of racism, the consistent breadwinners and family mainstays, while the men bolster their sagging egos with ''macho'' assertiveness (the situation attacked over and over again, for example, in the Broadway play, *For Colored Girls Who Have Considered Suicide When The Rainbow Is Enuf*). It is unfortunate that this is the subliminal model behind the children's relationship since it belies Johnetta's strength, and suggests to the reader that it is the place of the woman to shield the male's ego rather than to fight against racism with him.

Another false note is the instance of adult humor in the book. It is hard to believe that an eight year old girl, capable of the childish logic she demonstrates when she says her parents will get over the loss of their son, is also capable of a rather arch piece of humor based on a political allusion. . . . In addition to the incongruity created by the difference between her al-

lusion to King's words and her remarks on her parents' adjustment to their loss, the appropriateness of the humor is also questionable since it may go over the heads of most children.

Yet despite the rather contrived revelation that Baggy will be missed and that Johnetta has grown to need her brother, this book has its endearing moments, the best of which is Johnetta's discovery of her brother out on the stoop, followed by the return to their routine. (pp. 111-14)

> *Ellen Tremper, ''Black English in Children's Literature,'' in* The Lion and the Unicorn *(copyright © 1980 The Lion and the Unicorn), Vol. 3, No. 2, Winter, 1979-80, pp. 105-24.**

EVERETT ANDERSON'S FRIEND (1976)

How Everett makes friends with Maria—she invites him into 13A after school when he loses his apartment key—is unfolded in ten short rhymes that express his thoughts on Maria's Mama's *tacos*, his own Mama's scolding about the key, etc. More of a story, then, than Everett Anderson has given us before, and though it's a relatively skimpy one it's worked in neatly and unobtrusively.

> *A review of "Everett Anderson's Friend," in* Kirkus Reviews *(copyright © 1976 The Kirkus Service, Inc.), Vol. XLIV, No. 8, April 15, 1976, p. 462.*

Old friends of Everett Anderson will be disappointed with this uninspired picture book about the danger of making snap judgments. The premise is based on a stereotyped conception of girl/boy relationships: Everett dismisses the possibility of becoming friends with the new girl next door until, of course, he discovers it's fun playing with her and eating the tacos Maria's Mama makes. . . . [Ann Grifalconi's drawings] cannot compensate for the cliched story line or constrained rhyming verse. (pp. 96-97)

> *Karel Rose, in a review of "Everett Anderson's Friend," in* School Library Journal *(reprinted from the September, 1976 issue of* School Library Journal, *published by R. R. Bowker Co./A Xerox Corporation; copyright © 1976), Vol. 23, No. 1, September, 1976, pp. 96-97.*

Clifton's poem has a nice easy swing to it, forced only in a few places, which is unusual for a rhymed story. Children may have trouble making point-of-view jumps between character and author, and there is one difficult transition from general thoughts to the specific development of Everett's locked-out situation. Still, Everett's friends will be glad to see him again. . . .

> *Betsy Hearne, in her review of "Everett Anderson's Friend," in* Booklist *(reprinted by permission of the American Library Association; copyright © 1976 by the American Library Association), Vol. 73, No. 1, September 1, 1976, p. 34.*

Everett Anderson's story is told in a verse which is generally clever and lively, but which at times becomes dull because of predictable mechanics. However, the excitement and the curiosity of a ''someone new'' who ''has come to stay in 13A'' should be a sure winner with youngsters who live in apartments. Feminists will be pleased that Everett learns to respect and to accept his new neighbor, Maria, and sociologists will appreciate the bi-ethnic approach that manages, through Maria's

Mama, to include a few words of Spanish: *tacos, muchachos, Dios.*

> *Mary Agnes Taylor, in her review of "Everett Anderson's Friend," (copyright 1977 by the International Reading Association, Inc.; reprinted with permission of the International Reading Association and Mary Agnes Taylor), in* The Reading Teacher, *Vol. 30, No. 8, May, 1977, p. 947.*

THREE WISHES   (1976)

An urbanized version of the traditional tale in which the first wish reveals the power of the magic object—in this case a penny found "on the New Year Day with your birthday on it"—the second wish is a mistake, and the third wish undoes the second. Too few children's books for blacks justify their ethnicity, but this one is a winning blend of black English and bright illustration [by Stephanie Douglas].

> *Christopher Lehmann-Haupt, in his review of "Three Wishes," in* The New York Times *(© 1976 by The New York Times Company; reprinted by permission), December 20, 1976, p. C21.*

This beautifully illustrated book depicts a warm and loyal friendship between two Black children. That they are of the opposite sex is yet another plus. Victor is Zenobia's confidant and she points out that he has "*always* kept her secrets." Since there is a general dearth of books that show a positive relationship between male and female children, this one is welcome as is its useful lesson—the value of true friendship. Consider *Three Wishes* for your second or third grader. (pp. 19-20)

> *Lynn Edwards, in her review of "Three Wishes," in* Interracial Books for Children Bulletin *(reprinted by permission of* Interracial Books for Children Bulletin, *1841 Broadway, New York, N.Y. 10023), Vol. 8, No. 1, 1977, pp. 19-20.*

[In **"Three Wishes"**] . . . the text (not to mention spelling and grammar!) [is] softened by the depths of affection springing from the heart of America's black culture.

What would Mama want if she had just one wish?

"'Good friends, Nobie. That's what we need in this world. Good friends.'"

So Zenobia used her "lucky penny" not to get things but to re-find her good friend Victorius. And that's a lesson in priorities that all children need to learn as soon as they can—perhaps with gentle assistance from this book.

> *David Anable, "Please Don't Scare the Monsters," in* The Christian Science Monitor *(reprinted by permission from* The Christian Science Monitor; *© 1977 The Christian Science Publishing Society; all rights reserved), May 4, 1977, p. B5.**

EVERETT ANDERSON'S 1-2-3   (1977)

Everett Anderson's 1 2 3 has a narrow purpose, but should nonetheless prove useful in many communities. It provides the means for a single parent to introduce the idea of enlarging the family. (p. 78)

The rhymes are sometimes awkward, but in general the verse contributes that lightness of tone that such explicit bibliotherapy needs. (p. 79)

> *Barbara Dill, in her review of "Everett Anderson's 1-2-3," in* Wilson Library Bulletin *(copyright © 1977 by the H. W. Wilson Company), Vol. 52, No. 1, September, 1977, pp. 78-9.*

Lacking some of the emotional . . . impact of the early books about the small Black boy, the new story-in-verse succeeds, nevertheless, in treating an important theme with a combination of delicacy and childlike candor. Previous books contained wistful references to Everett Anderson's absent daddy; the latest one tells how the worried little boy gradually became reconciled to the idea of a new father joining the family.

> *Ethel L. Heins, in her review of "Everett Anderson's 1-2-3," in* The Horn Book Magazine *(copyright © 1977 by the Horn Book, Inc., Boston), Vol. LIII, No. 5, October, 1977, p. 552.*

In a continuing juvenile soap opera series, our young hero ponders the advantages and disadvantages of his mother's pending remarriage. . . . While the problem is real and the book "useful," the verses are not up to Clifton's standards. . . . For Everett Anderson's fans only.

> *Ruth M. Stein, in her review of "Everett Anderson's 1-2-3" (copyright © 1978 by the National Council of Teachers of English; reprinted by permission of the publisher and the author), in* Language Arts, *Vol. 55, No. 1, January, 1978, p. 43.*

In a simple, light-hearted, rhyming text, *Everett Anderson's 1 2 3* handles the subject of remarriage as a small boy considers the numbers one, two, and three, whether they're lonely or crowded or just right. The book could be useful in helping young children to understand and accept a new parent, while incidentally promoting number recognition and stimulating auditory discrimination of rhyming words.

> *A review of "Everett Anderson's 1-2-3" (copyright 1978 by the International Reading Association, Inc.; reprinted with permission of the International Reading Association), in* The Reading Teacher, *Vol. 32, No. 1, October, 1978, p. 93.*

AMIFIKA   (1977)

Amifika overhears Mama's happy news that his father is coming home from the army—and her comment that she will "just get rid of something he won't miss" to make space for him in their two rented rooms. As Amifika doesn't remember his father very well, he figures the reverse is true; hence Amifika is what Mama will get rid of. He runs away (as far as the front fence), falls asleep, and wakes up to a joyous reunion. Predictable, but sympathetically based on a very likely sort of misunderstanding.

> *A review of "Amifika," in* Kirkus Reviews *(copyright © 1977 The Kirkus Service, Inc.), Vol. XLV, No. 22, November 15, 1977, p. 1192.*

There is a time in every child's life when he is convinced that his parents want to get rid of him. That is Amifika's terrible fear. . . . A marvelous marriage of sensitivities, Lucille Clifton and [illustrator] Thomas DiGrazia have produced a book that is warm and special.

> *Nikki Grimes, in her review of "Amifika," in* Children's Book Review Service *(copyright © 1977 Chil-*

dren's Book Review Service Inc.), Vol. 6, No. 4, December, 1977, p. 31.

With the logic of a small boy, Amifika is sure that because he doesn't remember his father, his father won't remember him, and, therefore, he'll be the first to go (ridiculous to an adult—but enormously frightening to a young child). . . . Clifton's perceptive prose, written in the Black vernacular, will appeal to any youngsters afraid they may be expendable.

> *Marjorie Lewis, in her review of "Amifika," in* School Library Journal *(reprinted from the December, 1977 issue of* School Library Journal, *published by R. R. Bowker Co./A Xerox Corporation; copyright © 1977), Vol. 24, No. 4, December, 1977, p. 44.*

EVERETT ANDERSON'S NINE MONTH LONG   (1978)

Everett Anderson's well-loved Mama is pregnant and Mr. Tom Perry, "almost a dad," accepts and helps with some of the feelings aroused by these circumstances. The establishment of an active, effective, and supportive male figure is an important part of this story. So is its tacit acknowledgement that, for the younger child, a mother's pregnancy means disturbing changes now as well as a sibling later. . . . [The rhymed yet conversational verses of Clifton's style] are well displayed. (pp. 39-40)

> *Joan W. Blos, in her review of "Everett Anderson's Nine Month Long," in* School Library Journal *(reprinted from the February, 1979 issue of* School Library Journal, *published by R. R. Bowker Co./A Xerox Corporation; copyright © 1979), Vol. 25, No. 6, February, 1979, pp. 39-40.*

As warm, gentle, and therapeutic as this is, it's been done before, and Clifton's verse is not memorable in its own right.

> *Denise M. Wilms, in her review of "Everett Anderson's Nine Month Long," in* Booklist *(reprinted by permission of the American Library Association; copyright © 1979 by the American Library Association), Vol. 75, No. 11, February 1, 1979, p. 864.*

Despite all the closeness and hand holding, Everett still calls his stepfather Mr. Perry, and Clifton's jarring affectation of poetic enjambment is even less in synch with her mushy messages. . . . Expectant parents might welcome the soft-focus treatment, but these are not among Everett Anderson's best days.

> *A review of "Everett Anderson's Nine Month Long," in* Kirkus Reviews *(copyright © 1979 The Kirkus Service, Inc.), Vol. XLVII, No. 3, February 1, 1979, p. 120.*

[The] newest story poem about the small black boy who has accepted a loving stepfather [has a tender quality]. . . . A very nice handling of the dethronement problem, and—as always—nicely honed writing that seems deceptively smooth and casual.

> *Zena Sutherland, in her review of "Everett Anderson's Nine Month Long," in* Bulletin of the Center for Children's Books *(reprinted by permission of The University of Chicago Press; © 1979 by The University of Chicago), Vol. 32, No. 8, April, 1979, p. 132.*

This book, written in wonderful poetic style . . . , projects a warm, loving, understanding and supportive family. Many children will love having it read to them. . . . It would especially benefit teachers and parents who want to stimulate conversations with children about different family life styles in positive ways.

When reading the book aloud, adults may want to change some of the words because the text raises but does not address some very serious issues. For example, Everett describes Mr. Perry as being "almost a dad," a concept that might confuse or disturb children. And, in a discussion about how different his mother seems to him, Everett is told that he shouldn't worry about the new baby because "You know you are her special one, her firstborn Everett Anderson." While saying this may help Everett feel better, doesn't it set up a false sense of superiority towards the baby—and what about the effect hearing this will have on non-firstborn children? Overall, however, the book is a positive one. (p. 18)

> *A review of "Everett Anderson's Nine Month Long," in* Interracial Books for Children Bulletin *(reprinted by permission of* Interracial Books for Children Bulletin, *1841 Broadway, New York, N.Y. 10023), Vol. 10, No. 5, 1979, pp. 17-18.*

THE LUCKY STONE   (1979)

Lucille Clifton has written another really fine story for young children. The concept of past and present is usually hard for children to grasp but this book puts the passing of time in a perspective that children can understand. . . .

This book contains information on various aspects of Black culture—slavery, religion and extended family—all conveyed in a way that is both positive and accurate.

This book is a must!

> *A review of "The Lucky Stone," in* Interracial Books for Children Bulletin *(reprinted by permission of* Interracial Books for Children Bulletin, *1841 Broadway, New York, N.Y. 10023), Vol. 11, Nos. 1 and 2, 1980, p. 28.*

[*The Lucky Stone*] is at once talisman and anthology: over the years it has gathered unto it story after story, episodes indicating its power, both as a charm and as a unit of oral tradition. Clifton has a knack for projecting strong positive values without seeming goody-goody; her poet's ear is one factor in this, her sense of humor another.

> *Michele Slung, in her review of "The Lucky Stone," in* Book World—The Washington Post *(© 1980, The Washington Post), February 10, 1980, p. 9.*

Four short stories about four generations of Black women and their dealings with a lucky stone, . . . aimed at independent reading by older children, although younger children will enjoy hearing one story at a time. . . . Clifton uses as a frame device a grandmother telling the history of the stone to her granddaughter; by the end, the granddaughter has inherited the stone herself. The plot is necessarily episodic, spanning the period from just before the Emancipation Proclamation to the present, so that we see slavery, a revival meeting, and a traveling circus; but the orderly passing on of the stone ties it all together. The story is written in Black dialect, but the language is not obscured so that "it wondered me" and "howdyin'" are understandable from the context.

Ruth K. MacDonald, in her review of "The Lucky Stone," in School Library Journal *(reprinted from the March, 1980 issue of* School Library Journal, *published by R. R. Bowker Co./A Xerox Corporation; copyright © 1980), Vol. 26, No. 7, March, 1980, p. 119.*

MY FRIEND JACOB (1980)

[A story with a gentle tone] in which a black child speaks with affection and patience of his friendship with a white adolescent neighbor (Jacob is seventeen, Sam eight) who is retarded. Jacob is Sam's "very very best friend" and all of his best qualities are appreciated by Sam, just as all of his limitations are accepted. This isn't structured, it has no story line and little action, but it is strong in the simplicity and warmth with which a handicapped person is loved rather than pitied, enjoyed rather than tolerated.

Zena Sutherland, in her review of "My Friend Jacob," in Bulletin of the Center for Children's Books *(reprinted by permission of The University of Chicago Press; ©1980 by The University of Chicago), Vol. 34, No. 1, September, 1980, p. 4.*

The warm interracial friendship shows understanding, tolerance, and respect for retarded people; Sam's affection for Jacob is genuine, and through his eyes one learns that Jacob is a very fine friend.

Christine McDonnell, in her review of "My Friend Jacob," in The Horn Book Magazine *(copyright © 1980 by The Horn Book, Inc., Boston), Vol. LVI, No. 5, October, 1980, p. 511.*

My Friend Jacob is a special book about a very special friendship. . . . The two boys have a strong relationship filled with trust and affection. The author depicts this relationship and their everyday adventures in a way that is unmarred by the mawkish sentimentality that often characterizes tales of the mentally disabled.

Sam resists the gentle opposition of both sets of parents, who feel he spends too much time with Jacob. Sam sees their friendship as mutually beneficial. . . . There are some activities in which Sam takes the leadership and some in which Jacob leads.

This sensitive portrait of two engaging young people should charm and instruct young readers. African American children will certainly appreciate Sam's guiding and instructional role.

Ismat Abdal-Haqq, in his review of "My Friend Jacob," in Interracial Books for Children Bulletin *(reprinted by permission of* Interracial Books for Children Bulletin, *1841 Broadway, New York, N.Y. 10023), Vol. 12, No. 2, 1981, p. 20.*

Another winner is **My Friend Jacob**. . . . In a matter-of-fact, low-keyed style, we discover how [Sam and Jacob] help one another grow and understand the world. . . . It takes Sam's mother a while to appreciate her son's fortunate friendship, and this is realistically portrayed. A must.

A review of "My Friend Jacob" (copyright 1981 by the International Reading Association, Inc.; re-

printed with permission of the International Reading Association), in The Reading Teacher, *Vol. 34, No. 6, March, 1981, p. 735.*

SONORA BEAUTIFUL (1982)

In a spare evocative reflection on life that forgoes plot to emulate simple feelings, a young girl expresses personal as well as universal teenage concerns about herself and her family. . . . [A] realistic and loving portrait of a family's relationships, which, because it revolves around sentiment rather than action, excitement, and character should challenge teenage girls with reading difficulties by providing them with a different kind of book experience.

Ilene Cooper, in her review of "Sonora Beautiful," in Booklist *(reprinted by permission of the American Library Association; copyright © 1982 by the American Library Association), Vol. 78, No. 10, January 15, 1982, p. 644.*

For older reluctant readers, this is written in short sentences and fragments and designed with lots of pictures and more space than text on every page. Without the space, the text would take up about four skinny pages. It is not a story and it is not a prose poem. It is more like a complaint that turns into a loving affirmation. Just because the author wants it to end that way. First Sonora tells how some mornings she wakes up believing she has "got real ugly" during the night. But her mother always assures her that she's beautiful. She also complains of her name. Of her father's weird way of making a living (he's a poet). And of their house which doesn't have "regular" rooms like other kids'. Sonora's mother thinks the name, occupation, and house are all beautiful. (Most poets would wonder how Daddy maintains the house.) The family also goes for walks a lot, at dawn. Sonora says this is crazy but changes when she tells of the three of them sitting in the park and hugging. This she too finds beautiful. In the short text, Sonora says "I'm not joking" ten times. Alas, neither is Clifton.

A review of "Sonora Beautiful," in Kirkus Reviews *(copyright © 1982 The Kirkus Service, Inc.), Vol. L, No. 4, February 15, 1982, p. 207.*

[This] is one of the current YA hilo adolescent novels. . . . **Sonora Beautiful** emphasizes the simple qualities of life and why they are beautiful in the personification of Sonora, an adolescent girl who feels insecure and unsatisfied. Believing that she has been shortchanged in a lot of ways and convinced that her type of life is unusual because it is different than the typical middle class "way", Sonora is constantly being reassured by her gentle and loving mother. Told in the first person by Sonora, the book moves to a soft, satisfactory ending as she gradually comes to realize that her family and their life together is indeed beautiful in its closeness, its strength in the intangibles. Clifton writes smoothly. . . . The message is very clear if not new.

Rosemarie Melesh, in her review of "Sonora Beautiful," in Voice of Youth Advocates *(copyrighted 1982 by Voice of Youth Advocates), Vol. 5, No. 1, April, 1982, p. 33.*

Joanna Cole

1944-

American author of nonfiction and fiction.

A well-known science writer for younger children, Cole presents involved topics simply and accurately. Her works demonstrate the ability to challenge readers without overwhelming them. Throughout most of her career she has collaborated with Jerome Wexler, whose distinguished photographs and drawings complement her texts.

Cole began writing in 1971, following training in psychology and elementary education. She centers her attention most often on the field of zoology, but also creates works of fiction: *The Secret Box,* for example, considers the subject of theft and its repercussions without being didactic. Critics note Cole's ability in her nonfiction to express many facts clearly and in an interesting way. Perhaps the most frequent negative criticism regards her occasional use of a more advanced vocabulary than the reader might understand, though critics agree that she generally gears her information and examples to the child's intellectual level. The concensus is that many of Cole's books stand among the best contemporary science books for children.

COCKROACHES   (1971)

To know the cockroach is, *mirabile dictu,* to admire him: a living fossil, he has endured unchanged because, flat, he can slip into narrow places; fast, and keenly sensitive to vibrations (via feelers) and movements (via compound eyes), he can elude capture; omniverous . . . , he can live almost anywhere. . . . Throughout, the structure and functioning of the cockroach is systematically set forth . . . simply in the text. . . . For the last word hear Don Marquis' inimitable archie: "one thing the human bean never seems to get into it is the fact that humans appear just as unnecessary to cockroaches as cockroaches do to humans." This is the necessary corrective.

> *A review of "Cockroaches," in* Kirkus Reviews *(copyright © 1971 The Kirkus Service, Inc.), Vol. XXXIX, No. 1, April 1, 1971, p. 371.*

Pointing out certain assets, including adaptability to environments of all kinds and the ability to learn, which have helped the cockroach to survive almost unchanged since prehistoric times, the author identifies various species and describes the physical features, habits, and life cycle of the cockroach. She disproves the belief that the roach is a health hazard and discusses the use of the cockroach as an experimental animal in scientific research. Clearly written . . . , the brief study is absorbing despite its unpopular subject.

> *A review of "Cockroaches," in* The Booklist *(reprinted by permission of the American Library Association; copyright © 1971 by the American Library Association), Vol. 67, No. 18, May 15, 1971, p. 797.*

The author wisely had a competent entomologist check the manuscript; as a result, errors of fact are few. The worst error is the statement (page 56) "scientists have studied cockroaches for years and have found that they carry no germs harmful to man." It is established that cockroaches can transport numerous bacterial pathogens including those that cause dysentery,

typhoid, diarrhea, pneumonia, and gastroenteritis. Also, a disservice is done by underplaying the role of roaches in the home as a thoroughly unpleasant nuisance. This book is recommended as well written and informative.

> *A review of "Cockroaches," in* Science Books *(copyright © 1971 by the American Association for the Advancement of Science), Vol. VII, No. 3, December, 1971, p. 245.*

THE SECRET BOX   (1971)

In sentient words and pictures Anne Marie is projected whole: she lives in a city housing project with parents who work and sisters who need looking after; she "wanted to have something all to herself. So she made a secret box, which she kept under her bed." She has a best friend Vanessa and an understanding teacher Mr. Freeman . . . ; Mr. Freeman has "a pencil that was red on one end and blue on the other" and one day Anne Marie "looked at it for a long time." "Mr. Freeman was in the closet getting paper. The other children were writing. . . . Anne Marie picked up the pencil and slipped it into her pocket. It would be wonderful for the secret box." . . . There's an unreflective upbeat ending, intentionally and intelligently equivocal: each episode of theft has its roots in the ongoing organic context of an unassuming story, nicely modulated.

A review of "The Secret Box," in Kirkus Reviews *(copyright © 1971 The Kirkus Service, Inc.), Vol. XXXIX, No. 12, June 15, 1971, p. 637.*

[*The Secret Box*] tells a compelling story with which urban third graders can identify. . . . The book deals with the problem of stealing, and the child's "conversion" at the end is convincingly managed. Another plus—bad as well as good teachers are depicted. This open treatment may help children who must develop their own values in an unsympathetic or hostile environment.

A review of "The Secret Box," in School Library Journal, *an appendix to* Library Journal *(reprinted from the December, 1971 issue of* School Library Journal, *published by R. R. Bowker Co./A Xerox Corporation; copyright © 1971), Vol. 18, No. 4, December, 1971, p. 71.*

The reader is left with the feeling that Anne Marie has learned a painful lesson and that she will probably never again take anything that doesn't belong to her. The events are realistic, and the story is told without moralizing. Children might read this book independently, or it could be read aloud in a group.

Sharon Spredemann Dreyer, in her review of "The Secret Box," in her The Bookfinder: A Guide to Children's Literature about the Needs and Problems of Youth Aged 2-15, Vol. 1 *(© 1977 American Guidance Service, Inc.), American Guidance Service, Inc., 1977, No. 219.*

TWINS: THE STORY OF MULTIPLE BIRTHS **(with Madeleine Edmondson, 1972)**

How twins and "supertwins" (triplets, etc.) occur, why multiple births are less rare than they used to be (fertility pills), how it feels to be a twin, what accounts for the seemingly uncanny understanding between some twins, and how twins are used in heredity-enviroment studies: these and other likely questions are duly considered in comfortable prose that is supported by available research, pertinent anecdotes [and] examples. . . .

A review of "Twins: The Story of Multiple Births," in Kirkus Reviews *(copyright © 1972 The Kirkus Service, Inc.), Vol. XL, No. 4, February 15, 1972, p. 196.*

A clearly written . . . account of the biological causation of multiple births as well as their sociological and psychological implications. The authors challenge myths which associate ESP with multiple births and explain the contribution of multiple births to scientists' understanding of the roles of environment and heredity in human personality formation. Twins are covered briefly in general books on human reproduction, but the exclusive focus here on multiple births will be of interest to children.

A. C. Haman, in a review of "Twins: The Story of Multiple Births," in School Library Journal, *an appendix to* Library Journal *(reprinted from the February, 1973 issue of* School Library Journal, *published by R. R. Bowker Co./A Xerox Corporation; copyright © 1973), Vol. 19, No. 6, February, 1973, p. 57.*

All kinds of facts about twins are presented using identical and fraternal twins as examples. . . . The twins' importance to

science is stressed, particularly identical twins who have been separated as babies and raised in different environments. Such studies can help to answer the old question about which is more important, heredity or environment. A clear, matter-of-fact style plus an interesting topic make this good reading.

Elizabeth Gillis, in her review of "Twins: The Story of Multiple Births," in Appraisal: Science Books for Young People *(copyright © 1973 by the Children's Science Book Review Committee), Vol. 6, No. 2, Spring, 1973, p. 8.*

The book begins with a clear and simple explanation of the twinning phenomenon and continues to expand on its importance as a field of science. But the vocabulary, which may be difficult for second-to-fourth-grade readers, and the failure to hold interest mark this book with mediocrity. It is an easily readable, basically informative account, lacking interest or significance.

Robert J. Stein, in his review of "Twins: The Story of Multiple Births," in Appraisal: Science Books for Young People *(copyright © 1973 by the Children's Science Book Review Committee), Vol. 6, No. 2, Spring, 1973, p. 8.*

FLEAS **(1973)**

The life cycle and appearance of the flea . . . are followed by his tragic effect on human history as a spreader of the plague and the more elegant methods our ancestors had of combating infestation. . . . Cole serves up a nice blend of biological fact and curiosities (what a flea circus is and how it works)—all in simple, straightforward language. . . .

A review of "Fleas," in Kirkus Reviews *(copyright © 1973 The Kirkus Service, Inc.), Vol. XLI, No. 5, March 1, 1973, p. 256.*

A detailed, interesting description of the evolution, life cycle, and life style of the ubiquitous parasite, the flea. . . . A clear and complete treatment of the subject and an invaluable addition to any science collection.

Shirley A. Smith, in her review of "Fleas," in School Library Journal, *an appendix to* Library Journal *(reprinted from the May, 1973 issue of* School Library Journal, *published by R. R. Bowker Co./A Xerox Corporation; copyright © 1973), Vol. 19, No. 9, May, 1973, p. 70.*

This well written book for youngsters on the life and times of the flea outlines its probable evolution and describes various kinds of fleas now in existence. The author has neatly included several examples of the scientific method in a form palatable to the elementary level student. There is a remarkable amount of information in this simple text, and children intent on collecting small mammals such as gerbils and white mice (prime flea hosts) will benefit from the advice given.

A review of "Fleas," in Science Books *(copyright © 1973 by the American Association for the Advancement of Science), Vol. IX, No. 2, September, 1973, p. 167.*

Fleas deals with an unusual subject and will probably intrigue some children. The text has interesting information and a variety of topics. . . . Since there still is some health problem with fleas, such basic information for all children is important.

It could be one of the basic books for an elementary school library.

> Anne E. Matthews, in her review of "Fleas," in Appraisal: Science Books for Young People (copyright © 1974 by the Children's Science Book Review Committee), Vol. 7, No. 1, Winter, 1974, p. 12.

In spite of the spine chilling title this is a fascinating book, even for those of us who would really rather not know about these delectable creatures. . . .

The author makes them look most attractive and writes with sympathy of them in the "order of things." "Is it safe to be a flea" is one intriguing chapter title, and the answer is no, in this modern chemically controlled world.

> A review of "Fleas," in The Junior Bookshelf, Vol. 38, No. 5, October, 1974, p. 292.

PLANTS IN WINTER (1973)

Reliance on a perfunctory dialogue between the botanist Dr. Owen and her young friend . . . [makes] for a routine question and answer session on what happens to plants during winter. Dr. Owen's lecture is substantial enough to start off a classroom discussion or a winter gardening project, but even at this level, alert teachers should anticipate many more questions about the differences between evergreens and leafy trees, annuals and perennials, and seeds and bulbs.

> A review of "Plants in Winter," in Kirkus Reviews (copyright © 1973 The Kirkus Service, Inc.), Vol. XLI, No. 21, November 1, 1973, p. 1205.

[Written] with simplicity, a brief text covers just enough material to explain what plants do in winter and why evergreens are able to keep their leaves. With no extraneous material, the book closes with the fact that "no one knows *all* about plants in winter—yet."

> Zena Sutherland, in her review of "Plants in Winter," in Bulletin of the Center for Children's Books (reprinted by permission of The University of Chicago Press; © 1974 by The University of Chicago), Vol. 27, No. 8, April, 1974, p. 126.

The author describes clearly and simply the different ways that plants have adapted for survival during the adverse conditions of winter. . . . The accuracy of the information is excellent. . . .

> A review of "Plants in Winter," in Science Books (copyright © 1974 by the American Association for the Advancement of Science), Vol. X, No. 1, May, 1974, p. 70.

The text is clear and simple. . . . Considering how slight a volume this is, it covers a wide range of plants from evergreen and deciduous trees to smaller plants, such as dandelion and snowdrop. The author also explains leaves, roots, shoots, seeds, and bulbs. This is an attractive and informative introduction to plant life.

> Beryl B. Beatley, in her review of "Plants in Winter," in Appraisal: Science Books for Young People (copyright © 1974 by the Children's Science Book Review Committee), Vol. 7, No. 3, Fall, 1974, p. 12.

MY PUPPY IS BORN (1973)

The process of birth is explicitly and accurately explained. . . . Sentences are short and simple, and more difficult terms like "umbilical cord" and "sac" are clearly explained. . . . Young readers, especially puppy lovers, will appreciate the matter-of-fact treatment of a newborn animal's development.

> Bonnie Tolman, in her review of "My Puppy Is Born," in School Library Journal, an appendix to Library Journal (reprinted from the January, 1974 issue of School Library Journal, published by R. R. Bowker Co./A Xerox Corporation; copyright © 1974), Vol. 20, No. 5, January, 1974, p. 38.

A simple story . . . of the birth of a dachshund puppy, and his progress and growth until he is eight weeks old. . . . The text is confined to the necessary minimum. . . . The whole is dealt with in a healthy manner with just the right amount of information sensibly given for the young child, and will serve as a useful introduction to the process of birth.

> A review of "My Puppy Is Born," in The Junior Bookshelf, Vol. 39, No. 2, April, 1975, p. 104.

DINOSAUR STORY (1974)

[Certainly] the same material has been presented to young readers before. Still, the fascination endures, . . . and—to cite the most recent competitor—Cole provides more information and more continuity, without being significantly harder to read, than Peggy Parish's *Dinosaur Time*. . . .

> A review of "Dinosaur Story," in Kirkus Reviews (copyright © 1974 The Kirkus Service, Inc.), Vol. XLII, No. 20, October 15, 1974, p. 1106.

Pedestrian text. . . . [makes] this one of the least interesting books on dinosaurs. For the same age level *Dinosaur Time* by Peggy Parish (Harper, 1974) is far more attractive even though it gives less information on the different species of dinosaurs.

> Margaret Bush, in her review of "Dinosaur Story," in School Library Journal, an appendix to Library Journal (reprinted from the November, 1974 issue of School Library Journal, published by R. R. Bowker Co./A Xerox Corporation; copyright © 1974), Vol. 21, No. 3, November, 1974, p. 45.

The author has subtly woven connections between paleontology and dinosaurs, between dinosaurs and other dinosaurs, and between dinosaurs' behavior and their natural environment—too subtly, I'm afraid. Most young readers are likely to perceive this as a collection of random facts about dinosaurs rather than a coherent "dinosaur story."

> Ronald J. Kley, in his review of "Dinosaur Story," in Appraisal: Science Books for Young People (copyright © 1975 by the Children's Science Book Review Committee), Vol. 8, No. 2, Spring, 1975, p. 12.

The author begins with a dinosaur bone extracted by archaeologists; she attempts to show how the age of reptiles has been reconstructed from such evidence. She covers an immense time period and enumerates many interesting facts, as well as postulations about dinosaur habits and the final disappearance of the giant reptiles. Although carefully worded so that the reader will not confuse fact and fiction, the prose is meandering and at times bland, bordering on patronizing. There is no key to the pronunciation of the various dinosaurs' names. . . . Much information is amassed here, but the style and organization render it difficult for small children to follow.

> *Debbie Robinson, in her review of "Dinosaur Story,"* in Appraisal: Science Books for Young People *(copyright © 1975 by the Children's Science Book Review Committee), Vol. 8, No. 2, Spring, 1975, p. 12.*

A short, clear, accurate retelling of the dinosaur story which can be read to the youngest group and which will hold their attention. The better readers in the first few grades can handle the easy text for themselves. In spite of the briefness of the account, there is an emphasis on the *time span* of dinosaur existence unusual in a book at this level.

> *Polly A. Toups, in her review of "Dinosaur Story,"* in Science Books & Films *(copyright © 1975 by the American Association for the Advancement of Science), Vol. XI, No. 1, May, 1975, p. 34.*

Dinosaur Story . . . gives some background to the dinosaur era, offers an abundance of clear information about dinosaur types, and contains the kind of specific detail children enjoy. The author demonstrates an understanding of children's intellectual development through her emphasis. For instance, she describes the size of the dinosaurs in detail, using examples such as larger than a truck or taller than a house. However, when she mentions that "Millions and millions of years went by" she makes no attempt to explain this time span, realizing that young children cannot comprehend such abstraction.

Dinosaur Story may be too complex for young children; in such cases the book can easily be adapted to their comprehension level.

> *Pamela R. Giller, in her review of "Dinosaur Story,"* in Appraisal: Science Books for Young People *(copyright © 1980 by the Children's Science Book Review Committee), Vol. 13, No. 1, Winter, 1980, p. 5.*

A CALF IS BORN (1975)

The text is lucid and literal, answering, in spite of its brevity, a surprising number of the questions young readers may have. Information on how cows eat and digest food and on the milking process is delivered in the same straightforward fashion as that of the narrative for the birth sequence.

> *A review of "A Calf Is Born," in* The Booklist *(reprinted by permission of the American Library Association; copyright © 1975 by the American Library Association), Vol. 72, No. 4, October 15, 1975, p. 307.*

Cole documents the entire birth process of Daisy's calf, Speckle, from first protrusion of the sac, to the calf's first amusing attempts to stand and nurse. In addition, the entire life of a dairy cow is covered. . . . Although the prose lacks the freshness and charm of Cole's **My Puppy Is Born** . . . , this will still be useful for presenting dairy material as well as animal reproduction to young children.

> *Juliet Kellogg Markowsky, in her review of "A Calf Is Born," in* School Library Journal *(reprinted from the November, 1975 issue of* School Library Journal, *published by R. R. Bowker Co./A Xerox Corporation; copyright © 1975), Vol. 22, No. 3, November, 1975, p. 44.*

For city-dwellers this will be a real eye-opener, but even children who have seen a cow "in the flesh" will undoubtedly gain some new knowledge. . . . In a very brief text the author has brought together a wealth of information. Here is everything you always wanted to know about cows—plus a lot you might never have thought to ask about.

> *Barbara Dill, in her review of "A Calf Is Born," in* Wilson Library Bulletin *(copyright © 1975 by the H. W. Wilson Company), Vol. 50, No. 3, November, 1975, p. 248.*

This doesn't have quite the appeal of the author's **My Puppy Is Born,** since the cow is a less familiar animal to many small children than the dog, but the book has the same combination of direct, conversational style of writing and accuracy in presenting the facts. The text is sequentially arranged, with no extraneous material. . . .

> *Zena Sutherland, in her review of "A Calf Is Born," in* Bulletin of the Center for Children's Books *(reprinted by permission of The University of Chicago Press; © 1976 by The University of Chicago), Vol. 29, No. 5, January, 1976, p. 75.*

A CHICK HATCHES (1976)

Cole's spare text introduces a few terms, such as *allantois* and *amniotic sac,* but it's no more difficult than the accompaniments to Wexler's more conventional views of puppy and calf births. And the final portrait of a self-satisfied two-day-old chick puts the whole process in perspective.

> *A review of "A Chick Hatches," in* Kirkus Reviews *(copyright © 1976 The Kirkus Service, Inc.), Vol. XLIV, No. 22, November 15, 1976, p. 1223.*

First-class scientific writing . . . [introduces] as clearly and simply as possible the development of a chick from fertilization to the end of its three-week incubation. Cole has predicted children's questions with logical thoroughly, yet there's never a wasted word. . . . Reluctant students will get so interested they'll forget they're reading, and young science fair enthusiasts will get right to work. Material for this age group—and exciting nonfiction to boot—is a rare find.

> *A review of "A Chick Hatches," in* Booklist *(reprinted by permission of the American Library Association; copyright © 1976 by the American Library Association), Vol. 73, No. 8, December 15, 1976, p. 604.*

The [chick's] growth is followed step-by-step with a minimum of description, but the explanation is both adequate and accurate for the intended audience.

Pre-readers should be able to enjoy and understand a great deal of this book if portions referred to are pointed out in the pictures when the text is read to them. Slightly older children should find pleasure and wonder in reading the book by themselves, although they may need occasional help with a few technical words. It is rare that so involved a subject is as clearly and simply presented.

> *Marie M. Jenkins, in her review of "A Chick Hatches," in* Science Books & Films *(copyright © 1977 by the American Association for the Advancement of Science), Vol. XIII, No. 3, December, 1977, p. 166.*

A finely developed knowledge of how to distill, organize, and present information is evident here. . . . The economy and force of this simple didactic book in its entirety are such as to repay study.

> *Barbara Bader, in her review of "A Chick Hatches,"* in Children's Book Showcase 1977, *Barbara Bader, Betty Binns, Alvin Eisenman, eds. (© 1977 The Children's Book Council, Inc.), Children's Book Council, 1977, p. 22.*

SABER-TOOTHED TIGER AND OTHER ICE AGE MAMMALS (1977)

Cole briefly spotlights each [prehistoric animal] in turn, and ends with a scenario of how several of them—plant-eaters attracting carnivores who succumb to the same fate—might have got stuck in the tar pits where the bones of many were found. Defining the Ice Age and noting that prehistoric people lived then too, this is a respectable sequel to *Dinosaur Story*, but—being chiefly a catalog of the separate species—with somewhat less dimension.

> *A review of "Saber-Toothed Tiger and Other Ice Age Mammals,"* in Kirkus Reviews *(copyright © 1977 The Kirkus Service, Inc.), Vol. XLV, No. 22, November 15, 1977, p. 1200.*

This book describes a variety of Pleistocene or "Ice Age" mammals, emphasizing behavioral characteristics, predator-prey relationships, and the sources of such paleontological information (including fossils, preserved organic remains, and analogies drawn from the physiology and behavior of related modern creatures). It may be unrealistic to expect a very young reader to grasp the potential richness of this information—but it is there nevertheless. The vocabulary and sentence structure reflect a concerted and effective effort to work within the framework of primary level readability.

> *Ronald J. Kley, in his review of "Saber-Toothed Tiger and Other Ice Age Mammals," in* Appraisal: Science Books for Young People *(copyright © 1978 by the Children's Science Book Review Committee), Vol. 11, No. 2, Spring, 1978, p. 8.*

The saber-toothed tiger poised in menace on the cover of this book is bait for those of us who still judge books by covers, but the interior is a great disappointment. Geared for young readers, the text simply describes mammals of the Ice Age, the saber-toothed tiger striding among them and creating a central theme. Though the language tends to stiffness, some scenes are potentially exciting (such as a description of a predator chain in action at La Brea tar pits). . . . However, the subject matter is nowhere else treated for such young readers and this book may fill a need in children's collections.

> *Carolyn Noah, in her review of "Saber-Toothed Tiger and Other Ice Age Mammals," in* Appraisal: Science Books for Young People *(copyright © 1978 by the Children's Science Book Review Committee), Vol. 11, No. 2, Spring, 1978, p. 8.*

A FISH HATCHES (1978)

Cole's readily accessible text and Wexler's imposing black-and-white photos result in one of this season's outstanding science books for beginners. . . . This is a valuable addition to any child's library and especially recommended for young naturalists.

> *A review of "A Fish Hatches," in* Publishers Weekly *(reprinted from the December 25, 1978 issue of Publishers Weekly, published by R. R. Bowker Company, a Xerox company; copyright © 1978 by Xerox Corporation), Vol. 214, No. 25, December 25, 1978, p. 60.*

A Fish Hatches is specific as it deals with trout, yet general in that the information covers the life cycle of many other species of fish. . . . Pleasantly the complicated content has been presented . . . for the novice in a very readable manner without being condescending.

> *F. Luree Jaquith, in a review of "A Fish Hatches," in* Appraisal: Science Books for Young People *(copyright © 1979 by the Children's Science Book Review Committee), Vol. 12, No. 1, Winter, 1979, p. 14.*

Despite the format (one sentence to a line), the writing tends to be a bit older than the book might appear to an inquisitive child. There are some slight inaccuracies (the lateral line of a fish is an organ, not a sense), but generally the text explains what the reader sees in the photograph in a simple, interesting way.

> *Seymour Simon, in his review of "A Fish Hatches," in* Appraisal: Science Books for Young People *(copyright © 1979 by the Children's Science Book Review Committee), Vol. 12, No. 1, Winter, 1979, p. 15.*

Freedman's *Getting Born* (1978) began with an arresting close-up of trout eggs; now Cole and Wexler, who have all along been offering separate, closer looks at several of the same animals Freedman covers, show us many more stages in the trout egg's growth and the fry's development, as well as many of the adult fish's physical features. . . . Human hands are . . . prominent in the picture of trout fertilization: in a hatchery, it is done by people squeezing eggs out of the female, then squeezing sperm-containing milt from the male into the same pan. Perhaps a word on how it happens in nature is also called for, but Cole's approach constitutes a dramatic reminder that natural life cycles are no longer the rule.

> *A review of "A Fish Hatches," in* Kirkus Reviews *(copyright © 1979 The Kirkus Service, Inc.), Vol. XLVII, No. 2, January 15, 1979, p. 68.*

The first half of the book is an excellent presentation of how a fish hatches. The author indicates clearly the relative size of trout eggs by comparing them through a microscope to unmagnified eggs placed next to a penny. . . . [The] text is clear and interesting. Perhaps because of the outstanding quality of the first pages, the second half of the book is a disappointment. Too many topics are covered (external anatomy, feeding, respiration, vision, hearing, sensory organs, locomotion and behavior) and the section is not integrated into the overall theme of the book. The material is superficial and could be easily gleaned from any good biology text or introductory ichthyology book.

> *Richard K. Keiser, in his review of "A Fish Hatches," in* Science Books & Films *(copyright © 1979 by the American Association for the Advancement of Science), Vol. XV, No. 3, December, 1979, p. 168.*

FIND THE HIDDEN INSECT (1979)

Because most insects are so vulnerable to attack by predators, they have evolved methods of hiding themselves or disguising their true natures. They may employ camouflage, imitate other species, spin coverings of threads from their own glands, or hide within rolled leaves or other shelters. This book communicates a sense of wonder about these remarkable adaptations. It is well-written at a low readability level.

> *Elliot H. Blaustein, in his review of "Find the Hidden Insect," in* Children's Book Review Service *(copyright © 1979 Children's Book Review Service Inc.), Vol. 8, No. 2, October, 1979, p. 15.*

A clear, simple introduction to the concept of animal camouflage. Although the title seems to indicate a guessing game approach, most of the text is a straightforward explanation of the various means by which insects interact with their environment in order to protect themselves from predators. . . . Many of the insects used as examples are intriguing in appearance or behavior. . . . Cole and Wexler live up to their earlier felicitous collaborations. . . .

> *Margaret Bush, in her review of "Find the Hidden Insect," in* School Library Journal *(reprinted from the January, 1980 issue of* School Library Journal, *published by R. R. Bowker Co./A Xerox Corporation; copyright © 1980), Vol. 26, No. 5, January, 1980, p. 55.*

Teachers will find this attractive and informative little science book about insect behavior useful for supplementing units on animal adaptations and camouflage. Five to eight year olds will find it fun. This reviewer finds it quite nicely done.

> *Diane Holzheimer, in her review of "Find the Hidden Insect," in* Appraisal: Science Books for Young People *(copyright © 1980 by the Children's Science Book Review Committee), Vol. 13, No. 2, Spring, 1980, p. 20.*

A FROG'S BODY (1980)

Once more, a sharp, clear presentation of essentials. Cole provides a viewing point at the start with the statement that a frog's body is "suited to a life half in and half out of water." She also notes that because the adult frog's organs are so much like those of other land animals, including humans, they are used by students to learn about the body—and then she is careful to point out, when each particular feature comes up, how frogs are different: they have no ribs, outside ears, or external sex organs; their long tongues are attached at the front, not the back of the mouth; and so on. . . . Overall, a well-focused introduction to the frog, and to the fit between body features and their functions.

> *A review of "A Frog's Body," in* Kirkus Reviews *(copyright © 1980 The Kirkus Service, Inc.), Vol. XLVIII, No. 9, May 1, 1980, p. 587.*

Cole and Wexler have constructed a superb introduction to the life processes and anatomy of the adult bullfrog. The author is exceptionally skillful at selecting interesting bits of information (the frog feels soft bellied because it has no ribs) and deftly combining explanations of fact and concepts in a simple, lucid text. . . . This will stand among the best of many fine books available on a subject popular with children.

> *Margaret Bush, in her review of "A Frog's Body," in* School Library Journal *(reprinted from the September, 1980 issue of* School Library Journal, *published by R. R. Bowker Co./A Xerox Corporation; copyright © 1980), Vol. 27, No. 1, September, 1980, p. 67.*

A handsome book with outstanding photographs and admirable text. . . . The book is an excellent complement to *Common Frog* (Putnam); quite different material is offered. . . . To simplify the meaning of cold-bloodedness, the text states that frogs "do not have any heat that is produced by their own body, as mammals and birds do." Since all living cells produce at least some heat at times, this statement should be qualified. Also, one of the diagrams would be better if the blood vessels were labeled; but one need not quibble over an essentially high-quality book.

> *Sarah Gagné, in her review of "A Frog's Body," in* The Horn Book Magazine *(copyright © 1980 by The Horn Book, Inc., Boston), Vol. LVI, No. 5, October, 1980, p. 545.*

There are many books for five to nine year olds about frogs, but this one is unusual in that it is an anatomy book. And a beautifully done one at that. Clear direct language and superb close up photographs . . . describe the frog's internal organs and skeleton as well as its external body and senses. Every part of this creature is examined with care. . . . The way in which the frog's particular anatomy enables it to function in its niche is made quite clear; for example, those bulging eyes and the long sticky tongue enable frogs to lie in wait for their prey rather than chase it. All in all, this is a terrific book, about a perennial favorite.

> *Diane Holzheimer, in her review of "A Frog's Body," in* Appraisal: Science Books for Young People *(copyright © 1981 by the Children's Science Book Review Committee), Vol. 14, No. 1, Winter, 1981, p. 21.*

The frog frequently provides youngsters with their initial introduction to nature, and is traditionally the animal studied in biology classrooms. In simple language, the author presents an informative discussion of how frogs breathe, move, regulate their body temperature, hide from predators, capture food, etc. . . . The result is captivating reading, and the book is an excellent introduction for young readers (aged 9-12) who have or have not had the opportunity to study frogs first-hand.

> *Robert J. Stein, in his review of "A Frog's Body," in* Appraisal: Science Books for Young People *(copyright © 1981 by the Children's Science Book Review Committee), Vol. 14, No. 1, Winter, 1981, p. 21.*

A HORSE'S BODY (1981)

This clear, elementary description of the horse's anatomy proves its theme, that the body is well designed for particular functions. . . . Special treatment of the senses of touch and smell and diagrams of sex organs are not found elsewhere. This can be read aloud to younger children and will attract older reluctant readers, too. It is for an older readership than Cole's ***My Puppy Is Born*** . . . and is useful for assigned research or for leisure reading.

> *Pat Harrington, in a review of "A Horse's Body," in* School Library Journal *(reprinted from the May, 1981 issue of* School Library Journal, *published by*

R. R. Bowker Co./A Xerox Corporation; copyright © 1981), Vol. 27, No. 9, May, 1981, p. 63.

"The horse is an animal that is perfectly suited for running over flat grasslands," observes Cole on page one, and the remainder of this streamlined volume specifies how its body has evolved for that purpose. . . . Ending with a look at the horse's sex organs and then a nursing foal, this becomes a complete checkup, sharpened by its focus on "the special body of an animal that was born to run."

A review of "A Horse's Body," in Kirkus Reviews (copyright © 1981 The Kirkus Service, Inc.), Vol. XLIX, No. 10, May 15, 1981, p. 634.

Well described are the intricacies of the various gaits; the influence of evolution on the digestive system; the reproductive system; and the keen senses of smell, hearing, touch, and sight. . . . All in all, the book is a sensible, straightforward, and comprehensive introduction to the anatomy of the horse. . . .

Ann A. Flowers, in her review of "A Horse's Body," in The Horn Book Magazine (copyright © 1981 by The Horn Book, Inc., Boston), Vol. LVII, No. 4, August, 1981, p. 444.

Through a combination of fine photographs, drawings, and simple text, Joanna Cole and Jerome Wexler have produced another excellent science book for the young child. . . . A superb blend of picture and word!

Althea L. Phillips, in her review of "A Horse's Body," in Appraisal: Science Books for Young People (copyright © 1982 by the Children's Science Book Review Committee), Vol. 15, No. 1, Winter, 1982, p. 23.

A splendid book! This overview of the anatomy of the horse provides a surprising amount of information (some of it was new to me). . . . The vocabulary strikes a good balance between technical accuracy and comprehension by secondary school readers.

Timothy C. Williams, in his review of "A Horse's Body," in Science Books & Films (copyright © 1982 by the American Association for the Advancement of Science), Vol. 17, No. 4, March-April, 1982, p. 215.

A SNAKE'S BODY (1981)

Never stooping to exploit the shuddering fascination of their subject, Cole and Wexler will nevertheless capture—and rechannel—the giddiest interest along with the most scholarly. (p. 1347)

A review of "A Snake's Body," in Kirkus Reviews (copyright © 1981 The Kirkus Service, Inc.), Vol. XLIX, No. 21, November 1, 1981, pp. 1346-47.

The hardest thing to understand about snakes is how they move, and the thing that repels and fascinates us about them is how they capture and devour their prey WHOLE. These, and all other aspects of a snake's life, are presented with great detail and clarity in an easy-to-read and inviting-to-look-at book. It's hard to believe that the author and illustrator have managed to pack so much information into so few pages and still maintain their record for uncluttered and meticulously well designed photo essays on animal lives.

Lavinia C. Dermos, in her review of "A Snake's Body," in Appraisal: Science Books for Young Peo-

ple (copyright © 1982 by the Children's Science Book Review Committee), Vol. 15, No. 1, Winter, 1982, p. 23.

The text is clear, forthright and interesting. Both photographs and text dwell on some of the most interesting questions that a child has about snakes such as body covering of scales, shedding of skin, movement, arrangement of internal organs, capturing and swallowing of food, elimination and hatching of eggs. . . . I feel this book is a good start for a young child interested in snakes and should stimulate enough interest in many children to lead them on to further investigating. (pp. 23-4)

Peter Stowe, in his review of "A Snake's Body," in Appraisal: Science Books for Young People (copyright © 1982 by the Children's Science Book Review Committee), Vol. 15, No. 1, Winter, 1982, pp. 23-4.

A Snake's Body . . . should fascinate youngsters, whether they are squeamish, nonchalant, or snake-crazy. Unlike most snake books, which emphasize poisonous species and record-breaking sizes, this one illustrates how a snake's body is adapted to cope with life's demands without the use of arms or legs. (pp. 75-6)

The highlight of the book is a series of ten photographs [by Jerome Wexler] of a chick being caught, constricted, and swallowed. Inevitably, one feels pity at the death of the gaping chick, and readers may gasp, almost as young people do, watching the real occurrence in a classroom; but this fact of nature is presented without comment—matter-of-factly, as is appropriate. Four types of locomotion are described with unusual clarity, the three parts of fecal droppings are shown, and the book concludes with reproduction—we even see a young python emerging from the egg. One photograph in the text is missing an arrow said to point to the prey in the throat, but that is a small matter considering the remarkable visual content, some of which is entirely new to children's books. (p. 76)

Sarah Gagné, in her review of "A Snake's Body," in The Horn Book Magazine (copyright © 1982 by The Horn Book, Inc., Boston), Vol. LVIII, No. 1, February, 1982, pp. 75-6.

The writing and choice of words is occasionally flawed. "In order to survive as a species, snakes must bear young." Not all snakes bear young. What seems to be intended is snakes must *reproduce* to survive as a species. Also Cole states, "Each baby is smaller than its parents, about two feet long." This could have been better expressed as, "Each baby is about two feet long at hatching." Careful editing and consultation could make this a superb book. Nevertheless, it is an adequate, informative text for young readers.

J. P. Kennedy, in a review of "A Snake's Body," in Science Books & Films (copyright © 1982 by the American Association for the Advancement of Science), Vol. 17, No. 4, March-April, 1982, p. 215.

Like other books in the author's anatomical series, this has a well-organized continuous text, careful integration of illustrative and textual material, and a direct style for the accurate information provided. . . . While this gives no facts on the mating process, it does discuss the way in which the python protects a clutch of eggs, and how those eggs hatch.

Zena Sutherland, in her review of "A Snake's Body," in Bulletin of the Center for Children's Books (reprinted by permission of The University of Chicago Press; © 1982 by The University of Chicago), Vol. 35, No. 8, April, 1982, p. 45.

A CAT'S BODY (1982)

Continuing the superior series that has so far considered the frog's, horse's, and snake's bodies as evolutionary adaptations determined by their wild origins, Cole and Wexler now take up the cat, whose nature and body are still geared to hunt. Thus for example the cat's strong muscles allow it to "slink rapidly," "pounce like lightning" with precise accuracy, and stalk in "slow motion." The eyes, facing forward, are a predator's eyes; the ears can hear high-pitched squeaks and turn to pinpoint sound . . . ; and so on for its teeth, paws, flexible spine, and other organs. In passing Cole points out that cats, built to hunt low to the ground, don't really kill as many birds as some people believe. . . . As usual, trim and to the point.

A review of "A Cat's Body," in Kirkus Reviews (copyright © 1982 The Kirkus Service, Inc.), Vol. L, No. 6, March 15, 1982, p. 348.

Cole and Wexler have created another clear and intriguing account of the way an animal's body fits its life style. Here they show how well designed and programmed a cat is to catch small rodents (but not birds) and how its abilities, instincts and ways of socializing with other cats fit into the domestic cat's life with humans. The brief, substantive text, clear, informative photos and open, welcoming layout will attract preschoolers, but equally well provide a fresh viewpoint for adults and everyone in between. Only one statement is debatable: that a cat's purr does not change tone as the cat breathes in and out. A Cat's Body complements standard pet books about cats such as the Silverstein's Cats: All About Them (Lothrop, 1978).

Margaret L. Chatham, in her review of "A Cat's Body," in School Library Journal (reprinted from the May, 1982 issue of School Library Journal, published by R. R. Bowker Co./A Xerox Corporation; copyright © 1982), Vol. 28, No. 9, May, 1982, p. 50.

GOLLY GUMP SWALLOWED A FLY (1982)

Beginning readers will be captivated by Golly Gump. . . . [His tale] is an expansion of There Was an Old Lady Who Swallowed a Fly. As Golly Gump grows larger and larger with a whole zoo inside him, he resorts to a threat, which makes all the animals run out of him. There are intriguing words like "flapping," "tickling," "buzzing," and "howling," which the early reader will latch onto with gusto.

Lois K. Nichols, in her review of "Golly Gump Swallowed a Fly," in Children's Book Review Service (copyright © 1982 Children's Book Review Service Inc.), Vol. 10, No. 10, May, 1982, p. 94.

Joanna Cole's story takes advantage of children's familiarity with the old rhyme, but varies the action and language enough to make it new and funny and simple enough for beginners.

Nancy Palmer, in her review of "Golly Gump Swallowed a Fly," in School Library Journal (reprinted from the May, 1982 issue of School Library Journal, published by R. R. Bowker Co./A Xerox Corporation; copyright © 1982), Vol. 28, No. 9, May, 1982, p. 77.

Carlo Collodi

1826-1890

(Pseudonym of Carlo Lorenzini) Italian author of fiction and nonfiction, journalist, critic, editor, and translator.

Collodi is the creator of Pinocchio, hero of perhaps the best puppet story ever written. Recently the subject of a two-year long centennial celebration in Italy, *The Adventures of Pinocchio* continues to fascinate children and adults with its accurate and amusing portrayal of childhood. Blending fantasy with reality, Collodi impresses the values of school, honest work, and proper companions on his readers. Children identify with Pinocchio's love for adventure and dislike of school, and they applaud the book's simple justice: every time the puppet lies, his nose grows longer. Without undue moralizing, Collodi points out that disobedience and pleasure-seeking lead to evil and unhappiness. Historically, *The Adventures of Pinocchio* marked a turning point away from overt didacticism in Italian children's literature towards the use of comedy and minimal adult intrusion. Since then, it continues to receive much critical attention; whether seen as folktale, fantasy, or allegory, it is decidedly a classic of children's literature.

Collodi's childhood personality displayed many of the characteristics he later gave to Pinocchio: impudence, mischievousness, and curiosity. After four years of seminary training, Collodi decided he was unsuited for an ecclesiastical career. He then immersed himself in journalism, where he championed liberal causes and founded two journals dealing with political satire and dramatic arts. He also wrote numerous books for adults on a wide variety of technical and literary subjects. Following his second stint as a volunteer in the Italian war against Austria, Collodi became a government official and inaugurated several educational reforms. During this time he translated three of Perrault's fairy tales and developed several textbooks which espoused his theory of making education entertaining. These works, together with his later stories for children, were available only in Italy, and have long since been out of print; only *Pinocchio* survives. In 1881, the editor of a new children's magazine invited Collodi to submit a story. Collodi did so, adding a note: "I send you this childishness to do with as you see fit. But if you print it, pay me well so that I have a good reason to continue with it." This first adventure of Pinocchio met with much success. Collodi then sent in sporadic chapters. After thirty-five episodes had appeared, the book was published in 1883. Collodi died unaware that he had produced an international favorite.

Critics see *Pinocchio* as a story rich in imagination and symbolism. They find Collodi interweaving his classical education with peasant folklore by combining mythological, psychological, and religious parallels to other cultures and personages with Tuscan speech and storytelling patterns. Others read the book as a social and political allegory, or as Collodi's attempt to recover his lost childhood. In a negative vein, some reviewers contend that *Pinocchio* consists of a weak string of escapades devised by Collodi merely to write a winning serial and reap financial gain. Few would quarrel with the book's enduring qualities, however, and most would agree with Benedetto Croce: "The wood out of which Pinocchio is carved is humanity itself."

THE ADVENTURES OF PINOCCHIO (1883; English edition as *The Story of a Puppet*)

Children are at once so independent and so conservative in their literary judgments that we hesitate before recommending books to them that are not so sanctified by custom and tradition. We think we might possibly be safe in this case, and if they would take our advice only for this once, they might spend even a merrier Christmas than otherwise, enlivened by the waggeries and the sprightly naughtiness of Pinocchio. But knowing the critical cast of their minds, we don't press the point. It is with their elders we have to deal, and with them we are on more certain ground. Children seeking gifts, therefore, for their sober-minded elders might do worse than choose this **'Story of a Puppet.'** Pinocchio is the most fascinating creature we have met with for a long time. He has a very distinct personality and most winning manners even in his depraved moments. But his greatest charm is a certain inexhaustable vitality. With his open-mindedness, curiosity, and scorn for the prosaic round of ordinary life, of course he is bound to have many adventures. Which of them excite us most is difficult to say. Our blood curdles at the assassins' terrible chase; it is warmed by Pinocchio's noble attitude towards Harlequin, before the Fire-eater's sneeze betokens the coming on of a milder mood. We confess to have started with him in full confidence and high spirits for the Land of Boobies, and when the awful consequences of his folly were revealed to us, we instinctively put our hands to our own ears to feel if they too had grown. The Fairy with the blue hair is charming, when she is herself. She is less agreeable in her other impersonations. But here we can only hint at one or two of the incidents and vicissitudes in this remarkable career, though we must not omit a reference to what is the real attraction to us elders—the clear, straightforward, and aboveboard character of the morals. There is never any doubt about them. . . . [The] story of Pinocchio is a work of genius.

"The Story of a Puppet," in The Bookman, *London, Vol. 4, No. 1, January, 1892, p. 148.*

Among the illustrious collection of illustrated books "every child should know," the Italian juvenile classic, **"The Marvellous Adventures of Pinocchio"** . . . is entitled to a place; if not a first place, at least one very near the top. . . .

The story of **"Pinocchio"** is an allegory, a guide to self-control, self-government, and self-determination in children. Its concise style and picture words are well calculated to hold the attention of children. A few scenes in the book, however, might be considered too gruesome for the child mind—such as the description of the young girl who died and was waiting for the hearse to come and carry her away. But the moral of the puppet who, by overcoming his evil influences and following the advice of his good fairy, changes into a "real boy," is admirable. Love and consideration for animals are taught among many other things.

"A Juvenile Classic," in The New York Times Saturday Review of Books *(© 1909 by The New York Times Company; reprinted by permission), April, 3, 1909, p. 192.*

Carlo Lorenzini himself died unaware of the fact that he had written a world's best seller, one destined to become a classic in Italian literature. His contemporaries considered him just another writer of children's stories. But the trend today among the more prominent Italian critics is to see in Collodi not only the Tuscan writer of color and wit, but also the affirmation of the goodness and realistic teaching of life. Pinocchio is a hero of the soul, who, like the characters of the "Divine Comedy" and "Faust," goes through life finally transformed by experience. It is the story of hope and fear, joy and disillusionment, death and transfiguration. From a marionette with inordinate instincts and desires, tumbling downward on the road to ruin, Pinocchio emerges from the trials and tribulations of life a real boy.

Of greater moment to the foreign reader, however, is the question of how the fame of Pinocchio and the obscurity of its author are to be reconciled; the international success of one of his writings and the total oblivion of all the rest. (pp. 14-15)

The answer usually given is that Lorenzini did not take his hero seriously; that he sat down to pen **"The Adventures of a Puppet"** in an indifferent state of mind, with no other end in view than that of being well-paid. By so doing, however, he unwittingly divested himself of all literary and pedagogic preoccupations. He felt himself at ease, perfectly free to roam the domains of his imagination for childhood memories and fairy tales told him by his mother in the fantastic garden of Collodi. In such a charmed state of detachment he was able to evoke and give expression to his own experiences as a boy, who perhaps used to play hookey or sneak into a puppet-show, or run from the sight of a policeman. The adventures of Pinoc-

chio fascinated because they recalled echoes of an unknown world of childhood, recorded in accents so familiar that every child could see himself reflected in them. Had Lorenzini thought of moralizing or giving out precepts, he would have given us another Little Joe or Tiny Morsel, false artificial creations of his first period. Instead he gave us Pinocchio, a creature unhampered by intellectual and moral considerations, and who by his spontaneous display of life, has endeared himself to the hearts of every man, woman, and child the world over.

Certainly Pinocchio is Italian or, rather, Tuscan, to be more exact. . . . But the Italian or Tuscan atmosphere portrayed there is not the precise historical one of Little Joe and Tiny Morsel, but the vague poetical one of fairy-land. Benedetto Croce, Italy's beloved philosopher and critic, in an essay written to explain Pinocchio's great appeal to children and grownups alike, has said of it:

> It is a human tale which finds its way to the heart. The author intended to narrate the extravagant adventures of a marionette to amuse the curiosity and imagination of the child, and at the same time administer, by means of that interest, moral blessings and admonitions: in fact here and there are still discernible slight traces of that didactic intonation. But soon he began to take interest in the character and in his vicissitudes as in the fable of human life fraught with good and evil, error and atonement, temptation and resistance, rashness and prudence, egoistic concern and generous thought for others. The wood out of which Pinocchio is carved is humanity itself, and he who is its representative marches across the scene of life as one bent upon a perilous journey: a puppet, to be sure, but thoroughly spiritual.

(p. 15)

Giuseppe Prezzolini, "The Author of 'Pinocchio'," in Saturday Review *(© 1940, copyright renewed © 1967 Saturday Review Magazine Co.; reprinted by permission), Vol. XXI, No. 17, February 17, 1940, pp. 14-15.*

Pinocchio is not only a symbol—he is a problem complete with its solution. The work of education has always been considered within the restrictive framework of a fundamental course of studies. Collodi's *Pinocchio* represents in the field of children's literature what the *Critica della Ragion Practica* represents in philosophy—the victory of self-government and liberty. *Pinocchio* tells us that education is creative: it draws from the void, from the inorganic, from the mechanical. But that which appears to us as empty, lifeless, mechanical possesses within itself its own reality of existence. (pp. 72-3)

Pietro Mignosi, in his extract from "'Pinocchio', 'Cuore' and Other Italian Books," translated by V. Melegari, in The Junior Bookshelf, *Vol. 19, No. 2, March, 1955, pp. 72-3.*

[*Pinocchio* is the] first book in Italy to be written wholly from a child's point of view. . . . (p. 111)

[Children] are enraptured when they see and recognize themselves in a book. They see themselves as though in a mirror. Pinocchio is not bad; and if it were enough to have good intentions to be perfect, Pinocchio would be a paragon. But he is weak. He declares openly that we ought not to resist temptation because it is a waste of time. What he is forbidden to do is always a little more attractive than what he is ordered to do. Repentance follows close on sinning, but sinning follows close on repentance. He would prefer to have knowledge without the effort of learning. (p. 112)

All the fixations which a child has, such as not taking medicine or not wanting to eat lentils, although he has never tasted them; all the little selfishnesses that cunningly grow strong roots if they are not pulled up before it is too late; all the good qualities of childhood also, the sincere and deep affection, a confiding heart as yet undeceived, the need of being loved which calls forth love: all that is so clear that even a ten-year-old reader could not fail to understand Pinocchio the clever, the subtle and the loving. (p. 113)

Pinocchio joyfully leads [children] on through the unexpected and the extraordinary. . . . Whatever happens, the story always rebounds, light and whimsical. It seems to stop, it starts off again. As Pinocchio himself would say, there are only beginnings, never endings, except on the last page. (p. 114)

Stretched out in a fairy coach drawn by a hundred white mice, carried through the air on a dove's back, shamefully dragged along by two policemen, in perpetual motion, Pinocchio travels the realms of imagination. . . .

[The] Italian imagination is a magnificent heritage of which Pinocchio has received his share and spent it profitably. His physical equipment which might bind him to the earth is reduced to a minimum; hard wood and springs; no weighty body to hold back his caprices. He is as light and lively as spirit. He is as little obedient to the laws of dull existence as an association of ideas is to those of logic. He has the mobility of the creatures that stir in our dreams, being himself a dream in the night of a child.

Before he was called Pinocchio and amused youngsters, he was Harlequin, Punchinello, or Stenterello. He was one of the *maschere*, changeless characters that served as a fixed point for improvisation. That sparkling Italian comedy, enjoyed and borrowed by the French for years because they could not imitate it, lives again in this nimble marionette. It reminds us of those comedies in which the ingenuity of the players, fragmentary action, hot-headed impulse, and *brio* are given a free field. (p. 115)

Let us admit that [Pinocchio's] morality is neither sublime nor even superior. It is practical. If we were to sum up the philosophy of the book, we should get something like this: There is an imminent justice that rewards good and punishes evil. Since good is advantageous we must prefer it. The child who fights with his comrades or who plays hooky, or who listens to the advice of chance friends rather than obey his parents, or who does not keep his promises, will be punished for his misdeeds. The chastisements will come in unexpected ways but without fail. The child who thinks only of drinking, eating, and being a vagabond all day long, ends in prison or in the hospital. Money does not fall from heaven. It must be earned painfully by work with the hands or mind. Only imbeciles can believe that it is acquired by easy processes. They are the dupes of rascals.

Social morality is reduced to a law of exchange. To show oneself to be nice, kind, generous, is to assure oneself of being repaid in kind. "The other person" is the innumerable and mysterious being who appears grateful when he has been well treated, but who forgets neither wrongs nor injuries. Two prov-

erbs keep recurring in the story: *quel ch'é fatto, é reso:* Tit for tat; *i casi son tanti;* No knowing what may happen.

This whimsical imagination, and this very practical sense of a way of life, are not necessarily incompatible. And we can very well conceive a psychology subtle enough to pass rapidly from the realm of dreams to that of concrete realities. These lively minds, who enjoy giving color to commonplace beings and things, are never deluded by the illusion that they create for themselves. They destroy it as easily as they create it, as is the case here. Can we be sure that this simple and practical way of understanding morality is not an attribute of the whole Italian nation? Could it be a special form of that "profound good sense" so often presented as one of the most fundamental traits of the race?

But Pinocchio is not only Italian; he is Tuscan, like his father Collodi. . . . I challenge you to find a Tuscan who is not witty and spirited. All of them, even the common people, even the peasants, even the youngsters, have a flair for detecting the ridiculous, seizing any chance to launch a witticism. Witticisms, absurd associations of ideas, humorous observations, are to be found on every page in *Pinocchio;* an exuberant imagination that is not only comical but keen; a mixture of apparent naïveté and caustic shrewdness. . . . (pp. 116-17)

"I have another hunger," cries Pinocchio, one day when he was insufficiently filled. In the same way Collodi always holds in reserve another kind of laughter and wit. (p. 118)

> *Paul Hazard "National Traits," in his* Books, Children and Men, *translated by Marguerite Mitchell, fourth edition (copyright © The Horn Book, Inc.; all rights reserved; reprinted with permission),* Horn Book, *1960, pp. 111-44.**

Collodi's *L'avventure di Pinocchio* . . . can be classed in this branch of literature only with reservations, but it is perhaps the best South European variant of the nonsense theme. A wooden puppet comes to life in a world where poverty and riches, ugliness and beauty can all be found—briefly, in the real world. But this imaginary fellow has not been chosen in order to embody a world of poetic dreams, like Peter Pan, but rather as a symbol of sharpness and down-to-earth human understanding and he further provides the excuse for giving an exaggerated plot to a story which does not lie too far from the world of reality. It is, however, precisely this singular mixture of passionately conveyed reality, schoolboy cheekiness, and pure imagination (fairies and a little wooden boy with too much to say for himself) which has given the book its permanent attractiveness. (p. 77)

> *Bettina Hürlimann, "Fantasy and Reality," in her* Three Centuries of Children's Books in Europe, *translated and edited by Brian W. Alderson (English translation © Oxford University Press 1967; reprinted by permission), Oxford University Press, Oxford, 1967, pp. 76-92.**

Pinocchio may be the most durable stick of wood in the literary world. . . . We tend to assume the story has always existed, like a folk tale.

In the last two decades, however, the mischievous marionette has been subjected to beatings and batterings far more drastic than in any of his original adventures produced in 1881: flattened into comic strips, cut into pop-up nonbooks, injected with a diet of solid sugar and turned into a Walt Disney musical film. But the sturdy puppet has survived it all. . . .

How will today's multimedia minis take to this old-fashioned tale? It seems so goody-goody. The naughty creature who doesn't want to go to school and do lessons turns literally into a donkey. Is it too moralistic in its don't-be-a-dropout message? Written originally in installments for a weekly children's paper, all the cliff-hanging elements are present—the puppet saved at the last possible moment from hanging, drowning, consumption by fire, death by frying pan, and escapes from the writhing green serpent and from the monstrous shark whose "tongue was so wide and so long that it looked like a country road." How pleasant to us oldsters are these touches of long-ago: country roads instead of super-lane highways, party treats of bread, an Italian detail—cups of coffee-and-milk. But will the age of Aquarius Jr. find it all too moralistic and slow-moving? Somehow I think that Pinocchio's personality will survive and that children will continue to identify with this unheroic hero who is greedy, lazy, stupid, forgetful and occasionally brave, loyal, enterprising, endearing: in short, a very human stick of wood.

Eve Merriam, "Tales of a Mischievous Marionette," in The New York Times Book Review *(© 1969 by The New York Times Company; reprinted by permission), November 9, 1969, p. 71.*

[Italy] gave to the world a book so universal in its appeal as to necessitate mention whenever fantasies for children are discussed. . . . This story of a puppet brought vividly and realistically to life is a triumphant landmark in the long line of tales which personify inanimate objects. Pinocchio's creator did more than merely endow the little wooden figure with life; he gave to Pinocchio individuality, an irrepressible, heedless, boastful, slightly wicked, and yet lovable individuality. With beautiful inevitability, the other unique qualities of the book stem from the personality of Pinocchio—the stern justice which makes the punishment fit the crime, the pervasive humor which prevents morality from becoming morbidity, the satisfying convincingness of Pinocchio's final and complete transformation. (p. 345)

Elizabeth Nesbitt, "A Rightful Heritage 1890-1920," in A Critical History of Children's Literature *by Cornelia Meigs, Anne Thaxter Eaton, Elizabeth Nesbitt, and Ruth Hill Viguers, edited by Cornelia Meigs (reprinted with permission of Macmillan Publishing Co., Inc.; copyright © 1953, 1969 by Macmillan Publishing Co., Inc.), revised edition, Macmillan, 1969, pp. 275-392.**

Collodi set out, at the urging of his publishers, to write a book for Italian children which should celebrate diligence, deplore idleness, and convey the idea that man is rationally happy only through work. He sought to caution the Italian child that pleasure-seeking leads to misery and a donkey's grave. He succeeded in writing a wry, elegant, comic, and wistful book, as universal as *Pilgrim's Progress,* which it resembles in structure, as Tuscan as a terraced vineyard and antic as the commedia dell'arte, which informs it. . . .

[At] the time of its appearance nothing like it had been seen in Italy. . . .

Pinocchio is as firmly rooted in Italian culture as Alice is in the English. He looks back to Dante and *Orlando Furioso,* forward to Pirandello and Federico Fellini. He is a descendant and an ancestor. He emerges from a log of wood and becomes a *"ragazzo per bene"* (a real boy). He faces death by fire, by hanging, and by drowning, and achieves at last the human condition, the unification of the flesh with the spirit. The con-

summation was no more than that which his author asked for his country. (p. 89)

[Collodi wrote *Pinocchio* as] a celebration of his Italy, its virtues and its flaws, its landscape, festivals, poverty, people, and puppets, its laws and legends. (pp. 89-90)

[Collodi] understood completely the implications of the new industrialism which would bring the young nation abreast of the modern world. *Pinocchio* is a children's story, but it is also a political comment, an interpretation of history, a document of man's search for his soul, and a sign of the shape of things to come.

As a children's story *Pinocchio* is quite matchless. The line is true as Giotto's, and the language is light as thistledown. The theme is probably the one which children most favor, the search by children for parents and by parents for children, a search which in this case ends in success and reunion. Like all good writers for children, Collodi lets his hero sin, suffer, and triumph strictly on his own recognizances and permits only minimal intrusion by the adult world. No book, to be sure, was ever harmed by a wicked uncle or Satan, but any gifted writer knows that adults or Olympians must be kept in their place—in the first chapter and the last.

Collodi manages his father figure beautifully. Gepetto, nicknamed Polendina because of his yellow wig—the color of cornmeal—appears a fully rounded character, crotchety, warmhearted, cynical, and selfless. He carves the puppet from a piece of wood, clothes him in scraps, and makes a little cap of bread dough for him. He embraces the marionette as a son and names him for a family of his acquaintance, Pinocchio. . . . He pawns his jacket to buy his son an alphabet book, and the marionette, after passionate protestations of affection and promises of good behavior—he took to lying upon emerging from the log of wood from which he was carved—runs away in search of pleasure and excitement. He finds plenty of both, and we never encounter Gepetto again until Pinocchio discovers him inside the belly of the sea monster. By this time he has almost ceased to be a parent and is but a pathetic dotard, entirely dependent on the marionette. The reunion is partly effected now, but it is not complete until the final chapter when the magic change takes place. "Through labor and through hope" Gepetto renews his youth and finds himself the happy father, not of a puppet, but of a beautiful boy with chestnut curls and sparkling blue eyes—a boy of roses. To be a human child is to Pinocchio what the Celestial City is to Bunyan's Christian.

Like the damned as seen from heaven, the marionette lies, a discarded husk, in a corner, and the living father embraces the living son, while blessings rain upon the house. The fairy with azure hair who has watched over and disciplined Pinocchio, as Beatrice watched over and disciplined Dante, has shown herself not dead but a living presence, and in a most practical and Tuscan manner. She has paid back the forty soldi which Pinocchio earned for her during the course of his metamorphosis from puppet to person.

As a political allegory *Pinocchio* makes an unequivocal statement. Collodi believed that two imperatives must govern the mind and spirit of Italy: the republican idea and the necessity for sacrifice and work. Mazzini himself never wrote a more commanding call to republican sentiment than the opening sentences of *The Adventures of Pinocchio:*

Once upon a time there was—
A king! my little readers will say at once.

No, boys and girls. You are wrong. Once upon a time there was a piece of wood.

Nowhere in *Pinocchio* do we find the traditional nobility of the fairy tale. The story is about the common people of Italy, the cobblers and carpenters, the puppeteers and circus touts, the fishermen and farmers, the dogs and donkeys, the cats and crickets, the fishes of the Mediterranean, and the leaden-eyed boys who slouch at street corners to prey upon and corrupt the unwary. The book rings with the salty speech of Tuscany, and its characters live with its sardonic proverbs.

The only "personage" in the book is the fairy with azure hair, the enchanted being who has lived many thousands of years in the neighborhood of Pinocchio's adventures, and she is not a mortal maiden. Even she does not maintain at all times an exalted station in life, although she occasionally resides in a castle. (p. 90)

In Collodi's book the highest level to which the human spirit may rise is humanity itself. The transcendent flaw in this spirit, as Collodi saw it, was pleasure-seeking. Pleasure is not happiness and pleasure is the business of puppets, but the business of men and of the Risorgimento was work, and it is through work alone that puppets become men.

"Open a school," cried Collodi, "and you will close a prison."

The foregoing describes the political atmosphere of Collodi's book, but if allegorical interest were its only merit it would have long been relegated to the remaindered list. *Pinocchio* is more than a puritan sermon by a conscientious patriot. It is a fragment of the commedia dell'arte. And for all that he reforms, ceases his lies and his follies, and learns wisdom and thrift Pinocchio is Harlequin. (pp. 90, 92)

Who is Harlequin? Some say that he is the spirit of the night, Hellequin, cousin to the devil, but time has robbed him of his satanic qualities. He is one of the foremost characters to animate the commedia dell'arte. . . .

A vivid artistry was lavished on the commedia, and from records kept by individual actors we can learn something of its voice. It bears some resemblance to aria and recitative in opera, but it keeps the rhythm of common speech, the short sentence, and the quick riposte. It is with this voice that Pinocchio speaks:

> "Good morning, Master Antonio, what do you do
> on the floor?"
> "I am teaching the ants their alphabet."
> "Good for you."
> "What has brought you to me, Father Gepetto?"
> "My legs. You must know that I've come to ask a
> favor."

It pours forth without benefit of intellect and is saved by brio, by dancing, tumbling, handstands, and snatches of music. Like Harlequin, Pinocchio never thinks before he speaks. He hasn't time. The book gives the effect of improvising itself. Pinocchio is a commedia character to the end of his long nose, which grows alarmingly whenever he starts to deal in falsehoods. His nose and the indestructible cricket are his conscience, and he can never escape them.

When Collodi wrote *Pinocchio* he was determined that no mention of religion should be made in the text. He was devout, and like Lewis Carroll he had a morbid dread of anything approaching irreverence. There should be no allusion to the Deity or to the Mother of God or her Son. But how remarkable is Mary, Star of the Sea, especially in Italy? Every Italian child wakes and sleeps, plays and works under the veil of the Madonna. With her magnificent hood of azure hair she sanctifies Pinocchio in the role of the fairy. She mothers him, nurses him when he is ill, rescues him from assassins, and punishes him as a wise and just mother punishes. She teaches patience, fortitude, and resignation, and rewards him in the end with her fragrant but invisible presence in his apotheosis. She is the great lady, the Madonna Coronata in her castle and the peasant Madonna of the hill towns. She is the suffering Madonna, full of animal grief, who stands on the rock when Pinocchio is engorged by the great fish. She is the blue and worshiped Italian sky.

When Federico Fellini made his remarkable film *La Dolce Vita*, he could not, whether or not he intended to, escape Collodi's story. He preaches the same sermon and makes use of both the devices and the symbols which inform Collodi's work. The film begins with the puppet Christ carried over the rooftops of Rome and continues as a polemic delivered against idleness, lies, corruption, both sexual and spiritual, and above all pleasure for pleasure's sake. Marcello, the hero, is a Harlequin, openhanded, irresponsible, changeless, a puppet whose strings are pulled by fear and lust. . . .

It is "the sweet life," Fellini tells us, which could destroy the republic, not crime, but acedia, the deadly sin of sloth. This is the rot which besets Harlequin, Pinocchio, Marcello. . . .

Harlequin, Child of the Sistine Chapel, Pinocchio stands at the center of Italy, "the terrible puppet of her dreams," a character forever "in search of an author." (p. 92)

> *Martha Bacon, "Puppet's Progress," in* The Atlantic Monthly *(copyright © 1970, by The Atlantic Monthly Company, Boston, Mass.; reprinted with permission), Vol. 225, No. 4, April, 1970, pp. 88-90, 92.*

In my naughty moments I'd like to shock some of my colleagues (especially Italian) with the following baited question: Which three books have most tangibly affected the imagination of the Italian people? Leaving the Gospel aside, here is my answer: Dante's Divine Comedy, Manzoni's *The Betrothed*, and Collodi's *Pinocchio*. . . .

My immediate reason for putting literary underdog Carlo Collodi . . . in the formidable company of his fellow Tuscan Dante Alighieri and of the half-Tuscanized Lombard, Alessandro Manzoni, is the impact he had on idiomatic speech. . . . *Pinocchio* has enriched the language since its first printing in 1880, as witness the fact that everybody in Italy will understand you right away if you refer to a pair of unsavory schemers with the Collodian label "il Gatto e la Volpe" (the Cat and the Fox). Nor is this the only instant reference to be gleaned from the book. . . . Characters like Master Cherry or Master Geppetto, those lovable craftsmen, Fire-eater the puppeteer, the Talking Cricket and Lamp Wick the naughty boy have escorted Pinocchio himself into the pantheon of popular myths, where, way beyond ethnic boundaries, he enjoys the company of Alice, Red Riding Hood, Gulliver, and the Cowardly Lion. (p. 50)

If the intentional audience contributes to the making of a work of art, and if the work itself—at least when words are its medium—can be seen as an open-ended transaction between author and audience rather than as an exclusively self-contained object, we should consider children's books as valid literature in their own right, provided the requirements of formal function (style and structure) are met. . . . *Alice in Wonderland* certainly is [literature], and so is *Pinocchio,* because each handles its language in the neatest way to create a mythical configuration that appeals to imaginative readers of any age, not just to those in their nonage—though the latter were the intentional audience to begin with. . . . A related problem is the hierarchy of value within the genre; there are "minor" and "major" works, good and better poems, and Shakespeare is obviously greater than Herrick. *Alice* towers above *Peter Pan, The Wizard of Oz* probably belongs somewhere between the two, and E. B. White's *Charlotte's Web,* while even better than Beatrix Potter's charming *Jeremiah Fisher,* pales by comparison with *Pinocchio.* (pp. 50-1)

[In *Gulliver's Travels,* Jonathan Swift] came to include children in his originally adult intentional audience, and the results justify this transgression of purpose and genre. A reverse transgression, with equally felicitous consequences, was committed by Rev. Dodgson when, under the mask of Lewis Carroll, he wove pointed topical references, many satirical, in the charmed fabric of his *Alice* books, which he notoriously conceived and wrote for children; we now have *The Annotated Alice* to prove it. Collodi's deft winks at a growing or grownup audience point the same way, and it may even happen that some sophisticated readers smell social or political allegory in *Pinocchio.* At the moment, the scent fails to alert my nostrils; I am fascinated, instead, by the spectacle of Carlo Lorenzini becoming Collodi, or Charles Dodgson becoming Carroll, in a ritual of impersonation that sets the stage for their magical act: the recovery of an ancestral mythical mode of communication suitable to the children they purposely chose as privileged audience. If you don't become like children, you will not enter the kingdom of Heaven, namely, free imagination.

In this domain perhaps Alice reigns supreme, even over Pinocchio, having attained the kind of metaphysical shudder that many a surrealist writer was to covet decades later, and yet without ever departing from the tone of effortless simplicity that marks the work as a genuine fairytale, primarily addressed to children. Well, this hierarchy may be negotiable after all, even though Pinocchio, a notoriously chivalrous marionette, would not mind taking a back seat to Alice. Pinocchio's wonderland markedly differs from Alice's, despite some overlapping. Hers is a dreamland where every law of time, space, and logic is or can be put in abeyance; Pinocchio inhabits a concrete world where identity resists metamorphosis, actions have measurable consequences, and reality incorporates magic. Carroll's fable dissolves the known world into phantasmagoria, while Collodi's points the way, via magic, to the reliability of existence. In an ideal series, you could place Pinocchio midway between Alice and Tom Sawyer. If so, my earlier classification should yield to a different one which recognizes *Pinocchio* and the *Alice* fables as complementary to each other, and on the same level of artistic dignity. (p. 52)

The strength of modern fairytales, *Kunstmärchen* like Dodgson's and Collodi's, is that they draw on the reservoir of living folklore and thereby reintegrate their audience into a lost unity. (p. 53)

Collodi's closeness to living folklore stands out particularly in his style, a terse Tuscan that always rings with the tone of a speaking voice. The oral quality identified by scholars in Homer's style is no less prominent (*si parva licet componere magnis*) in our modern Tuscan storyteller whose addresses to the reader, brief digressions, lively dialogue, and direct, fluent syntax so appropriate to an evocation of the marvelous, all

contribute to narrative effectiveness. Storytelling is a folk art in the Tuscan countryside, and has been for centuries; it was the seedbed of much renowned fiction from the Middle Ages down to the ripe Renaissance, for the *novella,* or short story, first blossomed there with the anonymous *Novellino* collection of the thirteenth century to become a distinct Tuscan genre with Boccaccio and followers. *Pinocchio*'s relentless variety of narrative incident, its alertness to social types, its tongue-in-cheek wisdom are of a piece with that illustrious tradition—less, of course, the rich erotic fare which spices up the work of Renaissance *novellieri* and would have been out of place in a modern book addressed to children. Collodi's Aesopian sententiousness comes through all over in the guise of numerous warnings to the reckless marionette from the magical animal friends Pinocchio repeatedly fails to heed, the Talking Cricket above all; and the proverbs the redeemed puppet quotes at his arch enemies, the Cat and the Fox, when they are finally reduced to an amply deserved abjection, are gnomic folklore of peasant extraction, of the kind you would still hear in a Tuscan village around the fireside:

> "Oh, Pinocchio," cried the Fox, "give a little charity to two old people."
> "Two old people," repeated the Cat.
> "Good-by, masqueraders," replied Pinocchio; "you deceived me once and now you are paying for it."
> "Believe us, Pinocchio, we are today truly poor and starving."
> "Truly," repeated the Cat.
> "If you are poor, you deserve it. Remember the proverb that says, 'Stolen money will never bear fruit.' Good-by, deceivers."
> "Have compassion on us."
> "On us," said the Cat.
> "Goody-by. Remember the proverb that says, 'Stolen wheat always makes poor bread.'"
> "Do not abandon us."
> "No, no!" said the Cat.
> "Good-by. Remember the proverb, 'Whoever steals the cloak of his neighbor usually dies without a shirt.'"

Pinocchio had indeed been duped, robbed and nearly killed by the Cat and the Fox, and he lives in no goody-goody world. The first of the proverbs he quotes gains additional relevance from the remembered episode in his early adventures when Messrs. Cat and Fox had persuaded him to sow his four pieces of gold in the so-called Field of Wonders so they could steal them while he waited elsewhere for a plant bearing gold fruit to grow. Pinocchio's foolishness, a natural consequence of his childish naïveté ever ready to fall for the lure of pure wonder, has now been tempered into hard-earned wisdom. The book has to do with the education of a child, both through the traditional humanist instrument of classroom and books (which he rather resents) and through the school of hard knocks—the resistance of reality to the boundless urge for freedom and (however innocent) pleasure that keeps getting the child into trouble. When he learns that there are limits to desire, and that nothing comes for free, Pinocchio becomes an adolescent boy in flesh and blood and the story is over; its only conceivable sequel would be Collodi's own autobiography, describing the way he learned to live in a harsh matter-of-fact world by dint of work, wit, and imagination.

But what a delight it had been to follow Pinocchio's vagaries in his unreconstructed phase, and how poetically providential his transgressions were! Life certainly would have been dull for him and for the readers if he had been tame from the start (not that his final condition upon learning his lesson can be really described as "tame," to be sure). How exciting it is to see him get out of scrape after scrape, whether by his own devices (there is a Huck Finn in him) or through magical assistance from the Blue-Haired Fairy, his sister and mother figure, or again thanks to the gratefulness of an animal friend (Aladdin the Dog, the Tunny Fish), or to the kind feelings of formidable Mangiafuoco, Fire-eater the puppeteer. The mixture of naïveté and shrewdness in Pinocchio's character makes him a significant type, for he has something of the waif who, though not utterly unprotected, often has to fend for himself. Waif and child of poor workers, and withal, elf-child, the changeling. He loves the sheltered life a family can provide, for he has a warm heart, yet he yearns for frequent escape from that shelter, and if he thereby gets in plenty of trouble, he also meets reality in so many forms that this alone will have been a rich education for him and for his young readers by the time he is through. The world of work, the world of crime, the world of entertainment and the world of nature alternate or fuse with the world of magic fantasy with surprising ease, thanks to Collodi's handling of his narrative strings. Pinocchio's world is a microcosm of the adult world as seen through the eyes of an enterprising child. The complexity of actual life dawns on the child's simple mind, and there is nothing wooden in that simplicity. Pinocchio is alive and kicking, and he never impresses us so much as when he recalcitrates (not just in his temporary asinine avatar) against impinging threats—whether the nocturnally disguised Cat and Fox, or the rioting schoolmates in the classroom and on the beach, or the ogre-like Green Fisherman, or the innocent worker who had bought him (when still a donkey) from the circus master for a quarter, to get his skin. Collodi's master stroke in this regard occurs in chapter XXXIV, when the marionette, after regaining his humanoid shape through the not quite selfless help of fishes which had gnawed him bare of his asinine flesh, down to the wooden bone, is swallowed by the huge Dogfish and has the following exchange with a fellow prisoner, the Tunny Fish:

> "Help! Help! Oh, dear me! Is there no one who can
> save me?"
> "Who wishes to be saved?" asked a voice that sounded
> in the darkness like a guitar out of tune.
> "Who is it that speaks like that?" asked Pinocchio,
> feeling himself nearly frozen with fear.
> "It is I. I am a poor Tunny Fish, who was swallowed
> at the same time you were. What kind of fish are
> you?"
> "I have nothing to do with fishes. I am a marionette."
> "Then if you are not a fish, why were you swallowed
> by the monster?"
> "It is all your fault. If you had not been there, I surely
> should have escaped. And now what can we do in
> this dark place?"
> "We must resign ourselves to our fate, and wait until
> we are digested."
> "But I do not wish to be digested," said Pinocchio,
> beginning to cry.

The Tunny Fish's philosophical reply, that it is more dignified to die under water than to soak in vinegar and oil, and Pinocchio's immediate rejection of such stoical philosophy, crown the passage with choice Collodian humor, but what I want to emphasize is the marionette's stubborn defense of his own identity and will to live, a defense which attains here comic

and epic proportion as a climax to all his escapades. When caught by the Green Fisherman, Pinocchio had likewise objected to being mistaken for a fish and so devoured; when changed into an ass, he had inwardly refused the punitive metamorphosis, and this came through in his recalcitrance onstage as well as, later on, in his recovery of the marionette form through submersion and nibbling by fish. He is so irreducibly himself that, though he repeatedly refuses being eaten, he accepts for once that uncomfortable fate when it's a question of his returning to his original shape. See his description of the procedure to the obtuse and incredulous buyer of donkey-Pinocchio at the outset of Chapter XXXIV.

Pinocchio's waywardness can also take a silly turn, notably in the medicine scene (Chapter XVI), when the good Fairy tries to cure him of his disease (the mania for telling lies) and he thinks up all sorts of tricks to dodge the bitter potion. It is easy to see how vividly this scene must register on the child readership, since it presents a familiar domestic experience in terms of the marvelous. Here too Collodian humor reaches an apogee, with the trio of doctors (the Crow, the Owl, and the Cricket) two of whom utter pompous Lapalissian inanities just to contradict each other while the third one, the Cricket, manages to talk some sense and health into the devious patient by bluntly telling him off. The fun Collodi obviously had in writing this episode, or the one of the Tunny Fish, bears comparison with the fun Lewis Carroll must have had in penning so many of his, and the comparison extends to the results, which make readers share the fun. Here as there, conventional reality is parodied by a playfully logical absurdity; yet in *Pinocchio*'s case we don't leave the shores of common sense, while *Alice* does. But then *Alice* is not a humanist fable. Pinocchio never really loses his bearings, no matter how strange and menacing the situation he encounters; Alice instead does, and this is her great dreamlike privilege, for, unlike Pinocchio, she discovers and inhabits an utterly unreliable world. Dodgson pushed his narrative experiment to a fascinating critical limit, while Collodi stuck to his solid Tuscan tradition, and it stood him in good stead. It also made allowance for a lot of imaginative capers which are the delight of any reader. Remember the Gorilla Judge who sentences Pinocchio to jail for having let himself be robbed (Chapter XIX)? And when the incautious marionette and his lazybone friend Lamp Wick, after a prolonged stay in the Country of Playthings (Chapter XXXII), begin to show symptoms of donkeymorphosis and try to conceal it from each other until the transformation becomes irrefutable, the adult reader laughs with Collodi while the very young reader shuttles between fear, wonder and amusement. If the adult has read or seen Ionesco's *The Rhinoceros,* he may wonder whether the French-Rumanian playwright brought it off any better than his Tuscan predecessor. I personally think Ionesco is more heavy-handed in his comparable metamorphosis scene.

Classical education strengthened, instead of stifling, the vein of peasant folklore that went into the making of *Pinocchio,* and both account for the growing dose of horse sense with which Pinocchio ultimately confronts reality. As I said before, this is a far cry from Carroll's wonderful penchant for Nonsense. Classical hints are planted throughout the story; for instance, to name just a few salient cases, when the Green Fisherman (Chapter XXVIII) tells the captured Pinocchio that he has the privilege of choosing the way he'll be cooked, out of respect for his rare and so unfishlike gift of articulateness, the incident is a superbly handled variation on a Homeric theme from the *Odyssey,* where giant ogre Polyphemus grants Odysseus the privilege of being eaten last. At the outset of Chapter XXXVI, when Pinocchio is carrying his old "father" Geppetto to safety through the boundless sea, the latter's anxious scrutinizing of the horizon is conveyed by a graphic simile straight from Dante's *Divine Comedy,* Inf. XV, 20-21:

> "But where is the shore?" asked the old man,
> becoming more and more uneasy and straining
> his eyes to see it, just as tailors do when they
> thread a needle.

The Dantesque lines in question translate thus:

> and they sharpened their eyebrows to descry us
> as an old tailor does at the needle's eye.

Interestingly enough, a father figure in trouble (Brunette Latini) is also involved in this climactic Dantesque episode, and in fact the whole incident of Pinocchio carrying his own father to safety may remind us of Aeneas shouldering father Anchises in his flight from burning Troy (*Aeneid,* Book II); for in Collodi's case the analogy has overwhelming chances of being deliberate.

A marked Homeric trait in narrative technique is Pinocchio's frequent verbatim repetition of message or incident in his accounts to friends, and that is further proof of the oral tradition which nurtured both authors, distant though they may be in so many obvious respects. The Blue-Haired Fairy's unfailing assistance to Pinocchio in so many tight situations, her very animal metamorphoses or use of animal messengers, her disguises or white lies (the feigned death), are of a piece with Athena Pallas' resourceful closeness to Ulysses and his son Telemachus in the *Odyssey.* Like Athena Pallas, the Blue-Haired Fairy embodies benevolent wisdom. Pinocchio's decisive *peripeteia,* his being swallowed by the huge sea monster in whose maw he will find his lost father Geppetto and then start the long trip back to homeland and mended ways, has a Biblical counterpart in the story of prophet Jonah; yet in fairness to Collodi we should not assume here a mere feat of literary imitation, for Collodi has a truly inventive imagination that can delve into archetypes. The Blue-Haired Fairy is a motherly *anima* figure, Geppetto is a father figure, and the ambivalent attitude of Pinocchio to them completes the archetypal picture. It is part of Collodi's astuteness to have left the Blue-Haired Fairy in her transcendental domain, instead of materializing the happy family reunion on a terrene level at the end, just as it contributes to his poetical success to have conceived of Pinocchio as a man-made creature that becomes self-reborn. Need I refer to the craftman's attitude toward his creation, whether a marble Moses or a piece of furniture? In a place like Italy, the cultural background would insure a deep response to this aspect of Collodi's myth, and guarantee its authenticity.

One final point about Collodi's ingrained affinity for classical tradition: just as in the *Iliad* nothing less than private devotion to his dead friend Patroclus could have pulled sulking Achilles back into battle, it takes nothing less than love for the Blue-Haired Fairy and Geppetto to make Pinocchio shed his incurable laziness and get him to work and study at the end. While seeming to make light of his literary sources, Collodi somehow revives them.

He certainly drew upon a rich store of available culture, not just the culture of books, and books accordingly became live sources, not deadening pedantry, in his process of literary composition. In having given the world a uniquely imaginative and educative story like *Pinocchio,* he ranks high among benefactors of children in all lands. Not the least of his benefactions is the resolute plea for, and exemplary use of, articulateness; an articulateness he would have imbibed with his mother's milk in the Tuscan countryside where the common people have always retained an authentic culture of their own. This much remains true even when we register on the debit side the undeniable fact that Collodi tilts the scales against the element of play in his treatment of plot and incident. In his fable, the urge to play can only lead to laziness and degradation; the Country of Playthings (as well as the Circus) provides a deplorable antithesis to the Country of the Busy Bees and to the Classroom. Art and Play have nothing to do with Work and Study; at times one is tempted to take sides with the unredeemed Pinocchio against the latter options. The consequence of such Victorian bourgeois dichotomy is that books (within the framework of the story) can only become fetishes to the rightfully alienated Pinocchio, while the world of school must appear as pure drudgery, implying chores to master for the sake of further advantages, never a fulfilling experience that can include fun. Collodi never shows the delight Pinocchio could get from books as such, or from the process of learning. Conversely, the Country of Playthings is wholly bad, and it never occurs to the author to shed on it a more favorable light. To do this, he should have been a Montessorian, but history handicapped him by placing him one generation earlier than Maria Montessori. I wonder what would have happened to his little masterpiece if he had rewritten it along Montessorian lines by showing that children first learn *by* playing and *from* their toys, and that play is the source of both learning and work. Maybe he needed the drastic antitheses of play versus work and play versus study to provide dramatic space for Pinocchio's adventures, and so his fable could not have taken shape if he had surrendered his bourgeois ideology. At any rate, the poet in him knew better than the ideologist, and he made ample room for *Homo ludens* in his historically conditioned fantasy. Thank God he did. Thank God for the pixy in him. (pp. 53-8)

Glauco Cambon, "Pinocchio and the Problems of Children's Literature" (originally an address given at the University of Connecticut on November 27, 1972), in Children's Literature: Annual of The Modern Language Association Seminar on Children's Literature and The Children's Literature Association, *Vol. 2, edited by Francelia Butler © 1973 by Francelia Butler; all rights reserved), Temple University Press, 1973, pp. 50-60 [the excerpts of Collodi's work used here were originally published in his* Pinocchio, The Adventures of a Marionette, *translated by Walter S. Cramp (copyright, 1904 by Ginn & Company; used with courtesy of the publisher), Ginn & Company, 1904].*

[The publication in book form of the *Adventures of Pinocchio*] was an event to be celebrated. Here was the final blow to didacticism in Italian children's literature and the birth of a world classic. . . .

It was plain that here was a story of universal appeal, a concoction of ingenious fantasy and humour, brisk as a circus and light as a bubble. What an amazing series of adventures befall this little wooden creature who has come to life in the making by old Geppetto to face a strange world full of danger and magic! Pinocchio may be only a puppet, but he has feelings to captivate the reader's sympathy. He tries hard does Pinocchio but rarely fulfils his good intentions. So a note of realism makes itself heard beneath the whirl of make-believe. . . . This blending of reality with high-spirited fantasy is perhaps the secret of the book's great success. (p. 249)

Mary F. Thwaite, "Children's Books Abroad," in her From Primer to Pleasure in Reading: An Introduction to the History of Children's Books in England from the Invention of Printing to 1914 with an Outline of Some Developments in Other Countries *(copyright © 1963 by Mary F. Thwaite), second edition, The Horn Book, Inc., 1972, pp. 225-74.*

Carlo Collodi's *The Adventures of Pinocchio* has to stand, along with Lewis Carroll's *Alice's Adventures in Wonderland,* L. Frank Baum's *The Wonderful World of Oz* and J. M. Barrie's *Peter Pan,* as one of the few truly classic pieces of children's literature. For whatever the fate of these authors has been in academic circles—where Carroll has understandably proved the most exciting of the lot—many of the characters they created have become independent entities with lives of their own, free of the vagaries of literary taste and opinion. They seem to have escaped the written page, disowned their makers and become part of the very fabric of twentieth century civilization, in much the same way as the fairies, heroes and ogres found in the folktales of the brothers Grimm, Perrault, Basile and Hans Christian Andersen have returned to the hearths, the taverns and the nurseries from which they were originally gleaned. To some extent theatrical productions, films, cartoon animations and the vast market of children's books have contributed to this process. Yet the resultant success could not have occurred were it not also for a certain profound and universal psychological appeal, transcending the powers of commercialism. A study of *Pinocchio* may, I think, shed some light on the dark forces of enchantment at work in such tales. (p. 23)

It is difficult to know just how to classify *Pinocchio* in terms of literary genre. Strictly speaking we cannot treat it as a folktale since it was not handed down from tradition but rather originated in the creative mind of its author. On the other hand, it would be equally unfair simply to class it as a piece of imaginative fantasy for children, since the little wooden marionette who wanted to become a real boy has *become* something of a folktale tradition over the years. What is more, there is much in Collodi's style which betrays a close affinity with the household tale and the apologue. And the problem of classification is further complicated by Collodi's introduction of certain social and political criticisms into the text which add an element of contextual reality foreign to the folktale. In short, *Pinocchio* seems to fall on the borderlands between a number of literary forms and therefore lends itself to a variety of interpretations, no one of which can be taken as exhaustive.

The unusual blend of fantasy and reality which so many critics have observed in *Pinocchio* stems in part, I think, from Collodi's intention to recover in imagination his lost childhood. The course of his career having been run, he now seeks in his mature years to relive his past creatively and thereby to pass judgment on it, to evaluate its influence on his personality. Indeed the very fact that he chose the role of a storyteller to achieve this anamnesis supports such a view, for already as a lad Collodi was beloved for his ability to fascinate other children with his stories. . . . He was an individual bordering on eccentricity, largely self-taught and always distrustful of status and rank. A true Florentine in spirit, Collodi was ever ready to mock what he saw about him, though always with affection and good humor. . . . These same qualities, by his own admission, were dominant in his childhood. . . . It does not take much effort to see in the puppet a mirror-image of the independent, indolent and self-reliant little Carlino who refused to listen to his elders. (pp. 24-5)

Unlike the adventures of Wendy Darling, Alice and Dorothy, the adventures of Pinocchio do not begin in the real world and progress to the fanciful. From the very outset we move in a land without time or geography. The color of Collodi's landscapes is of course unmistakably Tuscan . . . ; but it is so *typically* depicted that it is meant to be "everywhere and nowhere." Likewise there is an apparent disregard for season and time. It snows and rains to fit the occasion; fireflies appear months ahead of their season; the muscatel grapes are ripe in the middle of winter. . . . The spoken idiom and certain details of social structure and fashion belong to the lower and middle bourgeoisie of nineteenth-century Italy. Yet the story and its principal themes belong to that universal time which its opening words recall: "Once upon a time . . ."

Further, unlike Alice's "wonderland," the "wonderful world" of Oz and "Neverland," there is no dream-like quality to Pinocchio's world. The fantastical elements are always kept in check by the realistic environment. The miracle of a living puppet is balanced by Pinocchio's subservience to the nature of a little boy, just as the anthropomorphisms of the animal characters must submit to the laws of nature. Even the Blue Fairy, who works some splendid feats of disappearance and transformation, is nevertheless powerless against the superior force of Pinocchio's free will and susceptible to sickness. Indeed every trace of magic or surrealism is set against a backdrop of reality where magic is the exception and not the rule. . . . (pp. 25-6)

At the same time the book is full of factual inconsistencies of the sort frequent in fairy-tales but uncommon in authored children's books. For example, since Pinocchio does not go to school as he should he is unable to read the simple signs at the carnival, and yet somehow he succeeds in deciphering the more difficult text on the tombstone of the beautiful child. He has no ears, having escaped Geppetto's workshop before they could be added, and yet hears perfectly well. (It is conceivable, let it be noted, that Collodi may have intended a bit of irony here, because it is Pinocchio's inability to "listen" which causes him so much trouble.) Or again, Collodi seems to have forgotten that he gave his puppet a bread-crust hat and paper jacket for all the weathering that meagre wardrobe is made to suffer. That such slips are due merely to the carelessness of the author, who could after all have later corrected them, is unlikely. Even without their help the blend of the realistic and the fantastic would be dominant in the story.

Perhaps no aspect of *Pinocchio* is more striking than the role which animals play in the story. . . . Crickets, rabbits, dogs, apes, donkeys, birds and fish of various sorts; not to mention the fox, the cat, the eel, the snake, the snail, the fire-fly, the crab, the marmot, the calf and the little goat—all these characters and more figure in the world of Pinocchio as naturally and unpretentiously as if they were human. It may be the case that by means of such animal projections the child is led to recognize traits of personality and signs of virtue and vice which are as yet indistinguishable to him, or at least only vaguely discernible, in the adult world about him. If this is so, then from the very outset *Pinocchio* is a didactic venture, and the blend of fantasy and reality serves the higher purposes of a moral fable.

If *Pinocchio* is a fable in narrative, it seems to be one with a fundamentally conflicting moral to it, and this for reasons again of the mixture of fantasy and reality. The lesson for children is clear and forthright. Hardly is Pinocchio taught to walk before he runs away in disobedience; as a result he burns his feet and has to be repaired. Repentance is short-lived, however, and he takes off self-reliantly again and again, piling up a history of lies and broken promises, and involving himself with shady characters who promise to fulfill all his desires without his having to go to school or do a stitch of work. In consequence of his misdeeds Pinocchio is nearly used for firewood, is hung by the neck on an oak tree, finds his nose grown to immense proportions, loses his money to the fox and the cat and goes to prison, is caught in a trap and tied up as a watchdog, is forced to beg for food, spends a second term in jail, is almost fried as a fish in a pan, is transformed into a donkey, is sold to a circus and then to a man who decides to make a drum of his hide after drowning him, and is finally swallowed by the great shark. The moral is obvious: evil comes to those who disobey their elders. "Woe to little boys who rebel against their parents. . . . They'll come to no good in this world and sooner or later will live to regret their actions bitterly." Both the episodic style of the moral and the underlying metaphysic (virtue rewards, vice punishes) are close to the thought-patterns of the young child. It is, as Chesterton has wisely noted in his autobiography, the most spontaneously appealing world to the child who knows too little of hypocrisy and cunning to reject such moralizing. And perhaps the appeal of *Pinocchio* to older generations simply indicates a desire to return to that purity of ideals which one once enjoyed as a child at play in imagination.

Together with this unambiguous advice to children to obey authority we find Collodi's lighthearted but subtler mockery of civil authority. Three times it happens that innocent parties are cast into prison: Geppetto for chasing after Pinocchio, Pinocchio for being robbed of his money and again later for staying to help a wounded friend. In the town of Fools' Trap, the judge is a giant gorilla wearing gold-rimmed glasses without lenses and his police are great bulldogs. When a general amnesty is proclaimed by the mayor, Pinocchio manages to escape prison with the others only by admitting that he is a criminal, since the jailer wants to keep him locked up because of his innocence. Such parody works deceptively to undermine trust in lawful authority on the part of the young child, and hence stands in contradiction to the surface moral of the story. More importantly, it seems to suggest that in the *real* world there is no justice; that only in the world of *fantasy* does good come of good, evil of evil. On our earlier hypothesis this tension can be traced back to Collodi's intention to recapture his youth and its ideals as a means of reflecting on his past life with its political concerns. But the conflict is not Collodi's own; it is a paradigm of our very human condition.

We are compelled, therefore, to see in Pinocchio more than merely the ghost-image of Collodi. In the same way that Pinocchio learns the harsh truths of life through experience by leaving his father-creator behind and venturing out into the world alone, so also does he escape the control of Collodi himself. . . . [Pinocchio's lifelikeness means] not the concretization of an individual figure, but rather his universalization. Pinocchio represents man, *homo viator*. . . . This insight needs to be understood in turn on two levels.

On the first level, Pinocchio appears to us . . . as the personification of a life-myth which brings [natural] tendencies into harmony one with another. This Collodi achieves by depicting Pinocchio's progress as a quasi-Socratic version of the way to virtue. He learns the lessons of life not from abstract classroom theories, but from direct experience, the frequent repetition of which ends in true conversion. His latent sentiments of loyalty and altruism surface only as he slowly learns the need to trim his frenzied passions for independence and the sweet life. He is victimized by wicked and evil men not because of any real wickedness on his own part, but because of ignorance; and he disobeys his elders since he does not yet know any better. In short, Pinocchio's travels lead him from an ignorance of ignorance to a knowledge of ignorance and thence to a self-conscious trust in the wisdom of age and tradition. In contrast to the cat and the fox whose hypocritical masquerade brings them finally to misfortune, Pinocchio's innocence is educated by his adventures in a world (unlike that of Voltaire's *Candide*) where happiness is ultimately guaranteed to the pure of heart.

Of all the animals who assist in Pinocchio's self-education, the Talking Cricket merits special attention. As every schoolboy knows, he represents "conscience," the wee inner voice of warning, the bond between law and responsibility. At their first encounter Pinocchio falls into a rage with the "patient little philosopher" and flattens him to the wall with a wooden hammer from Geppetto's workbench. But the Cricket cannot be so easily disposed of and his ghost appears later in the story to haunt Pinocchio, though his advice is again ignored. Still later the Cricket is called in by the Blue Fairy for his opinion on the ailing puppet, whether he be dead or alive. And here, true to his function as a *psychic* censor, he refuses to say anything about Pinocchio's *physical* well being, but simply denounces him as a disobedient little rogue who is going to be the death of his good father by and by. It is only at their final meeting that Pinocchio addresses him as "my dear little Cricket" and follows his counsel. Thus Collodi embodies in the figure of the Talking Cricket the imperative to trust in those inner promptings of the mind which curtail and yet finally protect one's independence. (pp. 26-8)

The conflict in the moral of *Pinocchio* which was pointed up earlier. . . cloaks a deeper irony in the book. It is not merely the case that children seem to be required to have faith in an older generation which often turns out to be corrupt; but also that true maturity is a function of individual insight which cannot be learned except through personal experience and reflection. Likewise, when Collodi concludes his sketch of school memories with the advice that students should obey their teachers, we can only presume that he is writing tongue-in-cheek, perhaps somewhat fearful of enunciating his own life-myth into a general principle. In *Pinocchio* its signs are more apparent, though many have overlooked them and consequently have not understood the reasons (however mistaken) for which the book was condemned as immoral. . . .

Pinocchio stands before us as a reflection of our human condition on another level—one is tempted to say a "deeper" level to stress its greater distance from consciousness, though not necessarily to imply a greater importance as well—which complements and balances the level of moral self-affirmation. To appreciate this we may consider the figure of the Blue Fairy, who can serve as a sort of psychopomp into the nether world of primordial, archetypal images. To ignore her, or to dismiss her as a mere *dea ex machina* who directs the fate of Pinocchio to a happy ending in typical fairytale fashion, is in my view radically mistaken and a distortion of the textual evidence of Collodi's finished tale. (p. 28)

Now there can be little doubt about the central role which the Blue Fairy enjoys in Pinocchio's life-story. As soon as he meets the beautiful child, his aimless wanderings begin to have an object: he wants to be with her. She proves inspiration and goal enough temporarily to conquer his innate distaste for school and even to forget about his father. For it is she who promises to make him a real boy, something Geppetto could not do. As Collodi himself suggests, she is something *like* a little sister; or later, something *like* a mother. More than that he does not seem to know. Indeed one feels that as the story progresses, the author does little more than *record* the activities of the Blue Fairy, who spontaneously suggests the part she will play in Pinocchio's process of development.

At this point we are obliged further to clarify our original hypothesis and to see **Pinocchio** as an involuntary autobiography which covers not only Collodi's childhood and his public career, but his private adult life as well. He never married, though it seems he sired a "secret" daughter . . . , who would thus have been, for all practical purposes of reputation, "dead" like the beautiful child who could not communicate by word of mouth. But note the immediate transformation which the symbol undergoes once it has been introduced into the story. The child returns Pinocchio from the threat of death which he had incurred by choking on the money he refused to give up; and then she teaches him a lesson about lies, those with short legs (which do not carry one very far) and those with long noses (which are apparent for all to see). The connection with Collodi's gambling habits and the daughter he tried to keep hidden by deceit could not be clearer. The symbol becomes his savior both financially (the writing of the story provided him with an income) and psychologically (by reflecting him to himself).

The transformation continues and the child soon becomes the idealization of Collodi's own mother, for whom his respect seems to have been constant and unfailing, as hers had been for him. The link between the images of child and mother can only be guessed at. Perhaps, because rumor has left us little or no information about the mother of Collodi's daughter, it is the filial love—in the one case given, in the other received—which was more important to him than matrimonial love. In any event, the final import of the story is clear: Geppetto gives Pinocchio his body, but the puppet must search elsewhere for his soul, which he eventually finds in the healing power of a mother's love.

Here again **Pinocchio** as the story of man-writ-small rises to the stature of man-writ-large. Willy-nilly Collodi has fallen into a world of symbols whose psychic roots touch more than the personal history which occasioned them in the first instance, and even more than the typical human problems of ethical maturation considered earlier. In a word, Pinocchio has now to be understood as *archetype of the motherless child*.

Pinocchio's own description of the Blue Fairy—"She is my mamma, who is like all those good mothers who love their children deeply and never lose sight of them . . ."—tells only half the tale. Bernabei intimates the double entendre by referring to her description as the *Blue* Fairy: the color of her hair makes her as unmistakable to the puppet as each mother is to her children; but it is also the color of heaven, the seat of Providence, the mother of all. Thus Bernabei finds it natural that she disappears at the end of the story "since the rightful place of *that* mother is in heaven rather than on earth". . . . The point is well taken, though others less familiar with feminine forms of the divinity in the history of religions and myth, and in particular within the Judaeo-Christian tradition, might object to the inference.

To characterize Pinocchio mythologically as an archetypal motherless child is to classify his adventures psychologically as a quest for that which can transform a man from within,

heal his divided self, and restore him to a state of primordial wholeness. For as the ego emerges from its embryonic identity with the mother's womb, it finds itself in a state of ambivalence. On the one hand the expansion of consciousness and the affirmation of autonomy are highly desirable; on the other, the comforts of unconsciousness and the bliss of ignorance are less threatening. Pinocchio's search for a mother is a symbol of this fundamental dividedness. At one moment we see him stubbornly following his own will in deliberate disobedience of the Blue Fairy; at the next, eschewing all temptation to freedom in a frantic flight to her protecting arms. He is a puppet of contrary forces not yet integrated into his nascent ego. It is only after his final adventure with the giant shark, in which he successfully demonstrates mastery over himself, that Pinocchio assumes the form of a hero and the Blue Fairy disappears as an external reality. He ceases to be a puppet and becomes a real boy; she ceases to be a projection and becomes a dream-figure of the *scintilla divinitatis* dwelling within. The solution to the moral conflict met on the first level is therefore confirmed here on the second: personal consciousness and social obligation are harmonized through self-reflection, through union with but not absorption into the place of one's origins, the Great Mother, the realm of the unconscious.

Numerous other images and motifs in **Pinocchio** suggest similar mythological and psychological parallels which would add support to this interpretation of the tale. I would like briefly to consider two of them by way of illustration.

Let us first look at the unusual circumstances surrounding Pinocchio's birth. Master Cherry the carpenter wants to make a table-leg from an ordinary piece of wood, when he hears a voice crying out from it in protest. "Can it be that someone is hidden inside?" he asks himself, and hastens over to the house of his friend Geppetto, who has coincidentally been dreaming up a plan to make a puppet of wood and travel about with it to earn a living. Cherry parts with his log and Geppetto sets to work to carve himself a little marionette, with no further objections from the wood.

The scene immediately brings to mind Michelangelo's neo-Platonic *concetto* theory of art. According to this theory the true artist is one who discovers. He sees in a block of stone, for instance, an inner form which is hidden to the non-artist. His handiwork consists merely in chipping away what is extraneous in order that that form become visible to all. This theory is incarnated in Michelangelo's famous *Prigioni* in Florence's Academy of Fine Arts, figures struggling to get free of the rock which seems to hold them fast. This is also the image which Collodi creates—perhaps wittingly, being a Florentine himself and well acquainted with the art and theories of Michelangelo—in having the puppet *in potentia* (i. e. in a state of relative unconsciousness) cry out from a simple piece of wood, "a log like all the rest." From the very outset, then, the principle of self-realization, according to which everything must develop after its own ideal, not as a *product* of environmental tools and forces but as a *project* of consciously exercized free will, is articulated in mythopoetic imagery.

The creation of man out of wood is a theme found in a number of mythical traditions. For example, we read in the *Popul Vuh* of the Quiché tribes of southern Guatemale of the gods first creating man out of clay and, finding them blind and stupid, sending a flood to destroy them. Next they carved manikins out of wood; but these creatures had no heart, lacked insight and were forgetful of their creators. They too were destroyed by flood. And so on, until a satisfactory man was made. The parallel is striking (all the more so in that it is nearly impossible that Collodi could have known of it) and shows us the other side of the coin to Pinocchio's creation.

Both in **Pinocchio** and in the Quiché myth the relationship between creature and creator is so symbolized as to accentuate a broken rapport and its eventual restoration. If the wooden manikins turn out contrary to the expectations of the gods, so does Pinocchio show his independence in a manner which brings grief to his poor father. And just as the gods need to experiment with the work of creation in order to achieve success, so does Collodi, dissatisfied with what he has made of his own life, need to recreate himself in the figure of Pinocchio, who in turn has to be cast aside like dead wood to give way to a real boy. In each case the creature, intended as a *reflection* of its creator's best qualities, reveals itself rather as a *distortion*. Its freedom, or capacity for self-formation, frustrates the plans of the gods and requires the redemptive work of a new creation. (pp. 29-32)

Secondly, let us consider the figure of the giant shark who swallows first Geppetto and then Pinocchio. (p. 32)

The religious and mythical motifs at work here are immediately evident to the reader. Pinocchio's adventure with the giant shark calls to mind stories like that of the Hebrew prophet Jonah or the Algonquin warrior Hiawatha, both swallowed by sea monsters from whose bowels they emerge as heroes. This same motif is re-enacted ritually, with remarkable similarity of detail, among certain New Guinea tribes in their ceremonies of initiation. In addition various structural parallels are to be found in baptismal and penitential rites from a wide variety of religious traditions too numerous to mention. Pinocchio's transformation into a real boy takes the form of a double cleansing. First, the outer animal shell, the weaknesses of the flesh, is eaten away by a school of fishes. Second, the "old man" is devoured by the sea monster and is replaced by a "new man" spiritually reborn. In each instance the change occurs through the dark forces which dwell beneath the waters, the realm where the Blue Fairy is in command. It is she who sends the fish and who lures Pinocchio into the mouth of the giant shark in sirenic fashion by appearing as a little goat on a white rock. In other words, the imagery must be seen as a further elaboration of Pinocchio's archetypal character. By confronting the unconscious the ego is confirmed and enabled to embrace social tradition and personal freedom in one saving act of self-realization. Thus the whole magic lantern of adventures is swept up into this one final heroic gesture of Pinocchio carrying the aged Geppetto on his back across the sea to dry land.

If we are moved and enchanted by the story of Pinocchio it can only be in virtue of some underlying affinity with the material upon which the author has drawn for his tale. In struggling to recover his lost childhood through the symbols of imagination, Collodi refracts the reader's gaze inwards to the often faint and nearly imperceptible truths of his own nature. (pp. 32-3)

James W. Heisig, "Pinocchio: Archetype of the Motherless Child," in Children's Literature: Annual of The Modern Language Association Seminar on Children's Literature and The Children's Literature Association, *Vol. 3, edited by Francelia Butler (© 1974 by Francelia Butler; all rights reserved), Temple University Press, 1974, pp. 23-35.*

Like any genuine work of art, the **Adventures of Pinocchio,** presents the critics even of today with an inexhaustible mine

of interpretation problems—and will probably present more in the future. Recently the book has been read from the point of view of social dissent, of psychoanalysis and Marcusian philosophy, with the clear intent of presenting Collodi as precursor of particular related theories. As a matter of fact, he was a real contemporary of his world, but at the same time, irreducibly himself, faithful to that bizarre, free and easy originality apparent in all his writings. His originality becomes genuine poetry and lost-in-reverie story where conflicts are settled in such a way that they reflect his most intimate creative-affective world, instead of an editorial commission. The comic vein with its touch of melancholy reaches beyond the times of Pinocchio-Collodi. The truth which was given full reign in the narrative inspiration will always remain alive just because it is indefinite and not easy to pin down. (p. 26)

Enzo Petrini, "Collodi and His Times," in Bookbird, *Vol. XIII, No. 1 (March 15, 1975), pp. 24-26.*

The wit and charm of the story of the puppet seems as indestructible as his wooden body. There can be few stories which survive so well the indignity of cutting or re-writing. There is so much good humour and good sense in the story and such pertinent, man-of-the-world wisdom in the characterization of the fox and the cat, the Showman Fire-eater, old Gepetto and the scape-grace son, among others, that the most banal version cannot destroy its vitality. Pinocchio is always himself. In his utmost hunger he pettishly refuses to eat the skin of the pears which Gepetto has sacrificed for him; in direst poverty he still bargains for better payment from the kind woman who offers to pay him for carrying her water-bucket (like so many of his well-wishers, she is the fairy giving him one more chance to redeem himself). Although he does reform and becomes a contented, good-looking boy, readers will note with some relief that he does not change for the love of goodness but for the love of people—a distinction which not all moralists make when they write fantasy for children with a concealed lesson in it. (p. 283)

Margery Fisher, "Who's Who in Children's Books: Pinocchio," in her Who's Who in Children's Books: A Treasury of the Familiar Characters of Childhood *(copyright © 1975 by Margery Fisher; reprinted by permission), Holt, Rinehart and Winston, 1975, Weidenfeld & Nicolson, 1975, pp. 282-83.*

Collodi's book may . . . reflect an acquaintance with the work of [a] . . . classical writer, once widely taught in the schools, but today comparatively neglected: the second century rhetorician and satirist, Lucian.

Like Collodi, Lucian was both moralist and entertainer . . . Like Collodi, . . . Lucian wrote in part for an audience that could appreciate a more subtle kind of art. He enjoyed making learned allusions which his audience familiar with classical literature could enjoy; as in Collodi, there is a good deal of deliberate parody, and it constitutes an important part of the fun for the knowledgeable reader.

In this note I want to suggest that two of Lucian's stories contain elements resembling some parts of **Pinocchio.** . . . The first of these stories [*A True Story*], like **Pinocchio,** is a tall tale which ironically mocks and deplores the telling of tall tales. (p. 98)

Probably the most striking similarity between *A True Story* and **Pinocchio** comes in Lucian's use of the old folktale motif of the sailor swallowed by the sea-monster. . . . Deep inside the whale the sailors find a little island with hills and a forest on it. To their amazement, they discover the land to be under cultivation and come upon an old man and a boy who have set up housekeeping in the belly of the monster. They are father and son and had been shipwrecked some years before. They have learned to make a precarious living from their little island, but are, of course, anxious to escape. In Lucian, as in the Walt Disney version of *Pinocchio* and in the Maori myth cited by Father Heisig [see excerpt above] the great escape is made by way of a fire. (p. 100)

Another striking resemblance to Lucian can be seen in the sequence in which Pinocchio is turned into a donkey. To Lucian is attributed the story called *Lucius the Ass* in which the narrator, through his own folly and rashness, finds himself turned magically into an ass. In his new life he, like Pinocchio, is much abused and overworked and frequently threatened with death. Like Pinocchio, Lucius is at one point forced to perform as the star of a circus. Like Pinocchio, he there sees a beautiful woman who excites him, but he, like Pinocchio, can only find despair in this turn of events, for he is trapped in his animal identity. Unlike the Collodi story, Lucian's involves the furry hero in some striking sexual adventures before he is released from the spell that binds him. But finally Lucius the Ass nibbles on some roses and finds himself restored to his former shape.

Some of the similarities in theme and motif between Collodi and Lucian may stem from their similar rhetorical situation. Each was both moralist and entertainer and drew upon a similar heritage of popular folklore, tall tale, wonder story, and anecdote to create stories which would at once charm, tease, and teach his audience. Some of the similarities in tone and manner between Collodi and Lucian may stem from similarities in temperament and outlook. Each seemed wry, skeptical about human pretensions, but not harsh in his criticism of men or manners, save when rank inhumanity or hypocrisy was involved. But since Lucian's works, though currently neglected, had long been staple elements of a classical education, they may well have been encountered by Collodi and have influenced him as they have influenced the work of many other writers in the Western tradition whose work combines elements of folktale, moral apologue, and fiction—writers ranging from Cyrano de Bergerac, Baron Munchausen, and Jules Verne to More, Erasmus, Swift, and Voltaire. (p. 101)

> Susan Gannon, "A Note on Collodi and Lucian," in Children's Literature: Annual of the Modern Language Association Group on Children's Literature and The Children's Literature Association, Vol. 8, *edited by Francelia Butler (copyright © by Children's Literature An International Journal, Inc.), Yale University Press, 1980, pp. 98-102.**

[Collodi] needed only two pieties: boys love to be disobedient, and disobedient boys get into trouble. . . . Collodi developed a formula. If people enjoy seeing Pinocchio flee Gepetto's house because he does not want to go to school, and have misadventures in trying to get home once he gets into trouble, then in every episode Pinocchio will get into trouble from being willful or impetuous, and in most there will be a sermon about being obedient to wise elders and going to school.

The result is that, as a story **"Pinocchio"** is awfully weak, a thin tissue of inevitable scrapes, inevitable rescues and inevitable sermons. The whole business about Pinocchio's being a puppet who wants to be a real boy is in jeopardy every time Collodi makes him able to be hungry, cold or killable by hanging while he is still a piece of wood. (p. 71)

Roger Sale, "Babar at 50, Pinocchio at 100: 'The Adventures of Pinocchio'," in The New York Times Book Review (©1981 by The New York Times Company; reprinted by permission), November 15, 1981, *pp. 49, 71.*

Some of the reasons for [*Pinocchio*'s international] success seem obvious enough. Collodi's style is delightful, and much of its earthiness and pungent wit survive translation quite well. The story also lends itself wonderfully to illustration. . . . But Pinocchio has emerged relatively unscathed even from the pastel attentions of the Disney organization. The undeniable mythic appeal of the story's basic premise is probably a crucial factor in its universal popularity, but equally important, I think, is the vivid personality of the central character. From the moment he speaks from the heart of Master Cherry's block of wood, Pinocchio is an original—spontaneous, unpredictable, springing to life as though from some urgent inner necessity.

The story in which Pinocchio comes to life is not without its flaws, of course. Collodi's book works toward a combination of aesthetic, mimetic, and illustrative effects which are often at cross purposes. His satiric indictment of a corrupt society and his painful picture of the psychological tensions in the parent-child relationship are strangely at odds with the overt message of the book. And the mythic symbolism of the fairy tale plot undercuts both the moral pessimism of the satire and Collodi's relentless insistence on docility and obedience. The very texture of the book is a puzzle. Much of the time it has the verve and spontaneity of a masterful improvisation, but now and again it becomes repetitious, saccharine, or heavy-handed.

Roger Sale recently pointed out the repetitiveness of what he thinks Collodi's "awfully weak" story, terming it "a thin tissue of inevitable scrapes, inevitable rescues and inevitable sermons" [see excerpt above]. Sale suspects that the impulse which motivated Collodi to "spin out the story to 36 episodes" was "the desire to capitalize on something popular and profitable." Collodi's writing formula was simple: "in every episode Pinocchio will get into trouble from being willful or impetuous, and in most there will be a sermon about obeying elders and going to school." Serial publication, as studies in the nineteenth century novel have suggested, does tend to lead to repetition, parallelism of incident and character, and a reliance on literary formula and traditional motifs. And it is true that *The Adventures of Pinocchio* relies heavily on such devices. But it also embodies an appealing and familiar overall pattern: the hero goes forth to seek his fortune, encounters unforeseen perils, undergoes metamorphosis and trials, descends into dark and dangerous nether regions, and emerges one of the twice-born, ready to ascend to a higher plane of being and to achieve his heart's desire.

On the aesthetic level, the book appeals to the mythic imagination. For one critic, Pinocchio is the "archetype of the motherless child," and his adventures constitute "a quest for that which can transform a man from within, heal his divided self, and restore him to a state of primordial wholeness" [see excerpt above]. Another critic has interpreted Pinocchio's progress from block of wood, to puppet, to free human being as a parable of the Jungian process of individuation and self-realization. However one may question the complete success of the story, its basic action, while repetitive and episodic, does offer the excitement of dangers dared and overcome, and the finale is an eminently satisfying one, offering all the joy and consolation and escape any true lover of fairy tales could wish.

While the basic pattern of *The Adventures of Pinocchio* may be the stuff of romance, the tale takes place in a realistic and rather satirically conceived world teeming with vividly described and recognizable psychological and social types. Pinocchio, as rebellious child, is locked in conflict with a series of alternately indulgent and tyrannical parent-figures who exploit him unmercifully when they are not bathing him in sentimental tears. Gepetto has a violent temper and no discernible sense of humor. He is a kind father in some ways, but when Pinocchio foolishly falls asleep with his feet on the stove this kind parent is capable of teaching him a lesson by letting him wait quite a while for a new pair. It is true that Gepetto sacrifices his coat to buy his son an A B C book, but there is something bullying in his very love. His behavior seems to say to Pinocchio: ''I love you so much! How can you fail to obey my slightest wish?'' When Pinocchio goes off to school, he yields to the temptation to sell his A B C book in order to buy a ticket to the Marionette Theatre. Here, he is hailed as a brother by the puppet actors. (The puppet, ordinarily a stringed creature doomed only to counterfeit independent action, is an effective symbol of the young child who must be completely dependent on adults, however eager he may be to explore the world for himself.) The terrible-tempered Fire Eater, impresario of the puppet troupe, is a bully and a tyrant who at first wishes to use Pinocchio for firewood. Fortunately, Fire Eater takes a whimsical fancy to him instead. The question this sequence in the story seems to ask for Pinocchio is a painful one: ''How can someone who is willing to destroy me as a free agent still love me as a person?'' Fire Eater, who is almost as alarming in his maudlin fondness for Pinocchio as he is when he wants to make kindling of him, is obviously a nightmare image of Gepetto.

The role the Blue Fairy plays in Pinocchio's life is also rather ambivalent. On a symbolic level she may serve as an anima figure, and she is an extremely useful didactic device, representing a voice of the highest authority in the moral universe of the story. She is the only significant female character in the story, and appears in a variety of guises. But the primary relationship developed with Pinocchio is the maternal one. As mother she is nurturer, healer, teacher, bringer of life and comfort. And yet, she, like Gepetto, can be very cruel. When the weak and starving Pinocchio begs at her door for food he must wait for hours. When the food comes (brought by a snail servant) it is stage food, made of plaster. The Blue Fairy's pretended death breaks Pinocchio's heart, and her sickness and poverty at the end of the story are yet another pious fraud to wring his feelings. Oddly enough, this figure who tries so hard to teach Pinocchio the value of telling the truth, rarely tells him anything of the kind. She is a tease, a flirt, a manipulative deceiver, and beyond that, she is a mysterious and rather terrifying figure, arbitrary, powerful, unquestionable as a force of nature.

The social world in which Pinocchio moves is a dangerous place, crowded with predators. The Fox and the Cat swindle Pinocchio and leave him hanging by a rope from an oak tree—a marvelous image of his foolish ''dependency'' on their lies and false promises. When the rascally little coachman sells Pinocchio and Lampwick into a degrading slavery, their metamorphosis into donkeys also images the extent and nature of their folly. Pinocchio's is a world in which a great deal of power is concentrated in the hands of the stupid and unfeeling. The ignorant and pompous Owl and Crow who are called in as doctors to pronounce on Pinocchio's case, the teachers who apparently make the schoolroom a dreary obstacle course, and

the bullying roughnecks determined to get Pinocchio in trouble all share an aggressive and willful incompetence. On the other hand, the heartlessness of the efficient and self-righteous is dramatized in the way the people on the Island of the Busy Bees can ignore Pinocchio's suffering if he won't work for his bite to eat. The impossibility of obtaining justice in a world where too many people are stupid or unwilling to fight for their rights is shown in the state of affairs in the City of the Simple Simons, where justice is administered by a gorilla judge who claps the victims of crime in jail and throws away the key. It is interesting to observe, in a story which stresses the importance of truth telling, that the only way Pinocchio can get out of prison in this city of thieves and liars is to claim that he, too, is a thief, and therefore eligible for an amnesty.

Pinocchio's story is as much fable as it is myth or satiric fiction, and it uses many familiar devices of didactic fiction: direct authorial commentary, the citation of pithy proverbs and neatly phrased generalizations about human conduct, and endless sermons delivered by the Blue Fairy and the Talking Cricket who constitute the ''divine machinery'' of the story. The Cricket, who performs on the mythic level the function Northrop Frye assigns to the ''demonic accuser'' who accompanies the hero engaged in a journey of descent, is on the didactic level the voice of Pinocchio's conscience. The gradual change in Pinocchio's attitude toward the Cricket is a good index of the marionette's moral growth. It is when he tells Gepetto of how he had thrown the hammer at the Cricket that we first see Pinocchio conclude that what happens to him in life is somehow connected with what he has done. He tells Gepetto how frightened he was by the darkness and the thunder, and claims (incorrectly, as it happens) that the Cricket said he deserved it, since he was bad. Certainly authorial manipulation of plot in order to stress the inevitability of retribution for moral offenses is a common device in didactic fiction. And in this story which overtly teaches the virtues of docility, obedience to parents, hard work, and truthfulness, deviation from the strict path of virtue seems to bring instant punishment. The disobedient runaway's feet are burned off, and in parallel episodes the rebellious child's ''father'' and ''mother'' disappear, leaving him cold and hungry. When he lies, his nose grows and must be pecked down to size by thousands of birds; when he chooses a life of fun and games instead of schoolwork, he turns into a donkey and enters a life of drudgery. Considering the objectively minor nature of most of Pinocchio's crimes, one might be surprised at the enormous burden of guilt imputed to him, and the cruelty of the punishment inflicted on him; but then his failures are seen in the didactic scheme of the book as failures in love—and so as grave sins, indeed.

Recently, a colleague asked me ''Why is it that children, with their keen sense of justice, don't reject the book?'' I think there may be several answers to that question. One might be that children, especially the well brought up children of loving parents, find it hard to defend themselves against the kind of guilt-trip *The Adventures of Pinocchio* offers. Perhaps they simply acquiesce in it, or perhaps they find relief in observing—with a certain aesthetic distance—the all-too-familiar psycho-pathology of family life. But there is another possibility, too. Perhaps the very flaws in the book work to its advantage: the positive thrust of the mythic plot undermines Collodi's narrow didacticism and qualifies the rather cynical view of the world he tries to project. I suspect much of the book's positive appeal is to be found in the way it fosters, in a sly and subversive way, the healthy independence of the child who cannot learn how to live in a treacherous and unjust world just by being told about it, but who must try his luck. Survival in such a world can depend on courage, independence, curiosity—even a certain recklessness—more than on docility and obedience. At the most crucial moment in the story, the incorrigibly life-oriented Pinocchio refuses to follow the advice of his despairing elders. Ignoring the fatalism of the wise old Tunny Fish and Gepetto's resignation, Pinocchio insists on trying to find a way out of the great Shark's belly. Against all odds, he flings himself recklessly into the sea—and his daring saves them all.

Pinocchio's story shows how a puppet—an instrument designed to be manipulated by others—can become a powerful independent source of life. Why does this happen? Not because the puppet is a good puppet, doing what his masters would have him do, but because he respects both the spirit of the moral code of his "parents" and his own inner obligation to his real self. In the opening pages of the story, Pinocchio seems to be an anarchic, almost demonic figure. He must learn to control his impulses, his curiosity, his boldness, his imagination, so that they will be sources of independent strength to him, rather than weaknesses which the adults around him can only exploit or deplore. He must also learn how to handle failure, guilt, and punishment. Again and again Pinocchio accepts responsibility for his errors without bitterness or complaint. When an error on his part has brought some dreadful metamorphosis upon him, he patiently accepts his new state and is willing to suffer any pains to effect a cure and a return to himself: he is happy to have his nose pecked down to size, relieved to have his donkeyskin nibbled off by fishes. Pinocchio's story is that of a series of symbolic deaths and rebirths until the figure who emerges from the donkeyskin is truly heroic. From this time forward Pinocchio doesn't make a single false step. He can address the Talking Cricket now as "Dear Cricket" because the Cricket has nothing to reproach him with except errors he has left behind. And when, at the end of the story, Pinocchio as a real boy looks about the room and sees his old self lying on a chair, we have reached a mythic moment of undeniable delight. Here, for the first time, Pinocchio speaks with contempt, saying: "How ridiculous I was as a marionette! And how happy I am, now that I have become a real boy!" . . . Collodi, himself, wasn't sure as he looked back on it that this priggish sentiment wasn't added by his editor, and I would rather like to think that this was so. For Collodi's little woodenhead, with all his flaws, is surely one of the most satisfyingly *human* characters in all of children's literature. (pp. 1, 5-7)

> *Susan R. Gannon, "Pinocchio: The First Hundred Years," in* Children's Literature Association Quarterly, *Vol. 6, No. 4, Winter, 1981-82, pp. 1, 5-7.*

[Since 1892, *Pinocchio*] has held a place in the affections of American children and has undoubtedly influenced American writers. . . .

This is the children's own epic, presenting young readers with themselves in wood, full of good resolutions, given to folly, sliding through somehow, but with one difference—Pinocchio always comes out on top and never quite loses face. But he does learn his lesson, and readers never doubt it.

> *Zena Sutherland, Dianne L. Monson, and May Hill Arbuthnot, in their review of "The Adventures of Pinocchio," in their* Children and Books *(copyright © 1981, 1977, 1972, 1964, 1957, 1947 by Scott, Foresman and Company; reprinted by permission), sixth edition, Scott, Foresman, 1981, p. 235.*

Pinocchio is a character immediately recognizable to children. His naughtiness has the broad humor of a child's joke and the consequences that follow upon his misdeeds evince the simple justice of the folktale, so understandable to children. Pinocchio behaves like an ass and becomes one; he lies and his nose grows longer. He is continually undone by his own selfishness and thoughtlessness, but he has a good heart which enables him to win through. And the tale of his winning through offers the child reader of today a good deal of fun and excitement.

But when *Pinocchio* appeared in its English translation in 1892, it had an effect that went beyond mere delight. At that time English children's literature had reached its First Golden Age and was almost beginning its descent into the age of sentimentality. With the exception of Edward Lear's nonsense verses (1846) and the sophisticated humor of *Alice's Adventures in Wonderland* (1865), the best literature, especially fantasy, was very serious stuff indeed. *Pinocchio* certainly did not throw out the moral tradition in children's literature, but it did something of almost greater consequence; it lightened it with childlike humor rather than with the parody of a Lewis Carroll or the allegory of a George MacDonald. *Pinocchio* represented a breakdown in the strict rules of conduct and order so dominant in English and American children's books of the day. (pp. 278-79)

[It] was Collodi's genius that he found such a holdable middle ground between didacticism and pleasure. *Pinocchio* has taken on an almost legendary quality and he still would be more easily recognized by children today than most characters in Walt Disney film and, of course, the pervasiveness of the Disney illustrations in most available editions. However, the recent reissue of the first English edition with the original illustrations may well restore *Pinocchio* to the status he deserves—literature and art rather than cartoon. (p. 279)

> *Sheila A. Egoff, "The European Children's Novel in Translation," in her* Thursday's Child: Trends and Patterns in Contemporary Children's Literature *(copyright © 1981 by the American Library Association), American Library Association, 1981, pp. 275-96.**

To consider the status of a book which has survived for a hundred years and is generally acknowledged to be a classic is scarcely to give it a second look. *The Adventures of Pinocchio*—like other children's books which have continued to be read and remembered—has attained a kind of folklorish immortality, which has been partly fostered by a sentimental appeal to popularity, as in Walt Disney's animated version of the story. It is valuable, however, to look again—whether for the second or the hundredth time—to discover what can be found in the story of the improvident puppet which can account for its longevity and popularity.

In *From Primer to Pleasure* (Horn Book) Mary Thwaite notes that *The Adventures of Pinocchio* signaled "the final blow to didacticism in Italian children's literature and the birth of a world classic" [see excerpt above]. This historical evaluation is more than merely factual; it is like a signpost facing in two directions. Pointing to what had come before, it reminds us of an obvious element of didacticism in the story of the lively, mischievous, carefree puppet and looks ahead to the story's abiding reputation as well as to its international fame. Pinocchio's creator . . . really wanted to impress on [children] the importance of school, the merit of an honest occupation, and the virtue of good human relationships; but with a sudden quirk of genius he borrowed the mask of comedy and covered the face of didacticism. . . . All through the book Collodi has granted Pinocchio free rein, but the author catches hold of himself—as it were—and renounces his creative act, reminding us of Prince Hal's repudiation of Falstaff at the end of *Henry IV, Part II*.

But Collodi's act of repudiation merely serves to bring the curtain down on his comedy even while satisfying his pedagogical intention. Glancing back to what has gone before, one finds a series of slapdash adventures—often preposterous by the standards of probability—and a rogue of a protagonist whose antics are characterized by irresponsibility and tempered with pathos. . . . It is significant . . . that *The Adventures of Tom Sawyer* . . . appeared in 1876 and *The Adventures of Huckleberry Finn* in 1884. Mark Twain was, of course, more frankly antiestablishment than Carlo Collodi, but both writers employed an ancient traditional form—the picaresque novel—and produced entertaining narratives.

Mark Twain was content to stretch the realism of his narratives to include the spirit of the American tall tale; but Collodi worked with a stranger, stronger mixture of elements. One is tempted to say that he created a minestrone of a narrative. Satisfied that he had included a dollop of didacticism to allow for moral nourishment, he added ingredients from ancient classical and Italian sources. (pp. 200-02)

But Collodi was not interested in a fixed point for improvisation. His book, of course, is full of improvised events—one has only to think of Geppetto and Pinocchio in the belly of the fish or of the four black rabbits carrying a coffin on their shoulders. A more important element than improvisation is his use of metamorphosis; in addition to the transformations undergone by Cricket and the Blue Fairy, there are the transformations of Pinocchio himself. He begins life as a stick of wood, and in the course of his adventures he assumes not only the form of a marionette but is turned into a donkey and once again returns to puppethood before he finally attains the human state.

There is still another ingredient in the fantasy world of *Pinocchio*. It is peopled with a variety of characters drawn from many sources. While Geppetto is a recognizable human being, Fox and Cat are drawn from the realm of the animal fable. The Blue Fairy smacks of the sentimentalized delicacy of nineteenth-century fairy lore, and the Green Fisherman seems to be a reincarnation of Polyphemus, the Cyclops. The huge fish that swallows Pinocchio suggests his archetype in the Book of Jonah.

Collodi's initial creative act injected fantasy into the real world simply by endowing a billet of wood with a voice; and everything that happens after the creation of the marionette endows the rascals, cheaters, and unruly boys of the real world with an element of unreality. Despite his serious purpose the author allowed himself to write an entertaining story—a story that holds the reader by its very improbabilities, not to say impossibilities. But Collodi knew where he was going. Pinocchio, as unreliable as Till Eulenspiegel, is not permitted to remain the archetypal rogue but suffers a moralistic apotheosis. After reading the book, however, who lingers over the ending? What remains in our minds is the zany, myriad-mooded puppet who constantly deceives himself but never the world, engaging our sympathy and interest, ever vibrantly alive. (pp. 203-04)

Paul Heins, "A Second Look: 'The Adventures of Pinocchio,'" in The Horn Book Magazine (copyright © 1982 by The Horn Book, Inc., Boston), Vol. LVIII, No. 2, April, 1982, pp. 200-04.

What is the cruelest fate a literary classic might suffer? To be neglected, forgotten, or lost? No. To be debased and trivialized and then remembered is crueler still. Such is the fate of *Pinocchio*. The irony is that everyone knows about *Pinocchio*, yet what many people know is not the original book but some adaptation confused with the original. The newer *Pinocchio* is tolerated as a cute or idle children's tale and nothing more, because that is just what it has become in the popular mind. Perhaps simple ignorance explains this circumstance, but the original is available in many editions, and probably no library is without a copy. Then what is the explanation?

In our view the social definition of childhood has changed since the 1880s, and *Pinocchio* has been changed to accommodate it. As a sociological study, *Pinocchio* is unique: There is the original work as well as a series of adaptations marking and dating the transformation of accepted images. Collodi's original has often been rejected because it portrays an older view of childhood—a view defining children as little adults or adults-in-becoming. Such a definition, however, allows children to have emotions and concerns which contemporary psychology attests they actually do have.

Unfortunately, for a long time beginning in the earlier part of this century, the more unacceptable psychological realities—such as hatred, jealousy, unbridled aggression, sexual desire—were considered exclusively adult characteristics. But the change in the image of childhood—that is, the adult view of how children understand themselves and their world—now exhibits itself in a wide range of modern children's books. Thus, psychological realism appears in children's literature in the works of writers such as Maurice Sendak, Louise Fitzhugh, and Judy Blume, but it failed to manifest itself in the facile truncations of Collodi's masterpiece.

In an attempt to understand *Pinocchio*'s evolution we reviewed scores of translations and adaptations; in addition, we conducted a survey of several hundred liberal arts college students in an effort to learn how they, as products of American culture, perceive *Pinocchio*. From these studies we know that the book was transformed gradually and systematically and that this change was a response to an emerging definition of children and to what was deemed appropriate for them. It is sometimes contended that Walt Disney's film created the later changes in *Pinocchio*. But the transformation began before Disney; the fundamental changes often attributed to him were created independently by others, and most later adaptations do not demonstrate his influence.

For Collodi the world of children is as complex and challenging as the world of adults; in fact, it is the same world seen from a different perspective. The popularity of the original *Pinocchio* in Italy and the subsequent success of faithful translations in Britain and North America show that in the 1890s and for some time thereafter the reading public shared Collodi's view of childhood. During the 1920s, however, a newer concept of childhood began to emerge in America, one in which children were believed to live in Elysian fantasy, insulated from external and internal reality. As a result, *Pinocchio* changed in three distinct ways. First, childhood terrors were modified or expurgated. Second, the image of the child, as represented by Pinocchio, was simplified to remove strong antisocial tendencies. Third, the image of the parent, exemplified in Geppetto, was idealized so as not to provide the young with too realistic a glimpse into the world of adult responsibilities.

Like his spiritual forebear Odysseus, Pinocchio faces genuine terror and experiences a full range of emotions. Collodi's big fish, *il pescecane*, is a threat the magnitude of which falls somewhere between Jonah's whale and the killer-shark of *Jaws* (Doubleday). Over the years Collodi's fearsome fish has been domesticated by a succession of adapters. When we asked the college students what kind of fish or sea creature swallowed Geppetto and Pinocchio, sixty-nine percent said whale, twenty-nine percent didn't know, and only six students answered shark or dogfish. Collodi's *prescecane* is, of course, a shark or a dogfish; and what Collodi actually depicts is a terrible, frightening shark that eats up little children who, disobeying their parents, swim out too far in the water. *Il pescecane* is a nemesis to bad boys and provides a necessary symbol for the child's most disturbing fears.

Modern American children, however, apparently did not have any troublesome fears; thus, truly foreboding worries, such as those symbolically embedded in *il pescecane*, were often expurgated from children's books. The American child was inherently happy, and, furthermore, must not be frightened. Therefore, a symbol that expressed or projected childhood fears must wither and vanish. Although Pinocchio might yet be swallowed, no longer may *il pescecane* do the swallowing. Consequently, Collodi's fish underwent a curious metamorphosis over the years.

Early translations rendered *pescecane* as *dogfish,* and many adaptations retain this term. Few people today, however, understand it. What does *dogfish* actually convey to those ignorant of the word? The term happily permits fanciful notions. After all, dogs and fish are both generally benign; but a comparison of illustrations suggests that early translators knew that Collodi meant his fish to be a full-fledged shark. (pp. 205-07)

So the use of *dogfish* after 1920 probably tended, through ambiguity, to minimize the threat. If that were not enough, some adaptations used the even more nebulous term *sea monster,* and Remo Bufano in his 1929 dramatization was the first to introduce the more gentle word *whale.* In various versions from 1930 to 1938 there was only one shark in contrast to "Attila the Sea Monster" and four dogfish. Yasha Frank in his 1939 dramatization substituted "Monster Whale"; Roselle Ross in her 1939 adaptation used "Sea Monster"; and Walt Disney, "Monstro the Whale." In the forty-year period from 1939 to 1979 we found only one monster shark—but six whales, four dogfish, two sea monsters, one great fish; five adaptations dropped the episode completely. Although the shark did reappear in 1979 and 1980, the versions restoring it conformed in every other respect to the newer portrayal of childhood.

Taken by itself the change in *pescecane* might be attributed to linguistic confusion. But the symbolic impact of this single change is amplified by other changes, all of them aimed at undermining psychological realism. Hence, as the image of the terrible fish has evolved, so has that of Pinocchio as the archetypal child.

Collodi's Pinocchio is a complex figure. Although he does many bad things, Collodi's Pinocchio is not inherently evil. Rather, he is thoroughly egotistical and self-centered. His behavior is consonant with contemporary psychology; he cannot anticipate the consequences of his actions, nor does he want to. Pinocchio is frustrating; he will not learn. He is a woodenhead, a marionette—all the worse for a spirit of independence—and cannot distinguish well-intentioned advice from confining restraint. Pinocchio is intractable, impudent, and rude, flying into a rage when he cannot get his way. In fact, he intentionally causes hurt and provokes conflict. Even as an uncarved piece of wood, he instigates two rough-and-tumble

fights between a pair of old men. While being carved into a marionette, Pinocchio plays mocking pranks on Geppetto and will not stop no matter what Geppetto says. As soon as he is carved, he runs away, and when Geppetto catches up with him, he throws a temper tantrum and refuses to budge. A crowd gathers to watch. A policeman arrests Geppetto to protect Pinocchio, who is then freed to do what he likes. How does one describe such a child? He is a brat. He does not warrant sympathy or love; he prompts anger.

In Collodi's original these tendencies are not irremediable failings but a natural stage of child development. Pinocchio simply is not prepared to recognize that other people have needs and feelings as important or valid as his own. Like Sendak's Max, he is on a journey of psychological discovery and reconciliation; he is the image of the child in contemporary psychology. Nevertheless, Pinocchio and his journey have been distorted and trivialized over and over again for seventy years. The best way to show how he has been changed is to lay out individual episodes from the original book and from subsequent adaptations, letting them speak for themselves.

The first stage of Pinocchio's transformation—1911-1938—weakens his egotistic nature and misbehavior. Condensed and abridged editions accomplish this by omitting various episodes entirely or by drastically cutting them. Incidents that Collodi develops over several pages are sometimes reduced to a summary sentence or two. The result is to change the significance of both Pinocchio and his activities. His mischief becomes a series of disconnected pranks, and even if these are not amusing, they provoke very little anger. They become the pranks we expect of any boy; mischief we outwardly scold but inwardly approve of. The dramatizations of the book—1929-1936—follow the same pattern; the later the play, the more amusing and endearing the puppet becomes.

In her adaptation of the book Roselle Ross explicitly made Pinocchio lovable—perhaps like Peter Rabbit—because of his mischief. Her character reinterpretation is striking. Recall that when Collodi has Geppetto carve Pinocchio, the puppet's eyes stare at him almost menacingly, and Geppetto is upset and angry. But for Ross the puppet's eyes wink merrily, and Geppetto is astonished.

The ultimate transformation is to cleanse a child even of mischief, to make him inherently obedient, totally innocent, and thoroughly well-intentioned. Dorothy Coit's ballet of *Pinocchio* in 1938 is very close to this concept. The full transformation is presented unambiguously in Yasha Frank's play and in the 1940 Disney film. Here Pinocchio displays no mischief whatsoever. He is totally loving and trusting, and it is these characteristics, along with his inexperience, that get him into trouble.

The portrayals of Frank and of Disney had virtually no impact on subsequent plays or adaptations. The chief exception is Brian Way's play—1954—which has been exceedingly popular and is now in its eighth printing. Although Pinocchio's mischief grows progressively milder, virtually all of the plays and the adaptations published through 1980 retain some element of mischief and recalcitrance. Occasionally, elements of Disney's story line are substituted for the original, but this is quite incidental to the issue: the changing portrait of Pinocchio.

Thus, the image of child Pinocchio meant one thing in 1881, something different through 1938; and it was radically altered from 1939 on. If children have, in fact, not changed over this long period, the presentation of them certainly has. In 1881

Pinocchio was egotistical and infuriating. Now he is either innocuously mischievous and therefore cute—or innocent and trusting and therefore lovable.

Geppetto, the image of the parent, has also undergone change. In the original book Geppetto is a truly human figure. He displays anger, rage, and frustration when Pinocchio is stubborn or disobedient; warmth, support, love, and sacrifice when Pinocchio is contrite or in need. Collodi captures the inherent ambivalence in parent-child relationships. The parent loves, but the parent also becomes angry and punishing. Raising a child, Collodi shows, is no easy matter.

Parents, however, by this time no longer punished; towards the child they displayed only love, warmth, support, and self-sacrifice. And so, as with Pinocchio, Geppetto as a character is weakened throughout the 1930s. Coit, Frank, Ross, and Disney completed his transformation and made him a pasteboard figure; Geppetto has never been the same since. Even Geppetto's reason for wanting Pinocchio must be purified; of our students, eighty-two percent thought that he wanted a son. Only nine students chose "he wanted a puppet so he could perform puppet shows and earn some money"; money, of course, *was* Geppetto's motive. Only in the 1930s does Geppetto begin to feel lonely and seek a son—but without ignoring economic need. Ross subordinated the financial aspect; Frank and Disney removed it entirely. From that point on Geppetto expresses the only appropriate motive for having children.

The idealization that distorts the image of child and adult in revised or adapted editions of *Pinocchio* has sapped the richness of many of Collodi's most dramatic and significant scenes. Pinocchio's violent meeting with Cricket is a case in point. From the revisions one would suspect that children never feel uncontrolled rage, never wish anyone ill, nor display anger towards parents. But real children do these things, and so does Collodi's Pinocchio. His first encounter with Cricket can be interpreted in this way: Rather than symbolizing Pinocchio's incipient conscience, Cricket is an adult figure. Pinocchio culminates his heart-to-heart talk by squashing Cricket dead with a mallet.

How does Cricket fare historically? Through 1940 all the retellers and adapters have him killed. Dramatic versions of *Pinocchio* in the 1930s, however, introduced uncertainty. Sometimes Cricket escapes unharmed; sometimes he is killed or simply hurt. In one version Cricket is killed, but now at least Pinocchio must pause and reflect on the gravity of his deed. Ross's book also made Pinocchio reflect and then absolved him of guilt. Colt and Frank avoided the problem by excluding Cricket as a character. Disney transformed the relationship completely: Pinocchio's violent act is inconceivable, and Cricket becomes his helpmate and conscience. (And it was Walt Disney, of course, who was not content with mere Cricket but added the totally inappropriate Jiminy.)

Yasha Frank seems to have been the first one to redefine Pinocchio and Geppetto thoroughly. His Pinocchio is the naïve, innocent child, quite incapable of discomfiting mischief. Plays of this kind, however, are usually performed, tested, and developed before they are published. While Frank's play was not published until April 1939, it opened on Broadway on January 2, 1939, and was performed at least as early as June 1937 in Los Angeles. Although Walt Disney had registered his intention to do *Pinocchio* in 1934, he did not become active on the project until he saw Frank's production. Story meetings began around November 1937.

Disney consciously created a story line different from Frank's but took the new image of Pinocchio and Geppetto from Frank. Disney's decision was deliberate and well thought out. Furthermore, Disney was clearly conscientious in his endeavor to know Collodi's tale. Not only did he acquire the Italian original and various editions and adaptations of the translations, but—perhaps to be sure of the material—he also contracted for his own translation. It is conceivable that he delayed the project until Frank offered the key he sought: concepts to which contemporary parents would be more receptive. With a major financial stake—and his reputation—involved, Disney's choice was not made lightly. He perceived, correctly, that his new definition of child and parent would be far better received than Collodi's. It was closer to what parents preferred to believe about their own children and to what they felt appropriate for children to know.

It is necessary to return to our opening thesis: Changes in *Pinocchio* manifest changes in the social definition of childhood. And thus a literary classic, written in terms of one perception, has been tragically rejected and rewritten to conform to another. (pp. 207-11)

Richard Wunderlich and Thomas J. Morrissey, "The Desecration of 'Pinocchio' in the United States" (reprinted by permission of the authors), in The Horn Book Magazine, *Vol. LVIII, No. 2, April, 1982, pp. 205-12.*

Although Ms. Gannon [see excerpt above] offers perceptive insights into the book's aesthetic successes, especially its mythic overtones, she nevertheless falls victim to two common critical misconceptions about the novel. The paramount fallacies of *Pinocchio* criticism are as follows: (1) "*Pinocchio* has emerged relatively unscathed" (Ms. Gannon's words), and (2) the book is a literary success in spite of glaring defects in the form of inconsistencies and archetectonic sloppiness. In fact, Collodi's masterpiece has been ruthlessly tortured by a parade of meddlesome adaptors and publishers. Furthermore, though there are some anomalies of plot, *Pinocchio* is a classic work of epic fantasy—not a lucky stab in the dark but a well crafted epic journey in the tradition of Homer, Vergil and Dante.

Pinocchio survives by the force of its greatness despite the ill-spent efforts of errant revisionists. Since 1892 . . . hundreds of versions have appeared, the vast majority unfaithful in significant ways to the original. Professor Richard Wunderlich and I present an overview of this sad publication history in "The Desecration of *Pinocchio* in the United States" [see excerpt above]. . . . (pp. 37-8)

Most critics of *Pinocchio* recognize the book's aesthetic successes. Unfortunately, Ms. Gannon pays too much attention to Roger Sale's negative comments about the novel and fails to cite the very positive view of Glauco Cambon, who regards *Pinocchio* as one of the three pieces of Italian literature that has "most tangibly affected the imagination of the Italian people." Ms. Gannon does not fully subscribe to Mr. Sale's assertion that Collodi offers a "very weak" story, but she does describe the texture of the book as a "puzzle" and sees it as at once "masterful improvisation" and "saccharine, or heavyhanded." She gets closer to the truth when she considers the novel's mythic motifs. Mr. Cambon and Fr. Heisig (whom Ms. Gannon does cite) are sensitive to Collodi's awareness that he is writing a myth. Indeed, he writes in a mythic tradition that includes the *Odyssey, Aeneid* and *Divine Comedy*. The fact that he does so does not preclude his writing for children, just as the fact that he writes for children does not prevent his speaking to adults with allusive erudition.

Pinocchio's mythic fabric features a number of major threads, one of the most important of which is the theme of the death and rebirth of the hero. Pinocchio's search for self-actualization is comic and haphazard because he is a wooden-head: he lacks the brawn and guile of Odysseus, the solemnity of *pius* Aeneas, and the Christian spirituality of Dante the Pilgrim, but he does undergo a symbolic journey to the realms of death and his *Angst* is as real as theirs. . . . Collodi's puppet undergoes symbolic death and resurrection by suffering a series of near-deaths, by journeying to a metaphorical underworld, and by his eventual metamorphosis, the shedding of his puppet-self in exchange for human form.

Death, real and symbolic, is a ubiquitous element in *Pinocchio,* and it is through these encounters with mortality that the puppet assimilates the truths about human existence that make it possible for him to become a real boy. Although Mr. Sale and, to a lesser extent, Ms. Gannon find Collodi overly didactic, the lessons his hero learns are pretty much the same as those that come to the classical figures who are Pinocchio's adult forerunners. Despite the comic, even slapstick settings, Pinocchio faces death on many occasions. He is nearly burned, stabbed, hanged, cooked and drowned. He himself kills the Cricket, grieves at the Fairy's pretended death, assists at the passing of his comrade Candlewick, and fears that Gepetto might have died at sea. Furthermore, he travels with other lost souls in a hearse-like coach with a Charon-like driver to the Land of Boobies, where heedless boys are changed into donkeys as punishment for slothful ways. Pinocchio is slow to learn from these glimpses at death and perdition, but learn he does. His laughable gullibility, frenetic impatience and anarchistic egoism give way to sound judgment, patience, filial piety and a sense of mutual interdependence. Like Odysseus he learns to distrust those unworthy of trust, like Aeneas he dedicates himself to the care of an infirm parent, and like Dante's Pilgrim he comes to recognize the place and power of love in human affairs, for he eventually adopts the credo of the loyal dog who saves him from the Green Fisherman: "You know that we must all help each other in this world." Clarifying his attitudes towards these ancient values is the goal of his picaresque journey to boyhood.

Writing a children's novel in which death is so important a feature without making the book morbid is a difficult matter; making the book humorous at the same time is a triumph of craftsmanship. But such an undertaking is not without unavoidable risks. What some have called the novel's uneveness of texture results in part from the complexity of its fictive world and tonal ambiguity. Take, for example, Collodi's manipulation of audience response to the puppet's chronic disobedience. The punishment for ignoring his mentors—Gepetto, the Fairy and the Talking Cricket—is usually death, exile from loved ones or involuntary imprisonment or servitude. But the death threats are stylized and the other punishments are temporary because Pinocchio's innocent rebellions are appealing and necessary. Not all adult authorities are to be trusted: the Fox and Cat, the Gorilla judge, the infernal coachman are corrupt and dangerous. Collodi clearly distinguishes between authority that deserves scorn and that which merits obedience. Pinocchio must learn to discriminate among the possible objects of allegiance. The novel's texture is sometimes strained by the abrupt juxtaposition of greed, malevolence and stupidity with beatific good will and preternatural intervention. Such is an occupational hazard of blending verisimilitude with fantasy.

There are, of course, some real inconsistencies of plot. How, for instance, can Pinocchio read the Fairy's tombstone when he has refused to learn to read? The answer might lie in the book's serial genesis, but Collodi has no monopoly on such anomalies. In Faulkner's *Absalom, Absalom!,* one of the great masterpieces of modern fiction, the creator of Yoknapatawpha County outdoes Collodi by a long shot. At the end of the book Sutpen's great brick mansion suddenly becomes wood in order that the old South can go out in a blaze of glory. Sutpen, the would-be patriarch, had to build his house of bricks, but in the end Faulkner needed a house of wood. Thus logical inconsistency sometimes yields to imagistic truth. Pinocchio must refuse to learn to read, but he must suffer the lesson that reading the stone provides. Both Collodi and Faulkner could have found ways to reconcile these factual slips: that they did not do so can be taken as a sign of sloppiness, but it is, I think, more profitable in the long run to see their "errors" as opportunities to watch the inner workings of creative minds at work. Is the glass half empty or half full?

It is fortunate that Ms. Gannon and others have used the *Pinocchio* centennial as an opportunity to focus attention on Collodi's classic; however, the novel's history, impact and meaning have yet to be explored fully. (pp. 38-9)

> *Thomas J. Morrissey, "Alive and Well But Not Unscathed: A Reply to Susan R. Gannon's 'Pinocchio at 100'," in* Children's Literature Association Quarterly, *Vol. 7, No. 2, Summer, 1982, pp. 37-9.*

Ed Emberley
1931-

Barbara Emberley
1932-

Ed—American author/illustrator of fiction and nonfiction.

Barbara—American adapter and author of picture books.

The Emberleys's picture books are recognized for their successful integration of text and artistic technique. Ed's use of woodcuts, pen and ink, and pencil combine with his imagination and sense of humor to produce illustrations which richly complement the texts with which they are paired. Five of these have been written by Ed's wife, Barbara, who uses a crisp, relaxed prose style for her adaptations of nursery rhymes, folk songs, and folk tales. Since 1969, Barbara has been involved with behind-the-scenes work on Ed's books, leaving active authorship to him.

Ed's knowledge of printing and production techniques makes him particularly aware of the overall design of a book. Critics compliment both his concepts and their execution. They are especially impressed with the originality of his presentation of

the alphabet in *Ed Emberley's ABC* and the animal menagerie in *One Wide River to Cross*, as well as the sensitivity of *Drummer Hoff*'s illustrations to the rhythm of its text. *Ed Emberley's Drawing Book of Animals* began a succession of how-to-draw books which reviewers regard as clear and entertaining. These books utilize step-by-step drawings of a wide variety of subjects using basic shapes, numbers, letters, and flourishes. Critics applaud the ease with which almost anyone over the age of eight can become an instant artist, but suggest that Ed has now exhausted his formula and should pursue something other than his drawing books. Nevertheless, Ed continues to be one of the most celebrated author/illustrators on the American scene, and his individual and collaborative works appeal in both picture and word. Ed received the *New York Times* Choice of Best Illustrated Children's Books of the Year award in 1961 for his first book, *The Wing on a Flea*, and in 1965 for *Punch and Judy; Wing* was also an ALA Notable Book. *One Wide*

River to Cross **became a Caldecott Honor Book in 1967, and another collaboration,** *Drummer Hoff,* **earned the Caldecott Medal and the Lewis Carroll Shelf Award in 1968.**

(See also *Contemporary Authors,* **Vols. 5-8, rev. ed.;** *Contemporary Authors New Revision Series,* **Vol. 5; and** *Something about the Author,* **Vol. 8.)**

GENERAL COMMENTARY

Two of Ed Emberley's outstanding assets as an illustrator of children's books are a strong sense of design and a prolific imagination. He is developing both at a rapid pace.

His sense of design shows most noticeably in his thoroughly stylized illustrations, especially those in bold patterns of flat color, always emphasizing simplified form. His 1966 *Rosebud,* for instance, shows strikingly how he can reduce an object to its simplest and most significant essentials, omitting whatever is not expressive for the purposes of the moment.

Again, his design sense is exemplified in the layout of pages as he effectively adjusts a variety of arrangements of type and illustration on successive page spreads. (p. 54)

As for imagination, this shows in Ed Emberley's exuberant building up of themes with copious commentary. We see it . . . in *The Parade Book,* where bystanders watching the drum major pass with pronounced verve include every conceivable type of human being in a multiplicity of delightfully expressive attitudes, with balloons, flags, cameras, opera glasses, pipes, dogs, and cats.

Ed's imagination is strongly colored by an active sense of humor. This may express itself in mountain climbers exerting prodigious effort, or in a dancing child who flings one hand high in abandonment, while with the other she catches a back-kicking ankle as seen in *The Wing on a Flea.*

Exaggeration is, of course, a basic ingredient in humor. We find it in this same "Flea" book (a playful commentary on simple forms, such as the triangle of a flea's wing or a boat's sail, and so on) when we view two drawings of a paunchy pirate leveling first a telescope, then a pistol, peering shrewdly along either from under the very edge of a floppy hat brim. We find it in *Punch & Judy* in the large, innocent goggle-eyes of a toothy saddle horse decoratively caparisoned, contrasted with the glowering squint eyes of a magenta devil wielding a villainous pitchfork and quirking a malevolent tail. (pp. 54-5)

Thus we have imagination humorously employed by means of exaggeration of *form,* giving us the pirate's . . . exalted characterization; and we have humor achieved by imaginative extension of subject matter. (p. 55)

With his flat color patterns Ed often combines areas of mottled color, produced by rendering them with crosshatching. *Punch & Judy* gives us our best examples of this. Line drawings often supplement the flat and mottled color areas in integrated combination with them. Ed's line is usually free and easy, though never merely careless. When necessary it is strictly controlled.

For his flat color work . . . , he sometimes uses a frosted acetate film that is double-layered. The upper layer is a very thin sheet of dark orange plastic held lightly by adhesive to a stiff, translucent lower layer. (p. 56)

The woodcut is another favorite medium of expression with Ed Emberley. He uses ordinary pine plank obtained from a local lumber yard. He pulls his proofs of the completed blocks in black printers' ink on domestic rice paper. For the proving

he uses three small hand presses of different sizes. Often he locks up lines of type with the woodblocks. Thus the layout for a book page or jacket can be made complete, with type in place with the illustration, ready for the engraver. (p. 58)

Texts for a number of Ed's books have been either his own or by his wife, Barbara, who has a sensitive skill with words, as delightfully evidenced in *The Story of Paul Bunyan.* (p. 60)

> *Dorothy Waugh, "The Meteoric Career of Ed Emberley," in* American Artist *(copyright © 1966 by Billboard Publications, Inc.), Vol. 30, No. 9, November, 1966, pp. 54-61.*

An Ed Emberley picture book leaves one with a strange feeling of predestination. It is as if to say, "Why, of course. It had to be done that way because no other way could be right."

Ed Emberley's ability to create a "just right" picture book can be attributed partly to his keen graphic sense and his imaginatively conceived and skillfully rendered artwork. But there is another dimension to his ability, elusively present in all of his work. He is not only an artist, but an illustrator as well. It is the artist who renders each page of a book, embellishing and extending the text to form a picture which pleases the eye and stimulates the imagination, but it is the illustrator who creates the book. The illustrator is aware of over-all design, the total book as opposed to what might be a series of successful spreads. He sees the entire product from the time of its conception through the end of its production.

In considering a project, Ed Emberley is always aware of the cold practicalities of bookmaking. Having studied printing and production techniques, he applies his knowledge in the development of any new style. An artist might feel that a given text would make a perfect 48-page book in a 9" x 12" format rendered in pencil line and full color. But an illustrator knows better. An extra-long, oversized, process color picture book would create enormous pricing problems for the publisher, and the technique of pencil and process color would be virtually impossible to reproduce properly. When an Emberley dummy is submitted, all such problems have been considered, and there is no necessity to compromise the artist's original conception of the book because of technical problems.

It is the illustrator in Ed, too, that can be credited with the subtle touches that make even the simplest texts exciting. This effect is evident in the cumulative build-up of *Drummer Hoff* as well as in his earlier book *One Wide River to Cross.* There are small details in the latter volume which are not really even noticed on the first or second reading, yet they serve to make a simple rhyme into a book. The colors are bright and gay at the beginning; then they suddenly darken as a small patch of cloud appears at the top of the page. The clouds become larger on each successive page while the colors become still darker. The end of the flood and the arrival of sunshine are a dramatic event as the color suddenly brightens again. *One Wide River* was actually a full-color book and the color was available for every page. It was the skill of the illustrator which opted to ignore the artistic potential of the available color and create an effective book rather than more effective pages.

The unusual way that *Drummer Hoff* came about is again an example of Ed Emberley's awareness of what a book should be. Its technique was developed long before the text was discovered. The style that was later to become *Drummer Hoff* was based on Ed's thought that there was no rule that a woodcut had to look like a woodcut. His past three Prentice-Hall books, all very different from one another, had been rendered in the same medium. With his typical aversion to repeating a style he had mastered, he decided to use the woodcut as a line drawing, dropping small patches of color into the open spaces in the cuts. The advantage of this technique was that it allowed great variety in the possible combinations that could be created from four basic colors. One color could be printed over another to create a third color without the inevitable danger of slips in the registration as the book was printed. The heavy black line of the woodcut would be able to absorb any stray colors that slipped out of position.

It was a simple idea and yet a highly original one. Compared with line drawings, woodcuts require a tremendous amount of time and effort. Ed's concern for the quality of the finished book, however, made him willing to put the extra work into the book to achieve the bright, varied colors that come from preseparated art, while at the same time avoiding the disadvantages of the process.

While the technique was being established, Ed's wife and co-author, Barbara, and I agreed that the next book should be a picture-book adaptation of a fairy tale [Jean Reynolds is children's book editor at Prentice-Hall]. The text was given to Ed and he prepared the first dummy. It was a glorious work, each page full of bright colors and bustling activity. And therein lay the problem. The over-all effect was too powerful. The strong story line competed with the robust style of the artwork and though the dummy was lovely, it was not a book.

Seeing the new technique in dummied form made the need for a simple text very obvious. Since woodcuts had the advantage of being able to be repeated on subsequent pages, a cumulative verse was indicated. So the fairy tale was discarded and *Drummer Hoff* came into being. The technique of the artist combined with the cold eye of the illustrator who could stand back and look at his own book had actually dictated the form of the text. (pp. 113-14)

The deceptive simplicity of the finished book makes the exact basis for its lively appeal difficult to describe. The key seems to lie in that integration of technique, art work, and text that consistently marks an Ed Emberley picture book. (p. 114)

> *Jean Reynolds, "Ed Emberley," in* School Library Journal, *an appendix to* Library Journal *(reprinted from the March, 1968 issue of* School Library Journal, *published by R. R. Bowker Co./A Xerox Corporation; copyright © 1968), Vol. 14, No. 7, March, 1968, pp. 113-14.*

In the hands of a gifted artist, often the frailest of literary wisps is turned into a visually rewarding picture book. Ed Emberley is one such illustrator, and his rich, inventive woodcuts provide many moments of pure aesthetic delight both in *One Wide River to Cross,* a free-wheeling adaptation of an old folk song on the Noah's Ark theme, and in *Drummer Hoff.* . . . As graphic work, both are virtuoso performances, full of visual wit, and they provide a wonderful means of honing observant eyes to the subtlest of visual changes. Words are barely necessary and linger not at all once the books have been closed. (p. 57)

> *Selma G. Lanes, "Blow-up: The Picture-Book Explosion," in her* Down the Rabbit Hole: Adventures and Misadventures in the Realm of Children's Literature *(copyright © 1971 by Selma G. Lanes; reprinted with the permission of Atheneum Publishers, New York), Atheneum, 1972, pp. 45-66.**

Ed Emberley . . . produced a pair of very clever and engaging books recently: *A Birthday Wish* and *Ed Emberley's ABC.* Like *Drummer Hoff,* both books are superficially simple, but each has a subtlety which will be appreciated by the young reader who takes the time to peruse each drawing. In *A Birthday Wish,* a poor little mouse blows out a candle on his cake (cheese, of course), and in so doing starts a chain of events which leads to his wish coming true. In blowing out the candle, he also blows his father's cap out the window; this causes a bird to fly into a tree, knocking an acorn loose and onto the head of a woodpecker, and so forth. The chain of cause and effect is often ludicrous and the individual situations are of the slapstick variety. The achievement of this wordless picturebook is found not only in the quality of the individual drawings but also in the sense of movement created by the sequences of pictures, often four on a two page spread. This is not a profound book, but it is a very clever one.

Ed Emberley's ABC is one of the most delightful and original ABCs to appear in recent years. Each of the letters is given a two page spread containing four pictures, each picture marking a stage in the formation of the letter. Thus an ant in a skywriting airplane forms the letter A. Often there are several objects with the featured letter; for example, one finds eleven G words. (And if you can't find them they're listed at the back.) An interesting, although perhaps slightly confusing feature, is the inclusion of three letters not found at the beginning of the words. *I* is represented by Pig, Pin, Pink, and Ribbon; *X* by fox, box, and six. Here the principle is that the specific letter is always in the same place within the words. At the end of the book, there is a chart showing how to print the words. The book thus teaches not only recognition, but also printing.

> *Jon C. Stott, in his review of "A Birthday Wish," in* The World of Children's Books *(© 1978 Jon C. Stott), Vol. 3, No. 2, Fall, 1978, p. 25.*

THE WING ON A FLEA: A BOOK ABOUT SHAPES (by Ed Emberley, 1961)

An attractively illustrated book. . . . The jacket is much less appealing than the pictures inside, and booksellers might do well to display to customers some of the good-looking double-page spreads in the book. It is, perhaps, unfortunate, that Mr. Emberley has written his text in rhyme. His rhymes are sometimes forced and for the sake of them he has included some illustrations that four and five-year-olds may not understand.

> *A review of "The Wing on a Flea," in* Publishers Weekly *(reprinted from the April 3, 1961 issue of* Publishers Weekly, *published by R. R. Bowker Company; copyright © 1961 by R. R. Bowker Company), Vol. 179, No. 14, April 3, 1961, p. 49.*

Gay rhymes and lively green-and-blue drawings show children how to identify triangles, circles, and rectangles in the everyday objects around them. Though some of the examples are a little far-fetched, this should prove effective in nudging boys and girls toward more intelligent observation. Recommended.

> *Anne Izard, in her review of "The Wing on a Flea," in* Junior Libraries, *an appendix to* Library Journal *(reprinted from the April 15, 1961 issue of* Junior Libraries, *published by R. R. Bowker Co./A Xerox Corporation; copyright © 1961), Vol. 7, No. 8, April 15, 1961, p. 38.*

This book begins with a white triangle on a pedestal and ends with the blue roundness of a little girl's eyes. On the expertly and amusingly designed pages in between, the shapes of triangles, rectangles, and circles are deftly highlighted—by means of color or the sudden absence of it—as they appear in the four-year-old's world. . . . Parents may see a bit of Steinberg in the drawings of this gay guide to awareness of form.

> *Pamela Marsh, "Pages of Pictures That Talk and Sing and Shout and Tell a Story," in* The Christian Science Monitor *(reprinted by permission from The Christian Science Monitor; © 1961 The Christian Science Publishing Society; all rights reserved), May 11, 1961, p. 2B.**

[Something] to build on: Ed Emberley's fresh and imaginatively illustrated primer, **"The Wing on a Flea"**. . . . This is a book about shapes. . . . And Mr. Emberley does a marvelous job in making sure they are seen, setting off, by the use of bright color, each shape from the rest of the page. Only a real square would deny that here is a wonderful, lively way to learn.

> *A review of "The Wing on a Flea," in* The New York Times Book Review, *Part II (© 1961 by The New York Times Company; reprinted by permission), May 14, 1961, p. 35.*

THE PARADE BOOK   (by Ed Emberley, 1962)

Ed Emberley has set himself a difficult task in **"The Parade Book"** . . . : attempting to convey the atmosphere, sights and sounds of a parade and describing specific parades such as New York's Thanksgiving, New Orleans's Mardi Gras, Pasadena's Tournament of Roses. His book is a grand, gay and colorful procession filled with neat rows of small marching figures, but the umpah-pah-pahs and the excitement don't really come through. There's no substitute for being there. (p. 57)

> *George A. Woods, "In the Hour between the Dark and the Daylight Comes a Pause for the Picture Book," in* The New York Times Book Review, *Part II (© 1962 by The New York Times Company; reprinted by permission), November 11, 1962, pp. 56-7.**

Gay color and slight humor do little to enhance this static book which seems to be a hasty grouping of various kinds of parades with little continuity and very limited appeal. Mr. Emberley's audience for **"Wing on a Flea"** will be disappointed.

> *Peggy Sullivan, in her review of "The Parade Book," in* School Library Journal, *an appendix to* Library Journal *(reprinted from the December 15, 1962 issue of* School Library Journal, *published by R. R. Bowker Co./A Xerox Corporation; copyright © 1962), Vol. 9, No. 4, December 15, 1962, p. 36.*

A circle is
Your eye, which can find
All sorts of shapes.
Now you'll know the kind.

Triangles, rectangles,
Circles, all three,
You'll know which is which
If you just look AND SEE.

From The Wing on a Flea: A Book about Shapes, *written and illustrated by Ed Emberley.*

From the very first "There's going to be a parade," Ed Emberley's illustrations, more effective than his text, lift anyone (from about four years old) into a hooraying mood. His quick, lively sketches making an unexpected and effective contrast with his bright range of poster type colors, show regular parades, and special ones, too.

> *Pamela Marsh, "Widening Horizons," in* The Christian Science Monitor *(reprinted by permission from The Christian Science Monitor; © 1963 The Christian Science Publishing Society; all rights reserved), January 31, 1963, p. 14.*

A book which little children will surely enjoy poring over and one which should be very useful in library exhibits all through the year. Everything about the book—long, narrow shape, bright colors, and brief, direct text—is just right for its subject.

> *Ruth Hill Viguers, in her review of "The Parade Book," in* The Horn Book Magazine *(copyright © 1963, by The Horn Book, Inc., Boston), Vol. XXXIX, No. 1, February, 1963, p. 51.*

NIGHT'S NICE   (by Barbara Emberley, 1963)

Really effective illustrations illuminate this book of night's attractions and lead the young child to consider the myriad beauties of his world at night. There is an unusual and subtle use of color here: the darkening of reds, oranges, yellows, and greens to effect a definite feeling of night while retaining the full array of colors a child loves so much. This book shows a fuller use of the [illustrator's] talents than his previous *Wing on a Flea* and *Parade Book.*

> *Eileen Lampert, in her review of "Night's Nice," in* School Library Journal, *an appendix to* Library Journal *(reprinted from the October, 1963 issue of* School Library Journal, *published by R. R. Bowker Co./A Xerox Corporation; copyright © 1963), Vol. 10, No. 2, October, 1963, p. 190.*

THE STORY OF PAUL BUNYAN   (adapted by Barbara Emberley, 1963)

Exploits of Paul Bunyan are told in anecdotal picture-story form with no real feeling or flavor of a tall tale. Exaggerations in narrative are excessive, with doubtful appeal for small children. The woodcuts in brown with blue accents are massive and burlesqued. Bunyan appearing almost troll-like. Color is good. Ida V. Turney's *Paul Bunyan the Work Giant* (Binfords) is a much more satisfactory abbreviated or simplified version.

> *Teresa Anne Fehlig, in her review of "The Story of Paul Bunyan," in* School Library Journal, *an appendix to* Library Journal *(reprinted from the November, 1963 issue of* School Library Journal, *published by R. R. Bowker Co./A Xerox Corporation; copyright © 1963), Vol. 10, No. 3, November, 1963, p. 54.*

A compilation of some of the anecdotes that are contained in the Bunyan legendry. The woodcuts that illustrate the book are effective and lively, although some of the pages seem overfilled with detail. The style of writing is good, occasionally achieving the traditional tall-tale flavor, but occasionally, also, dropping into a flat, prosaic phrase or sentence. While the illustrations are not appropriate for younger children, the text may be so used.

> *Zena Sutherland, in her review of "The Story of Paul Bunyan," in* Bulletin of the Center for Children's Books *(reprinted by permission of The University of Chicago Press; copyright 1964 by the University of Chicago), Vol. XVII, No. 5, January, 1964, p. 76.*

In **"The Story of Paul Bunyan,"** . . . the comic exaggerations of the tall tale are beautifully rendered. Written in an easy, yarn-spinning prose, this rambling saga follows the gigantic lumberjack as he digs the Mississippi River in an afternoon, clears the entire West, reads all the books ever written and finally retires with his huge ox, "Babe," for a well earned rest. Ed Emberley's woodcuts, robust and joyful, serve the story well.

> *Barbara Wersba, in her review of "The Story of Paul Bunyan," in* The New York Times Book Review *(© 1964 by The New York Times Company; reprinted by permission), January 26, 1964, p. 26.*

Bold woodcuts in brown and blue interpret a succession of tall anecdotes. . . . Set in short lines of large type and so enjoyably enhanced by the lusty drawings, this selection of legendary bits about Paul should prove an easy-to-read, happy introduction to the tall-tale heroes. A striking graphic arts achievement.

> *Virginia Haviland, in her review of "The Story of Paul Bunyan," in* The Horn Book Magazine *(copyright ©1964, by The Horn Book, Inc., Boston), Vol. XL, No. 1, February, 1964, p. 48.*

[Ed Emberley's] interpretation of the blue ox, Babe, is too coy for our taste but Paul himself is properly overwhelming with his huge size set off by the puniness of trees and ordinary people. (p. 18)

> *"Granddaddies of All Our Stories," in* Book Week—The Washington Post *(© 1964, The Washington Post), May 10, 1964, pp. 18, 32.**

PUNCH AND JUDY   (by Ed Emberley, 1965)

This is humor at an elemental, physical level, but in a form which anyone can enjoy. On every other page Punch and one of the other eight characters is provided with the text of a scene, each complete with a smack in the kisser, blow on the beanie, or the equivalent. The colorful pictures on the facing pages show a four part sequence of the action. The hand puppets, stage and props can easily be approximated. An excellent outlet for exuberant young comedians, and an ideal introduction to the always popular art of puppetry.

> *A review of "Punch and Judy," in* Virginia Kirkus' Service, *Vol. XXXIII, No. 5, March 1, 1965, p. 240.*

The puppet-play is presented here ready for a performance by young puppeteers. A brief history of Punch and an illustrated cast of characters introduce the play. The gay illustrations are a show in themselves. Recommended.

> *Hope H. McGrady, in her review of "Punch and Judy," in* School Library Journal, *an appendix to* Library Journal *(reprinted from the April, 1965 issue of* School Library Journal, *published by R. R. Bowker Co./A Xerox Corporation; copyright © 1965), Vol. 11, No. 8, April, 1965, p. 56.*

Here enacted—scene by scene, four scenes to the page—is a Punch-and-Judy puppet play with all its slapstick merriment.

Decorative type appropriate to the particular personality introduces each character, and a ''short history of Mister Punch'' precedes the play. Breezily drawn figures, crosshatched with jarring colors, go whacking and smacking their way through a performance crowded with fast-swinging comedy. The action is uproarious, the effect ridiculously funny. Quite likely this will be the inspiration for a multitude of Punch-and-Judy productions; but even if a child never sees or engages in a play, he will have met Punch and all the other puppets in a really representative version. (pp. 295-96)

> *Priscilla L. Moulton, in her review of ''Punch and Judy,'' in* The Horn Book Magazine *(copyright © 1965, by The Horn Book, Inc., Boston), Vol. XLI, No. 3, June, 1965, pp. 295-96.*

An extremely lively and decorative presentation of the puppet show about the famous baby-beating couple, which has lasted 400 years in many countries (see the preface).

Shall we turn this terrible couple loose on the children? At the risk of being thought a sadist, I say ''Yes.'' The ending is ferociously moral and leaves nothing misunderstood. Seriously, I think older children can enjoy making and using the puppets and knowing something of their history.

> *A review of ''Punch and Judy,'' in* Saturday Review *(© 1965 Saturday Review Magazine Co.; reprinted by permission), Vol. XLVIII, No. 25, June 19, 1965, p. 41.*

ROSEBUD (by Ed Emberley, 1966)

This supplies an imaginative, adventurous life history for one of the most familiar and most phlegmatic of children's pets—the 5 & 10¢ store's handpainted turtle. . . . Emberley's cool green and blue water world and his animals are handsomely stylized but static, except in the baboon scenes.

> *A review of ''Rosebud,'' in* Virginia Kirkus' Service *(copyright © 1966 Virginia Kirkus' Service, Inc.), Vol. XXXIV, No. 2, January 15, 1966, p. 53.*

A handsome picture book. . . . The futile attempts of the turtle to become one of the jungle animals or birds are lightly humorous and should appeal to children. . . . Emberley's stylized illustrations, primarily in bold blues and greens with touches of rosy pink, are excellent.

> *Patricia Allen & others, in their review of ''Rosebud,'' in* School Library Journal, *an appendix to* Library Journal *(reprinted from the March, 1966 issue of* School Library Journal, *published by R. R. Bowker Co./A Xerox Corporation; copyright © 1966), Vol. 12, No. 7, March, 1966, p. 225.*

Any child who has ever brought a turtle home from a ten-cent store will enjoy this fantasy of a plain Jane turtle who wanted to be a painted lady. Not as distinguished as Mr. Emberley's **''Parade Book,''** but a bright picture book that will delight all turtle-fanciers.

> *A review of ''Rosebud,'' in* Publishers Weekly *(reprinted from the April 4, 1966 issue of* Publishers Weekly, *published by R. R. Bowker Company; copyright © 1966 by R. R. Bowker Company), Vol. 189, No. 14, April 4, 1966, p. 62.*

ONE WIDE RIVER TO CROSS (adapted by Barbara Emberley, 1966)

Ed Emberley bridges *One Wide River* . . . with his striking woodcut prints—an accompaniment to the folksong favorite about Noah and his ark (the music is included at the end). Visually, the book has as much verse and rhythm as the rousing song. . . . The stylized figures are all in black, but highly varied in their singular details and activities. The color is in the pages themselves, each in a different, brilliant tone. It's the kind of a book that can be looked at repeatedly—buy it in twos, be prepared to have it reread in tens.

> *A review of ''One Wide River to Cross,'' in* Virginia Kirkus' Service *(copyright © 1966 Virginia Kirkus' Service, Inc.), Vol. XXXIV, No. 14, July 15, 1966, p. 683.*

From strong figures on the pages that read ''The animals came in one by one, / And Japheth played the big bass drum,'' one progresses to the intricate repetitive design spreading across the pages reading ''The animals came in ten by ten, / Let's go back and start again.'' At last, against the multicolors of the rainbow, the ark, laden with a toylike village, rests between the peaks of Ararat. Unfortunately, credit is not given in the book to the traditional source of the wonderful song. . . . Only the jacket blurb refers to the text as ''an old folk song.'' The stunning visual experience can be given an extra dimension if the children are familiar with the music.

> *Ruth Hill Viguers, in her review of ''One Wide River to Cross,'' in* The Horn Book Magazine *(copyright © 1966, by The Horn Book, Inc., Boston), Vol. XLII, No. 5, October, 1966, p. 559.*

Ed Emberley puts the verses into illustrative form with masterly woodcuts, inked on brightly colored soft-grained pages that are a perfect mix of idea and image.

> *Barbara Novak O'Doherty, in her review of ''One Wide River to Cross,'' in* The New York Times Book Review *(© 1966 by The New York Times Company; reprinted by permission), October 16, 1966, p. 38.*

Any child will have a giggle over such lines as: ''The animals came in four by four, the hippopotamus blocked the door.'' The animals are depicted with equal wit. ''I can count'' children will relish checking the artist's number accuracy on each page and be awed by the 34 columns of animals on the last pages intricately arranged 10 by 10.

> *Kent Garland Burtt, ''The Mouse Was a Film Buff,'' in* The Christian Science Monitor *(reprinted by permission from* The Christian Science Monitor; *© 1966 The Christian Science Publishing Society; all rights reserved), November 3, 1966, p. B3.**

This is Noah's year—he and his Ark have had three interpretations. I think he would have been pleased with all three. The Emberleys' one, with Mrs. Emberley's crisp adaptation of the old folk song for the story and with Mr. Emberley's handsome woodcuts for the illustrations, might well be the one that would have pleased him most of all.

> *A review of ''One Wide River to Cross,'' in* Publishers Weekly *(reprinted from the December 26, 1966 issue of* Publishers Weekly, *published by R. R. Bowker Company; copyright © 1966 by R. R. Bowker Company), Vol. 190, No. 25, December 26, 1966, p. 99.*

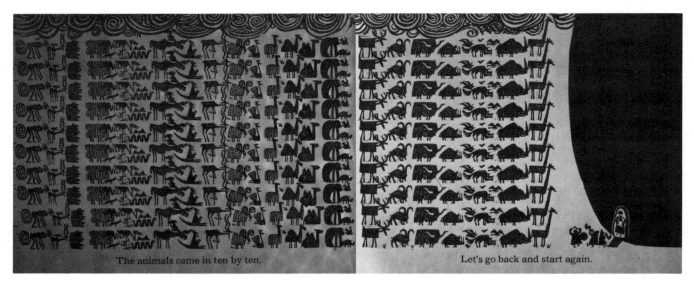

The animals came in ten by ten,   Let's go back and start again.

From One Wide River to Cross, *adapted by Barbara Emberley, illustrated by Ed Emberley.*

Ed Emberley's woodcuts . . . are extremely clever. Variety is given by printing on pages of different colours, the cuts themselves being black. Children old enough to examine Egyptian tombs in the British Museum will recognize the patterns.

A review of "One Wide River to Cross," in The Times Literary Supplement (© Times Newspapers Ltd. (London) 1969; reproduced from The Times Literary Supplement by permission), No. 3513, June 26, 1969, p. 695.

DRUMMER HOFF (adapted by Barbara Emberley, 1967)

AUTHOR'S COMMENTARY

Since the announcement of the Caldecott Award, my wife, Barbara, and I have often been asked about the preparation of *Drummer Hoff.* How was the technique developed? What steps were taken to turn a simple folk rhyme into a picture book? How does the adaptation differ from the original? And, surprisingly, what does it mean?

The drawings in *Drummer Hoff* are woodcuts. They were drawn on pine boards, all the white areas were cut away, ink was rolled on the remaining raised areas, and a set of prints was pulled on rice paper. The colors were added by using a technique I first tried in *One Wide River to Cross.* Although only three inks were employed—red, yellow, and blue—we were able to create the impression of thirteen distinct colors. This effect was accomplished by taking advantage of the fact that the inks with which most picture books are printed tend to be transparent. Therefore, by printing one ink over another, or "overprinting," a third color is made. For instance, if blue ink is printed over yellow ink, the yellow ink shows through and turns the blue ink green. Blue ink printed over red makes purple, and so forth. A separate drawing has to be made for each of the three colors, to show which color went over which color to make what color.

Since both the method of making the black line drawings and the method of coloring them seem unnecessarily complicated and time consuming, you may properly ask: Why bother? Why didn't you just draw the pictures instead of carving them and then just color them with water colors and send them to the printer?

Why I cut the pictures in wood instead of using a faster method like pen-and-ink drawings is hard to explain in a few words, but I suppose the most important reasons are that the pictures looked better and the method pleased me. It is easier to explain why we decided to use that particular method of printing the color. The sharpness and brilliance of the color in *Drummer Hoff* cannot be duplicated by any other practical printing process, including any "four color-full color" process.

You may have guessed by now that there is more to illustrating a picture book than knowing how to draw pictures. To an illustrator the picture on the drawing board is merely a means to an end. The end is the printed picture. An illustration could be defined as a picture that can be printed. A good picture is a bad illustration if it cannot be printed well.

And, of course, a bad picture is a bad picture no matter how well suited it is to the printing process.

I work in many different techniques when preparing illustrations—woodcuts, pencil, pen and ink. But as varied as they are in appearance they have one thing in common—the illustrations are meant to be printed. Although I am primarily an artist and not a printing expert, the necessity to be both dreamer and realist is what fascinates me most about picture-book making.

The original rhyme from which *Drummer Hoff* was evolved came from the *Annotated Mother Goose* by William S. and Ceil Baring-Gould. Entitled "John Ball Shot Them All," the verse [was] about the making of a rifle. . . .

In the adaptation, we first turned the rifle into a cannon to provide a more dramatic center of interest. The change led naturally to others. Military titles were substituted for the name John, since the gradations of rank from drummer to general accentuated the cumulative pattern of the book. Also, military uniforms provided the opportunity to make full use of the bright colors which the technique allowed. John Ball shooting them all did not seem an appropriate ending to the tale, so the refrain was changed to "Drummer Hoff fired it off." The name Drummer Hoff was selected (instead of Private Hoff or John Ball)

Captain Bammer
brought the rammer,
Sergeant Chowder
brought the powder,
Corporal Farrell
brought the barrel,
Private Parriage
brought the carriage,
but Drummer Hoff fired it off.

From Drummer Hoff, *adapted by Barbara Emberley, illustrated by Ed Emberley.*

because of its rich sound, and the "KAHBAH-BLOOM" was added just for fun, to give the book a good strong climax. The verse now reads:

> General Border gave the order,
> Major Scott brought the shot,
> Captain Bammer brought the rammer,
> Sergeant Chowder brought the powder,
> Corporal Farrell brought the barrel,
> Private Parriage brought the carriage,
> But Drummer Hoff fired it off.

The book's main theme is a simple one—a group of happy warriors build a cannon that goes "KAHBAHBLOOM." But, there is more to find if you "read" the pictures. They show that men can fall in love with war and, imitating the birds, go to meet it dressed as if to meet their sweethearts. The pictures also show that men can return from war sometimes with medals, and sometimes with wooden legs.

The book can have two endings. Many people prefer to stop at the "KAHBAHBLOOM" page. And for some purposes that is where the story should end. But others prefer to go on to the next page, which shows the cannon destroyed. The men have gone, and the birds and flowers that appear to be merely decorative through the first part of the book are in the process of taking over—again. The picture of the destroyed cannon was purposely put on a half page to keep it in its proper place as a minor theme. The main theme of the book is, I repeat, a group of happy warriors building a cannon that goes "KAHBAHBLOOM." The book's primary purpose is, as it should be, to entertain.

After I had been working less than two years as an artist, I started on my first children's book. I felt at the time that if I could inherit a million dollars on the condition that I stop doing art work of any kind, I could accept it with no regrets. As I started, I thought I was working at merely another job. Little did I know that I really had a tiger by the tail. For here I am, eight years and twenty-seven books later, not knowing who is the master, the art or the artist, and not caring. (pp. 200-03)

You might be interested to know how 'we' (Prentice-Hall, Barbara and I) felt about *Drummer Hoff*. We had no idea that it would ever become a popular book. It was designed for a

very few special (unknown) children. We thought the story line was too simple and naive and the art work too complicated and sophisticated to interest more than a very few. We were wrong. We still don't know why, even with the Caldecott, so many have found it interesting. (p. 204)

> *Ed Emberley, in his Caldecott Award acceptance speech in 1968, in* Newbery and Caldecott Medal Books 1966-1975, *edited by Lee Kingman (copyright © 1975 by the Horn Book, Inc.), Horn Book, 1975, pp. 199-204 [the excerpt of Barbara Emberley's poetry used here was originally published in her* Drummer Hoff *(© 1967 by Edward R. Emberley and Barbara Emberley; reprinted by permission of Prentice-Hall, Inc., Englewood Cliffs, New Jersey 07632), Prentice-Hall, Inc., 1967].*

On the first reading kids will join in the refrain; on the second they'll repeat the whole verse with you; on the third, with any encouragement, they'll reenact the entire procession—and explode at the end. The spark comes from the match of illustrations to text. They're wildly patterned, wildly colored woodcuts always under control until the grand and glorious blast-off, and then even Drummer Hoff burns.

> *A review of "Drummer Hoff," in* Kirkus Service *(copyright © 1967 Virginia Kirkus' Service, Inc.), Vol. XXXV, No. 20, October 15, 1967, p. 1264.*

[A] perfect wedding of text and pictures can be found in **"Drummer Hoff"**. . . . Irresistible for reading aloud, for memorizing, for pointing out all sorts of jolly details in the drawings. You don't have to be married to produce this wry, well-bred humor, but in the Emberleys' case, it doesn't hurt.

> *Eve Merriam, in her review of "Drummer Hoff," in* The New York Times Book Review *(© 1967 by The New York Times Company; reprinted by permission), November 5, 1967, p. 71.*

Stylized woodcuts in brilliant hues develop this martial folk rhyme into a sprightly book which the young child will enjoy again and again. The pictures are to be re-examined for their entertaining details (birds, ladybugs, and flowers appear and reappear), and the lines of the brief text are to be chanted for their alliterative nonsense. . . . An interesting contrast to the artist's more quietly charming *London Bridge Is Falling Down*. . . .

> Virginia Haviland, in her review of "Drummer Hoff," in The Horn Book Magazine *(copyright © 1968 by The Horn Book, Inc., Boston), Vol. XLIV, No. 1, February, 1968, p. 53.*

Ed Emberley has style. He has originality, superb technique and a lively sense of humor. All of these qualities find rich expression in this colorful picture book rendition of a cumulative folk verse. . . . No small boy should be able to resist this one.

> Polly Goodwin, in her review of "Drummer Hoff," in Book World—Chicago Tribune *(© 1968 Postrib Corp.; reprinted by permission of* Chicago Tribune *and* The Washington Post*), February 4, 1968, p. 22.*

The artist's unerring sense of design enables him to pace the text as it moves in snappy tempo. The brilliant colors over bold woodcut lines delineate the characters and their actions and the remarkable machine, which goes Kahbabloom!

> Sally Heifman, "Ed Emberley," in Top of the News *(reprinted by permission of the American Library Association), Vol. 24, No. 3, April, 1968, p. 274.*

[*Drummer Hoff*] is really just a song and is probably far more satisfying for the grown-up to read than for the child to listen to. . . . Though the pictures are amazingly bright and brilliant, and in the best possible (who am I to say) taste, they are really no more than carefully contrived graphic design; great on a Christmas card or a dishcloth, but not alive enough to hold a child's attention through a book. It was awarded the Caldecott Medal by the American Library Association for the most distinguished picture book in its year of publication, but I'm not sure that English children at any rate are after distinction in their reading matter. (p. 620)

> Candida Lycett Green, "Rich and Rare," in The Spectator *(© 1970 by* The Spectator; *reprinted by permission of* The Spectator*), Vol. 224, No. 7402, May 9, 1970, pp. 620-21.**

LONDON BRIDGE IS FALLING DOWN   (by Ed Emberley, 1967)

In the gaggle of Mother Goose volumes is Ed Emberley's "**London Bridge Is Falling Down**". . . . That venerable structure tumbles into a frothy current of curls and swirls. . . . Mr. Emberley offers a variety of verses, the music, a short history and instructions for playing the game of London Bridge along with his decorative and delicate pastel illustrations.

> George A. Woods, "A Gaggle of Goose and Grimm," in The New York Times Book Review *(© 1967 by The New York Times Company; reprinted by permission), October 29, 1967, p. 42.**

Ed Emberley's pictures in pale pinks, greens, blues, and yellows are imaginative rather than factual, with bewigged soldiers parading, a Heath Robinson iron bridge, and delicate little flowers cropping up unexpectedly.

> Patience M. Daltry, "Back to Olden Rhymes," in The Christian Science Monitor *(reprinted by permission from* The Christian Science Monitor; *© 1967 The Christian Science Publishing Society; all rights reserved), November 2, 1967, p. B3.**

Ed Emberley's *London Bridge Is Falling Down: The Song and the Game* has a bright, stylized flavor to it, the rhyme being illustrated with drawings that are as crisp and brittle as a bright, shiny whirligig. The book has a fine sense of immediacy, as well as humor—and Emberley's inclusion of the game is a special bonus. (p. 3)

> John Gruen, "Wild, Crazy, Mixed-Up Mother Goose," in Book World—Chicago Tribune *(© 1967 Postrib Corp.; reprinted by permission of* Chicago Tribune *and* The Washington Post*), November 5, 1967, pp. 2-3.**

[The] river scene is rendered in stylized fashion, a sense of movement being created by swirling concentric lines, and a feeling of period by meticulous domestic details. Quiet in effect, with pastel tones in its four-color art, this book may less directly attract a child [than Peter Spier's *London Bridge Is Falling Down!*].

> Virginia Haviland, in her review of "London Bridge Is Falling Down," in The Horn Book Magazine *(copyright ©1967, by The Horn Book, Inc., Boston), Vol. XLIII, No. 6, December, 1967, p. 743.*

GREEN SAYS GO   (by Ed Emberley, 1968)

This picture book attempts to say about colors what the author's *The Wing on a Flea* . . . said about shapes, but it is not nearly so successful. It is illustrated with poorly reproduced colors (red is fuschia on one page, almost orange on another) that combine unattractively with heavy, curlicued silhouettes. The last few pages, which attempt to define and show how colors invoke various moods and characteristics (yellow means cowardice, green means envy) are more in the style of *The Wing on a Flea*, but are offered with no textual discussion. Elsewhere, the text is also too cursory to be of any value: it is explained that on a ship red means port and green starboard, but these terms are not related to left and right. Mr. Emberley's previous successes were characterized by more care in conception and execution than is this unfortunate jumble.

> Marjorie Lewis, in her review of "Green Says Go," in School Library Journal, *an appendix to* Library Journal *(reprinted from the November, 1968 issue of* School Library Journal, *published by R. R. Bowker Co./A Xerox Corporation; copyright © 1968), Vol. 15, No. 3, November, 1968, p. 76.*

For the companion to his earlier, notable concept book about shapes, *The Wing on a Flea*, the author-illustrator uses disks of color, overlaid to explain secondary colors, or darkened or lightened to show the effects of mixing them with black or white. Other circles of color are given specific meaning: traffic lights, car headlights, ship lights. Finally, color is shown in amusing examples of speech and custom: A purple face on a fuchsia page screams, "I'm purple with rage," while a scowling coward opposite says, "I'm yellow." The book is effective because the illustrative examples are clear; and a final page, which notes "These are not all the things that colors say," raises questions a child should be able to answer. (pp. 681-82)

> Virginia Haviland, in her review of "Green Says Go," in The Horn Book Magazine *(copyright © 1968 by The Horn Book, Inc., Boston), Vol. XLIV, No. 6, December, 1968, pp. 681-82.*

SIMON'S SONG (adapted by Barbara Emberley, 1969)

Simon's Song relates the further follies of the simpleton who sought to buy a pie but hadn't any penny. . . . Accompanying are woodcuts in persimmon, spring green and sailor blue with figures that look like snap-ons and decorations that look like stick-ons—but the best accompaniment will be a teacher at the piano. This because the illustrations, though delightful, are disjointed and show to better advantage at a distance, and because, with the appended music, the whole could spark a lively sing-along session. (pp. 848-49)

> *A review of "Simon's Song," in* Kirkus Reviews *(copyright © 1969 The Kirkus Service, Inc.), Vol. XXXVII, No, 16, August 15, 1969, pp. 848-49.*

The disappointment of this quartet [of books being reviewed] is *Simon's Song,* in which Ed Emberley illustrates the venerable adventures of Simple Simon in stark greens, blues, and oranges that sometimes work but sometimes resolutely refuse to come together into a total conception.

> *Clifford A. Ridley, "Artists Add a Colorful Touch to Lear Nonsense," in* The National Observer *(reprinted by permission of* The National Observer; *© Dow Jones & Company, Inc. 1969; all rights reserved), November 3, 1969, p. 21.**

An exuberant adaptation of the Simple Simon nursery song, illustrated with fanciful woodcuts in bright orange, blue and green. The figures, reminiscent of old-fashioned jointed wooden dolls, are composed of many unconnected shapes, and sometimes the parts are easier to see than the whole. However, the pictures have so much movement that they almost seem animated. Also, the designs are well adapted to the medium and to the rollicking fun of the silly rhymes. Mrs. Emberley has added several delightful, generally unfamiliar verses to the well-known first four and thereby prolonged the enjoyment. The musical notes for the song are given at the end along with a listing of all the verses. Decorated as it is here, this rhyme will become a favorite for looking as well as for listening and reciting.

> *Anne Greenwood, in her review of "Simon's Song," in* School Library Journal, *an appendix to* Library Journal *(reprinted from the December, 1969 issue of* School Library Journal, *published by R. R. Bowker Co./A Xerox Corporation; copyright © 1969), Vol. 16, No. 4, December, 1969, p. 40.*

Ed Emberley has illustrated this book with woodcuts which very much resemble those in *Drummer Hoff*. . . . The humorous verses and the unique woodcut technique combine to make the book a delightful one to read to small children or to let them read for themselves when they are able.

> *A review of "Simon's Song," in* Catholic Library World, *Vol. 41, No. 9, May-June, 1970, p. 593.*

ED EMBERLEY'S DRAWING BOOK OF ANIMALS (by Ed Emberley, 1970)

Here is a winner for any book department—it can't help selling. For Caldecott-winning Ed Emberley has made a drawing book that makes drawing fun, or makes it look like fun. So stock up on this one, and listen to the music of the busy cash register.

> *A review of "Ed Emberley's Drawing Book of Animals," in* Publishers Weekly *(reprinted from the February 2, 1970 issue of* Publishers Weekly, *published by R. R. Bowker Company, a Xerox company; copyright © 1970 by Xerox Corporation), Vol. 197, No. 5, February 2, 1970, p. 90.*

There are things I could have been doing today. . . . Nothing was done because I got bogged down in **"Ed Emberley's Drawing Book of Animals"**. . . . The book told me that if I could draw simple shapes (triangle, rectangle, circle), a few numbers, letters and "things" (dots, curlicues and scratchy scribbles), then I could draw the animals here—over fifty—from ants and alligators to whale, worm and wolf running.

Well, it worked. I followed the step-by-step diagrams—. . . added a "thing," a shape or a number here and there and *voila!* a fat cat, a turtle skating in the rain, a pig with trousers. Of course I didn't have the benefit of the colors used in the book, so my giraffe's a little limp, my tiger too plain, but I've got a pad full of impressive doodles and drawings and my kids think I'm a genius!

> *George A. Woods, in his review of "Ed Emberley's Drawing Book of Animals," in* The New York Times Book Review *(©1970 by The New York Times Company; reprinted by permission), March 1, 1970, p. 34.*

Out of a basic vocabulary of forms, an infinite number of things . . . from the single dot that's an ant to the successive steps and many shapes that go into making a dragon. It's fun to see each figure come into being, circle by wedge by stroke, fun too to see them take off—turtle turns into "turtle sleeping," "turtle dancing," "turtle skating in the rain." Likewise there's more than one way to look at "dog"—as bulldog, dachshund, shaggy dog. "Notes, hints and suggestions" for change append (best are the gamut from grumpy to laughing faces, front and side) but there's a spontaneity that resists standardization anyhow—and why concentrate on copying what you can so easily approximate? Of its sort, the most entertaining, the least circumscribed.

> *A review of "Ed Emberley's Drawing Book of Animals," in* Kirkus Reviews *(copyright © 1970 The Kirkus Service, Inc.), Vol. XXXVIII, No. 8, April 15, 1970, p. 459.*

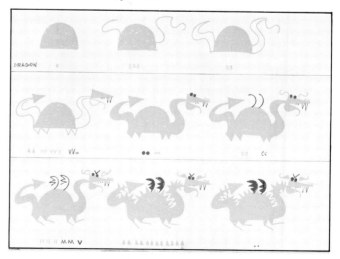

From Ed Emberley's Drawing Book of Animals, *written and illustrated by Ed Emberley.*

["**Ed Emberley's Drawing Book of Animals**"] can turn anyone over the age of eight into an instant artist. It works with me, so it will work with anyone. . . . His book has no literary pretensions at all and may well offend the free-drawing advocates, but it makes an encouraging book for those, adults included, who imagine they can't draw for toffee. It's a splendid book for whiling away a dull afternoon.

> *Pamela Marsh, "Shopping a Child's World," in* The Christian Science Monitor *(reprinted by permission from* The Christian Science Monitor; © *1970 The Christian Science Publishing Society; all rights reserved), May 7, 1970, p. B1.*

[*Ed Emberley's Drawing Book of Animals*] is that all but unheard-of success, a "how-to-draw" book that really works. Nearly everyone would like to be able to sketch a grumpy spider, a smiling octopus, or a porcupine jumping over a stone. Now, it turns out, nearly anyone from the age of five up can do just that. . . . With clear, entertaining verbal instructions, visual examples lead easily from simple dots to scaly dragons. The book is a splendid departure for Emberley, who has previously won readers and prizes for brisk, handsome woodcuts and brief texts. . . . (p. 68)

> *Timothy Foote, in his review of "Ed Emberley's Drawing Book of Animals," in* Time *(copyright 1970 Time Inc.; all rights reserved; reprinted by permission from* Time*), Vol. 96, No. 25, December 21, 1970, pp. 68, 72-4.*

ED EMBERLEY'S DRAWING BOOK: MAKE A WORLD   (by Ed Emberley, 1972)

Ed Emberley's smart and simple *Animal Drawing Book* . . . was a disarmingly contemporary example of the popular if not quite respectable add-a-line drawing lesson. There are not only more animals here but all sorts of cars, trucks, planes, boats, wagons, furniture, buildings, people, and "this and that." The crowding of each page with ten to 30 items and up to nine steps in the construction of each item makes the book less attractive than its predecessor, but the great variety of objects may be just what devotees of the animal book have been waiting for. Emberley invites junior cartoonists to take off on their own from the basics he supplies, and he makes it seem so easy and enjoyable that they're bound to go on to more creative doodling. (pp. 65-6)

> *A review of "Ed Emberley's Drawing Book: Make a World," in* Kirkus Reviews *(copyright © 1972 The Kirkus Service, Inc.), Vol. XL, No. 2, January 15, 1972, pp. 65-6.*

A welcome companion volume to *Ed Emberley's Drawing Book of Animals.* The young artist has been given enough instructions and items to draw to make his own world. Each page is covered with pictures—ambulances, cranes, train stations, gondolas, robots, anteaters, flags, faces—and provides hours of drawing delight. The final three pages, which supply suggestions for making comic strips, posters, mobiles, and games, help make the volume particularly appealing. For all developing artists and even for plain scribblers.

> *A review of "Ed Emberley's Drawing Book: Make a World," in* The Horn Book Magazine *(copyright © 1972 by The Horn Book, Inc., Boston), Vol. XLVIII, No. 2, April, 1972, p. 164.*

Emberley gives directions for drawing, among a myriad other things, 10 different kinds of cars, 16 varieties of trucks, and animals of all species including anteaters and dinosaurs. The drawings are emblematic rather than realistic—and can be executed by any child who has mastered the formation of a circle, triangle, rectangle, the numeral 3, and the letters Y, L, C, S, V, W, and U. Children are likely to be surprised by the things they *can* draw just by following ingeniously simple, step-by-step directions. For those who would protest that such instruction stifles a child's creativity, it should be noted that rules and manuals have long been a part of formal art study. Ed Emberley makes no claim that his schema are the only way to draw.

> *Helen Andrejevic, "Child's Play," in* Book World— Chicago Tribune *(© 1972 Postrib Corp.; reprinted by permission of* Chicago Tribune *and The Washington Post), May 7, 1972, p. 14.*

The book is colorful; while it can give children ideas about the use of shapes in space, it probably teaches them to copy rather than to draw. Double-page spreads are devoted to topics (animals, boats, "inside stuff," "outside stuff," etc.) with each page divided horizontally into narrow bands, each filled with a series of progressive drawings, so that the pages are gay but are crowded with tiny pictures, too small-scale to be very useful, save for adults working with bulletin boards. (pp. 154-55)

> *Zena Sutherland, in her review of "Ed Emberley's Drawing Book: Make a World," in* Bulletin of the Center for Children's Books *(reprinted by permission of The University of Chicago Press; © 1972 by The University of Chicago), Vol. 25, No. 10, June, 1972, pp. 154-55.*

KLIPPITY KLOP   (by Ed Emberley, 1974)

With no introduction nor any need for one, "Prince Krispen and Dumpling went for a ride." Then in a solid minimum of words and expertly unsophisticated fine line drawings on tan paper, the small toylike prince and his almost hobby-horsy steed ride over a bridge (KLUMP KLUMPITY KLUMPITY KLUMP), across a stream (KERPLASH KERPLOSH), through a field (KWISH KWASH) and so on to a cave where a dragon "looked out and yelled at them! KARRRRAAA-AGGGGAAHHHH"—sending Prince Krispen and Dumpling back the way they came. KLLLANG! The final slamming of the castle gate behind them is visibly loud and all the klumps and krunches are integrated not with the text but with the pictures—to be discovered independently by beginning readers or recited by a story hour chorus (though the scale and absence of color calls for a small group).

> *A review of "Klippity Klop," in* Kirkus Reviews *(copyright © 1974 The Kirkus Service, Inc.), Vol. XLII, No. 18, September 15, 1974, p. 1004.*

Pencil drawings on buff colored paper are rich in detail (animals and monsters, which are hardly visible in the journey to the cave, are seen running for cover on the return trip). A rollicking ride for primary graders.

> *Helen Gregory, in her review of "Klippity Klop," in* School Library Journal, *an appendix to* Library Journal *(reprinted from the December, 1974 issue of* School Library Journal, *published by R. R. Bowker*

Co./A Xerox Corporation; copyright © 1974), Vol. 21, No. 4, December, 1974, p. 36.

Line drawings, black on beige pages, include on almost every page a narrow frieze of onomatopoeic words that imitate the various sounds made by a horse's hooves as it goes at various paces and over various surfaces. . . . The reversing of pattern appeals to children, as does the opportunity to participate in making the hoof sounds, and the book has a blithe simplicity that is engaging—yet it has an adventure, a climax of action, and a satisfying, problem-solving ending. (pp. 111-12)

> *Zena Sutherland, in her review of "Klippity Klop," in* Bulletin of the Center for Children's Books *(reprinted by permission of The University of Chicago Press; © 1975 by The University of Chicago), Vol. 28, No. 7, March, 1975, pp. 111-12.*

ED EMBERLEY'S DRAWING BOOK OF FACES (by Ed Emberley, 1975)

Emberley's step-by-step cartoons of human and animal faces are far less varied and versatile than his *Make a World* [and *Animal*] drawing books. However, if this results in just a fraction of the creative doodling that the previous books inspired (even though it won't appeal to as wide an age range), it's worth the purchase.

> *A review of "Ed Emberley's Drawing Book of Faces," in* Kirkus Reviews *(copyright © 1975 The Kirkus Service, Inc.), Vol. XLIII, No. 9, May 1, 1975, p. 509.*

Emberley shows how to embellish a simple shape so that it becomes an amusing character—e.g., Doctor Diane, Eagle Earnest, Lion Leonard. One row of instruction shows what to draw and one row shows where to put it. Most people and animal faces are accomplished in six to eight steps and the author maintains that if children can "draw 7 things, they can draw all kinds of faces." A concluding section includes helpful hints on changing any face to a new personality, and an index is appended. Simple instruction for beginners, this is a worthwhile addition to school and public libraries.

> *Deborah S. Karesh, in her review of "Ed Emberley's Drawing Book of Faces," in* School Library Journal *(reprinted from the October, 1975 issue of* School Library Journal, *published by R. R. Bowker Co./A Xerox Corporation; copyright © 1975), Vol. 22, No. 2, October, 1975, p. 98.*

[*Ed Emberley's Drawing Book of Faces* shows] any child how he, or she, can draw faces that look like something, with recognisable expressions. All they need to be able to do is to draw moderately straight lines and half circles, triangles, squares and squiggles. It is not possible to count up just how many different faces, expressions and positions the author has illustrated but it is prodigious and a real eye opener as to how simple the process is. This book should appeal to every child and to most adults too.

> *A review of "Ed Emberley's Drawing Book of Faces," in* The Junior Bookshelf, *Vol. 42, No. 2, April, 1978, p. 87.*

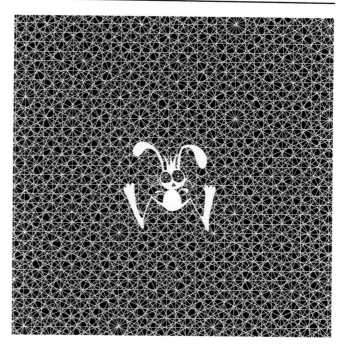

From The Wizard of Op, *written and illustrated by Ed Emberley.*

THE WIZARD OF OP (by Ed Emberley, 1975)

[In "**The Wizard of Op**"] Ed Emberley makes magic using a palette of glorious black and white. The pages are laid out comic book style with asides and exclamations that are par for the genre; "Huzzah," "BONK" and "oogly boogly" abound. A prince is turned into a frog. To de-frog him a bumbling wizard produces a series of optical tricks. Squares seen as curves, colors that bloom where there is only black and white and other such visual delights are put before us. The story plus special effects is original and dizzying.

> *Karla Kuskin, in her review of "The Wizard of Op," in* The New York Times Book Review *(© 1975 by The New York Times Company; reprinted by permission), November 16, 1975, p. 58.*

Would you like to have spots appear before your eyes? How about swirling lines or twirling circles? An intriguing and amusingly disturbing collection of optical illusions, this book is a good children's version of a "coffee table" book. . . . This story is well told with entertaining cartoons and imaginative vocabulary. However, the illustrations, each of which is spread over two pages, are the true highlight. This book is sure to appeal to adults, as well as to selected children.

> *Ellen M. Davidson, in her review of "The Wizard of Op," in* Children's Book Review Service *(copyright © 1976 Children's Book Review Service Inc.), Vol. 4, No. 5, January, 1976, p. 42.*

Many of the book's busy black-and-white comic strip-style pictures are very small, and much of the story (what there is of it) is contained in little signs. The dizzying effect of the Wizard of Op's spells, which are drawn as optical illusions, might be enjoyed by older children, but the attention of young children will not be held by the story.

Catherine A. Coté, in her review of "The Wizard of Op," in School Library Journal *(reprinted from the February, 1976 issue of* School Library Journal, *published by R. R. Bowker Co./A Xerox Corporation; copyright © 1976), Vol. 22, No. 6, February, 1976, p. 38.*

This picture book combines a funny strip cartoon story successfully with a convincing series of optical illusions, showing the reader how to reproduce them for himself. . . . [*The Wizard of Op*] works with op-tickle illusions. The Prince is his first ever customer, so he has to find the right spell by trial and error, the latter producing an hilarious series of transformations, until the Prince regains his shape, though still given to frog-like leaps, while the Wizard disappears—where? Ah! The double-spread black-and-white patterns are startlingly effective: the reader, aided by the wizard's hints, "sees" all kinds of non-existent things: an ingenious source of amusement and delight.

A review of "The Wizard of Op," in The Junior Bookshelf, *Vol. 41, No. 5, October, 1977, p. 275.*

ED EMBERLEY'S GREAT THUMBPRINT DRAWING BOOK (by Ed Emberley, 1977)

In a style similar to *Ed Emberley's Drawing Book of Animals* [and *Ed Emberley's Drawing Book: Make a World*], the artist shows how to combine thumbprints and simple lines to create a multitude of animals, people, birds, and flowers. In the "people" section, the artist uses short strokes to show action, change facial expressions, add hats, and make a variety of hair styles. Combining thumbprints results in flower gardens, trains, dragons, and butterflies. Final directions, which might have been more helpful placed in the beginning, show how to make the prints. Although artistic purists might find this stultifying, young readers will be sure to branch out and experiment with their own thumb smudging.

Barbara Elleman, in her review of "Ed Emberley's Great Thumbprint Drawing Book," in Booklist *(reprinted by permission of the American Library Association; copyright ©1977 by the American Library Association), Vol. 73, No. 18, May 15, 1977, p. 1419.*

Another Emberley gem, this begins with a thumbprint and, following his standard format, shows how a few simple lines can turn the print into animals and people in various poses. The step-by-step method is easy to follow, and Emberley's uncomplicated stylized drawings can be attractively reproduced by young children, even pre-readers. Some of the thumbprint figures are similar to those in Marjorie Katz's *Fingerprint Owls and Other Fantasies* (Evans, dist. by Lippincott, 1972) but the format of the books differs; Katz shows only the finished figure, while Emberley more wisely demonstrates methods.

Lynn S. Hunter, in her review of "Ed Emberley's Great Thumbprint Drawing Book," in School Library Journal *(reprinted from the September, 1977 issue of* School Library Journal, *published by R. R. Bowker Co./A Xerox Corporation; copyright © 1977), Vol. 24, No. 1, September, 1977, p. 106.*

Simple thumbprint drawings and instructions on how to make them are presented in a readable and understandable format. The cheery illustrations may encourage children to design their own original thumb creatures, which can then serve as story starters.

Ann Terry, in her review of "Ed Emberley's Great Thumbprint Drawing Book" (copyright 1978 by the International Reading Association, Inc.; reprinted with permission of the International Reading Association and Ann Terry), in The Reading Teacher, *Vol. 32, No. 1, October, 1978, p. 30.*

A BIRTHDAY WISH (by Ed Emberley, 1977)

Children will enjoy figuring out how one accidental incident leads to the next in this wordless picture book featuring a young mouse who makes a silent birthday wish for ice cream. Through an unlikely and humorous chain of events, the wish comes true. Emberley pays great attention to small comic details (e.g., an ant fire department, a business partnership between a woodpecker and a beaver called "Peck n' Chaw Builders," etc.) which should make this a popular book.

Micki Nevett, in her review of "A Birthday Wish," in School Library Journal *(reprinted from the November, 1977 issue of* School Library Journal, *published by R. R. Bowker Co./A Xerox Corporation; copyright © 1977), Vol. 24, No. 3, November, 1977, p. 46.*

Ed Emberley wrote and drew *A Birthday Wish,* but he didn't write too much—and that is an important part of the joke. . . .

Soft color enhances the easy-to-understand drawings of familiar children's books types—ducks, moles, frogs, pigs, cats, fish, bugs, and even a fox dressed up as Robin Hood.

For a good read without words, wish for *A Birthday Wish.*

Gene Langley, "Pull Up Your Argyles and Try the Turtle Trot," in The Christian Science Monitor *(reprinted by permission from* The Christian Science Monitor; *© 1977 The Christian Science Publishing Society; all rights reserved), November 2, 1977, p. B8.**

ED EMBERLEY'S A B C (by Ed Emberley, 1978)

"Ed Emberley's A B C" will be a hard act to follow. The book is an eye-dazzler—from its orange, purple and olive-drab endpaper swirls right on through each near psychedelically-bright color spread. Every letter gets star billing: two full pages in which to present its own evolving portrait via an ingenious, four-frame, animated mini-drama. Take B, for example: the letter is formed by a ladybug placing blueberries in precisely the sequence of line and half-circles it properly takes to print that letter. A *b*ear wearing bifocals and watching the proceedings provides the B word. Mr. Emberley is full of surprises: he throws in a family of *p*igs to represent I, a fo*x* for X.

Unorthodox, but why not? At the book's end, the artist reviews the sequence of strokes forming each letter and suggests more things to be found representing each letter in his illustrations. And if he spells daisy and zeppelin wrong, an artist who suggests an unguiculate for U can be forgiven. It's an alphabet not to be missed.

Selma G. Lanes, in her review of "Ed Emberley's A B C," in The New York Times Book Review *(© 1978 by The New York Times Company; reprinted by permission), July 2, 1978, p. 11.*

[The] artist has accepted the challenge of the alphabet book and has created a substantial and original piece of work. Each double-page spread shows several items representing a letter, and every one of the twenty-six characters is generated right before the reader's eyes by an animal's activity depicted in four separate panels. For example, . . . a contented horse munches hay while a literate hen weaves some of the stalks into an *H;* and a robot propelling a paint roller fashions a large letter *R.* The pictures are filled with enough goings-on and detail to invite concentrated examination; indeed, a few of them are almost too jammed with energetic busyness. But the pages show great ingenuity of conception and design, the color work is strikingly beautiful and subtle, and the whole book—including jacket, binding, end papers, and hand-lettered text—constitutes a handsome, unified production. In the catalog of "some things for you to find" several errors occur: A yellow and a black ukelele are listed, but only a yellow one is visible; and the words *daisy, fireflies, jackknife,* and *zeppelin* are misspelled. (pp. 386-87)

> *Ethel L. Heins, in her review of "Ed Emberley's A B C," in* The Horn Book Magazine *(copyright © 1978 by The Horn Book, Inc., Boston), Vol. LIV, No. 4, August, 1978, pp. 385-87.*

This intriguing alphabet book will surely be a hit with the concept book crowd. Like *Anno's Alphabet: an Adventure in Imagination* by Mitsumasa Anno (Crowell, 1975), Emberley's book pays great attention to detail; the formation of the letters is emphasized and readers are encouraged to find numerous examples of objects that begin with the featured letter within the pages of the book (e.g., "G" not only stands for geese, but for golf, grass, green, grapes, geraniums, etc.). A listing of these words appears at the end of the book. Unlike Mitsumasa's book, however, this one will rarely sit proudly on a coffee table. Rather, it will be snatched up by children eager to peruse its colorful, fun-loving, action-filled pages. Each letter is humorously and imaginatively drawn in four sequences which present the actual steps in printing the letter (e.g., a tiger and a turtle construct the letter "T" on a tray out of tinker toys). A must purchase for every children's collection.

> *Gemma DeVinney, in her review of "Ed Emberley's A B C," in* School Library Journal *(reprinted from the September, 1978 issue of* School Library Journal, *published by R. R. Bowker Co./A Xerox Corporation; copyright © 1978), Vol. 25, No. 1, September, 1978, p. 107.*

[*Ed Emberley's A B C*] is rather elaborately designed but static. Each spread consists of four pictures in saturated colors in which the letter is built either positively or negatively. . . . It's all very handsomely done, very ornamental, but seems too contrived—more clever than fun.

> *Burt Supree, in his review of "Ed Emberley's A B C" (reprinted by permission of* The Village Voice *and the author; copyright © The Village Voice, Inc., 1978), in* The Village Voice, *Vol. XXIII, No. 52, December 25, 1978, p. 99.*

This is not a book for really young children. While the figures on each page tell a story or present a situation, often amusingly, the art is sophisticated, and such difficult words as 'Ukelele', 'Unguiculate', 'Zeppelin' are used. 'N' is represented by words *ending* in 'N', 'I' by words *containing* the letter 'I'. The letter 'X' is particularly puzzling for a child, for again it comes at the end of the words given, one of which is in American spelling, 'Ax'.

For most children this will be more of a puzzle book than an alphabet book.

> *A review of "Ed Emberley's A B C," in* The Junior Bookshelf, *Vol. 43, No. 6, December, 1979, p. 316.*

ED EMBERLEY'S AMAZING LOOK THROUGH BOOK   (by Ed Emberley, 1979)

A neat trick of a nonbook—which might serve incidentally as an early reading lure. Each right-hand page shows an enigmatic cluster of shapes, a clue . . . , and one or more letters of the name of the animal—which, when the page is held to light, emerges complete. . . . Nifty design? Natch. Gimmick? To be sure.

> *A review of "Ed Emberley's Amazing Look Through Book," in* Kirkus Reviews *(copyright © 1979 The Kirkus Service, Inc.), Vol. XLVII, No. 9, May 1, 1979, p. 513.*

The stylized, semi-completed pictures in shades of pink and blue are built via use of only two shapes, something not readily apparent until a hard-to-read, gridded notice. They start out with an easily identifiable cat and gradually escalate in difficulty. Young children will enjoy the ferreting out—this will get plenty of use as a novelty item. . . .

> *Denise M. Wilms, in her review of "Ed Emberley's Amazing Look Through Book," in* Booklist *(reprinted by permission of the American Library Association; copyright © 1979 by the American Library Association), Vol. 75, No. 18, May 15, 1979, p. 1438.*

Each page has an abstract, cut paper, geometrically shaped illustration of an animal. . . . As a teaching aid, the idea might have some use, but as a picture book the gimmick isn't very interesting and the format seems crowded and forced. Not on a par with *Emberley's A B C* . . . or his shapes book, *The Wing on a Flea.* . . .

> *Hara L. Seltzer, in her review of "Ed Emberley's Amazing Look Through Book," in* School Library Journal *(reprinted from the September, 1979 issue of* School Library Journal, *published by R. R. Bowker Co./A Xerox Corporation; copyright © 1979), Vol. 26, No. 1, September, 1979, p. 109.*

Something new, a book that has a strong game element, can be used by beginning spellers to reinforce their efforts. . . . All of the pictures are of animal forms, and each recto page (the missing details are on the reverse of the page) carries a clue above the identifying word; these clues are the one weakness of the book, for two reasons: one is that they are a bit cutesy (dog is "a fuzzy roofer," owl is "he who hoos," and mice are "three wee squeakers") and the other is that some of the clue words may be difficult for a child who's spelling "cat" and "dog." (pp. 26-7)

> *Zena Sutherland, in her review of "Ed Emberley's Amazing Look Through Book," in* Bulletin of the Center for Children's Books *(reprinted by permission of The University of Chicago Press; © 1979 by The University of Chicago), Vol. 33, No. 2, October, 1979, pp. 26-7.*

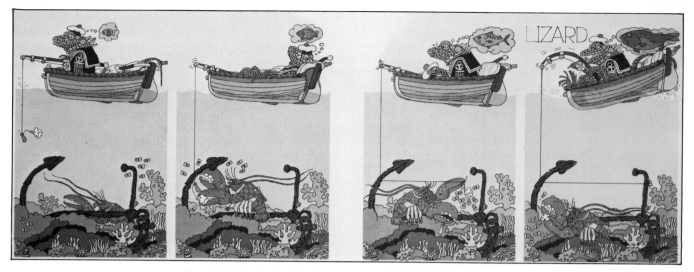

From Ed Emberley's A B C, *written and illustrated by Ed Emberley.*

ED EMBERLEY'S BIG GREEN DRAWING BOOK (by Ed Emberley, 1979)

Kids warm to Emberley's doodle-it-yourself lessons even if art-minded adults don't. (He's inserted Van Gogh's musing "Lots of people copy, lots of people don't copy. I copy. I find it teaches me things and above all it gives me consolation.") This time it's "práta people" (Prata is the old Irish name for the potato) and other creatures kids can draw, each made essentially by putting together basic shapes. Easy-to-follow, step-by-step drawings (all in green) guarantee successful results. If Emberley's drawing books are popular, put this one alongside them.

> *Denise M. Wilms, in her review of "Ed Emberley's Big Green Drawing Book," in* Booklist *(reprinted by permission of the American Library Association; copyright © 1979 by the American Library Association), Vol. 76, No. 1, September 1, 1979, p. 42.*

Emberley hasn't lost his talent for providing an enjoyable, frustration-free drawing experience for children. Here he combines basic shapes (circles, triangles, lines, squiggles) to create a variety of cartoon people and animals. The crisp green-and-black illustrations on a white background are large and well spaced, thus avoiding the cramped appearance of *Ed Emberley's Drawing Book: Make a World*. . . . As in his other drawing books, Emberley's wordless step-by-step method is easy to follow; even very young children can successfully reproduce the simple but appealing figures.

> *Lynn S. Hunter, in her review of "Ed Emberley's Big Green Drawing Book," in* School Library Journal *(reprinted from the November, 1979 issue of* School Library Journal, *published by R. R. Bowker Co./A Xerox Corporation; copyright © 1979), Vol. 26, No. 3, November, 1979, p. 64.*

Once you have joined two circles that look like a práta (pronounced "pray-tee"), you can advance to more ambitious projects: connecting circles and lines to form Irish men, women, lads and lassies, St. Patrick, etc. But Emberley's generous compendium of things green also features instructions on how to create catalogs (cats out of log shapes), crocolators (combined crocodiles and alligators) and many more comic critters, including beings on the alien planet Zort: the Zortian horse Woofler, the wild Fwaap and the dreadful Rok.

> *A review of "Ed Emberley's Big Green Drawing Book," in* Publishers Weekly *(reprinted from the December 10, 1979 issue of* Publishers Weekly, *published by R. R. Bowker Company, a Xerox company; copyright © 1979 by Xerox Corporation), Vol. 216, No. 24, December 10, 1979, p. 70.*

[Emberley] explains in the front endpapers (there is no paper wasted here) that *prata* is an old Irish name for potato, but these cartoon figures might just as well be based on peanut forms. Departing from *pratai*, Emberley also has some fun with . . . dressed-up tracings of hands, and with other more complicated figures including a Jekyll-Hyde head that flips personalities as you turn it upside down. . . . [This] seems to be a catchall for Emberley's odds and ends—not as basic and nifty as some of his drawing books, though ingenious enough to amuse.

> *A review of "Ed Emberley's Big Green Drawing Book," in* Kirkus Reviews *(copyright © 1980 The Kirkus Service, Inc.), Vol. XLVIII, No. 3, February 1, 1980, p. 129.*

ED EMBERLEY'S BIG ORANGE DRAWING BOOK (by Ed Emberley, 1980)

Like Emberley's **Big Green Drawing Book** . . . , this starts with a basic shape—a potato in the previous book, here a carrot that can become a clown, mouse, bird, bee, or rocket—but then settles into a series of step-by-step drawings. Most of these are geared to Halloween . . . , but Emberley also throws in a lobster and a lobster boat, a ship, and some mechanical space creatures. Like the green book, it's second-class Emberley, but good for some doodling diversion—and this one can help to satisfy some of that Halloween fever.

> *A review of "Ed Emberley's Big Orange Drawing Book," in* Kirkus Reviews *(copyright © 1980 The Kirkus Service, Inc.), Vol. XLVIII, No. 21, November 1, 1980, p. 1390.*

As in his other drawing books, Emberley shows children how to progressively build a picture by adding simple shapes: lines, dots, circles, etc. Because instructions are almost entirely visual, even prereaders can draw many of the characters. The "orange" of the title is a broad umbrella under which Emberley puts together a potpourri of cartoon-like sketches. . . . Similar in format to the well-spaced [*Green Drawing Book*], this offers an enjoyable and successful drawing experience for children.

> *Lynn S. Hunter, in her review of "Ed Emberley's Big Orange Drawing Book," in* School Library Journal *(reprinted from the February, 1981 issue of* School Library Journal, *published by R. R. Bowker Co./A Xerox Corporation; copyright © 1981), Vol. 27, No. 6, February, 1981, p. 56.*

ED EMBERLEY'S CRAZY MIXED-UP FACE GAME (by Ed Emberley, 1981)

The latest of Emberley's original productions is a rib-tickler that should become a favorite of both fun-seekers and budding artists. Bold, red-and-black checkerboard patterns carry out the theme, forming a background for drawings and directions on playing a novel game. . . . The result is "crazy, mixed-up" faces indeed: an ominously smiling Lucretia, a stuffy fellow staring at a butterfly perched on his big nose, a Wagnerian soprano, a madly extroverted cat, a sorrowing clown, etc.

> *A review of "Ed Emberley's Crazy Mixed-Up Face Game," in* Publishers Weekly *(reprinted from the March 13, 1981 issue of* Publishers Weekly, *published by R. R. Bowker Company, a Xerox company; copyright © 1981 by Xerox Corporation), Vol. 219, No. 11, March 13, 1981, p. 88.*

You've probably seen those split-page picture books that invite kids to line up unmatching tops and bottoms to create unheard-of creatures, faces, landscapes, or whatever. Emberley makes a more complicated game of this pastime by asking groups of "players" to fold a paper in four, then take turns drawing the first, second, third, or fourth quarter of a face. What each player draws is determined not by his or her own whim but by the number he or she draws: thus the first player might draw number seven, turn to the "first player's pages" in the book, copy the designated seventh pate from a total of twelve step-by-step drawings of head tops (rabbit ears, a Viking hat, etc.), then pass the paper on to player number two. Of course kids can and have played similar games without such lockstep instructions; and though some of Emberley's step-by-step drawing books have worked like sparks, this one will only stifle whatever spontaneous hilarity the pastime might ordinarily allow.

> *A review of "Ed Emberley's Crazy Mixed-Up Face Game," in* Kirkus Reviews *(copyright © 1981 The Kirkus Service, Inc.), Vol. XLIX, No. 7, April 1, 1981, p. 426.*

Ed Emberley's newest uses the same drawing tricks that he employs in all his books: the breaking down of figures to their simplest lines and circles in a particular order. . . . As always, Emberley provides all the lines, squares, dots and circles under each step so that the face is broken down into its simplest forms. The youngest children can play, with good results, since the directions are complete, clear and concise. Since the game is meant to be played on separate sheets of blank folded paper, the book is well suited for library circulation.

> *Patricia Homer, in her review of "Ed Emberley's Crazy Mixed-Up Face Game," in* School Library Journal *(reprinted from the August, 1981 issue of* School Library Journal, *published by R. R. Bowker Co./A Xerox Corporation; copyright © 1981), Vol. 27, No. 10, August, 1981, p. 54.*

ED EMBERLEY'S BIG PURPLE DRAWING BOOK (by Ed Emberley, 1981)

Emberley starts this off with some water play—a "Nessie" family, alligators looking up out of the water, a person (a pair of upside-down legs) diving into the water, and so on—and, as step-by-step drawing books go, the sequences are jaunty and clever. Pandas, poodles, and a few more animals made with circles complete this latest, unexceptional installment in Emberley's seemingly endless series.

> *A review of "Ed Emberley's Big Purple Drawing Book," in* Kirkus Reviews *(copyright © 1981 The Kirkus Service, Inc.), Vol. XLIX, No. 21, November 1, 1981, p. 1338.*

This most recent addition to the Emberley drawing shelf would have us believe that it is centered around a theme of purple things. Unlike the . . . *Orange Drawing Book* . . . , which did seem to bear some relationship to the color associated with Halloween, the purple book includes only a tiny percentage of objects, creatures, or people who ought to be purple. Grapes take the lead, but there seems no necessity for purple pandas, bees, crickets or pick-up trucks. The pedagogical method is exactly what we have come to expect. The inclusion of subjects such as "Lolita," "Froo," "Frooter," "Trakir," etc. makes one suspect that the artist's imagination is as exhausted as his style. (pp. 51-2)

> *Dana Whitney Pinizzotto, in her review of "Ed Emberley's Big Purple Drawing Book," in* School Library Journal *(reprinted from the December, 1981 issue of* School Library Journal, *published by R. R. Bowker Co./A Xerox Corporation; copyright © 1981), Vol. 28, No. 4, December, 1981, pp. 51-2.*

In an approach identical to *Ed Emberley's Big Green* and *Big Orange* drawing books . . . , the artist here uses eight simple shapes to draw yet another batch of creatures, animals, people, and objects. These range in complexity from a bunch of grapes made by a simple cluster of circles to a complex pirate ship that utilizes a whole network of tiny circles, lines, and triangles for its busy design. Notes or special advice from the artist pop up intermittently; it's all more fun for fans of Emberley's step-by-step methodology.

> *Denise M. Wilms, in her review of "Ed Emberley's Big Purple Drawing Book," in* Booklist *(reprinted by permission of the American Library Association; copyright © 1982 by the American Library Association), Vol. 78, No. 9, January 1, 1982, p. 596.*

Muriel L. Feelings

1938-

Tom Feelings

1933-

Philadelphia Tribune; courtesy of Muriel Feelings

Photograph by Don Lynn

Muriel—Black American author of fiction and nonfiction.

Tom—Black American author/illustrator and illustrator of fiction and nonfiction.

The importance of the Feelings's African heritage and their experiences of living and working in East and West Africa compelled them to create their books for children. They believe that young Afro-Americans are interested in stories of today's African children and desire information on their own historical background. *Zamani Goes to Market,* the Feelings's first collaboration, takes a reader through a day in the life of a young East African boy. The following two books, *Moja Means One* and *Jambo Means Hello,* introduce children to Swahili numbers and words, utilizing African geography, people, and objects as corresponding examples. *Black Pilgrimage,* written and illustrated by Tom Feelings, is an autobiographical work which traces Tom's life from his beginnings in the Bedford-

Stuyvesant area of New York through his South American and African travels.

Some critics have mentioned that the illustrations for *Moja Means One* may be too involved to allow a young child to readily find the specific item being enumerated. However, most reviewers consider the illustrations of Tom Feelings to be soft, realistic portrayals of African people and life and the texts by Muriel Feelings to be interesting introductions to African language and culture.

Moja Means One was designated a Caldecott Medal Honor Book in 1972 and *Black Pilgrimage* received the Woodward School Annual Book Award in 1973. *Jambo Means Hello* won the *Boston Globe-Horn Book* Award in 1974, the Caldecott Medal Honor Book award in 1975, and was included in the International Board on Books for Young People (IBBY) Honor List in 1979.

(See also *Contemporary Authors*, Vol. 49 and *Something about the Author*, Vols. 8 and 16.)

ZAMANI GOES TO MARKET (by Muriel L. Feelings, 1970)

"Zamani" in Swahili means "the first one." Anyone who reads Muriel Feelings' first book, with her husband's illustrations that are a perfect complement to her gentle text, will hope her first story will not be her last, for she has revealed with affectionate skill a day in the life of a small boy in East Africa today.

> *A review of "Zamani Goes to Market," in* Publishers Weekly *(reprinted from the February 9, 1970 issue of* Publishers Weekly, *published by R. R. Bowker Company, a Xerox company; copyright © 1970 by Xerox Corporation), Vol. 197, No. 6, February 9, 1970, p. 83.*

A measured glow pervades Zamani's first trip to market and the pictures which do not so much accompany as quite literally convey it—on softly tinted pages of umber and old gold. Until almost the last the matrix of East African life—filial respect, regret at selling a calf offset by confidence that others would replace it, pride in his father's bargaining power, delight at the many goods on display—supplies the impetus; then Zamani, rewarded with two coins, foregoes a kanzu (gown) for himself in favor of a necklace for his mother. Her pleasure completes his, but when everyone has returned to work Zamani finds a new kanzu with orange braid—Father's surprise gift of the very kanzu Zamani coveted. On the next market day he'll earn something for father. Slow, certainly, but not ponderous or self-important, and Zamani prancing in his new kanzu is a fitting finale, not the ultimate purpose. (pp. 321-22)

> *A review of "Zamani Goes to Market," in* Kirkus Reviews *(copyright © 1970 The Kirkus Service, Inc.), Vol. XXXVIII, No. 6, March 15, 1970, pp. 321-22.*

The author, who taught for two years in Uganda, East Africa, and her husband, who has visited there, have created a harmonious and unified picture storybook. The soft browns and golds of the pencil drawings convey a gentle, pleasant atmosphere of African village life, with its spirit of family closeness. . . . Smoothly told and produced with distinction.

> *Virginia Haviland, in her review of "Zamani Goes to Market," in* The Horn Book Magazine *(copyright © 1970 by The Horn Book, Inc., Boston), Vol. XLVI, No. 4, August, 1970, p. 381.*

A quiet book, both in tone of the story and in the modest plot, is appropriately echoed by softly executed and simply composed illustrations. . . . [A] contemporary story that gives a warm picture of family life. (pp. 6-7)

> *Zena Sutherland, in her review of "Zamani Goes to Market," in* Bulletin of the Center for Children's Books *(reprinted by permission of The University of Chicago Press; © 1970 by The University of Chicago), Vol. 24, No. 1, September, 1970, pp. 6-7.*

The greatest strength of the work is the unity between the description of a very normal, happy day in the life of a culturally different child and the softly rendered but strong illustrations that show the dignity, pride and beauty of the family and that life.

> *Lynne Stewart, in her review of "Zamani Goes to Market," in* School Library Journal *(reprinted from the November, 1970 issue of* School Library Journal,

published by R. R. Bowker Co./A Xerox Corporation; copyright © 1970), Vol. 17, No. 3, November, 1970, p. 98.

MOJA MEANS ONE: SWAHILI COUNTING BOOK (by Muriel L. Feelings, 1971)

Primarily a Swahili counting book, **Moja Means One** is also meant to be a gift of heritage, a glimpse at what is unique about East Africa. Each double-page spread hosts a Swahili number, from 1 to 10, and its pronunciation, a brief, simple sentence with the object to be counted printed in reddish brown, and a grey and white painting depicting that object. For instance, for "1 moja (mo-jah)," there is the statement, "Snowy Kilimanjaro is the highest mountain in Africa." The beautiful, warm-looking picture, with its rounded shapes and subtle shading, accordingly shows a single lofty peak. Throughout, the pictures accurately detail life in East Africa: e.g., readers see the three stages of growth in a coffee tree, four mothers in various stages of wrapping a baby to carry, six different kinds of clothing, nine musical instruments, etc. A short introduction explaining the importance of Swahili and providing a map of the areas in which it is spoken expands the book's use beyond the preschool level of the text into the first three school grades.

> *Vicki Merrill, in her review of "Moja Means One: Swahili Counting Book," in* School Library Journal, *an appendix to* Library Journal *(reprinted from the December, 1971 issue of* School Library Journal, *published by R. R. Bowker Co./A Xerox Corporation; copyright © 1971), Vol. 18, December, 1971, p. 52.*

This handsome picture book may indeed lead children of African origin to "enjoy learning to count in Swahili," or Kiswahili, which we learn is the proper name for this language spoken by forty-five million people. Moreover, the artist's powerful drawings will evoke the unique atmosphere of East Africa, important for non-African children as well.

> *Lois Belfield Watt, in her review of "Moja Means One: Swahili Counting Book," in* Childhood Education *(reprinted by permission of the Association for Childhood Education International, 3615 Wisconsin Ave., N.W., Washington, DC 20016; copyright © 1972 by the Association), Vol. 48, No. 5 (February, 1972), p. 260.*

[**Moja Means One: Swahili Counting Book** is a] counting book with a plus and a minus. On the plus side, illustrations in shades of brown and smoke evoke the beauty of rural Africa. On the minus side, the counting device is confusing: The Swahili name for each number is printed in red, and the accompanying English sentence also contains a word printed in red—the name of the object to be counted. But in many of the illustrations, the objects are part of a larger scene and locating them may be difficult for the novice enumerator. (pp. 40-1)

> *Sidney D. Long, in his review of "Moja Means One: Swahili Counting Book," in* The Horn Book Magazine *(copyright © 1972 by The Horn Book, Inc., Boston), Vol. XLVIII, No. 1, February, 1972, pp. 40-1.*

None of my critics [two schools' worth of four-to-nine-year-olds] showed any interest in **Moja Means One** . . . , Muriel and Tom Feelings's Swahili counting book, although they very politely sat through one reading of it. But the gray drabness of pictures and presentation appealed to them not at all.

From Moja Means One: Swahili Counting Book, *written by Muriel Feelings, illustrated by Tom Feelings.*

Jennifer Farley Smith, "Books before a Moppet Jury," in The Christian Science Monitor *(reprinted by permission from* The Christian Science Monitor; © 1972 The Christian Science Publishing Society; all rights reserved), April 4, 1972, p. 6.**

Swahili for numbers one to ten is given in a counting book illustrated with softly drawn pictures, strong in composition, that show aspects of East African life. The digits are followed by the Swahili word, its phonetic pronunciation, and a sentence in which the names of objects that are to be counted are printed in the same dark red as the Swahili word, the rest of the print in black. "Snowy Kilimanjaro is the highest *mountain* in Africa. . . . Many kinds of *animals* roam the grassy savannah lands. . . . The Nile River, which flows between Uganda and Egypt, is filled with *fish* . . ." (one mountain, five animals, seven fish). Although such references to river boundaries or to mountains may mean little to children young enough to be learning to count, the setting, the use of Swahili words, and the serenity and dignity of the pictures make this an impressive addition to the genre.

Zena Sutherland, in her review of "Moja Means One: Swahili Counting Book," in Bulletin of the Center for Children's Books *(reprinted by permission of The University of Chicago Press; © 1972 by The University of Chicago), Vol. 25, No. 10, June, 1972, p. 155.*

BLACK PILGRIMAGE   (by Tom Feelings, 1972)

The artist's account of the experiences that have shaped his decision to spend the rest of his life in Africa. . . . [Feelings concludes *Black Pilgrimage*] with his prescription for getting black art "back to the people," his affirmation that "I am an African," and his belief that "the only ideology that will liberate Black people is one which involves the linking up of African people throughout the world." This last section in particular may be of little interest except to aspiring black artists, but it is the drawings on every page, documenting

Feelings' developing intentions and reflecting his world, that provide an eloquent expression of one man's pilgrimage.

A review of "Black Pilgrimage," in Kirkus Reviews *(copyright © 1972 The Kirkus Service, Inc.), Vol. XL, No. 8, April 15, 1972, p. 489.*

In this moving word-and-picture autobiography, Tom Feelings describes how he grew to maturity as a black man and artist. Born and brought up in Brooklyn's Bedford-Stuyvesant ghetto, Feelings came out of the U.S. Air Force and entered art school in the late 1950s. But his preoccupation with drawing black people was seen both by his instructors and later, art directors, as an aberration. So Feelings took himself off to Ghana, where the faces of the children he drew were free of the "layers of frustration and alienation" he found in young American blacks, and where the beauty of the people and the land warmed his soul.

Feelings talks convincingly about his work, the responsibility of the black artist, and the strengths of African society. But his "return to Africa" advice—if it is meant for all young blacks —is naïve, as his own ouster from Ghana, when the Nkrumah government was overthrown, should have made clear. Africans have trouble accommodating Africans of other tribes, let alone permitting the settlement of large numbers of people from outside the continent. Feelings cannot be faulted, however, on the strength of his handsome color and black-and-white illustrations. His Afro-Americans and Africans alike breathe the vigor and beauty of a diverse and dynamic people.

Ernest Dunbar, "Worth Singling Out," in Book World—Chicago Tribune *(© 1972 Postrib Corp.; reprinted by permission of* Chicago Tribune *and* The Washington Post), Vol. VI, No. 19, May 7, 1972, p. 13.**

Tom Feelings nearly produced a great book, **"Black Pilgrimage"**. . . . Instead, he has written and illustrated a loose autobiography of a black artist (himself) whose historic and ethnic awareness is somewhat ahead of his critical sense. He fails to submit to the axiom he himself establishes. "Black artists must rethink the whole idea of 'art.' Their work must be given back to the people it comes from.''

If the black artist must rethink the whole idea of art, he must not simply rethink it while he wrestles the concept away from centuries of domination. He must rethink and rethink again. He must also rethink other ideas. In Tom Feelings's case, he must reexamine his whole idea of culture. ''The life style that comes out of mere survival should not be mistaken for 'culture,''' he writes ''for it could lead to romanticizing misery and could cloud the truth of our situation,'' and ''real culture comes from a people who are free.'' Only a white-dominated idea of culture can lead to such conclusions. He does, however, offer a stunning portfolio of art worth looking at.

> *Fred Clifton and Lucille Clifton, ''A Little Bit about Black Folks,'' in* The New York Times Book Review, Part II *(©1972 by The New York Times Company; reprinted by permission), May 7, 1972, p. 30.**

Feelings's candor and his bitterness about the stultifying treatment of the black artist in America (white publishers, he says, have recently issued books by and about black people only for profit) give his book an application and implication broader than the experience of one man. The illustrations, some in color, are beautiful.

> *Zena Sutherland, in her review of ''Black Pilgrimage,'' in* Saturday Review *(© 1972 Saturday Review Magazine Co.; reprinted by permission), Vol. LV, No. 21, May 20, 1972, p. 82.*

[In **Black Pilgrimage**, Tom Feelings] has created what can only be termed a spiritual autobiography. . . . The artist, who plans to return to Africa to live there permanently, reveals his experiences superbly by means of pencil and brush, and significantly tells how he ''began to play down *accuracy* for an overall *feel*.'' The drawings and the paintings reproduced in the volume progress from the sad realism of his observations in the rootless Bedford-Stuyvesant community to the open, free beauty of his African productions. In them, his joy in a traditional way of life is embodied in the dignified joy of his art. (pp. 380-81)

> *Paul Heins, in his review of ''Black Pilgrimage,'' in* The Horn Book Magazine *(copyright © 1972 by The Horn Book, Inc., Boston), Vol. XLVIII, No. 4, August, 1972, pp. 380-81.*

JAMBO MEANS HELLO: SWAHILI ALPHABET BOOK (by Muriel Feelings, 1974)

The Feelings, author and artist of **Moja Means One: Swahili Counting Book** . . . have now sired a superb follow-up—an African ABC. The format is essentially unchanged: for each letter in the alphabet (there's no q or x) a word is selected and spelled phonetically; defined in one or two sentences; and depicted in a double-spread. Yet whereas the earlier book was a beautiful but subdued hymn to East African heritage, **Jambo** . . . is more exuberant—a lyrical song of Swahili life. Arms outstretched, the jacket's grinning imp of a cover girl seems to be inviting readers to try out the rhythmic Swahili words and travel through the panoramic paintings. Feelings' grey-and-white compositions have a natural fluid movement; his drafting is detailed and inventive (e.g., using his charcoal to pick up the texture of the paper, he creates wrinkles in an old man's face or cracks in a clay jar); and, even in repose, his figures possess a lithe power and grace. Above all, the drawings

and text show this society as a community whether at work, at worship, or even at a wedding feast where the bride and groom figure no more prominently than the other guests because their marriage is ''an important event'' for the entire village. It is to this circle of life that the Feelings pay tribute. From their *heshima* (respect) comes much *uzuri* (beauty).

> *Jane Abramson, in her review of ''Jambo Means Hello: Swahili Alphabet Book,'' in* School Library Journal, *an appendix to* Library Journal *(reprinted from the May, 1974 issue of* School Library Journal, *published by R. R. Bowker Co./A Xerox Corporation; copyright © 1974), Vol. 20, No. 9, May, 1974, p. 47.*

Jambo Means Hello is an excellent book. It will introduce small children (and adults) to the African language of Swahili. It is a picture dictionary of the language with a word, its pronunciation and its meaning for each of the 24 letters of the Swahili alphabet.

The definitions are an important element in the excellence of this book. They are not *just* definitions; rather they tell how the word relates to the people and they describe a way of life. . . . The entire book evokes a feeling of community—Black community—and I recommend it highly.

> *Ed Celina Marcus, in his review of ''Jambo Means Hello: Swahili Alphabet Book,'' in* Interracial Books for Children Bulletin *(reprinted by permission of The Bulletin—Interracial Books for Children, 1841 Broadway, New York, N.Y. 10023), Vol. 5, No. 5, 1974, p. 7.*

The words of this Swahili alphabet book speak of respect and friendship, mothers and fathers and children, worship and celebration, succulent food, majestic animals, and of greetings to companions and strangers. But the beautiful vision of African life in the text merely hints of the community breathtakingly captured in the illustrations, which draw on the ambience of the words but move into the realm of the sublime. . . . With great vibrancy and rhythm, tremendous subtlety in the variation of light and shade, the illustrations magnificently contrast the white, shimmering heat of the African sunlight with the supple, black bodies of the natives. . . . Integrated totally in feeling and mood, the book has been engendered by an intense, personal vision of Africa—one that is warm, all-enveloping, quietly strong, and filled with love. (pp. 367-68)

> *Anita Silvey, in her review of ''Jambo Means Hello: Swahili Alphabet Book,'' in* The Horn Book Magazine *(copyright ©1974 by The Horn Book, Inc., Boston), Vol. VI, No. 4, August, 1974, pp. 367-68.*

Do not neglect the introduction when you read the book aloud, for it presents important information about the people who speak Swahili. You can also use it to acquaint children with the fact that an introduction is an important part of many nonfiction books. As you read the book, show the pictures so that children can see how the pictures help to develop word concepts. You may want to let children speak some of the words together, pantomiming the concepts as they say the new words. That is an effective procedure for words like *heshima* (respect), *jambo* (hello), *rafiki* (friend), and *Karibu* (welcome).

Responses to be sought and encouraged are, of course, enjoyment of the language and curiosity about word meanings, responses which touch on emotional reaction, interpretation, and attention to literary qualities. Children may show interest in

U **uzuri** means beauty
(oo·zoo·ree) Beauty means different things in different parts of Africa. In one it is a woman with a clean-shaven head; in another it is a great crown of braided hair.

From Jambo Means Hello: Swahili Alphabet Book*, written by Muriel Feelings, illustrated by Tom Feelings.*

similarities between Swahili and English, evident in words for father, mother, and school. Discussion may lead children to seek other information about how words enter a language. (p. 560)

> *Zena Sutherland, Dianne L. Monson and May Hill Arbuthnot, "Introducing Literature to Children," in their* Children and Books *(copyright © 1981, 1977, 1972, 1964, 1957, 1947 by Scott, Foresman and Company; reprinted by permission), sixth edition, Scott, Foresman, 1981, pp. 543-63.**

In ***Jambo Means Hello*** . . . , Tom and Muriel Feelings show that an alphabet book can be much more than just a represen-

tation of letters. Their book gives Swahili words and concepts for the letters and develops a sense of the majesty and dignity of the people who created the Swahili language. The magnificent illustrations extend the meanings of the words and convey the warmth and sense of community felt among these African people. (p. 75)

> *Bernice E. Cullinan, with Mary K. Karrer and Arlene M. Pillar, in their review of "Jambo Means Hello: Swahili Alphabet Book," in their* Literature and the Child *(copyright © 1981 by Harcourt Brace Jovanovich, Inc.; reprinted by permission of the publisher), Harcourt Brace Jovanovich, 1981, pp. 71-114.**

Kenneth Grahame

1859-1932

English writer of fiction, fantasy, short stories, and essays.

Grahame is regarded as a brilliant prose stylist whose crowning achievement is *The Wind in the Willows*. Although considered professionally successful by his contemporaries, he was uncomfortable with adulthood and its responsibilities and found refuge in nature and memories of childhood; his writings on these topics communicated inner longings which reality could not satisfy. Grahame's early experiences largely shaped the subjects and philosophy of his works. When he was five his mother died and his father abandoned the family, entrusting them to their disinterested maternal grandmother. Grahame became disillusioned with adult rigidity, dishonesty, and lack of imagination and turned away from human relationships to the freedom and honesty of nature. He claimed to remember everything from the ages of four to seven and nothing much thereafter; it is perhaps this factor that gives credibility to his writings for and about children.

Grahame's deepest desire was to attend Oxford and pursue an academic career. An uncle who controlled the family finances refused to give his approval, so Grahame was forced to accept a position as a clerk in the Bank of England; at thirty-nine he became its Secretary. Grahame began to publish essays and short stories in literary magazines which increasingly reflected his personal vision. In his first collection, *Pagan Papers*, he introduced his first retrospective analysis of the joys of childhood versus the limited world of adults, "The Olympians," a subject he examines fully in *The Golden Age* and *Dream Days*. In these works Grahame combines an adult perspective with a child's perception through his young anonymous narrator, who serves a dual purpose as both a character and the mouthpiece for Grahame's satirization of adulthood. The books were immediately popular, and are now considered remarkable for their time: Grahame is among the first Victorian writers to present accurate, detailed descriptions of childhood without sentimentality. Adults were attracted to the nostalgic aspects of the books, although many of them missed the underlying satire. Children related to Grahame's natural characterizations of the narrator and his four brothers and sisters, although both groups occasionally disliked his combination of child and adult sensibilities in them. The books were generally so successful that when *The Wind in the Willows* appeared, the public was somewhat disappointed to read about animals.

The Wind in the Willows evolved as a series of bedtime stories and vacation letters for Grahame's young son, Alastair. In *First Whisper of 'The Wind in the Willows'*, Grahame's wife Elspeth reports the evening a friend stood outside Alastair's bedroom door listening in awe: "It sounded like music, and every word slid just into the rightful place. There was magic in it, there was sense in it, and above all there was beauty in it." These attributes epitomize the work, which charms readers with its warmth and humor while touching deeper senses through Grahame's satisfaction of the basic needs for friendship and security. *Wind* is seen as a book for all ages and moods, one of those unique works that gains new meaning each time it is read. Children are often drawn to the adventures

of the wayward but likable Toad, while adults generally find the reflective personalities of Rat and Mole more appealing. Some critics state that while *Wind* is essentially a children's story, the reader needs maturity to comprehend the book fully and to appreciate its "spirit of divine discontent and longing," as Grahame described it. The work is considered a masterpiece of English prose; "Dulce Domum," "Wayfarers All," and "The Piper at the Gates of Dawn" are particularly noted for their eloquence and effect and for the skill with which Grahame uses language.

The Wind in the Willows and *The Reluctant Dragon*, a humorous folk tale from *Dream Days* about a philosophic dragon, a gallant shepherd boy, and St. George, have retained their popularity with succeeding generations. The majority of critics consider *Wind* a timeless classic, but a few criticize it as sexist, escapist, outdated, and lacking in technical unity; some consider *The Reluctant Dragon* to be the superior fantasy. *The Golden Age* and *Dream Days* are often seen as period pieces, and have little audience today among children. However, Grahame is universally regarded as a master of characterization and a painter of vibrant word images whose place in children's literature is assured. Though his literary output was relatively small, what Grahame produced was of such quality that Anthony Hope's epitaph—he left "childhood and literature through him the more blest for all time"—still seems applicable. Grahame's awards include the Lewis Carroll Shelf Award in 1958 for *The Wind in the Willows* and in 1963 for *The Reluctant Dragon*.

(See also *Yesterday's Authors of Books for Children*, Vol. 1.)

AUTHOR'S COMMENTARY

[Clayton Hamilton:] I had known, of course, for years, that all of Kenneth Grahame's work had been posited upon the opening stanza of that great Ode of Wordsworth which is one of the saddest, as it is one of the wisest, utterances of mankind. It was, therefore, not merely for information that I asked him why he had written mainly—almost only—about children and about animals. I cannot, of course, report his words with absolute fidelity; but I can recover at least the gist of his reply.

[Kenneth Grahame:] "The most priceless possession of the human race is the wonder of the world. Yet, latterly, the utmost endeavours of mankind have been directed toward the dissipation of that wonder. Everybody seems to cry out for a world in which there shan't be any Santa Claus. Science analyzes everything to its component parts, and neglects to put them together again. A barefoot boy cannot go wading in a mountain stream without being told that he must no longer spell the fluid that sings trickling round his feet by the age-old school-house lettering of W-A-T-E-R, but must substitute, for the sake of scientific exactitude, the symbol H_2O. Nobody, any longer, may hope to entertain an angel unawares, or to meet Sir Launcelot in shining armour on a moonlit road. But what is the use of living in a world devoid of wonderment? You have quoted Wordsworth:—'It is not now as it has been before'. But the poet *began* by reminding us that, 'There *was* a time'. . . . It is *that* time which I have attempted to recapture and commemorate in *Dream Days* and *The Golden Age*.

"Granted that the average man may live for seventy years, it is a fallacy to assume that his life from sixty to seventy is more important than his life from five to fifteen. Children are not merely people: they are the only really living people that have been left to us in an over-weary world. Any normal child will instinctively agree with your own American poet, Walt Whitman, when he said: 'To me every hour of the day and night is an unspeakably perfect miracle'.

"In my tales about children, I have tried to show that their simple acceptance of the mood of wonderment, their readiness to welcome a perfect miracle at any hour of the day or night, is a thing more precious than any of the laboured acquisitions of adult mankind. . . .

"As for animals, I wrote about the most familiar and domestic in *The Wind in the Willows* because I felt a duty to them as a friend. Every animal, by instinct, lives according to his nature. Thereby he lives wisely, and betters the tradition of mankind. No animal is ever tempted to belie his nature. No animal, in other words, knows how to tell a lie. Every animal is honest. Every animal is straightforward. Every animal is true—and is, therefore, according to his nature, both beautiful and good. I like most of my friends among the animals more than I like most of my friends among mankind. (pp. 71-2)

I doubt very much if I shall ever write another book. . . . A certain amount of what a countryman of yours called *life* must go into the making of any page of prose. The effort is enormous." (p. 73)

"A sentence that is easy to read may have been difficult to put together. Perhaps the greater the easiness in reading, the

harder that task in composition. Writing is not easy: I need not tell you that. There is always a pleasure in the exercise; but, also, there is always an agony in the endeavour. If we make a formula of those two motives, I think we may define the process. It is, at its best, a pleasurable agony.

"I am not a professional writer. I never have been, and I never will be, by reason of the accident that I don't need any money. I do not care for notoriety: in fact, it is distasteful to me. If I should ever become a popular author, my privacy would be disrupted and I should no longer be allowed to live alone.

"What, then, is the use of writing, for a person like myself? The answer might seem cryptic to most. It is merely that a fellow entertains a sort of hope that, somehow, sometime, he may build a noble sentence that might make Sir Thomas Browne sit upward once again in that inhospitable grave of his in Norwich.

"But language—before this ancient world grew up and went astray—was intended to be spoken to the ear. We are living now in an eye-minded age, when he who runs may read and the average person glimpses his daily reading on the run. What is the use, any longer, of toying with the pleasurable agony of attempting stately sentences of English prose? Apart from you and myself, who sit alone upon this ancient barrow, there are not more than six men in the United Kingdom who have inherited an ear for prose. (pp. 73-4)

"And all that agony, for half a dozen readers."

[Hamilton:] "The lovers of *The Wind in the Willows* have been counted by the thousands. . . . "All of them are eagerly awaiting another book by the same author."

[Grahame:] "They liked the subject-matter. . . . They did not even notice the source of all the agony, and all the joy. A large amount of what Thoreau called life went into the making of many of those playful pages. To toil at making sentences means to sit indoors for many hours, cramped above a desk. Yet, out of doors, the wind may be singing through the willows, and my favourite sow may be preparing to deliver a large litter in the fullness of the moon." . . .

[It] is a truth that, on [the day Kenneth Grahame died], the translators of the King James version of the Bible, seated at an eternal council-table, admitted to their fellowship the last great master of English prose, and that Great Britain lost the loveliest of all her living souls. (p. 74)

> Clayton Hamilton, "Frater Ave Atque Vale: A Personal Appreciation of the Late Kenneth Grahame," in The Bookman, New York (copyright, 1933, by George H. Doran Company), Vol. LXXVI, No. 1, January, 1933, pp. 69-74.

GENERAL COMMENTARY

The charm that is Carroll and the charm that is Barrie—yes, but these charms are already taken for granted. But the charm that is Grahame is not, perhaps, so popularly known and acknowledged. . . . [Not] the least important channels for conveying [the reflections of the child's mind and the child's way of looking at things] are the works of Mr. Kenneth Grahame. (pp. 125-26)

It was by his far-famed **"The Golden Age"** . . . that Mr. Kenneth Grahame's powers rose to pre-eminence. It was hailed by Swinburne as "one of the few books which are well-nigh too praiseworthy for praise.'' He remarked that ''the fit reader finds himself a child again while reading it. Immortality should be the reward—but it must have been the birthright—of this happy genius. . . . Praise would be as superfluous as analysis would be impertinent.'' That criticism places Mr. Grahame very high indeed, but by no means too high. Any one who is capable of revelling in the music and beauty of the elements will readily understand how Swinburne would appreciate, for instance, **''A Holiday,''** with the magnificent rush and sweep in the opening description of ''the masterful wind and awakening Nature.'' It is in this first scene that Mr. Grahame introduces us to the little girl, Charlotte, one of the four children who form the character-group in both this book and the almost equally superb **''Dream Days,''** the other children being Edward, Harold, and Selina—not to speak of the unobtrusive part of brother played by the author himself in the first person singular. The idiosyncrasies of each child are clearly presented without any undue insistence on the part of the author. (pp. 129-30)

In the pages of these two books we live over again our erstwhile manly attitude of revolt and our glad, precipitate escape to day dreams. . . . (p. 133)

[In] **''Dream Days''** Mr. Kenneth Grahame takes us so near to the tender hearts and wondering minds, the adventurous spirits and whimsical humours of children that after we have read the last words of the book we feel we have to rub our fists against our eyelids or pinch ourselves at some part of our person to realize if we are really awake in a material world or if it be true that we are once more the children of fleeting days of glory. Who is not the richer spiritually for having read **''Its Walls were as of Jasper,''** **''The Magic Ring,''** and **''The Reluctant Dragon''** in **''Dream Days''**? Mr. Kenneth Grahame draws upon a furtive, insinuating winsomeness, and the tablets of his memory are deeply engraved with words and notes of sweet music that chime again and again the rose-winged hours of eternal childhood, be it in . . . **''The Golden Age,''** in **''Dream Days''** or in his latest book, **''The Wind in the Willows.''**

For the most part, Mr. Kenneth Grahame's backgrounds are, first, a pastoral landscape that is replete with here a saturnalia of whirling leaves and there an orgy and riot of spring-blossom on the laughing hedgerows, and, secondly, a quiet pleasaunce with visions that lurk among the garden shadows, and dance upon the lush grass and round the mignonette or the meadowsweet—a homely, old-world seclusion at peace with its sometimes noisy inhabitants. . . . Of course, there may always be the chance, in Mr. Kenneth Grahame's books, that the Olympian ''gulfs will wash us down,'' but it is far more frequent that in children's company ''we touch the Happy Isles.'' Even on a day of pitiless rain there are pranks enough and to spare to while away the time in forgetful mood, absorbed in make-believe argosies and pirate escapades, in visions of dream palaces, or in the quaint spectacle of Harold as a muffin-man. . . . (pp. 134-36)

Mr. Grahame's humour is light and subtle, yet shining clear as a crystal. His prose combines in an exceptional way an unrivalled spontaneity of vision with a mature command of the most gracefully resilient style imaginable. Not only so; there is woven into the prose-texture innumerable tenderly poetic imageries and figures of speech that entrance and enthral to the utmost degree. . . . In fine, the ''bright-enamelled'' pageantry of Nature when related so harmoniously and so intimately, so nearly and so humanly to child-life must ever ring

a responsive echo in us—that is to say, if beneath our breasts a child's heart beats out its exultations and its despairs, if in our minds a child's imagination plays out its long games of delight and hides those sensitive, hidden sufferings that only children and the child-like among us experience in their journey, be it ever so rough, through the world towards the ultimate Hills of Joy. It is on the crest of these Hills that Mr. Kenneth Grahame has erected his triumphal arch, and upon its rich stonework are inscribed the indelible letters to be seen by all who come there to understand—The Triumph of the Innocents. (pp. 137-38)

W. M. Parker, ''The Children's Advocate: Kenneth Grahame,'' in his Modern Scottish Writers, *W. Hodge & Co., 1917 (and reprinted by Books for Libraries Press, 1968; distributed by Arno Press, Inc.), pp. 125-38.*

Kenneth Grahame seems to have been one of those people who may be delightful in the flesh, but whose literary conception of themselves is most unhappy. He was fond of loafing—the praise of idleness creeps into all his books; yes, but he loafed rather self-consciously along the hedgerows. He was a passionate bibliophile; yes, but he was one of the first humanists to sandwich quotations from Rabelais into his essays—Rabelais, who has since been so thoroughly appropriated by the beerier kind of British wit. He wrote of memory leading back to ''relinquished fields and wider skies''; yes, but he also wrote of ''strepitant metal'' when he meant a bicycle bell, and peppered his sentences with flat little archaisms—''yon town,'' ''lift you your eyes''—and with the neat rule-of-three of the imaginative historian: ''As this child . . . peeps at you from under her sun-bonnet, so may some ancestor have watched with beating heart the Wessex levies.''

From these, and other small indications, we may have a clear enough picture of him strolling about with a pipe, a sensitive, pleasant, uneccentric, very English Englishman, a sentimental ''hearty'' if you like. . . . (p. 446)

What saved Kenneth Grahame was a hard foundation. He was sentimental only in the best sense. His own childhood . . . was not a happy one, and so there are no concealing mists round the children he wrote about. It seems only by accident that they are children; one might say that his instinct for creation happened to be awakened by people who were not grown up. There is no patting of the head, no tedious, no gratuitous sympathy with the ''dear little creatures.'' They are meant to be looked at, tenderly it is true, by grown-ups; above all to be unconscious of themselves. And so their age is incidental. They are not even made to talk like children. The lisps and misspellings which are half the business of books about children, are rare; the test word, '''cos,'' scarcely appears at all. For childhood appeared to Kenneth Grahame, as he very brilliantly said, as ''the days when one was young and godless, and went to church.'' Not the sweets and the hoops, but the terrifying obtuseness of the drawing-room, the stuffy smells of the house, are the beginnings of being young. However unpleasant the realisation may be, he sees that the main stream of childhood is rebellious and only the backwaters occasionally idle and perfect.

Dream Days and *The Golden Age* are not easy books to write about. Their quality is sufficiently hinted at by their titles. In one or the other he writes:

> Instead of active ''pretence'' . . . how much
> better—I hold—to be at ease and pretend to

oneself, in green and golden fancies, slipping
the husk and passing, a careless lounger, through
a sleepy imaginary world all gold and green!

No literary enterprise could be more dangerous than this, no
colours more treacherous than green and gold. But he carries
it off; he manages to create a world as sleepily luminous as
the minute forest which appears only when one buries one's
face in long sunny grass. New perspectives, a new sort of hurry
and work, are found to be peculiar to that miniature kingdom
where a great human face trespasses among insects; and in the
same way the family of children about whom *Dream Days* and
The Golden Age are written go about their business. . . .

The style in which this business is recorded fits it admirably.
It is, in *The Golden Age* . . . still a little uncontrolled; but a
year or so later, in *Dream Days,* Kenneth Grahame reaches the
high-water mark of his prose—a neat, musical, instrument, not
too "literary," but always unhurried enough to be exact. It is
very easy to quote . . . and it is easy to find the sharp overtones
which are the leaven of both books—the children taking advantage of the fact that their elders, the "Olympians," are
"always open to sentiment of a treacly, woodcut order"; or
to find a phrase which can stand on its own legs, such as: "the
sort of set smile that mountebanks wear in their precarious
antics, fixed painfully on the face, as with pins."

But these felicities are only the frame of Kenneth Grahame's
personal genius. Anybody may write intelligently, or wittily,
but not anybody can make free with dream-days and yet be
not ridiculous. The atmosphere of these essays can scarcely be
criticised; it makes a clear case for rhapsody. Those who love
Kenneth Grahame pay him the compliment, so maddening to
non-bookish persons, of remembering and extolling the smallest incident, the obscurest character. Do we not love the pig?
Is not October 21, whatever may happen in the full-size world
on that day, chiefly the pig's anniversary? Yet the pig scarcely
comes into the story; he is a very incidental pig, with no
undoubted attribute, so far as I can remember than that he was
black. Nevertheless we can never hope to know a pig better,
and it is the same with Augustus the cat. That engaging animal
is as perfect a creation as Joseph Andrews, whom he much
resembles. And Rosa and Jerry, the dolls. The passage in which
Selina is playing with them on the stump of a tree is one of
the most exquisitely subtle records of the commonplace in
modern literature. We know exactly how they almost came to
life, how in her mind they existed on two planes at once, human
with half her mind and dolls with the other. And all the time
the imperceptible grown-up, the reader himself, is watching,
half-convinced when the dolls tumble together that they do it
from malice, and simultaneously contemptuous of the existence
of dolls, an amused, unwillingly fascinated grown-up. The few
pages on Rosa and Jerry, scattered through two books, sum
up all that a right thinking person need know about dolls. Even
the casual grown-ups are brightly visible. On the day of the
"battle," a day so nearly disastrous, when Harold and his elder
brother run after the soldiers too far and have to be rescued by
the doctor, we only have one glimpse of the doctor in his
carriage, while he tells the tired children on the way home
stories of bloodthirsty adventures all over the world. But I
think I should recognize his voice if I heard it. And who can
forget the scene when one of the children—the one who tells
the stories in his own person—goes upstairs to get a new bootlace from Martha, and finds her in tears over the news that
Billy, the sailor brother, has been drowned?

There had never been anyone like Billy in his
own particular sphere; and now he was drowned,

they said, and Martha was miserable and—and
I couldn't get a new bootlace.

Such claim to immortality as Kenneth Grahame possesses rests
on his ability to write the last clause of that sentence.

The faults in these books are inconspicuous. Kenneth Grahame
limited himself so strictly to what he knew he could do that
there is no room for faults. Few artists ever worked on a smaller
canvas, and the particular nature of his work means that it is
hit or miss; faults cannot impair. Evidently, though, he could
not have carried through a larger attempt. There is nothing
noble or passionate in what he has given us, nor any hint of
a capacity for such qualities. He might, had he attempted a
novel, have given us what is called an "unpleasant" novel,
for Rabelais occasionally shows himself among the children;
and, if one must discover a fault, it is probably one to make
the children fall in love so consciously with neighbouring children.

I suppose the most popular of his books is the latest, *The Wind
in the Willows.* . . . It is no less charming than the others but,
for me at any rate, too elaborate an artifice. I think Mr. Earle
Welby has already pointed out its fault: that Kenneth Grahame
had succumbed to writing for children instead of about them;
and consequently he could not avoid being pretty every now
and again, since children are not remarkable for good taste.
But from any adverse criticism Mole must be excepted. He is
a reincarnation of Harold, the most enchanting of the children
in *Dream Days* and *The Golden Age,* Harold, who is so perfect
a child that even his author weakened towards him into a
forgivable sentimentality, Harold, whom I suspect of being the
author's idealized memory of himself. Harold and Mole are
exchangeable, but Mole has no equal to Harold's solitary games
and beautifully calculated tempers. But I have no wish to read
The Wind in the Willows again, and still less wish to read
Kenneth Grahame's only other original novel, a small pamphlet
called *The Headswoman,* an inept little story about those French
middle ages appropriated, in the same lot with Rabelais, by
our beery wits. That he wrote *The Headswoman* shows, what
is surprising in Kenneth Grahame, that he, who ought in theory
to have been so aethereal was, apparently, so ordinary an Englishman, so good an example of the constant, and purely
English, contradiction that an author can swig off his beer,
stuff a pipe in his mouth and then create something of the most
sensitive beauty. Only in this country does it seem to pay to
be disrespectful to the Muse, and to one who has been brought
up in a different tradition it is extremely irritating that it should
pay at all. In Kenneth Grahame, however, we are forced to
see just such a man—an artist who was not less a banker, a
loafer and a "good fellow." (pp. 447-49)

Alan Pryce-Jones, "Kenneth Grahame," in The
London Mercury, *Vol. XXVI, No. 155, September,
1932, pp. 446-49.*

Kenneth Grahame was not a prolific writer. Two volumes of
miscellaneous pieces including short stories and essays, three
books for children, a few prefatory notes to other men's work—
such was his range and limit. Yet, small as this output was,
in all his writing there is apparent a most meticulous and musical care in his choice of every word. An eaves-dropper, who
had once listened to him telling his son a story, said afterwards
to Mrs. Grahame: "It sounded like music, and every word slid
just into its rightful place. There was magic in it." The judgment is impossible to better; it can only be enlarged upon. For
music, magic, and beauty—those are the three qualities which

distinguish him from so many of the other Yellow Book contributors, who, so often rich in one or other of these qualities, lacked the other two. (p. 11)

[In his long short story for adults, *The Headswoman*,] Grahame is able to maintain [a] paradox since what he is concerned with presenting is that point of truth where everything which seems clearly incredible is also incredibly clear: it is what made his subsequent books so popular with children. He does not appeal to their imagination because he is at one with their imaginations: he is meeting them on their own level so that what he asks of his listeners—and his books cry out to be read *aloud*—is not the suspension of doubt, but faith; and on this level his work is best summed up in Browning's line as "Infantile Art divinely artless." Only scrutiny on another level reveals his meticulous and musical artistry. . . .

[The] public greeted *Dream Days* with none of the enthusiasm which they had given to its predecessor, *The Golden Age,* and one of the reasons for this (apart from the fact that in nine cases out of ten sequels fail) may have been because Edward had gone to school. The children that he had played with as a boy were growing up and, as boys grow up, so there tends to be a declension in the heroic. . . . [Grahame] had, too, a growing son and, coupling these factors together, I would submit that they played no small part in his turning his attention to the animal kingdom. There, for adults as for children, dream days remain dream days; the golden age is endless. (p. 12)

He believed that people had lost their sense of wonder; that nobody any longer expected to meet Sir Launcelot in shining armour on a moonlit road, or an angel unawares behind a thicket. Such things belonged to the realms of poetry, not sense; they were fantasies, not realities. . . . He saw no reason why a man's life from sixty to seventy should be more important than his years from five to fifteen. . . . [In] wonderment Grahame saw truth. In the animal world that truth was natural; in the children's world it was miraculous, or supernatural. (p. 13)

Men had belied their natures; they had suffered the domestication of the miracle of life. In children the sense of the miraculous remained, and through them it *might* be restored. The waterways that led to Toad's Hall were also symbolic: they were the springs of life. (p. 14)

The Nineties was a period of transition, and it was against this transition that *The Wind in the Willows* was composed. . . . The England of which Grahame was writing was a changing England and, in so localizing the scene and playing tricks with time-sequences, he was able, steering between reality and fantasy, to play the satirist—though this was not his primary role. It was incidental to his main intention which was to restore sound to prose; to make words something more than sentences glimpsed "on the run" by men travelling up and down to the City. This meant capturing the music, magic, and beauty of the world; of transposing the taken for granted with the literal; of letting the miraculous re-appear where custom has dulled wonderment. The stress is on *being*. "I'm going to make an *animal* of you, my boy," says Toad to Ratty in just the same way as a father will say to his son "this—or that—is going to make a *man* of you." "Every animal, by instinct, lives according to his nature": the characteristics of Grahame's different animals are built up on this principle, so that before the grand Banquet begins which is to celebrate the defeat of the weasels and stoats it is not surprising to find that Toad "dipped his hairbrush in the water-jug, parted his hair in the middle, and plastered it down very straight and sleek on each side of his face": the action is in keeping with the character.

Doubtless it is touches such as these which eventually won such popularity for the book after a slow start. . . . [Some] recognized Grahame's own cadenced prose and hailed it: but they were few. Most people came simply to be fascinated by the subject matter, and because the artistry was so exquisite they mistook it for being "divinely artless." That was their compliment—a children's compliment which time has endorsed. (pp. 14-15)

> *Neville Braybrooke, "Kenneth Grahame—1859-1932: A Centenary Study" (copyright © 1959 by the National Council of Teachers of English; reprinted by permission of the publisher and the author), in Elementary English, Vol. XXXVI, No. 1, January, 1959, pp. 11-15.*

Kenneth Grahame's is a strange magic, and hard to describe; just as hard as the song of Pan proved when the Rat tried to retell it to the Mole. It is easy to speak of the perfection of style, a clear harmony of words falling upon our ears as naturally as "bird-song at morning" which sets Kenneth Grahame high among even the greatest writers of English prose. It is not hard to perceive the clear vitality of every character who passes before us by down and dale as he describes them—be they Edward and Harold and Selina, be they Badger or Mole, a Water Rat or a Reluctant Dragon. It is possible, also, to state that Kenneth Grahame was a true poet, though his vehicle was prose, who saw more deeply into nature than most of us do. But it is easiest of all to read what Kenneth Grahame wrote . . . and find each for ourselves what it is that the wind says among the reeds or over the downs, find what echoes his bright word-hoard can wake in each heart, and decide how high in our literature Kenneth Grahame's place should be. (pp. 47-8)

[Kenneth Grahame] wrote for the sheer joy and delight of expressing himself in beautiful and harmonious phrases, of capturing in the bright ring of words a golden memory of childhood, or a golden afternoon in his chosen country. (p. 48)

[We] seem to know the child Kenneth better than most other children of fact or fiction. The tales and sketches in *The Golden Age* and *Dream Days* may not be accurate as an historical account of his childhood: we must not assume too readily that the unnamed "I" was christened Kenneth, and the unmentioned surname of Edward and Charlotte, Harold and Selina, was Grahame. But none the less every sentence rings with the absolute truth of knowledge and experience, welded by the power of the true poet into the eternal likeness of that truer world in which we, as he, have also played our tiny parts. (p. 49)

In after years *The Wind in the Willows* came, with many readers, to usurp the place of *The Golden Age*—which we may consider as one book with its sequel *Dream Days*. . . . Yet some of us would still hesitate to set it above the adventures of Edward and Harold, Charlotte and Selina, and their unnamed companion, the poet of childhood and the springtide of the world, whom we would fain believe to be Kenneth Grahame himself.

And there had been nothing before it quite like *The Golden Age*. In the early 'Sixties Dickens experimented with happy childhood in *Holiday Romance;* Mark Twain had written convincingly of Tom Sawyer and Huckleberry Finn. . . . Mrs. Molesworth had woven many exquisite tapestries of child life, and S. R. Crockett with sentiment spread thickly over dry bones had managed to sell his first "Christmas Story," *Sweetheart Travellers,* through many editions. But both the new and the old, the good and the indifferent, turned, consciously or unconsciously, to *The Golden Age* for example and inspiration. (pp. 52-3)

[Emphatically] *The Golden Age* is for the adult reader. Misguided parents sometimes inflict it upon the young, and it was, as far as I remember, the only book which, as a child, I really and violently hated. The reason seems to be that Kenneth Grahame, like Prince Prigio, "knew too much." Here, though we could not then put the thoughts into words, was an adult writing in an adult style about things which touched the very heart of our mystery. He was profaning the holy places; perhaps (for his manner was elusive) he was laughing in some detestable Olympian fashion at the things which really mattered.

"*The Golden Age,*" commented one of E. Nesbit's children in *The Would-be-Goods,* "is A.1—except where it gets mixed with grown-up nonsense." I venture to think that even E. Nesbit did not quite realise where the difference lay.

Some of the adventures may appeal to children, but the adventures are only means to an end. And that end cannot be described adequately in words of this world: it is to capture for us of years mature the shadow of our own half-forgotten days . . . it is to forget—only that we may see the more clearly.

Besides his feeling for words and his unerring choice of them, Kenneth Grahame developed also that perfect blend betwixt the Puckish humour and the serious humanity which made the earliest of *The Golden Age* stories, "**A White-Washed Uncle**" . . . as finished and perfected a piece of work as "**A Departure**" which closed the series six years later at the end of *Dream Days.* (pp. 53-4)

The same mastery of humour, together with the fullest power of expression, and this time inspired throughout with the vision of a true poet, is shown in "**The Reluctant Dragon**" . . . , perhaps the most perfect star in Kenneth Grahame's crown: the jewel without any flaw. In this his understanding of childhood and his insight into the working of a child's mind are exemplified more subtly than in any of the other stories. It is at once a new folk-tale told by a master story-teller in language simple enough for the child reader, and a prose-poem whose charm does not pass with the passing of the years. In many ways it represents the culmination of Kenneth Grahame's art, and may well be accepted as his supreme achievement. (pp. 54-5)

Perhaps as a whole [*The Wind in the Willows*] lacks unity and a concentration of purpose, passing with breathtaking transitions from a child's fantasy among the creatures that people the fastnesses of dreams to the adult's poetic joy in all the life and nature round about us—but we cannot criticise it thus as we read it: then it also is "too praiseworthy for praise." Possibly some children reading it may find that too often it gets mixed with what Oswald Bastable [of *The Would-be-Goods*] called "grown-up nonsense," but many will read or listen to the difficult passages with a deep, part-comprehending awe, and the charm has worked.

But it is far more than an inspired nursery tale to those who read it in later life. At its face value it is a picture and an interpretation of the quiet things of every day as we may know them still in the country places. They are true animals, Toad and Mole and Badger and Rat, though at times they may step out of the picture to clown joyously for the children of men; and their world of wood and water is truer yet. The Thames murmurs through the book to the tune of the wind among the willows, and the grey waters shine silver and gold in the spring sun beneath the slender branches, making it a book of atmosphere, a thing of many beauties and a joy for ever. (pp. 57-8)

Roger Lancelyn Green, "The Magic of Kenneth Grahame," in The Junior Bookshelf, *Vol. 23, No. 2, March, 1959, pp. 47-58.*

[Grahame] was not, in the normal sense of the word, a children's writer at all; . . . he crystallized, in his life and writing, many profoundly important changes which affected English society towards the close of the nineteenth century.

Grahame described himself as a 'mid-Victorian'. This indicates, as it were, his natural centre of gravity. We are inclined to forget that he was a young man before 1880, and middle-aged by the turn of the century. He was, therefore, caught up emotionally in the events connected with Mid-Victorianism—the Industrial Revolution and its by-products, middle-class mercantilism and the collapse of agricultural society, scientific evolution and religious doubt. Like many other sensitive young men, he watched the decay of rural England with bleak horror, having been born early enough to understand just precisely what was being lost as railways and factories multiplied over the ravished countryside. He felt the tyrannous emptiness of a society which was rapidly losing all spontaneity, and which combined the pursuit of money with a rigid and authoritarian moral code.

Despite this, however, he (like many others in similar cases) not only continued to honour the obligations imposed by the hierarchy of family and society, but in some sense actively needed them; and thus two powerful elements were permanently at conflict in him. He compromised: outwardly he conformed with his society. But his inner self took revenge in satire and fantasy: at first openly, then by more oblique and subtle methods. Like Lear and Carroll, he found relief in the world of childhood, the animal fable, the potent symbols of fantasy. (pp. 1-2)

We can assume . . . that in a broad sense the 'I' of *The Golden Age* and its sequel at least represents Grahame's early attitude to life as he himself later recalled it.

This boy has a strongly marked and individual character. He simultaneously resents and envies the arbitrary power exercised by his elders. He has the emotional precocity often to be found in orphans, foster-children, or young D.P.'s. His tendency to solitariness is pronounced, and causes him some twinges of conscience; these children live by a positively hierarchical common code, and the individualist is not encouraged: 'I waited until they were both thoroughly absorbed, and then I slipped through the hedge out of the trodden highway, into the vacant meadow spaces. It was not that I was unsociable . . . but the passion and the call of the divine morning were high in my blood.' This is the authentic Wordsworthian note; Kenneth was to wander 'lonely as a cloud' for the rest of his life. From the beginning his love of Nature—that ambivalent abstraction—was considerably higher than his love of humanity. . . .

The *alter ego* of *The Golden Age* also goes out of his way—beyond the normal derision natural to a young boy—to mock and sneer at girls in general and the whole network of personal social relationships they involve one in. Girls are the inferior sex in every way. (p. 21)

His natural temperament is conservative; he has an absolute passion for stability, discipline, the sense of a fixed order in life; and his worst fits of brooding and misery are provoked by such occasions as the departure of a governess, or Edward's metamorphosis into an alien schoolboy—when he is left to contemplate the 'raw new conditions of our changed life'. (p. 22)

Some of these qualities may derive from adult *arrière-pensées;* but in general they square very well with what we know about the conditions of the Grahames' existence at Cookham Dene. They suggest how violent in fact was the emotional wrench that uprooted these children from their family atmosphere and transplanted them to the thin soil of relatives' charity. Nevertheless, the 'Olympians' that Kenneth actually knew were far from being monsters; at the worst they were unimaginative and irritable. There is every reason to suppose that he later fictionalized them almost completely in order to extend his satirical attack to a specific class of contemporary English society. (p. 23)

Whom, in fact, *was* he attacking? There can be no doubt about his resentment and hatred of relatives as a class; however hard he tried to disguise it as comedy, there are times when this resentment rises almost to pathological levels—openly in *Pagan Papers,* with greater art and discretion in *The Golden Age* and *Dream Days.* Perhaps it was provoked simply by emotional stupidity, unimaginative treatment, the unwillingness or inability of these adults to enter into a child's world. The core of Grahame's complaint really seems to be that they allowed the young no seriousness, no dignity, no warmth or colour, no *meaning* in life. For a foster-child such treatment would have been doubly destructive.

Whatever the cause, Grahame hit back, thirty years later, with every weapon at his disposal. The Olympians in general were materialistic, dull, anaemic, listless, wilfully stupid, stickily sentimental, stereotyped in their thought, unambitious in their actions. (pp. 24-5)

A modern reader will not be surprised to find that these spiritual oafs provoked elaborate revenge-fantasies, which culminated in visions of a triumphant child bestowing charity and forgiveness on the by now contrite aunt or uncle concerned. (p. 25)

[When] Kenneth Grahame came to create the idealized picture of his childhood, his main object was to preserve something essentially transient from oblivion, a talisman against time and change. Each successive blow at his sense of permanence and stability drove him further in upon himself. In *The Golden Age* and *Dream Days* he set down the vision he had had before, like Traherne, he was 'corrupted by the dirty devices of this world'; they are his bulwark, the fragments he has shored against his ruins. The quality he values above all is timelessness. Time destroys legends, puts children beyond the reach of fantasy, gives no warning of coming bereavement. (p. 31)

[The] thought of children summing up their elders with such cool and precocious contempt struck at the very heart of the Victorian child-myth. Children were supposed to be innocent, unthinking, all-adoring, uncritical; grateful acolytes sunning themselves in the benevolence of an omniscient father-figure. Grahame destroyed the whole myth at one stroke. He scaled adult pretensions and sentimentalities down to life-size; he showed that children not only possessed a private life of their own (which was romantic) but a mordant eye for the weaknesses of their elders (which was highly embarrassing). (p. 162)

The originality, if not the creative achievement, of Kenneth Grahame's short stories about children is often under-rated today. A post-Freudian epoch has accustomed us to the child's-

eye view of things; we are prepared to accept the unpalatable truth that children of a certain age dislike and despise adult concepts. We are no longer either so complacent or so psychologically naïve as to saddle our offspring with our own sentimental yearnings, and call them 'the pure vision of childhood'. In Grahame's day the situation was radically different. There were plenty of books both for and about children; indeed, the market was swamped with them. But their picture of the childish mind remained alarmingly unreal.

It is true that the old-style moral tracts, heavy with morbid Sabbatarianism, were by 1870 on the decline. . . . This revolution was due in great measure to the two *Alice* books; yet, despite their imaginative freedom and volcanic subconscious imagery, Alice herself remained a copybook child, a two-dimensional moral prig. (pp. 173-74)

Carroll, nevertheless, . . . shows us another use to which fantasy or children's literature could be turned in a morally repressive age. It served as an unconscious safety-valve for desires and feelings which the writer would not care to admit even to himself. (pp. 173-74)

There were only two other attitudes which the rebel could adopt. . . . The first, and rarest, is direct retaliation. . . . The more common and simple is retreat, in one form or another. . . . (p. 175)

Grahame's retreat to the world of childhood is especially adroit. Hitherto this had largely been a sentimental stamping-ground for the Olympians themselves, where they could indulge their mawkish imaginations with myths about Unspotted Innocence and Adoring Little Girls. Even Carroll was not exempt from this weakness. What Grahame did was to sneak a Trojan Horse inside the citadel; his children could get away with the kind of ferocious outspokenness that would not be tolerated from an adult. The Olympians were hoist with their own myth.

This, of course, largely accounts for the intrusion of adult opinions and behaviour in the children of *The Golden Age:* in one sense they are being used as stalking-horses, to put across their creator's satirical message in such a way that he himself remained unscathed. But quite apart from this, the effect on the Victorian child-myth was revolutionary. (pp. 176-77)

[After *The Golden Age* and *Dream Days*] the fictional child was never quite the same again. In all probability Grahame had no clear idea in his conscious mind of what he was doing. Half his imagination, throughout his adult life, remained that of a child: he simply wrote, as an artist, what he remembered and felt, moving effortlessly between the 'divided and distinguished worlds' of mature awareness and innocent vision. That the results (however familiar in essence and technique they may be to us) puzzled Grahame's contemporaries it is easy to deduce from his reviewers. The two things they all stuck on with virtual unanimity were, first, the scornful attitude to the adult world of Grahame's children; and second, the way in which Grahame himself shifted with fluid ease from the rôle of grown-up commentator to childish narrator, and even on occasion maintained both rôles simultaneously. Such tricks of psychological and stylistic technique do not bother us in the least; we have had half a century and more in which to absorb them. But to Grahame's early critics they were, obviously, startling innovations. . . .

The anonymous critic of the *Spectator* [see excerpt below] is typical. It does not occur to him that the double angle of vision produces a focused, stereo-scopic picture; that the child's-eye view is given fresh depth and solidity by the adult commentator. (p. 177)

Today, since we have absorbed the double-level technique so thoroughly that we are hardly aware of it, we would probably claim ['**Sawdust and Sin**' and '**The Roman Road**'] as the most brilliant in the book. In no other way could the gaps between adult and childish imagination have been so dramatically highlighted; in no other way could Grahame have explored each situation at all its contrasting levels, or analysed the *internal* changes which his narrator underwent between boyhood action and mature recollection.

'**Sawdust and Sin**' multiplies these levels of awareness in a most extraordinary way: it resembles a nest of psychological Chinese boxes. Here, through the narrator's eyes, is presented an account of Charlotte's dealings with her dolls over a tea-party. In addition to Grahame's own two *personae* there is also Charlotte's; and, to cap all, the dolls themselves (through a combination of Charlotte's imagination and the narrator's) behave, or seem to behave, in a quasi-human manner which parodies adult as well as nursery behaviour.

To bring this juggling act off so brilliantly required a technical *tour de force* of the first order. . . . (p. 178)

Psychologically, the effortless skill with which this sort of thing is done probably hints at Grahame's own emphatic duality of outlook; but the result in literary terms is almost unique. Throughout the book his best effects are due to some variant on the same double approach: the two halves counterpoint each other perfectly. (pp. 178-79)

At first ['**The Finding of the Princess**'] appears to be an elementary exercise in appearance-and-reality, with adult narrator and adult characters sharing the same superior knowledge, smiling tolerantly at the child for whom the footman behind his chair is a taciturn lord and the whole house a fairy palace. Then we realize that for the adults—though in a different sense—the fairy-tale is true too; *they* see the world, and the child, through the enchanted eyes of love. Each of them understands the other, but each in his own way: it is a situation worthy of Pirandello.

Here, for once, the adult world and the child's fantasy meet without disillusion. The words they use may carry completely different connotations to speaker and hearer; yet each has seen an aspect of the same universal truth, caught something of that imaginative wonder which for Grahame is man's supreme experience. A similar effect is produced by the scene between the boy-narrator and the aged, scholarly, gentle clergyman of '**A Harvesting**': superficially they are at cross-purposes, but at a deeper level they have an intuitive knowledge of their common temperament.

Normally Grahame uses the double-level technique in order to gloss his narrator's attitude to the adult world with the satirical voice of experience. The Prologue to *The Golden Age* is written throughout from the adult viewpoint in retrospect; after that the satirical *persona* only intrudes intermittently in a direct way. More often it is half-concealed in an ambiguity, and its tone ranges from the comic to the macabre. (pp. 179-80)

In . . . '**The Roman Road**', this method acquires additional depth and power from the fact that both the protagonists, boy and artist alike, represent different aspects of Grahame's own personality. This fictional diffusion of the ego is a common phenomenon: in Grahame's case, however, it has especial interest. The 'I' of '**The Roman Road**' is Grahame as a child, still undisillusioned by experience, always mentally pacing 'down

a delectable street of cloud-built palaces'. The Artist is Grahame the adult, who has actually been to magic places like Piccadilly, who has followed the road to Rome—and in a subtle way, has lost some part of his vision by so doing. The interaction of these two selves gives the story its peculiar power.

The whole point of '**The Roman Road**' is that it is the child who, all unknowing, offers salvation to the older man. The Artist can quote Marcus Aurelius and Aristophanes, but somewhere he has lost a dream. (pp. 180-81)

This sense of failure and disillusion runs [deep] in *The Golden Age.* . . . '**The Roman Road**' symbolizes the solution which Grahame adopted. It was the child in him that rescued the artist from that worst of all disappointments—experience. The glamour of being grown-up, independent, a free agent, of travelling to all those Chimborazos and Cotopaxis of one's dreams, had proved largely illusory. The real Rome could never hope to match the Golden City of Grahame's young imagination: that gleaming mirage which both his childish and his adult self needed so desperately. (p. 181)

This crystallization of Grahame's split desires into opposed fictional characters repeats itself throughout his work, and greatly heightens its dramatic tension. He is both Rat and Seafaring Rat in '**Wayfarers All**', both Rat and Mole in '**Dulce Domum**'. At other times his two protagonists share a basic identity of purpose; especially is this so in *The Golden Age* and *Dream Days,* where the innocent 'I' is a childish analogue to scholarly Rector or Bohemian artist, and only differs from them in clarity of vision.

The most complex example of ego-diffusion is to be found in that enchanting tale '**The Reluctant Dragon**'. This, it should be noted, does not really belong in the Edward-Harold-Selina canon at all: Grahame seems to have felt this himself, since he adopts the transparent device of turning it into a story-within-a-story to bring *The Golden Age* children in somehow. Yet even so he contrives, by so doing, to add to its subtlety, since he is not only all three major characters in the tale itself, but also audience and story-teller.

Taken at its face-value, '**The Reluctant Dragon**' is, of course, a satirical fable, rather in the gently debunking manner of *Don Quixote.* The dragon is a peaceable creature that only wants a quiet life; St. George is only anxious to do the decent thing, and quite happy to come to a private arrangement with his opponent; between them moves the innocent Boy, as a kind of go-between, oscillating from fantasy to disillusion and back again. The real villains are the villagers: and their basic crime is ingrained convention and habit. Dragons are pestilential scourges, everyone knows that; therefore this specimen *is* a pestilential scourge, whatever their senses tell them to the contrary. If St. George turns up, there *has* to be a battle. And so on. In the end, of course, they are defeated: St. George, the Boy, and the Dragon all walk off amiably arm-in-arm. The whole thing is beautifully done; the construction tight and economical, the humour delicately tinged with irony, the point made unmistakably yet without fuss, and a perfect balance struck between fantasy and farce.

Yet it is almost impossible to avoid reading it, at a deeper level, as the reconciliation (for the time being, at any rate) of Grahame's conflicting selves: it is no coincidence that the story was written in the year of his appointment as Secretary. St. George is the side of Grahame concerned with Honour and Duty: the public servant, the national figure, the representative of what we have come to know as the Establishment, the champion of convention. The Boy, of course, is the recurrent 'I'-figure of farsighted childhood, 'wonderful knowing about book-beasts, as everyone allows', transferred for the occasion to a more exotic setting. But it is the Dragon whose character is drawn in greatest detail, for whom Grahame obviously felt most affection and sympathy; and the Dragon, beyond any reasonable doubt, is a living portrait of Grahame's anarchic, artistic, anti-social, irresponsible, indolent self.

It is an interesting Dragon who—at this juncture in Grahame's life—remarks that 'one must look about and reflect and consider before settling down. It's rather a serious thing, settling down.' The obliging beast continues with his self-revelation. He is bone-lazy by nature, he says, while 'all the other fellows were so active and *earnest* and all that sort of thing'. But then there was an earthshaking catastrophe:

> 'I suppose . . . the bottom dropped out of something. Anyhow there was a shake and a roar and a general stramash, and I found myself miles away underground and wedged in as tight as tight. . . . So I scratched and burrowed, and worked this way and that way and at last I came out through this cave here.'

The symbolism could hardly be plainer: Grahame's creative mind, driven inward by the drudging, conventional duty required of him, has at last, with great effort, broken free. (The same symbolism, of course, was to be repeated in the first chapter of *The Wind in the Willows*.) His dilemma is plain: can he risk driving it back underground by going over to the forces of convention, *i.e.* by accepting the office of Secretary? The Dragon doesn't mean Them any harm; he only wants to read Them his poems; but They (as the Boy reminds him) regard *him* as an enemy of the human race. There he sits, a 'happy Bohemian', in Grahame's give-away phrase, enjoying the sunsets, telling stories, and polishing up his gorgeous blue scales (Grahame was a tremendous dandy), while all the time St. George is preparing for a battle royal. He can't be bothered to face the problem; he leaves the Boy to fix it. And fixed it is, as we might expect, with a great show of fighting; and ends with the Dragon painlessly transfixed, by arrangement, through an insensitive part of his neck, while all the villagers cheer. Then St. George (carefully side-stepping requests to finish the job properly) ends up, after the inevitable banquet, by helping the tipsy Dragon home, with the Boy in attendance. A compromise has been reached; the public decencies have been observed. (pp. 181-84)

'Olympians' and 'grown-ups' are not, as is sometimes supposed, interchangeable terms. When it comes to the point, 'Olympians' are middle-class relatives and their middle-class friends; Aunts, and, less often, Uncles, who impose their deadening will on the imaginative young according to some inscrutable canon of behaviour. . . . (p. 184)

The Olympians, then, stood for bourgeois society at its most materialistic, mean-spirited, and (worst of all) unimaginative. Incapable of enjoying life themselves, they were determined to deprive those who could of the chance to do so. . . . They were the great-grandparents of the Hollow Men.

Grahame hits off their foibles with deft economy of characterization and an acute psychological eye for the significant trait. Perhaps Uncle Thomas is his most devastating portrait. Detail is added to detail in each successive story: the senseless adult jokes at the children's expense, the fear of being left alone for a single minute, the superficial omniscience, the

petulant outbursts of anger, the ridiculous self-importance. Yet, and this is of the essence, Uncle Thomas is not a two-dimensional monster, but, reading between the lines, a pathetic and unhappy human being, the victim of his own Olympian condition. In one story he is laboriously mocking psychical research; but soon enough, as we might expect, he is dabbling in it himself. . . . We end by becoming rather sorry for Uncle Thomas: he is so utterly lacking in beliefs or purpose. Spiritually null, he suggests a premature victim of social *Angst*. (pp. 184-85)

Grahame's highest gift was for characterization; and in *The Golden Age* he made children live as they were, not as their elders would wish them to be. This was a completely new achievement. . . .

[His] two volumes of short stories must stand or fall, in the last resort, by the childish family quartet round whom they are built: Charlotte, Harold, Edward, Selina, with the personality of the narrator omnipresent in the background. His success may be gauged from the fact that these prototypes have left their mark on almost every subsequent fictional family of the kind, from E. Nesbit's *The Railway Children* to Arthur Ransome's *Swallows and Amazons*. This is all the odder since we know practically nothing about them in the way of external detail: they are never physically described, and their background is of the sketchiest. (p. 191)

[In] seizing on those perennial traits which embody the whole essence of childhood, he created a minor classic. The social evils he attacked have long since passed away: it does not matter. Grahame's children are timeless: yet each remains a sharply differentiated individual. (pp. 191-92)

His inner purpose throughout [*The Wind in the Willows*] was threefold: to satirize contemporary society, to sublimate his personal fears, and to construct an ideal model of the Good Life. (p. 240)

The River is perhaps the most all-persuasive symbol running through the book; and it is interesting to measure the degree of idealization which Grahame imposed on his Thames-side setting in order to achieve that timeless, drowsy beatitude. The River acts as a boundary, to begin with; beyond it lie the Wild Wood and the Wide World, with which it is several times contrasted. It is a symbol of rural traditionalism, faithful, steady-going, reliable. . . . Water stands for purity, natural life, lushness, the slow, peaceful, primitive tempo of existence; the river-god's rhythm, as Mr. T. S. Eliot aptly reminds us, was present in the nursery bedroom. There is a hint of mysticism in its whispering reeds, so closely connected with the pipes of Pan. It is the perfect background for a reaffirmation of all Grahame's values.

The actual river, of course, . . . was not like that at all, and Grahame, as a keenly observant naturalist, knew it perfectly well. His symbolism demanded that animals should show themselves as more natural, more peaceable, and (oddest of all) less concerned with sex than humankind; and therefore the whole Nature-red-in-the-tooth-and-claw concept, not to mention the mating season, had to be rejected. Furthermore, since the River Bank was to stand for idyllic peacefulness, another very material element had to be suppressed [the death of the animals]. (pp. 240-41)

Nothing of this appears in *The Wind in the Willows:* the terrors lie elsewhere, and this is Arcadia. . . .

This idealization of the River Bank had very deep roots in Grahame's past. All his life, as we know, he had fought with nostalgic doggedness to preserve his faith in a pre-industrial, agricultural, essentially aristocratic society. But as early as 1890 it was becoming uncomfortably clear that the rural squirearchy was collapsing (or at least being profoundly modified) under economic pressure from the Machine Age and slowly increasing political infiltration by Radicals. (p. 242)

The result of this social upheaval was a violent, often unformulated nostalgic urge for 'escape', which—oddly enough—cut across political denominations: even the early Radicals yearned for lost rural innocence. . . . There is no reason to suppose that Grahame was immune from this infectious emotional apprehensiveness; and a good deal which indicates that *The Wind in the Willows* was, *inter alia,* a subconscious defence against it, a fantasy in which country gentlemen finally triumphed over the unprincipled radical *canaille.* . . . The lurking lawless terror of the Wild Wood, the open anarchy when Toad Hall is usurped by stoats and weasels—all this is Grahame's minuscule projection of his own social fears. (pp. 242-43)

The social picture which *The Wind in the Willows* presents is not life as Grahame thought it was, or once had been: it is his ideal vision of what it *should* be, his dream of the true Golden Age. It is precisely because he knew at heart that the dream was lost beyond any hope of realization that his imaginary world acquired such compulsive fascination for him. (p. 244)

Throughout the whole book there runs the *leitmotif* which may be roughly described as the conflict between Us and Them—or more specifically, the attempts made by Grahame's ideal rural society to defend itself against encroachment. (The curious thing is that though Grahame set out to create a trouble-free Arcadia he could not stifle his private anxieties: the Wild Wood loomed menacingly across the River, stoats and weasels lurked ready to invade Toad's ancestral home.) This society is specifically identified with the River-Bankers: Rat, Mole, Badger, Otter, and their friends form a close-knit community of leisured landowners who observe an extremely strict code of responsible behaviour.

The paramount virtue in this code, emphasized over and over again, is loyalty to one's own caste: and in this, of course, the animals come very close to their human counterparts. The whole moral and ethical point about Toad's behaviour is that he has *let the side down.* . . . The stoats and weasels are enabled to gain possession of Toad Hall precisely because Toad has neglected his property and gone gallivanting on unbecoming picaresque adventures. (pp. 244-45)

Toad, of course, stands for a figure who was becoming increasingly prevalent after the turn of the century: the landed *rentier* squandering his capital on riotous pleasures. This kind of irresponsibility provided the best possible propaganda for radicals who wanted to bring the whole system of inherited wealth and traditional class-values crashing down. In this sense the Adventures of Toad constitute a social object-lesson. If you neglect your responsibilities, Grahame proclaims in effect, you are letting in the enemy and betraying your own friends. And what happens as a result? You are 'handcuffed, imprisoned, starved, chased, terrified out of your life, insulted, jeered at, and ignominiously flung into the water—by a woman too!' You return home to find your country house occupied by insolent riff-raff. Only the loyalty of your friends finally contrives to restore the traditional *status quo.*

Examined from this point of view, the whole business of the Wild Wood and Toad Hall's capture takes on an unmistakable

social symbolism. The Wild Wooders, stoats, weasels, and the rest, are clearly identified in Grahame's mind with the stunted, malevolent proletariat of contemporary upper-middle-class caricature. (pp. 245-46)

It is a characteristic touch of Grahame's that when the invaders are finally ousted, the first thing they are made to do is sweep under the beds, change the sheets, and supply each room with 'a can of hot water, and clean towels, and fresh cakes of soap'. What could better symbolize the triumph of the *ancien régime* over the upstart Unwashed . . .? . . .

Thus the nagging terror of the mob . . . has been exorcized by the most time-honoured reactionary's recipe of them all—physical violence. The paternal squirearchy is restored in triumph, and Wild Wooders gaze in respectful admiration as the Old Order, safely restored to its traditional authority and privilege, goes swaggering by on the last page. In this sense *The Wind in the Willows* was provoked by Grahame's need to combat his ever-increasing fear (shared by many of his class and period) that the structure of society might be destroyed through social revolution. (p. 247)

[The] hint of things to come, the ultimate triumph of mechanical progress over rural traditionalism, is sounded very early in *The Wind in the Willows*—'The Open Road' deals with it in unmistakable terms. The destruction of the caravan—which Grahame associated symbolically with untrammelled country Bohemianism—by the inhuman and somehow monstrous motor-car: this is the core of the matter. Into that chapter Grahame packed a whole social revolution, focused and scaled down into an episode at once fabulous and beguilingly familiar.

The most interesting thing about Grahame's Arcadian animal society is that it has more in common with the rich bourgeoisie than the aristocracy. All the River-Bankers are of apparently independent means; their life seems to be one unending holiday, boating, tramping round the countryside, eating enormous meals, and getting caught up in occasional adventures. They don't run farms or administer big estates; Toad is blamed, not for neglecting his duties as a landlord, but for behaving badly. What Grahame has done, of course, is to project his own private dream on to a social pattern which he admired, but to which he did not belong.

Nothing brings this home so sharply as Grahame's attitude to money. At first one suspects that, like so many rural Utopians, he wants to dispense with it altogether, or has left it out for the benefit of his childish audience. Then comes a revealing little episode which aligns Grahame more nearly to his middle-class banking forebears than to the aristocratic ideal he so admired. Toad at the booking-office in his washerwoman's disguise, without a penny to his name, is a bourgeois anxiety-dream incarnate. . . . (p. 248)

This incident suggests what one of the underlying emotional driving-forces of *The Wind in the Willows* may have been. For all his Scottish pedigree, Grahame, like Mr. Salteena, felt 'rather mere' about his lack of inherited wealth. (p. 249)

Grahame compounded more and more with respectability as he grew older: but the public figure, though it might overshadow the anarchic Id, could not wholly destroy it. What provided the tension, I suspect, was the new *persona's* terror that at any moment the old Adam might disgrace it. There was a time when Grahame had wanted nothing so much as to contract out of Society into Epicurean idleness: and deep down this was what he still wanted. But he had learnt—from Wilde's example above all—how mercilessly Society dealt with any infringement of the unwritten laws. Taken in this context Toad's adventures make considerably more sense; they represent Society's ruthless pursuit of the nonconformist, the heterodox, the *déclassé*.

Grahame's attitude to Toad is extremely ambivalent. He is ostensibly on the side of the angels, yet shows very little sympathy for Authority as such. While condemning Toad's excesses, he has, one suspects, a sneaking urge to behave in exactly the same way: Toad, in fact, is a sublimation of all his own unrecognized desires, and is harried by all the forces which Grahame himself found particularly terrifying. There is no one so congenitally scared of a magistrate as your thoroughgoing romantic Bohemian: he has nightmares about prisons, pursuit, disgrace, the ineluctable hand of the law.

This kind of compulsive terror permeates all Toad's adventures. (pp. 250-51)

[What '**The Piper at the Gates of Dawn**' and '**Wayfarers All**'] have in common is an overwhelmingly violent emotional experience, which in both cases can be related with some confidence to Grahame's own life. If, at one level, *The Wind in the Willows* subsumes the totality of its author's life—his fears, passions, pleasures, disappointments and beliefs—into a timeless myth, '**The Piper at the Gates**' and '**Wayfarers All**' crystallize, mythically, the most intimate and intensely felt experiences that Grahame ever sustained. The first forms a mystical testament to his *fin de siècle* faith in the beneficent, personalized powers of Nature; the second enshrines what he felt—and had felt for many years—to be his betrayal of that gleaming sunlit dream, and hints fairly clearly at the compromise he finally settled on. (p. 252)

It is significant that . . . Pan's last and most welcome gift (which he never had in antiquity, and which seems to be a creation of Grahame's own) is forgetfulness. The awe of that ultimate revelation was too much for the small creatures who inhabited Grahame's fantasy-world: it may have been too much for Grahame himself—or he may have shrunk from the recognition of its transience.

But there were other things, too, that he wished to forget: all his lost aspirations, the life he might (or dreamed he had) have led if things had turned out differently. . . . '**The Piper at the Gates**' celebrates a vision; but in the very *O altitudo* of participation Grahame is already begging for the release which oblivion brings. What he cannot bear to remember is his own denial of the light. Like Edmund, he had the white vision in the meadow, but he compromised and was lost. And for that he never quite forgave himself.

'**Wayfarers All**' deals with the same essential problem in slightly different terms. (pp. 253-54)

Clearly, in this private drama, all three participants represent aspects of Grahame's own personality. Rat is the repressed Bohemian Ulysses, fretting in London and at Cookham Dene, feeling an unformulated migrant urge in the blood. The Sea Rat speaks with the inner voice of the self-tempter: every voyage, each landfall from Corsica to Alassio and Marseilles was one Grahame had already made himself. Mole here is the respectable, conformist side of Grahame: conscientious, practical and loyal, he stands for all the domestic and public virtues.

It almost looks as though in 1907 Grahame was on the edge of leaving Elspeth. We remember the long period of separation:

and had not Grahame's father, forty years earlier, vanished in precisely the same footloose way? (p. 255)

But, as we know, the step was never taken. The struggle may have been an internal one: its reality and agonizing force cannot be in doubt. The entranced, spellbound Rat was defeated: once again, and for the last time, Grahame compromised. The dream of the solitary traveller was abandoned for ever. There would be no escape now, no enchanted and lonely pursuit of the warm, elusive Southern mirage, no miraculous new life. It was over and finished. And yet not quite finished: for one outlet still remained through which Grahame could obtain the emotional release he so desperately needed. Like Rat, he took a pencil and a few sheets of paper; he sucked and he scribbled; and out of his despair and yearning a classic was born. (pp. 255-56)

If Grahame had never married [Elspeth] it is extremely doubtful whether [*The Wind in the Willows*] would ever have been written: it needed exactly the emotional shock she provided for the creative flash-point to be reached. Repressed, unhappy, driven in on himself, badly bruised by contact with adult passion, Grahame turned—without being aware for one moment of what he was about—to the world of symbol and myth. In so doing he released the full strength of his genius. (p. 265)

Grahame can be more nearly identified with Mole than any other of his characters: the patient, tunnelling, laborious Mole who suddenly bursts through into the sunlight and the leisurely life of the River. Like Grahame, he is tactful, wide-eyed, a little naïve, content to play Watson to Ratty's Holmes; like Grahame again, he develops a violent, aching nostalgia for his old home—and goes back to it. . . . All the other animals reveal similar constituent elements—natural observation of the beast in question; literary associations; underlying symbolism; a degree of self-portraiture. They also incorporate features borrowed from Grahame's friends.

But—and this is the important point—their final realization is completely individual. They are not patchwork or *pointilliste* portraits: the material has been absorbed into a new entity. Just as in his children's stories Grahame experimented with fluid levels of awareness, so here he has contrived matters in such a way that animal, human, and symbolic traits co-exist, without any sense of incongruity, in the same character.

Rat is more complex altogether. He is a handyman, but also a dreamer; a man (or rat) of action and a poet; cool-headed in a crisis, yet liable to mystical seizures and symptoms indicative of hysteria. In the autobiographical sense he stands for Grahame's emotional extremes—at one end of the scale the practical businessman and freshwater sailor; at the other the volatile, highly imaginative, psychologically disturbed Celt. It may be Rat who supports Mole in his emotional crisis of longing for Mole End; but the rôles are reversed when Rat hears the call of the South and marches out, for all the world like a hypnotized zombie. . . . And the 'seizure', we should note, is cured by—creative writing. There could hardly be a closer parallel. (pp. 279-80)

[That friendship is higher than love] is one of the unspoken motifs running through *The Wind in the Willows,* where nobody who matters is married, or needs to work, and where the *summum bonum* is loyalty, with creature comforts a close second: an apologia, in fact, for the country bachelor's life. (p. 281)

One of the most curious (and least commented-on) features of *The Wind in the Willows* is the frequency with which characters indulge in violent, eccentric, and near-pathological emotions or actions. This psychological ferment is in striking contrast to the rural tranquillity of the setting. We would expect Mole and Rat, at least, to behave with 'English self-restraint'; but not a bit of it. Mole goes into hysterical sobs at a whiff of his old home, while Rat . . . is hypnotized into a kind of hysterical trance by the Seafarer. But it is, of course, in Toad that such phenomena reach a peak of intensity; at times his behaviour almost suggests that he is, as it were, the Id personified. (p. 282)

[For the most part, indeed,] Toad's behaviour is irresistibly suggestive of an adult manic-depressive. His entire life is a series of violent excesses matched by balancing moods of black and lachrymose despair; he shows the classic symptoms of irresponsibility, faddishness, bombastic fantasizing, tearful but impermanent repentance. (pp. 282-83)

[Toad is perhaps] the symbol of Grahame's urge towards swashbuckling action and Romantic heterodoxy. (p. 284)

Just as in his earlier books Grahame had achieved a convincing fluidity of viewpoint, which shifted without effort from child to adult, so with *The Wind in the Willows* he takes the process one step further. All the animal characters veer constantly between human and non-human behaviour. Rat lives in a river-bank hole, and also writes poetry. Mole burrows underground, but is capable of rounding up a horse from the paddock. (pp. 284-85)

There is no *stability* in Grahame's dream-world, and no incongruity. Human magistrates of a highly contemporary nature try and condemn toads to imprisonment in mediaeval dungeons guarded by halberdiers. The same toad can bargain with a gypsy for a horse, and ride off on it. Most curious of all, a humanized Rat and Mole can walk through a village on a winter's night, and still consider its inhabitants somehow alien—including their dogs and cats. This interchangeability of essential nature is Grahame's hall-mark; and the oddest thing about it is that it still leaves every character sharply defined and psychologically consistent. Perhaps only a writer who combined a satirist's talent with the imperturbable vision of a child could have managed it. (p. 286)

> Peter Green, in his Kenneth Grahame 1859-1932: A Study of His Life, Work and Times *(reprinted by permission of Harold Ober Associates Incorporated; copyright © 1959 by Peter Green), John Murray, 1959, 400 p.*

[What Grahame captured so successfully in *The Golden Age* and *Dream Days*] were the changeless elements of childhood, the outward signs and the child's hidden response. There have always been children who could appreciate that detachment, and so enjoyed them: and always adults taken back so inescapably to their own early days that it seemed to them incredible that other children could not see them with their eyes.

The childhood of which he was writing now lies a hundred years behind us, yet the books are not dated, nor have they become period pieces. They remain vigorously alive, created so clearly, with such certainty that they can still be explored, not merely with the questing eyes of childhood, but with the critical mind of the adult. (pp. 31-2)

Kenneth Grahame had himself suffered all the small injustices, wrongs and humiliations endured by most children of his day, but he looked back on them without anger, without self-pity, and escaped sentimentality, surely, by a miracle. (p. 32)

What has so endeared [*The Wind in the Willows*] to all sorts of people of all ages for the last fifty years and more?

First and most important it was told and written for one beloved child whose reactions, as the story shaped, checked and confirmed it at every turn. Then, it was told by a man who remembered with particular vividness all he had felt when he was just that child's age. In general practice, of course, it is not specially or precisely for children of four to seven. Kenneth Grahame was not writing for an age, but for one child, who hung on his words, and followed wherever his father's invention led him. What held and comforted Mouse all those years ago, still gets across and holds the child of today. And because the author was accustomed to living in different worlds at the same time, on different levels, he twined all kinds of extra threads in and out of the simple story he was telling, so that there is something in it for old as well as young. (pp. 48-9)

For many children, the appeal is felt right at the start with Mole, so simple and sensible, innocently ignorant, impulsive. From the moment he flings down his brush and rushes out of the house, sympathy is with him, and when he routs the obstructively inclined rabbits with his jibing, '*Onion sauce, onion sauce!*' he is already established as first friend. . . . For others Rat is the link which holds most strongly: Rat the capable, managing, knowledgeable, indulgently protective, elder brother of the party. Badger shapes the background with his dignity and authority, a creature of dry humour and sound judgement on most things, having much in common with the better kind of Victorian father, never easy of access, even slightly Olympian (in Grahame's special sense) yet melting so warmly when hospitality was clearly needed. Why he has such a curious obstinacy about words not usually counted as King's English is not plain.

Then there is the river itself, Rat's river, on and in and by which he had been born and bred, his faithful, steady-going old river which never played tricks on him, never packed up and flitted like the migrant swallows, nor tucked itself away unsociably in winter quarters like the hibernating animals. Rat's love of the river is sound, giving a sense of permanence, stability, and safety, so that almost anything that may happen can be accepted on trust. (pp. 49-50)

Toad is the always popular bad boy, the wild boy, boastful, blustering, full of swagger, so head-in-air that he misses what lies at his feet and falls over it. Like toads in general, he is quickly puffed up, and deflates as quickly to just the small, insignificant size of the common toad. But even at his lowest ebb, his spirits are wild and volatile, already soaring upwards even before he has touched bottom, restoring his confidence that he will always be cunning enough to find a way out. Then Toad, with his passions for the latest craze, is a familiar figure to all generations and it is Toad who attracts all the adventures, with the barge-woman, the gipsy, the police, the jailer's daughter. It is Toad who goes to jail, and escapes. Careless Toad who leaves all his money and papers behind, so losing his identity and being seen to be nothing after all but a common toad, and as such is thrown into the water.

Toad is never really the hero. Rather, he is a will-o'-the-wisp careering across the scene, drawing a trail of incidents behind him. But Rat, Mole and Badger are strong, permanent realities.

Deeply embedded in the story is the warm feeling of home. Three times over is a home described, always with loving care as though Kenneth Grahame wanted to make sure of passing on to his son his own cherished memory of a happy home-coming. (pp. 50-1)

Yet the cosiness does not devitalise. On the contrary, it rounds off and sustains the powerful feeling of reality which binds the scenes together into that happy world which is not wholly fantasy, but often so like a reflection of a child's groping awareness of a world beyond the family circle, an ordered world. In this case a *benevolently* ordered world with the Piper at the Gates, the goat-footed Pan, as the great power. Frightening things do happen but without giving rise to alarm. There is an implicit assurance—to the reader—that all will be well. Be brave like Rat, it seems to say, persevere like Mole. Trust Badger. (p. 53)

> *Eleanor Graham, in her* Kenneth Grahame *(© The Bodley Head Ltd 1963; reprinted by permission of the author), Henry Z. Walck, Incorporated, 1963, 72 p.*

[Why does *The Wind in the Willows*] survive in the competitive markets of the twentieth century? Why have countless readers loved it enough to bring it to the bedsides of their own children?

The Wind in the Willows sings out from a loft of its own. The writing, unmistakably Kenneth Grahame's, is word music to match the wind's song. Characters are so distinctly drawn that they dwell in the memory and shun imitation. The unusual tales enchant the reader and call him to its pages again. Yet more than all this accounts for the book's enduring quality. It is its life blood—the implicit meaning—that keeps *The Wind in the Willows* eternally contemporary.

The well spring of this vitality is the author. No man ever had greater affinity for the good earth or more respect for the integrity of nature. The man is the book; the book is the man. (pp. 1032-33)

In *The Golden Age* and *Dream Days* there are vignettes of the days and doings in Grahame's early years—yearnings and disappointments; anticipation and discovery; gay abandon and necessary nods to Olympian demands. Shifting patterns of introspection and retrospection create the meaning and spirit of that time before 'the gate' swings to and the 'golden age' flickers away. The vivid recollections stir the subconscious of adults who have forgotten. . . .

No psychological probe is needed to determine the origin of the essays in *The Golden Age* and *Dream Days*. Their birthplace is that attic playroom and the grounds around Granny Ingles' ancient, rambling house. The early years in that place were trying ones for the orphaned Kenneth. It was then that he came to view adults as ones who sit, preoccupied, on their own Olympus. Left alone, he lived out childhood with an intensity which made it a dynamic part of him forever. Clearly he is the narrator, I, recalling those impressionable four-to-seven years—". . . those days of old ere the gate shut to behind me."

Studies in child development were fast at Kenneth Grahame's heels when he pulled aside that veil to reveal the true nature of children and, more than that, the children's views of adults. It is surprising that the writings of this literary Spock caught on before Victorian notions about childhood had been destroyed. The universalities which emerge through those pages keep *The Golden Age* and *Dream Days* as contemporary as childhood itself. (p. 1034)

> *Kathryn A. Smith, "Kenneth Grahame and the Singing Willows" (copyright © 1968 by the National Council of Teachers of English; reprinted by permission of the publisher and the author), in* Elementary English, *Vol. XLV, No. 8, December, 1968, pp. 1024-35.*

Kenneth Grahame in *The Golden Age* . . . and *Dream Days* . . . , essays originally written for adults, but treated as children's books, though in fact their archly ponderous style makes them quite unsuitable, created children not only without any sense of sin, but without a sense of honour either. They have no ethical boundary. As long as they are undetected they have no scruples about what they do. They live in a permanent state of antagonism with the adult world—the Olympians, they call its inhabitants, whom they regard as born directly into middle age through their own choice. They are wild, destructive and disobedient, of course, but they also outrage the gentlemanly code by stealing, lying, and ill-treating animals. But Kenneth Grahame evades the issue of direct defiance of parents. 'To children with a proper equipment of parents,' he says at the outset, 'these things would have worn a different aspect. To those whose nearest were aunts and uncles, a special attitude of mind may be allowed.' Even Kenneth Grahame would hardly have dared imply that a mother could be a natural enemy like the rest of the adult world. (pp. 159, 161)

> *Gillian Avery, "The Innocents: 1880-1930," in her* Childhood's Pattern: A Study of the Heroes and Heroines of Children's Fiction, 1770-1950 *(copyright © 1975 Gillian Avery), Hodder and Stoughton, 1975, pp. 143-63.*

[*The Wind in the Willows* seems] like a shift in Victorian consciousness. Lewis Carroll, born in 1832, grew up as the Victorian cult of childhood was first taking shape; . . . the adored child for Lewis Carroll and his generation was a preadolescent girl, while the awkward, unpleasant thing to be was an active boy. Grahame, born a generation later in 1859, grew up as the cult was in full flower, and the central figure was more and more apt to be a boy. . . .

Grahame's first books . . . were published when this new version of the ideal person had gained a firm grip on the English imagination, a hold it would not lose until World War I, when the boy, slightly older, gained his apotheosis as a young victim in Flanders. (p. 166)

The Golden Age and *Dream Days* were immensely popular books because they fitted so easily into this new phase of the cult of childhood. These books are almost unknown today, except perhaps for **"The Reluctant Dragon,"** but we will understand Grahame much better if we see why his early books were so popular, and how *The Wind in the Willows* is a transmutation of his earlier materials into ideal and enduring shape. It too is about boyishness, or, more properly, boyish manhood, about being free of adult restraint and responsibility and sex. Furnivall appears as Rat, messing about in boats and taking along good food; the rural god Pan reappears, still idolized; Oscar Wilde appears in Mr. Toad's adventures in jail. *The Wind in the Willows* goes *Peter Pan* one better; Barrie and Peter Pan acknowledge in the very act of saying what they want that it is impossible, while Grahame's ideal world on the river seems more palpable, more fully realized, more truly desirable, than *Peter Pan*. As a result, *The Wind in the Willows* lives today, perhaps more popular now than it has ever been, part of its time but blessedly not limited to it. It is loved by lovers of children's books, and also by many who care little for, or even positively dislike, most children's literature. Its pleasure is the pleasure of enclosed space, of entering a charmed circle, of living in a timeless snugness. It takes so little to turn snugness into smugness that it is no wonder that many books that seem to resemble *The Wind in the Willows* are tiresome and even objectionable. If it did not exist it might rightly be claimed that a good book with its essential emotional bearings could not be written. . . . Grahame's was not a distinctly original genius, like Lewis Carroll's or Beatrix Potter's, and it takes some stretching to call *The Wind in the Willows* a great book. But its best pages are magical, fringed with joy, and therefore irreplaceable. (pp. 167-68)

The crucial fact in Grahame's life is that he did not become the Oxford don he wanted to be and seemed suited to be. Had he done so he could have retired early into a quiet single life, and, lacking Lewis Carroll's genius and urgencies, he might never have been heard from again. Thrust into the city, he found in the Bank of England an institution in which he could believe sufficiently to make him persevere successfully in his work, but for which he was sufficiently unsuited that he had to seek escape from it constantly. The more successful he became, the more he wanted to give a form to this constant need to escape. . . . When he knew he would soon be appointed Secretary, he became an author; when he realized his marriage was also something from which he needed to seek refuge, he began *The Wind in the Willows*. Never having the permanent haven Oxford might have provided, he had to invent it in his books. (p. 169)

[For Grahame] freedom was all one needed to be at the heart of all fantasy and escape. (p. 170)

That Grahame was not really seeking a realistic version of childhood in *The Golden Age* and *Dream Days* is most evident in his narrator, who experiences all the joys and dark gloom of the other children but who is frankly free to become an adult narrator whenever Grahame wishes. The result is a kind of double perspective: here is a child telling a story, building a fortress against adults; here also is an adult narrator authorizing and supporting that fortress in his nostalgia for its having never been, or its having been lost. The results tend to be unpleasant a good deal of the time. For instance, in a famous story, **"Sawdust and Sin,"** the younger sister, Charlotte, is trying to make two dolls named Jerry and Rosa sit still so she can tell them stories, while the narrator watches from a convenient hiding place [and discovers "the full measure of Jerry's infamy"—Jerry collapses forward, and is propped on Rosa's shoulder by the innocent Charlotte.] . . . On the one hand the narrator can share with Charlotte the presumption that the dolls have ears, eyes, and intentions. On the other, he can laugh at Charlotte for not understanding what Jerry's "real" intentions are. It is a convenient perch. (pp. 170-71)

Charlotte is condescended to as the little girl who plays with dolls, so absorbed in telling her stories and "getting them to listen" she doesn't know what is "really" going on. She is hardly a worthy victim of any but the briefest sally, one would have thought, but Grahame and his narrator get much mileage out of her innocence. The narrator is of course male, and superior to the girl's naïveté, and by believing in Charlotte's fantasy that the dolls are real, by poking fun at Charlotte, Grahame can simultaneously indulge his sexual fantasy and deny it is fantastic.

Thus when, a moment later, Rosa falls "flat on her back in the deadest of faints," Grahame can giggle at the doll's orgiastic swoon and poke an elbow in a reader's ribs with double

entendres: "'It's all your fault, Jerry,' said Charlotte reproachfully, when the lady had been restored to consciousness: 'Rosa's as good as gold except when you make her wicked. I'd put you in the corner, only a stump hasn't got a corner—wonder why that is.'" Ostensibly, one presumes, this is Grahame's joke on "the sacred cause of childhood," or that part of it that elevated the purity and innocence of Alice and Rosa. But in his licentiousness Grahame only reveals *his* innocence. He and Charlotte mean different things by "good" and "wicked," but he accepts the equation of goodness and sexual purity just as much as Charlotte accepts the equation between goodness and correct manners. What makes Grahame's innocence all the more culpable is that it is all done with an ostensibly adult snicker that shows he would not have dreamed of giving a copy of **"Sawdust and Sin"** either to Charlotte or to her older brother. (pp. 171-72)

But the stories are seldom as bad as **"Sawdust and Sin,"** and Grahame can occasionally use his blend of child and adult narrator to real advantage. (p. 172)

The style [of **"Dies Irae"**] includes the gardener's boy rather than ridicules him, and so everything that shows the narrator is an adult as well as a boy shows only the boyishness of both.

In **"Sawdust and Sin"** the hierarchy makes a leer, while in **"Dies Irae"** it celebrates release, the fantastic becomes real, the gods become defenders in which anyone might wish to believe. With a writer like Lewis Carroll, leering can be a fascinating and poignant activity—as with Alice and the Duchess, or the Gnat—but with Grahame it is only a nasty trifling. He needed situations and materials in which he could be more open, where the pleasure of creating hierarchies was mostly the pleasure of being inside a charmed circle, as with the gentleman lad in **"Dies Irae,"** and thus beyond care, however momentarily, and beyond snobbery or snickering. In these early books, or so it seems to me, only in **"Dies Irae"** and **"The Roman Road,"** where a boy and a man discuss the places they'd like to go, does the open enjoyment of wanting bring pleasure free from any attendant restrictive absorption with victims, or from a nostalgia where there is no circle and the charm is all a blur. (p. 173)

It is not pleasant to think of *The Wind in the Willows* as the work of a man becoming increasingly miserable, but such seems to have been the case; he began the work as stories told in letters to Alastair to placate him and his mother for Grahame's spending so much time away from them.

Since *The Wind in the Willows* did begin in this fashion, it superficially resembles Milne's Pooh books and J.R.R. Tolkien's *The Hobbit*, all being stories fathers told their sons, written by men who never thought of themselves as authors of children's books. The resemblance, however, may be one reason people have been mistaken about *The Wind in the Willows*. Ostensibly Grahame is inventing a world to enchant his son of six or seven, but actually he is describing a world he himself had lived in so completely that it seems false to say he invented it; he had been Rat, Mole, Badger, and Toad. Somewhat nervous about its reception, Grahame himself wrote on the dust jacket that the book is "perhaps chiefly for youth," but it was really written for himself and it usually fails to please a child who has just been delighted by the Pooh books and *The Hobbit*. But thereby lies the reason for its superiority to these other books: it has none of the superior tone that mars Milne's book or the smugness that hurts Tolkien's. It is *about* coziness, but it never seeks an uncomfortably cozy relation with its reader or listener. Its best audience is certain children, or adolescents, or adults, people of a particular sort or in a particular mood. If there is a "good age" to give a "child" *The Wind in the Willows,* it is not the age of Alastair Grahame when he first heard it, but twelve- or thirteen-year-olds, boys especially, who need to be told or reassured that the demands of adult life—work, sex, family, aging—which loom so frighteningly for them are in fact capable of frightening everyone. If one is rather doubtful about one's suitableness as an adult, one can be enthralled by *The Wind in the Willows.* . . . Like the *Alice* books, it is too personal, too signed by the needs of its author, to be a children's book as the Pooh or Oz books are.

By the time Grahame wrote *The Wind in the Willows* he was almost fifty and able to see that he was, in certain important respects, never going to "grow up." He also could see the ways in which the demands of maturing could no longer levy on him as strongly as they once had. He was what he was, he loved what he loved, which is why this book is much less self-conscious and satiric than the earlier ones. . . . In one particular way, it seems a ripe book, mature: it has an unerring sense of season and of the effect certain seasons can have on us irrespective of the demands of work or school. **"The River Bank"** in early spring, **"Wayfarers All"** in October, **"Dulce Domum"** at Christmas, are perfect expressions of a seasonal mood. If for no other reason, *The Wind in the Willows* is part of the ongoing emotional equipment of those who love it; there are many times and situations that recall its characters and scenes with vividness and fondness. Its sense of fun carries with it a sense of belonging, of the deep rightness of this kind of pleasure. (pp. 174-75)

[The book is divided] into something like two halves. Up to chapter 7, **"The Piper,"** everything is of a very high order, and the early Toad episodes blend splendidly with those centered on Rat and Mole. After **"The Piper,"** Grahame seems less certain, more forced into letting Toad dominate and into letting plot play an unwontedly large role. Ask any lover of the book to name the most memorable parts, and the answer will invariably be scenes from the first half, even though the halves were never constructed as such by Grahame.

The special and enduring pleasure of *The Wind in the Willows* is an invitation into an enclosed space, and from its first pages Rat is the essential inviter, and Mole the essential enterer. . . . (p. 176)

What difference does it make that these characters are a rat and a mole? They speak, wear clothes, scull, pack cold lunches, and wish they could afford black velvet smoking jackets. They are much more like human beings, and individual human types, than Beatrix Potter's animals. Yet it will not do to say they are human beings, because Grahame's fantasy depends on his being able to give them so much because they are not human, because he does not have to give them an age, a biography, a past for which they might have to feel guilty, or a future they must anticipate. These are the basic freedoms which then create the possibility of [other freedoms] . . . : messing about in boats, enjoying a full larder, making a new life, for oneself, for someone else.

So Rat and Mole are not human, for all their human apparatus. They are also, in a dimmer sense, animals, as Rat reveals when he begins to describe what lies outside the charmed circle, starting with some residents of the Wild Wood. . . . Rat here resembles an Englishman describing French and Germans, but what he says is also based on the natural fact that weasels,

stoats, and foxes all kill rats, so that when Rat says these others "break out sometimes," he is being English, politely understating the nasty truth, but without any taint of English insularity or prejudice. Mole then remembers "it is quite against animal etiquette to dwell on possible trouble ahead, or even to allude to it." . . . Grahame wants to have it both ways, to elevate both animal and human possibility. It is fun, but irresponsible, for human beings to ignore the future, especially the natural fact of death. Animals have, on the other hand, only the most instinctive sense of any future, nothing more than a pregnant female preparing a home, or birds migrating. Grahame's animal etiquette resembles English manners in insisting on the virtue of understatement, but it carries with it something much more important to Grahame than that: the freedom to ignore the future by not speaking of it, so that if this weekend must end, or if weasels kill rats, it is best we not even think of it. The abolition of worry about the future without abolishing the knowledge that day will break, or that summer will follow spring, encloses Grahame's animals in a secure present where all time is rhythmic time, and rhythmic time brings all the changes one needs. (pp. 178-79)

In the opening chapter, one of the finest openings to any book, Grahame keeps inviting, drawing a boundary, making those pleasures into relief and release. After sculling, lunch; and after lunch, meeting the society of the river. . . . All the while we understand, as Mole does, that we are learning about the limits of enclosed space without ever arriving at a definition of what belongs inside it. But we understand more than Mole does about all this. This is the greatest day of Mole's life, and **"The River Bank"** is also one of the great opening chapters of any reader's reading life. But what is to follow? . . . All too often, we know, the original sensation of release—how wonderful to be free to do this, to leave all that behind—is followed by other feelings—that the space is too narrow, the blessed activity too repetitive, such that we long to return to uncertainty, hope, doubt, and despair, the future even. If Grahame's opening chapter is exhilarating, he succeeds in it in ways others have succeeded too.

Sensing his situation and its problem, Grahame introduces us to the perpetually outside insider, Mr. Toad. We know, of course, that Grahame began with Toad when writing to Alastair, but when he made a book that could embody his own deepest longings, he rightly shifted Mr. Toad from the center of attention and placed him to one side. We hear of him first from Otter's announcement that he is out on the river: "Such a good fellow, too, but no stability—especially in a boat." The phrase "good fellow" reads like a code word here, an insider's phrase, such that neither we nor Mole expect to understand it fully the first time around. We do gather, though, that "no stability" is a pun, of Grahame's and perhaps of Otter's, because not only is Mr. Toad liable to tip over in a boat, but he also is always searching for new things to do. He has sailed and houseboated in the past, and the other animals expect he will soon tire of sculling, and before he learns to manage the oars. To reinforce his point about the virtues of stability, Grahame has Mole suddenly imagine he has become a master of the oars after only one afternoon; he soon tips the boat over, and Rat has to haul him out. But Mole is a "good fellow," and learns his lessons quickly. Mastery comes through repetition, and repeated actions are the best because they teach you how to live in your landscape. (pp. 180-81)

When Rat described the stoats and weasels he drew a boundary—"They're all right in a way" but they "break out"—and we and Mole could see where and why the line is drawn so stoats and weasels will be on the other side. . . . Rat is inside the circle, but we cannot see if Toad is inside or outside it. So we need to go see him, and for at least two chapters Grahame does marvelously at placing and re-placing Toad for us.

Toad is "Mr. Toad," he lives in magnificent Toad Hall, but no one ever condemns him for being rich and living ostentatiously. . . . It is the instability that is bothersome; when Rat and Mole first visit Toad Hall the boathouse has "an unused and a deserted air," because Toad has given up boats altogether. But Toad greets his visitors like "the best of animals," gives them lunch, and exultantly shows them his new toy, a gypsy caravan. . . . The life of the open road might seem to embody instability as a principle, but clearly, also, it resembles messing about in boats; you go, and it doesn't matter where you get to because there is so much to see and do all the time. Mole, always eager to be invited, longs for the open road as he longed for the life on the river. . . . Toad's search, we see, is for "real life," while Rat's is not a search at all. Presumably he does not talk about the river because that would make him boastful, like Toad, a possessor of activities and places; presumably, too, he does not think about the river *all* the time, but it is always there, inside him, defining him. (pp. 181-82)

Toad's conceit lies in his being unable to consider anyone but himself, his pleasure lies in his easy willingness to share his joy, even to give Rat credit for it. Unstable he is, . . . but constant he is too, in the innocent friendliness with which he conveys and shares his passions.

It is easy, we now see, to exclude the Wide World; one just messes about in boats or has lunch and all thought of it is gone. It is not difficult, apparently, to exclude weasels and stoats, because their natural instinct is to be predators, and to "break out," water rats being their prey. If all animals were simply to obey their instincts, however, then Rat and Mole would never meet, and there would be no holiday. To enjoy their lives the animals must not just professionally do as they are naturally fitted to do; they must also be amateurs, more "human," and lead life as a series of charmed possibilities. For precisely these reasons Toad cannot be easily excluded. He cares nothing for the Wide World, he is a gentleman, an amateur above all, fully enjoying what he does. He shares easily, he goes his own way, he never pries into the private concerns of others. Grahame presents him so that in a great many ways he resembles Rat. To rule him out would be most unfriendly, since it would in effect be insisting that everyone be like everyone else.

Yet Toad is dangerous. We may think at first that his defect is flightiness and faddishness as he goes from one exciting activity to the next, always scorning everything he did previously. But after Toad discovers automobiles he never develops another interest, because Grahame wants to define the problem involved here more precisely. Toad buys cars, he wrecks them, he is a menace on the highway, but he is constant to his love. His dangerousness lies in the source and the uncontrollableness of his passion. He has no natural instinct to guide him, and he has a profound and pathetic inability to resist what he mistakenly assumes are his greatest inner needs. Thus, in chapter 6, **"Mr. Toad,"** after Badger, Rat, and Mole incarcerate him in Toad Hall, and after Toad himself seems willing to admit he has been victimized by a terrible malady, his passion leads him to escape from the others and then to become a car thief. . . . It is one of the best moments in the book, Grahame's version of hell. Like all well-conceived hells, it closely resembles

heaven. Every gesture here invites, draws a boundary, and excludes the unwanted outside world, so that the grammar of hell and heaven are precisely the same. Thus Toad can never be excluded from the society of the other animals. What differentiates heaven from hell is what is excluded and included. Inside Toad's passion there is only Toad. In this passage we focus first on the car, the handle, the driver's seat, the ignition; but gradually the car disappears, having succeeded in obliterating everything else in the world: "he was Toad once more, Toad at his best and highest, Toad the terror." . . . "The car responded with sonorous drone, the miles were eaten up under him as he sped he knew not whither"; that *seems* like "whether you arrive at your destination or whether you reach somewhere else . . . you're always busy and never do anything in particular," and Grahame never once implies Rat is better because he does not play with complicated twentieth-century machines. But Rat is always looking outward, . . . delighting in whatever the river and its banks happen to show him, which is why it is possible for him to say "I think about it—all the time!" Toad is concerned with his own pulse rate and delights only in whatever can raise it to new heights; he is bored and twitchy all the rest of the time, since now he has found his "real life." Passion, the great excluder, is thus for Grahame the great enemy, because its dangers lie within us and can never be ruled out just by drawing a boundary or evolving an etiquette that agrees not to discuss the future. To be free, to be released, to live in the present—these are crucial for both Rat and Toad. Toad's is a perversion of a way of life of which Rat is the deepest embodiment.

But here, in this passage, Grahame reaches one of his limits. It is the nature of passions that, once their temptations have been given in to, little good can result for very long, so Toad soon ends up in the dock. It is also the nature of passions to become repetitive, so that once Toad has become "Toad at his best and highest," neither Toad nor Grahame can do more than to try to climb the mountain again and again, so the adventures of Mr. Toad must become the further adventures of Mr. Toad, and these must consist mostly of the frustrations and miseries of Toad as he is kept from getting into cars. When such passions are the subject of works whose scale is larger than Grahame's they are the stuff of high tragedy. . . . The trouble is that after this moment of Toad's fulfillment all we can have is Toad in jail, . . . Toad with the barge woman, Toad regaining Toad Hall from the weasels and stoats. Perhaps he is chastened at last, but the book must end lamely since a chastened Toad is of no interest; and the unchastened Toad has had too many tales told of him already. . . . He belongs, to repeat, over to one side, and Rat and Mole belong at the center.

We have hardly done enough thus far, however, to celebrate Rat and Mole. If *The Wind in the Willows* were only the stunning opening chapter, and the two chapters with Toad before he reaches the height of his passion, the book would not be the irreplaceable work I think it is. But this is not all, and in the other non-Toad chapters Grahame tries to find ways to keep his animals inside their boundaries and, at the same time, describe their responses to impulses as powerful in their way as Toad's. Of the five chapters involved at least three seem totally successful: **"The Wild Wood," "Mr. Badger,"** and **"Dulce Domum."** The other two, **"The Piper at the Gates of Dawn"** and **"Wayfarers All,"** are very attractive in part, but in them Grahame is trying to do what is really beyond his capacities. . . . **"Dulce Domum"** [is] the gem of the book, Grahame's wonderful story of Rat's success at the apparently impossible task of inviting Mole into his own home.

Caught in the "rapid nightfall of mid-December," far from their river home, Rat and Mole trudge through a village where a canary in a cage reminds them of how snug and warm it is to be indoors. As they go on, Rat in the lead, Mole is struck and then overwhelmed by a series of scents that come over him. He soon interprets them to mean home, his home, his old home in the ground: "Poor Mole stood alone in the road, his heart torn asunder, and a big sob gathering, gathering, somewhere low down inside him, to leap up to the surface presently, he knew, in passionate escape." This designedly resembles Toad's response when he first hears the "poop-poop" of the automobile, but it is noteworthy that Mole is not so much excited as made miserable: "But even under such a test as this his loyalty to his friend stood firm. Never for a moment did he dream of abandoning him. Meanwhile, the wafts from his old home pleaded, whispered, conjured, and finally claimed him imperiously. He dared not tarry longer within their magic circle." The word "imperiously" is an important one for Grahame. He uses it in the opening pages to describe the way Mole is commanded by the spring to leave his housecleaning and come above ground and go to the river. There, as here, the power that does the commanding is every bit as great as the passion of Toad, but it is located outside the characters, in the world, as part of the great creation of nature. The imperious command to return to one's natural habitat is made stronger here because it is December, and cold, and all living things are seeking home as their refuge.

Mole breaks away from the magic circle of the imperious smells, catches up with Rat, but then breaks down:

> "I know it's a—shabby, dingy little place . . . , but it was my own little home—and I was fond of it—and I went away and forgot all about it—and then I smelt it suddenly . . . and everything came back to me with a rush—and I *wanted* it."

This is the perfect speech to contrast with Toad's triumphant conversion to the automobile. Mole is not in heaven here, but he is a candidate for admission. What shames Mole is a power strong enough to break down his duty as Rat's friend to keep up and not to bother anyone else with his private troubles. The network of pleasures and loyalties the animals work so hard to build cannot resist such power, which is why Mole is so miserable. But Rat, best of animals, knows the crucial difference between seeking passion as a form of excitement and giving into imperial powers naturally greater than oneself. The opposite of the amateur pleasures is not anything professional, but a power essentially religious. So, insisting that Mole blow his nose to keep it keen so it can guide them, Rat takes over, himself having only to obey the need to be loyal to his friend.

When they arrive at Mole's house Mole must go on being ashamed, because all he can see is a "poor, cold little place." Rat, however, kind beyond thanks, dissolves Mole's shame, not by cheering him up but by discovering the pleasures of Mole End. . . . Rat keeps on drawing the circles, inviting Mole across his own threshold, recreating the splendors of home and thereby recreating the purpose and possibility of friendship. . . . In these pages Grahame makes home both richly nostalgic and actively alive in the present. One wants to keep cheering Rat on to find more things to love, and one wants also to weep, as one's gratitude for Rat reveals the knowledge that no homecoming, no friendship, could ever quite be this good. (pp. 183-88)

What begins as the summons of an imperial power ends as the relaxed intense excitement of giving to a friend what he could not, were he the mightiest or most wealthy, give to himself.

But this sense of imperious powers in nature haunted Grahame, and he could not rest content with having that power be whatever drove Mole up out of his hole and then drove him back down into it. Grahame came to his world of the river and the woods with thanksgiving, he entered its courts with praise, and so he wanted to name its god. Thus, after the splendid burrowings into the houses of Mr. Badger and Mole, he makes an attempt to soar, in **"The Piper at the Gates of Dawn,"** as high above the earth as the other chapters go beneath it. This chapter divides the book; before it we have Grahame at his very best, in all the ways we have seen thus far, and after it we have the later and less interesting Toad stories. In **"The Piper"** Grahame rather self-consciously tries to justify his excursions into cozy fantasy when, in fact, no such justification was needed.

It is a summer evening, and it feels, even late at night, as though the sun has never quite left this spot of earth. Rat and Mole hear that Otter's son Portly is lost, and, worried and unable to sleep, they set out to try to find him. As they row up the river, it begins to get light in the east, and Rat hears a noise, a bird maybe, the wind in the reeds: "'Now it passes on and I begin to lose it,' he said presently. 'O Mole! the beauty of it! The merry bubble and joy, the thin, clear, happy call of the distant piping! Such music I never dreamed of, and the call in it is stronger even than the music is sweet!'" Once again, the imperious power. Mole, who only smells his powerful callers, hears only "the wind playing in the reeds and rushes and osiers," but Rat needs more, a religious summons. This is a strain in Rat that has been there all along—in his dreaming off at the very beginning while telling Mole about messing about in boats, in his writing poetry when the fit seizes him—but it seems more a part of Grahame himself than something he can make actively a part of Rat's character. We can concede Rat's "I think about it—all the time!" certainly, but this more ethereal propensity seems just not to belong. Thus, when Rat and Mole, following the piping music only Rat hears, arrive at their destination, it does not sound like Rat who is speaking: "'This is the place of my song-dream, the place the music played to me,' whispered the Rat, as if in a trance. 'Here, in this holy place, here if anywhere, surely we shall find Him.'" We hardly seem to be in *The Wind in the Willows* at all. (pp. 189-90)

As Rat and Mole come to the island to which they have been summoned, they see "the very eyes of the Friend and Helper," complete with horns and rippling muscles and shaggy limbs. Then: . . . last of all, nestling between his very hooves, sleeping soundly in entire peace and contentment, the little, round, podgy, childish form of the baby otter. All this he saw, for one moment breathless and intense, vivid on the morning sky; and still, as he looked, he lived; and still, as he lived, he wondered.

> "Rat!" he found breath to whisper, shaking. "Are you afraid?"

> "Afraid?" murmured the Rat, his eyes shining with unutterable love. "Afraid! Of *Him!* O never, never! And yet—and yet—O Mole, I am afraid!"

No one not already a worshipper of Pan would actually prefer this Rat, this Mole, this writing, to **"The River Bank"** or

"**Dulce Domum.**" The adjectives—"very," "entire," "unutterable"—all show a straining toward a feeling that by its thrilled vagueness makes us remember how much, elsewhere in the book, Grahame can convey with language only slightly more pinned down. Grahame may say Mole and Rat are afraid, but he himself is not; he is only thrilled at the possibility of feeling such fear.

The trouble is the context, or, in this case, the feebleness of the context. . . . [We] must try to look at Pan himself to see what Grahame is caring about, and of course Pan himself is, and probably must be, vague. The young otter is there, protected by Pan the Friend and Helper, but even he, the most clearly seen figure in the scene, is only putative; we know nothing of him, and Rat and Mole are looking for him mostly because it is a restless summer night, not because they know where or how to look for him. In other words, the imperious command does not arise out of anything, or, really, lead to anything beyond a rescued Portly. Pan simply is, and we must take him or leave him. Even the relation of Pan to the dawn is more suggested than carefully realized.

I don't for a minute think that in any serious way Grahame believed in Pan or in any other deity. What he knew was the intensity of his own longings to live life as an escape, as holiday, as Rat and Mole can live it and Toad cannot. He was not ashamed either of the feelings or of the intensity. Still, one of the secrets of the power of the release was some sense that grown people are not supposed to yearn that much for something that many other grown people see as the yearnings of a child. . . . [The] greater part of [Grahame] felt himself to be an exile from a world, a childhood, a Thames life, he had never quite lived in. Lonely and unhappy, possessed by longings, he was driven to justify them. The first six chapters of *The Wind in the Willows* were the only justification he needed, but he was driven to insist on more than this. There is no radical defect involved here, only a reminder that books like this one are often written by huddled, self-protective people who can be driven toward a definition of a vaguely understood "higher experience."

How odd, thus, that someone whose writing was so personal should ever have been thought of essentially as a writer for children. If Grahame "understood children," it was not because he liked them, enjoyed their presence, or even thought about them. Rather, because he was deprived of much that goes into the usual experiences of a childhood, he remained something of a child throughout his life, perceptibly more so than the rest of us. . . . [It] is usually very difficult to tell stories that take place in ideal worlds. But Grahame did just this, and in its finest moments *The Wind in the Willows* creates and sustains a genuine ideal, one that is going to continue to appeal strongly to many people, for centuries perhaps. To be rid of the cares of personality and responsibility, to forget or never know yesterday's wrongdoings or tomorrow's needs—it is a great wish, close to universal perhaps. . . . Most writers and most people find that when they have tossed off adult tasks and human curses they have, left over, only a rather empty space. But Grahame could fill that space and invite us into the charmed circle he thereby created. He could make little sounds seem like bustle, make gestures of invitation seem like love, make food and fire feel like home. (pp. 190-93)

> Roger Sale, "Kenneth Grahame," in his *Fairy Tales and After: From Snow White to E. B. White (copyright © 1978 by the President and Fellows of Harvard College; excerpted by permission), Cambridge, Mass.: Harvard University Press, 1978, pp. 165-94.*

THE GOLDEN AGE (1895)

The Golden Age is, as all know, the period of childhood. . . . [The] "grown ups" are nicknamed the "Olympians," and such is the title of the Prologue, which one reads with that delightful sensation—as of a mental cold-water bath—which is occasioned by dipping into a fresh and sincere bit of writing. The author is, evidently, one of those who speak in their natural voice, the ring and the music of it unextracted by any consideration as to whether the output will be "marketable". . . . The water-mark of spontaneity in literature, though hard to describe, is unmistakable, and it is stamped on every story in *The Golden Age.* In the Prologue the reading Olympian is forced to see himself as the children—the children of this volume at least—see him, "stiff and colourless, . . . equally without vital interests and intelligent pursuits." This criticism of the Olympians is, from a youngster's point of view, logical enough, but it is not childlike. Children, fortunately, take people very much as they find them, and they are far more charitable than are the Olympians themselves. (pp. 48-9)

Save in this hostile attitude of his young heroes and heroines, Kenneth Grahame interprets child life with striking sympathy and truth, and at this point it is only fair to quote the author himself. He opens the book by saying : "Looking back to those days of old, ere the gate shut to behind me, I can see now that to children with a proper equipment of parents these things would have worn a different aspect. But to those whose nearest were aunts and uncles, a special attitude of mind may be allowed." However, the explanation hardly explains, since the children of these stories are pictured as happy, healthy youngsters, debarred from no natural pleasures, and even treated with a degree of indulgence, considering their roguish tendencies. Yet this note of criticism and hostility is sounded throughout the volume, marring an otherwise strong and true representation of child nature.

So delightfully genuine are the sympathy and liveliness with which the exploits of these children are recorded that the reader must needs hark back to his own childhood, and then look with kindlier eyes on the pranks and freaks of those who dwell in the Golden Age. Herein lies the true value of the book: it puts the Olympian in the child's place, so that he catches once more that "visionary gleam" which has faded out of his own life. . . . *The Golden Age* is an enlightener of adult stupidity.

Several of these stories are fine studies of the workings of a child's imagination, reproducing the very glamour in which the Golden Age is bathed. The best of these are "**Alarums and Excursions**" and "**The Finding of the Princess.**" "**Alarums and Excursions**" is a charming bit of word painting. We see the children playing at Knights of the Round Table, and following far a band of exercising cavalry, in the hope of seeing a very bloody battle. (p. 49)

The first story, "**A Holiday,**" is one of the best in the volume. "A boy's will is the wind's will," and the boy, lightly following the wind whithersoever it leads him, runs up against the hard fact that law and license are incompatible. In this chapter, as in several others, there is a delicate touching on the problems of life, an outreaching and a questioning, which lend a world-wide interest to the unpretentious tale of a boy's doings. In "**The Secret Drawer**" and "**The Roman Road**" we find again that suggestion of something deeper than childish adventure—a momentary, shadowy glimpse, as though a mist had lifted and quickly fallen again. **"The Burglars"** and **"The Blue Room"** are full of young laughter and roguery, while **"The Whitewashed Uncle"** throws out a pretty broad hint to any Olympian who would fain be popular with the little people.

"Young Adam Cupid" and **"What They Talked About"** show the author so wise in the lore of child nature that the chapter **"Sawdust and Sin"** is simply amazing in its error. Here a conceit possible to an adult only is foisted on the mind of a child with a result which is far from pleasing. . . . Children do indeed have ideas about love and love affairs, but they are so deliciously, so alarmingly innocent and quaint in their conception of such matters! There is nothing innocent about this passage.

"A Falling Out" and **"Exit Tyrannus"** are the only stories which could send a lump to the most sensitive throat; indeed, the author seems rather to have missed his opportunities for tenderness and pathos. His chief power lies in fitting to the reader's eyes those glasses through which the little ones look out upon this world of ours—glasses made largely of imagination and innocence and ignorance, and all shot with rosy and golden lights, but sometimes dimmed by the ruthless fingers of stupid Olympians. And would any such know how the universe looks to children, he is recommended to see it through the pages of *The Golden Age*. (pp. 49-50)

Virginia Yeaman Remnitz, in her review of "The Golden Age," in The Bookman, New York *(copyright, 1895, by George H. Doran Company), Vol. II, No. 1, August-September, 1895, pp. 48-50.*

We are a little tired of the child in fiction, but these papers record the doings of a group of children with much humour and generally with much truth to nature. . . . Mr. Grahame looks through both ends of the telescope, and writes as a small boy with the knowledge and experience of a man, and this causes a sense of artificiality and incongruity about some of the sketches, such as **"Sawdust and Sin"** and **"The Roman Road,"** and also there is a decided touch of burlesque in the amusing chapters headed **"The Blue Chamber"** and **"The Burglars."** But the humour of **"The Whitewashed Uncle"** is delightful where the children sit in judgment on a stranger uncle, and with the intolerance and ignorance of youth, condemn him for his air of false geniality, making no allowance for the shyness of a bachelor unused to the right methods of conciliating childhood. . . . Some of the incidents have an air of truth about them that lead us to suspect Mr. Grahame of having drawn a good deal on his own boyish reminiscences; the love of "pretending" that is inherent in children, . . . the thirst for adventure, the charm that overlays the search for a "secret drawer," will all find echoes in the hearts of those who remember their own youthful days. There is pathos as well as humour in the account of the departure of the governess. . . . One of the best sketches in the book is the story of a **"Falling-Out,"** in which the narrator has remembered or imagined, with no adornments of false sentiment, the feelings of a small boy who had, in a momentary fit of sulkiness, repulsed the kind overtures of an elder sister. . . . "A boy's will is the wind's will," and this is fully exemplified in the chapter entitled **"A Holiday,"** where the thoughtless joyousness of youth has seldom been recalled to older minds with a more vigorous and breezy sense of elation. (p. 140)

[There] is something healthful in the tone of the book, which is to be welcomed as a breezy spring morning is welcome after the heavy fogs of winter; there is no special grace of distinction,

but the author has shown decided promise of literary power, and we shall look with interest for further essays. (p. 141)

A review of "The Golden Age," in The Spectator *(©1896 by The Spectator; reprinted by permission of* The Spectator*), No. 3526, January 25, 1896, pp. 140-41.*

Quite lately more than one serious attempt has been made to give childhood its due in fiction. A notable instance is Mr. Kenneth Grahame's pictures from child-life [*The Golden Age*]. The book has been praised on high authority as a new revelation of childhood. . . . (p. 225)

[The] critical attitude towards the elders as a "strange anaemic order of beings" is bold, and gives a tone of engaging smartness to the narrative. Yet it may be conjectured that Mr. Grahame carries his idea too far for the best kind of effect. Children's passion for play leads them, no doubt, to resent the customary limitations as highly inconvenient. But this resentment is a long way from the development of a cut-and-dried theory of the relation of older people's doings to young inclinations, such as is here formulated in rather high-flown adult language. It would surely be nearer the mark to say that a child never fully thinks out the relation of his play to the serious concerns of life as the adult understands them. . . . Mr. Grahame's remarks about promotion to the tooth-brush . . . are a complete refutation of his theory that children look on the adult and his ways as something hopelessly foreign. The tooth-brush, with its monotonous return of irksome duty, is welcomed only because it is a visible sign of an approach to the status of the "stupid" and "anaemic" grown-up.

The adventures of this small child-community in its quest of new sensation, and its pathetic attempt to press elders into its service are agreeable enough reading. There is here the breeziness of true play, of play in the country. The children are individualised with a skilful hand, and the most is made of those collisions of young wills which keep play from growing tame without undermining its solidarity.

Yet there are drawbacks serious enough to make one doubt whether the book is, after all, a new revelation straight from the children's world. Mr. Grahame carefully omits to give a hint as to ages. As, however, all are as yet in the hands of a governess, and the narrator includes himself among the "three younger ones," one may safely set him down to have been not above ten. He is child enough, at any rate, to enjoy strumming, to take a toy-snake to bed with him, and to be addressed by strangers as a water-baby. Yet this small person not only gives himself now and again an air of superiority to the others' play, wandering forth into the fields alone to indulge in precocious poetic raptures, but shows himself capable of reading into a scene in which figure his little sister and her two dolls, a significance which surely could only have occurred to an experienced adult. It is one thing to have the vague stirring of instinct, quite another to see what this child is said to have seen. As this chapter now stands, it must, I fear, appear to many a dishonour done to the sacred cause of childhood.

The chapter is merely the exaggeration of a tone of cynical superiority which runs through the volume and gives it its peculiar cleverness. It has its advantages: it is an admirable safeguard against a feeble sentimentalism. There is, however, another safeguard in the humour (not Mr. Grahame's caustic variety), which can find room for sentiment and at the same time restrain it from ever swelling into ridiculous bulk. And perhaps, after all, a treatment at once tender and humorous is what best does justice to the subject. (pp. 226-27)

J. Sully, "The Child in Recent English Literature," in The Fortnightly Review, *Vol. LXI, February, 1897, pp. 218-28.**

One charm of **The Golden Age** is its felicity in combining the philosophy of a man of the world, blessed with more than a dash of poetry and romance in him and a pretty taste for paganism, with the philosophy of the thoughtful boy. By a remarkable feat Mr. Grahame has been able to remember his childhood, and preserve it sweet and unsullied alongside his maturer wisdom. The-first-person-singular of **The Golden Age** is charming and unique in its mixture of grave juvenility and whimsical humorous manhood. We never confuse the dual character of the historian: we see him as boy and listen to him as man, and both boy and man are a delight; one for his boyishness, his mischief, and his proprietary sense (common to all adventurous boys) with respect to the world; the other for his humour, his sympathy, his literary distinction. All the children are life-like. By a thousand minute touches Mr. Grahame establishes their reality. So typical are their thoughts and actions, misgivings and ambitions, that **The Golden Age** is to some extent every reader's autobiography. Everything is slightly "toned up"—the duty of the romanist as opposed to the realist—but truth is never violated. Mr. Grahame's deftness in selection is remarkable. As a short story **"The Burglars,"** for example, is truly excellent. And his style is so fresh and buoyant. "The masterful wind was up and out, shouting and chasing, the lord of the morning"—how strong and communicative, this opening sentence! The joy of living has at the moment in Mr. Grahame an exponent of rare sympathy. . . . [**The Golden Age**] is written with the golden pen. After all, it matters very little whether or not Mr. Grahame writes any more. In **The Golden Age** he has given us a book, a four-square piece of literature, complete in itself. Many a literary man writes hard all his life, and never a book—in the best sense of the word—is forthcoming. Mr. Grahame made one the first time.

"Some Younger Reputations: Mr. Kenneth Grahame," in The Academy, *No. 1335, December 4, 1897, p. 493.*

DREAM DAYS (1898)

[**Dream Days**] must be considered a collection of stories about children for grown-up people. There are eight of these tales, all well written and some very amusing. Sketches of incidents in child-life often assume graphic forms in Mr. Grahame's volume. . . . The book is full of quaint things, but few of them will be pleasing to children.

A review of "Dream Days," in The Athenaeum, *Vol. 115, No. 3719, February 4, 1899, p. 142.*

Our old friends of the Golden Age are all here, as full of life and fancy and rebellion as ever. We do not tire of their fresh company; and if Mr. Grahame spin still more yarns about Selina and Edward and the incomparable Harold and the others, we shall read them with a twinkle of sympathy. A close examination of the two books is highly favourable to the second; and if we receive it the more coolly, it is only because the children's very decided characters and manner of playing were pretty fully defined in the first. The development is not surprising, but it is excellently amusing. **"The Twenty-First of October,"** which is Selina's special Saga . . . ; the incident of the Death-Letter,

where Harold is the hero, and the tale of the pilfering and burial of two dear memorial trophies from the parcel about to be sent by thoughtful relations to the Children's Hospital, are beyond praise. Childhood, at once imaginative and lusty, is in his pages made very living to us. We think there is just one blunder. The average child is brutally obtuse, and when Martha locked herself into her room on hearing of her brother's death, it would have struck him "as a funny sort of proceeding." But the child who was afterwards the recorder of all these tales, the child of the sensitive eye and memory, would not have thought it "funny." In the midst of our amusement and admiration we must own that it is not in every aspect a general picture he draws of the relations between the grown-up world and children. As a rule, children are in half their being enthusiastic admirers of the grown-up world, and in the other half supremely indifferent to it. The critical, scornful attitude of Mr. Grahame's children is quite exceptional.

A review of "Dream Days," in The Bookman, *London, Vol. XV, No. 90, March, 1899, p. 190.*

There is no book about children like **"The Golden Age,"** unless it is Kenneth Grahame's present volume, which is chiefly divided between their adventurous happenings in daily life and sundry exploits in worlds which they have shaped to their own imagining. An illustration of the former is called **"The Magic Ring"**—in reality a first visit to a circus. We are back in our own childhood, amidst the old delight and dazzlement. A certain **"Saga of the Seas"** is the crowning instance of the second: it is an ecstasy of pirate hunting. There is, however, an extra which belongs to neither class, a story told by a grown-up concerning **"The Reluctant Dragon,"** no other than that of the Seven Champions myth and St. George of England. But a change and a new spirit has come over all; the dragon is really the desirable acquaintance, while the champion earns his laurels by coming to a good understanding with the enchanting beast. One expects that **"Dream Days"** will appeal as strongly to all between nine and ninety as did—and indeed does—**"The Golden Age."**

A review of "Dream Days," in The Bookman, *London, Vol. LXII, No. 375, December, 1922, p. 187.*

THE WIND IN THE WILLOWS (1908)

[If] Mr. Kenneth Grahame's **"The Wind in the Willows"** . . . should fall into the wrong hands it might suffer great indignities. Such, for instance, as being termed "an allegory," or, worse still, a "nature book." It might even be banished into the nursery, where it would simply be wasted, if it were not actively dangerous.

Imagine children reading such heresies as this: "The Rat . . . during his short day sometimes scribbled poetry or did other small domestic jobs around the house." Or this: "On the walls hung wire baskets, alternating with brackets carrying plaster statuary—Garibaldi and the infant Samuel and Queen Victoria and other heroes of modern Italy." And these are not the worst by any means!

You must be quite grown up to appreciate the thrilling adventures of Mr. Toad, who would a-motoring go, even to the extent of stealing a car. For this rash act he was thrown into a deep dungeon, rescuing himself after sundry encounters with a fat barge woman, a gypsy, and a captured engine. The Toad is much more human than many people we read of in novels nowadays. Really, the story's chief characters are the Rat and the Mole, but no reviewer could attempt to describe them— you must get them at first hand.

"The Wind in the Willows" is a worthy companion to **"The Golden Age"** and **"Dream Days."** It is whimsical, fascinating by its apparent seriousness and that sense of underlying poetry which Mr. Grahame somehow manages to convey through all his nonsense. When the poor little Rat and Mole come to the enchanted isle, and, drawn by mysterious music, find themselves in the presence of the great God Pan himself, refuge and savior of weary, stricken wild creatures—well, you hope it is all true, and you know it is very beautiful.

Some may call it nature faking of the baldest sort, but such pedantry carries its own punishment. The book is not easily classified—it is simply destined to be one of those dog-eared volumes which one laughs over and loves.

> *"'The Wind in the Willows','' in* The New York Times Saturday Review *(© 1908 by The New York Times Company; reprinted by permission), October 24, 1908, p. 593.*

I should describe [*The Wind in the Willows*] as a sort of irresponsible holiday story in which the chief characters are woodland animals, who are represented as enjoying most of the advantages of civilisation—shopping, caravanning, motoring, travelling by train, and so on—apparently on terms of more or less equality with the human world. Some grown-up readers may cavil at this, others may find in the story a satirical purpose which its author would probably disclaim. But children will, I think, accept Mr. Grahame's Rat, Mole and Badger as personal friends, and enjoy Toad's adventures and mishaps with a heartiness untroubled by any such curious considerations.

> *"Our Booking-Office," in* Punch *(© 1908 by Punch Publications Ltd.; all rights reserved; may not be reprinted without permission), Vol. CXXXV, November 11, 1908, p. 360.**

[*The Wind in the Willows*] rambles along in a vein of delightful extravagance, the misfortunes and ultimate reformation of the wayward Toad being among its most pleasant and stirring episodes; but the author seems not to have given himself up whole-heartedly to his fantasy, and is apt to hinder the charm of his incongruities by spasmodic efforts to make them congruous. These cavillings apart, the book, with its scenes of river, forest, and field, and its whimsical incursions into the human world, forms an all but perfect blending of idyll and inconsequence.

> *A review of "The Wind in the Willows," in* The Athenaeum, *No. 4230, November 21, 1908, p. 643.*

[*The Wind in the Willows*] for me is notable for its intimate sympathy with Nature and for its delicate expression of emotions which I, probably in common with most people, had previously believed to be my exclusive property. When all is said the boastful, unstable Toad, the hospitable Water Rat, the shy, wise, childlike Badger, and the Mole with his pleasant habit of brave boyish impulse, are neither animals nor men, but are types of that deeper humanity which sways us all. To be wise, an allegory must admit of a wide application. . . . And if I may venture to describe as an allegory a work which critics, who ought to have known better, have dismissed as a fairy story, it is certain that *The Wind in the Willows* is a wise book. It is wise, moreover, with that simplicity which has its appeal to children as well as to grown-up folk. Just as young

people read *The Pilgrim's Progress* and *Gulliver's Travels* for the story, so I fancy they will find Mr. Grahame's book a history of exciting adventures, and value it in this aspect no less than we, who find it a storehouse of glowing prose, gracious observation, delicate fantasy, and life-like and even humorous dialogue. (pp. 127-28)

I confess, though it is some ten years since I first read them, that I still find Mr. Grahame's *Dream Days* and *The Golden Age* as perfect as when they first taught me what my boyhood meant. *The Wind in the Willows* is a wider, fuller book than these, and yet I believe that Mr. Grahame has accomplished the harder task with no less sureness of touch, with no less qualified a success. And I think it will be time to lay down my pen, when I shall be able to review soberly a book that gives me such unalloyed pleasure at the first reading. (p. 128)

> *Richard Middleton, in his extract from "'The Wind in the Willows'" (originally published in* Vanity Fair, *1908), in* Kenneth Grahame: Life, Letters and Unpublished Work *by Patrick R. Chalmers, Methuen Co. Ltd., 1933, pp. 127-28.*

Mr. Kenneth Grahame's reputation is indissolubly connected with children, but not with children's books. His delicate art of wistful retrospect makes children real to grown-up people, and gives dulled hearts a breath from forgotten childhoods, but it is not an art that can be enjoyed by any one still so fortunate as to be a child. Its appeal is not only to imagination, but to knowledge. Mr. Grahame writes for people who have passed the barriers, and look affectionately back at their little dead selves playing in the meadows behind them. They know that they are different, now. But the very secret of childhood is a feeling of eternal age. . . . As soon as a child thinks he is a child he is so no longer. . . . [A] little boy would find Mr. Grahame's books incomprehensible, for in them there is always the consciousness of a gulf between childhood and manhood, a gulf it is a sorrow to have passed, a horrible chasm between dream and reality. Their motive is the pathos of retrospective life in which no child can possibly believe.

"The Wind in the Willows" is an attempt to write for children instead of about them. But Mr. Grahame's past has been too strong for him. Instead of writing about children for grown-up people, he has written about animals for children. The difference is only in the names. He writes of the animals with the same wistfulness with which he wrote of children, and, in his attitude towards his audience, he is quite unable to resist that appeal from dreamland to a knowledge of the world that makes the charm of all his books, and separates them from children's literature. The poems in the book are the only things really written for the nursery, and the poems are very bad.

If we judge the book by its aim, it is a failure, like a speech to Hottentots made in Chinese. And yet, for the Chinese, . . . the speech might be quite a success. Mr. Grahame's book is quite a success from the point of view of the people for whom it was not written. When the grown-up reviewer, after his annoyance with Mr. Grahame for having chosen the wrong language, makes up his mind to think of the book as if it were meant for himself, and grants its author a fairy-story licence he would have done better without, he finds himself reading page after page to the end and spending his time quite happily. A toad, for example, must be allowed to live in large houses, to be imprisoned in gaol, to drive motor-cars, to wear the clothes of an ordinary-sized washerwoman, and yet to consort upon terms of equality with a mole, whose attributes are merely those of nature. A greater man than Mr. Grahame would not have asked so much. But we would willingly have granted Mr. Grahame even more for the sake of **"Dulce Domum,"** that delicious little picture of the rat and the mole in the mole's house, mulling ale on Christmas Eve for the field-mice waifs who have come, in red worsted comforters, to sing their Christmas carols. (pp. 190-91)

Arthur Ransome, "Betwixt and Between," in The Bookman, *London, Vol. XXXV, No. 208, January, 1909, pp. 190-91.*

The bother about most books is that they endeavor to explain away the wonder of the world. . . . But the books of Kenneth Grahame may be safely read, because they are haunted by the visionary gleam. He knows things simply, like a child; and he loves them for the great reason that they are wonderful.

The Wind in the Willows is a poem in praise of the glory that can never really pass away from the earth, unless we allow ourselves to grow up and forget. . . . It reveals anew the miracle of out-of-doors. The romance of the river, the allurement of the open road, the tremulous ecstatic terrors of the wild wood, the sad sweet tug of heart-strings by the sense of home, the poignant wander-longing, the amusement of adventure,—all these moods of simple wonderment are told and sung in its enchanting pages. (pp. 84-5)

In the original and undefiled sense of the word, Mr. Grahame's work is worthy mainly because it is irradiated by the spirit of the *amateur*. He writes because he loves to: he is too child-like and playful to subside into the mere professional man of letters. *The Wind in the Willows* is fun to read because the author wrote it for fun. It ranges through all the moods of natural enjoyment: it is humorous and beautiful, it combines satire with sentiment, it is serious and jocund. An uproarious chapter, which satirizes the modern subservience to the latest fad, is followed by a chapter in which, mystically, we are brought face to face with the very God of out-of-doors. Mr. Grahame talks in whatever mood most enchants him at the time: his range is as various and as free as the aeolian breathing of the wind in the willows.

The actors in the present rambling narrative bear the names of animals; and a certain inconsistency may be noted in the handling of them. At times they are endowed with human traits and used to satirize the foibles of mankind; and at other times they are exhibited as animals indeed, and are used to reveal an infra-human view of life. This inconsistency is sometimes jarring; and as a consequence, the critic is moved to set the book on a plane a little lower than that of the perfect expositions of the mood of wonder,—like *Alice in Wonderland*, for example.

Ten years ago, before his disquieting silence, Mr. Grahame demonstrated that he held command of the most finished and perfected English prose style that had been listened to since Stevenson's. *The Wind in the Willows* is written in the same style, ripened and matured. To be a great artist is, of course, a lesser thing than to be an undiscouragable child; but it is reassuring to record that Mr. Grahame is the one as well as the other. We need him, both to play with and to listen to. Those of us who refuse to grow up and forget are banking on his future. May he fulfil his future, even if he has to neglect his Bank! (p. 85)

Walter Clayton, "An Interrupted Pan Resumes His Piping," in Forum *(copyright, 1909, by Events Pub-*

lishing Company, Inc.), Vol. XLI, No. 1, January, 1909, pp. 83-5.

"The Wind in the Willows" does not disappoint. Here, indeed, we have the work of a man who is obviously interested in letters and in life, the work of a fastidious and yet a very robust artist. But the book is fairly certain to be misunderstood of the people. The publishers' own announcement describes it as "perhaps chiefly for youth," a description with which I disagree. The obtuse are capable of seeing in it nothing save a bread-and-butter imitation of "The Jungle Book." The woodland and sedgy lore in it is discreet and attractive. Names of animals abound in it. But it is nevertheless a book of humanity. The author may call his chief characters the Rat, the Mole, the Toad,—they are human beings, and they are meant to be nothing but human beings. Were it otherwise, the spectacle of a toad going through the motor-car craft would be merely incomprehensible and exasperating. The superficial scheme of the story is so childishly naïve, or so daringly naïve, that only a genius could have preserved it from the ridiculous. The book is an urbane exercise in irony at the expense of the English character and of mankind. It is entirely successful. Whatever may happen to it in the esteem of mandarins and professors, it will beyond doubt be considered by authentic experts as a work highly distinguished, original and amusing—and no more to be comprehended by youth than **"The Golden Age"** was to be comprehended by youth. (pp. 57-8)

Arnold Bennett, "Kenneth Grahame," in his Books and Persons: Being Comments on a Past Epoch, 1908-1911 *(copyright, 1917, by George H. Doran Company; reprinted by permission of the Estate of the late Arnold Bennett), Doran, 1917, pp. 57-8.*

[I am going to speak] of a book which should be a classic, but is not; of a book of which nobody has heard unless through me. (p. 86)

[One] cannot recommend a book to all the hundreds of people whom one has met in ten years without discovering whether it is well known or not. It is the amazing truth that none of those hundreds had heard of *The Wind in the Willows* until I told them about it. Some of them had never heard of Kenneth Grahame. . . . But most of them were in your position—great admirers of the author and his two earlier famous books, but ignorant thereafter. . . . Indeed, I feel sometimes that it was I who wrote *The Wind in the Willows,* and recommended it to Kenneth Grahame. . . . (pp. 87-8)

I shall not describe the book, for no description would help it. But I shall just say this; that it is what I call a Household Book. By a Household Book I mean a book which everybody in the household loves and quotes continually ever afterwards; a book which is read aloud to every new guest, and is regarded as the touchstone of his worth. But it is a book which makes you feel that, though everybody in the house loves it, it is only you who really appreciate it at its true value, and that the others are scarcely worthy of it. It is obvious, you persuade yourself, that the author was thinking of you when he wrote it. (pp. 88-9)

But I must give you one word of warning. When you sit down to it, don't be so ridiculous as to suppose that you are sitting in judgment on my taste, still less on the genius of Kenneth Grahame. You are merely sitting in judgment on yourself. . . . You may be worthy; I do not know. But it is you who are on trial. (p. 89)

A. A. Milne, "A Household Book," in his Not That It Matters, *eighth edition (reprinted by permission of Curtis Brown Ltd., London), Methuen & Co. Ltd., 1927, pp. 85-9.*

I believe that [*The Wind in the Willows*] will live when *The Golden Age,* already dated, is dead. For children to-day do not of necessity see their elders as The Opposition. But *The Wind* is artless and nursery-ageless and it, probably, is the work by which its author would best wish to be remembered. For since that long ago day when the Kings of the East came to the manger, bringing with them their gold and frankincense and myrrh, surely all men, Kenneth Grahame among them, give of their heart's best only when they give to a child. (p. 148)

Patrick R. Chalmers, in his Kenneth Grahame: Life, Letters and Unpublished Work, *Methuen & Co. Ltd., 1933, 321 p.*

Does anyone believe that Kenneth Grahame made an arbitrary choice when he gave his principal character the form of a toad, or that a stag, a pigeon, a lion would have done as well? The choice is based on the fact that the real toad's face has a grotesque resemblance to a certain kind of human face—a rather apoplectic face with a fatuous grin on it. This is, no doubt, an accident in the sense that all the lines which suggest the resemblance are really there for quite different biological reasons. The ludicrous quasi-human expression is therefore changeless: the toad cannot stop grinning because its 'grin' is not really a grin at all. Looking at the creature we thus see, isolated and fixed, an aspect of human vanity in its funniest and most pardonable form; following that hint Grahame creates Mr Toad—an ultra-Jonsonian 'humour'. And we bring back the wealth of the Indies, we have henceforward more amusement in, and kindness towards, a certain kind of vanity in real life.

But why should the characters be disguised as animals at all? The disguise is very thin, so thin that Grahame makes Mr Toad on one occasion 'comb the dry leaves out of his *hair*'. Yet it is quite indispensable. If you try to rewrite the book with all the characters humanized you are faced at the outset with a dilemma. Are they to be adults or children? You will find that they can be neither. They are like children in so far as they have no responsibilities, no struggle for existence, no domestic cares. . . . But in other ways it is the life of adults. They go where they like and do what they please, they arrange their own lives.

To that extent the book is a specimen of the most scandalous escapism: it paints a happiness under incompatible conditions—the sort of freedom we can have only in childhood and the sort we can have only in maturity—and conceals the contradiction by the further pretence that the characters are not human beings at all. The one absurdity helps to hide the other. It might be expected that such a book would unfit us for the harshness of reality and send us back to our daily lives unsettled and discontented. I do not find that it does so. The happiness which it presents to us is in fact full of the simplest and most attainable things—food, sleep, exercise, friendship, the face of nature, even (in a sense) religion. . . . [The] whole story, paradoxically enough, strengthens our relish for real life. This excursion into the preposterous sends us back with renewed pleasure to the actual. (pp. 84-5)

C. S. Lewis, "The Reader and All Kinds of Stories: On Stories," in Essays Presented to Charles Williams *(reprinted by permission of Oxford University Press),*

Oxford University Press, London, 1947 (and reprinted in The Cool Web: The Pattern of Children's Reading *by Margaret Meek, Aidan Warlow, and Griselda Barton, The Bodley Head, 1977, pp. 76-90).*

The first essential of a bedside book is that it should tranquillize the mind. What better bedside book could there be, then, than one which mingles universal truth with fancy, and at imperceptible points crosses the boundary between the world we know and the world of dreams? I know of none. I know that in reading Kenneth Grahame's *The Wind in the Willows* I recapture childhood's delight in fairy tales, that I am taken into delicious little odd corners of understanding and fun, and that while I sometimes laugh aloud at what I read the effect of the book as a whole is one of such smiling happiness that I can close my eyes, see and think of nothing but half-poetic images, and fall blissfully asleep.

For other moods, of course, and for other natures, books of a different order must be found; and to relish *The Wind in the Willows* at all one must certainly possess the English kind of humour, a love of small and young things, and a willingness to yield to fancy. The logical mind, which says 'Who ever heard an animal talk like this?' or the glib modernist mind, which calls every ascent of the imagination 'escapism,' might well fail to be amused by a tale of three or four animals who live underground, row boats, write poetry, go caravanning, drive motor-cars, get put into prison, and in times of battle carry lethal weapons. There are more things in heaven and earth than are dreamt of in the philosophies of these superior spirits.

But I have committed treachery to *The Wind in the Willows* by calling its heroes 'three or four animals.' One does not so think of them. They are Mole, Ratty, Toad, and Mr. Badger; and while Mole, simple and likeable, and Ratty, shrewd to the bone in spite of his habit of 'doing poetry,' are sometimes little animals and sometimes children and sometimes well-grown schoolboys camping and pretending, there can be no doubt, I think, that Toad—some call him Mr. Toad—is in a sense all mankind.

I mean that he is all of us at our most unguarded, our most impulsive, boastful, and collapsible. He escapes from trouble only to become idiotically conceited; and in the grip of conceit he plunges dementedly into a more ghastly scrape than the last. From all these plunges, these fortunate rescues, and these lessons he buoyantly emerges, full of self-reproach and self-complacency, and he learns nothing from experience. As a result his life has the variety of a kaleidoscope, and it needs the concerted effort of his three devoted but critical friends, Mole, Ratty, and Badger, to save him from the consequences of his own folly. They do this from love, which shows how excellent some of Toad's traits are; and they do it from duty, for they are noble animals; and they do it for fun, because that is the kind of creature each one of them is. (pp. 175-76)

It is with the introduction of Toad that *The Wind in the Willows* becomes unique, as bed-book, children's book, or any other kind of book; for Toad is a character drawn in the grand manner by a master. (p. 177)

[I have] a number of favourite passages in *The Wind in the Willows* which are ideal reading for the end of the day. . . . There is Rat's meeting, for example, with the Seafaring Rat. . . . I could read it for ever. . . . And there is Toad's brief conversion to sorrow for his own misdeeds. He is withdrawn for reproof by Badger; his sobs are heard by the listeners; he is quite cured—Badger thinks.

'I have,' says Badger, reappearing with a limp and dejected Toad, 'his solemn promise to that effect.' . . . [When] asked to repeat his expression of sorrow Toad, after looking desperately this way and that, revolts. . . . In all of us sorrow for misdeed has given way to defiance. It is in such a passage as this, therefore, that Toad ceases to be merely Toad, and becomes epitomized human nature.

Many other passages throw equally searching light into character; still others express and fulfil our younger dreams. And, above all, the entire book is filled with the silent laughter, the gravity, and the mocking nonsense of true English humour. To read *The Wind in the Willows* is to be very profoundly amused, to have the mind set free for unlimited speculation, and to be brought, as I have said, to dreamland itself. You read a chapter, you switch off the bedside lamp, and you find yourself listening to the ripple of the river, hearing again the conversation between Toad and the washer-woman, the carol sung by the little fieldmice at Mole's front door, and the Seafaring Rat's account of halcyon nights in the Mediterranean. Gradually these sounds blend and fade. Memories blur. Still smiling, you are asleep, tranquil and content; to awaken in the morning as refreshed as you would be after a summer night in the open air. What more can a bedside book do for you than that? (pp. 180-81)

> Frank Swinnerton, "A Bedside Book," in his Toke-field Papers: Old and New, *revised edition, Hamish Hamilton, 1949, pp. 175-81.*

The Wind in the Willows is a wise book; it is a complicated book; yet it has given more pleasure to children than almost any other. Firm and strong it certainly is in its implications, but it is a long way from the derisive and shattering propaganda of Erich Kästner's *The Animals' Conference* or George Orwell's *Animal Farm*, in which animals stand for so much of human error that they have almost ceased to be animals at all. Grahame's story will not push philosophy or satire at a child. It will rouse in him, at different times, pity and anger, enjoyment and laughter; it will satisfy the desire for these things as it satisfied Grahame when he wrote it; and it will leave the animal world where it was, untouched by human sentiment or speculation. The animals return to the river and the wood unchanged; but the reader, young or old, can never again feel blank or indifferent towards them. (p. 64)

> Margery Fisher, "Mrs Bunny and the Rabbits: Animal Stories," in her Intent Upon Reading: A Critical Appraisal of Modern Fiction for Children *(copyright © 1961 by Margery Fisher), Hodder & Stoughton Children's Books (formerly Brockhampton Press), 1961, pp. 50-68.*

There are many enchanting things in this great work, but undoubtedly part of its continual fascination for children lies in the character and adventures of Toad. For Kenneth Grahame too, Toad was the first inspiration for the whole work. It is in letters to his son, Alastair, that we first hear stories about "this wicked animal", long before mention of the other riverbank characters. (p. 160)

It says a great deal about children's reading tastes that they should so take to this "bad, low animal", in Grahame's own words, rather than to some of the more exalted characters that have appeared in children's books. In many ways, of course,

Toad is the personification of the spoilt infant and is generally shown to glory in this, despite naggings from Badger and others. Adults who look to children's books for their generally improving qualities will find very little support in this character, which is perhaps why children enjoy him so. With his abundant flow of cash, Toad revels in his own omnipotence, buying house-boats, caravans and motor cars at will, just as in any childish fantasy, and for good measure steals on impulse as well. He is, as Piaget says of infants in general, in the classical egocentric stage; self-willed, boastful, unable to share the limelight, but basically insecure in strange situations, as in the fearful Wild Wood. He is a skilful liar too, but again, like so many infants, Toad seems almost to believe in his own fantasies, and perhaps cannot help treating the truth in such a relative way. When corrected, Toad can be quite genuinely sorry, but his sobs never last for very long, and cannot disguise his basic single-minded obstinacy. Indeed, this can result in the most violent infantile tantrums, where it takes two other animals to haul him upstairs to bed in disgrace. . . . (pp. 160-61)

There is one especially interesting way in which Toad comes close to the hearts of today's children, and in a manner that Grahame could hardly have predicted. Toad was, perhaps, the first of the demon car drivers. . . . Children still warm to this fearful example far more than to any respectable puppet or policeman demonstrating the canons of road safety. (p. 161)

Finally, of course, Toad renounces his old self, just as his audience one day will have to turn away from childhood. But typically, and consistent with Toad's almost irrepressible high spirits, this personal transformation is only wrung out of him extremely unwillingly after a final fling where Toad shows that he has no intention at all of learning any lessons from his previous bad behaviour. (pp. 161-62)

In his admirable biography, *Kenneth Grahame* [see excerpt above], Peter Green traces the origin of Toad to Grahame's son, Alastair, along with touches of Horatio Bottomley and Oscar Wilde in Toad's penchant for loud clothes, after-dinner speaking and final downfall and imprisonment. There is also a certain ludicrous resemblance to the adventures and return of Ulysses. But there is surely another literary origin that must be mentioned, both in his likeness to Toad's actual shape and in his general effect upon the other characters. Grahame himself was for some time Honorary Secretary to the New Shakespeare Society, and Shakespeare was always one of his favourite authors: surely, when writing about Toad the image of Falstaff must have had some influence over him too. As it is, both characters have an intimate, although enforced, connexion with laundry, which finally results in their being thrown into the Thames. They each dress up as somebody else's aunt, and make a presentable, if finally unsuccessful, shot at passing off as an elderly lady. But more importantly, of course, through both of them runs the spirit of personified Riot, a perpetual and irrepressible threat to the status quo both of their friends and of the rather stuffy society outside that condemns them so freely. Falstaff torments the Lord Chief Justice, while Toad, never short of repartee, receives fifteen years' imprisonment for his "gross impertinence" to the rural police. Although Grahame described *The Wind in the Willows* as "Clean of the clash of sex", Toad alone has an eye for the women and takes it for granted that the Gaoler's daughter has fallen in love with him, in spite of the social gulf that also separates Falstaff from Doll Tearsheet. Toad's version of his escape from prison improves with each telling very much like Falstaff's Gadshill exploits, and while Falstaff is renounced at the end of the play, the riverbank animals renounce the old Toad, and the book itself goes on to assure us . . . that the new Toad goes on to win the universal respect of all local inhabitants around him. Falstaff, in spite of or possibly because of what Tolstoy described as his "Gluttony, drunkenness, debauchery, rascality, deceit and cowardice", is probably Shakespeare's most popular comic character; Toad, that "dangerous and desperate fellow", has always been an especial favourite with children. (pp. 162-63)

For children themselves, *The Wind in the Willows,* and especially the adventures of Toad, constituted one of those few books written not at them but for them. Toad himself was a character who dared do and express many of the things they may often have felt like doing, and such children could both feel superior to Toad's obvious deficiencies and excesses and also revel in them at the same time. With any amount of opportunity for moralizing, Grahame leaves the field mercifully clear to a few, largely unsuccessful efforts by the other riverbank animals to get Toad to mend his ways.

In fact, all the characters Grahame created are real and alive and in Toad he gave us a character who was even larger than life and in this sense, surely, becomes the children's Falstaff, whether Grahame consciously intended the connexion or not. We do not find in these pages any of those miserable creations who are merely the mouth-pieces for an adult's stereotyped vision of what is considered to be especially suitable for children. And in this, as in so many other things, *The Wind in the Willows* continues to be an object lesson for many of those who are writing for children today. (pp. 163-64)

> *Nicholas Tucker, "The Children's Falstaff" (originally published in* The Times Literary Supplement, *No. 3513, June 26, 1969), in* Suitable for Children? Controversies in Children's Literature, *edited by Nicholas Tucker (copyright © 1976 by Nicholas Tucker; reprinted by permission of the University of California Press; in Canada by Sussex University Press),* University of California Press, Sussex University Press, 1976, pp. 160-64.

The only one of Grahame's books that will last is *The Wind in the Willows.* (p. 318)

[In] all his work, and particularly in *The Wind in the Willows,* Kenneth Grahame was revenging himself on the adult world which he had been forced to join and on the century whose materialism his sensibility could not accept. He said once that he was 'not a professional writer'. It is true; he was a confessional one. The book that he stoutly protested he wrote for children was a letter written in invisible ink to himself. (p. 319)

> *Clifton Fadiman, "Professionals and Confessionals: Dr. Seuss and Kenneth Grahame" (reprinted by permission of the author), in* Only Connect: Readings on Children's Literature, *edited by Sheila Egoff, G. T. Stubbs, and L. F. Ashley, Oxford University Press, Canadian Branch, 1969, pp. 316-22.*

Frank and generous friendship is [one of the themes which gives *The Wind in the Willows*] its lasting appeal. Indeed it is the only quality which makes Toad tolerable at all. . . . It is probably best seen . . . in the loyalty which induces Mole, Rat and Badger to put up with Toad, to attempt to reform him, and, when he proves incorrigible, to restore him to Toad Hall. . . . (p. 26)

It is always difficult to separate such a quality from the revealed character of the animals themselves, but if they are on the whole stereotypes of vanity, judicious good sense and good nature yet the developing character of Mole is always interesting. On however small a scale Mole is the true adventurer for he has to learn the life of the river bank and the hostility of the Wild Wood. Rat's friends have to be met and relations with them established. It is all done with a becoming modesty. . . . The way that Mole progresses from river bank apprenticeship under Rat to be Badger's first lieutenant at the recovery of Toad Hall places him, however humbly, in the line of the unregarded younger sons of folk tradition who find fortune and a sense of their own identity by remaining true to their own natures. In Mole's case this is accompanied by a sensible awareness of his own limitations. . . . (pp. 26-7)

[Any] appreciation must take into account the variety of style in the book and the resolution of this variety into convincing and colloquial dialogue. If the present reader now responds to the quieter presentation of Mole, where the schoolboy once revelled in the adventures of Toad, this, too, is evidence of the book's capacity to grow with the reader. So, today, it has taken on an additional authentic period appeal, being part of the larger scene of Jerome K Jerome and W S Gilbert. . . . (p. 27)

There are destroyers of the social contract about, but, like the weasels and the stoats, they can take over for a while but lack the fibre to defend their conquest for long against the wrath of the rightful owners. In 1908 such stability may well have seemed assured, though a teacher reading to a class today may feel that the fate of those rightful owners has been other than Kenneth Grahame supposed, and reflect that it is always educative to counter the prejudices of today with those of yesterday. But that is far too sententious a thought with which to leave a book which makes its points more indirectly, and is founded on the pleasures of companionship and home, whose author knew that there are more ways of looking at an adventure than one, and that glory for the victors may also become a cautionary tale for the losers. . . .

Part of the deeper attraction of *The Wind in the Willows* will always lie in this individual presentation of some of the faces of truth. (p. 28)

> *Kenneth Sterck, "Rereading 'The Wind in the Willows'," in* Children's literature in education *(© 1973, Agathon Press, Inc.; reprinted by permission of the publisher), No. 12, (September), 1973, pp. 20-8.*

Not long ago, while I was being third-degreed by a group of determined teachers (in England . . .) about writing for children, I was asked to say, as an author, which children's book I myself thought most interesting from a technical point of view. I think I alarmed most of them by naming *The Wind in the Willows.* I could see the contempt on many faces—"That old thing, that product of the upper middle-class nursery, that whimsical bit of outdated fantasy?" I stick by my guns. In spite of the many excellent contenders, I still find *The Wind in the Willows* a mine full of rich and thought-provoking veins.

In the first place, it is important to understand that *The Wind in the Willows* is not really a fantasy. And secondly, that it has certain universal qualities which elevate it above its age and class and still keep it circulating from library shelves, if not quite as enthusiastically as a few years ago.

And before going any further, I ought to deal with that "not quite as enthusiastically". I think it's because there is a certain resistance to it on the part of some librarians and teachers, who have told me that it is "sexist" and "bourgeois". The argument goes that, since it deals with a romantically bucolic world in which the motorcar was new and there were still washerwomen, it has no point of contact with the real problems of today's children. But it seems to me that there is a danger implicit in such an argument. Because the condition of some children has until recently not been treated in children's books, the pendulum is swinging sharply in their direction, and some librarians seem to feel that *all* children belong to minority groups or working-class families, or that if they don't, they ought to. The corollary is that children will not want to read about anything outside their own class interests, and that, for instance, to give them fairy tales about princes and princesses is a kind of betrayal. Well, Bruno Bettelheim has shown, in terms that are difficult to dispute, that the fairy tale has an important psychological effect on all children regardless of their class. (pp. 103-04)

That said, it must be admitted that *The Wind in the Willows* is a book about a lovely, easy-going rural paradise, a gentlemanly dream of country pleasures in which there are only bachelors, set in an England which perhaps never really existed. . . . Nobody takes Kenneth Grahame's England as a real place. What children see in it is cosiness, snug little houses underground, a lazy river, dark woods, plenty of space for play. (p. 104)

Technically, Grahame's book shouldn't work. It appears to violate the primary canon of a book: unity. It is, in fact, three books pasted together, the adventures of Toad, the tale of the friendship of Rat and Mole, and two prose-poems about the English countryside ("**Wayfarers All**" and "**The Piper at the Gates of Dawn**"). Nevertheless, the book does play, as we used to say in show business, and it plays for the same theatrical reason that Shakespeare's plays do, or that a good musical comedy does—routining. Everybody in the theatre knows that you should follow a tender boy-girl number with a rousing production number, that a lyrical song should be followed by a fast comedy bit. It is the arrangement of the parts that keeps things moving in *The Wind in the Willows:* a bucolic opening, followed by the introduction of the clown, Toad, followed by the dangerous Wild Wood, and so on. I am aware that it wasn't altogether Grahame's skill that was responsible for this; the book was pieced together like a variety programme, but like a good variety programme, it works.

It also works because of something which has all but vanished from literature, an economic climate that could allow an author to ramble along to his heart's content without having to worry about the cost of paper or production, and in the full knowledge that children will skip over anything that bores them but will plough on through the book to find out what happens to the people who interest them. (pp. 104-05)

One reason that girls like it as much as boys, even though there are only two minor female characters in it, is that the characters are animals. And so, in an odd way, although they are also Englishmen (and of a certain class—even Mole, shabby genteel as he is, is the sort of chap you wouldn't hesitate to invite to dinner), they are as asexual as Peter Rabbit. Grahame never lets the reader forget their animalness. . . .

It is precisely because there are no mothers, no girlfriends, no wives, that the neuter quality of the animals is preserved. They are not anthropomorphized, as are the rabbits in *Watership Down,* nor are they exactly people wearing animal masks, like Stuart Little or Paddington. They are a careful blend which manages to retain the character of each side. More to the point, they are alive, fully realized, and living in a world that is detailed with such precision and love that it forces belief in itself and in them. (p. 105)

And because they are drawn from reality, and the characters are so consistent and have their feet so firmly planted in everyday life, the book can hardly be called a fantasy. It is, rather, a series of stories about a group of interesting people who just happen to be rather out of the ordinary—I suppose "eccentric" is the word. Technically, the balance between their real and unreal aspects is maintained so well that it is beautiful to contemplate. It is done so delicately that none of the children I've ever talked to about it saw anything at all unusual in the discrepancies of size between Toad and motorcars, or Mole and the horse he walks beside.

In addition to their animal-human aspect, the creatures have still a third—they are children. It is only a subtle shading, but it is enough to produce a kind of ambiguity about them which, I think, explains something more about the book's attraction. Toad's swagger, his thoughtlessness, the wildness of his adventures, are not too remote from Tom Sawyer; he is more like a mischievous boy's idea of what he'd like to be than a country gentleman, and when Badger scolds him he bursts into tears as a child might. Mole's exclamations of delight are those of a child, as are his timorousness and his easy weeping. (p. 106)

And everything in the book lies well within a child's own make-believe; it is full of play, in which there may be fright but no ultimate disaster. I am not saying that children today aren't familiar with violence. . . . The vast majority of kids do a lot of fighting, but in the end, although they may be banged up a bit, nobody gets killed. The battle with the stoats and weasels at the end of *The Wind in the Willows* goes just that way. . . . And in the Wild Wood, although ominous whistles draw near, nothing appears; the terror is as real as when children play ghosts and monsters to scare themselves, but it's the imagination which has to be used—nothing is spelled out explicitly. That restraint is missing from a lot of children's books these days, and I think it is a loss.

I am convinced that *The Wind in the Willows* does have a universal appeal rather than one only to well-brought-up youngsters with nannies. Its low comedy is among the best ever written for children, and if its high-brow sections are sometimes a bit over their heads they are no more so than the more opaque parts of *Watership Down,* or *Earthfasts,* or *The Owl Service.* Its key word, perhaps, is "snug"—it is full of people finding their way home to jolly dinners and comfortable beds after adventures, which is, it appears to me, what most children want most. It may not have invented the form, but it was the precursor of a whole swarm of books in which human-animals (as distinct from human-minded animals, or the talking beasts of fables) appear. . . . (pp. 106-07)

Yet even if its day is done, even if it has nothing to say to modern children, it has, I think, like every true work of art, most of all to say to the artist. (p. 107)

Jay Williams, "Reflections on 'The Wind in the Willows'" (copyright © 1976 Jay Williams; reprinted by permission of the author and The Thimble Press, Lockwood Station Road, South Woodchester, Glos. GL55EQ, England), in Signal, *Nos. 19, 20, 21, September, 1976, pp. 103-07.*

THE RELUCTANT DRAGON (1938)

[For its enduring humor and charm, *The Reluctant Dragon*] is a title for every child's library. And a good many adults, if they do not already know him, will be delighted with this delectable dragon who had a kind heart. No attempt should be made to grade or pigeonhole this book. It belongs to wherever it finds a kindred spirit.

> *Marjorie F. Potter, "Fiction: 'The Reluctant Dragon'," in* Library Journal *(reprinted from Library Journal, February 1, 1939; published by R. R. Bowker Co. (a Xerox company); copyright © 1939 by Xerox Corporation), Vol. 64, No. 3, February 1, 1939, p. 118.*

Once the introductory paragraphs which preface it are put aside, the story of Boy, Dragon, and St. George unfolds fluently.

Strong contrasts create the story's essential meanings. There is the faith and vision of Boy and the literalness of his shepherd father; the prejudice and naivete of village folk; the benign Dragon and its wistful protector. Boy's compassion and unblemished vision lead him to that sound resolution.

Grahame knit the tale tightly. His moral commitment and rare humor permeate the fantasy. . . .

The little book is a gem that will enchant any hour. (p. 1035)

> *Kathryn A. Smith, "Kenneth Grahame and the Singing Willows" (copyright © 1968 by the National Council of Teachers of English; reprinted by permission of the publisher and the author), in* Elementary English, *Vol. XLV, No. 8, December, 1968, pp. 1024-35.*

The Reluctant Dragon . . . is the prototype of most modern story-book dragons that are, in theory, possible to live with. Its sting has been removed. . . . This one has all the proper attributes, with one more—a *fin de siècle* weariness; he has lived too long and reacted against being intense and taking all those pre-Raphaelite knights in armour seriously. He is an Edwardian dilettante who likes company and composing a little verse and has left fighting to all the other fellows who were so active and *earnest* and all that sort of thing. Unfortunately, he would probably have been just in time to enlist in the First World War. (pp. 117, 119)

The medieval setting is quite illusory. The boy, who, although he is supposed to be living in the middle of it, is obviously going to grow up with exactly the same social manners as the dragon, complains aggrievedly that the whole affair of the challenge is being treated 'as if it were an invitation to tea and croquet'. The amusement of the narrative is that child, knight and monster *do* behave as if tea and croquet were being discussed, with perhaps a few amateur theatricals added. Nothing is what it seems; the fight is rigged, the dragon is the life and soul of the subsequent party—and when dragon, knight and boy set off for home arm in arm afterwards, the dragon appears to have diminished in size, the boy and knight have grown, and the three revellers seem oddly similar.

This near-perfect story is just long enough. (p. 119)

> *Margaret Blount, "Dragons," in her* Animal Land: The Creatures of Children's Fiction *(reprinted by permission of the author; copyright ©1974 by Margaret Ingle-Finch), William Morrow & Company, Inc., 1975, pp. 116-30.*

BERTIE'S ESCAPADE (1949)

This story, which Kenneth Grahame wrote for a magazine "edited" by his own son (then in the nursery) and a little girl, was first published in Elspeth Grahame's illuminating memoir of her husband, **"First Whisper of 'The Wind in the Willows.'"**

Here, indeed, one sees the fore-shadowing of one of the most beloved of children's books of all time. It is not, of course, so finished a creation as any one of the chapters in **"The Wind in the Willows."** But in the merry Christmas Eve antics of Bertie the pig, the rabbits, Peter and Benjie and the unnamed mole are found that bland mixture of fantasy and reality, the same childlike sense of fun and that deep, unobtrusive tenderness. Children will delight in Bertie and his friends singing carols (off-key) in their discomfiture, their breathless retreat and in their Gargantuan feast. It ends with that wonderful feeling of well-being which is not the least among the charms of **"The Wind in the Willows."** Because it is simpler in content than **"The Wind in the Willows"** it will make a fine introduction to the enchantment of that book. Read it aloud to 5- and 6-year-olds, give it to 7-to-9-year olds to read to themselves.

> *Ellen Lewis Buell, in her review of "Bertie's Escapade," in* The New York Times Book Review *(© 1949 by The New York Times Company; reprinted by permission), October 24, 1949, p. 28.*

The slight story tells how Bertie the pig, with Peter and Benjie Rabbit, went to sing Christmas carols, had no luck, returned to Mr. Grahame's house and feasted on the best from his pantry, meanwhile causing him funny and unpleasant dreams. However slight, it has all of this author's special style, charm and wit. [It] becomes a "must" for the Christmas stockings of all who love this author. . . . This great company by now includes many ages. Age has nothing to do with the privilege of peeping in on a funny bad dream of Kenneth Grahame's, or loving a pig and two rabbits. . . .

Bertie's feast in the inner pigsty, his face as he proposes a toast to Mr. Grahame, Mrs. Mole waiting up with a candle for Mr. Mole—we didn't know how much we needed this at Christmas of 1949.

> *Louise S. Bechtel, "My Four Favorite Authors," in* New York Herald Tribune Book Review *(© I.H.T. Corporation; reprinted by permission), November 13, 1949, p. 7.**

[Before] he drafted *The Wind in the Willows* in its final form, Grahame composed that curious little fragment, '**Bertie's Escapade**'. This was a *jeu d'esprit* for domestic consumption, full of private allusions. (p. 270)

It is the incidental oddities which are most revealing in this sketch. The first place the animals go to is that highly-charged and recurrent symbol in Grahame's mythology—the chalk-pit. They pull out a piece of chalk, and behold! a tunnel. At the end of the tunnel is a lift operated by—inevitably—a mole, which rapidly shoots them up and out into the moonlight. Later the mole is brought back for the feasting, and returns home in the small hours to find 'Mrs. Mole sitting up for him, in some uneasiness of mind'. There follows immediately the long and detailed anxiety-dream experienced, it is stated, by Grahame himself. . . .

This dream has personal as well as social implications. To begin with, the entire sequence—not merely the final fantasy—has every appearance of being transcribed from a genuine nightmare. The dream-symbolism is both classic and transparent. The chalk-pit stands for the creative, sub-conscious self, where . . . not only the imagination but also all emblems of despair, nostalgia, failure, and resignation have their home. The tunnel, as we know from **'The Reluctant Dragon'** no less than **'The River Bank',** is the outlet for the creative force; and the Mole—another symbol for the subterranean, upthrusting, blind imagination—is, of course, an aspect of Grahame himself. (p. 271)

> *Peter Green, in his* Kenneth Grahame 1859-1932: A Study of His Life, Work and Times *(reprinted by permission of Harold Ober Associates Incorporated; copyright © 1959 by Peter Green 1959), John Murray, 1959, 400 p.*

Maria Gripe

1923-

Swedish author of fiction and fantasy and scriptwriter.

Gripe is one of Sweden's most distinguished writers. Reviewers compare her to Hans Christian Andersen for her sensitivity, her strain of melancholy, and her presentations of timeless themes in contemporary settings. Her ability to enter into the joys and sorrows of children and to portray them in sensitive relationships has earned her an international following. Critics feel that Gripe's stories are expressed with the imagery of a poet, and that such motifs as appearance versus reality, fate versus free will, parental abandonment, and changing roles in life contribute to the high caliber of her work. Though sometimes difficult to comprehend, her books are generally rewarding and stimulating.

Gripe's early exposure to literature consisted of listening exclusively to Andersen's fairy tales. According to her father, Andersen was the only person worthy of being called an author. His works inspired Gripe to write on her own; when her father read these stories, he informed her that if she wished to write, she must have something to write about and learn how to say it. It wasn't until her own daughter began asking for stories that she had the motivation to become an author. Her husband, Harald, has illustrated all of her works.

Because she remembers her childhood so vividly, Gripe portrays realistic characters who are considered childlike but not childish. She uses a direct style, lightened by occasional humor, to produce poignant stories whose introspective protagonists have much dignity, but live in an atmosphere of loneliness and isolation. Gripe frequently criticizes adult treatment of children. In the *Elvis* series, Elvis's mother is too preoccupied with her own life to care properly for her son, and, in *Pappa Pellerin's Daughter*, three children are deserted by their parents. Critics believe that the *Hugo and Josephine* trilogy accurately depicts a child's mentality and conveys a sense of universal childhood, but consider Gripe's use of the present tense to be annoying. They commend *The Glassblower's Children* for its delicate imagery, while finding *The Land Beyond* too obscure and abstract even for adults. Reviewers praise the *Elvis* books for their perceptive characterization of the title character, but comment that children old enough to appreciate the books would not want to read about a precocious six-year-old. The international success of her works, however, proves that Gripe has met the challenge of her father's advice, and in the process has created books that are considered classics. She has adapted several of her books into plays for movie, television, and radio presentation. Gripe's numerous awards include the Nils Holgersson Plaque in 1963 for *Hugo and Josephine* and the Heffaklumpen Award in 1966 for *Hugo*. *Pappa Pellerin's Daughter* earned the Lewis Carroll Shelf Award in 1966 and the New York Herald Tribune Children's Spring Book Festival Honor Book award. Other honors include the Astrid Lindgren Prize in 1972 and the Hans Christian Andersen Medal in 1974.

(See also *Contemporary Authors,* Vols. 29-32, rev. ed. and *Something about the Author,* Vol. 2.)

AUTHOR'S COMMENTARY

Many people have said to me, "You who can do such wonderful children's portraits, why do you sometimes write such strange, melancholy books?" I think it's time I tried to answer this question.

My spontaneous reaction is naturally that I don't find these books strange nor the least bit melancholy. Writing them was pleasant and I felt myself present; it left me with a rare feeling of perfection. In my opinion they were positive. That's all.

But, of course, this is a sort of defense mechanism because I really do not feel like going any deeper into the problem. It's hard for me. First of all because I can never find it natural to go back to things which are finished. By uncovering such buried things one can destroy the desire to go on further. But also because I must rummage in my childhood and my earliest fascinations in order to grasp this side of me at all. That increases the risk for rationalization later on very much. The difficult thing with early experiences is that one rarely really knows what one really experienced and what is merely the story. For the very small child the story becomes a direct experience, especially when one was involved oneself. The narrative situation is not kept in mind, it is not the words and who said them, but rather all the pictures, events, feelings, etc. which come to life.

Much of that in my books which can be considered fleeting can be traced back to my repeated efforts to show our various views of reality—that of the child going far beyond the borders of that of adults. Every experience of reality depends on knowledge and information, and those things for which we have no knowledge from without, we complement with an inner testimony, with that which we believe with the help of our fantasy. That is certainly why children seem to have more fantasy than adults. They know so little, but believe so much. Genuine reality consists of pieces, fragments; but that which fills it out is also reality, perhaps just as valid. One creates the relation which is needed for the current situation for oneself. I have also tried to study this model on myself with the help of my childhood. By means of conscious perception of these phenomena one can sometimes discover the causes. Later I experimented in my books with some of my experiences, and it seemed to be neither an end in itself nor alien to me. Many people only remember their childhood vaguely, but I happen to have mine within reach. It is easy for me to bring events, moods and even thoughts from this time back to life. Childhood is in one way perhaps the only place where people can meet openly. It is a state before corruption, before the "fall" and therefore for everyone the most valid. . . . [I now want to say] a few words on another stumbling block—the language.

Adults speak about mutual experiences and think they have read and seen the same things, but they can never be sure they understand one another, not even when they use the same words. Hardly an idea has the same meaning for you as for me. Every word we speak is filled with our very own private experiences, emotions, memories, desires, phobias, dreams, aggressions, etc. The older we become the more different meanings the words take on. One comes further and further from the original values. This state of affairs should make us think when we speak to children. Does the child possess the simple, correct and straightforward word? In our efforts to meet the child it therefore happens that we limit and simplify the concepts but forget the whole time that we do so due to our present, muddled relationship to them and that we actually have no idea where it will lead us. That can fall flat. (pp. 4-5)

I discovered my shadow early in life. . . . A sort of friendship developed between my shadow and me. In one period I tried to ask everyone about their shadow, but I never got satisfactory answers from the others. I found out more myself. I don't know how, but it was through the shadows that I came into relationship with the world of fantasy.

The first thing I discovered was that shadows always faced the back. Nobody knew what its face looked like. Why? Was it against people? Of course not—but it couldn't turn around because then its ability to see a world much different than ours would be lost. It could see things we couldn't see and had no idea existed. It could see the backside and the inside of everything. It had seen the inside of the earth and the backside of the moon and sun. It had looked into the flowers, inside God and the devil. Through the shadow I could therefore gain insight into everything unfamiliar and into things I would never see myself, just like the shadow could not see me and my world since it was doomed to face the backside forever. We each had something we could tell the other about, my shadow and I, and I had the feeling that there wasn't so much to say to the others. But on the other hand, it is natural for children to share their experiences. One doesn't even think about being alone with something, and one therefore doesn't know when one should keep still. This did not lead so much to conflict with

my environment—in spite of everything I adjusted immediately when I noticed I was casting aspersions on myself—as to conflicts within myself. Inside of me things were a bit confused until a very concrete experience helped me break the contact with my shadow and everything it stood for. As I think about it now I see that it was a very small thing, but at that time it was decisive. I was the oldest child in the family and obviously ready to do anything not to be considered childish. I therefore turned my back to my shadow as unrelentingly as it had to me and decided to let myself go. I played the wildest games with the rascals in the neighborhood—I changed my personality completely within the shortest time. I was deathly afraid that someone might catch a glimpse of my inner life, and whenever I got a hint that it might happen I merely stuck out my tongue. I scoffed at my earlier self and began to speak in a new and more effective way. Undeniably, I was more successful. I became popular and that was a most welcome change. I had no intention of falling back upon my old ways.

But I no longer felt so naturally happy, although I behaved as though I did. In order to feel joy one suddenly needed such a mightly apparatus, and as the laughter died down there was nothing left. I felt strange. I think I was on the way to become alienated.

Surrendering myself to reality nevertheless did not make the reality more real. One would have thought so—but it seemed rather less real, less explainable and more fathomless. It hung in the air. That hadn't been the case before. Before it had been as though the shadow world and my world confirmed and complemented one another so that everything fit together. Now the reality was really split. One felt uncertain in it. But there was nothing to do except go on. I went on by reading fairy tales—something still permitted back then. Today it is more dubious—today when fairy tales are so necessary. But adults said often enough that fairy tales are nothing for modern children, that the children soon believed it themselves. The inside of a child is merely a little conformity machine which can be very easily manipulated. And if everything just functions as it should in society and the result seems satisfactory from without, the rest will take care of itself later—especially if everyone learns as early as possible what they should experience and what they should not.

As I said, I read fairy tales. Again and again I read H. C. Andersen's "The Travelling Companion" and "The Shadow". (It is, by the way, a strange feeling to read them again as an adult and to discover that I no longer see what I did then, but also that I now see things I did not then. . . .) (pp. 6-8)

And every time I read about the learned man who lost his shadow one night to the poesy which he had perceived for a moment in the house across the street, I got goosebumps. The man had ordered the shadow to go there. Years later the shadow returned as a human being who had seen everything no one else could see or should see, everything no one should learn about, but desires to so badly.

The shadow has only one problem: it doesn't have a shadow. It demands of the learned man who is growing weaker and weaker and will soon die that he become his shadow. This is an unbelievably pointed dramatic situation which moved me indescribably. Sometimes I didn't dare to read the end. But I couldn't keep from repeatedly returning to some parts of the text. Did they perhaps remind me of that which I had done? I don't know . . . I hardly drew consciously any deep parallels to my own lost shadow, but the idea certainly lingered in my subconscious. And although I hadn't lost my shadow to the poesy, I had let it be swallowed by—let's call it the juggernaut as in the Old Testament, the foreign deity who was honoured with child sacrifices in Gehenna. Or—not to become ambiguous—the social claim to better conformity with reality. There is more to say, but this is perhaps enough for an explanation that three of my 18 books—and that is all, I don't believe *Glasstunneln* belongs here—can be seen as taking place in a "social vacuum". (pp. 8-9)

Perhaps it is an illusion, but it seems to me that just as the shadow world and reality give strength to one another, the same is true of the realistic and the "metaphysical" books—if one questions the one way of writing, the whole building topples. And when Hugo goes out in the end to find out where the waters of two rivers merge, perhaps it is just to find out how the currents of two realities can be brought together. "I must know how it's done," he says. That's why his eyes are bluer than ever. They see something others don't see.

Is it then feasible that I write these books due to egoistic motives? In order to recapture something I lost as a child?

No and no again. If that were the case, I would keep them for myself. I write them because I simply believe that they are necessary—these books too. Otherwise I wouldn't keep on. I don't do it to confuse adults.

But the difficulty for a children's book author is that one cannot reach one's public directly. Besides his own inner resistance, which can be difficult enough, there are four hindrances to overcome: the publishers, critics, parents and finally the children. Each barrier is different. . . . The children themselves cannot formulate their wishes. It might be assumed that the authors and the children have the most in common, but they never reach one another—there is too much in between. Therefore, the author must write in a way that he can win over the publisher, the critics and the parents so that the child must not suffer for it and really try to save as much as possible for the child when he finally gets ahold of the book.

One more thing which cannot be repeated too often: children differ from one another, immensely. . . . The child who feels himself different doesn't know why and merely conforms more and more. That is the situation. (p. 10)

Maria Gripe, "A Word and a Shadow," in Bookbird, *Vol. 12, No. 1 (March 15, 1974), pp. 4-10.*

GENERAL COMMENTARY

Maria Gripe's child portrayals are always impressive. In [*Josefin* and *Hugo och Josefin*], fairy-tale and fantastic elements predominate, while her later stories are rather more realistic. Maria Gripe very quickly rose into the front rank of Swedish authors for children. She is both a realistic painter of memorable child characters and an original story-teller. (pp. 52-3)

"Recommendations for Translation," in Bookbird, *Vol. VII, No. 2 (1969), pp. 44-61.* *

The author of *Hugo and Josephine* has given each of her characters a book of his own. . . . All three books show a gentle humour and an interest in the complexities of human relationships. This interest is most developed in *Hugo. Josephine,* the weakest of the three books, suffers from an almost sentimental sweetness in places and also has a less coherent plot than the other two books. Children who enjoyed *Hugo and Josephine* will find more satisfaction in *Hugo,* who is, in any case, the

more unusual character. *Josephine* doesn't hold the attention so well without him.

Susan Stanton, in her review of "Hugo" and "Josephine," in School Library Journal, *an appendix to* Library Journal *(reprinted from the November, 1970 issue of* School Library Journal, *published by R. R. Bowker Co./A Xerox Corporation; copyright © 1970), Vol. 17, No. 3, November, 1970, p. 108.*

The finest evocation of real life in [the 7-12 age range] at the moment must surely be the *Hugo and Josephine* trilogy. Maria Gripe's tales of a Swedish primary school have delicacy, insight and a warmth the more intense for being carefully banked and covered. Every sensitive little girl will recognise Josephine's misery at being '*nearly* like everyone else' and share her passionate admiration for Hugo who, in his complete naturalness, frankness and courage, is quite different from everyone else. But perhaps these books are even more for educators than for children: certainly Hugo does more than Ivan Illich to call in question the usefulness of school. (pp. 662-63)

Audrey Laski, "Magic and Misery" (© British Broadcasting Corp. 1971; reprinted by permission of Audrey Laski), in The Listener, *Vol. 86, No. 2224, November 11, 1971, pp. 662-63.* *

The story of [Hugo and Josephine] is admirable and could have been absorbing and enjoyable. It is quite incomprehensible that the author of *Pappa Pellerin's Daughter* should have chosen to tell this story in such a style. All three books are written in the present tense and supposedly from a child's point of view, but the mixture of childishness and totally adult understanding, inevitably creates a feeling of contempt, similar to that felt when listening to an adult indulging in baby-talk. (p. 192)

Sylvia Mogg, in her review of "Josephine" and "Hugo," in Children's Book Review *(© 1971 by Five Owls Press Ltd.; all rights reserved), Vol. I, No. 6, December, 1971, pp. 191-92.*

[This trilogy, *Josephine, Hugo and Josephine,* and *Hugo,*] appears to be translated most intuitively, for the distinctive style plays a large part in its impact: the short sentences and use of the present tense which gives immediacy, the colloquial, utterly natural dialogue. The brief, telling descriptions of weather or scene appear as through a child's eyes, often echoing Josephine's mood or difficulties. She is the youngest daughter of a Swedish vicarage. Her father is remote but obviously excellent at his job (though his unpopularity rubs off on Josephine), her mother gentle and harassed. The grown-up brothers and sisters are all too preoccupied with their own world to understand the extent of Josephine's solitary worries and self-dramatisation. Confused between fact and fantasy, she becomes ill with the strain of being naughtier and naughtier, until her father succeeds in making things clear.

The second volume gains a new dimension with the arrival of Hugo, who for some weeks never reaches school because there is so much of greater importance to be attended to on the way. He is the son of a charcoal burner, a creature of the woods, with a self-assured disregard of conventional standards. The account of Josephine's beginning school is amusing and perceptive: the awful return to her real name Anna (so well dealt with by the teacher), the village children who are, with one charmingly depicted exception, indifferent or hostile to her till Hugo appears as her protector. The last book shows Hugo as the young reader's ideal even more: there is nothing, not even journalism, to which he cannot turn successfully. At the end, he leaves (because school interferes with the many things to be learnt in the world) in search of a confluence, since it must be "something terrific, tremendous". By contrast, Josephine seems more waif-like. The adults, the other children, even Hugo, who helps another girl in greater need, seem to threaten the security of her world. One longs to know more of her. There seems no doubt that, even in translation, these books will win a place as children's "classics". (pp. 97-8)

A review of "Josephine," "Hugo and Josephine," and "Hugo," in The Junior Bookshelf, *Vol. 36, No. 2, April, 1972, pp. 97-8.*

[Maria Gripe] made her debut in 1954 with *I var lilla stad,* which told the story of a small town inhabited by humanized animals. During the next few years, this book was followed by two more books in the same style. In 1956 she published **Kvarteret Labyrinten,** which depicts the budding friendship of a boy and a girl living in the same block. We also meet an unknown, almost mystical boy, who appears from nowhere and foreshadows similar characters in later books. Many of these books have an atmosphere or an attitude which she was later to develop more deliberately. . . . *Pappa Pellerin's Daughter* . . . is definitely something new in her development as a writer. The main character is Loella, a gaunt, patient figure continually battling with inward weaknesses and outward adversities. . . . Loella is a child of impeccable integrity but devoid of humor or of any sense of security.

[*Josephine*] is also about a lonely, insecure child. This was the book which made Maria Gripe's reputation. It is a restrained portrait of childhood in the realistic vein; the author tries to penetrate the mentality of the child to a greater depth than is commonly undertaken in children's books. Accordingly, *Josephine* is not so much about adventures and funny incidents as it is about the threads joining the comprehensible and the remote. (p. 122)

Apart from her realistic books, Maria Gripe has also written a series of others, including **Glasblasarns barn.** . . . The whole of this fairy tale is interwoven with a pattern of poetry, magic, mysticism, and shifts in time. At the bottom of it all is a fight between good and evil, life and death. *Glastunneln* . . . combines both realism and fantasy. The book is about an ordinary Swedish boy who runs away from his family to Stockholm and makes friends with a blind girl, but the actual story is written in an elusive, almost surrealistic fairy-tale manner.

The basic theme of Maria Gripe's books—at least those written since 1960—is the relationship between people and their role in life. In all her books she seeks opportunities of self-realization and liberation for her characters; she is constantly probing the boundaries constricting our lives. She is highly critical of the way in which adults treat children. (p. 124)

Mary Orvig, "A Collage: Eight Women Who Write Books in Swedish for Children, Part II," in The Horn Book Magazine *(copyright © 1973 by The Horn Book, Inc., Boston), Vol. XLIX, No. 2, April, 1973, pp. 119-26.**

Maria Gripe has just handed in the manuscript of her third book about Elvis: *Elvis, a child of the Seventies.* Read it! But be prepared to cry!

For few have described the relationship of a thoughtless, unaware mother and her child as Maria Gripe has. . . .

Maria Gripe has described mothers in several books, one kind in the Elvis books and another, the efficient, brisk, dominating dentist in **The Green Coat,** who gives you the shivers. (p. 4)

[As a child, Maria] felt as if she had almost lost her shadow, she realised later, just like the man in Hans Andersen's story [see author's commentary above]. Luckily she found it again; they found each other. That could be one of the explanations for the two paths that Maria Gripe has taken as an author which have puzzled some of her critics (not the children!) because they seem so dissimilar. In one, she has written down-to-earth, realistic books, in the other, ones which are timeless and mystical. She writes for the whole child, who has one foot in reality and one in dreams and stories so that the child can know that everything is equally real and permissible. And equally important to develop! (p. 6)

Lena Rydin, "Childhood: The Universal Experience—A Profile of Outstanding Swedish Author, Maria Gripe," in Books for Your Children *(© Books for Your Children 1978), Vol. 13, No. 3, Summer, 1978, pp. 4-7.*

[Maria Gripe is a] writer whose stories, realistic and fairytale alike, express the imagery of a poet. Without sentimentality or cliches she writes books with psychological connotations and with a true understanding of children. Usually writing in the present tense, she manages to convey warmth and freshness in a language, while vivid, that is still understandable and readable by children. Her ability to combine symbolism, humor and the theme of loneliness and lack of communication in her books makes her an artist in the craft of writing.

The symbolism used by Maria Gripe has a sustaining continuity throughout her books. The symbols of angels, the changing of given names and the use of animals as hats or head coverings are used with delicate precision in many of her books. . . .

Angels first appear in *Josephine,* Mrs. Gripe's first translation into English. Josephine is concerned that God, in the disguised person of a bearded gardener, has come to take her away. She is extremely concerned and relates: "*And since she isn't even allowed to play with the village children, she certainly won't be allowed to play with the angels.*" After a long spell of psychosomatic illness, she receives a gift of a sheet of bookmarks depicting angels sitting on wooly clouds. When her father comes into the room, he sees her asleep. "*She is holding a pair of scissors in her hand, and all round her lie lots of little angels without heads. She's sniped off all their heads, every one of them. Curly little angels' heads lie all over the floor.*" The destruction of the angels symbolizes Josephine's rejection of what she feels is the calling of God to take her to heaven to make her an angel. By snipping off their heads and being naughty she can remain on earth.

In the book **Hugo and Josephine** the description of the role of the angel in a Christmas play and the use of bookmarks are again used to develop an atmosphere of good versus evil. In the book **The Night Daddy** there is another mention of angel book markers and a reference to the death of Martin Luther King. Cleverly, little Julie tells a story of a Negro King who died, turned into a cross among the "flowers" and then flew out a church window to be with all the people waiting for him. Therefore, with imaginative poetic creativity, Maria Gripe has developed an aura of heavenly awareness in the symbol of the angel. . . .

In four of Mrs. Gripe's books the loss of identity and the rejection of the role one has to play in life is symbolized by the changing of the character's name. In *Josephine* the little six-year-old heroine refuses to use her real name "Anna Grae" because she cannot accept the role in life she has been born into. She writes her name on a box and buries it in the backyard and assumes the name Josephine.

In *Hugo and Josephine* the little girl goes to school still using the ficticious name and it is not until the last chapter that she becomes Anna Grae. (pp. 447-48)

In the *Glassblower's Children* two children lose their identity in the house of his Lordship. They assume different names and very gradually they are turned into puppets, dressed in velvet and silk, who can't see their reflection in a mirror. Gradually, they just disappear altogether and it is only through the love of their parents and the aid of a wise and gentle old woman that they are saved from eternal death. The struggle of good and evil is resolved by disclosing death as an inevitable fact thus giving life its fullest meaning.

In the book *The Night Daddy* Julia refuses to tell her new babysitter her name. By withholding her name she feels he cannot know her. . . .

The final symbolic writing tool that will be discussed is the appearance of animals and birds on peoples' heads. Three books, *Julia's House, The Night Daddy* and *Elvis and His Secret* have illustrations on the front covers depicting an animal on the head of a human. In *The Night Daddy* the character, Peter, explains the symbolic meaning when he says:

> *"He* (the owl, Smuggler) *settled down on my head to supervise the job. He knows I like that. He's just about the right weight, and the pressure seems to hold down my thoughts so that they don't fly off in all directions . . . I can think better with Smuggler sitting on my head and he is aware of that."*

Thus, animals and birds symbolically serve as an organizing control to the humans in Maria Gripe's books, along with the symbols of angels and name changes.

Humor abounds in all of the books. Even the most somber book, *The Glassblower's Children* carries some humor. The terrible Nanny is described in horrid but humorous detail. The character Hugo, in three of the books, is so independent and eccentric that many of his experiences blend satire with humor. (p. 448)

The tragic depression of loneliness and the lack of communication are prolifically distributed throughout Maria Gripe's works. In *Elvis and His Secret*, little Elvis is determined to be himself in spite of parental opposition and lack of attention. When parental attention is finally given to him, it is in the form of dictatorial demands and his parents don't listen to him whenever he tries to appeal these demands or voice an opinion. Alone and introspective, Elvis wanders the streets with only his shadow for company.

In *Pappa Pellerin's Daughter*, three children are deserted by their parents and face life alone in the woods near a small village in Sweden. All the main characters, in all of Maria Gripe's books, are alone and introspective. Hugo's mother is dead and his father is in jail. Josephine feels left out of the adult world even when she is at home at the vicarage. Julia is rejected by her school friends and neglected by her mother. Loneliness pervades all the books and the inability of the child and the parent to communicate casts shadows of despair on the characters until they are symbolically saved by some caring person with affection and tender humor. Thus, the humor proves to be the uplifting element in these books that would otherwise be somewhat depressing to a young reader.

Maria Gripe's stories can be read at any age level with enjoyment because of the many levels of understanding the author has attained in her writings. Early readers can enjoy the books for their story line and gradually, as age and maturity is attained, the reader can see the increasing depths of understanding and psychological interplay which is present and well developed.

Finally, the motifs such as: good versus evil, changing roles in life, animals assuming almost lifelike characteristics, shattering mirrors, unfulfilled wishes, and parental abandonment make the fairy-tales and realistic stories of a high caliber indeed. While the young reader does not recognize these motifs, they are valuable in the construction of good children's literature.

Clearly, Maria Gripe is deserved of the many awards she has been given. However, her fiction seems to be directed more to the discerning reader than to the very young reader. Thus, while a book seems to be written for a certain age group, an older age is necessary to read the book with any understanding. As an example, *Hugo* is supposedly written for beginning readers, however, the language which might have been distorted through translation, is too difficult, for instance: *"Hugo has an enigmatic smile"* . . . *"As soon as you're involved yourself it becomes confusing."* The idea and vocabulary are too difficult for a beginning reader. This does not mean that an older reader would not find this story of great interest.

Another point to consider is the universality of Maria Gripe's books. While the themes and motifs are universal there is doubt about whether these books would be acceptable throughout the world. Realistic stories about children without known parentage, born out of wedlock are not acceptable in some countries. In the midwestern United States, the adult relationships in *The Night Daddy* made the book unacceptable to an elementary book review committee.

In addition, the ethnic atmosphere and vocabulary might not be acceptable to some young readers. (pp. 448-49)

While the universality and Hans Christian Andersen qualities of *The Glassblower's Children* cannot be disputed, Maria Gripe's other books do not display the same characteristics. However, this lack of universality on the part of the realistic fiction in no way detracts from the imaginative, poetic qualities of Maria Gripe's books which are a joy to read, young and old alike. (p. 449)

> *Lorraine Stanton, "Shadows and Motifs: A Review and Analysis of the Works of Maria Gripe," in* Catholic Library World, *Vol. 51, No. 10, May-June, 1980, pp. 447-49.*

In her stories about Swedish children, Maria Gripe has shown us that children have similar problems, no matter what their country of origin. . . .

Gripe is distinguished for the depth of her characterizations and the sensitivity with which she portrays relationships. She has the rare ability to be childlike without being childish; she understands the children and so do we. We enter willingly into their joys and sorrows, defeats and triumphs.

> *Zena Sutherland, Dianne L. Monson, May Hill Arbuthnot, in their review of "Hugo and Josephine" and "The Night Daddy," in their* Children and Books *(copyright © 1981, 1977, 1972, 1964, 1957, 1947 by Scott, Foresman and Company; reprinted by permission), sixth edition, Scott, Foresman, 1981, p. 329.*

Maria Gripe's delicate fantasy, *The Glassblower's Children*, has two doll-like children who are just as charmingly wooden at the end of the story as at the beginning. But in its sophisticated portrayal of adult human needs and desires it is reminiscent of the literary fairy tales of Hans Christian Andersen and Oscar Wilde.

[While] European novelists still hold to the traditional view of childhood as a separate state from adulthood, they usually add to that view the modern understanding of the basic need for a child's sense of self. Both these concepts are prominent in the works of Maria Gripe, who is deservedly considered a "classic" writer in her own time. In her childhood trilogy *Josephine, Hugo,* and *Hugo and Josephine* . . . , Gripe remembers the simple anxieties and uncertainties of childhood as well as the great flashes of joy. She remembers her own reactions to colors, tastes, and sounds, and the intensity of all feeling. . . . (p. 288)

Maria Gripe's subtle art in these books lies in her style. With utter simplicity and restraint she evokes the interior thoughts of the child Josephine—her earnest sensitivity and clear common sense—as she gropes toward an intellectual understanding of herself, her friends, and the adults around her. Somehow, in a gentler, purer manner, she recalls the musings of Salinger's Holden Caulfield. Gripe's is the greater triumph, for a child's mind is more closed from this kind of keen comprehension than is that of a teenager. In both her allegorical fantasies and realistic tales, her human relationships are handled in a delicate, almost ritualistic way and the very writing about them suggests a ceremonial act.

The *Hugo* and *Josephine* books are unique in modern children's literature because they deal so perceptively with such *young* children and because, although both Hugo and Josephine are individual characters, Gripe still manages to convey through them a quality of universal childhood. There are few English-language writers today who share either of these qualities with Gripe, even though their writing may be every bit as literary and sensitive. Most explore their concepts with older children or young teenagers as the protagonists, and the coloration given to the traumatic and specific events of the stories lessen the attention paid to the nature of the child's reactions—the commonality of childhood.

Gripe's books are not laden with either national or local color. The King does come to Josephine's town; her life as a parsonage child does set her off from other children; but there is no overt quality of foreignness in Gripe's books. She translates well in this respect, and if her popularity does not equal that of Astrid Lindgren with *Pippi Longstocking,* she is still a favorite among English-speaking children. (pp. 289-90)

> *Sheila A. Egoff, "The European Children's Novel in Translation," in her* Thursday's Child: Trends and Patterns in Contemporary Children's Literature *(copyright © 1981 by the American Library Association), American Library Association, 1981, pp. 275-96.**

JOSEFIN [JOSEPHINE] (1961); **HUGO** (1966)

Hugo himself (and he is eminently himself) is a grand conception, his own man at seven: "No one knows anything about him. And no one asks questions. You wouldn't get an answer if you did. Besides, there's no need to ask. You are happy that he exists. That's enough." Which same could be said for [*Hugo*]—as it was for *Hugo and Josephine* . . .—whenever he's the pivot. But he isn't always: sometimes he's a sort of

absolute, a yardstick to which others never measure up, as when Hugo alone relates to Miriam, the icy new girl. He doesn't judge or classify, he meets things as they are, even his mother's death: "Angel? No, I hope she isn't, because she wouldn't like it—it wouldn't suit her either." Later, needing to earn money, Hugo's blithe about the problem, serious about the solution; refusing a party invitation, equally direct, and respectful gossip hums "Imagine not wanting to! And then just saying so!" He towers awesomely above the teacher, calmly transcending stupid regulations in the first episode and speaking his mind—not rebellious, just honest—and afterwards says it's sheer mockery to sing *Thy Bright Sun* every cloudy Swedish morning. When spring comes, he solemnly takes his leave: "I'm going to look for a confluence. . . . The waters from two rivers, you see, they join together and flow into one. I've got to find out how it happens. . . ." And thus the story fades, back into the vapor it sprang from—mystifying, moment-satisfying, faults and all.

> *A review of "Hugo," in* Kirkus Reviews *(copyright © 1970 The Kirkus Service, Inc.), Vol. XXXVIII, No. 13, July 1, 1970, p. 680.*

From the sometimes sublime (*Hugo* . . .) to the subliminally grotesque [in *Josephine*] . . . a troubled little girl of six experiments with good and evil under the guises of mischief and self-pity. The leavening characteristic of the trilogy is deceptive—as in the opening presentation of this parson's daughter who first seems to be just another terpsichorean sprite: "Actually her name isn't Josephine. Her name is Anna Gra. It's rather a lovely name, if it happens to suit you. But she feels too small for it. To be called Anne Gray—because that's what the name means in Swedish—is rather like wearing shoes that are too big. . . ." Until the very end when Josephine's "Papa-Father" puts God back in heaven and everything on earth is as it should be, she exists in unhealthy symbiosis with the witchy scandalmonger Granny Lyra (who feeds on her exaggerated woes while Josephine feeds on her candy), and in mortal terror of gardener Anton *God*marsson lest he take her for an angel and carry her from her not-so-unhappy-after-all home. Adventures (as a social outcast, meeting the King) and cute quips notwithstanding, Josephine is not to be trusted any more than the falsely pristine jacket picture of her, blonde and innocent. (pp. 680-81)

> *A review of "Josephine," in* Kirkus Reviews *(copyright © 1970 The Kirkus Service, Inc.), Vol. XXXVIII, No. 13, July 1, 1970, pp. 680-81.*

Josephine's story is simultaneously the account of a small Swedish girl's misadventures (suggestive of Beverly Cleary's *Ramona the Pest* . . .) and an exemplification of the universality of childhood experience. . . . The use of present-tense narration gives a sense of immediacy to a subtle story.

> *Mary M. Burns, in her review of "Josephine," in* The Horn Book Magazine *(copyright © 1970 by The Horn Book, Inc., Boston), Vol. XLVI, No. 5, October, 1970, p. 478.*

Some time ago we reviewed Maria Gripe's charming, unlikely, perceptive, daydreamy, adult-seen, child-felt **"Hugo and Josephine."** Now we have a prelude and a sequel. . . .

The plot [of **"Josephine"**] is slightly more fey than the plots of the other two thirds of the trilogy. Readers who love **"Hugo and Josephine"** probably will enjoy **"Josephine."**

They may enjoy **"Hugo"** rather more, even though the book is really about Josephine. . . .

It is all very feminine, lit with the author's understanding humor and compassion. Adults blessed with the same qualities may read both these little novels with profit and appreciation.

Will children find them equally rewarding? Perhaps, especially if the children are girls.

Neil Millar, "Moles—The Whole Story," in The Christian Science Monitor (reprinted by permission from The Christian Science Monitor; © 1971 The Christian Science Publishing Society; all rights reserved), February 20, 1971, p. 15.*

HUGO OCH JOSEFIN [HUGO AND JOSEPHINE] (1962)

Sympathetic 8-12's will recognize their own distant youth here, and they may feel for Josephine who detests and passionately rejects the name Anna, by which she was christened. All readers, surely, will rejoice in Hugo. By his sheer honesty, directness, and empathy he sets many a wrong right and many a school rule on its head.

Here are the youngest scholars, especially girls, sensitively and shrewdly observed and recorded, often with delight.

Neil Millar, "Pre-Teens for Tolstoi," in The Christian Science Monitor (reprinted by permission from The Christian Science Monitor; © 1969 The Christian Science Publishing Society; all rights reserved), November 6, 1969, p. B4.*

[Hugo] is the most convincing example of self-possession to come along in many years of childrens' books, and the quiet, episodic story of his and Josephine's friendship has an innocent charm. There's a Swedish flavor, but the appeal is universal, with thanks to the translator [Paul Britten Austin] who preserved the artless, direct style of the author.

Zena Sutherland, in her review of "Hugo and Josephine," in Saturday Review (© 1969 Saturday Review Magazine Co.; reprinted by permission), Vol. LII, No. 45, November 8, 1969, p. 67.

The story is written in the present tense throughout, and this style is often awkward and annoying. However, the characters are believable, and the story has enough warmth to make it appeal to some middle-grade girls.

Susan Stanton, in her review of "Hugo and Josephine," in School Library Journal, an appendix to Library Journal (reprinted from the January, 1970 issue of School Library Journal, published by R. R. Bowker Co./A Xerox Corporation; copyright © 1970), Vol. 16, No. 5, January, 1970, p. 57.

Criticism is stilled almost entirely by . . . **Hugo and Josephine**. . . .

[It is] a return to the purest kind of enjoyment. . . . All one can say of the book is that it is even better [than the film of the same name]—despite being written entirely in the present tense, usually of all tricks of style the most irritating. Here, after a time, you do not notice it. It simply seems right.

The generation gap—the way children misunderstand adults and adults children is caught exactly . . . , so are the terrors and enmities of children in the ordinary world. This is more, though, than just a sensitive chronicle of everyday experience—it sits a little aside, restates and illuminates, because of the character of Hugo himself, . . . who is far from ordinary. He is, as Josephine comes to recognize for herself, a "natural spirit". He is an original, just like the book itself.

"Pure Enjoyment," in The Times Literary Supplement (© Times Newspapers Ltd. (London) 1971; reproduced from The Times Literary Supplement by permission), No. 3605, April 2, 1971, p. 391.*

PAPPA PELLERINS DOTTER [PAPPA PELLERIN'S DAUGHTER] (1963)

Loella is a fiercely independent 12 year-old, and this story . . . makes her come alive in a very real way. . . . This book is the first to be published in England; we hope for more.

A review of "Pappa Pellerin's Daughter," in The Junior Bookshelf, Vol. 30, No. 2, April, 1966, p. 121.

Children differ little enough, all in all, whatever their time or clime. It is the prevailing rules and codes, the immediate landscapes, the degrees of comfort or poverty, and other social differences that affect the course of fiction. Thus, in **Pappa Pellerin's Daughter**—a book of exceptional quality—the two main scenes (a remote Swedish village on the edge of a forest; a modern Swedish orphanage in the city) must each add point to the story—an intensity, too, that their equivalents here might seem to the English reader to lack. Yet the heroine herself would stand out whatever the setting.

"Same Faces, Other Scenes," in The Times Literary Supplement (© Times Newspapers Ltd. (London) 1966; reproduced from The Times Literary Supplement by permission), No. 3351, May 19, 1966, p. 43.*

"Papa Pellerin's Daughter" is a study in character and temperament of a child coping with adult problems. . . . Although the author writes in a realistic style, she stresses the warm human aspects of a twelve-year-old mind and presents unusual figures and epithets. Comparable to "Heidi", this unusual book delves into a child's imaginary world and will delight children from 9 to 15 years and, indeed, can be enjoyed by everyone.

Sr. M. Denis, in her review of "Pappa Pellerin's Daughter," in Best Sellers (copyright 1966, by the University of Scranton), Vol. 26, No. 9, August 1, 1966, p. 174.

[An] interesting story for girls. . . . The book has an unusual situation, an interesting setting, good characterization, and a candid treatment of relationships and conflicts. It is weak, not in the happy ending, although that is a little pat, but in the areas it leaves unexplained: the relationship between Loella's parents, the mother's casual abandonment of three children, the future relationships between the father who appears at the end of the book and the mother. . . . There is a reference to the fact that the small twin brothers "Have a different father, after all."

Zena Sutherland, in her review of "Pappa Pellerin's Daughter," in Bulletin of the Center for Children's Books (reprinted by permission of The University of Chicago Press; copyright 1966 by the University of Chicago), Vol. 20, No. 1, September, 1966, p. 11.

[The] author has taken a severe, straight look at personality—of a lonely child and an apparently irresponsible mother—and the book has a keen edge and a particular flavour rarely to be found in our own children's stories.

Margery Fisher, in her review of "Pappa Pellerin's Daughter," in her Growing Point, *Vol. 5, No. 4, October, 1966, p. 777.*

Loella and one of the other girls in the orphanage emerge as fairly well realized characters, with plausible adolescent feelings, hopes, and daydreams and annoying faults as well as virtues, but the rest of the characters have no reality, and the plot falls down badly. Some girls who like introspective stories or stories about orphans will be interested in Loella, but the story will not have general appeal.

Lillian N. Gerhardt, in her review of "Pappa Pellerin's Daughter," in School Library Journal, *an appendix to* Library Journal *(reprinted from the October, 1966 issue of* School Library Journal, *published by R. R. Bowker Co./A Xerox Corporation; copyright © 1966), October, 1966, p. 229.*

GLASBLASARNS BARN [THE GLASSBLOWER'S CHILDREN] (1964)

Unlike Gripe's contemporary Hugo and Josephine books, *The Glassblower's Children* is a fairy tale, with remote storybook settings, mythic themes and archetypal rather than realistic characters. The first chapters, drenched in Germanic folklore, are dominated by an almost tangible sense of foreboding which peaks at the country fair when Albert the glassmaker confronts the clairvoyant Flutter Mildweather, who weaves uncanny tapestries on Gallows Hill where she lives with a one-eyed raven. Then, in keeping with Flutter's prophecy, the glassmaker's beautiful children are kidnapped and carried across the river of forgotten memories into an altogether more elegant (and perhaps more French than Teutonic) but just as menacing fairy-tale world, linked with Albert's only by Gripe's dazzling but artificial glass imagery. Here the rich young Lord of All Wishes Town and his unhappy Lady hire a governess for the children, and Nanny's consuming evil presence and grotesque proportions introduce a third note, that of surreal extravagance. Unfortunately the shifts in scene and focus tend to dissipate the tension and instead of mounting revelation and convergence the climactic Flutter-Nanny confrontation (they turn out to be twin sisters) simply makes the previously mysterious Flutter a more and more conventional figure. Despite the seams and weak spots, however, Gripe polishes each separate scene to fine perfection and makes each development more chilling than the last. (pp. 515-16)

A review of "The Glassblower's Children," in Kirkus Reviews *(copyright © 1973 The Kirkus Service, Inc.), Vol. XLI, No. 9, May 1, 1973, pp. 515-16.*

The story of the poor glassblower's children . . . is an extended fairy tale in the manner of Hans Christian Andersen; for the straightforward, simple style is threaded with allegory and symbolism. But even more important than the skillfully patterned plot are the images, moods, and emotions, which add to the intensity of the storytelling. (p. 365)

In the manner of a true fairy tale, the children are restored to their rightful forms and returned to their parents. And justly so; for the good and the evil, the simplicity and the mystery of the events are so tightly woven together that each detail in the plot is significant in itself and, at the same time, linked to all of the other details. After the frightening premonitions of the opening of the story and the Kafkaesque nightmare quality of the central portion, the author has—with magical sensitivity—evoked a satisfying conclusion. (p. 366)

Paul Heins, in his review of "The Glassblower's Children," in The Horn Book Magazine *(copyright © 1973 by The Horn Book, Inc., Boston), Vol. XLIX, No. 4, August, 1973, pp. 365-66.*

Maria Gripe deals in archetypal truths—a dangerous business, as nothing, paradoxically, leads more easily to truism and banality. Her preoccupations in **"The Glassblower's Children"** are more naked and central than ever, good and evil no less, and the nature of happiness and despair, with despair, perhaps, having the best of it. This is strange, because the rare triumph of her earlier books about Hugo and Josephine was the way they caught happiness—a very fragile and very threatened happiness perhaps—but happiness all the same.

This book is more distanced, too. It is an allegorical fairy tale, portraying characters with whom we are not expected to identify as closely as before, and reminding me of Andersen's "The Snow Queen." . . .

The story's progression is altogether Blakean—a mental as much as an actual journey (the lord and lady can be seen as Albert and Sofia themselves, rendered joyless by experience); from blind innocence through blind despair, to a knowledge and acceptance of coexisting good and evil. . . .

A lot of this is superb; beautiful and terrifying by turns. But I am left uneasy. The overtness and clarity must be deliberate in a book where the main symbol is glass—but at what point does overtness become overstatement, and clarity reveal only the obvious? Puzzling over it, I am driven back to "The Snow Queen" as a comparison. It shows, after all, a very similar progression, and has rather more insistent undertones of sadism and sentimentality. But finding such nice detail as where Gerda takes the message written on a dried stockfish to the Finland woman, who once having memorized it, "threw the fish into the porridge pot . . . for she never wasted anything," I am left concluding tentatively that in a final analysis it is just such particularity and unexpectedness—humor if you like—that **"The Glassblower's Children"** lacks, for all its power. Curious, when it was precisely that which made **"Hugo and Josephine"** so good.

"The Glassblower's Children" is a brave book, nonetheless, to which some children will, I hope, respond thoroughly.

Penelope Farmer, in her review of "The Glassblower's Children," in The New York Times Book Review *(© 1973 by The New York Times Company; reprinted by permission), September 2, 1973, p. 20.*

The Glassblower's Children is Gothic in setting and in atmosphere. The rural Scandinavian setting of country fair and remote mansion is deepened by images which rouse deep-rooted associations in the mind. A talking raven, a closed black carriage, dark forests, cold hearts and cold, echoing rooms—Maria Gripe uses these stage-properties with conspicuous skill and judgment so that we are drawn gradually and willingly into the mood of her fiction. (p. 2568)

Like Hans Andersen, Maria Gripe has embedded in the sustained sensuous atmosphere of her story nuggets of psychological truth. (pp. 2568-69)

In this parable of human relationships the innocent neither suffer nor learn. . . . [The final impression of Maria Gripe's fantasy is] its essential optimism. In its Gothic trappings there is no Gothic horror. . . . Poetic intensity and pictorial detail, plain statement and veiled emotion, are fused magnificently in this book. (p. 2569)

Margery Fisher, in her review of "The Glassblower's Children," in her Growing Point, Vol. 13, No. 8, March, 1975, pp. 2568-69.

Not quite a folk tale, not quite a fairy tale, **The Glassblower's Children** . . . is a beautiful book and a disturbing one too. In her style of writing Maria Gripe combines simplicity with poetic intensity, and she has the ability to capture the poignancy of emotional experience familiar from memories of childhood. Prising beneath the surface of the family situation she discovers lurking unhappiness and lack of fulfilment: situations are created which convey different psychological states: of pride, of lassitude, and of isolation, for instance. Happiness, the author is suggesting, is as fragile as glass, and unless sorrow and evil are faced too, it is not really happiness, it is superficiality. . . .

This is a book to be read and returned to: it touches one deeply before the full pattern of meaning becomes clear, but, when it does, every detail is seen to have its place.

Lesley Croome, "Dangerous Wishes," in The Times Literary Supplement (© Times Newspapers Ltd. (London) 1975; reproduced from The Times Literary Supplement by permission), No. 3813, April 4, 1975, p. 365.*

I KLOCKORNAS TID [IN THE TIME OF THE BELLS] (1965)

Thirteen-year-old King Arvid is not interested in power over his people; in fact, it makes him uncomfortable. Philosophy is his forte; solitude his favorite state. Into Arvid's life comes Helge, a wise, regal, peasant boy who'd make a perfect king. Gripe tells a much more readable story here than in her . . . wishy-washy **Night Daddy;** but the dark, forbidding medieval atmosphere that is created by the presence of a vicious siamese cat and an evil dwarf is not sustained. This parable of power might have been a magnificent tragedy, but is just an entertaining (and forgettable) fairy tale.

Joyce W. Smothers, in her review of "In the Time of the Bells," in Children's Book Review Service (copyright ©1977 Children's Book Review Service Inc.), Vol. 5, No. 5, January, 1977, p. 46.

The author's latest story offers sharp characterization in a philosophical fairy tale full of discussion of determinism and free will. . . . The exploration of distinctive secondary characters, such as the sharp-witted dwarf and the ethereal queen-to-be, add to the richness of the tale; and when the author strays from the main plot, she does so to enlarge upon her philosophical theme. The story, not quite as allegorical as **The Glassblower's Children** but more similar to it than to any of her other books, is enjoyable on many levels.

Sally Holmes Holtze, in her review of "In the Time of the Bells," in The Horn Book Magazine (copyright © 1977 by the Horn Book, Inc., Boston), Vol. LIII, No. 1, February, 1977, p. 51.

[The plot] is admirably devised and highly economical and . . . moves to a surprising and effective dénouement. Maria Gripe never lets the reader off lightly, and here she demands close attention and an unusual degree of involvement. Interest is shared between Helge, the man of action, Atlas the dwarf, a Freudian creature, all malice and fear, and the king himself, a Hamlet-like character in his mistrust of action.

Marcus Crouch, "Rule of the Boy Kings," in The Times Literary Supplement (© Times Newspapers Ltd. (London) 1978; reproduced from The Times

Literary Supplement by permission), No. 3979, July 7, 1978, p. 767.*

What a strange tale. Maria Gripe is one of the world's great writers, . . . but she is never easy. . . .

Very slowly, and with many a pause for reflection and description, the plot unfolds to its notable climax.

What English children will make of this I do not know. It is a fine strong story, full of wisdom and shrewd observation. The characters are revealed with great subtlety. . . . One would hope that a story so fine in conception, so beautiful in execution, would find its readers anywhere in the world, and no doubt it will do so. I fancy that in this country those readers will be devoted but few in numbers.

A review of "In the Time of the Bells," in The Junior Bookshelf, Vol. 42, No. 5, October, 1978, p. 268.

This highly charged existential novel contains themes and dilemmas unique in juvenile literature. It questions the purpose of life and love; it deals with illusion and reality and whether the latter can be known with certainty; it concerns problems of personal need and philosophical commitment in conflict with socially imposed destiny, of public expectations, and of private, idiosyncratic needs.

While the story is compelling in its thematic treatment, it is even more so in terms of its literary structure. The author's manipulation of symbols and incidents with myriad meanings is skillful and complex. Death makes a multitude of appearances in various guises: left to die by his mother, herself a suicide, Helge is raised by the court executioner—a man who speaks of the covenant between executioner and condemned; the brothers first meet in front of a tapestry showing a unicorn, the symbol of death; Helge escapes to the city where he passes a priest on his way to administer the last rites. . . . (pp. 144-45)

This gripping, somber, and overpowering work can be expected to have a limited audience, in part because of the unresolved and unresolvable questions it poses, but also because of its relentlessly depressing tone. (p. 145)

Barbara H. Baskin and Karen H. Harris, "A Selected Guide to Intellectually Demanding Books: 'In the Time of the Bells'," in their Books for the Gifted Child (reprinted with permission of the R. R. Bowker Company; copyright © 1980 by Xerox Corporation), Bowker, 1980, pp. 143-45.

LANDET UTANFOR [THE LAND BEYOND] (1967)

Even more ethereal than last year's **Glassblower's Children,** this concerns a clear-eyed explorer, a young skeptic king and a misfit princess (she is both near-sighted and left-handed) who discover for themselves, and metaphorically in themselves, a land beyond any charted on maps or globes. To make the most of her symbolic "land beyond," Gripe gives us two versions of the same story: first, a shimmering but rootless fairy tale, then a much longer retelling—no less polished and abstract but laced with metaphysical asides which reveal the young king particularly as a sort of restless philosopher and the princess as a solitary late bloomer. . . . After the princess releases the explorer who has been imprisoned by an old king, her father, and runs away to seek the unknown land, the explorer brings news of that land to the young king—a ruler disgruntled with his advisers because they will not give him an honest answer to a question as simple as "how many people they think pick their noses.'' In both variations of the tale the young king discovers the land and the questing princess as well, but not, on the second time around, until there has been a great deal of speculation all round on Gripe's favorite topic, the split between the inner individual and his public, social persona. At one point, the young king uncharacteristically refuses to elaborate on his unease because ''that really gets us into mysticism and identity and all that sort of thing. And it's so damn boring anyway.'' Indeed, that's exactly what Gripe does get us into and this mirrorlike tale is definitely not for those who find ''that sort of thing'' a bore. Her exploration of this land, which so many find invisible or even ''nonexistent'' is witty, glancingly profound, elegantly framed into a fable that uses familiar metaphors with a knowing lightness—for the uncommon reader who can find growing space in a mythical kingdom where, on the surface, nothing happens. (pp. 949-50)

> *A review of ''The Land Beyond,'' in* Kirkus Reviews *(copyright © 1974 The Kirkus Service, Inc.), Vol. XLII, No. 17, September 1, 1974, pp. 949-50.*

Throughout the reading of this book I felt as though my mind were wrapped in a sweater. I simply could not get things straight—story, plot, setting, characters or theme. It is possible that this is because **''The Land Beyond''** is translated from the Swedish. It is also possible that the book is wildly obscure.

The author's idea is promising enough: she will tell the same story twice, once as a child's fairy tale and once as an adult allegory. But, to my distress, I found both fairy tale and allegory the same. No new secrets were revealed by the latter (though it abounds in metaphysical hints) and the former was rather a bore. The plot also bothered me in its monumental vagueness. . . .

I found it difficult to *care* about the discovery of a land whose marvelous properties are never once described by the author. Then there is the old king's daughter, who drifts away from the castle and aids the young king in his search. Why? And the land itself—a continent which seems to be growing into the heavens—what does it represent? Imagination? The part of the human spirit which is still untamed? I do not know. And to add to my confusion the author has divided her chapters with quotations from Lord Acton and the Beatles.

> *Barbara Wersba, in her review of ''The Land Beyond,'' in* The New York Times Book Review *(© 1974 by The New York Times Company; reprinted by permission), October 6, 1974, p. 8.*

More abstract than in her previous titles, Gripe gets wordy when exploring the evils of labeling, the many ways of seeing, the nature of reality, the moral issues of capital punishment, etc. However, the symbolism in the story is riveting—the spider's crown of eyes, the young king's fire fountain in Holy Wrath Square, the snake which becomes a stream. An often powerful exploration of a very personal vision, but most readers will be stumped by this complicated allegory. (p. 56)

> *Ruth M. McConnell, in her review of ''The Land Beyond,'' in* School Library Journal, *an appendix to* Library Journal *(reprinted from the November, 1974 issue of* School Library Journal, *published by R. R. Bowker Co./A Xerox Corporation; copyright © 1974), Vol. 21, No. 3, November, 1974, pp. 55-6.*

Although the author tries to [tell this story] in a narrative that introduces elements of satire as well as of fantasy, her concept overburdens the storytelling. Unlike the parables of the New Testament or *Animal Farm,* in which ethical and social concepts are embodied in the interplay of characters and events, this psychological or metaphysical allegory . . . does not measure up to the requirements of effective, not to mention absorbing, fiction. The story is inferior to both *The Night Daddy,* with its subtle yet realistic relationship of personalities, and *The Glassblower's Children,* with its nightmarish atmosphere and its articulated narrative flow. (p. 153)

> *Paul Heins, in his review of ''The Land Beyond,'' in* The Horn Book Magazine *(copyright © 1975 by the Horn Book, Inc., Boston), Vol. LI, No. 2, April, 1975, pp. 152-53.*

Maria Gripe's **The Land Beyond** is [an] essay on the nature of imaginative truth, and [a] very difficult book. She tells a fairytale as it was told to her as a child. Even in this form there are puzzling elements. What is the land which the explorer discovered and which, freed from its tethering bridge, floats into the sky? What do the spider and the toad and the snake who help the myopic princess on her path mean? Maria Gripe then tells the story all over again, exploring its depths and releasing new ideas latent in it. The exploration is fascinating, the details enchanting, but the mysteries only deepen.

When logic retires defeated it is best to look for present delights rather than hidden meanings. On this level **The Land Beyond** is a most beautiful and delicately told story. The author . . . has some of Andersen's sensitivity and his gift for giving a contemporary air to a timeless theme. Like Andersen too she has a touch of satire and an underlying strain of melancholy. Her story is exquisite, elusive, and strangely unmoving.

> *Marcus Crouch, "An Elusive Menace," in* The Times Literary Supplement *(© Times Newspapers Ltd. (London) 1975; reproduced from* The Times Literary Supplement *by permission), No. 3847, December 5, 1975, p. 1457.**

NATTPAPPAN [THE NIGHT DADDY] (1968)

In its concurrent projection of the piquant and the pathological, this autobiography-of-a-relationship—a dialogue in the form of alternating journal entries composed by the girl he calls ''Julia'' and the man she calls her ''night daddy''—is reminiscent of the variously unsettling **Hugo** and **Josephine** books. Whether the realm be reality, fantasy, or an internally logical combination of both, the voices don't change: ''My mommy isn't married,'' writes Julia, explaining why she doesn't have what *they* think of as a *real* daddy; the night daddy is in fact a hired baby sitter (Julia's mother works until six A.M. as a nurse)—or is he, the two of them muse on occasion, invented? dreamed? by her? by himself? by Captain Janssen who gave him Smuggler the personable night owl and the extraordinary vanilla plant, Queen of the Night? While Julia is surely precocious and the night daddy is somewhat un-matured—i.e., uncorrupted by being grown-up—the more important feature of their sharing the same wave lengths is that they are complementary eccentrics: he the nearly dried-up puddle, she the rain, as he once puts it. (Parables are convenient and mutually congenial—if obfuscatory to young readers . . . but then no more so than the very strange rest). The schizophrenia represented by Julia's special, separate night-name and by all the yin-yang night business cannot be facilely indulged as fantasy: the 'real' world is too much with them, the leap unfaithful, the break unclean.

> *A review of ''The Night Daddy,'' in* Kirkus Reviews *(copyright © 1971 The Kirkus Service, Inc.), Vol. XXXIX, No. 1, January 1, 1971, p. 2.*

The story includes an ornithologically unlikely pet owl, called Smuggler, and a botanically incredible plant called the Queen of the Night. Both are important to the sense of the story. Julia's classmates refuse to believe in the whole set-up, and so may many readers. Perhaps the story should be taken as a fantasy, expressing a child's emotional deprivation and longings. Then it makes an impression, but one far less deep than the care in structure and writing would lead one to hope for. Something is missing: either imaginative intensity, or common sense.

> *"Something Missing," in* The Times Literary Supplement *(© Times Newspapers Ltd. (London) 1973; reproduced from* The Times Literary Supplement *by permission), No. 3719, June 15, 1973, p. 674.**

Maria Gripe's characters always have great personal dignity and *The Night Daddy* is impressive in its recognition of a child's right to keep her own counsel and her own identity. . . . In allusive, elliptical prose Maria Gripe shows through the diaries of these two natural loners how they gradually edge together. . . . The young man's preoccupations and the child's fancies match as each gives a version of the same discussion, midnight meal, approach. . . . Pointed and intricate, this is a fine piece of writing whose style adds its own element to the implicit argument of the book.

> *Margery Fisher, in her review of "The Night Daddy," in her* Growing Point, *Vol. 12, No. 3, September, 1973, p. 2209.*

As with any real relationship there are problems and difficulties to be surmounted, but the author does not fall into the all too common trap of dismissing them too easily or allowing the whole thing to develop too simplistically. Instead these real people, with their own idiosyncrasies, hang-ups, and needs, form a relationship which is eventually based on mutual trust and affection. Reminiscent of Webster's *Daddy-Long-Legs*, this is a powerful book, now amusing, now sad, but never overstepping the line between real feelings and mere sentimentality. . . . [The] book . . . may be warmly recommended for children of ten up.

> *Vivien Jennings, in her review of "The Night Daddy," in* Children's Book Review *(© 1973 Five Owls Press Ltd.; all rights reserved), Vol. III, No. 6, December, 1973, p. 178.*

This book is not a factual or didactic book exploring solutions to the problem of the single mother. The imagery and emotional content of the man and child's relationship are the most important factors in the book. It is not a book that will appeal to every reader—some may find the mood and the happenings too vague or tenuous for their taste. But for those who are ready to appreciate the sustaining quality of the relationship and the seemingly small but actually very important adventures that these two share, the book will provide a tender and memorable experience.

> *Masha Kabakow Rudman, in her review of "The Night Daddy," in her* Children's Literature: An Issues Approach *(copyright © 1976 by D. C. Heath and Company), Heath, 1976, p. 55.*

JULIAS HUS OCH NATTPAPPAN [JULIA'S HOUSE] (1971)

A sequel to *The Night Daddy* is in the same format, with chapters written alternately by Julia and by Peter, the young man who stays with her each night while her mother is on night duty as a nurse. Julia is older now, her affection for Peter complicated by some ambivalence about their relationship. This is a less cohesive book than the first one, with Julia's loyalties divided between Peter and her teacher and friends at school, with Peter's interest caught by a small, silent boy who watches him; each is a little jealous of the other's divergent interests. There is just enough of this conflict to impinge on the major plot line, the threatened demolition of Julia's house. Albeit less cohesive, the writing evinces such a genuine understanding of a child's concerns, it is so fluent and perceptive, that the book makes an incisive impact. (pp. 113-14)

> *Zena Sutherland, in her review of "Julia's House," in* Bulletin of the Center for Children's Books *(reprinted by permission of The University of Chicago Press; © 1975 by The University of Chicago), Vol. 28, No. 7, March, 1975, pp. 113-14.*

Ms. Gripe's new novel is bound to appeal to her fans. We must add that, innovative and gifted as she is, the author comes nowhere near achieving the marvels she offered in **"The Glassblower's Children."** Julia is a bit too saccharine, the writing fussy.

> *A review of "Julia's House," in* Publishers Weekly *(reprinted from the March 31, 1975 issue of* Publishers Weekly, *published by R. R. Bowker Company, a Xerox company; copyright © 1975 by Xerox Corporation), Vol. 207, No. 13, March 31, 1975, p. 49.*

Something in this book has gone awry: the underdevelopment of some interesting new characters; the total absence of Julia's mother; soppy and flowery love-in house-party as the finis. In spite of Gripe's ability to portray her sensitive, introspective characters truly and honestly, this is not a great story—only a good one.

> *Marjorie Lewis, in her review of "Julia's House," in* School Library Journal *(reprinted from the May, 1975 issue of* School Library Journal, *published by R. R. Bowker Co./A Xerox Corporation; copyright © 1975), Vol. 21, No. 9, May, 1975, p. 55.*

As you'd expect there are nice touches throughout but there's something a bit coy in the two narrators' early explanations and disclaimers as to why they are again putting pen to paper, something a bit odd in Peter's total immersion in the affairs of children, and something wistfully '60's-ish in the flower power ending. (p. 604)

> *A review of "Julia's House," in* Kirkus Reviews *(copyright © 1975 The Kirkus Service, Inc.), Vol. XLIII, No. 11, June 1, 1975, pp. 603-04.*

Like all Maria Gripe's books, the plot consists of a circling movement round a few salient points rather than a continuous forward march through logically connected events. . . . [The neighbourhood party is a symbol]—perhaps of the need to understand one another, perhaps just Maria Gripe's way of saying that, in the hands of the innocent, failure can turn out to be a kind of success. However we choose to interpret the story, it is full of the sharp idiosyncratic details, the sound, solid wisdom and the spontaneous humour that marks her entirely individual work.

> *Margery Fisher, in her review of "Julia's House," in her* Growing Point, *Vol. 14, No. 7, January, 1976, p. 2799.*

ELVIS KARLSSON [ELVIS AND HIS SECRET] (1972); *ELVIS! ELVIS! [ELVIS AND HIS FRIENDS]* (1973)

It is difficult to conceive of an audience for these books. The central character, Elvis, moves from preschool into early school experiences, articulating every minute detail of these experiences, making adult-sounding judgments and ascribing motives to his parents. Older children, those who could read the 300 pages of this milk-toast tale, wouldn't be interested. His peers would find him either a puzzle or a bore. I opt for the latter.

> *Marion Carr, in her review of "Elvis and His Secret" and "Elvis and His Friends," in* Children's Book Review Service *(copyright © 1976 Children's Book Review Service Inc.), Vol. 4, No. 9, April, 1976, p. 79.*

Maria Gripe has created another memorable character in startlingly mature six-year-old Elvis Olsson. . . . The simplicity of Gripe's style complements Elvis' outspoken, blunt, and independent nature. Elvis and his family and friends emerge subtly, without complicated metaphor or elaborate description. There is not much plot, however: the only moment of real action in either book occurs when Elvis and Peter defend Julia's home from vandals. The drawing card in both books is Elvis himself, busy, self-reliant, sports-hating, and full of life. The drawback is that children old enough to read these books may not be attracted to such a young hero.

> *Carolyn Johnson, in her review of "Elvis and His Friends; Elvis and His Secret," in* School Library Journal *(reprinted from the April, 1976 issue of* School Library Journal, *published by R. R. Bowker Co./A Xerox Corporation; copyright © 1976), Vol. 22, No. 8, April, 1976, p. 74.*

The strange, silent little boy who hung around *Julia's House* . . . has his say here, and though we would have thought him older than six (and would here too, from some of his observations), we're easily drawn into his very individual, often mistaken view of things. In *Elvis and His Secret,* . . . Elvis has all he can do simply to justify his separate identity. First, he's not at all like his namesake, "the real ELVIS," his mother's "idol," and what's more, Mom says he's here as a punishment for her sins. Dad's displeased because he can't learn soccer, and even Elvis' clothing once belonged to his dead uncle Johan, on whose birthday Grandma doles them out. But by the end it's clear even to Elvis that he is very much his own person, and if the appearance and support of Peter, Julia's *Night Daddy,* is a bit fortuitous (as is the second rescue, this time from vandals, of Julia's now abandoned house), this sober little boy who can't seem to do anything right, and whose lonely but purposive behavior is so often misunderstood, is for real. In *Elvis and His Friends,* Elvis starts to school—though, after wetting his pants the first day, he drops out for a while until it's time to "take another chance"—and there he meets Annalisa, who brings him home and introduces him to Old Granny, who thinks on Elvis' wavelength, and to a very different, casual kind of household of which Elvis' mother strongly disapproves. The misunderstandings with Mom continue, but at last, at a family Christmas celebration, he learns how to win her with cuteness: "Since he obviously couldn't be himself at home anyway, why not act childish instead of making a nuisance of himself?" Thus, appropriately for an ending, Elvis loses his innocence. It had to happen, and meanwhile he's provided a touching and amusing window on the solemn misconceptions of childhood and the troubles they engender.

> *A review of "Elvis and His Friends; Elvis and His Secret," in* Kirkus Reviews *(copyright © 1976 The Kirkus Service, Inc.), Vol. XLIV, No. 8, April 15, 1976, p. 469.*

While it is possible that children old enough to cope with the vocabulary may need persuasion to read about a child of six, those children who have already been captivated by the small, solitary figure that appeared in *Julia's House* . . . always hovering on the outside of any action, will be a ready audience. These two books about Elvis are touchingly poignant and imbued with a wry humor. . . . What is most remarkable about these books is the consistency with which the author describes everything that happens from Elvis's viewpoint. The stories are written with perception in a style that is both ingenuous and graceful.

> *Zena Sutherland, in her review of "Elvis and His Secret; Elvis and His Friends'," in* Bulletin of the Center for Children's Books *(reprinted by permission of The University of Chicago Press; © 1976 by The University of Chicago), Vol. 29, No. 11, July-August, 1976, p. 174.*

The theme of [*Elvis and His Secret*]—one cannot call it a plot—is elusive and is about identity and the growing awareness of self. It has many strands, woven with the utmost care and sensitivity by the sure hand of the author. She is a craftsman of the highest order and she is also a marvellous observer of human behaviour and of the minutiae of everyday life. She has written a book which any critic could safely pronounce good. It is not easy to predict how a child will react to it. Apparently, the hundreds of letters received by the author were largely from teenagers and parents, and perhaps this points to its being a book which adults can enjoy by identifying retrospectively with Elvis but which children will find unsatisfying and perplexing—even dull. Most under tens are too busy *being* themselves to reflect unduly on who they are and why.

> *Ann Evans, "Home of Your Own," in* The Times Literary Supplement *(© Times Newspapers Ltd. (London) 1977; reproduced from* The Times Literary Supplement *by permission), No. 3931, July 15, 1977, p. 865.**

Maria Gripe has deliberately isolated a small boy in the centre of *Elvis and his Secret.* . . . This kind of book, intense and allusive and relatively lacking in event, needs a particular kind of reader, rather as Paula Fox's tales do—a reader certainly no younger than ten and one who has some inkling of the craft of fiction, the way dialogue and description can be used to suggest feeling and character without any direct explanation. . . . Reading between the lines, older children may discern how and why this self-centred [mother] finds Elvis's literalness so devastating and may see the story as a demonstration of a lack of understanding between the generations. People are Maria Gripe's concern, the clash of identities and the need to relate to others on their terms. Her books are not easy to read properly but they are always rewarding and stimulating with their subtle blend of comedy and sympathetic comment.

> *Margery Fisher, in her review of "Elvis and His Secret," in her* Growing Point, *Vol. 16, No. 3, September, 1977, p. 3167.*

ELLEN DELLEN [THE GREEN COAT] (1974)

Again Maria Gripe has created a child struggling with her own conflicts to grow and change. In two years time, and in the inevitably irregular manner of adolescents, Frederika changes. Burdened with an adoring friend Britt, Frederika must show Britt her own worth so that they may be individuals and not shadows. A self-confident mother who seems to need no one complicates life by saying goodbye to her ineffectual husband, Frederika's beloved father. Frederika experiences girlhood crushes, physical change and its accompanying sexual curiosity, and new self-awareness regarding motivations and relationships. With subtlety and sensitivity, Gripe again writes from the child's point of view, this time producing an exceptionally fine story about the uncertain search of an adolescent for confidence. Gripe's subtlety makes Judy Blume's work seem didactic and over-written.

> *Rebecca Lukens, in her review of "The Green Coat,"
> in* Children's Book Review Service *(copyright © 1977
> Children's Book Review Service Inc.), Vol. 5, No.
> 12, Spring, 1977, p. 119.*

Though it is not projected from the inside as are *Elvis* and Gripe's other, intimate portraits of younger children, an obviously autobiographical charge crackles throughout this odd, intense, introspective story of pre-adolescent Frederika. And though it is less polished and less structured than the author's other fiction, the fierce emotional reality more than compensates—even when it gets knotted up in minute analyses of the heroine's motives and her devious manipulation of petty schoolyard politics. . . . There are pages of obsessive self-questioning—about why she had changed, how she had changed, why she helped Britt, was she really bright? And it all takes her back to her mother—whose almost venomous characterization is the weakest, least convincing piece of the picture. However, resolved or not, the force of Frederika's feelings is impressive. And, sublimated or not, this is surely Gripe's most direct expression of her longtime concern with roles, masks, and layers of the self.

> *A review of "The Green Coat," in* Kirkus Reviews
> *(copyright © 1977 The Kirkus Service, Inc.), Vol.
> XLV, No. 9, May 1, 1977, p. 493.*

It must be difficult, nay impossible, for Maria Gripe to write a *bad* story, but in **The Green Coat** she presents a less than sterling effort. . . . At a critical point in the story, Frederika receives a coat identical to that worn by a paragon of virtue in the neighborhood, and mysterious changes occur. From a shy underachiever, she blossoms into a leader par excellence, gathering a follower reminiscent of her own weak "older self." Maturity does sometimes come as sudden as the dawn to an

adolescent, but this suggests magic! No one can fault Ms. Gripe's character etchings, though, even in a weak story. Frederika's day-dreaming father is a real pearl; her liberated mother would set women's liberation back years by association, and *every* child has been a victim of the "perfect" girl down the street. . . .

> *Mrs. Hildagarde Gray, in her review of "The Green
> Coat," in* Best Sellers *(copyright © 1977 Helen Dwight
> Reid Educational Foundation), Vol. 37, No. 5, August, 1977, p. 141.*

Gripe is wonderfully perceptive in depiction of character, especially biting in the case of the ruthless mother. However, the pace of the book is so deliberate and the tone so introspective that the book's appeal to some readers will probably be limited. (p. 16)

> *Zena Sutherland, in her review of "The Green Coat,"
> in* Bulletin of the Center for Children's Books *(reprinted by permission of The University of Chicago
> Press; © 1977 by The University of Chicago), Vol.
> 31, No. 1, September, 1977, pp. 15-16.*

Award-winning Swedish author Maria Gripe is one of those rare adults who retains a child's-eye view of the world, squint and all. . . . Gripe's story has all the virtues and faults of childishness: flashes of intuition rising out of a desert of tedious self-absorption. Fredrika is a potential soul-mate for all unreconstructed introverts, but only adventurous and skillful readers need apply. (pp. 40, 42)

> *Joyce Milton, in her review of "The Green Coat,"
> in* The New York Times Book Review *(© 1977 by
> The New York Times Company; reprinted by permission), September 18, 1977, pp. 40, 42.*

In dealing with adolescence, the author of **The Night Daddy** and **The Glassblower's Children** shows the same kind of sensitivity she manifested in depicting younger children. The confidential tone of her style avoids any possible suggestion of coyness, and, as always, her observation of character is noteworthy for its humor as well as for its keenness. In one episode of the novel, adolescent sexuality is frankly suggested, but it is kept from blatancy by Fredrika's thought that "it was more important to keep working at being a human being rather than a female." (pp. 539-40)

> *Paul Heins, in his review of "The Green Coat," in*
> The Horn Book Magazine *(copyright © 1977 by the
> Horn Book, Inc., Boston), Vol. LIII, No. 5, October,
> 1977, pp. 539-40.*

Jill Krementz

1940-

American author/illustrator of nonfiction.

Krementz blends her experience as a photojournalist and her expertise as a photographer of authors for their book jackets to create children's books in a documentary format. Most of these books belong to the "A Very Young . . ." series which depicts a brief period in a child's struggle to achieve an athletic goal. Krementz is noted for capturing the emotion of the children and the impact of their experiences through her photography; her attention to detail in both illustration and text is also recognized.

Krementz began her career as a news and candid portrait photographer. She is known nationally for her photographs of literary figures such as Kurt Vonnegut, Jr., P. G. Wodehouse, Henry Miller, and Marianne Moore. She became a children's author with *Sweet Pea: A Story of a Black Girl Growing Up in the South,* which is applauded for its insight and vivid picture of rural life. While some reviewers state that Krementz's focus on Sweet Pea's positive attitude will make children see poverty as an acceptable lifestyle, others say that by allowing children to identify with Sweet Pea through her joys, they will understand the reality of her environment. Krementz wrote *Sweet Pea* as a narrative in the voice of her heroine and she receives praise for the accuracy of this technique; some critics have mistakenly assumed that her books are written in the child's own voice.

A photographic session with a child acquaintance inspired Krementz's idea for a book concerning a young girl's experiences at The School of American Ballet. *A Very Young Dancer* is based on Krementz's notes and background research and documents conversations with Stephanie, her classmates, and her teachers, as well as her growth as a dancer from initial training to her leading performance in *The Nutcracker* at the New York City Ballet. It is noted for giving an interesting, subtly detailed account of the labor and rewards of ballet and for Krementz's high-quality photographs. These, like the text, catch the details and atmosphere of the ballet school and its classes. Although Krementz's first-person narrative is praised in her early books, critics state that the children in her succeeding athletic books seem to be prototypes of the first: determined, successful, and dedicated to perfection. Some critics dislike her concentration on goals which are financially inaccessible to the average reader, while others state that children need Krementz's idealistic athletes as positive role models.

How It Feels When a Parent Dies differs from Krementz's earlier books by covering the experiences of several children dealing with their parents' death. She is praised for her sensitive approach and for her correlation of photographs with the serious but optimistic tone of the book. Many critics state that Krementz's talents as a photographer reach their potential through her children's books. Her technique of presenting actual children and situations in a first-person narrative tend to make her works unique additions to children's literature. In 1976 *A Very Young Dancer* was named to the American Institute of Graphic Artists Fifty Books of the Year, *School Library Journal* Best Books of the Year, and the *New York*

© Kurt Vonnegut

Times Best Seller List of Children's Books; it won the Garden State Children's Book Award for nonfiction in 1979. *School Library Journal* selected *A Very Young Rider* as best book of the year in 1977 and *A Very Young Gymnast* in 1978.

(See also *Contemporary Authors First Revision Series,* Vols. 41-44 and *Something about the Author,* Vol. 17.)

SWEET PEA: A BLACK GIRL GROWING UP IN THE RURAL SOUTH (1969)

On most pages, [Sweet Pea] is laughing or smiling, and one gets a sense of unremitting joy—even though Sweet Pea lives in a wooden frame house that looks like it's falling apart and wishes that her family had a new one with a toilet inside and running water in the sink.

The photographs do what the book jacket claims—"provide insight into a cultural pattern of life in the rural South." But one never really gets a feeling of just how horrid the whole existence is. What's it like, for instance, to have to use an outdoor toilet? Is it worse in the winter than it is in the summer? Will a young child, in the urban north with no sociological background in poverty understand that this is a dreadful existence when she sees Sweet Pea's mamma, who has eight children and no man in the house, smiling happily on the front porch? And her sisters and brothers doing the same thing on the next page? How will it affect the argument against the Stennises and the Eastlands, who claim that "those people" are happy and don't need the meager poverty funds they already have and certainly no new legislation to change their way of living?

Charlayne Hunter, "Home Sweet Home," in The New York Times Book Review *(© 1969 by The New York Times Company; reprinted by permission), November 9, 1969, p. 50.*

Jill Krementz has drawn for us a portrait of Sweet Pea, a young black girl who lives in Montgomery County, Alabama, in a dilapidated house owned by "some people in Detroit." Her camera illuminates the particular circumstances of Sweet Pea's life—many of them strange to city and country children in other parts of the United States. But Sweet Pea and her brothers and sisters share the hopes and fears, the delights and disappointments of American children everywhere, at home, at school, at church, at Christmas. Americans everywhere, adults and children, know what it is like to get a whole family dressed at once and will chuckle over Jerry, who lost his own shoe and insisted his mother's would do. Every child who feels that his home isn't quite what he sees on television will sympathize with Sweet Pea's wish for a house with running water and a bed for each of her brothers. And every child who has had a happy Christmas will share her happiness at the end of the day when each of the children got a "wheel," for which their mother had saved all year.

The third quarter of the twentieth century has seen a tremendous widening of peoples' knowledge of each other as photographs, films, and television have presented vivid pictures of how other people live. And today all of us, wherever we live, have the task of bringing our children closer to people in other towns and states and nations, on the six continents and the islands of the seas. This book will help.

But Jill Krementz has also given us a picture of a particular child with a quality of joyousness all her own—who, in spite of some sad and frightening dreams, feels she would be happy if she were just in the twelfth grade.

Margaret Mead, "Foreword" (reprinted by permission of Mary Catherine Bateson as Executrix of the Literary Estate of Margaret Mead), in Sweet Pea: A Black Girl Growing Up in the Rural South *by Jill Krementz, Harcourt Brace Jovanovich, 1969, p. 5.*

One of the better books in the past year's crop of photo-documentaries about black children, **Sweet Pea** has the double advantage of a highly photogenic protagonist and a text in which the casual conversational tone seems genuinely that of a ten-year-old. . . . [Sweet Pea] gives a vivid picture of the fullness and dignity of her community.

Zena Sutherland, in her review of "Sweet Pea: A Black Girl Growing Up in the Rural South," in Saturday Review *(© 1970 Saturday Review Magazine Co.; reprinted by permission), Vol. LIII, No. 19, May 9, 1970, p. 44.*

Jill Krementz's clear black-and-white photographs portray the poverty conditions, but they also show a lively girl as she goes to an all-black school and church, works and plays at home, and mixes with friends and relatives; as in all families, there are both humorous and somber moments. This book is longer and has more depth than *A Week in Robert's World: the South*, written for a younger audience. . . . **Sweet Pea** is a superior

book because it offers a realistic picture of a black girl living in the rural South in the same way that Sandra Weiner's *It's Wings That Make Birds Fly* (Pantheon, 1968) believably reveals the life of a black boy in a New York City ghetto.

Merrilee Anderson, in her review of "Sweet Pea: A Black Girl Growing Up in the Rural South," in School Library Journal, *an appendix to* Library Journal *(reprinted from the September, 1970 issue of* School Library Journal, *published by R. R. Bowker Co./A Xerox Corporation; copyright © 1970), Vol. 17, No. 1, September, 1970, p. 162.*

Sweet Pea, who narrates the story, gives the reader a specific and vivid picture of her life. . . . She tells in detail of one of her school lessons about the "Indians." In the lesson, one member of the tribe says "that the settlers had helped them [the Native Americans] with better ways of farming and had made the Indians richer with trade and had taught the Indian children how to read and write and the women how to keep better homes and that they shouldn't have a war." Sweet Pea seems to have no perception that the lesson she is learning is a distorted view of history. She accepts whatever exists in her life with the same calm, coping attitude. She mentions at one point that she often has nightmares, but does not bother her mother with them. She rarely has good dreams.

This book graphically demonstrates the poverty level of many rural black families. It conveys the idea that this family works hard, enjoys what is enjoyable, and cares very much for each family member and each member of the community. None is self-pitying; none is defeated. One of the daughters goes to college. The family will endure. (pp. 189-90)

Masha Kabakow Rudman, in her review of "Sweet Pea: A Black Girl Growing Up in the Rural South," in her Children's Literature: An Issues Approach *(copyright © 1976 by D. C. Heath and Company), Heath, 1976, pp. 189-90.*

A VERY YOUNG DANCER   (1976)

When an outstanding photographer has an equally remarkable subject, the result is a rare treat—for all ages. Children who respond to the beauty and excitement of ballet will love this book with exquisitely detailed scenes depicting the budding career of 10-year-old Stephanie. . . . The text is a running account in the girl's own words: she describes her joy at being chosen to play a leading part in "The Nutcracker" and includes anecdotes about other dancers, teachers including George Balanchine and the many behind-the-scenes workers responsible for the company's performances. The book is instructive as well as a delight to look at and read, for it spells out clearly the message that intensive hard work and a continual striving for improvement (not to mention aching bones and muscles) are the price paid for professionalism.

Jean Mercier, in her review of "A Very Young Dancer," in Publishers Weekly *(reprinted from the October 18, 1976 issue of* Publishers Weekly, *published by R. R. Bowker Company, a Xerox company; copyright © 1976 by Xerox Corporation), Vol. 210, No. 16, October 18, 1976, p. 63.*

Jill Krementz remembers wondering, when she was taken to the *Nutcracker*, how all those children got on that stage. Others like her, and all those little girls taking ballet, or wishing they could, will no doubt envy ten-year-old Stephanie. . . . Putting

Krementz's words in Stephanie's mouth doesn't really bring her closer as her statements all seem so calculatedly conventional, and Stephanie's bandbox looks and perpetual poise don't help either. (We can't help comparing the scene to the twirling tournaments of less privileged princesses). Impressively packaged, this has the air of a too well-rehearsed production—but that certainly won't dim the stars in the eyes of Stephanie's audience.

> A review of "A Very Young Dancer," in Kirkus Reviews (copyright © 1976 The Kirkus Service, Inc.), Vol. XLIV, No. 21, November 1, 1976, p. 1172.

There are two reasons—or if one is counting scrupulously, perhaps three—for the initial prospect of Jill Krementz's book **"A Very Young Dancer"** to fill me with misgivings. First, following an overdose of seasonal exposure to The New York City Ballet's "The Nutcracker" has left me perceptibly cool to anything to do with that ballet. . . . Second, I am antipathetic to dance books for children. This is merely a blind prejudice. Finally, I am not all that keen on ballet students.

Yet Miss Krementz's story and pictures carry all before them. It is quite the best ballet book ever written for children, partly because it is not really a ballet book but a book daringly written in the first person about an enchanting girl called Stephanie.

The first person device could have been horrifically coy. Yet somehow Miss Krementz has caught the very tone and manner of a 10-year-old girl. Her story opens with total simplicity. It is a picture of a grave little girl in a leotard doing her *barre* work—a ritual that will be with her for as long as she is in the dancing profession. . . .

Miss Krementz—well-known for her photographs of writers—also has a documentary eye. She catches the atmosphere of classrooms and locker rooms, of rehearsals and even, less interestingly and, for that matter, less surely, performances. It is a world of make-believe and ritual. Of sweat and effort. Of tinsel and spotlights. . . .

Stephanie tells us: "Mr. George Balanchine is the head of the New York City Ballet. The School of American Ballet was started by a friend of his named Lincoln Kirstein because Mr. Balanchine wanted a place where he could train dancers to do the kind of dancing he likes." There have been more wordy, but few shrewder insights into the history of American ballet.

The book has been beautifully produced—the picture reproduction and layout are splendid—and the impression left is overwhelmingly of a pretty little girl going through some professional rite of passage.

> Clive Barnes, in his review of "A Very Young Dancer," in The New York Times Book Review (© 1976 by The New York Times Company; reprinted by permission), December 26, 1976, p. 11.

According to Miss Krementz' view, not a harsh word was spoken nor a tear shed throughout the entire process [of the routine from classroom through auditions to Stephanie winning the role of Mary]. I wonder if everybody was on best behavior for the photographer? In any case, this book is a visualization of the fantasy of how-many-thousand little girls and their mothers. It certainly does show what it looks like to be a ballet student at Lincoln Center in New York City.

> Douglas Blair Turnbaugh, in his review of "A Very Young Dancer," in Dance Magazine (copyright 1977 by Danad Publishing Company, Inc.; reprinted with

From A Very Young Dancer, *written and illustrated by Jill Krementz.*

> permission of Dance Magazine, Inc.), Vol. LXII, No. 5, January, 1977, p. 16.

The intimate quality of [Krementz's] art invites the viewer to linger over her pictures, and nowhere is this quality more evident than in her extraordinary new book about a student in George Balanchine's School of American Ballet. . . . Information about the process of training children to become disciplined dancers is unobtrusively provided, and the memorable photographs in the beautifully designed book precisely illustrate Stephanie's story and offer a fascinating perspective on the School.

> Sally Holmes Holtze, in her review of "A Very Young Dancer," in The Horn Book Magazine (copyright © 1977 by the Horn Book, Inc., Boston), Vol. LIII, No. 2, April, 1977, p. 173.

Krementz's book is uncompromisingly American, told in the imagined words of a ten-year-old, choosing only to see the glamour, a few simple sentences to each page. It will appeal to young children, but it will give them a totally false impression.

> B. J. Martin, in a review of "A Very Young Dancer," in The School Librarian, Vol. 27, No. 4, December, 1979, p. 381.

A VERY YOUNG RIDER   (1977)

In a strikingly designed photo-essay produced with all the skill and care of her **A Very Young Dancer** . . . , Krementz follows ten-year-old Vivi Malloy who owns her own horse and, with her sister, competes in major regional horse shows. . . . Although **A Very Young Rider** is above all Vivi's story and is told in her own words, it contains a wealth of basic information about horses and their care and training (readers learn what a ferrier is, for example, and are shown the several steps involved in properly grooming a horse). Riders and daydreamers alike will enjoy this fascinating glimpse into Vivi's world which captures beautifully her dedication and willingness to strive for perfection as well as the great joy she finds in her sport.

> Whitney Rogge, in his review of "A Very Young Rider," in School Library Journal (reprinted from the December, 1977 issue of School Library Journal, published by R. R. Bowker Co./A Xerox Corporation;

copyright © 1977), Vol. 24, No. 4, December, 1977, p. 49.

A Very Young Rider is the dream come true of every juvenile interested in horses and equitation. . . .

I think this would be a good book for a horse-minded youngster, especially the individual who would like to own a horse but doesn't know about the responsibility that goes along with it. . . . We see what it means to be responsible for a horse of one's own—the hard work and the dedication required.

Jill Krementz does a wonderful job explaining the various events and episodes that might take place in the wonderful world of horse showing.

> *Gail Gougeon, in her review of "A Very Young Rider," in* Best Sellers *(copyright © 1978 Helen Dwight Reid Educational Foundation), Vol. 37, No. 10, January, 1978, p. 335.*

[*A Very Young Rider*] chronicles the day-to-day life of a ten-year-old girl who aims to become a member of the United States Equestrian Team and also makes clear the enormous financial investment which must accompany her activities. The photographic essay and the first-person narrative convey the rigors of horse care and training and the joys and fears of competition. An effective balance between pictures and text makes the book an artistic achievement worthy of the author's reputation.

> *Karen M. Klockner, in her review of "A Very Young Rider," in* The Horn Book Magazine *(copyright © 1978 by the Horn Book, Inc., Boston), Vol. LIV, No. 1, February, 1978, p. 65.*

The sense of happy dedication that was part of the charm of *A Very Young Dancer* is present here. . . . Although the photographs can't capture an equivalent of the beauty of ballet, as they did in the earlier book, they do convey the pleasures and rigorous discipline of Vivi's equestrian passion; technically they are outstanding.

> *Zena Sutherland, in her review of "A Very Young Rider," in* Bulletin of the Center for Children's Books *(reprinted by permission of The University of Chicago Press; © 1978 by The University of Chicago), Vol. 31, No. 9, May, 1978, p. 144.*

[*A Very Young Rider*] reveals the reality and hopes of a youngster and her preoccupation with and love of horsemanship. Her family and her pony are also well portrayed. Youngsters, especially girls from 9 to 13, will savor the easy reading and pleasant viewing. (p. 138)

Respect and responsibility toward one's domesticated pet is the theme with a strong definition of the reward of self-satisfaction that comes from proving you have treated another creature well. The practical aspects of caring for a horse are clearly outlined in words and pictures, as is the bond of love that develops between youngster and animal. It also serves as a good manual on show care for ponies. (p. 140)

> *Diana L. Spirt, "Respecting Living Creatures," in her* Introducing More Books: A Guide for the Middle Grades *(copyright © 1978 by Diana L. Spirt; reprinted by permission of the author), R. R. Bowker Company, 1978, pp. 121-43.*

A VERY YOUNG GYMNAST (1978)

[A] beautifully photographed, expertly produced study of a young athlete. While the text (in the young Torrance York's own words) is lively, it is the photographs which most movingly capture the vibrant personality of the very engaging little girl featured. Not an instructional book, but a title certain to please young readers while leading them to new insights and fresh perspectives.

> *Richard Luzer, in his review of "A Very Young Gymnast," in* School Library Journal *(reprinted from the December, 1978 issue of* School Library Journal, *published by R. R. Bowker Co./A Xerox Corporation; copyright © 1978), Vol. 25, No. 4, December, 1978, p. 71.*

Young fans of Jill Krementz's two previous books, "**A Very Young Dancer**" and "**A Very Young Rider**," will not be disappointed by her latest addition to this popular series. Like its predecessors, "**A Very Young Gymnast**" uses copious photographs and a clear first-person text to document a year in the life of a talented young girl. . . . Thanks to Miss Krementz's miraculous organizational talent, the young reader is allowed to enter every aspect of Torrance's gymnastics life. . . .

As usual, Miss Krementz's photographs are eye-catching and appealing; she has an uncanny gift for bringing out the best in all her subjects. . . . The text, written as if in Torrance's own words, is witty and informative; and the more competitive aspects of gymnastics are sensibly played down. I can't imagine any child—well, any girl between the ages of 8 and 12, anyway—not wanting to own this book; meeting Torrance York through its pages and getting to know her practically as a friend is worth the whole price of admission.

> *William Jaspersohn, "Girl Wonder," in* The Christian Science Monitor *(reprinted by permission of the author), in* The Christian Science Monitor, *December 4, 1978, p. B19.*

In many ways, this new book is the most alarming and disturbing of the series.

In barest outline, these books are black-and-white photo essays about beautiful, rich little girls who have passionate, expensive, family-absorbing hobby interests. In terms of other little girls' daydreams and longings, they are large-format photographic substitutes for fairy-story heroines or paper dolls. The "**Very Youngs**" lead, or seem to lead, perfect lives. They dance in "The Nutcracker," get new horses for Christmas, go to Germany for competitions. No one insists that they make their beds, help with the dishes, or do anything for anyone else or anything that isn't related to their hobby interest. They also have enough pocket money and perfect preppy clothes.

What is somewhat alarmingly different about Torrance York, the gymnast, is that she is training for Olympic gymnastic competition and, in effect, gearing up to be "A Very Young Celebrity." The most dazzling dancers don't get hyped into stardom until their late teens, and the riders stay off the television talk shows and out of People magazine. But the gymnasts? Alas.

While some Americans are learning and using gymnastic routines as a pleasant kind of individual noncompetitive exercise, millions more, captivated by the nymphet charms of Olga Korbut and Nadia Comaneci, have begun watching gymnastic competition as a spectator sport. The most graceful gymnasts are the nubile young girls, but there hasn't been a real American star. Yet.

Enter 10-year-old Torrance, followed by Miss Krementz and her camera. Torrance may make it. She's being groomed like a horse, trained like a fighter; use whatever cliché you like. And part of the training is getting ready for the publicity. Everything we know about child prodigies and stars suggests that in later years they pay a terrible price for the performance skills that are outgrown before they are worn out. I wish Torrance York well. She may be A Very Young Gymnast. She is still a little girl.

> *Eden Ross Lipson, "Olympics in Sight," in* The New York Times Book Review *© 1978 by The New York Times Company; reprinted by permission), December 10, 1978, p. 84.*

As her followers already know, Krementz is an excellent photographer, and, in following the format of the texts of *A Very Young Dancer* and *A Very Young Rider,* she has again achieved the casual intimacy of a child's conversation. . . . The author spent a year with Torrance, so the coverage is full; an appended author's note includes the information that Torrance qualified for the A.A.U. Junior Olympics just as the book was going to press, and the quality of the book is such that many readers will feel a sense of gratification that someone they know has made it.

> *Zena Sutherland, in her review of "A Very Young Gymnast," in* Bulletin of the Center for Children's Books *(reprinted by permission of The University of Chicago Press; © 1979 by The University of Chicago), Vol. 32, No. 6, February, 1979, p. 101.*

[Torrance York] is quite desperately appealing: the subject of **"A Very Young Gymnast"** . . . , she is already a top junior performer in a sport that has now swept the west: her evenings and mornings are spent practising, her weekends in competition. Horribly chilling is the visit to a top sportsmen's doctor for X-rays, so that if—more like when—she hurts herself, they will know what her frame looked like before. Only the spontaneous brightness of this child stifles the uncomfortable sensation of perfection pursued at a too-high price.

> *A review of "A Very Young Gymnast," in* The Economist *(© The Economist Newspaper Limited, 1979), Vol. 273, No. 7112, December 22, 1979, p. 86.*

A VERY YOUNG CIRCUS FLYER   (1979)

To echo the ringmaster, this documentary is for "children of all ages," likely to outdo Krementz's other best selling **"A Very Young . . ."** books. Tato Farfan, born into the circus, is thoroughly at home with Ringling Bros. and Barnum & Bailey, as a nine-year-old trapeze artist. He and his older brother and parents are the world-famous Flying Farfans, a close-knit and loving family. Tato seems to be speaking directly to readers as he describes long practice sessions with his strict father (the act's catcher) and the circus children's academic tutor. Obviously, Tato has earned star status by hard work and absorbing his father's teaching: "Responsibilities are the difference between the professional and the amateur." . . . Splendid photos record the troupers' daily lives in black-and-white, and there are 15 glittering, full-color shots of a performance under the Big Top.

> *A review of "A Very Young Circus Flyer," in* Publishers Weekly *(reprinted from the April 2, 1979 issue of* Publishers Weekly, *published by R.R. Bowker Company, a Xerox company; copyright © 1979 by Xerox Corporation), Vol. 215, No. 14, April 2, 1979, p. 73.*

Krementz' latest very young star is a nine-year-old boy, and he can't be called privileged in the way that her dancer and rider were; nevertheless this has the same synthetic quality as its predecessors. In fact other youngsters can get closer to a young circus performer in Powledge's far less classy *Born to the Circus* (1976). . . . Appropriately, Krementz bursts into splendid color for a fifteen-page center spectacular showing the full circus cast performing in all their glitter. Hers is a less upfront type of razzle-dazzle.

> *A review of "A Very Young Circus Flyer," in* Kirkus Reviews *(copyright © 1979 The Kirkus Service, Inc.), Vol. XLVII, No. 8, April 15, 1979, p. 454.*

With Tato's commentary and Ms. Krementz' camera, the reader moves through the world of a "Very Young" circus star. One becomes aware of Tato's responsibilities, his friends, his joys, and his concerns. As the circus is about to begin, the marvelous black-and-white glossy photographs change to color. Ms. Krementz shows the reader the "Greatest Show On Earth" in all its glory. The book is a masterpiece of visual thrills. It is a superb addition to Ms. Krementz' "Very Young" series.

> *Madge M. Dhus, in her review of "A Very Young Circus Flyer," in* Children's Book Review Service *(copyright © 1979 Children's Book Review Service Inc.), Vol. 7, No. 10, May, 1979, p. 98.*

Readers follow [Tato] through his daily rounds, building up to the glorious spectacle itself, displayed in a perfectly placed color section of photographs . . . Cleverly, Krementz doesn't end on this technicolor note but, after stepping from behind-the-scenes Kansas into Oz, takes her audience back to black-and-white for the Flying Farfans in action, offering all the details from the last minute blast of hair spray, dab of rouge, and resin rubbed on hands to the final prayer before "going up" . . . As with her other Very Young books, the author gives the glitter of a pro performance well done its due, at the same time revealing the required care, patience, and faith. (p. 64)

> *Laura Geringer, in her review of "A Very Young Circus Flyer," in* School Library Journal *(reprinted from the May, 1979 issue of* School Library Journal, *published by R.R. Bowker Co./A Xerox Corporation; copyright © 1979), Vol. 25, No. 9, May, 1979, pp. 63-4.*

A VERY YOUNG SKATER   (1979)

Youngsters hooked on Krementz' photo-journalistic portraits of talented young athletes will readily pick up this latest. It pictures Katherine Healy, a skater since age three, who loves performing and wants her own ice show when she grows up. . . . Aside from the letdown of what is now a formula package, the chief problem here is the quality of the photographs. Many are grainy, some are poorly focused, and others badly composed. Krementz is capable of much sharper work. This will appeal because of subject and series momentum, but technically it is below par.

Denise M. Wilms, in her review of "A Very Young Skater," in Booklist *(reprinted by permission of the American Library Association; copyright © 1979 by the American Library Association), Vol. 76, No. 8, December 15, 1979, p. 613.*

The latest of Krementz' very young competitor/performers takes us through the rigors, intricacies, and consuming demands of career-oriented ice skating. At ten, Katherine Healy is as pretty, personable, and self-possessed as Krementz' other subjects, and seemingly as single-minded. . . . For better or worse, the whole package is proficiently trim and polished as always.

A review of "A Very Young Skater," in Kirkus Reviews *(copyright © 1980 The Kirkus Service, Inc.) Vol. XLVIII, No. 2, January 15, 1980, p. 69.*

A Very Young Skater, cast in the familiar and successful format of its four predecessors in the series, is a handsomely produced book, profusely illustrated with photographs in black and white, featuring a confident ten-year-old for whom skating is the hub of existence. . . . Although the search for perfection is not minimized, the emphasis is on triumph rather than on trials. (p. 72)

Mary M. Burns, in her review of "A Very Young Skater," in The Horn Book Magazine *(copyright © 1980 by The Horn Book, Inc., Boston), Vol. LVI, No. 1, February, 1980, pp. 72-3.*

HOW IT FEELS WHEN A PARENT DIES (1981)

Psychoanalysts disagree about the ability of children to grasp the concept of death. This affecting collection of statements by children between the ages of 7 and 16, each of whom has suffered the loss of a parent, strongly supports the argument that they both understand the concept of death and are capable of the necessary work of mourning. They address themselves openly to the facts: how their mothers or fathers died, the reactions of other family members and friends, and the physical details of the funerals. . . . Extraordinary events are recorded with striking simplicity. . . .

Several children mention discomfort in being treated differently by their peers after the death. And some of them talk about the surviving parent's remarriage with a mixture of relief and guilt. But each child speaks in his or her own voice. In every piece the grief is fresh and palpable. (p. 8)

It is obvious that children mourn in many of the ways that adults do, and this lovely book has relevance for readers of all ages. But it should offer particular solace and reassurance to those young people who cannot articulate their grief and who are confused and terrified by what has befallen them. . . . [Krementz's] sensitive photographs are a perfect accompaniment to the honest testimony of the text. In most of them, the children are seen going on with their lives. (p. 9)

Hilma Wolitzer, "Children in Mourning," in The New York Times Book Review *(© 1981 by The New York Times Company; reprinted by permission), July 19, 1981, pp. 8-9.*

I read Jill Krementz's *How It Feels When A Parent Dies* with a wonder of recognition, the relief of affirmation, and the serenity of acceptance. Now there is room in the world for the mourning of the young. The book is both evidence and model of our own maturity in dealing with death. It is a labor of love. Sensitive to the unspoken needs of a friend's son after the death

of his mother, Jill Krementz was moved to collect the personal stories of eighteen children who had lost a parent. They speak openly of their sorrow, their anger, their questioning, their resolution. The telling is enriched with personal photographs, informal portraits of the authors, at home, with friends, caring for pets, alone in thought. This is a helping book; for the bereaved, their families, their friends, and for all who would share this moment with children.

Carolyn S. Lembeck, in her review of "How It Feels When a Parent Dies," in Best Sellers *(copyright © 1981 Helen Dwight Reid Educational Foundation), Vol. 41, No. 5, August, 1981, p. 197.*

There's a similarity of tone to all these accounts—perhaps it's the format—but the kids' individual reactions register nonetheless, as do their common pain and sense of loss. Others in the same situation may find comfort in their company and assurance that one does survive, stronger or not; kids who haven't lost a parent may be drawn to musing on the subject.

A review of "How It Feels When a Parent Dies," in Kirkus Reviews *(copyright © 1981 The Kirkus Service, Inc.), Vol. XLIX, No. 15, August 1, 1981, p. 937.*

Children are often more honest and open—and blunt—when it comes to discussing subjects like death, and Krementz has

From How It Feels When a Parent Dies, *written and illustrated by Jill Krementz.*

155

wisely chosen to let these 18 children tell in their own words about the death of a parent. Their accounts of pain, sadness, fear, guilt and anger may seem depressing, but their strength and spirit of sharing could greatly comfort other children in the same situation. . . . The photographs are excellent and often show the child with brothers and sisters or with the surviving parent, relaxed and smiling—graphically demonstrating that it is possible to learn to enjoy life again. This is quite a different approach from other recent nonfiction books on death. . . .

> *Karen Ritter, in her review of "How It Feels When a Parent Dies," in* School Library Journal *(reprinted from the September, 1981 issue of* School Library Journal, *published by R.R. Bowker Co./ A Xerox Corporation; copyright © 1981), Vol. 28, No. 1, September, 1981, p. 127.*

This is a sad book, and there is some question of how helpful it will be to a bereaved child to read 18 others' experiences of parental death in an unrelieved documentary row. However, this is also a hopeful tribute to the healing power sustained by young survivors, who are competently interviewed and photographed in their widely varied reactions and situations. . . . Adults helping children through a hard time will better understand their charges' problems through the honest opinions expressed here, and young readers might feel less alone.

> *Betsy Hearne, in her review of "How It Feels When a Parent Dies," in* Booklist *(reprinted by permission of the American Library Association; copyright © 1981 by the American Library Association), Vol. 78, No. 1, September 1, 1981, p. 48.*

When speaking to a trusted adult who is not his parent, a child can be remarkably candid and articulate about his experiences. The eighteen children . . . who talk about their feelings after a parent's death show that mourning is as individual and as complex for youngsters as it is for adults. There are no laws governing how anyone traverses the unfamiliar territory of loss, and the editor intends to validate all the feelings a bereaved child may have—the ambivalence, anger, and guilt as well as the grief. While the book is meant to help children and surviving parents discuss their personal situations, it offers more than sensitive usefulness. The presence of the interviewer is effaced almost completely, leaving each child's statement as a direct narrative, so that the reader perceives distinct personalities and glimpses various separate approaches to family life. By offering no commentary and drawing no conclusions, the editor conveys the impression that each story is as equally important an account as any other. The black-and-white photographs, which show the children and their families in a variety of moods—sober and playful—contribute to the serious but hopeful tone. Not intended as a scientific study, the book, however, is a compelling human document.

> *Holly Willett, in her review of "How It Feels When a Parent Dies," in* The Horn Book Magazine *(copyright © 1981 by The Horn Book, Inc., Boston), Vol. LVII, No. 5, October, 1981, p. 553.*

Arnold Lobel

1933-

American author/illustrator of poetry, fiction, and nonfiction.

Lobel's personable characters, comfortable domestic settings, and meaningful stories make him one of the most popular contemporary writers for children. His works include modern fairy tales, historical fiction, and animal stories. Lobel is best known for his characters Frog and Toad, who share a warm friendship and adventures which are skillfully written in an easy reading format. These books are highly popular with children and have received both the Caldecott and Newbery Honor Book selections—awards rarely given to works of this type.

The Frog and Toad series is unique for creating lifelike characters and relationships with a minimum of words. Lobel's themes are welcomed for their childlike sensitivity and logic. Frog and Toad are child-substitutes with simple, honest emotions who take pleasure in the kinds of activities that children enjoy. They have individual yet complementary personalities—this friendship is another important way in which Lobel reaches into the child's world. His settings are rustic, timeless, domestic atmospheres which exclude telephones, automobiles, and electricity; they are valued for their relevancy to children of all cultures and lifestyles. Frog and Toad also have a universal appeal because they do not portray a specific race, class, or age. All the characteristics of Lobel's works are enhanced by his illustrations. Critics commend his portrayal of Frog and Toad's personalities through mild caricatures which are expressive without losing the natural qualities of their subjects. Lobel's realistic animals and environmental settings are often compared to those of Beatrix Potter. His use of varying degrees of browns and greens softly reflect the gentle mood of the stories. Lobel states that he keeps his illustrations simple in these and other "I Can Read" books so that they lend to, rather than distract from, the reading of the story. His technique of using two or three colors of varying shades is also seen in works such as *Mouse Tales*, *Owl at Home*, and *Grasshopper on the Road*.

Lobel's modern fairy tales are noted for their versatile use of text and illustration which is adjusted to reflect the mood of the story. When he began to create books in the folktale tradition, many critics found his texts to be trite and forced. With works like *A Treeful of Pigs* and *Fables*, Lobel proved that he has come closer to a mastery of the genre. With *Fables*, he has produced a collection of contemporary allegories which are praised for being written at a level children can understand and enjoy; his illustrations for *Fables* are noted for their rich color and original animal characters. Lobel uses Chinese folklore as the inspiration for *Ming-Lo Moves the Mountain*. Most critics concur that while this book reflects the art and fables of China, it remains a distinctively personal interpretation. Lobel is a talented contributor to children's literature who is sensitive to both the needs of childhood and the qualities of each style he employs. He has won numerous awards for his children's books, such as the 1971-72 American Institute of Graphic Arts Children's Book Show selection for *Frog and Toad Together* and *The Ice-Cream Cone Coot and Other Rare Birds*, the American Library Association Notable Book selec-

Photograph by Tom Wommack; courtesy of Arnold Lobel

tion in 1971 for *Frog and Toad Are Friends* and in 1973 for *Frog and Toad Together* and *On the Day Peter Stuyvesant Sailed into Town*, the National Book Award and a Caldecott Honor Book selection in 1971 for *Frog and Toad Are Friends*, the Newbery Honor Book selection in 1973 for *Frog and Toad Together*, the Christopher Award in 1973 for *On the Day Peter Stuyvesant Sailed into Town* and in 1976 for *Frog and Toad All Year*, the George G. Stone Center for Children's Books Recognition of Merit Award in 1978 for the *Frog and Toad* books, and the Caldecott Award in 1981 for *Fables*.

(See also *Contemporary Authors*, Vols. 1-4, rev. ed. and *Something about the Author*, Vol. 6.)

AUTHOR'S COMMENTARY

[*Geraldine DeLuca*]: How did you begin writing for children?

[*Arnold Lobel*]: Well, I began writing for children because I couldn't do anything else. I had gone to art school, started working in advertising agencies, and hated it. This was in the mid 50's, at which time there really was not a children's book market, strangely enough. . . . It was really a very small field, and I said, "Well, perhaps I would like to try that." I would go to employment agencies and say, "I think I would like to try illustrating children's books," and they would say "Oh no, you can't do that. There's no money in it" and since I had a family to support I said, ''Well there's no money in it.'' But I finally decided that I could not get on the subway every morning and face the workaday world so I had to try freelancing in children's book illustration. . . . I turned to writing only as a kind of economic expediency, because you quickly learn that when you're illustrating for another author you get 5% royalties and when you're writing your own story you get 10%. That makes a big difference. . . . I feel that I'm a trained illustrator and a lucky amateur in terms of writing.

[*Roni Natov*]: That's very interesting. I don't feel that way about your work.

[*AL:*] Well, apparently nobody does, but I feel that way about myself. I'm really rather insecure about writing, which is why I always write my stories complete before I draw pictures. Drawing the pictures is nothing for me. I know how to draw pictures. With writing, I'm in quicksand a bit. I don't really know what I'm doing. It's very intuitive.

[*GD:*] How do you come upon an idea for a story?

[*AL:*] Oh, heaven knows. Well, how does an adult author come upon an idea for a story? It's lifetime experience. It's just that I transmogrify everything to children because that's my particular medium. You know, if an adult has an unhappy love affair, he writes about it. He exorcises it out of himself, perhaps, by writing a novel about it. Well, if I have an unhappy love affair, I have to somehow use all that pain and suffering but turn it into a work for children. The children don't know, but the truth of the story, whatever gives it validity, is its truth to me, as an adult. It's kind of complicated and rather difficult to articulate, and for many years I didn't know that. When I first started writing, I would begin by writing stories *for children* that were really outside my own feelings. I would ask myself, what would the children like. I was writing fairly charming little books, but they really didn't have any kind of weight to them. And then I suddenly realized that if I was going to be a writer, I was going to be a writer like any writer and it was going to come from myself. All of the *Frog and Toad* stories are based on adult preoccupations really. I was able to tilt them somehow so that a child could appreciate them too, but I think that adults also enjoy them—and I think that's probably why. It's because they're really adult stories, slightly disguised as children's stories.

[*RN:*] They may be, but my son, who's eight, also enjoys them.

[*AL:*] Oh sure, I mean they are children's stories, and they've been very successful. Obviously children love them because they're very popular. But I was at the Bank Street School of Education once for some sort of function they had for authors, and this very large, formidable teacher there sat down and said, ''Now how do you do that? How do you write those stories? How do you zero in?'' You know, I didn't know what to say. I said, ''I don't know.'' And I think that was a very truthful answer. I'm a sort of amateur writer and I write in a very intuitive way. And I can't be very articulate as to how those stories are evolved. They are based on adult preoccupations.

[*RN:*] It's interesting because a lot of the themes that I see, in the *Frog and Toad* stories especially, feel adult, but they feel like the child part of the adult. . . .

[*AL:*] Well, of course, you could ask, ''What is the difference between a child and an adult?'' I think a child probably goes through all the same kind of struggles. I don't think we lose anything when we grow up. We think that we're adults and

that our emotions are adult, but we're really just going through the same kind of thing that we went through as children. Maybe we were more open about revealing our feelings when we were children.

[*GD:*] Have you ever tried writing for adults?

[*AL:*] No. People keep telling me, ''You should write a longer novel for children,'' and I keep arguing and saying, ''Well no, I'm a picture book person.'' Maybe some day when the eyesight fails and old age comes in, maybe I'll try. I don't really think I could write a novel for adults. (pp. 72-5)

[*RN:*] Your stories feel like little glimpses of life.

[*AL:*] That's what they are, I suppose.

[*RN:*] Rather than a whole development. Except that when Geri and I were looking at *Frog and Toad Together,* we noted that the last story, **''The Dream,''** felt like the culminating story about Frog and Toad. Did you have a sense of that?

[*AL:*] Well it isn't the culmination because I have another *Frog and Toad* coming out. There is, after that, more. Whether they're as good as the first two. I don't know, but there is more. No, that particular story was based on a very particular relationship I have with a friend who tends to be an expert in one-upmanship. . . . If you really like the person, you submit to that. You don't fight it; Frog submitted to it. He just got smaller and smaller.

[*GD:*] Do you see yourself more as Frog than as Toad?

[*AL:*] Both, both. I think everybody is both. But I think characters that are particularly valid for children, that live for children, are characters that are so clearly defined that they seem to be alive even when the child is not reading the book. They seem to have a life outside of that book, so that when the child gets back to the book, he refreshes his memory, he reunites himself with it. But when he closes the book, they're still there. Those are the characters that live. Stuart Little—I can't think of many offhand, but we all know them really. They exist outside of the framework of the books that they're in because they're very clear. That's the secret I guess. One works with these books for a long long time. From the time one begins to write to the time one finishes the sketches for the dummy—as an illustrator, I go right on. I finish with the writing; then I go on with the sketches for the dummy. Then I bring the thing into the publisher: then we make changes; then I bring it home; then I take those sketches; then I make original artwork; then I do color overlays. . . . My point is that it takes a year, maybe two years sometimes: if these stories don't have a germ of humor that is appealing to me as an adult, then they'd become too stale for me to work on. So that's one reason why I throw away a lot of stuff. Because I realize that a lot of the ideas I get are not amusing enough to me to sustain my interest for the long period of time that I'm going to have to have my interest sustained, and perhaps that's another reason why they are valid. But it's hard for me. When I wrote the first *Frog and Toad,* I had done quite a number of books and I didn't think that was anything special. Obviously it had more impact than anything I'd ever done and I hadn't really expected that. So, you know, I really don't quite know what I'm doing.

[*RN:*] Some part of you knows.

[*AL:*] No, really not. I can tell when I'm working that the thing is good—I usually can tell, this is good, this is bad . . . on my own level. I really don't know whether it's good or bad for the world. Sometimes I'll do a book that I'll think is terrific.

Then it'll come out and nothing will happen to it. There's no way of telling. It's all very unpredictable. I did a book a few years ago that I thought was just splendid and it died.

[RN:] Which one was that?

[AL:] Well, it was called *The Man Who Took the Indoors Out*. Do you know it?

[RN:] No.

[AL:] No, you see you don't know it because it died. And I thought, this is really a sensational book. It's doing okay but. . . . Well, of course, the "I Can Read" books are marvelous. I'm delighted to be connected with them because they're cheap. Therefore, they're so available to so many kids that can't. . . . What is the average picture book going for now, $5.95? The "I Can Read" books are splendid because they do get to the kids. The kids can afford them, the schools can afford them, so I feel very delighted to be a part of that. (pp. 77-9)

[RN:] How does the controlled vocabulary . . .

[AL:] I don't use a controlled vocabulary at all. I wouldn't dream of it. There are some publishers, I've heard, that impose that on their authors. I don't know how it works. When I'm writing, I know I'm writing an early reader and I think about it all the time. I think of trying to express myself in the simplest fashion I can, but I won't stop and not use a word that is a little longer, if there's not a simpler word. In the third *Frog and Toad* book I get to a sentence—it's a Christmas story—"Toad decorated the tree." Well, decorate is not an "I Can Read" word but I thought "trimmed the tree," "put balls on the tree. . . ." So I went back to "decorate" because even though it was a longer word, it was the word that was most functional and simple. I think that if it fits well in the story and the children are going along and very interested in their reading, they're going to have that, they're going to read it, they're going to grab it. I've used words like "avalanche," "beautiful," because there just isn't another word that I could gracefully exchange them for. And a word like "avalanche" is a great word for a child to have. Once he learns it within the context of a story that he loves, why he'll always have it, I think. . . . Once they bite into reading, they'll read anything. Once they are enjoying it, nothing stops them, even if they come to a word that they have to sort of sound out and fight with a bit. They just kind of devour it very quickly. So I don't worry too much about that.

[GD:] Do you get a response from kids?

[AL:] Oh yes. I get lots of letters. (pp. 80-1)

[AL:] I've gone to different parts of the country and it's marvelous to have some kid come up and say, "Got your letter." The response is exciting. But people assume that because you write children's books you have a special rapport with children. It's not so. Some of the greatest people in children's books, both past and present, have never been near a child. . . . Writing is something else again. You take it out of the child in yourself. It doesn't mean to write a children's book you have a special rapport with children on a social level. (pp. 81-2)

[RN:] I wanted to ask you some more about the themes because what struck me with the *Frog and Toad* books especially, as well as with the story **"Very Small Mouse and Very Tall Mouse,"** was that there was something in them that felt very fresh, that I hadn't seen before in children's books. . . . Did you have a sense that that was fresh, that "this is something

I'd like to write about, not only because it comes from myself but because I haven't seen that"?

[AL:] No, I don't think I work for originality when I write. I think it's kind of dangerous to do that because if I started to be terribly original, I would end up with crazy things that I would have no contact with. The *Mouse* stories—I wrote lots and lots and lots of them and I threw away lots and lots, but I do seem to be able to know when something is working dramatically. I began with the abstract idea of a very tall something and a very short individual and kind of thought about all of it; I guess that's the way any artist would work. The process is probably the same with adult literature too. A person could write about two men, one of whom was very short and one very tall and wind up with an adult novel about that, thinking about all the emotional ramifications of this relationship, of course, going into a deeper, wider range because he was writing for adults. I have to take the same thing and simplify it, you know, "Hello raindrops, hello mud puddles," because that's the kind of thing a child will understand. When I wrote that story, I knew it was working dramatically, beginning with the idea that a tall person was up higher than a short person and a short person had a different point of view from the tall person as they walked along the street. Sometimes I do start with an idea. In the same book, there's a story about a mouse whose pants fall down and I'm very intrigued by the idea you're talking about comedy . . . it seems to me the one thing that doesn't change much as we grow older is our sense of humor. I think a child's sense of humor and an adult's sense of humor are rather the same. And if you don't have a sense of humor when you're a child, you're not going to have one when you're an adult. We've all met children who don't seem to have a sense of humor and they grow up to be adults without a sense of humor. The same situations strike us funny when we're older, except we laugh at different things—we can laugh at sexual things; our points of reference become larger. But the basics: we laugh at incongruity and we laugh at lack of dignity. If a man's pants fall down, everybody laughs, children, adults. There's a sudden incongruity. He's lost his adult dignity. That's funny to everybody. And when I wrote, I did want to bring that out somehow. This very pompous, unpleasant person was reduced to something comical, and indeed, that's when children were able to relate to him and they did and they helped him and he began to love them. I don't know if you remember the story, but he holds up his pants with chewing gum, or something like that. In that case, perhaps I do think there was something I was trying to get across, but very often I'll begin a story and have no idea what the ending is going to be and that's why I throw away a lot. If I can't resolve it, if I can't bring it to some fruition, I'll just throw it out or put it away.

[GD:] The nice thing about the humor in your stories is that it doesn't distance too much. It's possible to identify with those characters and sympathize with them and still recognize the humor in them. . . .

[AL:] All the *Frog and Toad* stories are based on specific things in my life. I don't think I've ever written one that was arbitrary. You know, silly things, like the story about the cookies. Well, there was a cookie that I had a lot of trouble with—not eating it, that is. So you begin with something like that. Here's this cookie that if you eat you're going to get heartburn and gain a lot of weight and get pimples, and you've got to stop eating it. And, of course, when you take a simple situation like that, trying to check a compulsion really, you touch on the whole range of things. Somebody put that chapter in a Weight Watchers' publication. I guess it lends itself very perfectly to a whole aspect of fighting with oneself and that can be for any kind of habit, gratification that one feels is bad for one. We all go through that, and children go through it too. They feel a little less compelled to do anything about it than we do, but they have it. (pp. 82-5)

[*RN:*] **"The List"** has that quality too.

[*AL:*] Well again, that's very personal because I'm a compulsive list writer. I've had the experience of writing long lists and losing them and then having no mind because it was all there on the list. I learned at some point to take things out of myself and turn them into stories rather than just pull things out of the air, as it were. I think one of the most personal books I've ever written was *Owl At Home.* It came out last year. It's more personal than any of the other books.

[*GD:*] Can you identify with your characters in terms of style, their vision of the world? in *Frog and Toad* there's a muted quality both to the language and to the illustrations. Do you feel particularly identified with that?

[*AL:*] I suppose so. I'm really a very domestic kind of person. I guess that comes through in the illustrations, in most of my work. It's all very bourgeois. There's a lot of furniture, a lot of accoutrements of the home, because that's what I am. I'm really not much of a traveller or wanderer or adventurer and I think that feeling certainly comes into my books. I notice that all of my books are rather homebound.

[*GD:*] Also the colors are muted.

[*AL:*] Yes, well, that comes from experience. You have to do these separations in the "I Can Read" books—that green and the brown in *Frog and Toad*—and you learn that if the color gets too strong for those little books—this is an artistic, visual kind of thing . . . with those little books, and that big type, if you use bright colors, it looks lousy. And I've done it. In my early years I used to do bright colors in those things and I really wasn't happy with them, so I gradually got muter and muter and became more pleased with the aesthetic result. Those things you just learn through doing. I've been doing it since 1960 so I've learned a few things about how to make a book look good. It just happens naturally that you do.

[*RN:*] The domestic thing is interesting because the stories feel like they're about human relationships and tenderness and warm people—not huge adventures but nuances.

[*AL:*] Yes that's true. Well, that's very much me. I'm a small adventurer. Another thing is I'm not a particularly demonstrative person. I grew up in a very stoic household. I was raised by my grandparents who were German Jews. When I was little, there was laughter in the house but I don't remember any discord, any crying. It was all very very stoic and I'm not the kind of person who embraces people easily. I'm rather reserved. That I think comes across, a certain reticence in my work. I see it. It isn't as obvious to others as it is to me.

[*RN:*] I didn't pick that up especially. There was a calm, a feeling of assurance. Not bravado, but "it will happen, it will get worked out." Frog and Toad do care about each other. They can help each other. It felt optimistic to me. It didn't have that thing that Sendak does with the nightmare and the fear and the terror. It seemed to come from a more pleasant, more even vision of life.

[*AL:*] Well, that may be because I have been a parent, and I think if you have children, you kind of adapt that for them.

You create a feeling of well-being, whether or not you feel it. After awhile it becomes second nature. But you do that for your children. No matter how horrible, no matter how nightmarish you feel the world is, you kind of hide that for them and, after awhile, it becomes a part of you. (pp. 85-6, 88)

[*GD:*] Toad, though, comes fairly close to a lot of nightmarish things.

[*AL:*] Well, it's interesting, because Toad is a neurotic and Owl is a psychotic. Toad is like most of us. He knows the limits. He never goes over the line. There's always a certain logic to everything he does. He's irritated because he's looking for something that he hasn't found. He's the kind of a person who, if something goes wrong, goes to bed. We all do that occasionally. That's a very rational way of dealing with one's problems. You go to bed and you wake up. But Owl is a complete psychotic. His grasp of reality is gone. In one chapter he tries very desperately to be in two places at once, and doesn't make it. You know, that kind of thing. There's no sense of gravity to his thinking. It kind of completes the whole thing. I haven't done any writing in a long time, and all writers have this period when they feel like magicians pulling rabbits out of a hat. All of a sudden you look in the hat and there are no more rabbits. And I've sort of had that lately.

[*GD:*] How long does it take you to write a story or a vignette, once you get started on it?

[*AL:*] Well, there's no way of telling. I've written very good books in a week and I've written books that have taken me six months. It just depends on how it's going. And sometimes I'll write something and I'll think, "This is great" and I'll bring it in to my editor and she'll look at it and say, "Are you sure you can't do better" and I'll go home and I'll struggle with it. So there's a lot of back and forth. It does take a long time sometimes. Other times no. In *Mouse Tales,* some of those stories took a long time to work out. Others I sat down and the whole thing was done in five minutes.

[*RN:*] Which one, do you remember?

[*AL:*] Yes, the one about the mouse who travels to his mother. I wrote that in five minutes and never changed a word. I don't know. They say the subconscious is always working and helping one. Even before one does these things, it's all worked out up there. I don't know whether that's true or not. When I'm not writing, when I can't write, I really don't have any basic method of getting into it. I just have to sit down and throw away a lot of stuff and hope that eventually it will begin to flow and I'll begin to do something that pleases me. (pp. 88-9)

[*GD:*] It's in you and it's going to come out and you're just waiting for it to happen.

[*AL:*] Right, and the other factor is that a picture book is an audio-visual thing. It's both, and in a good picture book you shouldn't know where the words stop and the pictures begin. Certainly a child doesn't, particularly a small child who's being read to. He looks at the picture and hears the words from the parent's mouth, or somebody reading, and I don't think he dissociates the two. It comes to him as we'd watch a movie. We see an image and we hear a voice. It's one thing. And that makes it a whole different cup of tea.

[*RN:*] I want to ask you about poems. Did you write poems?

[*AL:*] I've written in verse. I love writing in verse. It's very hard but I love doing it.

[GD:] *Martha the Movie Mouse.*

[AL:] Yes. And I did something about Peter Stuyvesant in verse that I liked very much. And *The Man Who Took the Indoors Out* is a book that I did in verse. I like writing in verse. It's like doing the *New York Times* crossword puzzle. It's sort of a game I like to play. I don't think I'm particularly good at it. . . . [But] I will do some others because it is fun.

[GD:] How do you like Dr. Seuss?

[AL:] I like Dr. Seuss. I was about 8 or 9 in 1939 when his first books came out and I loved them. *The 500 Hats of Bartholomew Cubbins,* I was just the right age when that hit the market. It probably was one of the decisive books of my life. Later on, of course, he became like Walt Disney. He turned out these things and some of them were good, some of them were bad. He was grinding them out one after another, and of course the quality went down. Graphically, his pictures were always sort of ugly. I'm sure children loved them. But it's all very complicated because you know when you're writing books for children, you're also writing books for your peer group. There are design shows in New York. There's the Children's Book Showcase at the American Institute of Graphic Arts where they pick a certain number of books every year for a show, and you want your books to be in them. They look at the books and they look at the type and the paper and the style, and it's an art show. If you don't get into these shows, you begin to feel rather bad. If several years pass by and you don't make these shows, you think there's something wrong with your work. It has nothing to do with children. Children don't know from beautiful art styles. They want a book that's going to be pleasing for them on another level. Not that it would hurt them to see a beautiful book, of course, illustrated with exquisite taste and beautiful type. I mean, why not? There was a theory that if a child sees a book like that, if you put a beautiful book in the hands of a small child, it will develop their tastes so that when they get older, they will be able to buy all the beautiful and proper furniture, have all the right pictures on the walls, love Matisse. I don't know if that's true. But as an artist, I want my books to be beautiful and wonderful on that level. So it's complicated. It's a very schizophrenic thing. You have to think of all kinds of things at once. You have to please the kids, you have to please the librarians, you have to please the art directors. Sometimes you make the mistake of going too far. Sometimes your books are too designed, too sophisticated. Sometimes they're too screwy and cartoony. Those are the kinds of things that go wrong. And they go wrong with me frequently. One interesting thing, and I haven't really thought about this—you ask how did I get into writing children's books—when I was about seven or eight, I started telling stories. At the time it seemed perfectly natural, though now, it's quite extraordinary I guess. I'd tell stories extemporaneously and children loved them. If the teacher had 20 minutes she didn't know what to do with, she'd say: "Well, Arnold is going to tell a story." And everybody yelled and screamed, and I would get up and I would tell stories. They had conversations—I don't remember any of them—they had plots. When I started, I didn't know how they were going to end but they just came out of me. And I would draw pictures to go with them. When I got to be an adolescent I got very ashamed of that. That was part of my childhood. So I never thought about it. I just buried it. And then later I thought about it and thought, well, I was writing children's books even then. And I've never heard of another child who was able to do that. I really wonder—they didn't have tape recorders in those days—what the hell were

those stories like? Do you know how hard it is to hold kids' attention for twenty minutes? They loved them! And I don't know what I did. Fortunately, it just happened that I was able, by a succession of accidents and necessities, to have to go back to it. Like I had to eat, and it was one thing I thought I had a feeling for. (pp. 90-2)

[RN:] Do you have any favorites?

[AL:] Of my own work? Well I always say, when I'm asked that, "My next book." And that's true. There's a certain sense of letdown. You work on a book for sometimes as long as two years on and off and you think, oh it's a fantastic book, and then it comes out and it's just another book. There it is, put in on the shelf with the others. And there's a certain not exactly disappointment with it. Although sometimes if you get a few bad reviews, you are disappointed. But I don't really think I have any top favorite. I guess the *Frog and Toad* I feel very close to, and the *Owl At Home* too. (p. 93)

[GD:] Do you feel any . . . sense of going back to a better age? I think Kenneth Grahame was doing that. He was retreating in a way.

[AL:] I think that's part of all children's literature; there's an element of that in my work. The domesticity is a kind of going back to a time when one was dependent on the security that one's parents could provide. . . . I myself had a rather physically pleasant and emotionally unpleasant childhood. My surroundings were rather convivial to happiness. I wasn't so happy for other reasons, but I lived in a nice house with nice furniture, a nice backyard with trees and everything. I think that probably comes into my work.

[GD:] Is there any reason why you use animals?

[AL:] Yes. When you write about children, you usually wind up writing about a certain kind of child. I think it's unavoidable. You either write about poor children, the ghetto. Or you write about middle-class children. . . . But by using animals, by pulling it away from everybody, everything, you bring it to everybody. I mean, Frog and Toad belong to no one but they belong to everyone, every sector: rich children, poor children, white children, black children. Everybody can relate to Frog and Toad because they don't exist in this world. And I'm very careful in the stories not to make any direct allusions to modern life. That's something I just sense not to do. Frog and Toad don't call each other on the telephone. Toad takes a walk, and he visits Frog. He could, I suppose, pick up the telephone and call, but that would be too much, the world would be too much with them. And I do that purposely because I feel that it really creates a wider audience. Another reason I use animals is because you can give animals the freedom of adults while they still maintain the attitudes of children. I think children feel very restricted in their lives. They're surrounded by boundaries. Life is a prison really, for most children. And rightly so, I guess, but they still feel it, and they feel a release when they read stories about Frog and Toad who do not have parents—but who are children, really. Their preoccupations are those of children. They like cookies, they like ice cream, they like to go swimming, just as children do. Yet they have the freedom of adults. They live in separate houses, they can come, they can go. I couldn't do that with children. I suppose I could write a story about two old gentlemen but it would be sort of peculiar. Suddenly they would be human beings, and you'd have to write about why they were eccentrics. (pp. 94-6)

[GD:] And there's a kind of droll quality that I don't think you could get if you were writing about children.

[*AL:*] Some artists though, can. . . . But I, myself, don't particularly do that kind of thing. It's very difficult right now because editors are very hung up on ethnic themes; and the overwhelming thing right now is sexism.

[*GD:*] Do you ever find yourself censoring things in any way?

[*AL:*] How do you mean "censoring"? I don't deal with much that has to be censored.

[*GD:*] I mean cutting out things which might be questionable in some way.

[*AL:*] No, I don't think so. I'm a fairly conservative writer. That's another reason why I use animals. I don't have to deal with those problems. Frog and Toad live in a world where these things don't exist. (p. 96)

> *Roni Natov and Geraldine DeLuca, "An Interview with Arnold Lobel," in* The Lion and the Unicorn *(copyright © 1977 The Lion and the Unicorn), Vol. 1, No. 1, 1977, pp. 72-97.*

GENERAL COMMENTARY

Frog and Toad . . . lead lives of comfort and mild eventfulness in a world that relates without fuss jackets and teapots, a cycle and a writing desk with the natural form and some of the natural avocations of a frog and a toad in nature. Glass-paned windows and bullrushes, an umbrella and a clover-head combine just as easily in the precise, exquisite water-colour illustrations, with their gradations of green and brown, and their skilful suggestion of personality and animal form.

With Frog as the responsible, somewhat dictatorial brain of the duo and Toad as the emotional, nervous, wayward one, the two animals are endearing, comical and perhaps a shade touching in their leafy lives. There can have been few writers since Beatrix Potter who use snatches of talk so subtly to indicate the human type within a true animal and few artists who so wittily, meticulously and sympathetically suggest personality through the entirely natural movements of animals.

> *Margery Fisher, "Who's Who in Children's Books: Frog and Toad," in her* Who's Who in Children's Books: A Treasury of the Familiar Characters of Childhood *(copyright © 1975 by Margery Fisher; reprinted by permission), Holt Rinehart and Winston, 1975, Weidenfeld & Nicolson, 1975, p. 113.*

[Arnold Lobel] is versatile in his technique. . . . Although occasionally his work is too decorative, he approaches most problems with honesty and feeling. Invariably his artwork extends the dimension of the text and he is able to capture the individual mood of the writing. . . . Anyone who has read the **Frog and Toad** stories must feel he personally knows those two as individuals, through Lobel's sensitive portrayal of their character. (pp. 17-18)

> *Walter Lorraine, "Book Illustration: The State of the Art," in* Illustrators of Children's Books 1967-1976, *Lee Kingman, Grace Allen Hogarth, Harriet Quimby, eds. (copyright © 1978 by The Horn Book, Inc.), Horn Book, 1978, pp. 2-20.*

To romantic temperaments, the great tragedy of life is not growing old but growing up—away from "the hour / Of splendor in the grass, of glory in the flower," as Wordsworth mourned. The lucky few, however, never really grow up at all: they retain the ability to see the world with childlike wonder. One

such blithe spirit is Arnold Lobel . . . , creator of Frog and Toad, two of the most beloved animal characters to appear in children's books in recent years. Through their simple adventures together, from flying a kite to eating cookies, Lobel has brought young readers a world as warm, comforting—and enduring—as the land of Winnie-the-Pooh.

> *Annalyn Swan, "An Aesop for Our Time," in* Newsweek *(copyright 1980, by Newsweek, Inc.; all rights reserved; reprinted by permission), Vol. XCVI, No. 7, August 18, 1980, p. 78.*

The illustrations for Lobel's books are his own, deft and direct and carefully placed on the pages so that they present no visual barrier to the print. *Mouse Tales* is a series of bedtime stories told by a father mouse to his young; it is simply written and engaging, but it was with **Frog and Toad Are Friends** that Lobel established himself as master of this form. . . . What Lobel achieves in **Owl at Home, Mouse Soup, Grasshopper on the Road,** and **Days with Frog and Toad,** is a pervasive feeling of amused affection blended with a wry appreciation of the foibles of the creatures in the stories. The pictures are appealing, but the smoothness of the writing and the establishment of personalities in so limited a space are the strongest aspects of these animal stories. (p. 103)

Arnold Lobel's **Frog and Toad Are Friends,** has become a minor classic, with the sequel, **Frog and Toad Together,** not far behind. The stories are short and simple enough for a beginning reader but flow smoothly for reading aloud, and they have a humorous, ingenuous style. (p. 108)

Arnold Lobel believes that a good illustrator should have a wide repertory of styles at command, and his work shows this whether he uses wash, pencil, or pen and ink, which is his favorite medium. (p. 146)

> *Zena Sutherland, Dianne L. Monson and May Hill Arbuthnot, "Books for the Very Young" and "Artists and Children's Books," in their* Children and Books *(copyright © 1981, 1977, 1972, 1964, 1957, 1947 by Scott, Foresman and Company; reprinted by permission), sixth edition, Scott, Foresman, 1981, pp. 78-123, 124-55.**

Arnold Lobel made beginning reading more fun when he created Frog and Toad and, in doing so, loosened the restrictions of the easy-to-read form. His two amphibian friends evoke unrepressed giggles from beginning readers who view Frog and Toad's naiveté with a feeling of superiority. (p. 87)

> *Bernice E. Cullinan, with Mary K. Karrer and Arlene M. Pillar, "Expanding Language through Literature," in their* Literature and the Child *(copyright © 1981 by Harcourt Brace Jovanovich, Inc.; reprinted by permission of the publisher), Harcourt Brace Jovanovich, 1981, pp. 71-114.**

For beginning readers there is no better present than [the] Frog and Toad tales—stories that are funny, easy to read and above all illustrated throughout at exactly the right points to encourage fluency.

> *A review of "Frog and Toad Tales," in* Books for Your Children *(© Books for Your Children 1982), Vol. 17, No. 1, Spring, 1982, p. 7.*

A ZOO FOR MISTER MUSTER (1962)

A wonderfully funny picture book with an absurd story about a man who loved the zoo. One day, all the animals leave their cages and go to visit him. Obviously, this is an idea that will be hilarious to little zoo-goers. The pictures, done in black and white and a tawny shade which is about the color of a lion, are very funny, too.

> *A review of "A Zoo for Mister Muster," in* Publishers Weekly *(reprinted from the January 29, 1962 issue of* Publishers Weekly, *published by R. R. Bowker Company; copyright ©1962 by R. R. Bowker Company), Vol. 181, No. 5, January 29, 1962, p. 122.*

Mister Muster is a kind of professional zoo-goer. Daily the elephants trumpet him in the gate at opening time, mournfully they honk him out at night. The trouble is, on rainy days Mister Muster has to stay at home with only two goldfish and a canary to give him that public gardens feeling. Mr. Lobel leaps far into fantasy for a solution to Muster's problem. But his engaging orange cartoons should be able to get young logic to go along with him.

> *Melvin Maddocks, "I Never Saw Purple Quetzal," in* The Christian Science Monitor *(reprinted by permission from* The Christian Science Monitor; © 1962 *The Christian Science Publishing Society; all rights reserved), May 10, 1962, p. 3 B.**

Stories about zoos appear for the very young as regularly as spring, and often enough in other seasons. They are enormously popular with the nursery and kindergarten children who sympathize with the animals, always longing for love, and with the human characters, always eager to love and be near the animals. Mister Muster and the animals in his favorite zoo are no exceptions. . . . This is a very slightly new twist on an old theme, but it provides a simple framework for the forceful, humorous drawings of Mr. Lobel. The animals are comical without slavishly following the Disney and cartoon tradition.

> *Margaret Sherwood Libby, in her review of "A Zoo for Mister Muster," in* Books *(© I.H.T. Corporation; reprinted by permission), June 10, 1962, p. 18.*

PRINCE BERTRAM THE BAD (1963)

One of the best of recent "mean" stories which third-grade youngsters will enjoy, a new fairy tale they can read. Smaller fry, whose punishment is more traditional, will be entranced by the pictures.

> *Eloise Rue, in her review of "Prince Bertram the Bad," in* School Library Journal, *an appendix to* Library Journal *(reprinted from the March, 1963 issue of* School Library Journal, *published by R. R. Bowker Co./A Xerox Corporation; copyright © 1963), Vol. 9, No. 7, March, 1963, p. 165.*

There will be no doubt in the minds of the very young set who see this book that Prince Bertram earned his title "the Bad." He kept right on earning it until the day he aimed his slingshot at a big black bird that wasn't a bird at all but a respectable witch peaceably riding her broomstick and in no mood for nonsense. How this incident changed the course of Bertram's ways makes a hilariously funny little tale; and the pictures are wonderful.

> *S.B.B., "Knight Time," in* The Christian Science Monitor *(reprinted by permission from* The Christian

Science Monitor; © 1963 The Christian Science Publishing Society; all rights reserved), May 9, 1963, p. B3.*

A bad child, who manages to do a lot of mischief before he is properly punished, is always a popular subject for children's reading. The Prince Bertram in this picture book turns out to be as satisfactorily mean as any virtuous child could wish. . . . The medievally garbed members of the court with their comical cartoon-like faces, and the imaginative designs of the cradle, the castle and various group scenes are very funny and exactly in the mood of this mock serious cautionary tale. Fun all the year and not to be forgotten at Halloween.

> *Margaret Sherwood Libby, "Beware the Errant Slingshot," in* Books *(© I.H.T. Corporation; reprinted by permission), July 7, 1963, p. 9.**

Children of four to six will like to read or hear about Prince Bertram who enjoyed being as horrible as it is possible for a small boy to be. . . . The illustrations, in red and mauve, are amusing and there is nice detail in the text which is kept short and within the grasp of the under-sevens.

> *V. A. Bradshaw, in her review of "Prince Bertram the Bad," in* Children's Book News *(copyright © 1970 by Baker Book Services Ltd.), Vol. 5, No. 5, September-October, 1970, p. 229.*

GIANT JOHN (1964)

A contrived story which retains none of the humor or imagination of the folk tales after which it is styled. Pleasant illustrations do not compensate for poor text. Not recommended.

> *Marguerite A. Dodson, in her review of "Giant John," in* School Library Journal, *an appendix to* Library Journal *(reprinted from the September, 1964 issue of* School Library Journal, *published by R. R. Bowker Co./A Xerox Corporation; copyright © 1964), Vol. 11, No. 1, September, 1964, p. 169.*

The comic charm of Mr. Lobel's **"Mr. Muster"** illustrations is in his new picture book. Although the text is not as amusing as the pictures, five-year-olds will love a young giant, whom the fairies make dance and a king makes serve.

> *Jane C. Morse, in her review of "Giant John," in* The Horn Book Magazine *(copyright © 1964, by The Horn Book, Inc., Boston), Vol. XL, No. 5, October, 1964, p. 491.*

[The over-used characters of kings, queens, and princesses] are made tolerable by Mr. Lobel's slight touches of pictorial whimsicality. (pp. 24, 26)

Giant John is endowed with a childlike and appealing humor that grows on you. (p. 26)

> *Fritz Eichenberg, "Familiar Themes and Variations," in* Book Week—The Sunday Herald Tribune *(© 1964, The Washington Post), November 1, 1964, pp. 24, 26.**

Really bad books, like ***Giant John***, have a charm all of their own. There is a blundering naivety about these drawings, as about the hero himself, which is, near enough, irresistible.

> *A review of "Giant John," in* The Junior Bookshelf, *Vol. 29, No. 5, October, 1965, p. 278.*

There is nothing fearsome about Giant John; he is young, good-natured, and gentle. Geared to young children the simple story and comical pictures are more homely than imaginative and will appeal to some for this reason.

"Easy and Picture Books," in Books for Children 1960-1965 *(copyright © 1960, 1961, 1962, 1963, 1964, 1965 by the American Library Association),* American Library Association, *1966, pp. 358-94.**

THE BEARS OF THE AIR (1965)

This is what a good bear should do: go for walks, take naps, catch fish, climb up and down trees. At least that's what it said in Grandfather's heavy, embossed leather volume of "Things a Good Bear Should Do." "Things a good bear should do are not much fun" argued his four young grandchildren, who proceeded to demonstrate that juggling, lassoing, somersaulting and fiddling are really much more useful arts. It takes some stretching to get to the proof, but then the audience shouldn't require much more convincing. The brown on brown coloring of the illustrations is visually bland, but a second glance shows up some attractive details, like the Tiffany glass decorations in the bears' cozy cave.

A review of "The Bears of the Air," in Virginia Kirkus' Service, *Vol. XXXIII, No. 11, June 1, 1965, p. 529.*

A moralistic story that seems pointless and unchildlike. The creatures with large, bulbous noses in the illustrations have no resemblance to bears. Not recommended.

Margaret Poarch, in her review of "The Bears of the Air," in School Library Journal, *an appendix to* Library Journal *(reprinted from the September, 1965 issue of* School Library Journal, *published by R. R. Bowker Co./A Xerox Corporation; copyright © 1965), Vol. 12, No. 1, September, 1965, p. 191.*

Arnold Lobel's *The Bears of the Air* are such cuddly-wuddly butterballs that I wish the hunting season were on. His renderings seem to derive from Maurice Sendak's *Where Wild Things Are.* The bears' most prominent feature are big black rubberball noses, which I'd like to punch, they're so cute. The point of the story, as I get it, is that misbehaving bears know what's good for them better than their old-fashioned grandfather. I'm on grandfather's side. (p. 16)

Richard Kluger, "Hi-Jinks, and Low," in Book Week—The Sunday Herald Tribune *(© 1965, The Washington Post), October 31, 1965, pp. 6, 12, 16.**

The Bears of the Air . . . is a tedious brief tale illustrated with revolting coyness. Arnold Lobel's technique is just reminiscent of the Hobans' in the Frances books for us to realise how precisely right the latter are and how easy it is to slip into "cuteness."

A review of "The Bears of the Air," in The Junior Bookshelf, *Vol. 31, No. 1, February, 1967, p. 33.*

The Bears of the Air . . . could also be read as a moral tale for adults. But it's a moral that children appreciate too—and Lobel, if anyone, writes for children.

Lobel's brown and white pictures convey the bears' feelings, and back up the story perfectly.

Virginia Makins, "Lollipops," in The Times Educational Supplement *(© Times Newspapers Ltd. (London) 1978; reproduced from* The Times Educational *by permission), No. 3308, November 24, 1978, p. 46.**

SMALL PIG (1969)

Try these words of small pig's on your 4-to-8-year old's reading ability: "Ouch!" "Oops!" "Yow!" No trouble? Then he'll do fine with this new book in the I CAN READ series. But what brings these yelps from small pig? Trouble. Farmer's wife has been on a cleaning binge, tidying up the barnyard, pig and pigpen, too, and since pigs aren't meant to be neat and shiny this little piggy has gone wee-wee-wee all the way to where he can wallow—like in fresh cement. Mr. Lobel, as always, is adept at plotting amusing predicaments and putting woebegone expressions on illustrated animal faces. If the story isn't likely to join the ranks of classic accounts of pigs in literature, remember, it's only about a small pig for small ones.

George A. Woods, in his review of "Small Pig," in The New York Times Book Review *(© 1969 by The New York Times Company; reprinted by permission), March 30, 1969, p. 28.*

Small Pig's saga grows funnier by the episode as he scrambles from swamp, to city ("'Even the air is dirty here,'" he says hopefully), to cement. . . . In a year that has seen a profusion of picture-book pigs, Small Pig is one of the most endearing.

Sidney D. Long, in his review of "Small Pig," in The Horn Book Magazine *(copyright © 1969 by The Horn Book, Inc., Boston), Vol. XLV, No. 4, August, 1969, p. 403.*

The *I can read* series from America has come up with some zippy books and this is a notable addition. . . . This witty and pithy narrative makes the most of words easy enough for a six-year-old to read and the mildly caricatured figures of farmer and wife, pig and citizens, are extremely funny.

Margery Fisher, in her review of "Small Pig," in her Growing Point, *Vol. 9, No. 2, July, 1970, p. 1565.*

This is Early Reader's delight—fascinating story and pictures and clever vocabulary whereby the child reads difficult words easily. This is also a first-rate picture book, calling the young child from play. I read it to a playgroup of nineteen two to four-year-olds, with immediate impact. I read it twice and eighteen stayed the course enthusiastically. A week later, they are still asking for the picture of the mud disappearing into the vacuum cleaner and of Small Pig balefully chewing his blue ribbon.

S. Irvine, in her review of "Small Pig," in Children's Book News *(copyright © 1970 by Baker Book Services Ltd.), Vol. 5, No. 4, July-August, 1970, p. 183.*

MARTHA, THE MOVIE MOUSE (1966)

A slight, purposeless story with an inexplicable ending told in stilted verse and rather nicely detailed three-color pictures. Large picture book collections might like to try it out.

Elva Harmon, in her review of "Martha, the Movie Mouse," in School Library Journal, *an appendix to* Library Journal *(reprinted from the September, 1966 issue of* School Library Journal, *published by R. R. Bowker Co./A Xerox Corporation; copyright © 1966), Vol. 13, No. 1, September, 1966, p. 236.*

Arnold Lobel's cartoonlike drawings of winsome Martha snoozing forlornly near a garbage pail, smiling gratefully at a friend, or doing the twist endear us to her at first glance. And the poetry swings along at a jaunty pace.

> *Kent Garland Burtt, "The Mouse Was a Film Buff," in* The Christian Science Monitor *(reprinted by permission from* The Christian Science Monitor; *© 1966 The Christian Science Publishing Society; all rights reserved), November 3, 1966, p. B3.**

FROG AND TOAD ARE FRIENDS (1970)

Another happy book, this collection of five stories that recount the adventures of two best friends. The illustrations that accompany them are so enticing that they will lead any child into learning to read the words they illustrate—again and again and again. You'll see.

> *A review of "Frog and Toad Are Friends," in* Publishers Weekly *(reprinted from the August 3, 1970 issue of* Publishers Weekly, *published by R. R. Bowker Company, a Xerox company; copyright © 1970 by Xerox Corporation), Vol. 198, No. 5, August 3, 1970, p. 60.*

The artist has done nothing more attractive than these spirited portraits of animal characters whose unaffected relationships make this I Can Read story akin to *Little Bear.* Also one sees a relationship to Caldecott's animal drawings in the animation of clever Frog and tired, somewhat inept Toad. . . . The five separate adventures have freshness, humor, and a beguiling childlike simplicity. (pp. 475-76)

> *Virginia Haviland, in her review of "Frog and Toad Are Friends," in* The Horn Book Magazine *(copyright © 1970 by The Horn Book, Inc., Boston), Vol. XLVI, No. 5, October, 1970, pp. 475-76.*

It is true that toads don't go swimming in striped bathing suits or fuss about lost buttons nor would one expect a frog to write his toad friend a letter so that for once his letter-box won't be empty. All these things and more happen in *Frog and Toad are friends,* but there is verisimilitude all the same in this comic little book. Designed for easy reading, the narrative is extremely simple but a surreptitious wit lifts it out of the ruck and the absurdity of each episode is balanced by a moderate degree of accuracy in zoological terms. The illustrations enforce this accuracy in their own way. On each page minute landscapes or garden corners, endearing amphibian figures, all in brown and green with black, exhibit nuances of shade and design which in an odd way take one back to *Jeremy Fisher.* The style is different but the attention to detail and the absorption are the same. Beginner readers will be lucky to find (and I suggest, to keep) this unassuming, delightful book.

> *Margery Fisher, in her review of "Frog and Toad Are Friends," in her* Growing Point, *Vol. 10, No. 4, October, 1971, p. 1802.*

Five very short stories in a direct and ingenuous style, appealing because of their ease and the familiarity of the situations, translated into animal terms. The mild humor that permeates the tales . . . adds to the value of some of the concepts obliquely presented (differences in shape and size in **"A Lost Button"**;

time concepts in **"Spring"**) and the give-and-take of a fast friendship is gently affectionate.

> *Zena Sutherland, in her review of "Frog and Toad Are Friends," in* The Best in Children's Books: The University of Chicago Guide to Children's Literature, 1966-1972, *edited by Zena Sutherland (reprinted by permission of The University of Chicago Press; © 1973 by The University of Chicago), University of Chicago Press, 1973, p. 256.*

Arnold Lobel's books about Frog And Toad give the lie to the theory that books which teach reading have to be boringly repetitive. They may, long ago, perhaps have derived from Ratty, Mole and Toad of Toad Hall but Frog And Toad have distinct personalities of their own; and above all they are funny. Here are five of the best stories about them, ideal for reading aloud but also beautifully presented in big type for children to learn from. Part of an excellent I CAN READ series, the short sentence structure in no way takes away the amusement. . . .

> *A review of "Frog and Toad Are Friends," in* Books for Your Children *(© Books for Your Children 1982), Vol. 17, No. 2, Summer, 1982, p. 12.*

THE GREAT BLUENESS AND OTHER PREDICAMENTS (1968)

The text has rhythm, and the associative properties of the colors are matched in the experience—favorable on the first two-page spread, less pleasing on the second. Primarily coloring the world in shades of meaning that show and tell at the same time.

> *A review of "The Great Blueness and Other Predicaments," in* Kirkus Service *(copyright © 1968 The Kirkus Service, Inc.), Vol. XXXVI, No. 19, October 1, 1968, p. 1107.*

A very new story to explain the proliferation of color in our world is told by Arnold Lobel in *The Great Blueness and Other Predicaments.* . . . The world began by being all gray until 3the great wizard discovered first blue, then yellow, then red. The world's reactions to each complete change of color was understandable and is detailed in crowded pictures that cry out to be studied. (p. 5)

> *Anne Izard, "And Best of All, There Are Lots and Lots of Pictures," in* Book World—The Washington

From Frog and Toad Are Friends, *written and illustrated by Arnold Lobel.*

Post (© *1968 Postrib Corp.; reprinted by permission of* Chicago Tribune *and* Washington Post*), November 3, 1968, pp. 4-5.**

[Arnold Lobel, in **"The Great Blueness and Other Predicaments"**, never forgets the importance of telling a good story.] His fantasy about the wizard who introduced color to the world in the far-off time of "The Great Greyness" hasn't a single drab moment.

Selma G. Lanes, in her review of "The Great Blueness and Other Predicaments," in The New York Times Book Review *(© 1968 by The New York Times Company; reprinted by permission), November 3, 1968, p. 69.*

The sorry-looking gnome-like people that crowd the pages of this picture book are as lackluster as the slight text. . . . Pencil drawings with appropriate color washes are monotonous as the text, so color this drab. (pp. 287-88)

Eleanor Glaser, in her review of "The Great Blueness and Other Predicaments," in School Library Journal *(reprinted from the January, 1969 issue of* School Library Journal, *published by R. R. Bowker Co./A Xerox Corporation; copyright © 1969), Vol. 15, No. 5, January, 1969, pp. 287-88.*

ON THE DAY PETER STUYVESANT SAILED INTO TOWN (1971)

Puffed-up, peg-legged, hawk-nosed Peter Stuyvesant, a feather in his wide-brimmed hat, a buckle on his boot, could be the Captain of the Pinafore the way he self-asserts: he makes a great, grand entrance and Lobel makes it rhyme. . . . For those who don't know about the order he made out of the chaos that was New Amsterdam, Mr. Lobel provides a factual preface, but this Peter Stuyvesant is no textbook governor: no, no textbook governor would sit in the street ("a goat from behind, in a manner unkind, / Gave Peter a push on his seat"). "'This New World is a mess!' Peter cried in distress. / 'These animals need gates and fences. / Take these birds to a cage!' Peter shouted in rage. / 'Oh, good Dutchmen, let's come to our senses!'" They do, after hemming and hawing (it's all in the drawing), and then "'Let us have a big Dutch celebration!'"— at which "Someone asked, 'Will the town stay as small as it is?'" and old Stuyvesant uses his bedtime imagination. He "knew he was dreaming" and what does he dream but Manhattan today (again, pictured); and what indeed could better consummate what is what else but the jauntiest Pilgrim's Progress on record? Droll, too.

A review of "On the Day Peter Stuyvesant Sailed into Town," in Kirkus Reviews *(copyright © 1971 The Kirkus Service, Inc.), Vol. XXXIX, No. 17, September 1, 1971, p. 936.*

Come along with Arnold Lobel, who definitely proves that history can be entertaining as well as informative. His imaginative interpretation of historical events when Peter Stuyvesant came to the Dutch colony of New Netherlands in 1647 as Director-General and issued a series of proclamations and laws to improve safety and health is portrayed in rhymed verses and droll illustrations. A delightful voyage into history, with a surprise ending guaranteed to bring laughter.

A review of "On the Day Peter Stuyvesant Sailed into Town," in Publishers Weekly *(reprinted from the October 4, 1971 issue of* Publishers Weekly, *pub-

lished by R. R. Bowker Company, a Xerox company; copyright © 1971 by Xerox Corporation), Vol. 200, No. 14, October 4, 1971, p. 59.*

Children should enjoy the fun of seeing pictured (in Stuyvesant's dream) the New York of today, a punctuation mark to an ingenious presentation of a bit of colonial history, told in blithe verse and illustrated with pictures that are humorous and handsome.

Zena Sutherland, in her review of "On the Day Peter Stuyvesant Sailed into Town," in Bulletin of the Center for Children's Books *(reprinted by permission of The University of Chicago Press; © 1971 by The University of Chicago), Vol. 25, No. 4, December, 1971, p. 60.*

The illustrations, many framed like Dutch tiles, are done in yellow and blue and have a rhythm and humor that complement the verses exactly. The double-page spread at the end of the book—showing the future of Peter's tidy city—provides an unexpected shock of recognition. (p. 602)

Sidney D. Long, in his review of "On the Day Peter Stuyvesant Sailed into Town," in The Horn Book Magazine *(copyright © 1971 by The Horn Book, Inc., Boston), December, 1971, pp. 601-02.*

Lobel tells ["**On the Day Peter Stuyvesant Sailed into Town**"] simply, as an amusing story, without irony. He neither yearns for the easy solutions of the past nor suggests that the city be abandoned. Today Manhattan's inhabitants of all ages know that their home is in deep trouble. Lobel does not have to say that New York needs a strong hand again to save it; the kids already know it.

Paul Shepard, "The Circle of Life," in The New York Times Book Review *(© 1972 by The New York Times Company; reprinted by permission), January 2, 1972, p. 8.**

From On the Day Peter Stuyvesant Sailed into Town, *written and illustrated by Arnold Lobel.*

FROG AND TOAD TOGETHER   (1972)

Taking honors at the top of the list this season is *Frog and Toad Together*. . . . Once again, Arnold Lobel has created a masterpiece of child-styled humor and sensitivity in five short stories. . . . **"The Dream,"** in which Toad finds friendship more precious than fame and glory, admirably rounds out the selection. *Frog and Toad Are Friends* . . . is already a classic. This new offering continues a delightful tradition with good stories and pictures, the same easy reading level and satisfying relationship between these two who seem to be headed for seats beside Pooh, Wilbur, Petunia and other notables. Readers will readily identify with this perfect beginning-to-read book.

> *Evelyn Stewart, in her review of "Frog and Toad Together," in* School Library Journal, *an appendix to* Library Journal *(reprinted from the May, 1972 issue of* School Library Journal, *published by R. R. Bowker Co./A Xerox Corporation; copyright © 1972), Vol. 18, No. 9, May, 1972, p. 90.*

Arnold Lobel must be a toad in human disguise. Or perhaps just a child. In *Frog and Toad Together* . . . he shows once again how much further than Dick-and-Jane one can go with a simple vocabulary and a great deal of imagination. . . .

I could read these vignettes day after day, but my friends keep going off with the book. The last story, **"The Dream,"** is my particular favorite. Toad's simple boasts threaten to lose him the friendship of Frog, but reassurance is richly present at the end of the tale.

This kind of reassurance is one of the most precious qualities a book can give its small readers (or listeners)—if the story is well-done and the pictures imaginative and cheerful.

> *Jennifer Farley Smith, "A Marvelous Clutter of Tales: Fabulous Fish, a Returning Toad," in* The Christian Science Monitor *(reprinted by permission from* The Christian Science Monitor; *© 1972 The Christian Science Publishing Society; all rights reserved), May 4, 1972, p. B3.*

It's the simple things that are the hardest to say. And that's how it is with easy readers, where a too often limited vocabulary begets dull characters and too-concrete situations. Arnold Lobel is an exception to this dismal truism—first with **"Frog and Toad Are Friends,"** now in this second book of their adventures. . . .

Five separate stories lend themselves nicely to reading all-at-once or one-at-a-time. Each centers on some small incident in the lives of the two friends but reflects a larger fault, virtue or problem. Always, there's a trace of humor.

The best story is **"Cookies,"** in which the friends try hard to stop eating the wonderful things Toad has baked. . . .

In another tale, they put their courage to the test and encounter a hawk, a snake and an avalanche. When safely back home and "feeling very brave together" one is in bed under the covers, the other in the closet. (Mr. Lobel's humor is tongue-in-cheek but never cheeky.)

Abstract concepts and offbeat themes (rarely found in easy readers) are what lend this book flavor and substance. Frog grows smaller and smaller with Toad's increasing self-adulation (though it all turns out to be a dream). Inflexible Toad announces crossly that he can do nothing after the wind blows away his "list of things to do today." There are no cardboard

characters. No namby-pamby, this Toad says "Blah" when he wants to, sings to his newly-planted seeds and gives in to his gastronomic cravings. He is by far the less restrained of the two while Frog tempers all with reason. A welcome juxtaposition.

The child reading on his own will find that story has not been sacrificed for simplicity.

(The vocabulary does contain a few words to curl one's tongue around, like "trembling" and "avalanche.") He will find something gentle yet strong and appealing in the amphibious twosome, something very real in the large-mouthed, long-toed, brown-and-green way Mr. Lobel has drawn them. And when Toad, waking from a nightmare, says "Frog . . . I am so glad that you came over," and Frog answers, "I always do," the young reader will know what togetherness means.

> *Ingeborg Boudreau, in her review of "Frog and Toad Together," in* The New York Times Book Review *(© 1972 by The New York Times Company; reprinted by permission), May 7, 1972, p. 37.*

Two of the stories in this volume (**'The Garden'** and **'The Dream'**) scarcely even rank as incidents, being so exiguous as to verge on the invisible. Nevertheless, such is the quality of Mr. Lobel's illustrations—his expressive line, his virtuoso use of what appear to be utterly unpromising browns and greens—that he can conjure enjoyment and sympathy from the mere looks and posturings of his amphibious heroes.

> *Brian W. Alderson, in his review of "Frog and Toad Together," in* Children's Book Review *(© 1973 Five Owls Press Ltd.; all rights reserved), Vol. III, No. 4, September, 1973, p. 110.*

Toad is endearingly thick, Frog is nimble; this goes for wits as well as physique. Toad is clueless and directable; Frog is decisive, not to say bossy. In the first book of linked stories about these entertaining friends, their nicely opposed characters were firmly established; in the new book they are if anything more evident. Toad's alarmingly literal attitude to life makes a point of humour in the first story, *The list.* . . .

Frog and Toad together was named last year in America as a Newbery Honours Book. All honour to the selectors for making such an imaginative addition to a normally predictable list. Does this mean that in the future students will be writing theses on the psychiatric implications of the fable in reconciling the irresponsible and irrational impulses in all of us, or on the justification of dressing the animals in green and brown suits of clothes? Or there is the obvious thesis subject of the literary reminiscence in *The dream,* in which Toad is in danger of losing his friend because of a slavish, if unconscious, admiration for his distant relative from Toad Hall. I hope no such dreary academic fate is in store for these two splendid comedies. I hope readers will be content to share the sheer enjoyment behind the stories and appreciate the author's skill in devising rational absurdities with which to lure beginner readers towards fluency. Whatever Arnold Lobel may say (he has asserted that he did not set out initially to write a supplementary reader), the fact remains that the book is included among the "I can read" books. A series which has stimulated Nathaniel Benchley to demure wit surely need not be denied some of the credit for Arnold Lobel's superbly controlled, affectionately funny, supremely simple prose. (p. 2229)

Critics may note everywhere in this book the apt placing of a particular word, the unobtrusive variations of syntax within a repetitive framework. But, having noticed these literary points, they may join the multitudes of children who have taken the two heroes to heart because they are so amusing—and so real. Like Beatrix Potter, Arnold Lobel delineates his characters with a naturalist's care. His use of limited colour—green and brown with black ink lines and shading—is extended by his strong sense of design and his selective use of detail (look at Toad reading to his seeds, Toad climbing a ladder to put a batch of cookies out of temptation, the two friends colloguing over the garden gate). How much pleasure these books have to offer, to how many! (pp. 2229-30)

> *Margery Fisher, in her review of "Frog and Toad Together," in her* Growing Point, *Vol. 12, No. 4, October, 1973, pp. 2229-30.*

MOUSE TALES   (1972)

In quietly animated pink-toned pictures and resonantly simple words, Papa mouse puts his seven sons to sleep with seven bedtime stories. Lobel's handling of the cloud that becomes a cat and frightens little mouse until his mother reassures him is basic without banality; there is an affecting absurdity, reminiscent of Frog and Toad, in the two friends—one very tall and one very short—who see everything at different eye levels . . . but view a rainbow together; and the account of the mouse who floods a whole town with his bath water has a fresh if finely tempered silliness. Once again Lobel demonstrates that a beginning reader can be gentle in humor, resourceful with limited vocabulary, and even subtle in simplicity.

> *A review of "Mouse Tales," in* Kirkus Reviews *(copyright © 1972 The Kirkus Service, Inc.), Vol. XL, No. 19, October 1, 1972, p. 1142.*

Interspersed with the simple words—obviously repeated to encourage new readers—are words used only once: *castle, puddles, ceiling, rainbow, bloom, suspenders.* Even more important, the stories are touched with childlike humor. . . . Scattered through most of the cream-colored pages are small drawings in pastel tones of gray, brown, yellow, and magenta; and the joy of looking at the mice and their adventures equals the joy of reading about them.

> *Paul Heins, in his review of "Mouse Tales," in* The Horn Book Magazine *(copyright © 1972 by The Horn Book, Inc., Boston), Vol. XLVIII, No. 6, December, 1972, p. 591.*

Arnold Lobel scores again as illustrator and author. . . . Each tale is self-contained and can be read independently of the others. Among Lobel's ingenious witticisms, there is a wishing well that says "OUCH!" when a penny is dropped in it, an old mouse who resorts to chewing gum to hold up his pants, and a mouse who is so dirty he causes a flood when he takes a bath because of all the water he needs to get himself clean. *Mouse Tales* is somewhat easier to read than *Frog and Toad Are Friends* . . . but shares the same good humor and sense of the ridiculous. Excellent illustrations capture and extend the mood of the tales. If readers enjoyed the frog and toad stories, they won't want to miss *Mouse Tales.*

> *Carol Chatfield, in her review of "Mouse Tales," in* School Library Journal, *an appendix to* Library Journal *(reprinted from the December, 1972 issue of* School Library Journal, *published by R. R. Bowker Co./A Xerox Corporation; copyright © 1972), Vol. 19, No. 4, December, 1972, p. 70.*

[The stories are] crisp, witty and eminently well suited to beginner-readers; at the end the mouse-boys are sound asleep but this is no reflection on the liveliness and unexpected twists in the tales, or on the pictures, exquisite in their muted olive, pink, mauve and brown, skilfully inserting an element of caricature and wit (surely Papa has a look of his creator?) into scenes of tender delicacy. Right up to the standard of the Frog and Toad books, which is saying a lot.

> *Margery Fisher, in her review of "Mouse Tales," in her* Growing Point, *Vol. 12, No. 6, December, 1973, p. 2297.*

It really is very pleasant to read a book which, whilst making no claims for it as a masterpiece, is undoubtedly a little gem in which form, content, text and illustration combine into a delightful and amusing whole. . . .

Straight, deadpan delivery [by Papa Mouse] cunningly points up the dotty content of the tales. . . . But the text accounts for only half the delights, for each tale is enriched by droll illustrations which add much detail (don't miss the feet on the bath or the old mouse's candy-striped underpants) and character to the stories.

For those just beginning to read independently and for whom print size, spacing and sentence length is important, this is an excellent book for its rewards are far more satisfying than plain reading practice; but be prepared for others, both younger and older, to sneak a look and a laugh!

> *Robert Barker, in his review of "Mouse Tales," in* Children's Book Review *(© 1974 Five Owls Press Ltd.; all rights reserved), Vol. IV, No. 1, Spring, 1974, p. 16.*

THE MAN WHO TOOK THE INDOORS OUT   (1974)

"There was an old man / Who was named Bellwood Bouse. / He loved all the things / In his very large house"—and so one day he invites all of his furniture, pots, etc. . . . out into the sun and fresh air. . . . The concept of prodigal "mirrors and drapes" and teakettles is offbeat at the least, and it's harder to share Bouse's fondness for things than, say, Mister Muster's for his animals, but Lobel invests this with more of his own loving attention. The pictures, with fine black lines shading the subdued colors, glow with the quiet affection old Bouse has for his possessions and the significance he attaches to them. (pp. 737-38)

> *A review of "The Man Who Took the Indoors Out," in* Kirkus Reviews *(copyright © 1974 The Kirkus Service, Inc.), Vol. XLII, No. 14, July 15, 1974, pp. 737-38.*

A nonsense poem of great virtuosity. However freewheeling the work seems, it is, nevertheless, a tidily planned excursion in rhymes and pictures. . . . Every particular of each illustration fits the moods and details of the rhymes. The rhythm of the verse suggests chantable Clement Moore, while the sheer verbal nonsense brings to mind the great Edward Lear himself.

> *Virginia Haviland, in her review of "The Man Who Took the Indoors Out," in* The Horn Book Magazine *(copyright © 1974 by The Horn Book, Inc., Boston), Vol. L, No. 5, October, 1974, p. 131.*

An amusing though pointless fantasy highlighted by colorful, humorous, action-filled illustrations. Feeling sorry for his cooped up household goods while he enjoys the fresh air from his front porch, Bellwood Bouse invites his possessions outside. . . . The drawings of Victorian tables and chairs, pots and pans, shoes, etc. tumbling from the house and parading behind Mr. Bouse will divert young children, but the rhymes are sometimes forced, making the story awkward for reading aloud.

> *Judith S. Kronick, in her review of "The Man Who Took the Indoors Out," in* School Library Journal, *an appendix to* Library Journal *(reprinted from the October, 1974 issue of* School Library Journal, *published by R. R. Bowker Co./A Xerox Corporation; copyright © 1974), Vol. 21, No. 2, October, 1974, p. 106.*

A nonsense story in verse is illustrated with colorful, lively pictures that echo the daft momentum of the text. . . . [*The Man Who Took the Indoors Out* is not] substantial, since the plot is one extended idea, but it's silly fun, the pictures are attractive, and the rhyme has appeal.

> *Zena Sutherland, in her review of "The Man Who Took the Indoors Out," in* Bulletin of the Center for Children's Books *(reprinted by permission of The University of Chicago Press; © 1975 by The University of Chicago), Vol. 28, No. 5, January, 1975, p. 82.*

It is worth considering Arnold Lobel's latest full-colour picture book alongside *The Bed Book* [by Sylvia Plath] because he too is partly concerned with a strange domestic incident . . . and he has also cast it in a familiar doggerel ('Bellwood went to the door / And he opened it wide. / He Shouted, "Now, Indoors— / Please come outside!" '). Here, though, because of his graceful and imaginative illustrations, and because of a companionable sympathy which he calls up both for the eccentric Mr. Bouse *and* for his furniture, Arnold Lobel has produced a book that is at once amusing and touching. There is more here than the lines 'I will not let my Indoors / Run loose anymore' to remind the reader of Edward Lear.

> *Brian W. Alderson, in his review of "The Man Who Took the Indoors Out," in* Children's Book Review *(© 1976 Five Owls Press Ltd.; all rights reserved), Vol. VI, October, 1976, p. 27.*

OWL AT HOME (1975)

What seems at first to be the winter of Owl's discontent proves in the end, like all true melancholy, to have its sweet and ultimately contenting facets. Alone throughout, Owl invites "poor old winter" to come in and sit by the fire, but the "guest" behaves so wildly that Owl has to shut it out. Another night he makes tear-water tea by thinking of sad things (all subtly echoing his own loneliness); elsewhere he is driven to run madly upstairs and down in order to occupy both parts of his house at once, and in the end the moon accompanies him home from the otherwise unpopulated seashore. "'What a good round friend you are!' said Owl . . . (and he) did not feel sad at all." Nor will readers, for to add to the solo cast would clearly shatter the poignant perfection of Owl alone.

> *A review of "Owl at Home," in* Kirkus Reviews *(copyright © 1975 The Kirkus Service, Inc.), Vol. XLIII, No. 18, September 15, 1975, p. 1064.*

Owl is a sober-faced little homebody who lives alone in a comfortable house. Literal-minded and not very bright, he is,

nevertheless, altogether appealing. . . . There is security in the five economically told tales, and in the many enchanting illustrations which show stout little owl enjoying his creature comforts. A delightful addition to the I Can Read shelf.

> *Beryl Robinson, in her review of "Owl at Home," in* The Horn Book Magazine *(copyright © 1975 by the Horn Book, Inc., Boston), Vol. LI, No. 6, December, 1975, p. 588.*

Arnold Lobel is one writer who always seems to "make exciting things happen" in his "I Can Read" books (like *Frog and Toad Are Friends, Frog and Toad Together* and *Mouse Tales*). With the publication of *Owl at Home*, possibly Lobel's most splendid "I Can Read", it becomes imperative to examine the nature of his special talents, and to seek to place him among his contemporaries. *Owl* is five stories. **"The Guest"** introduces us to Owl, snug next to his blazing fireside, eating buttered toast and hot pea soup for his supper. Owl hears noises outside. Being hospitable by nature, Owl invites the noise inside. It is Winter that enters, and shortly turns Owl's home into a freezing and unsettled version of the chilly outside. Winter makes a terrible mess of Owl's home, filling it with snow. Finally Owl is forced to act against his nature, and he gives Winter the bounce, relights his fire and quietly resumes his supper.

The pictures, in greys and sepias, are alive with Owl's personality. The contrast between the beginning of Owl's supper and its end in two similar pictures is at once both funny and heartbreaking. Contented Owl has had an amazing adventure and he has become haggard and weary from it and, naturally, wiser!

The "essential" Lobel is in the last of the five stories, **"Owl and the Moon"**. Sitting one night at the seashore, Owl looks at the moon for a long time. "If I am looking at you, then you must be looking back at me. We must be very good friends," Owl says. Owl takes his leave, but notices that the moon follows him home, lighting his way. "Dear moon," Owl says, "you really must not come home with me. My house is small. You would not fit through the door. And I have nothing to give you for supper." When the moon disappears behind a cloud, Owl observes, "It is always a little sad to say good-bye to a friend." Then Owl goes to bed, only to find that his bedroom is filled with moonlight. "Moon, you have followed me all the way home." So Owl "put his head on the pillow and closed his eyes. The moon was shining down through the window. Owl did not feel sad at all."

What a satisfying book this is, and on several levels. It is suffused with warmth and coziness, yet is not for a second either self-conscious or cute. Owl is that most likeable of creatures: one filled with fallibilities, but with a candour and straightforwardness that excuse any stupidity with which he might be burdened. He is generous to a fault. He may seem to be naïve, but that is not the case: he is innocent and there is an enormous difference between the two qualities. Only an artist of the purest sensibilities can capture innocence and not turn it into something cloying and, ultimately, embarrassing. Lobel clearly has these sensibilities. As for his art, it extends and complements his storytelling, in the same way that Maurice Sendak's art does, and with the same results. Each, in his best books, looks inside: Sendak sees the dark and illuminates it, while Lobel sees the light and shares it. (pp. 42-3)

> *John Donovan, "American Dispatch" (copyright © 1976 John Donovan; reprinted by permission of the*

author and The Thimble Press, Lockwood Station Road, South Woodchester, Glos. GL55EQ, England), in Signal, *No. 19, January, 1976, pp. 40-4.**

In *Owl at Home,* as in his incomparable tales of Frog and Toad, Arnold Lobel places his hero in a delectable and exact domestic setting. In the case of Owl it is a home suitably old-fashioned, with fire-dogs, candle and carriage-clock all in keeping, and in this cosy habitat the amusing bird, belying tradition and the rows of learned-looking books on his shelves, demonstrates a naïve slowness of wit that reminds me of Lobel's Toad. Perhaps the best story in the set of five is **"Tear-water Tea."** . . . As in the Frog and Toad books . . . the Owl stories are as witty as they are brief, and Lobel's apt choice of words is matched by the artful way he chooses objects, facial expressions and colour (pink, brown, yellow and grey) to make pictures, small or full-page, which are beautiful, touching, funny and descriptive all at once. Fortunate the child who exercises an early reading skill on this book.

Margery Fisher, in her review of "Owl at Home," in her Growing Point, *Vol. 15, No. 2, October, 1976, p. 2966.*

Owl At Home is a . . . perfect example of the subtle use of simple language development linked to beautiful sepia pictures. A book which cannot be praised too highly for its warmth and reassurance. . . . A highly amusing book, which uses great economy of words in weaving its inventive tale.

From Owl at Home, *written and illustrated by Arnold Lobel.*

A review of "Owl at Home," in The Junior Bookshelf, *Vol. 40, No. 6, December, 1976, p. 333.*

Indeed Arnold Lobel's *Owl at Home* . . . has probably been eagerly awaited by many. Not since Minarik's "Little Bear" books have the children who can just read had such classic stories placed within their grasp, stories that are shapely, humorous, nonchalantly whimsical, yet written in simple language and illustrated with pictures that complement them by pointing up the fun.

Elaine Moss, "Solace for Spring," in The Times Literary Supplement (© *Times Newspapers Ltd. (London) 1977; reproduced from* The Times Literary Supplement *by permission), No. 3915, March 25, 1977, p. 355.**

From The Man Who Took the Indoors Out, *written and illustrated by Arnold Lobel.*

FROG AND TOAD ALL YEAR (1976)

Lobel's peerless, though much imitated, animal comrades do a little borrowing of their own here when Frog goes around the corner to look for spring, recalling Clifton's *Boy Who Didn't Believe in Spring* (1973); in this case we can't consider Lobel's more conventional rustic setting an improvement, but Frog does make the search his own. In fall Frog and Toad rake each other's leaves for a surprise, but the wind undoes the jobs before either is aware of the other's favor; elsewhere the friendship seems to have settled down to a kind of mellow harmony. . . . We miss some of the resonant psychological heft of this pair's previous experiences, but Frog and Toad can still transform the most ordinary seasonal activities into celebrations.

A review of "Frog and Toad All Year," in Kirkus Reviews *(copyright © 1976 The Kirkus Service, Inc.), Vol. XLIV, No. 12, June 15, 1976, p. 683.*

The book can help reinforce environmental concepts, and it's useful for augmenting a reading program, but these are tangential benefits. Like other books about Frog and Toad, it's the amusing illustrations and the ingenuous, affectionate tone of the writing that will appeal most to children.

Zena Sutherland, in her review of "Frog and Toad All Year," in Bulletin of the Center for Children's Books *(reprinted by permission of The University of Chicago Press; © 1976 by The University of Chicago), Vol. 30, No. 3, November, 1976, p. 45.*

Frog and Toad, those two gentle and endearing friends created six years ago by Arnold Lobel, are, with their third outing, in danger. They are in danger of becoming indistinct and forgettable, of fading away. The loss would be considerable. Which is to suggest not that **"Frog and Toad All Year"** is a bad book—it is, in fact, among the very best and nicest of new children's books, no surprise—but rather that one's expectations are way up there, and it falls a little short. (p. 30)

The illustrations [in the **"Frog and Toad"** series] one or two to a page, are immediately inviting—humorous, intelligent, gracefully ebullient—and are done in all three books with inked line and green, brown and gray wash. The stories are very simple—plain events in everyday situations—and told with an economy that is skillful because it seems so unhurried.

Lobel's achievement, really, is to make the friendship warm and cozy in its familiar routineness (it is not subject to any serious testing, beyond, say, Toad's being grumpy in winter and wanting to stay in bed—okay because toads hibernate) without ever being cute or coy or saccharine. Frog and Toad's friendship is not a thing; it is a mood. And it is known by the shared comfort it provides.

The order of Frog and Toad's friendship is elementary—rather vague, gentle, undemanding, supportive (Pooh and Piglet come to mind, though their adventures are more complex and passionate)—but in its very modesty it is both appealing and very comforting to young children, being within their own early and tentative concepts of what friendship is and means.

Why, then, the relative disappointment with **"Frog and Toad All Year"**? The illustrations are as delightful as ever. But the stories in the new book, all but one, tend to waver across the border of mildness into boredom.

The opening winter story repeats the hibernation theme of the very first story of the series: Frog persuades Toad to go sledding. Toad doesn't enjoy it and returns to bed. . . . The summer story is the weakest: Toad is buried under two melting chocolate ice cream cones. Aside from being pointless, the story raises problems about relative size that even young children may find distracting.

The story for fall, an O. Henry-type joke of intention and fate, is the most enticing in the book. . . . There's the appeal of symmetry here, as well as a laugh.

The book closes with Frog's being late to Toad's house on Christmas Eve. . . . Now, some smartypants youngster may point out that the implication at the beginning of the story is that Toad only thinks Frog is late (Toad's clock is broken), an implication reinforced at the end when Frog's present for Toad turns out to be a new clock. So why does Frog apologize? Was he late, or wasn't he?

The answer may be that even in Frog and Toad's warm and cozy world, perfection is a sometime thing—and that to nag too much at questions that can well be left moot is neither a sign of friendship nor fully expressive of the admiration one feels for an original and very fine creator of decent books for children, Arnold Lobel. Frog and Toad are a rare creation. The first two books are best; the third provokes a concern that can be, one hopes will be, alleviated by a fourth, fifth and more. (pp. 30, 32)

Eliot Fremont-Smith, in his review of "Frog and Toad All Year," in The New York Times Book Review *(© 1976 by The New York Times Company; reprinted by permission), November 14, 1976, pp. 30, 32.*

The amphibious duo returns in five easy-to-read celebrations of friendship. . . . The contrast between adventurous Frog and his more cautious companion is skillfully delineated in text and pictures. . . . Whether he is trying to carry two huge chocolate ice cream cones through the summer heat or imagining the dire circumstances which might have caused Frog's delay on Christmas Eve, Toad is endearingly inept, the slightly timorous type who manages to rise above dilemmas because of a friend's support. As inventive and original as its predecessors, the small volume is successful as a sequel or as a separate book. (pp. 621-22)

Mary M. Burns, in her review of "Frog and Toad All Year," in The Horn Book Magazine *(copyright © 1976 by the Horn Book, Inc., Boston), Vol. LII, No. 6, December, 1976, pp. 621-22.*

Each episode shows another dimension of their friendship, and, of course, there are the loving illustrations. This takes its rightful place beside ***Frog and Toad Are Friends*** . . . and ***Frog and Toad Together***. . . .

Alice Ehlert, in her review of "Frog and Toad All Year," in School Library Journal *(reprinted from the December, 1976 issue of* School Library Journal, *published by R. R. Bowker Co./A Xerox Corporation; copyright © 1976), Vol. 23, No. 4, December, 1976, p. 64.*

MOUSE SOUP (1977)

"'Ah!' said the weasel. 'I am going to make mouse soup.' 'Oh!' said the mouse. 'I am going to *be* mouse soup.'" But wait—"Mouse soup must be mixed with stories to make it taste really good," he announces from the pot. And so, looking so absurdly endearing that you know he must be spared, the mouse tells the gullible weasel four stories. In the first a mouse outsmarts some bees, just as *our* mouse will outsmart his captor in the end; the other tales are, in turn, a simple fable, a laughable instance of misunderstanding, and a fondly amusing correlative of good will. Small but satisfying, and all informed with Lobel's own gentle resonance.

A review of "Mouse Soup," in Kirkus Reviews *(copyright © 1977 The Kirkus Service, Inc.), Vol. XLV, No. 4, February 15, 1977, p. 165.*

[*Mouse Soup*] contains four understated and subtle tales that are lovingly illustrated. The stories are held together by an effective device. . . . Not quite as substantial as *Mouse Tales,* but it is still completely delightful.

Alice Low, in her review of "Mouse Soup," in Children's Book Review Service *(copyright © 1977 Children's Book Review Service Inc.), Vol. 5, No. 8, March, 1977, p. 76.*

Arnold Lobel is one of the few author-illustrators who has the magic touch. **"Mouse Soup"** . . . is his latest, an artistic triumph with enough suspense, humor and wisdom to hold any reader who has a trace of curiosity and compassion. Mouse outwits weasel by spinning four tiny adventure tales, for as everyone knows "Mouse soup must be mixed with stories." Thus the little one triumphs over the big one, and every child will rejoice. The exquisite wash drawings in mousey shades of grays, blues, greens and golds, have enough humor and pathos to exact repeated scrutiny. Like the stories, they improve with each reading.

Nancy Larrick, "Instead of Dick and Jane," in The New York Times Book Review *(© 1977 by The New York Times Company; reprinted by permission), May 1, 1977, pp. 29, 43.**

[*Mouse Soup* contains four] amusing brief tales . . . ; the final tale, about an old lady who found a thorn bush growing in her living room chair, is a stroke of pure genius. . . . Genial, artless nonsense, all contained in the snug, imaginary world of a Lobel I-Can-Read book.

Ethel L. Heins, in her review of "Mouse Soup," in The Horn Book Magazine *(copyright © 1977 by the Horn Book, Inc., Boston), Vol. LIII, No. 3, June, 1977, p. 308.*

A gentle kind of Scheherazade in mouse-land. . . . **"The Crickets"** is the most appealing of the tales within a tale—they get a little weak when stones become involved in philosophic speculation. But Lobel's mice are as winning in blue and yellow as his frogs are in brown and green.

Brigitte Weeks, in her review of "Mouse Soup," in Book World—The Washington Post *(© 1977, The Washington Post), June 12, 1977, p. E4.*

GRASSHOPPER ON THE ROAD   (1978)

[Grasshopper] is a venturesome character and his mind is wide. He takes to the road . . . and meets a series of friendly compulsives whose lives are narrow: a housefly who's a cleanliness fiend, a group of sign-waving beetles who're promoting the delights of morning over other parts of the day, dragonflies who pity him his inability to zip and zoom. Though charming and easygoing, Grasshopper's neither intimidated nor diverted from what he knows to be his path. The story follows him all day to a temporary bed in a soft place. Lobel's writing is rhythmic, spirited, and witty, and uses repetition as a source of that wit. But you never get that sense of *drill* that permeates some easy readers.

Burt Supree, "Books for Kids, Babe Ruth Too" (reprinted by permission of The Village Voice *and the*

author; copyright © The Village Voice, Inc., 1978), in The Village Voice, *Vol. XXIII, No. 46, November 13, 1978, p. 121.*

That searching for new adventures is more significant than stagnating is suggested in the episodic story of Grasshopper's determination to "'find a road [and] follow that road wherever it goes.'" . . . Although lacking the ingenuous humor of *Frog and Toad* . . . the contemporary version of the fable of the ant and the grasshopper is told in a repetitive I-Can-Read text and extended in three-color illustrations which delicately capture the grasshopper's microcosmic world view. (pp. 636-37)

Mary M. Burns, in her review of "Grasshopper on the Road," in The Horn Book Magazine *(copyright © 1978 by The Horn Book, Inc., Boston), Vol. LIV, No. 6, December, 1978, pp. 636-37.*

As with Frog, Toad, Owl, et al., Arnold Lobel again has created an endearing individual: Grasshopper. Grasshopper is the spirited one, the happy-go-lucky adventurer on a journey who (like Faust with strong back legs?) will follow the road wherever it goes. . . . Grasshopper is a loner, yes, and he knows that every morning the road will be there to enjoy. Mr. Lobel's inimitable gentle green-and-pink illustrations will continue to enchant beginning readers. (p. 82)

Margaret Klee Lichtenberg, "On This and That," in The New York Times Book Review *(© 1978 by The New York Times Company; reprinted by permission), December 10, 1978, pp. 82-4.**

Arnold Lobel is at his unbeatable best with *Grasshopper on the Road*. . . .

There are beetles who worship morning, a mosquito ferryman who works by the rule book, ritual-bound butterflies and other. It is very funny—thought-provoking for children who want to think, and an object lesson in how depth and wit can be injected into a simple text for beginning readers. The pictures are delicate, lively and very expressive, as Lobel's always are.

Virginia Makins, in her review of "Grasshopper on the Road," in The Times Educational Supplement *(© Times Newspapers Ltd. (London) 1980; reproduced from* The Times Educational Supplement *by permission), No. 3319, January 18, 1980, p. 37.*

GREGORY GRIGGS AND OTHER NURSERY RHYME PEOPLE (1978)

Lobel delights with his selections as much as his illustrations in these 35 lesser-known folk rhymes, all with human subjects. . . . There are some fresh, first-rate limericks, a twist on Miss Moffat, and a brisk ten lines on a "mad" family that could be ancestral Stupids. And all their foibles, talents, and comical conditions are keynoted with style and assurance in Lobel's solid little figures—as splendid in pastel rags (or, in one case, sprouting grass) as in 18th-century finery.

A review of "Gregory Griggs and Other Nursery Rhyme People," in Kirkus Reviews *(copyright © 1978 The Kirkus Service, Inc.), Vol. XLVI, No. 7, April 1, 1978, p. 367.*

["**Gregory Griggs and Other Nursery Rhyme People**"] eschews the pampered stars of Mother Goose land for such obscure but worthy plebeians as Terence McDiddler, "the three-stringed fiddler," tongue-twisting Theophilus Thistle, and Jerry

Hall ("He is so small / A rat could eat him / Hat and all"). For some reason, Mr. Lobel dresses up these meat-and-potatoes characters in cream-puff pastels. That isn't how I would have imagined them, though in every other respect, Mr. Lobel's paintings take the measure of the rhymes.

> Joyce Milton, in her review of "Gregory Griggs and Other Nursery Rhyme People," in The New York Times Book Review (© 1978 by The New York Times Company; reprinted by permission), April 30, 1978, p. 28.

The selector claims to have focussed attention on the "exuberant and courageous race of human beings" who . . . "in a nonsensical way . . . seem to mirror all of our own struggles with the rigors of contemporary living". So here are horror or ecstasy exemplified. Hannah Bantry is clearly worried about losing her marrow-bone even while she enjoys the taste: Theophilus Thistle seems to regard his role of sifting thistles as vastly important. Horror is relative, of course, as the illustrator demonstrates. The milkman in buttermilk up to his chin, Jerry Hall waiting to be devoured by a rat, look acquiescent and vaguely surprised. The use of successive framed pictures in sequence confirms the dotty action of these shrewdly chosen rhymes.

> Margery Fisher, in her review of "Gregory Griggs and Other Nursery Rhyme People," in her Growing Point, Vol. 17, No. 5, January, 1979, p. 3452.

The inhabitants of Nursery Rhyme Land are a queer lot and they make a strange community, not unlike that created by Edward Lear. One is reminded all the time of Lear in reading Arnold Lobel's splendid collection, featuring highly individual people flouting the conventions. . . .

The compiler's illustrations record this world in a dispassionate, timeless way, not presuming to criticise its mores or add a gloss to its history. A lovely book.

> A review of "Gregory Griggs and Other Nursery Rhyme People," in The Junior Bookshelf, Vol. 43, No. 1, February, 1979, p. 20.

Arnold Lobel speaks today's language, even when he sets his nursery rhymes in a vaguely olde-worlde never-never land. He has concentrated on the less familiar rhymes, mostly those which are portraits of strange and largely anti-social people. Here surely is the mother's milk which nourished Edward Lear. Mr Lobel's drawings are uninhibited and very funny. He may distress a few sensitive adults, but how the kids will love him!

> Marcus Crouch, in his review of "Gregory Griggs and Other Nursery Rhyme People," in The School Librarian, Vol. 27, No. 1, March, 1979, p. 36.

A TREEFUL OF PIGS   (1979)

Blessed with more optimism than energy, a lazy farmer cajoles his wife into purchasing a dozen pigs by promising to share the work they will bring. Unfortunately, his short spurt of ambition quickly dissipates, and he continues "to spend most of his time lying in bed, asleep with his head on the pillow." Again and again he refuses to help, until his wife causes the pigs to "disappear like snow in the spring"—a drastic move which brings instant penitence and reform. The cumulative structure is a felicitous choice for the droll tale, yet the repe-

tition, which makes the text relatively easy to read, is not labored or dull.

> Mary M. Burns, in her review of "A Treeful of Pigs," in The Horn Book Magazine (copyright © 1979 by The Horn Book, Inc., Boston), Vol. LV, No. 2, April, 1979, p. 184.

["A Treeful of Pigs" has a witty folk-tale plot]. This is clearly a tale of a marriage saved by the last-minute reform of a male chauvinist pig! . . . [The] text, while not so aphoristic and subtle as that of Arnold Lobel's brilliant Frog and Toad books, is full of piggy energy and fun.

> Harold C.K. Rice, in his review of "A Treeful of Pigs," in The New York Times Book Review (© 1979 by The New York Times Company; reprinted by permission), April 29, 1979, p. 29.

[A Treeful of Pigs has] a simple, easily understood text, and an interesting story-line makes this a happy choice for bedtime reading. Children will enjoy the lazy farmer and the devices that his wife uses to make him change his ways.

> A review of "A Treeful of Pigs," in The Junior Bookshelf, Vol. 44, No. 6, December, 1980, p. 285.

DAYS WITH FROG AND TOAD   (1979)

The glowing friendship of Frog and Toad continues, with Frog as the wiser, supportive partner easing Toad through his small frustrations and uncertainties. . . . Once more, Lobel leaves the two with their friendship reaffirmed, this time after Toad misinterprets his friend's desire to be alone for a while. As in Frog and Toad All Year . . . the relationship has settled into a comfortable, conflict-free pattern; but the complementary pair continues to delight and vulnerable Toad to invite sympathetic recognition.

> A review of "Days with Frog and Toad," in Kirkus Reviews (copyright © 1979 The Kirkus Service, Inc.), Vol. XLVII, No. 20, October 15, 1979, p. 1209.

Friendship, as always, is a comfortable thing with Frog and Toad, because they know when to tease (at least Frog does) and when to be sorry and when to be quiet. With "Days With Frog and Toad," their adventures may be becoming as predictable, and as comfortable, as their friendship, but it is a book that will be welcomed by fans. And for new readers, it provides an excellent reason to make the acquaintance of two of the most appealing figures in recent children's literature. (p. 54)

> David W. McCullough, "Arnold Lobel and Friends," in The New York Times Book Review (© 1979 by The New York Times Company; reprinted by permission), November 11, 1979, pp. 54, 69.

Again, five short stories about a friendship distinctive for its tolerance and stability; again, illustrations that echo, in soft tones of brown and green, the affectionate humor of the writing; again, as thousands cheer, Frog and Toad are together. In this distinctive series of books for the beginning independent reader, Lobel eschews didacticism and offers vignettes that, with artful simplicity, describe such small adventures as flying a kite or getting a birthday hat that doesn't fit; the dynamics of the relationship (Frog is sensible, Toad a reed in the wind) can easily involve the reader, as the popularity of earlier Frog and Toad books can attest.

Zena Sutherland, in her review of "Days with Frog and Toad," in Bulletin of the Center for Children's Books (reprinted by permission of The University of Chicago Press; © 1979 by The University of Chicago), Vol. 33, No. 4, December, 1979, p. 74.

[Days with Frog and Toad] presents five more stories featuring loyal, dependable Frog and naïve, endearing Toad. Frog helps Toad to cope with his neglected household chores, and later the pair successfully launch a kite; Frog whiles away a cold, dark night by telling a shivery ghost story, and in the funniest episode of all he deals ingeniously and tactfully with the over-large hat he has given Toad as a birthday present. The book ends quietly as the two companions reaffirm their affection for each other. Nowhere does Arnold Lobel display his artistry more fully than in his deceptively simple books for beginning readers; substance, humor, and definitive characterization are combined in beautifully fashioned stories told and pictured with economy and style. (pp. 659-60)

Ethel L. Heins, in her review of "Days With Frog and Toad," in The Horn Book Magazine (copyright © 1979 by The Horn Book, Inc., Boston), Vol. LV, No. 6, December, 1979, pp. 659-60.

The five stories in this welcome new book exhibit the anticipated dotty logic, or logical dottiness; whichever way you put it, the revelation of Toad's blundering good nature and Frog's affectionate tolerance are as telling as ever. . . . The green and brown illustrations as always have an offhand expressiveness in their firmly composed glimpses of wood and field, against which the animal characters come to life with minute alterations of posture and expression.

Margery Fisher, in her review of "Days With Frog and Toad," in her Growing Point, Vol. 19, No. 4, November, 1980, p. 3799.

FABLES (1980)

[Twenty] pithy fables—as memorable as Aesop's parables—are the stuff of Lobel's new creation. Handsome paintings in exuberant colors point up lessons in the experiences of anthropomorphs, making this the most remarkable of the author-illustrator's 60-plus, bestselling award winners and surely a chief contender for 1980's top literary prizes.

A review of "Fables," in Publishers Weekly (reprinted from the June 13, 1980 issue of Publishers Weekly, published by R. R. Bowker Company, a Xerox company; copyright © 1980 by Xerox Corporation), Vol. 217, No. 23, June 13, 1980, p. 73.

"Fables," written and illustrated by Arnold Lobel, held a surprise for me. In my own silent read-through, I decided I very much liked the illustrations but didn't think the text would hold up from a child's point of view. Because I did enjoy a couple of the fables and their morals, which appear at the end of each story, I decided to read the book to my 7-year-old son, Zach.

Zach asked me to read the fables in the order of the pictures he found most interesting. The one-sentence morals delighted Zach, even though I had thought they would go over his head. He found them amusing and understood each one, not only as it related to the story, but also as it might relate to him.

Each fable, one page in length, takes about five minutes to read and discuss. One of the more enjoyable aspects of this book is that the fables do lead to interesting discussions with the child.

Zach's favorite fable was about a cat who was fishing and had a vision of the fish he would like to catch. Zach admitted he felt his own cat probably daydreamed. He was quiet for a moment and then said, "You know, when I fish, I dream about the fish I'm going to catch."

The fable's moral was: "All's well that ends with a good meal." Zach added, "I really don't like to eat fish, but all's well that ends with a good hot dog."

The illustrations are quite beautiful. The pictures are well defined, so a child will know exactly what each is meant to convey. The colors are rich and accurate.

I recommend this book for children aged about 7 through 10. Even if the child can read alone, this book is most fun when shared with an adult.

Robin Pappas, "For Sharing with Ages 10 and Under," in The Christian Science Monitor (reprinted by permission of the author), August 11, 1980, p. B5.*

One might expect that the creator of Frog and Toad could, if he chose, give us fables with some subtlety and psychological depth. But there's not a jot of wit, wisdom, style, or originality in these 20 flat and predictable items. The illustrations could be animal companions to the human figures for *Gregory Griggs* . . . , Lobel's nursery rhyme collection; but these suffer for having less to illustrate. Lobel begins with the static portrait of a foolish crocodile, who prefers the patterned flowers on his bedroom wallpaper to the tangled profusion of his wife's real garden. And so? He simply stays in bed and turns "a very pale and sickly shade of green." Even the moral is redundant: "Without a doubt there is such a thing as too much order." The third fable is another platitude in story form: a little Beetle topples an imperious Lion King who demands respect. "If you look at me closely you will see that I am making a bow," says the Beetle, whereupon King Lion bends over and, top-heavy with jeweled crown and medals, loses his balance. Meanwhile, in the second entry, Lobel has added a twist of sorts, possibly for a joke; but it's counterproductive. It starts out with two duck sisters arguing about whether they will go to the pond by their usual route or try something new. "This road makes me feel comfortable. I am accustomed to it," says one. We're set up for a confrontation between the stodgy and the venturesome, right? But then instead of confirming, modifying, or exposing the expected conclusion, Lobel fudges the issue: a fox, who knows their habits, is waiting to bag them on their regular route. Moral: "At times, a change of routine can be most healthful." In another fable, Lobel evokes Aesop with a crane inviting a pelican to tea, only to set forth a cautionary lesson in table manners. (And the consequence of messy pelican's bad ones is merely that he isn't invited back.) All of which serves to confirm Lobel's moral for his story of **"The Frogs at the Rainbow's End"**: "The highest hopes may lead to the greatest disappointments." (pp. 1229-30)

A review of "Fables," in Kirkus Reviews (copyright © 1980 The Kirkus Service, Inc.), Vol. XLVIII, No. 18, September 15, 1980, pp. 1229-30.

Without apologies to Aesop, La Fontaine, or Krylov—and without imitating them, either—the author-illustrator has invented twenty animal fables with an original flavor. Each one starts in a classical storytelling manner. . . . But the simple introductions are followed by deceptively ingenuous narrative developments frequently embellished with preposterous situations and completed with a moral smacking of deliberately gleeful cynicism. The bear, for example, is convinced by the crow to cover himself with a sheet and wear paper bags on his feet and a frying pan on his head. Each miniature narrative occupies a page by itself and is balanced by a full-page picture which reflects the crucial event of the fable and portrays the joyfully conceived characters. Carefully composed, rich with modulated colors, the illustrations make their mark as works of art and offer visual correlatives for the tongue-in-cheek stories.

> *Paul Heins, in his review of "Fables," in* The Horn Book Magazine *(copyright © 1980 by The Horn Book, Inc., Boston), Vol. LVI, No. 5, October, 1980, p. 520.*

Aesop this is not, but Lobel is true to fable form, making his animals display human foibles and acquire human wisdom. The subjects are also traditional: rigidity, vanity or pride, posing (or lack of self-knowledge), foolishness. While the author, in the classic vein, attacks excess ("Too much of anything often leaves one with a feeling of regret."), he also permits himself some romantic and non-traditional maxims. . . . Lobel's maxims are all worthy, but their narrative vehicles are not all powerful. Fables should be single minded, and some of these are defective in that their "morals" are unclear until stated. As with most fables the appropriate audience is really adult (children do not need to be told that "Even the taking of small risks will add excitement to life."). Adult and child alike, however, will enjoy the large, droll pictures of kangaroos in Edwardian dress, a camel in a tutu, a wolf disguised as an apple tree, etc.

> *Patricia Dooley, in her review of "Fables," in* School Library Journal *(reprinted from the October, 1980 issue of* School Library Journal, *published by R. R. Bowker Co./A Xerox Corporation; copyright © 1980), Vol. 27, No. 2, October, 1980, p. 148.*

Arnold Lobel has consistently created with wit and style, and *Fables* . . . is to some extent no exception. It looks as handsome as can be; to turn the pages and gaze at Lobel's masterful, beautifully colored animal portraits is to feel pleasure. But the 20 fables themselves (more text than he has previously written) are another matter altogether. Something like brief shaggy-dog stories, something like Sufi tales, these are not fables that Aesop would recognize, as the morals are deliberately underwhelming, and there seems a lack of conviction in the telling. Deadpan humor that plays against itself for effect is a subtle form; Lobel has managed it before without seeming as lame as he does this time out. (p. 14)

> *Michele Slung, "The Artful Menagerie," in* Book World—The Washington Post *(© 1980, The Washington Post), November 9, 1980, pp. 14-15.**

UNCLE ELEPHANT (1981)

Nine gentle stories for the beginning independent reader; the soft grey, peach, and green tones of the deft pictures are an appropriate echo of the mood. The nephew and uncle may be elephants, but their relationship speaks effectively of the special bond between young and old and of the comforting fact that other family members can be as loving and supportive as parents are.

> *Zena Sutherland, in her review of "Uncle Elephant," in* Bulletin of the Center for Children's Books *(reprinted by permission of The University of Chicago Press; © 1981 by The University of Chicago), Vol. 35, No. 1, September, 1981, p. 12.*

A model uncle and a warming relationship, projected with a resonance that invites dwelling on, and re-reading.

> *A review of "Uncle Elephant," in* Kirkus Reviews *(copyright © 1981 The Kirkus Service, Inc.), Vol. XLIX, No. 19, October 1, 1981, p. 1234.*

It is hoped that any young elephant whose parents are temporarily lost at sea will be fortunate enough to possess an Uncle Elephant to give him a home. He is a very comforting fellow, full of diverting tricks, sustaining stories, and catchy songs. . . . And it is definitely a treat for the little one to see Uncle Elephant trumpet "'VOOMAROOOM'" to greet the dawn. . . . The illustrations showing the anxious, wistful young elephant and the affectionate, amusing older one complement a warm and delightful I-Can-Read story.

> *Ann A. Flowers, in her review of "Uncle Elephant," in* The Horn Book Magazine *(copyright © 1981 by The Horn Book, Inc., Boston), Vol. LVII, No. 6, December, 1981, p. 662.*

From Fables, *written and illustrated by Arnold Lobel.*

Uncle Elephant . . . entertains his nephew with his mild eccentricities and inventiveness. . . . The poignancy and humor of the world these two pachyderms create between them (in text and illustrations) warms the entire book. Though some episodes don't work as well as others, the whole is still a unique evocation of affection between old and young.

Nancy Palmer, in her review of "Uncle Elephant," in School Library Journal *(reprinted from the December, 1981 issue of* School Library Journal, *published by R. R. Bowker Co./A Xerox Corporation; copyright © 1981), Vol. 28, No. 4, December, 1981, p. 74.*

MING LO MOVES THE MOUNTAIN (1981)

The watercolors, in gentle greens and grays warmed with peach, allude in Lobel's own distinctive manner to Chinese landscape painting. This pleasantly foolish fable, with its low-key but most attractive illustrations, would make a good addition to the "fool's tales" shelf.

Patricia Dooley, in her review of "Ming Lo Moves the Mountain," in School Library Journal *(reprinted from the March, 1982 issue of* School Library Journal, *published by R. R. Bowker Co./A Xerox Corporation; copyright © 1982), Vol. 28, No. 7, March, 1982, p. 136.*

Ming Lo is told to bundle the household belongings, face the mountain with eyes closed, and begin a dance of putting his left foot in back of his right and his right in back of his left "for many hours." Then the mountain will have moved away. Indeed it has, as youngsters will see—while chuckling at such a fool's errand. Illustrated in earthy tans, grays, and greens for a subdued look that is a subtle counterpoint to the story's sharp wit.

Denise M. Wilms, in her review of "Ming Lo Moves the Mountain," in Booklist *(reprinted by permission of the American Library Association; copyright © 1982 by the American Library Association), Vol. 78, No. 15, April 1, 1982, p. 1019.*

Many good illustrators write their own books, but few of them do so well as Arnold Lobel. . . . [He] is a talented teller of slender, well-built tales. The latest is **"Ming Lo Moves the Mountain."**

Ming Lo in green and his wife in red have the grace of matched porcelain figurines. Perfectly suited, they would be perfectly happy except for the looming presence that casts rain, stones and a deep shadow on their dwelling and their lives. It is the mountain that towers over them. You must move it, his wife says, and acting on the advice of his wise man, Ming Lo tries. . . .

Using lightly curving lines and forms washed with a grayed rainbow of soft shades, Lobel decorates the horizontal pages with his own versions of Oriental landscapes. The tone of the story and the look of the book are as inseparable as Ming and the Mrs.: restrained and amusing, a measured dance to the accompaniment of gentle laughter. (p. 46)

Karla Kuskin, "The Complete Illustrator," in The New York Times Book Review *(© 1982 by The New York Times Company; reprinted by permission), April 25, 1982, pp. 31, 46.**

Arnold Lobel's **Ming Lo Moves the Mountain** is . . . an original story that is all of a piece with his pictures. It's a very funny story told in a solemn voice that is part of the humor and has, as well, a nice comment to make on faith in the pronouncements of sages. (p. 16)

This is a splendid story, seemingly simple, but finally full of subtleties. Ming Lo is not the fool of traditional tales. He goes for advice, follows it carefully, and his ingenuousness and faith are in the end rewarded.

To back it all up, Lobel has created a soft, pleasing green and brown Orient everywhere made up of curves and circles, and his wise man is just inscrutable enough without tipping over into stereotype. The pictures make it clear that between the wise man and Ming Lo there is a perfect understanding of the ritual of question and answer, a ritual full of mutual respect and formality. And I especially like the mountain, which has a sort of draped, implacable look to it as it looms on its haunches behind Ming Lo's house, wearing a halo of mist. It is only peripherally derivative of Chinese painting; mainly it is Lobel.

But to say that it is "Lobel" is misleading; one of the things that is admirable about Lobel's work is that he is able always to adapt his style to the demands of the story, and that is a rare quality. It demonstrates courage, flexibility, and responsiveness, three of the factors which contribute to his solid and well-deserved reputation. (pp. 16-17)

Natalie Babbitt, "Fairy Tales and Far-Flung Places," in Book World—The Washington Post *(© 1982, The Washington Post), May 9, 1982, pp. 16-17.**

An original tale utilizing folkloric motifs, the book is Chinese-like rather than Chinese, for the artist has created an imagined landscape. The setting, shown in flowing lines and tones of delicate watercolors, provides a source of inspiration drawn from an ancient artistic tradition; particularly effective in conveying a sense of distance are the panoramic double-page spreads. With gentle humor Ming Lo is shown not as a ridiculous figure but rather as everyman, who at one time or another solves a problem, not by surmounting it but by finding a way to escape it—which the wise man may have known all along. (p. 393)

Mary M. Burns, in her review of "Ming Lo Moves the Mountain," in The Horn Book Magazine *(copyright © 1982 by The Horn Book, Inc., Boston), Vol. LVIII, No. 4, August, 1982, pp. 392-93.*

Joan Phipson

1912-

(Pseudonym of Joan Margaret Fitzhardinge) Australian author of fiction and nonfiction.

The Australian countryside and the lifestyles of its people come vividly to life in Phipson's books for children. Her early works relate the experiences of youngsters in situations such as horse training, calf rearing, and sheep herding. Three of these books, *The Family Conspiracy, Threat to the Barkers*, and *Good Luck to the Rider*, revolve around members and close friends of the same New South Wales family. Often, the characters in these early books are shunned or ignored by their peers for walking with a limp, being shy and timid, speaking with an accent, or simply for being unattractive. Through the course of their stories these characters display particular talents or an awareness which the other characters come to rely on, thus signifying their acceptance. In these instances, Phipson earns praise from critics for her understanding and handling of the subject matter in a frank, realistic manner without resorting to unnecessary tragedy or melodrama. Reviewers have felt, however, that on other occasions Phipson fails to fully explain a situation or leaves out information which may alleviate or lessen a problem.

Phipson's later works often involve older children in urban rather than rural settings and tend to deal with more suspenseful and adventurous situations such as the crippling effects of a city-wide strike, a metaphysical journey through time, and a parapsychological struggle. While some of these books did not receive the same critical acclaim as Phipson's earlier works, most critics are generous in their praise of her ability to develop her characters's personalities and to maintain a high level of suspense throughout her stories. Long regarded by Australians as one of their major writers for young readers, Phipson is now universally recognized for her contributions to children's literature. Phipson received the Children's Book Council of Australia Book of the Year Award in 1953 for *Good Luck to the Rider* and in 1963 for *The Family Conspiracy*. The latter also received the New York *Herald Tribune* Children's Spring Book Festival Award in 1964. *The Boundary Riders* was honored with the Boys' Clubs of America Junior Book Award in 1964.

(See also *Contemporary Authors*, Vols. 15-16 and *Something about the Author*, Vol. 2.)

GOOD LUCK TO THE RIDER   (1953)

This is a book which might well be missed by many children's librarians, as it is published by an Australian firm (with a London branch) and has not received much publicity in this country. It was awarded first place in an Australian *Children's Book of the Year* competition, 1953, and certainly deserves this distinction. Although at first sight it seems to be just another pony book, it is in fact very much more than that. The young heroine lives on a large country property in N.S.W., with a pleasant and normal sort of family, and the everyday incidents of her life make up the background of the story— bush picnics, the local agricultural show, riding, mustering, going away to school. The main theme is the girl's attachment to a bush-bred foal which proves to be a veritable ugly duckling,

but through her faith in the horse and her desire to prove its worth, she herself outgrows her timidity and indecision and becomes a much more responsible and confident person. The Australian setting and way of life is vividly and convincingly described, without undue emphasis on natural calamities like floods and fires. The characters are lively and likeable and their relationships sound, though not sentimental. Girls who like outdoor stories, and who are interested in countries other than their own, should thoroughly enjoy this book.

A review of "Good Luck to the Rider," in The Junior Bookshelf, *Vol. 18, No. 1, January, 1954, p. 20.*

When uncertain girl meets unwanted horse, it's bound to be love at first sight, confidence in the last chapter, but with Joan Phipson putting the familiar plot through its paces almost every moment counts: twelve-year-old Barbara, ordinarily fearful and undecided, persuading her brothers and sister to save the brumby foal with the leer of a clown, persuading her even more skeptical father to let her raise him; the satisfaction of sitting quietly near him, of slipping a halter on him, eventually of riding him. . . . And he's a natural jumper, which encourages Barbara to school him for the hunts at the Bungaree meet. It's the commitment and the willingness to expose herself and Rozz that matters, of course, but readers will be cheering *good luck to the rider* as he approaches the hurdles. People and place have personality too, and after the cheering's over youngsters are likely to remember riding across the Australian plains with staunch friend Will and unlike twin brothers Clive and George. . . .

> *A review of "Good Luck to the Rider," in* Kirkus Service *(copyright © 1968 Virginia Kirkus' Service, Inc.), Vol. XXXVI, No. 5, March 1, 1968, p. 273.*

You'll be in Australia when you read this story, with a pro for a guide. If you've never been before, you'll enjoy your stay there on a ranch with a friendly family. You'll enjoy sharing with them the delight of watching the shy young daughter bloom, thanks to her affection for a stray foal—an endearing clown named Rosinante. If Joan Phipson has shown you Australia already in **"The Family Conspiracy,"** etc., you'll enjoy meeting the Barkers once again in this new book.

> *A review of "Good Luck to the Rider," in* Publishers Weekly *(reprinted from the May 27, 1968 issue of* Publishers Weekly, *published by R. R. Bowker Company, a Xerox company; copyright © 1968 by Xerox Corporation), Vol. 193, No. 22, May 27, 1968, p. 58.*

Children who enjoyed sharing the adventures of the Barker family on their sheep station in the western part of New South Wales in *The Family Conspiracy* and *Threat to the Barkers* will feel at home on the neighborhood sheep ranch of the Trevors. The same qualities distinguish all three works—a well-developed story, depth of characterization, and the vivid portrayal of the Australian sheep rancher's way of life.

> *M. M., in a review of "Good Luck to the Rider," in* The Horn Book Magazine *(copyright © 1968 by The Horn Book, Inc., Boston), August, 1968, p. 422.*

SIX AND SILVER (1954; British edition as *It Happened One Summer*)

An exceptional book, a joy to read and re-read and to recommend to others. It is difficult to refrain from quotation, and impossible to choose an isolated example from so well-integrated a text, its characters and their conversation caught so naturally and yet so skilfully that each statement seems to contribute to our understanding of these people and their background. They are very nice people, and their background is Australia, in several of its various aspects. The story opens and closes with Jack and Pat Steadman, 16 and 13, sharing a stretch of beach with Tess Moorland and her sister; in the opening incident they are unsure of themselves in the face of the Moorlands' competence in the water—in the last they feel as much at home as on their country sheep-ranch. . . . All the children and their families are unpretentious but beautifully observed full of individuality and humour; the adventures that come their way are not wildly exciting, but the book is exciting for its evocation of living, of being young and up on the mountain tops for the first time, or staying in a strange place and meeting a snake in the passage, or simply doing ordinary things in good company. Most children enjoy recognizing their own everyday reactions in book-characters, but it takes a very perceptive author to make those reactions really recognizable, by attaching them to characters with a life of their own instead of merely hanging them round the neck of a lay figure who then has to be pushed into violent action to give some impression of life. The Moorlands and Steadmans obviously have a very good, rewarding life of their own, and in the few months of

it presented here the reader shares not only their pleasures, but also something of their feeling for that strange vast country with its sea-shore and city life, its great open spaces and unexpected mountain heights. There is a completeness and serenity about the whole that makes the reading an Experience, as Tess herself would say. (pp. 152-53)

> *A review of "Six and Silver," in* The Junior Bookshelf, *Vol. 19, No. 3, July, 1955, pp. 152-53.*

Like everything else, terra firma is relative—per a counterpoint so docile that its peak episodes are no more than ripples on two Australian turfs. . . . There are some nice family moments—Pat is uncommonly personable and Jack is uncomplicatedly wholesome at sixteen—before Tess leaves for Sydney; somewhat the worse for saddle-soreness, she looks pluckily forward to September's mountain-climbing expedition which is when there are six, plus Silver, Jack's dog. But not even then does the tempo accelerate, and the imperturbable languor is pleasant only for a while.

> *A review of "Six and Silver," in* Kirkus Reviews *(copyright © 1971 The Kirkus Service, Inc.), Vol. XXXIX, No. 12, June 15, 1971, p. 677.*

[*Six and Silver* is] an earlier work than the author's well-known *Birkin*, *The Boundary Riders*, and stories about the Barker family. Yet it is characterized by the same feeling of strong family unity and love of the Australian outback found in the other books. . . . The story seems more episodic than the author's other stories; and perhaps a more careful editing might have eliminated the one or two phrases, such as "'negroid suntans,'" which may prove distasteful to American readers. However, the book is satisfactory as an adventure story, and an element of delight is provided by the pervasive character of the intrepid toy lamb Pinkie.

> *Sheryl B. Andrews, in her review of "Six and Silver," in* The Horn Book Magazine *(copyright © 1971 by The Horn Book, Inc., Boston), Vol. XLVII, No. 6, December, 1971, p. 615.*

THE BOUNDARY RIDERS (1962)

The Boundary Riders is about three children who set out to inspect the boundary posts on their Australian farm. . . .

The idea of the Australian bush has very little glamour, a story about children losing their way does not sound particularly exciting, and even the dust-cover is an unattractive khaki tan. But it is [one book] in which the interest depends on character. At the beginning it is the successful, popular Vincent who is in charge of the expedition. His younger cousin Bobby, an eleven-year-old with remote and calculating eyes, has never really liked him and when things become difficult, the balance of power changes. The relationship between the boys is the heart of the story and it is not at all exaggerated. Vincent is only just too patronizing and Bobby, until the crisis that brings out his courage and resourcefulness, not particularly attractive, but he is sufficiently the centre of the book to make us delighted at his success and, regrettably perhaps, equally delighted when Vincent finds himself less virtuous than his pretensions.

> *"Adventures in the Mind," in* The Times Literary Supplement *(© Times Newspapers Ltd. (London) 1962; reproduced from* The Times Literary Supplement *by permission), No. 3144, June 1, 1962, p. 404.**

This is a perfect example of the story in which the adventures come naturally from the setting and the characters. There is no invention, no dragging in of hazards to ginger up the plot, no crooks, no hidden treasure, not even a villain. . . . What [happens to the three children] is the core of an admirable story, completely convincing and most subtly imagined.

Of the many admirable features of the book, the most impressive is the character of Bobby, a boy whom "no motherly ladies longed to cuddle" and who "keeps his own counsel." Very quietly and almost in spite of himself Bobby takes control of the expedition from the extrovert Vincent.

A first-rate addition to the growing literature of Australia, and one which should find many friends in England.

> *A review of "The Boundary Riders," in* The Junior Bookshelf, *Vol. 26, No. 3, July, 1962, p. 140.*

So vivid are Australia's vastness and rugged beauty, so logical the disasters, and so natural the people that the reader feels he is sharing an actual experience.

> *Ruth Hill Viguers, in her review of "The Boundary Riders," in* The Horn Book Magazine *(copyright © 1963, by The Horn Book, Inc., Boston), Vol. XXXIX, No. 2, April, 1963, p. 177.*

Miss Phipson's account of the children's struggles to find their way home should be thoroughly absorbing fare for the 9-12's. She concentrates on building a solid picture of the country and its difficulties, and her youngsters come through as individuals and not stereotypes. The accent is on action and the reader is spared any contrived dissertations as to what the children were thinking during their wanderings.

> *Marian Sorenson, "Far Away, Far Back, and Down Under," in* The Christian Science Monitor *(reprinted by permission from* The Christian Science Monitor; *© 1963 The Christian Science Publishing Society; all rights reserved), May 9, 1963, p. 4B.**

THE FAMILY CONSPIRACY (1962)

This is in the great tradition of Victorian family stories—one of the chapter headings, **"Edward on Trial"**, is typical—but without Victorian priggishness. The Barkers know the loyalties but also the strains of real family life; and the parents are only more grown up than the children, not more angelic.

The Australian countryside of **The Family Conspiracy** is authentic and lively, because the Barkers make their living by it.

> *"The Good and the Dead: A Test of Quality for Teenagers," in* The Times Literary Supplement *(© Times Newspapers Ltd. (London) 1962; reproduced from* The Times Literary Supplement *by permission), No. 3169, November 23, 1962, p. 894.**

Throughout the real suspense the reader, following the children's efforts [to pay for an operation for their mother], runs the gamut of emotions from hope to dismay, and, eventually, to satisfaction. Although the earning-money motif has been overworked, and the children's sense of guilt for their mother's ill health seems strained, the characterizations of the members of the Barker family are so good that the reader is readily involved.

> *Ruth Hill Viguers, in her review of "The Family Conspiracy," in* The Horn Book Magazine *(copy-*

right © 1964, by The Horn Book, Inc., Boston), Vol. XL, No. 2, April, 1964, p. 179.

The competence, spunk and dogged perseverence of the youngsters of the Barker family of Western New South Wales arouse our admiration and interest immediately. . . .

The children all fail quite dramatically (and understandably) at first, almost despair, and then with grim determination tackle the tasks anew. Their experiences are sometimes touching, sometimes dangerous, often humorous and always completely real. You want to stop Belinda from chancing her hard-earned money on a lottery ticket, to warn Robbie when he crawls into that old mine shaft and, above all, to aid the indomitable Edward when singlehandedly he rounds up distantly-scattered cattle that stampeded during the night—a richly authenticated report of a drover's experience. We admired the author's **The Boundary Riders** as one of the notable books of last year but this prize winner from Australia, told with pace and economy, surpasses it. Though far more virile than the Alcott books it has the same ring of truth. These children live, struggle, fail and triumph before our eyes. To us it is the best family story we have read in years.

> *Elizabeth Enright, in her review of "The Family Conspiracy," in* Book Week—The Washington Post *(© 1964, The Washington Post), May 10, 1964, p. 3.*

As the story opens, the mother is having an "attack," of what we do not know and never find out. The doctor says she needs an operation. Because of financial difficulties she cannot have it, and goes on getting worse. Meanwhile the children try in various ways to earn money to pay for the operation. As Australia has a National Health Program, which went into effect in 1944, doesn't the plot fall apart if the author doesn't indicate that it happened before this? Or is it a protest against socialized medicine?

> *Alice Dalgliesh, in her review of "The Family Conspiracy," in* Saturday Review *(© 1964 Saturday Review Magazine Co.; reprinted by permission), Vol. XLVIII, No. 26, June 27, 1964, p. 44.*

The children in this book show exceptional unity among themselves and concern for their parents' physical and financial well-being. Although some of the words and phrases in the story may be unfamiliar to American readers, the delightful characterizations, the hilarious situations in which the children sometimes are involved, and the satisfying but unsentimental ending all add up to engrossing reading.

> *Sharon Spredemann Dreyer, in her review of "The Family Conspiracy," in her* The Bookfinder: A Guide to Children's Literature about the Needs and Problems of Youth Aged 2-15, *Vol. 1 (© 1977 American Guidance Service, Inc.), American Guidance Service, Inc., 1977, No. 708.*

THREAT TO THE BARKERS (1963)

In this author's previous books, which like this one have a New South Wales setting, she has conveyed a sense of the grandeur of the scenery and a feeling for the attitudes of the still pioneering settlers in the territory. The major emphasis in this sequel to **The Family Conspiracy** . . . is in following up the activities of the ample Barker family. Those readers who previously liked the six children and their parents will be pleased that they all continue to maintain their individual personalities. . . . The descriptions of sheep farming are enlivened by rumors of thieves, and there are some genuinely tense moments when 14 year old Edward discovers and is threatened by the band of juvenile sheep-nappers. The story is unnecessarily drawn out by the author's tendency toward elaborate descriptions of casual occurrences. It is still enjoyable for its warm picture of the closely bound family and for its moments of suspense.

> *A review of "Threat to the Barkers," in* Virginia Kirkus' Service, *Vol. XXXIII, No. 1, January 1, 1965, p. 8.*

"Vivid descriptions of remote countrysides, characterization in depth, and strong suspense are wonderful ingredients for any story. It is a special treat when these qualities combine to such a degree that one can actually feel dust and heat and the threat of trouble settle over an Australian sheep ranch. . . ." It is a rare book that can live up to its publisher's publicity, which makes **"Threat to the Barkers"** a rare book, because it *does* contain all the ingredients promised. Readers who met the Barkers in the prize-winning **"The Family Conspiracy"** will be eager to hear news of them; those who don't know them are urged to meet this doughty and exuberant family as fast as they can get to a bookstore.

> *A review of "Threat to the Barkers," in* Publishers Weekly *(reprinted from the January 25, 1965 issue of* Publishers Weekly, *published by R. R. Bowker Company; copyright © 1965 by R. R. Bowker Company), Vol. 187, No. 4, January 25, 1965, p. 316.*

A fine story. . . . All the family, from trumpeting, temperamental Mr. Barker down to the enigmate 3-year-old Fanny, are convincingly presented. So is Edward, the 14-year-old who is the principal figure, involved as he is in real danger. Edward's search for his dog in a dark, sleeping town is chillingly described; and it is his courage, ultimately, which prevents the theft of his brother's prized stud-ewes. An excellent sequel to . . . **The Family Conspiracy.**

> *Elizabeth Enright, in her review of "Threat to the Barkers," in* Book Week—The Sunday Herald Tribune *(© 1965, The Washington Post), May 9, 1965, p. 16.*

As the story of Edward's inner turmoil, **"Threat to the Barkers"** is a fine job; with style, understanding and humor, it makes each of the boy's successive moods credible and logical. As a mystery, it tips its hands early. Some suspense is also lost in repetition and dull detail.

The colorful Australian background is superbly presented; and characterization is full and most effective.

> *A review of "Threat to the Barkers," in* The New York Times Book Review *(© 1965 by The New York Times Company; reprinted by permission), May 9, 1965, p. 18.*

With a family as vivid and appealing as the Barkers, a story with the frailest plot should be able to grip the 9-12's. But Joan Phipson adds a gripping, dramatic one with almost adult ingredients—sheep-stealing gangs, blackmail, threats. And the boy who struggles to cope with them all is too convincing to allow tension to slacken. "Moral courage is to mere physical courage as the sun is to the moon. And a good deal more difficult"—the lesson is clear but unforced. And as to lessons,

this story's Australian setting makes the continent and its people far more vivid than geography books and atlases can.

> *Pamela Marsh, in her review of "Threat to the Barkers," in* The Christian Science Monitor *(reprinted by permission from* The Christian Science Monitor; *© 1965 The Christian Science Publishing Society; all rights reserved), July 29, 1965, p. 5.*

BIRKIN (1965)

This story is set in an Australian rural community. A group of children adopt a small calf and are then faced with the problems of feeding it as it grows. Time passes and the older children lose interest, but a younger girl and boy remain faithful to Birkin. Interwoven into this is the story of Angus, a Scottish boy, son of the head cattleman at the local big ranch. At first he is not accepted by the children at school because of his accent, but as they realise the value of his specialised knowledge, and that of his father concerning Birkin, he becomes an important figure in their community.

Miss Phipson is an Australian and obviously writes from experience. The story has an authentic air, but some of the descriptive passages are rather long and, for an English child, they do not really create a specific atmosphere. The story is in fact a succession of episodes in the life of Birkin without a really strong theme to hold it together. However, children love animal books and a calf is a refreshingly new kind of hero.

> *A review of "Birkin," in* The Junior Bookshelf, *Vol. 29, No. 2, April, 1965, p. 100.*

Joan Phipson always tells a rousing story in the framework of Australian physical space but sometimes oddly restricting codes and taboos. . . . **Birkin,** her latest story, has a theme that holds anywhere: what can you do with a calf or sheep that starts its life as a pet? . . . A good long eventful story, this.

> *"Man and Beast: Some Persistent Attitudes," in* The Times Literary Supplement *(© Times Newspapers Ltd. (London) 1965; reproduced from* The Times Literary Supplement *by permission), No. 3303, June 17, 1965, p. 497.**

The book is marred by too many indistinguishable and unmemorable characters, and more seriously by an infuriating style, mock-heroic, arch, and redundant. A boy with big eyes has "been granted two enormous, thick-lashed and limpid orbs." Going home from school, the children do not walk or bicycle; they "employ their various means of locomotion."

Children are too tolerant of style. If they find the going hard or fussy, they assume the trouble lies in their inadequacy as readers. They will get around or get over obstacles, as if they were so many rocks and strands of barbed wire between themselves and a promised swimming hole. I am not so generous myself. Why should any auto-intoxicated author presume upon the humility and good nature of the young?

Horses and dogs, mice, foxes, and cats make splendid heroes of fiction. But the languid genus Bos has rarely been chosen to bear the mantle of the chief protagonist. (Ferdinand is the glorious exception.) The truth is that a steer doesn't make a very good pet, much less a hero. And perhaps that's what's really wrong with this book, and why the pumped-up language is used to simulate drama and importance where none naturally exists.

Mary Nash, "Adventures of a Boy and His . . . ," in The Christian Science Monitor (reprinted by permission from The Christian Science Monitor; © 1966 The Christian Science Publishing Society; all rights reserved), May 5, 1966, p. B4.*

This begins as a lighthearted picture of village life in which the inter-relationships of older and younger brothers and sisters, friends and neighbors are beautifully realized. Gradually the story builds in intensity as the children are led into a series of crises which test their hardihood and loyalty. As we have come to expect from this author, the locale is compellingly lifelike and the children, with their grit and self-reliance, are totally winning.

Houston L. Maples, "Showing Their Mettle," in Book Week—The Washington Post (© 1966, World Journal Tribune, Inc.), May 8, 1966, p. 31.*

That the story of a pet steer could make absorbing reading seemed unlikely until I read this memorable book. Birkin becomes a personality (never anthropomorphised, however), but he serves mainly as catalyst in the story. If he had not demanded the children's devotion, Tony—with his lame leg—might not have found his place in the world; Scottish Angus might not have so soon been accepted as one of them by the children of Coolabin; and Frances might not have had her passion to manage difficult situations and to help the underdog so richly satisfied. So alive are the children—even minor characters like Frances' young brother who nips in and out of the story like the small imp he is—that in memory they will not be confined to the pages of a book. Not only is the story the author's best, it would be outstanding in any season. Seldom are vivid characterizations and reality of unusual setting teamed with so well developed a plot.

Ruth Hill Viguers, in her review of "Birkin," in The Horn Book Magazine (copyright © 1966, by The Horn Book, Inc., Boston), Vol. XLII, No. 3, June, 1966, p. 313.

This sensitive, old-fashioned story of considerable literary merit displays many themes common to this field: Outcasts together—Tony and Angus, the foreigner, are shunned by others and perforce become allies; the exceptional character as nature child—Tony has a special way with animals; and the Santa Claus theme—Mr. Mitchell provides direction and support for a career. Tony copes with pain, but it causes him to be testy and irritable. He is also courageous, intelligent, and tenacious. . . . [The] characterization gives some insight into his pride and his ability to manage the vicissitudes of life.

Barbara H. Baskin and Karen H. Harris, in their review of "Birkin," in their Notes from a Different Drummer: A Guide to Juvenile Fiction Portraying the Handicapped (reprinted with permission of the R. R. Bowker Company; copyright © 1977 by Barbara H. Baskin and Karen H. Harris), Bowker, 1977, p. 270.

PETER AND BUTCH (1969)

Butch is what cherub-faced, curly-haired Peter likes to be called so he won't be taken for a sissy. By any name he's Exhibit A of the boy who mistakes a rough, tough front for manliness—and unfortunately that's just what he is here, an exhibit: "There was no doubt that the worldly, confident manner had its attraction and especially for someone like Peter who wanted to prove his own toughness. But now that he knew what lay behind it, now that he knew, or guessed, this toughness was precisely what Raymond (who's goaded him into fury in a friendly boxing match) was also trying to prove, he began to see, as he had with Tex (who'd strung him along on a robbery), where the image was artificial." After the dawning comes the light of day, in the person of older teen David Miller: "His notions of right and wrong were firm and unshakable. It did not matter to him if people disagreed with him. He knew what he thought and why he thought it. For anyone as easily blown by the winds of chance, rumor, and current fashion as Peter, getting to know David was a salutary experience." Salutary perhaps for adults involved in child guidance (like the Police Boys Clubbers here) but too much clogged introspection and too many shafts of brilliant illumination for kids. Joan Phipson is usually more circumspect.

A review of "Peter and Butch," in Kirkus Reviews (copyright © 1969 The Kirkus Service, Inc.), Vol. XXXVII, No. 8, April 15, 1969, p. 453.

Joan Phipson's new book, **Peter and Butch,** is . . . ambitious but not entirely successful. . . .

There is no getting away from the fact that this is a moral tract; it is almost as improving a tale as one by Mrs. Sherwood. Alan Garner once said, "Didactic writing is unworked writing."

Joan Phipson has worked and worked on this, but some final alchemy is missing.

Peter's redemption comes when he can value success in a choral competition as greatly as success on the playing field, when he forgets to worry about what image he is showing to the world and when he can tolerate being addressed as Curly. It seems rather a pity, that in the final pages, when he is confronted with his old enemies, the youths he shopped, it is force that wins. Peter is now cleverer and stronger than they. Fighting is apparently all right if it is done in self-defence, but one can't help wondering what would have happened if Peter had not been good at boxing. Instead of going on happily to mend a spurting water tap for his grateful mother, he would have needed an ambulance. It's as if Joan Phipson suddenly changes her mind. "I've told you", she seems to say, "that music and bird-watching are fine manly pursuits, that real strength is in self-control, that there's nothing cissy about helping to dry the dishes—but I'm afraid in the end you won't get anywhere unless you can use your fists." (p. 693)

"Faraway Places," in The Times Literary Supplement (© Times Newspapers Ltd. (London) 1969; reproduced from The Times Literary Supplement by permission), No. 3513, June 26, 1969, pp. 692-93.*

Realistic enough, but the characters seem fashioned to fit the story rather than inspiring the action. The dialogue and setting are good, although they lack the color of the author's rural Australian stories. (p. 16)

Zena Sutherland, in her review of "Peter and Butch," in Bulletin of the Center for Children's Books (reprinted by permission of The University of Chicago Press; © 1969 by The University of Chicago), Vol. 23, No. 1, September, 1969, pp. 15-16.

The book has all the classic ingredients of a 'poor mixed-up kid' tale. The boy's father is dead, he is involved with a gang of petty thieves, without really understanding what he is doing he tells all to the police. Now the story turns the corner, he joins a boy's club run by the police, learns true values and all ends well. Joan Phipson is capable of much deeper writing than this, which is really a very commonplace little book. Who reads this kind of book? Certainly not the age group the author imagines, for fourteen or even twelve-year-old boys are far beyond it. Perhaps the ten to twelve year-olds . . . but when one thinks of books like *The Crew of the Merlin* one is sadly disappointed.

> *A review of "Peter and Butch," in* The Junior Bookshelf, *Vol. 33, No. 5, October, 1969, p. 314.*

It is a little sad to see such an honest and subtle writer of domestic novels yielding to the current demand for a sociological moral, especially when her central character emerges so well in the first chapters.

> *Margery Fisher, in her review of "Peter and Butch," in her* Growing Point, *Vol. 8, No. 5, November, 1969, p. 1427.*

Joan Phipson invests this simple story with great authority by the depth of her understanding. The efforts of the floundering adolescent to find his true personality, the import of the influences he encounters, are fully realized. A book to learn from.

> *C.E.J. Smith, in his review of "Peter and Butch," in* The School Librarian, *Vol. 17, No. 4, December, 1969, p. 401.*

BASS AND BILLY MARTIN   (1972)

Bass and Billy Martin by Joan Phipson follows the exploration of the east coast of Australia and the slightest deviation from fact is noted. The interest is slow to build up, but when the actual words of Bass's own Journal take over . . . the story leaps to life with the excitement of seeing for the first time the coast of Van Diemen's Land and New Holland. This is for [boys] who scorn fiction. . . .

> *"Fighting for Freedom," in* The Times Literary Supplement *(© Times Newspapers Ltd. (London) 1972; reproduced from* The Times Literary Supplement *by permission), No. 3687, November 3, 1972, p. 1320.**

Bass, who gave his name to a strait, and Flinders, who gave his to a river, are the authentic heroes of *Bass and Billy Martin.* . . . Billy was a 14-year-old servant of Bass's, here rescued from a vague documentary existence and given a Cockney sharpness and receptivity that make him the ideal centre of a tale of exploration: frail boats in immense Australian seas. Warmly recommended: it's lovingly done. (p. 694)

> *Edward Blishen, "Past Into Present," in* New Statesman *(© 1972 The Statesman & Nation Publishing Co. Ltd.), Vol. 84, No. 2173, November 10, 1972, pp. 692, 694.**

A 'leisurely' style is a damning handicap for a contemporary children's writer. A great majority of younger readers, nurtured on the instant response promoted by film and television, are not prepared to allow their novelists even a few pages of preparatory sparring. Consequently it is saddening to think that Joan Phipson's story of the exploration of the dangerous southern Australian coastline by George Bass and his boy servant in the 1790s will be lost to many prospective readers owing to the long introductory chapters.

The history and geography teachers, where they still survive in their independent roles, would do well to know the book

and to use it selectively. The author obviously knows her Australia and if at times her enthusiasm leads to some over-writing, younger secondary children could still appreciate a story of real adventure if skilfully introduced.

> *Gordon Parsons, in his review of "Bass and Billy Martin," in* The School Librarian, *Vol. 21, No. 2, June, 1973, p. 166.*

THE WAY HOME   (1973)

Although not excessively long in terms of pages, *The Way Home* feels a long, almost interminable tale because, possibly, it is very short on hope. After a motor accident three children (Australian) find themselves passing through illogical varieties of flora and fauna in combination with undefined and equally equivocal changes in time. There is always fear, always disappointment, always hardship, always distorted temperaments and a sense of doom. Miss Phipson deserves considerable credit for her descriptive writing and her imaginative composition of eerie landscapes. As the story proceeds, it becomes hazily evident that a question of faith is involved but one is left wondering at the end how far the "scepticism" of Richard affects his reception at the end.

> *A review of "The Way Home," in* The Junior Bookshelf, *Vol. 37, No. 2, April, 1973, p. 411.*

A wilderness journey becomes a sort of metaphysical adventure as well for Australian Prue, her seven year-old brother Peter and her teenage cousin Richard after the three youngsters are tossed over a cliff in an auto accident and then swept downstream into unknown country. . . . Admirers of didactic metaphysical adventure/fantasy will be impressed by Phipson's meticulously realized landscape and her skillful integration of different times and realities, but we can't help sympathizing with Richard's failure to intuit the relevance of all the prehistoric tumult or to trust the benign omnipotence behind it. (pp. 760-61)

> *A review of "The Way Home," in* Kirkus Reviews *(copyright © 1973 The Kirkus Service, Inc.), Vol. XLI, No. 14, July 15, 1973, pp. 760-61.*

Joan Phipson, a good writer, is almost lost in her own atmosphere in *The Way Home.* Three children, again well-characterized survive a motor-accident in the wilds of Australia. They wander for days—in Australia this seems possible, unnervingly—before they realize that they have begun to wander in time, as well as space. Mostly in a terrifying pre-history, with volcanoes and monsters. They have to run very fast for a good deal of the time, rather like Alice hand-in-hand with the Red Queen, in order to remain. Increasingly they are aware of a Presence, sometimes male, sometimes female, always gnomic, who literally holds them in the hollow of its hand. At the very end, the boy who was too rational and hadn't enough contact with Mother Earth (or perhaps Father Earth), is dead. The other two, and the readers, are worn out.

> *"Testing Quests," in* The Times Literary Supplement *(©Times Newspapers Ltd. (London) 1973; reproduced from* The Times Literary Supplement *by permission), No. 3734, September 28, 1973, p. 1114.**

The story . . . explores the idea of the alienation of man from nature; and [Phipson's] message is an ecological one. Yet, the fantasy is not forced; and the children's journey back in time, which happens on the symbolic eighth day of their search for civilization, conveys a powerful, almost poetic sense of the primeval. (pp. 52-3)

> *Sidney D. Long, in his review of "The Way Home,"*
> *in* The Horn Book Magazine *(copyright © 1974 by*
> *The Horn Books, Inc., Boston), Vol. L, No. 1, Feb-*
> *ruary, 1974, pp. 52-3.*

In **The Way Home** the time-dimension element is exploited imaginatively and the changes are sudden, wide-ranging and bewildering. . . . Some readers may possibly find the action too bewildering and the changes too abrupt and inexplicable for complete satisfaction, but the story and the intriguing symbolism will certainly provoke thought. (p. 77)

> *Robert Bell, in his review of "The Way Home," in*
> The School Librarian, *Vol. 22, No. 1, March, 1974,*
> *pp. 76-7.*

Reactions to this story are likely to tell less about the book than they are about the reader, for it is one of those weird and wonderful works full of strange undercurrents of which the reader makes what he will. . . .

Those who like their books self-contained with loose ends nicely parcelled up are unlikely to be impressed; those who like their books to act as a springboard to further thought will be well satisfied.

> *David L. Rees, in his review of "The Way Home,"*
> *in* Children's Book Review *(© 1974 Five Owls Press*
> *Ltd.; all rights reserved), Vol. IV, No. 1, Spring,*
> *1974, p. 21.*

POLLY'S TIGER (1973)

Joan Phipson's **Polly's Tiger** [is] about a lonely child faced with a new environment and a new school, and protecting herself with an imaginary tiger. It is unpretentious, quiet, but exact and convincing.

> *"Novellas for Under-Nines," in* The Times Literary
> Supplement *(© Times Newspapers Ltd. (London)*
> *1973; reproduced from* The Times Literary Supple-
> ment *by permission), No. 3709, April 6, 1973, p.*
> *387.**

[The] concepts of adaptability, conquering fear, and an imaginary companion are smoothly woven into the narrative. . . . [The story is not] dramatic, but there is a problem-solution structure, and the style of writing is natural and easy.

> *Zena Sutherland, in her review of "Polly's Tiger,"*
> *in* Bulletin of the Center for Children's Books *(re-*
> *printed by permission of The University of Chicago*
> *Press; © 1974 by The University of Chicago), Vol.*
> *27, No. 10, June, 1974, p. 162.*

HORSE WITH EIGHT HANDS (1974; British edition as *Helping Horse*)

Horse is the way "the eight hands" (Phipson's name for her four Australian school children) hear the name Horst, and everyone of those helping hands is needed to assist the shy, inarticulate German immigrant in turning his rundown cabin, formerly the haunt of the local bikies, into a successful antique store. Phipson reminds us, rather baldly at times, that the children's view of Horst is subjective, and even as he changes in their eyes from a prowling madman to a helpless near baby to

a solid friend, he remains the children's spiritual ward and a never failing source of entertainment. . . . At times Horse's bovine passivity and the children's protectiveness can be annoyingly condescending, but their partnership does generate a sustained and purposeful intensity—outside of fantasy and orphanhood, children their age rarely have so much opportunity to use their initiative. Old fashioned, but satisfying.

> *A review of "Horse with Eight Hands," in* Kirkus
> Reviews *(copyright © 1974 The Kirkus Service, Inc.),*
> *Vol. XLII, No. 15, August 1, 1974, p. 805.*

[A] character baffled, temporarily, by life in Joan Phipson's story is an immigrant German antique dealer, Horst (nicknamed Horse), starting Australian life helped by four local children and the cause of a good deal of "fun". The inverted commas are necessary, sad to say, because Mrs. Phipson seems to follow in the Blyton footsteps (one would have thought the tracks were fading by now) of portraying adults as easy meat for child manipulation: Horse, after all, had enough brains to get to Australia, but one would not think so from the children's determination to view him as helpless. The fun is facetious not humorous, the children lack true individuality and the only real thrill is a small piece of information about the aging of antique glass.

> *Barbara Britton, "Under Dogs," in* The Times Lit-
> erary Supplement *(© Times Newspapers Ltd. (Lon-*
> *don), 1974; reproduced from* The Times Literary
> Supplement *by permission), No. 3796, December 6,*
> *1974, p. 1376.**

Helping Horse [is] a cheerful tale, topical in its details and absorbing in its casual, easy, detailed progress. . . . It is in the nature of such stories to have a happy ending and this one does, after the usual vicissitudes. But its good humour and racy detail carry one through even the Dickensian conclusion of "What happened after that", and the young people—Hilary, the restless daughter of a doctor, Debby with her prosperous business background, athletic Bruce and Simon with his very English home life—are properly established, with their personalities suitably affecting the action.

> *Margery Fisher, in her review of "Helping Horse,"*
> *in her* Growing Point, *Vol. 13, No. 7, January, 1975,*
> *p. 2560.*

While the situation [in **Horse with Eight Hands**] seems a bit contrived . . . , each incident is convincing, and both the characters and their relationships are solidly drawn; the additional appeal of the story is in the satisfying development and completion of a project, as Horst and his eight helping hands turn a dilapidated house into an attractive and successful home and shop.

> *Zena Sutherland, in her review of "Horse with Eight*
> *Hands," in* Bulletin of the Center for Children's Books
> *(reprinted by permission of The University of Chi-*
> *cago Press; © 1975 by The University of Chicago),*
> *Vol. 28, No. 6, February, 1975, p. 98.*

Throughout the book the story develops slowly and at times the plot is barely strong enough to carry the reader on, in spite of some very obvious attempts by the author to stimulate flagging interest. It might have been more successful had the author concentrated on the group's activities to help a new neighbour and not tried to spice up an everyday (and nothing wrong with that) story with ghostly interference and gangs of delinquents.

Not knowing when to stop is in fact the downfall of the book. Nearly all events are unnecessarily heightened by the author's style as if overwork were the order of the day. The strain is too great and results in, for example, a disastrous attempt at slapstick and a highly artificial spread of characters for the sake of variety. The cumulative effect is contrived, irritating and eventually dull.

> *Robert Barker, in his review of "Helping Horse," in* Children's Book Review *(© 1975 Five Owls Press Ltd.; all rights reserved), Vol. V, No. 1, Spring, 1975, p. 21.*

___

THE CATS   (1976)

Few thrillers for young readers rival their television or film equivalent in tense narrative pace: an exception is **The Cats**. . . . Superficially the plot has much in common with a typical late-night movie. Two Australian teenage boys are kidnapped by a couple of delinquents, and imprisoned in a ruined house in the remote bush. The kidnappers' plans misfire and events reach a macabre climax when they are hunted by a pack of super-cats, which have grown to three times the size of their domestic cousins after running wild for several generations. In this conflict the kidnappers have to depend on their victims to rescue them.

In the hands of a less skilful writer this material could be crudely sensational; but Joan Phipson avoids cliché and with one exception, implausibility. It is perhaps surprising at the end that neither police nor doctors are curious about the severe injuries sustained from the cats by the main characters, though animals like these are unknown in the area. Here she sacrifices reality to plot; but her characters are three-dimensional and their moral conflicts are drawn with subtlety. Tension is handled expertly, particularly the claustrophobic horror of standing in a half-rotten house in pitch darkness; or being trailed in a fast enclosing dank mist. Perhaps most remarkable is her imaginative portrayal of the landscape and weather of the bush, which is never simply descriptive but used as an integral part of the plot and emotional atmosphere. This book will grip many readers. . . .

> *Laura Cecil, "Kidnappers and Super-Cats," in* The Times Literary Supplement *(© Times Newspapers Ltd. (London) 1976; reproduced from* The Times Literary Supplement *by permission), No. 3890, October 1, 1976, p. 1242.*

Like all Phipson's work, "The Cats" is set in Australia and the country itself plays a major role. Jim and Willy, teen-age brothers whose parents have just won a big lottery prize, are kidnapped by Socker and Kevin, two local "coves." The boys are driven to an abandoned farmhouse in the far reaches of the outback where the relationship between criminal and victim begins to change. . . .

After a series of calamities, it would be easy for Jim and Willy to escape, leaving Socker and Kevin to perish. They reject this idea and wind up not only saving their captors, but joining with them in a pact. Jim and Willy will tell no one about the kidnapping if Socker and Kevin tell no one about the cats. This is the one false note in an otherwise compelling and satisfying novel. I can buy the pact being made but can't quite believe that the boys' parents, the police, and the doctors who examine Socker, who has been mauled by the cats, would accept the false explanations.

And what about the cats? Well, that part is apparently true. The author includes an extract from a story in The Sydney Morning Herald. Gigantic wild cats are indeed roaming the central part of Australia. And you thought all they had down there were platypi and kangaroos and cuddly koalas!

> *Susan Meyers, in her review of "The Cats," in* The New York Times Book Review *(© 1976 by The New York Times Company; reprinted by permission), November 21, 1976, p. 63.*

The social theme of the book, the rootlessness and envy that drive Socker and Kevin to crime, is conveyed almost entirely in spontaneous and natural talk through which, over the few days of their ordeal, the two couples move towards some kind of understanding. The third element that defeats Socker's plan is an irrational one. The enormous cats which stalk the boys in the mist are real enough. . . . What is in doubt—putting a chill and suspense into the story—is Willie's influence. Is it merely a case of a boy who, exploring the hills on his bicycle, had convinced the cats of man's harmlessness? Is the bond a less explicable one? The reader must decide, taking into account the clear motivation and the compelling atmosphere of an outstanding novel.

> *Margery Fisher, in her review of "The Cats," in her* Growing Point, *Vol. 15, No. 6, December, 1976, p. 3019.*

The story is told chiefly from the point of view of straightforward, extroverted Jim, who is a foil for his brother, while Willy, an animal lover, enjoys an almost mystical feeling for the solitude of the wilderness. Brash Socker and pusillanimous Kevin are well-contrasted, too; and the narrative about the quartet of four skillfully individualized youths is effective for its combination of character portrayal, suspense, and irony.

> *Paul Heins, in his review of "The Cats," in* The Horn Book Magazine *(copyright © 1977 by the Horn Book, Inc., Boston), Vol. LIII, No. 1, February, 1977, p. 54.*

The story is at its best when it is factual, and Willy's superior knowledge of the environment constitutes the victims' trump card. Suggestions of the supernatural are less successful.

> *A review of "The Cats," in* The Junior Bookshelf, *Vol. 41, No. 2, April, 1977, p. 119.*

___

FLY INTO DANGER   (1977; British edition as *The Bird Smugglers*)

The author of many fine novels presents another which, like "The Cats," is rooted in cruel reality. Margaret, a 13-year-old, is on a flight from her beloved country home in Australia to London. She suspects that her seat mates, an elderly German couple, are smuggling wild parrots, a crime of which she has firsthand knowledge. In exciting episodes, the brave girl finds the concealed birds and proves the case against Theo and Maria. They are arrested. The birds that survive dope and lack of air are saved. Phipson gives readers a rousing thriller, but she does more. Revealing Theo and Maria as poor and lonely in a strange country, she explains why they succumbed to the offer of a free passage home to their families. The book is a plea for all victims of money grubbing higher-ups who profit vastly, in anonymous safety, at the expense of others.

> *A review of "Fly into Danger," in* Publishers Weekly *(reprinted from the August 1, 1977 issue of* Publishers Weekly, *published by R. R. Bowker Company, a*

Xerox company; copyright © 1977 by Xerox Corporation), Vol. 212, No. 5, August 1, 1977, p. 116.

Although an environmental message is explicit in the ranger's comments and Margaret's actions, didacticism is avoided by the author's skill in developing a taut plot line around a group of characters who are believable because they are ordinary people in an extraordinary situation—struggling against one another in a jumbo jet on a routine flight from Australia to England. The novel derives its vitality from the author's passionate concern for protecting the environment and her ability to tell a good story.

Mary M. Burns, in her review of "Fly into Danger," in The Horn Book Magazine (copyright © 1977 by the Horn Book, Inc., Boston), Vol. LIII, No. 6, December, 1977, p. 666.

The suspense potential of a mid-air drama has not been fully exploited, and the heroine is a bit wet, but this is an efficient enough story on a fascinating and unusual subject.

Cecilia Barkis, "Out in the Outback," in The Times Literary Supplement (© Times Newspapers Ltd. (London) 1980; reproduced from The Times Literary Supplement by permission), No. 4018, March 28, 1980, p. 362.*

Strict limits of time and place give shape and tension . . . to *The Bird Smugglers.* Though this more direct, less intense book might suit readers of ten or so, it is no less deeply felt and no less circumstantial in setting and plot than *No Escape.* A girl of thirteen, shy in disposition and country-minded, is travelling from Australia to London for an annual visit to her mother, a singer pursuing an international career. After an encounter on her father's property with poachers catching parrots for illicit sale, Margaret is hardly surprised when she finds herself sitting near an elderly German couple whom she had seen conferring with a pet-shop manager and whom she guesses are paying for their trip with the kind of smuggling the reserve-warden had described to her. But how can she make anyone believe her suspicions? And how can she get hold of Maria's overnight bag, in which the doped birds are probably hidden? The story moves slowly at first but the almost painstaking description of take-off and the Jumbo jet interior helps to create suspense as the pace increases in proportion to Margaret's difficulties. An authorial reflection makes Joan Phipson's realistic aim very clear. Margaret has become a public hero, but this will not last long, and in any case her fellow-travellers, student Stephen and elegant Stella, are far better candidates for fame:

> "In a world of artificial romance and artificial crime, with characters tailored to suit, Margaret simply had no place. She was too ordinary, just like anybody else. And after all she was only a child."

As for that very ordinary couple. Theo and Maria, whose longing to see their grand-children has over-ridden social discipline and good sense, they are far from being story-book villains. This adventure is firmly and honestly based on the world as it is.

Margery Fisher, in her review of "The Bird Smugglers," in her Growing Point, Vol. 19, No. 1, May, 1980, p. 3700.

WHEN THE CITY STOPPED (1978; British edition as *Keep Calm*)

Joan Phipson, the Australian writer, chooses to follow her treatment of kidnapping in *The Cats* with an even more chilling subject: the total breakdown of society. At the end of *Keep Calm,* the thirteen-year-old hero, Nick, reflects: "I'll always know it's nothing but an eggshell we're living on". What brings him to this frightening conclusion (one which many adults spend considerable energies in combating) is a strike, the result of a proposal by the Australian government to build a nuclear reactor at Botany Bay.

The strike in the end is effective—services are resumed and the government promises a referendum. But the story concentrates on the collapse of the normal things we all take for granted, and in particular the effect of the strike on Nick and his younger sister. Their mother is involved in a car accident, their father is abroad. The two children have to cope alone with the lifts that don't work in their tower block, the putrefying food in their refrigerator, the wild dogs in the streets, the police who are too tired and busy to help them find their mother.

The first section of the book is very well done; so long as the children and the city are the only characters, the tension is marvellously sustained. But from the time the children join up with others and start their trek out of the city, it becomes a more commonplace odyssey. It is an interesting story, but not the high achievement it gave promise of being.

Ann Thwaite, "Chills and Thrills," in The Times Literary Supplement (© Times Newspapers Ltd. (London) 1978; reproduced from The Times Literary Supplement by permission), No. 3991, September 28, 1978, p. 1082.*

There's a perennial appeal in stories of children who cope capably and believably with disaster, and in this tale of a general strike in an Australian city, Phipson has captured the tension and fear of Nick and his sister Binkie most vividly. . . . The book shows in credible fashion how such a situation brings out the best in some people, the worst in others, and it's a cracking good read.

Zena Sutherland, in her review of "When the City Stopped," in Bulletin of the Center for Children's Books (reprinted by permission of The University of Chicago Press; © 1978 by The University of Chicago), Vol. 32, No. 3, November, 1978, p. 50.

Joan Phipson has directed the events of *Keep Calm* firmly in terms of a boy of thirteen. It is through the eyes of Nick Lorimer, and to a lesser degree through the reactions of his younger sister, that we watch the events of three or four days in which a city comes near to chaos. . . . Looting and murder, fire and the threat of disease, all the possibilities are faced and their effect on the sheltered, dreamy boy are duly noted, but the effect of realism is counteracted somewhat by the easy way their problem is solved, by a kindly truckie and his hospitable wife, and even Jo's death is couched in softened, almost sentimental terms. If the final impression of the book is a serious one, it is perhaps because of the choice of certain unsensational but telling details—for example, the appearance of flocks of predatory gulls in the park. . . .

Margery Fisher, in her review of "Keep Calm," in her Growing Point, Vol. 17, No. 4, November, 1978, pp. 3412.

First, it's the electricity that goes off, so Nick and Binky, coming home from school, have to walk up the ten flights to their apartment. Then, Mrs. Piggott, who "does for" the Lorimers, is there briefly to greet them, not their mother; and by the next morning she still hasn't come. (Unbeknownst to them, she's unconscious after an auto accident.) Clutching at normalcy, Nick—usually a dreamy, drifting thirteen to Binky's assertive eleven—decides they should go into Sydney to school, only to find the building empty and a single teacher waiting with the news he didn't listen to yesterday: that utilities and transport workers have gone on strike to protest the nearby construction of a nuclear power plant, an action "in the interests of all." Quickly the ordinary turns ugly. . . . It's a large book, however brief, balancing fear and excitement and fellow-feeling, that the contrivance of the mother's accident doesn't diminish—the larger, indeed, for the insignificance her absence comes to assume.

> *A review of "When the City Stopped," in* Kirkus Reviews *(copyright © 1978 The Kirkus Service, Inc.), Vol. XLVI, No. 24, December 15, 1978, p. 1363.*

An ominous story—told with frightening plausibility—of the disintegration of a great city in a time of crisis. . . . The account of the refugees' agonizing journey to safety in the country and of their ultimate return to a recuperating metropolis would read like a mere documentary were it not for the beautifully defined personalities of the diverse characters and for the author's literate, sometimes even poetic, style.

> *Ethel L. Heins, in her review of "When the City Stopped," in* The Horn Book Magazine *(copyright © 1979 by The Horn Book, Inc., Boston), Vol. LV, No. 1, February, 1979, p. 65.*

[This story] has unusual potential which Joan Phipson exploits fully. The children's flight falls into fortunate patterns with the help of neighbours, friends and stray encounters, but there are obstacles and obstructions logically developed and intelligently chosen. Characters develop through contact with others and in the face of hardship and intimidation. Extremely well written.

> *A review of "Keep Calm," in* The Junior Bookshelf, *Vol. 43, No. 1, February, 1979, p. 38.*

A TIDE FLOWING (1981)

When Mark was only ten years old, he witnessed his mother's fatal slip off the deck of a sailboat in the sea between Tasmania and Australia. He was never sure whether it was accident or suicide, but his sense of despair and betrayal was exacerbated by the realization that neither his father nor his new stepmother wanted him and that his mother's English parents were content to wait to see him until he was older. The boy was taken to live with his grandparents in Sydney. . . . He suffered from loneliness and alienation almost to the point of total breakdown. Often, when walking home from school, Mark would see a woman pushing a girl in a wheelchair; one day he saved the girl's life by shoving her runaway chair out of the path of a car. He was severely injured, but his resulting friendship with the girl Connie continued until her inevitable death and ultimately helped him to mature. Together they explored his feeling that they and all the natural world were part of a great stream of life, symbolized by his fascination with the albatross, a notably solitary bird. Connie and her mother are so restrained their inner feelings are not revealed to the reader, and the author seems dispassionate and remote; but Mark and his grandparents are very real, and the boy's unhappiness is almost palpable. (pp. 311-12)

> *Ann A. Flowers, in her review of "A Tide Flowing," in* The Horn Book Magazine *(copyright © 1981 by The Horn Book, Inc., Boston), Vol. LVII, No. 3, June, 1981, pp. 311-12.*

A major Australian author writes with sympathy and insight about a child who feels doubly rejected, not sure that his mother's drowning hadn't been suicide and only too sure that his father is never going to send for him. . . . Phipson uses the sea and the rarely seen albatross as symbols of Mark's solitude and loss, but she uses them as poignant notes rather than the fabric of the story, so that there is no break in the smooth, strong narrative flow.

> *Zena Sutherland, in her review of "A Tide Flowing," in* Bulletin of the Center for Children's Books *(reprinted by permission of The University of Chicago Press; ©1981 by The University of Chicago), Vol. 35, No. 1, September, 1981, p. 13.*

This most moving Australian story is beautifully written, beautifully shaped, sensitively aware of emotions and natural surroundings. . . . This is a book of dramatic events, accidents and deaths, but also particularly observant of difficulties of communication among those who love one another, and conveys imaginatively that flowing tide of nature which can console the lonely. (pp. 215-16)

> *A review of "A Tide Flowing," in* The Junior Bookshelf, *Vol. 45, No. 5, October, 1981, pp. 215-16.*

An insightful story of an unlikely friendship in which adolescents, especially those from split families, will recognize a friend in Mark. Perhaps, also, they'll see friendship as a two-way street and not a one-lane highway.

> *Frank Perry, in his review of "A Tide Flowing," in* Voice of Youth Advocates *(copyrighted 1981 by Voice of Youth Advocates), Vol. 4, No. 4, October, 1981, p. 37.*

Phipson is as potent writing about water as she is writing of the Australian landscapes. Her seascapes charge the atmosphere with emotion. A fine piece of writing.

> *Ruth M. Stein, in her review of "A Tide Flowing," (copyright © 1982 by the National Council of Teachers of English; reprinted by permission of the publisher and the author), in* Language Arts, *Vol. 59, No. 5, May, 1982, p. 486.*

THE WATCHER IN THE GARDEN (1982)

Despite the "TRESPASSERS PROSECUTED" sign, fifteen-year-old Kitty Hartley frequently visited the extensive garden located on a ridge and separated from an Australian town by a deep gorge. Given to violent outbursts of temper and often a trial to her family, the girl considered the garden a place of refuge; she soon met its owner, old blind Mr. Lovett, and ultimately came to be on friendly terms with him. But when Terry Nicholson, whose family had a grudge against Mr. Lovett, began to appear, Kitty became apprehensive. . . . Seen through all seasons of the year, the garden uncannily reflects the benevolence or malevolence of its frequenters; and the psychological symbiosis, akin to ESP, which links the two chief characters, is instrumental in developing moral and physical tension and leads to a powerful but unexpected denouement.

Paul Heins, in his review of "The Watcher in the Garden," in The Horn Book Magazine *(copyright © 1982 by The Horn Book, Inc., Boston), Vol. LVIII, No. 5, October, 1982, p. 522.*

Hot-tempered, turbulent 15-year-old Kitty finds unexpected peace in the hilltop garden of blind, reclusive Mr. Lovett—the first person who understands her feeling that a part of her is somehow missing. Wise as he is, however, he does not defend himself against the violence of young hood Terry, and Kitty, watching over her friend, is drawn into bitter conflict. After Terry's motorcycle attack on her leaves them both unconscious, they find that they can (and must) read each other's minds, and the battle for the garden becomes a struggle for a soul. The story's allegorical force is strengthened by Kitty's isolation in the first scenes of the book; her family context and the content of her rages are filled in later and remain subordinate, although believable. The geography of the garden, with Mr. Lovett's two lookout rocks jutting up over the canyon and the sabotaged bridge between them, mirrors the division between Kitty and Terry without being intrusively artistic; the mental and physical upheavals of the climax are merged almost perfectly. This novel is serious, exciting and nearly a masterpiece.

Gale Eaton, in her review of "The Watcher in the Garden," in School Library Journal *(reprinted from the November, 1982 issue of* School Library Journal, *published by R. R. Bowker Co./A Xerox Corporation; copyright © 1982), Vol. 29, No. 3, November, 1982, p. 89.*

H(ans) A(ugusto) Rey

1898-1977

Margret Rey

1906-

Courtesy of Houghton Mifflin Company

Courtesy of Margret Rey

H. A.—(Also wrote under the pseudonym Uncle Gus) American author/illustrator of picture books, fiction, poetry, and nonfiction.

Margret—American author of fiction and poetry.

The Reys are the creators of the popular character Curious George, who first appeared in 1942 and has remained a favorite ever since. Children identify with the theme of the Curious George stories, stated simply in the first book: "He was a good little monkey, but he was always curious." George's innocent inquisitiveness takes him from one mishap to another throughout the entire series. As the works progressed, the Reys began including some elements of education in them without losing their basic entertainment value. Initially, critics saw the Reys's works as a welcome substitute for comic books. Today's critics especially appreciate the simplicity, strong colors, and European flavor of H. A.'s illustrations and the slapstick humor of the texts.

Both Reys grew up in Hamburg, Germany. H. A. began drawing at a very young age, his subjects consisting mainly of the animals he visited regularly at the Hagenbeck Zoo. He could not afford to attend art school and wound up selling bathtubs in Brazil until Margret convinced him to become her advertising partner in 1935. Although Margret has not illustrated any of their children's books, she attended various art schools and had several one-woman watercolor shows. She had been a reporter, a copywriter for an advertising agency, and a photographer before she met H. A. After about four months of of partnership, they became a husband and wife team and moved to Paris. The first Curious George book was published in the United States after the Reys fled from the Nazi invasion with the manuscript among their possessions. Although Margret's name is not seen on their early books, the Reys have assumed dual credit for the creation of the monkey and his stories.

Most critics say that *Curious George* summarizes the qualities that the Reys exhibit in all their picture books; a likeable main character and an absorbing story, accentuated by lively illustrations and bold colors. George's personality and charm attract children to these books as does the lack of adult restriction on his activities. The kindly parent figure, the man in the yellow hat, helps George out of his predicaments rather than blaming and punishing him for his curiosity. These stories contain adventures children can enjoy vicariously with no fear of the disapproval of their parents. H. A.'s active pictures complement the monkey's naive attitude toward his environment and problems with understanding and humor. With *Curious George Flies a Kite*, Margret changed the format from picture books which need to be read to the child to a simple text which can be read by the child; critics remarked on the smoothness of this transition while children continued to appreciate George's adventures.

Most of the Reys's other stories also focus on a main character who is a personable animal, with the exception of *Elizabite* the carnivorous plant. *Elizabite* is well received for its original story and illustrations, and many critics are especially impressed with the Reys's distinctive portrayal of Elizabite. *Pretzel* and *Spotty* focus on the themes of racial prejudice and individuality and receive praise primarily for their illustrations. H. A. wrote and illustrated *Find the Constellations*, a nonfiction book which is noted for its clarity and Rey's display of the star patterns through a stick-figure method which relates to the name and theme of each constellation. He also developed several toy books as Uncle Gus. The Reys are responsible for a body of work that both entertains and instructs children. Although Margret has not continued to write children's books since H. A.'s death, with Curious George they created a character whose personality and adventures have an immediate and lasting appeal. *Curious George* was among the New York Times Choice of Best Illustrated Children's Books of the Year in 1957 and *Curious George Goes to the Hospital* received a special citation from the Child Study Children's Book Committee at Bank Street College in 1966.

(See also *Contemporary Authors*, Vols. 5-8, rev. ed. and *Something about the Author*, Vols. 1 and 26.)

AUTHORS' COMMENTARY

Among children we seem to be known best as the parents of *Curious George*, the little monkey hero of some of our books. "I thought you were monkeys too," said a little boy who had been eager to meet us, disappointment written all over his face.

Not all our children's books are about George, but they are all about animals. We both love them, and one of the first things we do when we come to a new town is visit the Zoo. . . . Over the years we have owned an assortment of animals: turtles in Paris; monkeys in Brazil, which unfortunately died on a trip to Europe; alligators, chameleons and newts in New Hampshire, where we live in summer; and dogs, of course. We always have a cocker spaniel and H. A. generally manages to get him into some picture in each of our books.

H. A. also has written and illustrated two books on astronomy. One for children, which is written so simply that even adults can understand it; and one for adults, which today's children, growing up in the space age, often master better than their elders.

The books on astronomy are, in a way, a by-product of the First World War. There's no ill wind. . . . H. A., as an eigh-

teen-year-old G.I. in the German army, carried in his knapsack a pocket book on astronomy, the stars being a handy subject to study in those blacked-out nights. But the book was not much help for the beginning star-gazer, and the way the constellations were presented stumped him. So, many years later, still being dissatisfied with the existing books, he worked out a new way to show the constellations and ended up by doing his own books on astronomy. (pp. 359-60)

In Paris we did our first children's book. It came about by accident: H. A. had done a few humorous drawings of a giraffe for a Paris periodical. An editor at Gallimard, the French publishing house, saw them and called us up to ask whether we could not make a children's book out of them. We did and this became our first book, *Cecily G. and the Nine Monkeys,* one of the nine being George, incidentally.

Ever since we have done mostly children's books, and it seems to agree with us. (H. A. is still surprised that he is being paid for what he likes to do best and would do anyhow.) (p. 361)

How do we work together and who does what? Basically H. A. illustrates and Margret writes. But that is not the whole story. H. A. also has the ideas for a book which Margret then turns into a story. And Margret sometimes writes her own books, such as *Pretzel* and *Spotty*, and H. A. does the illustrations, at times changing the story a little to fit his pictures. And the astronomy books H. A. does all by himself—no, not quite. Margret sometimes rewrites parts of them to make them easier to understand for the layman. For Margret is a layman in astronomy, and H. A. by now is nearly a professional. So it is confusing and at times it confuses even us.

One thing is clear, though: doing a book is hard work for us. People sometimes think we dash them off. We wish we could. We work very long on each one, frequently over a year. We write and rewrite, we draw and redraw, we fight over the plot, the beginning, the ending, the illustrations—as a matter of fact our work is nearly the only thing we do fight about.

And where do the ideas come from? We wish we knew. Sometimes they don't come. Soaking in a hot bathtub—a news item in the papers—a piece of conversation at a party—it all helps. Once we heard a biochemist tell how, as a boy, he had made a bargain with his mother to give the kitchen floor a thorough scrubbing in order to get money for a chemistry set. So one day, while his parents were out, he sprinkled the contents of a large package of soap flakes on the floor, pulled the garden hose through the window and turned the water on. . . . In *Curious George Gets a Medal* George emulates this experiment with spectacular results. (p. 362)

> Margret Rey and H. A. Rey, "Margret and H. A. Rey" (reprinted by permission of Margret Rey), in Authors and Illustrators of Children's Books: Writings on Their Lives and Works, edited by Miriam Hoffman and Eva Samuels, R. R. Bowker Company, 1972, pp. 359-63.

GENERAL COMMENTARY

[H. A. Rey's] muse is of the lighter vein, he will admit, but still important enough because it captures the imagination of our children. He gallantly competes with Superman, and that shows courage. With taste, humor and some sophistication his books might lure our kids away from Mandrake, the Magician, and other gory subjects. His fine sense of line and color might even beat "Batman" or "Tillie the Toiler." . . .

From Curious George Gets a Medal, *written and illustrated by H. A. Rey.*

In another way I am sure his work can successfully compete with our funnies. It appeals to children and grown-ups alike. His success, 8 books in two years, shows that our publishers have good taste, and sales figures show they know good business when they see it. (p. 52)

Fritz Eichenberg, "Presenting Three Fine Artists to America" (originally a speech delivered on December 15, 1942), in Publishers Weekly *(reprinted from the January 2, 1943 issue of* Publishers Weekly, *published by R. R. Bowker Company; copyright © 1943 by R. R. Bowker Company), Vol. 143, No. 1, January 2, 1943, pp. 50-6.**

Rey is one of the most exuberant of the makers of picture books, with a fertile humour and a lively sense of colour. Connoisseurs will remember his pre-war study in heredity—*Zebrology*. In these two little books, he is provided by his wife with stories which are as good as such things usually are. *Spotty* is about a rabbit who becomes an outcast because he is covered with brown spots. The theme of *Pretzel* is the protracted courtship, as lengthy as the suitor, of an exceptionally elongated dachshund. The pictures are very much better than the story, which, in the case of *Spotty*, is so long that the printers have had to use an unreasonably small type. When good picture books are so rare, books like this are particularly welcome. . . . (pp. 133-34)

Marcus S. Crouch, in his review of "Pretzel" and "Spotty," in The Junior Bookshelf, *Vol. 14, No. 4, October, 1950, pp. 133-34.*

The dramatic quality in the illustrations of *Little Tim and the Brave Sea Captain* becomes a dynamic force in H. A. Rey's picture book *Curious George*. Their dramatic effect is gained by strong color, vividly seen action and irregular vignetting—

the exciting appeal of dark colors boldly brushed on white paper. The block formation gives an impact to the illustrations which is instantaneous in its appeal. Anyone, child or adult, is captivated by the skill with which the agility of the monkey, George, is caught and shown against a background of familiar scenes of city life. Rey's sense of dynamic design is easily seen in his pictures of the predicaments caused by a monkey's curiosity. No one could miss it, for example, in the group of policemen overturning the desk in search of Curious George.

The story has a breathless pace. The simplicity and brevity of the telling is rhythmic and dramatic. The sentences have space and shape. When Curious George finds himself in jail for his thoughtless misdeeds, his escape is told in words carefully chosen for their speed, animation, and sound. . . .

The tempo and drama of the story are accented in the illustrations so that they advance together as one. No wonder little children return to *Curious George* again and again, finding there a picture book of the kind they are looking for. (pp. 127-28)

Lillian H. Smith, "Picture Books," in her The Unreluctant Years: A Critical Approach to Children's Literature *(reprinted by permission; copyright © 1953, 1981 by the American Library Association), American Library Association, 1953, pp. 114-29.**

What makes George so popular? There are many reasons, but perhaps the most important is the ease with which the children can identify with him. He is an animal and, moreover, he is an animal who is doing the things that they would like to do but don't dare. One teacher commented very nicely, "George *could* be a child". . . . And that's exactly it. He doesn't mean to be bad, he's just "curious" and that's what gets him into trouble. . . . [Everything] he does, no matter how remote from the realm of everyday life of the children who are listening, stems from some simple shortcoming which the children might easily be guilty of. . . . So George is a kind of release for the children—while they themselves cannot do the things he does, they can "be" George, in a safe and acceptable way.

Another aspect of these books which helps maintain the image of George as a good, albeit curious, monkey, is the way in which he is portrayed in the illustrations. Studying these, you see a very likable monkey, with a very sweet, simple face. He can look happy or sad, or maybe surprised, but he never loses the sweetness in his expression. He is not in any way a demoniacal, evil monkey doing bad things; once again he is just curious. This is very important in helping the children understand that one can make mistakes and do things he is not supposed to, without entering the realms of being "bad" with all the unfortunate connotations it carries with it.

Parents would be mightily surprised if they had any idea of the things a child will worry about, and how his child-mind can magnify them way out of proportion to reality, and the problem of good and evil is one of the most important of these, indeed, as it is for all of society. George fulfills a real need for them: not only does he actually *do* the bad things, giving them the pleasure of the escapade, but he does them in a way which is clearly unintentional and not "bad," thus removing the fear of punishment which the children have. For George is never punished—at least not by being spanked or losing an adult's love—his punishments seem to fit more readily into the idea of poetic justice. If he doesn't watch where he is going, he has an accident on his bike. As he runs away from the lady whose apartment he has painted like a jungle, he hurts himself jumping off a fire escape. . . . (pp. 5-7)

The *George* stories are good stories, exciting, rather detailed, and the fours and fives seem to be ready for this. They combine realistic elements, such as telephones and balloons which get him into trouble, with fanciful ones, like George's becoming a movie star. Mr. Rey is one of the rare authors who actually hint that children might like to become movie actors; such a daydream would hardly be allowed by many parents.

In spite of George's seeming independence, he had an adult to whom he could turn—a combination mother-father-guardian angel, but mostly friend—in the Man with the Yellow Hat, who gets him out of trouble, and likes him so much he always keeps him. This is a new idea—could it be better to live with a friend like the "Man in the Yellow Hat" than with one's parents, who can sometimes be awfully difficult? (p. 7)

> *Margot Dukler, "Five Popular Children's Authors,"* in Elementary English *(copyright © 1958 by the National Council of Teachers of English; reprinted by permission of the publisher), Vol. XXXV, No. 1, January, 1958, pp. 3-11.**

Curious George's creator . . . combines text and illustrations to make George a lively and likable little monkey. The illustrations in strong, dark colors, full of action, on white paper mirror the agility of Curious George. The text and the illustrations move at a breathless pace.

Young readers have looked forward to more Curious George stories. The pattern remains much the same throughout the series. George's curiosity gets him into one precarious situation after another. He manages to escape in ways that add more hilarity to the stories. (p. 92)

> *Bernard J. Lonsdale and Helen K. Mackintosh, "Laughter in Literature," in their* Children Experience Literature *(copyright © 1973 by Random House; reprinted by permission of Random House, Inc.), Random House, 1973, pp. 77-106.**

The series of stories beginning with *Curious George* . . . by Margret and Hans Rey depend upon a number of hazardous episodes, as much as upon character, for their success. George the curious monkey is not as engaging as Kipling's curious Elephant's Child in *Just So Stories* (1912); the plot and style of the George books are rather undeveloped. George simply works his way from one scrape to another. Still, George's well-meaning mischief is what attracts children. (p. 103)

Dramatic elements are very strong in the first book in the series and help to establish the appeal of the character. By the second page, George has been momentarily blinded by a big yellow hat over his eyes and caught and tied up in a sack. He nearly drowns; then he's chased and locked up in jail. He escapes by walking along some telephone wires. Finally we see him sailing through the air with a handful of balloons and descending onto the top of a traffic light.

The style of writing in the George books is too often similar to the style of a first-grade primer: The sentences are short, uniform, and monotonous. But the perilous exploits and the slapstick humor redeem these stories in the eyes of children. . . . (pp. 103-04)

> *Donnarae MacCann and Olga Richard, "Outstanding Narrative Writers," in their* The Child's First Books: A Critical Study of Pictures and Texts *(copyright © 1973 by Donnarae MacCann and Olga Richard; reprinted by permission of The H. W. Wilson Company), Wilson, 1973, pp. 95-106.**

From Curious George, *written and illustrated by H. A. Rey.*

Curious George (called Zozo in Britain) is not curious in the English sense of 'peculiar' but in the sense found at the start of the first book about him—'but he was always curious'. Easy as it is to give a human twist to a monkey countenance, easy as it is to think of a million and one comic situations into which an inquisitive nature might impel a monkey as easily as a human child, nobody would deny Margret and H. A. Rey the credit for endless inventiveness and a sense of occasion as they involve George with stethoscopes and ink wells, wind and water, toy balloons and a space-ship, people and animals, in a series of minor accidents from which his friend the Man with the Yellow Hat is always able to rescue him.

> *Margery Fisher, "Who's Who in Children's Books: Curious George," in her* Who's Who in Children's Books: A Treasury of the Familiar Characters of Childhood *(copyright © 1975 by Margery Fisher; reprinted by permission), Holt, Rinehart and Winston, 1975, Weidenfeld & Nicolson, 1975, p. 77.*

Rey's "jolly bright pictures" were admired [in America] for their European manner—a central European manner, actually, that he shares with Bemelmans—but like Duvoisin and Rojankovsky (and unlike Bemelmans), his work is universal in outlook. Universal and uniquely versatile, for the same artistic shorthand—flexible outline figures, flat washes, a modicum of shadowing—serves him equally well in telling his own stories and in dramatizing the quite different texts of his wife and others. . . .

Curious George . . . is one of those creations that come to seem inevitable, so completely is he the-small-boy-who-gets-into-scrapes. Everyone knows that monkeys look like people. Disney avoided them as looking too much like people to caricature—that is, they were caricatures of people to start with. In Rey's work the problem doesn't come up. George doesn't feed himself bananas with his feet or swing by his tail (like many African monkeys, he has no tail). He does what any youngster can do or could, given sufficient agility; he is Tarzan, not one of the apes. Add a measure of deviltry and, presto, 'that boy is a little monkey.'

Rey has great fun with him, letting him scamper around the edges of the story, pantomiming relish, contentment, stupefaction to the workaday words, ''After a good meal and a good pipe, George felt very tired''. . . . But tomorrow is another day, a day for discovering the telephone, alarming the fire department, escaping from jail, walking the high (telephone) wires, surveying the city by balloon . . . , before settling down—momentarily—in the zoo. With balloons for all his new zoo friends, a buoyant end.

Rey is as flexible as his hero—or heroes: Cecily G. (for Giraffe), Elizabite the Carniverous Plant and Pretzel the dachshund are all long benders. When George is just monkeying around, Rey closes in on him; when he has a bird's-eye view, the artist 'takes' him from a high angle and the scene expands to fill the frame. The choice of movie terminology is deliberate. What film technique (live, before cartoon) did to expand the possibilities of picturebook illustration can be seen with exceptional clarity in *Curious George* and in Rey's work generally.

In successive stories George became a fixture, a guy who could be trusted to get out of whatever trouble he got into, so it was good news—for fearful kids, concerned parents, ministering librarians and booksellers—when word came that *Curious George Goes to the Hospital*. . . . If George could do it, so could Dick or Jane. (pp. 204-05)

Pretzel [is] Rey's first collaboration with his wife Margret and the beginning of the Harper picturebooks about the difficulties of being different. Not that there is anything glum about *Pretzel,* the story of an extra-long dachshund admired by everyone but the light of his life . . . ; but alongside the Munro Leaf-Ludwig Bemelmans dolors of a dachshund, *Noodle* (Stokes, 1937), it is a book of a different and tougher breed. The premise of *Noodle* is that just to be a dachshund is to be overlong—freakish and comical—and, when it comes to digging, an inconvenience. . . . Pretzel, on the other hand, is the rejected suitor who proves the value of his difference: ''I'll get you out of there,'' he shouts after Greta falls into a deep hole, and when he grabs her by the scruff of the neck—''How good that Pretzel was so long!''

More troublesome—even tragic—are Spotty's spots . . . ; and when Aunt Eliza's needling results in his being left at home and spot remover fails him (''And he had thought he was pretty!''), he runs away. . . . (p. 248)

Unmistakable as Aunt Eliza's hypocrisy is, or the identity of the spotted Browns (averse, in turn, to Whities), *Spotty* scores with youngsters because of the injustice to one bunny who is a brother under any skin. He has, besides, a sister who stands up for him, a mother who won't rest until he's found and—for safekeeping—the thought, before he leaves home, to ''take my breakfast along.'' (p. 249)

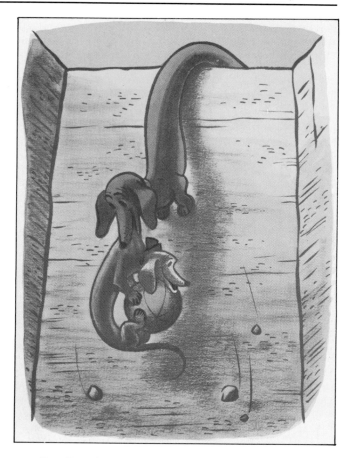

From Pretzel, *written by Margret Rey, illustrated by H. A. Rey.*

Barbara Bader, ''The Storytellers'' and ''The Emotional Element,'' in her American Picture Books from Noah's Ark to the Beast Within *(reprinted with permission of Macmillan Publishing Co., Inc.; copyright © 1976 by Barbara Bader), Macmillan, 1976, pp. 199-211, 241-64.**

The Curious George series . . . is a favorite with young children and features a monkey who is not only disobedient, but at times appears to have singlehandedly invented and popularized the phrase *monkey business.* (p. 336)

Myra Pollack Sadker and David Miller Sadker, ''Room for Laughter,'' in their Now Upon A Time: A Contemporary View of Children's Literature *(copyright © 1977 by Myra Pollack Sadker and David Miller Sadker; reprinted by permission of Harper & Row, Publishers, Inc.), Harper & Row, 1977, pp. 318-59.**

CECILY G. AND THE NINE MONKEYS (by H. A. Rey, 1939; British edition as *Raffy and the Nine Monkeys*)

H. A. Rey's spirited picture-story books have an unforced humor which is irresistible; while their grave attention to the matter in hand, their carefully worked out details, make the absurd so entirely logical and credible that the adventures of Cecily G. the amiable giraffe and her monkey friends have for children the absorbing interest of their own make-believe. . . .

[Cecily Giraffe is a lonely soul who] offers to share her house with the monkey family who have lost their home and are about to set forth in search of another.

It must be left to Mr. Rey's delightful drawings to show what a magnificent and patient playfellow Cecily G. became, how ingenious the monkeys were in finding ways in which Cecily G. could add to their and her own entertainment, and how cozily nine monkeys could sleep in a giraffe bed. The artist has included just the right kind and amount of detail to please the 4-to-6-year-olds, who are delighted by these pictures in clear strong color, which are full of action without being confused. A picture-story book that the youngest readers will promptly take to their hearts and that their elders will enjoy with them.

> *Anne T. Eaton, in her review of "Cecily G. and the Nine Monkeys," in* The New York Times Book Review *(© 1942 by The New York Times Company; reprinted by permission), November 15, 1942, p. 36.*

[The situation and the characters are] such fun to read about—and still more fun to look at in the pictures that are as important as the story. Be sure and read about George in his own book, if you haven't already, and don't miss meeting Cecily G. and her nine playmates. These are original, much-to-be-desired books for the picture book age and for children who like "funny books" whatever age they may be.

> *Florence Bethune Sloan, "Books Are Windows for You and Me," in* The Christian Science Monitor *(reprinted by permission from* The Christian Science Monitor; *© 1942 The Christian Science Publishing Society; all rights reserved), November 30, 1942, p. 14.**

[Good] nonsense. Mr. Rey's big, colored pictures of Cecily Giraffe are unexpected and laughable, and it's remarkable to how many surprising uses his nine young monkeys can put one obliging giraffe.

> *K.S.W. in a review of "Cecily G. and the Nine Monkeys," in* The New Yorker *(© 1942 by The New Yorker Magazine, Inc.), Vol. 18, No. 43, December 12, 1942, p. 89.*

CURIOUS GEORGE (by H. A. Rey, 1941; British edition as *Zozo*)

With its clear, bright colors, its simplicity that eliminates confusing details and the zestful activity of its hero, **"Curious George"** is an ideal picture book for the 3-to-5-year-old. . . .

The tide of fun for young readers rises higher and higher as Curious George, on reaching the city, experiments with the dial telephone and accidentally calls out the entire fire department, which charges across a double page spread with a fine effect of breathless hurry. . . .

The story is full of things that small children like, for the 3-to-5 year-olds not only take endless delight in the lively course of the story and in the boats, cars and fire engines, but throughout enjoy the details, the red, yellow, green and blue balloons, the small red and white chair which George sits in, his blue and white pajamas and the fact that he carries his own little bag off the boat. . . .

[Rey] understands the little child's interests, and we shall hope for other such lively picture books from his brush and pen.

From Cecily G. and the Nine Monkeys, *written and illustrated by H. A. Rey.*

> *Anne T. Eaton, in her review of "Curious George," in* The New York Times Book Review *(© 1941 by The New York Times Company; reprinted by permission), October 26, 1941, p. 10.*

More than once in this demure, jolly picture story a sense of Jean de Brunhoff hovers in memory. This naturalized Brazilian artist, newcomer to American picture books but well known in those of Paris and London, does not imitate the inimitable Babar, but his lookout on life is something the same, his drollery has the same affectionate tone and his style has much the same swing.

> *May Lamberton Becker, in her review of "Curious George," in* New York Herald Tribune Books *(© I.H.T. Corporation; reprinted by permission), November 2, 1941, p. 26.*

This satisfying funny book is about a monkey whose curiosity led him into all sorts of adventures. . . . Small children will wear the book out with affection for the story with its jolly bright pictures in the French manner.

> *Alice M. Jordan, in her review of "Curious George," in* The Horn Book Magazine *(copyrighted 1941, by The Horn Book, Inc., Boston), Vol. XVII, No. 6, November-December, 1941, p. 460.*

The story of *Zozo* is slight enough. It records the adventures one would expect to befall a monkey when given an opportunity of mischief. The pictures in colour have a boldness and simplicity that will appeal to young readers. They convey the humour of the tale admirably.

> *A review of* "Zozo," *in* The Junior Bookshelf, *Vol. 6, No. 3, November, 1942, p. 93.*

[An] outstanding book to use with [handicapped children] is *Curious George* by H. A. Rey. This is one book every special education teacher should have. A fairly simple story that is absolutely fascinating, it has an excellent vocabulary and sentence structure. But best of all, *Curious George* has humor—humor that is obvious, that the children respond to and are able to understand. This is important because mentally retarded children quite often are characterized as lacking a sense of humor.

> *Karen H. Harris, in her review of* "Curious George" *(revised by the author in February, 1983 for this publication), in* School Media Quarterly, *Vol. 8, No. 1, Fall, 1979, p. 25.*

ELIZABITE: THE ADVENTURES OF A CARNIVOROUS PLANT (by H. A. Rey, 1942)

Although she has milder relatives in real life, you will not find Elizabite in any handbook of the vegetable or animal kingdom. She is, fortunately, a unique creation from the unpredictable and always amusing brush of H. A. Rey, who has given us "Curious George" and other original picture books. . . .

This unruly creature gleefully nips her way through pictures which will rouse amazed guffaws from adults and the hardier-spirited youngsters as crisp rhymes outline her outrageous behavior. The whole adds up to a bright spot of hilarity in a darkened world.

> *Ellen Lewis Buell, "A Strange Plant" in* The New York Times Book Review *(© 1942 by The New York Times Company; reprinted by permission), April 26, 1942, p. 8.*

Elizabite is a carnivorous plant, a character new in children's picture books. With much humor, author-artist has imagined and pictured series of adventures a plant of this type might have. Illustrations are full page, in four colors, with rhyming couplet under each. Children will be quick to catch fun of story.

> *Eunice G. Mullan, in her review of "Elizabite, The Adventures of a Carnivorous Plant," in* Library Journal *(reprinted from* Library Journal, *May 1, 1942; published by R. R. Bowker Co. (a Xerox company); copyright © 1942 by Xerox Corporation), Vol. 67, No. 9, May 1, 1942, p. 416.*

Rey, who never sees things in everyday fashion, shows by many large, gayly colored pictures and a rhyming text how Elizabite began by snapping at a mosquito and came at last to the grand climax of catching a burglar. . . . The pictures of the eager and ferocious flower, happily bringing down its scarlet petals on anything handy, are funny in the hearty slapstick way little children enjoy. . . . Four years to six is the age for it; the couplets are to be read aloud by an older person who will enjoy it.

> *May Lamberton Becker, "Fun and Laughter for the Little Children," in* New York Herald Tribune *(©*

*I.H.T. Corporation; reprinted by permission), May 10, 1942, p. 17.**

The strangest character yet to be celebrated in a children's book is Mr. Rey's carnivorous plant, Elizabite. Elizabite's misdeeds . . . are recounted in rhymed couplets and hilarious four-color pictures calculated to amuse children from five years old up to almost any age.

> *A review of "Elizabite, The Adventures of a Carnivorous Plant," in* The New Yorker *(© 1942 by The New Yorker Magazine, Inc.), Vol. 18, No. 14, May 23, 1942, p. 56.*

CHRISTMAS MANGER (by H. A. Rey, 1942)

"A Christmas Manger" [is Mr. Rey's] most beautiful "punch-out-and-play book."

The covers, showing the thatched stable, with the Christmas star shining in the deep blue of the night sky, serve as a background, and when the Three Kings, their camels left at the entrance, the shepherds and the animals and four charmingly youthful angels are grouped about the Holy Family, the result is reverent and lovely, though Mr. Rey has caught the happy spirit of childhood and its joy in the Christmas festival. . . .

The four little angels show a childlike curiosity as well as joy, the camels are as supercilious in expression as camels invariably are, and there is a gentle dignity about Joseph and Mary and the Child. . . .

Mr. Rey has made an important and delightful addition to the pleasures of Christmas in the home.

> *Anne T. Eaton, in her review of "A Christmas Manger," in* The New York Times Book Review *(© 1942 by The New York Times Company; reprinted by permission), December 6, 1942, p. 9.*

TOMMY HELPS, TOO (by H. A. Rey, 1943)

"Tommy Helps, Too" is an admirably planned picture book, and though it uses a very simple toy device it still remains a real book, with a timely little story about a small boy who "helped, too" by collecting junk, delivering packages and taking care of a younger sister.

Mr. Rey has made each of Tommy's helpful activities personal and interesting by connecting it with some member of Tommy's family. One of his brothers drives a tank, and scrap metal is needed to make more tanks; the brother who patrols the coast in a blimp likes to read in his free time; the brother in the air force, like all pilots, needs gas for his plane; Brother Sam in the Marines drives a jeep, and his jeep and other jeeps need rubber for tires. Tommy's older sister has joined the Waacs, and so when Tommy looks after his little sister he sets his mother free for her A.R.P. duties. Old silk stockings help to make parachutes, and Tommy's father trains parachute troops; while the pennies that Tommy saves go for war savings stamps.

Facing each page of text, a picture of a tank, a jeep, a blimp, etc., pulls out to fill a space in an appropriate background. This little book suggests to young children in terms they can understand that they, too, can have a part in the war effort about which they hear so much. It will also give to the preschool child the feeling that he is actually reading a book for himself, a feeling which he invariably finds exhilarating.

Anne T. Eaton, "All-Out Tommy," in The New York Times Book Review (© 1943 by The New York Times Company; reprinted by permission), July 18, 1943, p. 10.

WHERE'S MY BABY? (by H. A. Rey, 1943)

So many people have written to compliment us on bringing this superb book for babies to their notice. . . .

The picture facing the verse shows mother pig but lift the flap, extend the page and there is mother pig and all her babies. Like all the best children's books this takes a very simple idea, open the flap and there are all the babies, close the flap and they've gone (the same principle as the peek-a-boo game). It has delighted generations of children and . . . it is still excellent value for money.

A review of "Where's My Baby?" in Books for Your Children (© Books for Your Children 1976), Vol. 11, No. 3, Summer, 1976, p. 14.

PRETZEL (by Margret Rey, 1944)

Pretzel was the longest dachshund in the world and therefore the handsomest but not the happiest. There was Greta, the cute little dachshund across the street, whom he loved but who simply didn't like long dogs. Pretzel literally tied himself into knots before he convinced her that handsome is as handsome does. The Reys, with blithe text and pictures, present such a good case for Pretzel that young readers, and older ones too, will take him to their hearts.

Ellen Lewis Buell, "Dogs, Cows, Brown Bears," in The New York Times Book Review (© 1944 by The New York Times Company; reprinted by permission), November 12, 1944, p. 10.*

"Pretzel" . . . is frankly a nonsense story. The very, very long dachshund . . . is an engaging animal from the time we first see him with his four brothers and sisters. The colors are bright and clear and the whole effect is jaunty and gay. Fun for four to six.

Frances C. Darling, "Let's Have Fun with Books," in The Christian Science Monitor (reprinted by permission from The Christian Science Monitor; © 1944 The Christian Science Publishing Society; all rights reserved), November 27, 1944, p. 12.*

This is the sort of picture book that the very young child or the very sophisticated adult will like. It is not a must, but with the . . . drawings, it is bright and amusing.

Siddie Joe Johnson, in her review of "Pretzel," in Library Journal (reprinted from Library Journal, December 15, 1944; published by R. R. Bowker Co. (a Xerox company); copyright © 1944 by Xerox Corporation), Vol. 69, No. 22, December 15, 1944, p. 1104.

SPOTTY (by Margret Rey, 1945)

A delightful picture book for any age from three up. There's plain delight in story and pictures—and a moral if you want it. Spotty, a brown and white bunny in a peaceful white and pink warren suffers loneliness when his family label him queer. He leaves home and finds a comfortable, welcome place in a forest of spotted rabbits. He learns, to his surprise, that a lovely pink and white rabbit is as unhappy in this setting as he was in his, and their mutual difficulties are solved with dispatch and joy. This is a sure favorite—both for libraries and bookshop customers. Lively, irrepressibly spirited drawings. . . .

A review of "Spotty," in Virginia Kirkus' Bookshop Service, Vol. XIII, No. 21, November 1, 1945, p. 491.

To the child this will be just another bunny story, but to the adult it will mean a lesson in spreading the gospel of international good will and fellowship or a token against racial prejudice.

Elsie T. Dobbins, in her review of "Spotty," in Library Journal (reprinted from Library Journal, December 15, 1945; published by R. R. Bowker Co. (a Xerox company); copyright © 1945 by Xerox Corporation), Vol. 70, No. 22, December, 1945, p. 1191.

A rather heavy-handed fable of tolerance for the picture-book age. . . . A large family of spotted bunnies which has hitherto looked askance at its white-furred brother provides a happy ending and plenty of scope for Mr. Rey's pictorial humor.

A review of "Spotty," in The New York Times Book Review (© 1946 by The New York Times Company; reprinted by permission), January 6, 1946, p. 8.

PRETZEL AND THE PUPPIES (by Margret Rey, 1946)

Pretzel was enormously popular—and "funnies" are the problem children of today's parents (who want to call a halt to their consumption but know of no wise method for so doing). The Reys . . . have produced this time a comic strip sequel to *Pretzel,* in which the adventures of this longest of all dachshunds prove again that though he is "so long" he is not always "so smart". Nonsense in good nature vein.

A review of "Pretzel and the Puppies," in Virginia Kirkus' Bookshop Service, Vol. XIV, No. 16, August 15, 1946, p. 382.

Each adventure takes up two pages of pictures by H. A. Rey, brightly colored, cleverly drawn, really amusing and a good substitute for the "funnies."

Gertrude Andrus, in her review of "Pretzel and His Puppies," in Library Journal (reprinted from Library Journal, October 1, 1946; published by R. R. Bowker Co. (a Xerox company); copyright © 1946 by Xerox Corporation), Vol. 71, No. 17, October 1, 1946, p. 1335.

Pretzel, the longest dachshund in the world, is always ready to try anything. His five puppies are full of admiration for their Daddy as he gets in and out of one funny scrape after another. . . . Using picture strips as in comic magazines, Mr. and Mrs. Rey have made a story that young children can follow by looking at the pictures. Older brothers and sisters will want to read the conversation and comments of this lively dog family.

L.P., in a review of "Pretzel and the Puppies," in The New York Times Book Review (© 1946 by The New York Times Company; reprinted by permission), November 10, 1946, p. 42.

CURIOUS GEORGE TAKES A JOB   (by H. A. Rey, 1947; British edition as *Zozo Takes a Job*)

No one who remembers George from the first book of his adventures could expect that irrepressible monkey to stay put for long—not even in a zoo. It was a simple matter for him to swipe the keeper's key and set out to explore the city. Investigation of a spaghetti pot led to a bout of dishwashing, an easy trick for one with four hands, and thus to a job of skyscraper window-washing. His curiosity grew by what it fed upon and one escapade followed another at a furious and funny pace. All this is told in a few well-chosen words and pictures which bear the author-artist's inimitable stamp. If you want to wean 4 to 8-year-olds away from the comics you might start with this.

> *Ellen Lewis Buell, in her review of "Curious George Takes a Job," in* The New York Times Book Review *(© 1947 by The New York Times Company; reprinted by permission), September 21, 1947, p. 37.*

That indefatigable little monkey George . . . continues his career in a tale of rippling fun and absurd color-pictures. George escapes from the Zoo, rides a bus-top through the city—this picture of traffic is lovely. . . . George sees interior decorators at work within, waits till they go to lunch, and then uses their paints to turn the room into an uproariously funny jungle. He finally gets into the movies and I don't wonder; I'd like to see him there myself.

> *May Lamberton Becker, in her review of "Curious George Takes a Job," in* New York Herald Tribune Weekly Book Review *(© I.H.T. Corporation; reprinted by permission), November 23, 1947, p. 8.*

The children who liked Mr. Rey's first story about George will find this one just as much fun with gay and realistic pictures of city scenes and a story full of unexpected happenings.

> *Alice M. Jordon, in her review of "Curious George Takes a Job," in* The Horn Book Magazine *(copyrighted, 1948, by The Horn Book, Inc., Boston), Vol. XXIV, No. 1, January-February, 1948, p. 34.*

BILLY'S PICTURE   (by Margret Rey, 1948)

Billy is a rabbit which starts to draw a picture of himself. No sooner has he started than each of his animal friends comes along and asks if he may work on the portrait a bit. Each animal adds to the picture his own favorite feature, the elephant a trunk, the mouse a long tail, the owl a pair of wings. When Billy finally solves his dilemma of figuring out a way to draw his own picture and entertain his friends at the same time, a three to five year old reader will still be grinning at the Rey's funny picture of the strange looking animal on Billy's drawing board.

> *Virginia H. Mathews, in her review of "Billy's Picture," in* New York Herald Tribune Weekly Book Review *(© I.H.T. Corporation; reprinted by permission), August 8, 1948, p. 9.*

Artists of the nursery set should find a new stimulus in the trials of Billy the Bunny, who set out to draw a self-portrait. . . . The net result of this composite portrait must be seen to be believed. The colors of the pictures are not as sparkling as the imagination which contrived them, but the humor will enchant any youngster with a fondness for animals and a taste for the ridiculous.

From Billy's Picture, *written and illustrated by Margret and H. A. Rey.*

> *Ellen Lewis Buell, in her review of "Billy's Picture," in* The New York Times Book Review *(© 1948 by The New York Times Company; reprinted by permission), August 15, 1948, p. 12.*

CURIOUS GEORGE RIDES A BIKE   (by H. A. Rey, 1952; British edition as *Zozo Rides a Bike*)

The only predictable thing about that dynamic monkey, Curious George, is his unpredictability. . . . His escapades aren't quite so furiously paced as in **"Curious George Gets a Job,"** but they are fast and funny enough to keep any youngster happy once he has glimpsed Mr. Rey's comic pictures.

> *Ellen Lewis Buell, in her review of "Curious George Rides A Bike," in* The New York Times Book Review *(©1952 by The New York Times Company; reprinted by permission), October 12, 1952, p. 26.*

The popular little monkey in a new series of misadventures, which make the kind of lighthearted sense only a four- to eight-year-old can fully appreciate. George's ultimate triumph this time is magnificent. . . .

> *Katherine T. Kinkead, in her review of "Curious George Rides a Bike," in* The New Yorker *(© 1952 by The New Yorker Magazine, Inc.), Vol. XXVIII, No. 42, December 6, 1952, p. 191.*

FIND THE CONSTELLATIONS   (by H. A. Rey, 1954)

An excellent introduction to the heavens, to satisfy and stimulate a child's interest. Known primarily for the *Curious George* and other picture books, H. A. Rey is a scientist too and offers his method of star study with a practical clarity. Familiar constellations are named and identified with interstellar lines drawn to make the figures. Seasonal panoramas of northern hemisphere skies place the stars and planets in relationship to each other and as the need arises, the physical facts—light years, planetary orbits, magnitudes and so forth—are explained. Index, sky schedules, bibliography, handlines for outdoor use, and the author's explicit, striking two tones are the further virtues of a very useful book.

A review of "Find the Constellations," in Virginia Kirkus' Bookshop Service, *Vol. XXII, No. 23, December 1, 1954, p. 775.*

An informative, lucid book designed to introduce readers in the middle-age group to the study of astronomy. The constellation designs are the same ones used in Mr. Rey's adult book, **"The Stars: A New Way to See Them."** They are remarkable pictures depicting the stars as they appear at different times of the year and showing by means of lines sketched from star to star, how such formations as the big dipper, the twins, etc., acquired their names. The origins of the many names taken from Greek mythology are explained, too. Once the reader has learned something about constellations, aided by Mr. Rey's text, diagrams and quizzes, the book goes on to discuss more complicated subjects including the solar system and space travel.

A review of "Find the Constellations," in Publishers Weekly *(reprinted from the December 25, 1954 issue of* Publishers Weekly, *published by R. R. Bowker Company; copyright © 1954 by R. R. Bowker Company), Vol. 166, No. 26, December 25, 1954, p. 2418.*

Whether or not a reader has ever wished to "find the constellations," he will certainly want to do so after he has read even a few pages of this enthralling book. Mr. Rey has the faculty of making star-gazing sound as if it were the most exciting and worthwhile hobby imaginable. And not only that— his directions for locating stars are so clear that practically anyone who can read can follow them. There are many diagrams and illustrations (including pictures of two little Gremlins who appear here and there on the pages making remarks that add to the book's gayety). . . . A "must" for public and school libraries and a wonderful book for an individual or a family to own.

Jennie D. Lindquist, in her review of "Find the Constellations," in The Horn Book Magazine *(copyrighted, 1955, by The Horn Book, Inc., Boston), Vol. XXXI, No. 1, February, 1955, p. 49.*

A minimum of simple text gives basic information about each constellation. The material centers around four seasonal sky views which plot the position of the constellations throughout the year.

This is an excellent book which should supply many fascinating hours for the embryonic astronomer if he is sufficiently blessed with that quality with which Mr. Rey has imbued his most popular hero, "Curious George."

Alice Brooks McGuire, in her review of "Find the Constellations," in The Saturday Review, New York *(© 1955 Saturday Review Magazine Co.; reprinted by permission), Vol. XXXVIII, No. 12, March 19, 1955, p. 41.*

To most beginners in the art of star-gazing the concepts of the Great Bear, the Twins, Andromeda and their heavenly companions seem rather like a bad joke on the part of the ancients. H. A. Rey, however, makes a diverting game out of finding them. . . . [He] gives recognizable line and form to the constellations—recognizable, that is, if one allows for just a little

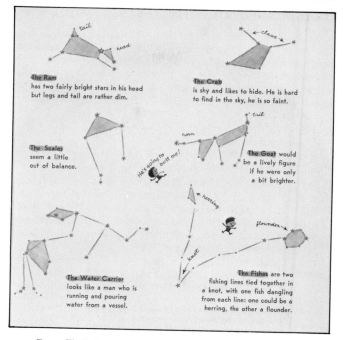

From Find the Constellations, *written and illustrated by H. A. Rey.*

poetic license. Four sets of "sky-views" show American children where to look for them in as many seasons, which also includes information on the planets and on certain aspects of space travel. His text, is clear, informal and has a gaiety which persuades the reader that astronomy is not only easy— it's fun.

Ellen Lewis Buell, in her review of "Find the Constellations," in The New York Times Book Review *(©1955 by The New York Times Company; reprinted by permission), April 3, 1955, p. 30.*

This excellent exposition of stargazing for young readers is a necessary addition to every elementary school library. Constellation diagrams are presented with and without connecting lines and are drawn for 40° N. Latitude to cover the continental United States. The use of color in these diagrams is a refreshing change from the black-and-white usually used. Key words in the text are also highlighted in color, and the text includes at critical points several self-tests with inverted answer keys. Scientific accuracy is stressed, stellar magnitudes are indicated on the diagrams, and the concept of light year is discussed. Some of the myths surrounding the names of the constellations are given. . . . The only defect in this otherwise excellent book is the use of English names for the constellations, with the Latin names given only in the glossary. Today the Latin names of the zodiac constellations are in the common vocabulary and these classical names should not be foreign to young readers.

Devlin M. Gualtieri, in his review of "Find the Constellations," in Science Books & Films *(copyright ©1977 by the American Association for the Advancement of Science), Vol. XII, No. 4, March, 1977, p. 210.*

SEE THE CIRCUS   (by H. A. Rey, 1956)

Rhymes and colored pictures, that fold open to reveal an extension of the original scene, give the young a provocative meeting with big top characters. Each verse is something to guess at—what will Kiki the clown do, who will walk the tightrope and so forth. The author's pictures are in the agreeably loose style of the illustrations for the *Curious George* books.

> *A review of "See the Circus," in* Virginia Kirkus' Service, *Vol. XXIV, No. 16, August 15, 1956, p. 569.*

It's been a long time since Mr. Rey has treated the nursery group to one of his fold-out flap books. The fortunate ones who grew up with **"Feed the Animals"** and **"Where's My Baby?"** know that these books include a simple but satisfying device, a picture with a folded flap which, when opened, reveals another picture where seemingly there was only one. Now Mr. Rey applies his ingenuity to the circus scene, supplying plenty of surprises under those flaps—a kangaroo boxer, for instance, and polar bears on a slide. Each picture page is faced with brief verses to pique one's curiosity. The entertainment value is enormous.

> *Ellen Lewis Buell, in her review of "See the Circus," in* The New York Times Book Review *(© 1956 by The New York Times Company; reprinted by permission), September 30, 1956, p. 46.*

The greatest fun for the very young will be found in the little cardboard book of H. A. Rey with a circus surprise under every flap. The creator of the *real* books on Curious George knows what children like.

> *"Horses, Colts, Crocodiles and the Whole Circus," in* New York Herald Tribune Book Review *(© I.H.T. Corporation; reprinted by permission), November 18, 1956, p. 35.**

CURIOUS GEORGE GETS A MEDAL   (by H. A. Rey, 1957; British edition as *Zozo Gets a Medal*)

For sixteen years now Curious George, that famous picture-book monkey, has been titillating children with his antics. This fourth prank begins when George receives a letter. He cannot read it, but, with a logic which small children will understand perfectly, he decides to write one. Forthwith he plunges into a pool of ink, then a roomful of soap suds, from which he emerges to make a wild dash through the countryside, on to a museum, finding temporary shelter with a stuffed dinosaur, and finally soars into the stratosphere in a space ship. It is all typical of George and, if it seems to adults a mite labored in comparison to earlier escapades, there is plenty of unexpected fun to keep children turning the pages as fast as they can to keep up with that monkey.

> *Ellen Lewis Buell, in her review of "Curious George Gets a Medal," in* The New York Times Book Review *(© 1957 by The New York Times Company; reprinted by permission), September 15, 1957, p. 30.*

In popularity, Curious George seems to be running a close second to the much-loved elephant, Babar, and children will welcome with great delight this fourth book about the engaging little monkey who is as good at getting out of trouble as he is at getting into it. . . . [George's attempts to clean up his mistakes] have as hilarious and far-reaching results as his projects

always do, and will please children as much as his earlier adventures.

> *Jennie D. Lindquist, in her review of "Curious George Gets a Medal," in* The Horn Book Magazine *(copyrighted 1957, by The Horn Book, Inc., Boston), Vol. XXXIII, No. 5, October, 1957, p. 392.*

Curious George has been a prime favorite of kindergartners for many years. Anything George does pleases them. [In **"Curious George Gets a Medal"**] George does plenty. . . . [After a series of misadventures] George then has "the happiest day of his life," receiving a medal and a title, a fine ending to satisfy his young fans. It is all rather breathless for the elderly, but they, like this reader, can be happy admiring George on the first (and only) calm page where he lies sprawled on his tummy on the floor, his thumb in his mouth. George can "explore with books!"

> *Margaret Sherwood Libby, in her review of "Curious George Gets a Medal," in* New York Herald Tribune, *Part 11 (© I.H.T. Corporation; reprinted by permission), November 17, 1957, p. 20.*

For plain, snowballing, slapstick farce, Curious George—literally and figuratively a monkey—deserves the medal he winds up with in this fourth picture adventure. It begins with spilled ink and includes an avalanche of pigs and a rocket flight, among other things, before youngsters with a broad sense of humor may be expected to stop laughing. The way one misadventure leads to another may not demand art, but it does demand skill, and this Mr. Rey has in plenty.

> *Roderick Nordell, "Widening Horizons," in* The Christian Science Monitor *(reprinted by permission from* The Christian Science Monitor; *© 1957 The Christian Science Publishing Society; all rights reserved), December 19, 1957, p. 11.**

CURIOUS GEORGE FLIES A KITE   (by Margret Rey, 1958; British edition as *Zozo Flies a Kite*)

The book's virtues are simple one and two-syllable words, a plot that doesn't out-distance a child's imagination and a full measure of colorful pictures.

> *George A. Woods, in his review of "Curious George Flies a Kite," in* The New York Times Book Review, *Part II (©1958 by The New York Times Company; reprinted by permission), November 2, 1958, p. 52.*

The Reys' popular monkey is at it again, still curious, still getting into scrapes. . . . The sequence here seems less contrived than in the last previous book and the result is that parents may be less puzzled at the appeal this little figure of farce has for their offspring.

> *Rod Nordell, "Big Pictures, Small Stories, and Easy Reading for Kindergarten and Up: Friendly Animals in Pages of Modern Design," in* The Christian Science Monitor *(reprinted by permission from* The Christian Science Monitor; *© 1958 The Christian Science Publishing Society; all rights reserved), November 6, 1958, p. 14.**

Another contender for the cheers of first readers, their parents and teachers, and one the odds all favor . . . is Curious George. . . . In a primer-like style, not noticeably different from the other books, and with H. A. Rey's same beguiling full-color illustrations three more of his adventures are told. . . . Just try to stop them from reading this one.

Margaret Sherwood Libby, in her review of "Curious George Flies a Kite," in New York Herald Tribune Book Review (© I.H.T. Corporation; reprinted by permission), November 9, 1958, p. 11.

Mrs. Rey's story suffers inevitably from the restrictions of a limited vocabulary, but then the words never counted for much in the Rey stories (in fact the most memorable of them, Ze-brology, had no words at all!). The new Zozo is pleasant enough. The monkey gets into mischief, as he has many times before, and he and the other animals (but not the humans), are drawn with a nice simple humour. Some of the colour-printing is less than good, and there are minor irritations, like the fish . . . who is described as "red" and who in the blue water turns mauve. Artistically and naturally defensible, but this is a book for small children to read for themselves.

A review of "Zozo Flies a Kite," in The Junior Book-shelf, Vol. 25, No. 2, March, 1961, p. 82.

CURIOUS GEORGE LEARNS THE ALPHABET (by H. A. Rey, 1963; British edition as *Zozo Learns the Alphabet*)

This is not an alphabet book for the very young children, but for those learning to read and write. Though irrepressible George and his creator may tweak a few educational whiskers with this one, they will satisfy many parents, and as always, entertain the children.

A review of "Curious George Learns the Alphabet," in Publishers Weekly (reprinted from the March 11, 1963 issue of Publishers Weekly, published by R. R. Bowker Company; copyright © 1963 by R. R. Bowker Company), Vol. 183, No. 10, March 11, 1963, p. 56.

Fun lies several ways here. George is still curious enough to get into mischief; and his artist-friend, the man with the yellow hat, discovering his interest in the little black marks in books, teaches him the letters of the alphabet by turning them into pictures. The game of learning becomes entertaining, for the letters are illustrated by words that start with the letters and look like those letters: F makes a fireman, D a dinosaur, h a horse, and so on. This should be as popular as the other picture books about the famous little monkey.

Virginia Haviland, in her review of "Curious George Learns the Alphabet," in The Horn Book Magazine (copyright ©1963, by The Horn Book, Inc., Boston), Vol. XXXIX, No. 2, April, 1963, p. 169.

Curious George the monkey is sure-fire for the 4-6's at least in this parent's household, and even the present longish excursion into education held in the 6-year-old all the way and the 4-year-old almost as far. The reason is that Mr. Rey "has mingled profit with pleasure," as Horace said, "by delighting the reader at once and instructing him." . . . A dab of color identifies the letter every time it appears in a sentence. As a learner George is a good teacher. After his hilarious biking, kiting, etc., this may be the beginning of a new career.

Roderick Nordell, "Pretending in Pictures—Beginning to Grow Up—Learning to Read: If I Were You," in The Christian Science Monitor (reprinted by permission from The Christian Science Monitor; © 1963

The Christian Science Publishing Society; all rights reserved), May 9, 1963, p. 2.*

H. A. Rey's irresistible simian scamp, Curious George, is back—and in an alphabet book outstanding in instruction and entertainment. . . . Mr. Rey supplements the teaching by using the letters alliteratively in parts of the text and outlining each appearance with a dab of color. And through it all are pauses for fun and frolic and George's wonderful monkeyshines. (p. 5)

George A. Woods, "A Growly Bear, Lovely Lioness—and Fun," in The New York Times Book Review, Part II (© 1963 by The New York Times Company; reprinted by permission), May 12, 1963, pp. 4-5.*

Curious George is as mischievous as ever. . . . The text is both informative and amusing. Children will love George and the highly entertaining illustrations every bit as much as his previous adventures. A delightful way to meet the alphabet.

Hope H. McGrady, in her review of "Curious George Learns the Alphabet!" in School Library Journal, an appendix to Library Journal (reprinted from the September, 1963 issue of School Library Journal, published by R. R. Bowker Co./A Xerox Corporation; copyright © 1963), Vol. 10, No. 1, September, 1963, p. 158.

CURIOUS GEORGE GOES TO THE HOSPITAL (by Margret Rey, 1966; British edition as *Zozo Goes to the Hospital*)

Hurrah! Curious George is here again, and let's throw in a couple of huzzahs because he visits a hospital, which makes his story about the most useful book you will be ordering for a long time. . . . [It] offers a bright way of preparing a child for his trip to a hospital. No book can keep his throat from aching after his tonsils are removed, but this one will go a long way in removing his fears—he will want to see the place where his friend, Curious George, had his fast and funny adventures.

A review of "Curious George Goes to the Hospital," in Publishers Weekly (reprinted from the January 31, 1966 issue of Publishers Weekly, published by R. R. Bowker Company; copyright © 1966 by R. R. Bowker Company), Vol. 189, No. 5, January 31, 1966, p. 100.

The nicest thing about the *Curious George* books is that while beginning readers are convinced that they are just enjoying themselves with George, their supervising adults are equally sure that they are learning something. Both are absolutely right. . . . Here, all of the hospital routines, from getting into bed to being taken to surgery are illustrated and described. George goes from being uncharacteristically subdued to a convalescence that is contagiously funny. . . . If your reader must be prepped for surgery, let George do it.

A review of "Curious George Goes to the Hospital," in Virginia Kirkus' Service (copyright © 1966 Virginia Kirkus' Service, Inc.), Vol. XXXIV, No. 3, February 1, 1966, p. 107.

As a book that prepares the child for the hospital this new **"Curious George"** is one of the best. . . .

There is truth and realism in the text as well as in the illustrations. George is apprehensive, tearful and uncomfortable. The book doesn't make going to the hospital a joyous thing, but its honesty will help dispel some of the fears and mysteries. Certainly it will speed the recovery process, when laughter is the very best of medicines.

> George A. Woods, in his review of "Curious George Goes to the Hospital," in The New York Times Book Review (© 1966 by The New York Times Company; reprinted by permission), March 20, 1966, p. 26.

Going to the hospital is a serious matter, and so this adventure is not as laughing-out-loud funny as other Curious George escapades. It is, however, a reassuring, realistic, and unsentimental treatment of the potentially frightening prospects of hospitalization. . . . A most appealing creature, even in his misery, George's health and spirit are ultimately restored by the cooperative efforts of the doctors and nurses. And, he is even able to cause a minor calamity in familiar Curious George style before going home.

> Nancy F. Paige, in her review of "Curious George Goes to the Hospital," in School Library Journal, an appendix to Library Journal (reprinted from the May, 1966 issue of School Library Journal, published by R. R. Bowker Co./A Xerox Corporation; copyright © 1966), Vol. 12, No. 9, May, 1966, p. 145.

How many of today's stories are designed to be read [again and again, bringing out different details and embellishments each time?] . . . Zozo, now on his seventh adventure, seems certain to survive the next generation.

In choosing a small, inquisitive monkey as their protagonist the Reys made a shrewd beginning. Zozo can plausibly be set to explore and find out about anything likely to impinge on the lives of the under fives; best of all, he fits in among the humans without jarring credulity, which is stretched beyond endurance in so many of the nursery tales. *Zozo goes to the Hospital* is a particularly successful adventure. . . . [He] is shown drinking barium, having an X-ray, sleeping in a children's ward, having injections, going to the operating theatre—everything, in fact, which could happen to a sick child. He gets into all kinds of mischief and makes the other children laugh; most blessed of all, he never actually speaks, he simply acts. There is an obvious benefit in writing so well and so wittily about the unfamiliar and potentially frightening world of the hospital, but the Reys' talents go far beyond this; their work shows real understanding of a child's mind.

> "Pictures Speak Louder than Words," in The Times Literary Supplement (© Times Newspapers Ltd. (London) 1967; reproduced from The Times Literary Supplement by permission), No. 3431, November 30, 1967, p. 1152.*

Not a classic of children's literature or children's book illustration, maybe, but in its own way this longish picture-story book is enormously successful. . . . [The] story is designed to give a cheering picture of hospital life, as well as providing comedy in the shape of Zozo's misadventures. It serves its purpose admirably; the reviewer's recently hospitalized four-year-old, and many of his envious friends, have all been enthralled by it.

> Anthea Bell, in her review of "Zozo Goes to the Hospital," in The School Librarian and School Library Review, Vol. 15, No. 3, December, 1967, p. 378.

Uri Shulevitz

1935-

American author/illustrator and illustrator of fiction.

Shulevitz, who began drawing at a very early age with the encouragement of his artistic parents, recalls much of his nomadic childhood in terms of colors and landscapes. Born in war-torn Warsaw, Shulevitz and his family wandered for several years, settled in Paris for a while, and moved to Israel when he was fifteen. It is no wonder, then, that Shulevitz's first three books, *The Moon in My Room, One Monday Morning,* and *Rain Rain Rivers,* involve travel by children; their travels, however, are imaginary flights out windows and across city and country.

Often called evocative, Shulevitz's illustrations detail city streets, country meadows, fabled forests, and their respective inhabitants with precision. He is constantly working with different methods of illustrating, including pen and ink, watercolor, Japanese reed pen, and Chinese brush. Some of his illustrations, it is said, have a very definite Oriental flavor. Many reviewers feel that Shulevitz's drawings often need no text, and if a story line is weak, the illustrations make up for it. Only in *Oh, What a Noise!* did critics find fault with both the text and illustrations.

Besides his own work, Shulevitz has illustrated works he has adapted from folk tales as well as works by other authors. Among these is Arthur Ransome's *The Fool of the World and the Flying Ship,* for which Shulevitz won the 1969 Caldecott Medal. Other awards include the 1974 Christopher Award and the 1976 International Board on Books for Young People (IBBY) Honor List for *Dawn,* and the 1978 *New York Times* Choice of Best Illustrated Children's Books of the Year, the Caldecott Medal Honor Book Award for 1980, and the award from the 1980 American Institute of Graphic Arts Book Show for *The Treasure.*

(See also *Contemporary Authors,* Vols. 9-12, rev. ed. and *Something about the Author,* Vol. 3.)

AUTHOR'S COMMENTARY

A picture book is not a silly little plaything. It is much more. Sometimes it can be everything to a child. A picture book can be a messenger of hope from the outside world. Its message, written in coded language, reaches the child in his prison, is understood by him while often hidden from the adult or the parent who is unwilling to listen to its true content or is simply insensitive to it.

It seems to me that in order to tune in on the wavelength that will penetrate prison walls and reach the child, all one has to do is tune in to a life-affirming attitude. Children are very sensitive to this, because their lives depend upon it. A destructive, life-negating attitude will not do. Neither will a saccharine approach. A picture book does not have to be deep, but it does have to be alive—whether it offers pleasure, joy, or sadness. I believe this point of view is essential to anyone interested in the field.

I first had the idea for my own picture book *Rain Rain Rivers* . . . about five years before actually starting on the illustrations;

Photograph by Leon Kotkofsky

it came and imposed itself on me in an unmistakable way. One evening I heard the patter of rain and simultaneously saw a series of images—impressions of which I immediately wrote down. This was the beginning. I thought that it was raining outside, since I could actually hear it. But when I looked out of the window, there was a clear night sky over the Greenwich Village rooftops. All this happened in a flash, and it was the seed of the future book. Subsequent work on the book—the unfolding, developing, extending, and organizing of the material—took considerably more time and effort. But everything was potentially there in the initial vision. The life substance of what was to come was there, provided I kept it alive by thought and care. As I worked on the pictures and the book gradually took shape, I began to distinguish in it the existence of different levels. In addition to the rhythm of rain, I felt in it the rhythmic beat of breathing. And so accordingly, I made the pictures large and small, small and large, as if breathing in and out; the energy accumulating, building to the final climax, and giving birth to splashes of joy. Colors in a rainbow, birds in the streets, children stamping in mud, the sky reflected in street puddles—a union of sky and earth through rain. When I reached the climactic double spread of the ocean, I felt like the ancient Greek philosopher who said: 'Everything is water,' meaning that everything in the universe consists of that substance in different states of consistency. In the ocean picture everything was brought back to its primordial state. As work was progressing, I felt that the little girl was making contact through the growth of the plant on the window sill of her room with the whole process of growth in the universe, and that in each drop of rain was contained a potential ocean, and in the child a potential of unlimited growth, energy, and freedom. All this had a definite purpose: to express what is real, to give hope, and to reinforce what is positive.

Unless we perceive and accept the fact that everything is related in a greater or lesser degree, nothing makes much sense and we are impoverishing our own resources. When I start on a new book, I try to see the images contained in the words of the story and to "listen" to the different pictorial elements and their impact, their orchestration, and whether they are expressing what I want them to. Although my natural way of thinking is through images, at some point there is a fusion of the different modes of expression. One "listens" with one's eyes, and "sees" through one's ears and fingers. For me, it is the small chaos preceding creation.

Ideas and thoughts make up our inner landscape and extend to what surrounds us. Life-affirming thoughts emanate energy that can stimulate the child to grow, expand, and even perform wonders. A picture book, like any other art form, has a life energy of its own. Take that away, and all you have left is an empty shell. Therefore, why not treat a picture book with care in order to make it grow—like a plant or an animal? One has to heed and nurture the something-that-is-there. Force it and it will die. For the process of artistic creation is an extension of the life process itself, and life itself is the supreme master. (pp. 311-12)

Uri Shulevitz, "Within the Margins of a Picture Book" (copyright © 1971 Uri Shulevitz; reprinted by permission of the author), in The Horn Book Magazine, *Vol. XLVII, No. 3, June, 1971, pp. 309-12.*

GENERAL COMMENTARY

[When he lived in Paris, Shulevitz] spent countless hours on the Quai de la Seine, browsing among the bookstalls. He was fascinated by the city, its streets, its architecture. This love of city-scapes is in his picture books; many drawings contain rich details of streets, rooftops, chimneys—the texture of a city.

At this time Uri became very much interested in movies and often sat through the same film two or three times. His books employ cinematic movement. He draws panoramic views and then focuses on portions of them. (p. 390)

Rain Rain Rivers . . . , which he both wrote and illustrated, exemplifies his realistic approach. Rainwater in its various aspects—pond, stream, river, ocean—derives its strength from being just what it is, and needs no embellishment.

Uri wants to give children stories and pictures that will be meaningful and enjoyable to them. He brings his total experience in art and literature to every book he does and considers the distinction often made between "children" and "people" as false. (p. 391)

Marjorie Zaum K., "Uri Shulevitz," in The Horn Book Magazine *(copyright © 1969 by The Horn Book, Inc., Boston), Vol. XLV, No. 4, August, 1969, pp. 389-91.*

ONE MONDAY MORNING (1967)

One rainy Monday morning in New York a small boy brightens the gray day by peopling his neighborhood with royal visitors from a thoroughly satisfying daydream. He tells how the king, the queen, and the little prince tried every day for a week to call on him. "But I wasn't home." Each day the royal party increased in number until Sunday when the entire retinue found him in. "So the little prince said, 'We just dropped in to say hello.'" The great dignity of it all is also the source of humor. The royalties and their court are immediately recognizable as playing-card figures. Their sumptuous clothes and stylized forms sparkle against accurately drawn interior and exterior views of crumbling, fading apartments. . . . [This] book provides the thoughtful adult with a commentary on the motive and substance of daydreams. Children will be able to find and under-

Oceans are swelling,
Melting the skies.

From Rain Rain Rivers, *written and illustrated by Uri Shulevitz.*

stand clues in the pictures to the way the boy transforms many real objects into dream material. Beautiful, easy to read and fun, with an interplay between text and pictures always sought for, seldom encountered. (pp. 64-5)

> *Lillian N. Gerhardt, in her review of "One Monday Morning," in* School Library Journal, *an appendix to* Library Journal *(reprinted from the April, 1967 issue of* School Library Journal, *published by R. R. Bowker Co./A Xerox Corporation; copyright © 1967), Vol. 13, No. 8, April, 1967, pp. 64-5.*

Is it a rainy Monday morning where you live? Do you have a rainy Monday morning compulsion to pull the covers over your head and forget about the whole thing? Look at **"One Monday Morning"** instead. If a small boy in a New York tenement can have kings and queens come to brighten his day by calling on his small boy's imagination, think of the people yours could conjure up: David Rockefeller if you're feeling broke: Yves Montand, if you're lonely. On second thought, you would be wise to call on Mr. Shulevitz to put on your fantasy; he's a great stage manager, as this delightful picture book testifies.

> *A review of "One Monday Morning," in* Publishers Weekly *(reprinted from the April 10, 1967 issue of* Publishers Weekly, *published by R. R. Bowker Company; copyright © 1967 by R. R. Bowker Company), Vol. 191, No. 15, April 10, 1967, p. 80.*

Mr. Shulevitz's illustrations are very much his own and he offers a colorfully pleasing contrast with his haughtily humorous entourage amid the drabness of crumbling tenement walkups.

> *George A. Woods, in his review of "One Monday Morning," in* The New York Times Book Review, *Part II (© 1967 by The New York Times Company; reprinted by permission), May 7, 1967, p. 53.*

The idea of the story is so childlike, the telling of it so effortless, and the book executed with such distinction that it belongs naturally among the true picture books we seem always to have had, like *Clever Bill* by William Nicholson, *Millions of Cats* by Wanda Gág, and *In the Forest* by Marie Hall Ets. A book no child should miss.

> *Ruth Hill Viguers, in her review of "One Monday Morning," in* The Horn Book Magazine *(copyright © 1967, by The Horn Book, Inc., Boston), Vol. XLIII, No. 3, June, 1967, p. 338.*

One of the nicest read-aloud books about the imaginative play of a small, solitary child to come along in a while. The setting is urban, inner city, lower class; a small boy is seen alternately engaged in such humdrum occupations as waiting at a laundromat or riding on a subway, and such a fanciful, glamorous one as being visited by a royal family whose party, cumulating through the week, is a startling, glowing, visual contrast to the realistic scenes.

> *Zena Sutherland, in her review of "One Monday Morning," in her* The Best in Children's Books: The University of Chicago Guide to Children's Literature, 1966-1972, *edited by Zena Sutherland (reprinted by permission of The University of Chicago Press; © 1973 by The University of Chicago),* University of Chicago Press, *1973, p. 362.*

From One Monday Morning, *written and illustrated by Uri Shulevitz.*

RAIN RAIN RIVERS (1969)

Very well, go ahead and sue me. I will still maintain (as of today—who knows what glories tomorrow's mail will bring?) that Uri Shulevitz's newest picture book is this year's loveliest picture book. It's so lovely that I don't want to spoil your delight by talking about it. As an old friend, I want you to be surprised by your joy when you look at it.

> *A review of "Rain Rain Rivers," in* Publishers Weekly *(reprinted from the September 15, 1969 issue of* Publishers Weekly, *published by R. R. Bowker Company, a Xerox company; copyright © 1969 by Xerox Corporation), Vol. 196, No. 11, September 15, 1969, p. 61.*

If the year were to end right here, Uri Shulevitz should win the Caldecott Medal for the most distinguished picture book. . . . In **"Rain Rain Rivers"** you can *feel* the dampness, the trickle running down your neck. There's contrast and cumulation. Shulevitz begins with the patter of little drops on windows and roofs, then the rain slants downward all over town against a background of huddling apartments, rushing and gushing out of downspouts. A few people scurry through the storm, a momentary suggestion of their passing reflected in the rain-swept street. And it's raining in the country, too, as Shulevitz shows, on hills and fields and ponds and mountain ranges. Now rills and rivers race to the sea where "Waves billow and roll, / Rush, splash and surge, / Rage, roar and rise."

The author-illustrator gets good mileage out of simple declaratives, although his text sometimes does tend to lapse into R.L.S. writing haiku verse—there is even a suggestion of Japanese art in those billowing waves. Yet over all there is beauty and exhilaration for after the rain, as children know, there's always sunshine.

> *George A. Woods, in his review of "Rain Rain Rivers," in* The New York Times Book Review *(© 1969 by The New York Times Company; reprinted by permission), September 21, 1969, p. 30.*

Uri Shulevitz . . . has picked a subject that limits his use of color but allows full scope to his gift with widespread views of the landscape. In **"Rain Rain Rivers"** . . . he takes that most desolate sight—a teardrop of rain drizzling down the window—and opens our eyes to a gleaming, freshening view of rain. . . .

> *Pamela Marsh, "A Glance at the Winners," in* The Christian Science Monitor *(reprinted by permission from* The Christian Science Monitor; *(© 1969 The Christian Science Publishing Society; all rights reserved), November 6, 1969, p. B1.**

Even more distinguished than his earlier Caldecott winning book, is this lovely buoyant hymn to the wonders of rain on cities, mountains, meadows, and sea. This lovely book brings a renewal of life and spirit—even as the rain itself.

> *Elizabeth Minot Graves, in her review of "Rain Rain Rivers," in* Commonweal *(copyright © 1969 Commonweal Publishing Co., Inc.; reprinted by permission of Commonweal Publishing Co., Inc.), Vol. XCI, No. 1, November 21, 1969, p. 253.*

OH WHAT A NOISE! (1971)

Another disappointment, considering Uri Shulevitz's recent achievements in "The Fool of the World and the Flying Ship" and **"Rain Rain Rivers."** He has departed from his usual style to create a pop art book in the vein of Maurice Sendak's "In

the Night Kitchen." The story is adapted from an English nonsense poem about a boy who tries to postpone bedtime by imagining a parade of noisy animals in his house. The result is not a book for parents and children to enjoy at bedtime reading.

> *A review of "Oh What a Noise!" in* Publishers Weekly *(reprinted from the October 4, 1971 issue of* Publishers Weekly, *published by R. R. Bowker Company, a Xerox company; copyright © 1971 by Xerox Corporation), Vol. 200, No. 14, October 4, 1971, p. 60.*

The verse is rhythmic but nothing extraordinary; the drawings, somewhat akin to those of Maurice Sendak, range from cute to grotesque. And why does the author offer advertisements for himself on the billboards in his sketches? (p. 3)

> *Michael J. Bandler, "Tried and True," in* Book World—Chicago Tribune *(© 1971 Postrib Corp.; reprinted by permission of* Chicago Tribune*), November 7, 1971, pp. 2-3.**

The descriptions of the rather commonplace noises and noise-making agents are not particularly original or arresting, while the visual accompaniment is more one of mindlessness than mirth: full-color tempera double-page spreads grate on readers' nerves with a cacophony of myriad neon colors and loutish figures bumping loudly together.

> *Melinda Schroeder, in her review of "Oh What a Noise!" in* School Library Journal, *an appendix to* Library Journal *(reprinted from the January, 1972 issue of* School Library Journal, *published by R. R. Bowker Co./A Xerox Corporation; copyright © 1972), Vol. 18, No. 5, January, 1972, p. 53.*

From Soldier and Tsar in the Forest: A Russian Tale, *translated by Richard Lourie, illustrated by Uri Shulevitz.*

SOLDIER AND TSAR IN THE FOREST: A RUSSIAN TALE (1972)

Spectacularly illustrated, the unspectacular tale of a runaway soldier's promotion to general after he spends a night in the forest with the disguised tsar, whom he saves from a band of robbers by whacking off the intruders' heads. There is both suspense and humor in the overnight adventure (to which Shulevitz gives an ominous intensity) but little of the rhythmic language or the richness of detail and diverting characters that distinguished Ransome's *The Fool of the World and the Flying Ship*. . . . Some of Shulevitz' outdoor scenes resemble those he did for the previous tale, but there are also views of the night forest with haunting blues and mauves added to the natural colors, and depictions of cottage and castle, with elaborated folk art figures and motifs, that make muted, shadowed use of the heavy black lines and fluorescent rainbow colors of *Oh What a Noise*. . . . Shulevitz brings all these styles together with aplomb and unabashed artifice, signifying a considerable advance over *Oh What a Noise* but perhaps a decadent departure from the exhilarating fresh air loveliness of *The Fool of the World*.

> *A review of "Soldier and Tsar in the Forest," in* Kirkus Reviews *(copyright © 1972 The Kirkus Service, Inc.), Vol. XL, No. 16, August 15, 1972, p. 937.*

Soldier and Tsar in the Forest [is] . . . a robust tale of a young man with common sense and luck who unknowingly befriends the tsar and lives to appreciate it. Shulevitz's lush green fields, glistening forests and cheerful interiors are those of an artist enamored of color. The book should be a strong contender in awards competitions.

> *Michael J. Bandler, "First to Look At . . . ," in* Book World—Washington Post *(copyright © 1972 The Washington Post Company), November 5, 1972, p. 3.**

A tale full of punishment and reward, of villainy and innocence, but the honors belong to Mr. Shulevitz, who makes you feel the rough planking inside a peasant's cottage, the pounding hooves of the Czar's retinue . . . the loneliness of the vast, dark woods.

> *A review of "Soldier and Tsar in the Forest," in* The New York Times Book Review, Part II *(© 1972 by The New York Times Company; reprinted by permission), November 5, 1972 p. 30.*

THE MAGICIAN   (1973)

In this happy retelling of an Isaac Loeb Peretz Yiddish folk tale, "The Magician," artist Uri Shulevitz will add lustre to that mysterious figure's elusive charm. . . .

Unlike much of his recent picture-book illustration, which has been large scale, bold in outline and intentionally strident in color, Shulevitz's drawings here are snapshot-sized, meticulously executed in black and white. Sometimes softened by delicate ink cross-hatchings, occasionally spotlighted by patches of untouched white paper, the pictures provide archetypal vignettes of a now-extinct Jewish community life. At once both somber and gay (Elijah's radiant smile could brighten all of East Europe), bleak yet exuding an ethnic warmth, the illustrations have a dreamlike, mythic quality. If the Shulevitz conception is at all flawed, it lies in the direction of over-generalization: we do not learn more than we had already pictured

in our mind's eye about life in the Old Country. Nonetheless, Elijah has at last made a welcome appearance at a fitting Passover feast—as the hero of a thoroughly happy Jewish holiday tale.

> *Selma Lanes, in her review of "The Magician," in* The New York Times Book Review *(© 1973 by The New York Times Company; reprinted by permission), April 15, 1973, p. 8 .*

Disarming in its simplicity, the quiet tale of faith tells of the visit of the prophet Elijah to a small village on the eve of Passover. Disguised as a ragged magician, he performed many wonderful tricks for the people, but most wonderful of all, he sought out the humblest home in the village and rewarded the faith of an old couple with a true Passover feast. Black-and-white drawings, effectively deepened with cross-hatching, illustrate the legend with a spare strength that is a perfect complement to the text.

> *Beryl Robinson, in her review of "The Magician," in* The Horn Book Magazine *(copyright © 1973 by The Horn Book, Inc., Boston), Vol. XLIX, No. 3, June, 1973, p. 262.*

[Shulevitz's] pictures in black and white capture the homely quality of peasant life and the raffish charm of the magician who comes to visit the village. . . . Nicely retold, handsomely illustrated, a story to read alone, read aloud, and tell.

> *Zena Sutherland, in her review of "The Magician," in* Bulletin of the Center for Children's Books *(reprinted by permission of The University of Chicago Press; © 1973 by The University of Chicago), Vol. 26, No. 11, July-August, 1973, p. 177.*

The wisdom and sincerity of Jewish folk tales is portrayed simply and descriptively. Essentially, this is a book to be ad-

From The Magician: An Adaptation from the Yiddish of I. L. Peretz, *written and illustrated by Uri Shulevitz.*

mired more by adults than children: the stylised black and white illustrations have a formal appeal to a sophisticated taste rather than to the enthusiasm of the young child. They are reminiscent of classic woodcuts, attractive in their restraint and formality. (pp. 26-7)

> *A review of "The Magician," in* The Junior Bookshelf, *Vol. 39, No. 1, February, 1975, pp. 26-7.*

DAWN (1974)

Shulevitz' deep-blue, oval watercolors draw you into the still, quiet spot "under a tree by the lake" where "an old man and his grandson curl up in their blankets." Gradually, as dawn approaches, the blues become lighter and the forms more distinct. Slowly the moonlit lake shivers, and "vapors start to rise." The man and boy get up, light a fire for breakfast, and roll up their blankets. As they move off in their rowboat, "suddenly the mountain and the lake are green" and the hushed, misty scenes give way to one double-page abstraction of the spectral response to sunrise that recalls Marvell's "annihilating all that's made / To a green thought in a green shade." Perhaps not every child will be receptive to this lovely impressionistic book, but on the ohter hand it is hard not to be enveloped by Shulevitz' mood of muted serenity.

> *A review of "Dawn," in* Kirkus Reviews *(copyright © 1974 The Kirkus Service, Inc.), Vol. XLII, No. 20, October 15, 1974, p. 1100.*

Evocative is the word for this briefly written impression of the dawn. The soft variety of blues pale and change the mood and color of a circumscribed world: a tree, a mountain, a lake to sudden brilliant morning. Although the two human figures at times lack the flow of their surroundings the total effect of these watercolors is gently oriental and satisfying.

> *Karla Kuskin, in her review of "Dawn," in* The New York Times Book Review *(© 1974 by The New York Times Company; reprinted by permission), November 3, 1974, p. 57.*

["Dawn"] is a series of marvelously evocative images. . . .

Really young children might pine for incident, but my paint-loving seven-year-old sits in hushed fascination over the color-shifts in each beautiful watercolor page.

> *Susan Cooper, in her review of "Dawn" in* The Christian Science Monitor *(reprinted by permission from The Christian Science Monitor; © 1974 The Christian Science Publishing Society; all rights reserved), November 6, 1974, p. 11.*

[Dawn] is the kind of children's book that may not break circulation records at the library desk, but is unquestionably destined for illustrator honors. . . .

The text . . . tells the simple story of an old man and his grandson waking, then rowing across a lake at morning. The blue and indigo sky lightens, birds stir, and the pictures open out before the eyes. The visual climax is truly stunning, and the last page almost sighs. "Ahhh . . .". (p. 7)

> *Pat Hyatt, "Kookie Monsters," in* Book World—The Washington Post *(© 1974, The Washington Post), November 10, 1974, pp. 5, 7.**

Beautiful, beautiful. A text as hushed and simple as the still, cool hour it describes is almost a poem of dawn. And the

A bird calls.
Another answers.

From Dawn, *written and illustrated by Uri Shulevitz.*

pictures, in soft, dark blue that springs into lush, brilliant green and blue when daylight comes, are lovely and evocative.

> *Zena Sutherland, in her review of "Dawn," in* Bulletin of the Center for Children's Books *(reprinted by permission of The University of Chicago Press; © 1975 by The University of Chicago), Vol. 28, No. 8, April, 1975, p. 138.*

The dust jacket states that the creator of this evocative mood book was inspired by the lines of an ancient Chinese verse. But he also must have been dazzled by the miracle of dawn breaking over a wooded lake, the sun suddenly bursting forth above a mountain that "stands guard" over the water. . . . The purity of the hues, well-produced on ample spreads, the subtle graphic development from scene to scene, and the sharply focused simplicity of the few words make this a true art experience.

> *Virginia Haviland, in her review of "Dawn," in* The Horn Book Magazine *(copyright © 1975 by the Horn Book, Inc., Boston), Vol. LI, No. 2, April, 1975, p. 141.*

THE TREASURE (1978)

A spare text and magnificent illustrations make Shulevitz's latest picture book a very special one. . . . The simple but dignified narrative provides the perfect frame for Shulevitz's pictures, which depict traditional eastern European cities and countryside in subtly glowing colors. The 17 paintings are of varying sizes, set off by ample amounts of white space, to reinforce the stately rhythm of the story. The perfect blend of words and pictures is supported by excellent bookmaking to make this one a must purchase for any picture-book collection.

Margaret A. Dorsey, in her review of "The Treasure," in School Library Journal *(reprinted from the April, 1979 issue of* School Library Journal, *published by R. R. Bowker Co./A Xerox Corporation; copyright © 1979), Vol. 25, No. 8, April, 1979, p. 48.*

Uri Shulevitz combines his superb talents as a folklorist and an illustrator to retell an age-old tale of quest and discovery. When a poor man named Isaac sets out to learn whether a recurring dream of his is true—that a treasure awaits him at the capital city's royal bridge—he does not know what to expect. But his journey leads him through apparent disappointment to a surprising revelation: that "Sometimes one must travel far to discover what is near". Once again, as in his earlier adaptation, **"The Magician,"** Shulevitz proves himself a storyteller loyal to the spirit of his tale. His unassuming text is wonderfully enhanced by illustrations of astonishing luminosity and richness. A crucial quality one finds in forming in many of Shulevitz's books is that of faith—in a just God, in humanity, in the possibility of dreams beyond a pinched and sometimes cruel reality. Here that faith is working in abundance. This book is a treasure.

William Jaspersohn, "Snatch Up, Catch Up, Match Up," in The Christian Science Monitor *(reprinted by permission of the author), April 9, 1979, p. B10.**

"The Treasure" . . . is a simple fable about a poor man from an Eastern European ghetto. . . . But so stiff and rudimentary is the tale that we never care very much about the traveler (we never see his face in close-up), and the careful illustrations, despite their fine craftsmanship and elegance, don't prevent the book from dwindling into boredom. (pp. 29, 46)

Harold C. K. Rice, "The Picture Books," in The New York Times Book Review *(© 1979 by The New York Times Company; reprinted by permission), April 29, 1979, pp. 29, 46-7.**

Rich, full-color illustrations provide a fresh and vigorous interpretation of the familiar story of a poor man who, inspired by a recurring dream, journeys to a far city to look for a treasure—only to be advised to return home and find it. Although the story is known in many cultures, the retelling suggests the Hassidic tradition, when the grateful Isaac, having found the treasure, builds a house of prayer and inscribes: *"Sometimes one must travel far to discover what is near."* The precept is logically integrated into the narrative, so the tale does not seem didactic. The eastern European influence is extended in the illustrations, which depict the aging Isaac against constantly changing backdrops while documenting his travels from crooked and crowded streets, through vast timberlands and fields, to royal dwellings. Each picture is an artistic entity, the gemlike colors recalling illuminated books of hours; yet in sequence the individual paintings are part of a whole which becomes a moving and dynamic series of images suggesting an imagi-

From The Treasure, *written and illustrated by Uri Shulevitz.*

native synthesis of cinematic and painterly techniques. Thoughtfully designed, the book is modestly scaled to suit the essential simplicity of the story. (pp. 295-96)

Mary M. Burns, in her review of "The Treasure," in The Horn Book Magazine *(copyright © 1979 by The Horn Book, Inc., Boston), Vol. LV, No. 3, June, 1979, pp. 295-96.*

Certainly one of the most beautiful books reviewed [by doctoral students at the University of Houston] was **The Treasure** by Uri Shulevitz. . . . In the illustrations, Shulevitz successfully blends the calm beauty of **Dawn** . . . with the more vibrant colors in *The Fool of the World and the Flying Ship.* . . . The result is one of the finest picture books published recently. (pp. 224-25)

A review of "The Treasure" (copyright 1979 by the International Reading Association, Inc.; reprinted with permission of the International Reading Association), in The Reading Teacher, *Vol. 33, No. 2, November, 1979, pp. 224-25.*

The spare sentences and delicately tinted drawings, intelligible to all but the youngest children, seem almost transparent. But their power of suggestion is remarkable.

Annalyn Swan, in her review of "The Treasure," in Newsweek *(copyright 1979, by Newsweek, Inc.; all rights reserved; reprinted by permission), Vol. XCIV, No. 25, December 17, 1979, p. 94.*

Shel Silverstein

1932-

(Also writes under the pseudonym Uncle Shelby) American author/illustrator, poet, cartoonist, and songwriter.

Silverstein combines humorous poetry and reflective prose with simple, skillful line drawings to interpret the moods of children and adults. Several of his books have been best-sellers, and publishers regard him as a phenomenon because of his appeal to all ages. In his poetry collections, carefree verse reveals Silverstein's ability to be funny, tender, philosophical, and ridiculous. At times he pokes fun at parental authority and often dares to treat bizarre topics such as a babysitter who literally sits on the baby, a camel who wears a bra, and a customer who orders broiled face for dinner. Silverstein's allegories *The Giving Tree, The Missing Piece,* and *The Missing Piece Meets the Big O* lend themselves to various interpretations and have received mixed reviews. In spite of some negative reception from critics, these works remain popular with children and teachers as well as with college students, who regard Silverstein as a literary cult figure.

A prolific artist, Silverstein also creates cartoons for *Playboy* magazine and writes humorous country-flavored songs such as the Johnny Cash hit, "A Boy Named Sue." Several poems in his books for children are adapted from his song lyrics. Reviewers feel that he obtains much of his inspiration from nursery rhymes, fairy tales, and such poets as Edward Lear, A. A. Milne, and Dr. Seuss, with whom they compare him. Although some critics regard his poetry as witty but minor, they consider Silverstein's insight into children's peeves, fears, and sense of silliness to be a rare gift. His black-and-white illustrations are described by reviewers as often delightful and sometimes macabre. Often they directly complete a poem, as in "The Loser": a boy who loses his head and can't see to find it decides to sit down on a rock and rest. The reader shares a joke with the author, who depicts the boy really sitting on his head. Silverstein also uses type and layout to increase the humorous effect of his illustrations.

Two of Silverstein's books revolve around simply drawn geometric shapes which critics feel sensitively represent human emotion. Widely accepted as parables of adaptation and growth, *The Missing Piece* and *The Missing Piece Meets the Big O* probe the quest for fulfillment in relationships. In the first book, a circle minus a pie-shaped wedge rolls along looking for its lost piece only to discover that it isn't needed, while in the sequel the pie-shaped wedge finds that it, too, can get along on its own. *The Giving Tree,* a fable in which a tree gives everything it has to a boy over the course of his lifetime, is perhaps Silverstein's most well-known work. Despite the public's initial lack of interest, the book eventually raised Silverstein's name to the best-seller list. It has recently fallen into some critical disfavor because of its theme of exploitation. Though popular, critics feel that these works present a negative attitude toward human relationships and may be too advanced for children. Nevertheless, many reviewers regard Silverstein, with his repertoire of hilarious nonsense, provocative fables, and expressive drawings, as unique in the children's literature of our time.

(See also *Something about the Author,* Vol. 27.)

AUTHOR'S COMMENTARY

[Silverstein has said that he] was happy to see the revival of his first children's book, "Lafcadio, the Lion Who Shot Back," which . . . "has more story" in it than his subsequent books. Indeed, two of them, "The Giving Tree" and "The Missing Piece," are almost parables, with a kind of wise-fool simplicity that leaves them open to a variety of interpretations. "The Giving Tree" tells of a boy and a tree. The tree keeps giving to the boy—first, her shade, then her fruit, then her branches, then her trunk, until finally there is only a stump left. The boy—by now a weary old man—sits on the stump: "And the tree was happy." . . .

Many readers saw a religious symbolism in the altruistic tree; ministers preached sermons on "The Giving Tree"; it was discussed in Sunday schools.

Now Mr. Silverstein says of the book merely that "It's just a relationship between two people; one gives and the other takes." Similarly, he resists reading a moral into "The Missing Piece," in which a sort of wheel with a slice taken out of it rolls along, singing a song, looking for the missing piece. After rejecting several bad fits, it finds a compatible wedge, only to realize it can no longer sing its happy-go-lucky song. "I could have ended the book there," he says, meaning where the piece seemed to have found its mate. "But instead it goes off singing: it's still looking for the missing piece. That's the madness of the book, the disturbing part of it."

Happy endings, magic solutions in children's books, he says, "create an alienation" in the child who reads them. "The child asks why don't I have this happiness thing you're telling me about, and comes to think when his joy stops that he has failed, that it won't come back." By the same token, creating mythic heroes "20 feet tall" places an impossible burden on the child, who feels he can never live up to the image. . . .

He does not object to fantasy for children, but it should be "fantasy presented as fantasy, not a life possibility."

Richard R. Lingeman, "The Third Mr. Silverstein," in The New York Times Book Review *(© 1978 by The New York Times Company; reprinted by permission), April 30, 1978, p. 57.*

LAFCADIO, THE LION WHO SHOT BACK (1963)

"And the young lion, he just yawned and picked up his gun." This particular jungle fellow, later to be known as Lafcadio the Great, had kept the gun from an encounter with a hunter and had, with practice, become quite a marksman. His post-jungle career with the circus leads him into some funny (and perhaps sad) affectations. A wild, free-wheeling, slangy tale that most children and many parents will enjoy immensely.

A review of "Lafcadio, the Lion Who Shot Back," in Publishers Weekly *(reprinted from the October 28, 1963 issue of* Publishers Weekly, *published by R. R. Bowker Company; copyright © 1963 by R. R. Bowker Company), Vol. 184, No. 18, October 28, 1963, p. 52.*

Daft, that's what. A nonsense story about utter success, illustrated by drawings that have a Thurber quality. . . . A most amusing book, written in an easy, mildly mad style. . . .

> *Zena Sutherland, in her review of "Uncle Shelby's Story of Lafcadio, the Lion Who Shot Back," in* Bulletin of the Center for Children's Books *(reprinted by permission of The University of Chicago Press; copyright 1964 by the University of Chicago), Vol. XVII, No. 5, January, 1964, p. 85.*

THE GIVING TREE (1964)

"The Giving Tree" begins "Once there was a tree . . ." (Dots Shel's) and goes on for 50 more pages with a simple tale, illustrated in graceful cartoon style by the author. There was a boy who played in the tree, gathering its leaves, swinging on its branches, eating its apples. When the boy grew older he lay in the shade of the tree with a girl and carved initials in a heart. Yet older—a young man—he took the tree's branches to build a house. As an old man he needed a boat to get away from it all, so the tree said cut me down and make a boat. So we have a stump. Along comes the boy, now an old, old man, and the ex-tree says, "Come, Boy, sit down. Sit down and rest." And the tree was happy.

My interpretation is that that was one dum-dum of a tree, giving everything and getting nothing in return. Once beyond boyhood, the boy is unpleasant and ungrateful, and I wouldn't give him the time of day, much less my bole. But there's a public out there who think otherwise. . . .

The book, to me, is simply a backup of "more blessed to give than to receive." My wife's interpretation, not surprisingly, is that the tree represents a mother, giving and giving with no expectation of return. Whatever it is, it touches a sensitive point clearly and swiftly. . . .

> *William Cole, "About Alice, a Rabbit, a Tree . . . ," in* The New York Times Book Review *(© 1973 by The New York Times Company; reprinted by permission), September 9, 1973, p. 8.* *

I've just discovered a new and . . . horrible example [of sexism] in Shel Silverstein's *The Giving Tree*. . . .

The Giving Tree has a broad appeal to readers. With its engaging drawings, seemingly sophisticated theme, and witty expression, it becomes a much more dangerous book than Whitney Darrow Jr.'s pedantic pre-school picture book [*I'm Glad I'm a Boy, I'm Glad I'm a Girl*]. . . . (p. 1)

Instead of being a "parable on the joy of giving," the book impressed me as a dressed-up version of the "happy slave" myth where the "good slave," "loyal dog" or "old family retainer" finds satisfaction by serving his or her master. Their service is doubly enobling—so goes the myth—since it requires them to sacrifice their own lives for their masters' well-being.

By choosing the female pronoun for the all-giving tree and the male pronoun for the all-taking boy, it is clear that the author did indeed have a prototypical master/slave relationship in mind. In this male supremicist's fantasy, we see the "idealized" relationship of mother/son, wife/husband, mistress/lover. . . .

I should add that I would find this book objectionable even if the author were to use a neutral "it" in referring to the tree. This is a tale of man's selfish plundering of the environment. The boy uses up every part of the tree; he feels no obligation to share [what he has with others nor to plant] another tree for future generations. . . .

How frightening that little boys and girls who read *The Giving Tree* will encounter this glorification of female selflessness and male selfishness! Hopefully a liberated adult will be nearby to help them discover ways of giving and loving that enrich *both* partners. (p. 8)

> *Barbara A. Schram, "Misgivings about 'The Giving Tree'," in* Interracial Books for Children *(reprinted by permission of* The Bulletin—Interracial Books for Children, *1841 Broadway, New York, N.Y. 10023), Vol. 5, No. 5, 1974, pp. 1, 8.*

A clever, unlikely and warm story about the relation between a human being and a tree, from boyhood until the end of life. Silverstein teaches his lessons gently and unobtrusively.

> *A review of "The Giving Tree," in* Book World— The Washington Post *(© 1978, The Washington Post), May 14, 1978, p. G1.*

Silverstein's story is widely appreciated as a glorification of the generosity of the tree which is always giving of itself for the life of another creature. On careful reading, however, the boy is pictured as totally self-centered and selfish. The tree, in its constant giving of itself, seems to be rewarding this selfishness in a kind of masochistic way. It passively allows itself to be used, even destroyed by the selfishness of the other. Children will invariably identify with the child-man who is like them rather than with the "generous" tree. The child is portrayed as callously using, using, using.

This book is widely used in classes and liturgies for children. Adults should be aware that the natural identification for the child is with the boy in the story, not the "generous" tree, and should handle the story accordingly.

> *Jean Marie Hiesberger and Pat McLaughlin, in their review of "The Giving Tree," in* New Catholic World, *Vol. 222, No. 1328, March-April, 1979, p. 92.*

A GIRAFFE AND A HALF (1964)

"Uncle Shelby" has done it again. With the delightful style and flair of "**Lafcadio, the Lion Who Shot Back**" we are treated to a delicious bit of nonsense. This book is definitely superior to the author's "**Who Wants a Cheap Rhinoceros?**" which enjoyed incongruity, but lacked sufficient story line. The present book has definite development which compels the reader to continue. The pictures are of the usual excellent quality. They reveal additional delightful details each time they are re-examined, and will charm the readers. Such items as the snake nibbling the dragon's tail and the Boy Scout Troop flag with at least 15 digits, the overpacked knapsack (including, among other items, a canoe complete with paddle), are just a few of the author's humorous touches. The rhymes, which are so wonderfully illustrated, are not in the least forced. . . .

Good nonsense books are always welcome, especially those that maintain interest upon repeated re-reading. "Uncle Shelby" has demonstrated considerable talent with this difficult form and "**A Giraffe and a Half**" will increase his troop of admirers. (p. 14)

> *A review of "A Giraffe and a Half," in* Young Readers Review *(copyright © 1965 Young Readers Review), Vol. 1, No. 7, March, 1965, pp. 14-15.*

[The very young] will know after the first glance at *A Giraffe and a Half* that giggles are in store. The strong black and white drawings are hilarious, showing on each successive page a new encumbrance added to the giraffe and a half. The brief cumulative rhyme builds up in a House-that-Jack-Built fashion, then shrinks again until nothing is left but the giraffe and a half. Children will grin happily and point out every change in the pictures. Good nursery fun.

> *A review of "The Giving Tree" and "A Giraffe and a Half," in* Book Week—New York Herald Tribune *(© 1965, The Washington Post), March 21, 1965, p. 17.*

Shel Silverstein has cunningly adapted old formulas to new uses in *A Giraffe and a half.* This is a cumulative nonsense story based on short, similar monosyllables. 'If you glued a rose to the tip of his nose you would have a giraffe and a half with a rat in his hat looking cute in a suit with a rose on his nose' and so on till a turning point is reached and the story unwinds again. This kind of humour, emphasised by the American-Mad illustrations, seems to me very adult, but I am always being assured that children love it. Anyhow, here is a book properly designed to make reading easy at the earliest stage.

> *Margery Fisher, in her review of "A Giraffe and a Half," in her* Growing Point, *Vol. 5, No. 1, May, 1966, p. 715.*

WHERE THE SIDEWALK ENDS   (1974)

Here's a volume of verse for children labeled "all ages." It's either the ultimate in silliness or the ultimate in good sense. Quite possibly the latter.

Take it from the top age group. There are a number of rollicking patter songs that a parent could well enjoy tripping off for a child audience. Consider ["**Sarah Cynthia Sylvia Stout**"].

A magnificent catalogue of garbage that's fun to read aloud and that should delight any youngster who's been collecting those unofficial camp and kindergarten chants on the side. In fact, for the younger members of "all ages" there's quite a bit of flouting of traditional niceties scattered throughout. Probably a good thing. For the middle members, things tend to go squishy. Take the opening stanza of the title poem. . . . (p. 24)

Echo of the Beatles.

Shel Silverstein is, in fact, a song writer himself (. . . several of the poems in this book are adapted from song lyrics). . . . And a cartoonist. . . . And a philosopher (author of a goopy morality lesson called "**The Giving Tree**" that has become a sort of second-string "Jonathan Livingston Seagull"). In short, what his press releases call a Renaissance Man.

The trouble is he isn't. Not even a 19th-century eccentric. He's a very facile 20th-century man with a sense of where the market is. The result is a sense of derivativeness. Sarah Cynthia Sylvia Stout, for example, despite the different nature of her problem, seems a descendant of A. A. Milne's James James Morrison Morrison Weatherby George Dupree, who took great care of his mother, though he was only 3. A poem called "**Dreadful**" (an outspoken working-off of sibling rivalries) is straight out of the "Ruthless Rhymes for Heartless Homes" . . . of Harry Graham. . . . (pp. 24-5)

The nonsense rhymes are reminiscent of Dr. Seuss (with perhaps a touch of Edward Lear, though I'll give points to the drawings of either Seuss or Lear). . . .

One last carping comment: Light verse—especially light verse that slides over into logical nonsense—has to be impeccable. And Shel Silverstein is very sloppy about false rhymes. Here's

a sequence from "**The Crocodile's Toothache**": "guess / West / address / less." And one from "**No Difference**" (I've reversed the order): "mite / light / white / light / right / light / giant / light." Ira Gershwin could do better than that without half trying.

But all that aside, there's some nice, lively stuff in here, good for reading aloud on a sleety weekend afternoon. Just don't make it the only book of verse on the children's shelves. (p. 25)

> *Sherwin D. Smith, in his review of "Where the Sidewalk Ends," in* The New York Times Book Review *(© 1974 by The New York Times Company; reprinted by permission), November 3, 1974, pp. 24-5.*

Classic children's books don't come along each season, but this book *is* one. . . . There are skillful, sometimes grotesque line drawings with each of the 127 poems, which run in length from a few lines to a couple of pages. The poems are tender, funny, sentimental, philosophical, and ridiculous in turn, and they're for all ages, including mine. There are occasional indelicacies, which are surprising to find in a children's book, such as an anti-nose-picking poem and one about belching—but that's life.

> *William Cole, in his review of "Where the Sidewalk Ends," in* Saturday Review/World *(© 1974 Saturday Review Magazine Co.; reprinted by permission), Vol. 2, No. 6, November 30, 1974, p. 26.*

The poems are raucous and zany, and the drawings sprawl delightfully across the page. In at least nine instances, poem and illustration are so interdependent that the child—or adult, for that matter—has the pleasure of making connections and sharing a joke with the poet. (p. 166)

Silverstein has gifts rarely found in children's poets, most particularly the gift of direct communication with the roguish, playful, and uncivilized tendencies of healthy children. In many of the poems he establishes a tone of delicious complicity with the child's disobedient, naughty, asocial, or even wicked impulses. (p. 167)

> *A. Harris Fairbanks, "Children's Verse: Four Styles," in* Children's Literature: Annual of The Modern Language Association Seminar on Children's Literature and The Children's Literature Association, *Vol. 4, edited by Francelia Butler (© 1975 by Francelia Butler; all rights reserved), Temple University Press, 1975, pp. 165-72.**

Steeped in folklore, fairy tales, and songs that sing themselves, Shel Silverstein spins out poems that giggle and snicker their way across the pages of *Where the Sidewalk Ends.* With creatures from the never-heard, Ickle Me Pickle Me, Tickle Me too, the Mustn'ts, Hector the Collector and Sarah Cynthia Sylvia Stout (who would not take the garbage out), Silverstein's funny bone seems to function wherever he goes.

This is an ideal book for teachers to have handy. It's a snatch-a-moment book, just right for those five minutes when the music teacher is late, when it's almost lunchtime, or when a dull day needs some seasoning. The poems lend themselves to chanting. Elementary youngsters will recognize the boa constrictor and the unicorn and chime right in. It's not a book for the prim and proper or the stodgy and the uptight. But if you want to ungloom your day, or show your youngsters that poetry isn't all daffodils and fluffy clouds, start *Where the Sidewalk Ends.*

Kay Winters, in her review of "Where the Sidewalk Ends" (copyright 1976 by the International Reading Association, Inc.; reprinted with permission of the International Reading Association and Kay Winters), in The Reading Teacher, *Vol. 29, No. 5, February, 1976, p. 515.*

An extensive collection of expert minor verse, verbally agile and with a touch of reflection and melancholy even in the lightest pieces. The forms used are diverse, ranging from epigram and exclamation to nonsense-narrative, and type and layout are occasionally used to increase humour, as in a poem written vertically on a giraffe's neck. The drawings are often used as a direct completion for a poem—as in **"Magical Eraser"**, **"Invisible Boy"** and **"Shadow Wash"**. Slyly and sardonically observed, the small accidents of everyday life are encapsulated here in stanzas shaped by rhyme of half-rhyme and enlivened by nuggets of unexpected words.

Margery Fisher, in her review of "Where the Sidewalk Ends," in her Growing Point, *Vol. 17, No. 5, January, 1979, p. 3453.*

[Silverstein's collection ***Where the Sidewalk Ends***] is credited with bringing more converts to poetry than any other volume; for many it is the turning point at which they first become poetry lovers. When a teacher reads aloud from it, children who think they don't care for poetry may listen suspiciously at first, then cautiously ask to "see that book." ***Where the Sidewalk Ends*** contains verse and illustrations that tickle the reader in weird and ridiculous ways: for **"Jumping Rope,"** a gangly girl is shown completely entangled in a jumping rope from head to foot. **"Band-Aids"** describes all the places a child needs band-aids, and the illustration shows head and torso covered with them. Silverstein shows no restraint in the situations he mocks to make things laughable. . . . Anything becomes the butt of Silverstein's humor, and he's on target about what makes children laugh.

In the gooey, smelly poem **"Sarah Cynthia Sylvia Stout / Would Not Take the Garbage Out,"** Silverstein piles up the pits, the rinds, the crusts, and bones to show what happened to a girl who would not take the garbage out. . . . By the time you finish reading the graphic details of Sarah's overflowing garbage pail, students are gagging and groaning in mock horror. Despite their pretense of utter disgust, the comment heard most often is, "Read it again." (pp. 265-66)

Bernice E. Cullinan, with Mary K. Karrer and Arlene M. Pillar, in their review of "Where the Sidewalk Ends," in their Literature and the Child *(copyright © 1981 by Harcourt Brace Jovanovich, Inc.; reprinted by permission of the publisher), Harcourt Brace Jovanovich, 1981, pp. 265-66.*

THE MISSING PIECE (1976)

The journey, not the arrival matters . . . to the extent that once Silverstein's freehand circular "it" finds the pie-shaped missing piece it's been seeking all along, it decides to do without it—for when the wedge-like gap that had functioned as a sort of mouth is filled in, "it" is unable to sing. The whole fable bears more resemblance to a Feiffer cartoon than to the fat book it appears on the outside; the "mouth" and a dot for an eye are all that make "it" a creature of sorts, and there's nothing else on the bare white pages but the line it rolls along, the small scale butterfly, flower, etc., it encounters on the way, and the various other "pieces" it tries before finding the

perfect one. However, the very childlike sparseness of words and lines at least leaves room for application without forcing any—and we'll take "its" approach to life over that of Silverstein's ***Giving Tree*** any day.

A review of "The Missing Piece," in Kirkus Reviews *(copyright © 1976 The Kirkus Service, Inc.), Vol. XLIV, No. 7, April 1, 1976, p. 387.*

An endearingly simple fable about "It" (a being that looks something like a pie but acts like a human) and "Its" quest for "Its" missing piece—ideal for storytime. The clean open pages and simple text leave lots of scope for questions, and endless repetition will not stale this quietly important book. . . .

Brigitte Weeks, in her review of "The Missing Piece," in Book World—The Washington Post *(© 1976, The Washington Post), April 11, 1976, p. E4.*

Aside from the late James Thurber, few artists have put so much verve and meaning into simple lines and circles as Shel Silverstein. Here, his adroit black pictures—set off by expanses of white—complement brisk verses which tell a story and also seem to express a philosophy. . . . An unusual and oddly appealing book, this will no doubt attract a large following.

A review of "The Missing Piece," in Publishers Weekly *(reprinted from the April 19, 1976 issue of* Publishers Weekly, *published by R. R. Bowker Company, a Xerox company; copyright © 1976 by Xerox Corporation), Vol. 209, No. 16, April 19, 1976, p. 85.*

Charm and a poignant honesty, an almost painfully real view of the world marks Shel Silverstein's fables for children of all ages. . . .

Like most fables, [this] story's meaning is better understood by emotionally weary adults than more literal young children whose capabilities for metaphor are still undeveloped. While finding it hard to resist the appeal of this story, I basically don't like some of the meanings I see. It seems to have all the winsomeness of the fellow at the singles bar explaining why life is better if you don't commit yourself to anyone for too long—the line goes that too much togetherness turns people into bores—that creativity is preserved by freedom to explore from one relationship to another. In this book the missing piece has a voice too and so we identify with it and feel rather badly that the circle never looks back or even says a tender goodbye. I really don't see why that sense of wholeness that comes from loving another person, completing the circle of yourself really has to be destructive, boring or limiting of creative possibility.

This fable can also be interpreted to mean that no one should try to find all the answers, no one should hope to fill all the holes in themselves, achieve total transcendental harmony or psychic order because a person without a search, loose ends, internal conflicts and external goals becomes too smooth to enjoy or know what's going on. Too much satisfaction blocks exchange with the outside.

I like the fable better when I interpret it this way but, after all, who's in danger of becoming complete? I wonder if this fable can really bring new truth to a reader—or is it a gimmick, a red herring or a straw dog disguised as a circle rolling over our better sense. The book is provocative, open to other interpretations besides mine and certainly original. It would be a perfect book to give a lover as a goodbye present . . . a nice way to say thank you but no more. As for little children I asked a lot of them and they think it's a book about a circle that likes to roll. That's something that happens all the time on Sesame Street.

Anne Roiphe, in her review of "The Missing Piece," in The New York Times Book Review *(© 1976 by The New York Times Company; reprinted by permission), May 2, 1976, p. 28.*

The Missing Piece by Shel Silverstein is a popular book which has been widely accepted as "a fable that gently probes the nature and quest of fulfillment." Instead, upon careful reading, it does exactly the opposite and presents a negative attitude toward relationships. . . . There is a clear implication that completeness is not desirable and that questing by oneself is preferable to commitment to another. One must think twice about presenting this model of rewarded selfishness to children.

Jean Marie Hiesberger and Pat McLaughlin, in their review of "The Missing Piece," in New Catholic World, *Vol. 222, No. 1328, March/April, 1979, p. 92.*

THE MISSING PIECE MEETS THE BIG O   (1981)

Silverstein's new opus should match the bestselling record of its companion, **"The Missing Piece,"** and his other phenomenal successes. . . . [The missing piece gives] readers much merriment and a lesson in self-reliance. It's remarkable how Silverstein can make a few straight or curved lines portray such meaning.

A review of "The Missing Piece Meets the Big O," in Publishers Weekly *(reprinted from the January 9, 1981 issue of* Publishers Weekly, *published by R. R. Bowker Company, a Xerox company; copyright © 1981 by Xerox Corporation), Vol. 219, No. 2, January 9, 1981, p. 73.*

[This] is a fable for those familiar with mate-seeking. . . . With little more than a low horizon line and the informally drawn geometric shapes, Silverstein pulls it off and will find an appreciative audience in college dorms and discussion groups for the divorced. This is a book peculiarly suited to our times and temper, but not suited to young children.

Mary B. Nickerson, in her review of "The Missing Piece Meets the Big O," in School Library Journal *(reprinted from the April, 1981 issue of* School Library Journal, *published by R. R. Bowker Co./A Xerox Corporation; copyright © 1981), Vol. 27, No. 8, April, 1981, p. 143.*

Part of Shel Silverstein's appeal undoubtedly lies in his penchant for wrapping allegories for adults in packages that look as if they were designed for children. His line drawings are simple and whimsical, his stories no more than a hundred words or so. But there's something pretentious about Silverstein, which may be more obvious to children than it is to many adults (although in this case the sexual allusion in his tasteless title will be blatantly obvious to adults).

Silverstein's insights into human nature are seldom original, but they do appeal to book buyers, that is, adults. Witness the perennial best-seller *The Giving Tree,* which discourses on the ingratitude of children and the selfless love of parents (symbolized by the tree).

Silverstein's latest homily is the story of a wedge-shaped object looking for some other object into which it can insert itself and get a free ride through the world. This is no easy matter and finally, acting on the advice of the Big O, this oddly shaped

piece discovers it is pretty mobile by itself. Voila! The missing piece becomes—here's the message!!!—*independent*. On the subject of independence, *The Wind in the Willows* has far better and more entertaining examples.

Alice Digilio, in her review of "The Missing Piece Meets the Big O," in Book World—The Washington Post *(© 1981, The Washington Post), April 12, 1981, p. 9.*

A delicious visual love story; a detailed and provocative exploration of the physical, emotional, spiritual, and mental processes involved in becoming whole. . . . Shel Silverstein's new eighty-eight page book is so immensely satisfying on so many levels that it truly can appeal to word-readers and picture-readers of all ages.

Leigh Dean, in her review of "The Missing Piece Meets the Big O," in Children's Book Review Service *(copyright © 1981 Children's Book Review Service Inc.), Vol. 9, No. 10, May, 1981, p. 83.*

Let's get one thing clear at the outset. The title of Shel Silverstein's new cartoon fable is definitely the best part. . . .

The ending is a surprise and not the one you might be anticipating either. Shel Silverstein is a witty man and if he's not so much an author of children's books as a publishing phenomenon, who's to complain? All a reviewer can do in this situation is to offer reassurance to nervous parents. Should this book happen to find its way from the local card shop to your house (chances are fair to good that it will), and should your children happen to see it, don't worry. It won't mean a thing to them.

Joyce Milton, in her review of "The Missing Piece Meets the Big O," in The New York Times Book Review *(© 1981 by The New York Times Company; reprinted by permission), October 11, 1981, p. 39.*

The deliberately paced story of the missing piece ". . . waiting for someone / to come along / and take it somewhere" is purposely slowed by almost-empty pages of space, with a continuous line leading the eye and interest. Assonance, alliteration, and rhythm raise the tale of taking charge of one's life to the poetic level, with design definitely affecting the story's timing.

Ruth M. Stein, in her review of "The Missing Piece Meets the Big O" (copyright © 1982 by the National Council of Teachers of English; reprinted by permission of the publisher and the author), in Language Arts, *Vol. 59, No. 1, January, 1982, p. 53.*

A LIGHT IN THE ATTIC   (1981)

This is a big, fat treasure for Silverstein devotees, with trenchant verses expressing high-flown, exhilarating nonsense as well as thoughts unexpectedly sober and even sad. For instance, the dialogue between a very old man and a small boy reveals that both sometimes drop their spoons, wet their pants and cry, and worst of all, grownups pay no attention to them. Silverstein's inspired ink drawings illustrate each poem, with an especially provocative scene accompanying his ideas on **"Rockabye Baby".** . . .

A review of "A Light in the Attic," in Publishers Weekly *(reprinted from the September 18, 1981 issue of* Publishers Weekly, *published by R. R. Bowker Company, a Xerox company; copyright © 1981 by Xerox Corporation), Vol. 220, No. 12, September 18, 1981, p. 155.*

Limericks, puns, riddles, cautionary tales, lyrics, verses serious and witty—there is a rhyme here for every occasion and taste. As fans of *Where the Sidewalk Ends* know, Silverstein is an outrageous and wise fellow whose words and drawings unerringly touch the child's heart and psyche. Elementary school teachers consider him the guru of their poetry unit. This collection of 136 poems makes a swell appetizer; I would encourage exploring other kinds of poetry and poets for the remainder of the five-course dinner.

> *Leigh Dean, in her review of "A Light in the Attic,"* in Children's Book Review Service *(copyright © 1981 Children's Book Review Service Inc.), Vol. 10, No. 3, November, 1981, p. 30.*

In his verse for children, . . . Shel Silverstein displays a certain startling quirkiness. . . .

There's a streak of the weird in Mr. Silverstein's fun. It turns up in a poem called **"Who Ordered the Broiled Face?"** and in another, **"Quick Trip,"** in which a couple of kids are swallowed by a colossal lizard, then immediately excreted to safety. Characteristic of Mr. Silverstein, too, is a vague and dreamy religiosity ("God says to me with kind of a smile, / 'Hey how would you like to be God awhile?'"). In some of his most memorable nonsense, Mr. Silverstein is playfully disruptive of parental authority. The natural joy that children take in testing their tethers to breaking point (for they don't, of course, want the tethers to snap) will be kindled and sustained in Mr. Silverstein's rhymes about Little Abigail, who dies because her parents won't buy her a pony, and about Clarence, who sends away for a new mail-order set of folks.

Like its forerunner, **"Where the Sidewalk Ends,"** this new book is physically ample. Its 175 pages supply droll black-and-white line drawings for most of its 136 poems. A Silverstein poetry book *looks* worth the money, as if it will last a child awhile; and, in fact, it gives excellent value. Both cartoons and verses in this new bunch seem just about as lively as those in **"Sidewalk."** Readers of any age may care to commit to memory the one about the sitter who sits on babies, and another about an infant bat who's afraid of the light. Personally, I'm memorizing **"In Search of Cinderella,"** a fresh view of the familiar tale. . . . (p. 51)

In this new book, I regret only a vein of platitudinous wisdom that recalls the late syndicated bard Edgar A. Guest: "How much good inside a day? / Depends how good you live 'em." Despite such moments of banality, and there aren't many, Mr. Silverstein's work remains a must for lovers of good verse for children. Quite like nobody else, he is still a master of delectable outrage and the proprietor of a surprisingly finely tuned sensibility. (pp. 51, 60)

> *X. J. Kennedy, "A Rhyme Is a Chime," in* The New York Times Book Review *(© 1981 by The New York Times Company; reprinted by permission), November 15, 1981, pp. 51, 60.**

This exuberant companion to *Where the Sidewalk Ends* . . . will delight lovers of Silverstein's raucous, rollicking verse and his often tender, whimsical, philosophical advice. If one could eliminate the precious, the straining for effect, the ubiquitous use of the dropped "g" . . . and the poor taste of one entry that describes a camel in a brassiere to hide her humps, this would be nearly perfect. From the list of frightening "what-ifs" ("Whatif I get sick and die? Whatif I flunk that test?") to the **"Prayer of the Selfish Child"** (a child prays that if death comes before waking, the Lord should break his toys so nobody else can use them), the poems are tuned in to kids' most hidden feelings, dark wishes and enjoyment of the silly. Mrs. Mc-Twitter, the baby sitter, who's confused enough to sit on the baby; Pamela Purse whose incessant demand, "Ladies first," leads to her uncomfortable end; Ticklish Tom, who literally laughs himself to an untimely death; and other cautionary characters may not be as memorable as "Sarah Cynthia Sylvia Stout who wouldn't take the garbage out," but they're all great fun. Make peace with the camel in the brassiere, and, too, with the man who has a library book overdue for 42 years, and enjoy it. The witty line drawings are a full half of the treat of this wholly satisfying anthology by the modern successor to Edward Lear and Hilaire Belloc.

> *Marjorie Lewis, in her review of "A Light in the Attic," in* School Library Journal *(reprinted from the December, 1981 issue of* School Library Journal, *published by R. R. Bowker Co./A Xerox Corporation; copyright © 1981), Vol. 28, No. 4, December, 1981, p. 57.*

A fat volume of small illustrated rhymes from Silverstein, who gets down to the level of kids' peeves, spooks, and sense of silliness often enough to score a collective hit. . . . There are some funny twists and take-offs on familiar rhymes and tales—such as a speculation on what would happen if Captain Blackbeard shaved, and a warning to the "Rockabye" baby that a treetop is no place to rock. . . . There are also a number of typical twist endings, many of them lame or predictable—but then you can't expect 168 laughs in 168 pages. For undertow, there's the eyeball in the gumball machine (a sentinel reminder that "I" have had enough gumballs) and the fearful "Whatifs" that climb into "my" ear at night. All in all, bright and knowing nonsense.

> *A review of "A Light in the Attic," in* Kirkus Reviews *(copyright © 1982 The Kirkus Service, Inc.), Vol. L, No. 1, January 1, 1982, p. 10.*

Scratchy line drawings, occasionally macabre and usually humorous, illustrate a robust collection of entertaining poetry. Little of this is sensitive, and some of it is more slapstick than subtle, but there's a sense of fun and nonsense that should appeal to most children. Many of the selections have a memorable lilt, some almost like jump-rope rhymes. . . . Not great poetry, but likely to be popular.

> *Zena Sutherland, in her review of "A Light in the Attic," in* Bulletin of the Center for Children's Books *(reprinted by permission of The University of Chicago Press; © 1982 by The University of Chicago), Vol. 35, No. 6, February, 1982, p. 117.*

Peter Spier

1927-

American author/illustrator and illustrator of picture books.

Spier's creations enjoy international popularity with readers of all ages for their meticulous detail, historical accuracy, and charm. His works include several books of Americana, books of sounds, and the acclaimed Mother Goose Library series, which is noted for its original portrayals of four popular rhymes and songs. He has also created a set of board books depicting various buildings which form a village when placed upright.

Born in Holland, where his father was a prominent Dutch illustrator and journalist, Spier has had a lifelong interest in art. Following an early stint as a junior editor in Holland, he came to the United States and began working in publishing and illustrating magazines and children's books. A prolific artist, Spier illustrated over one hundred books prior to his career as an author/illustrator. As preparation for his illustrations, Spier travels to the book's locale and draws numerous sketches. He later renders these in ink and colors them with delicate watercolors.

Spier's most applauded work is *Noah's Ark*, which realistically depicts the plight of the doomed animals and the monumental task of providing for those safe on the ark. Critics consistently praise Spier for his panoramic scenes, such as those in *To Market! To Market!*, where the reader can delight in the minute details, bustling activity, and authentic freshness of a nineteenth-century Delaware marketplace. In order to make a scholarly presentation, Spier often includes historical notes, diagrams, and other informative addenda to his books. Humor also characterizes Spier's pictures, such as the whimsical house-painting spree in *Oh, Were They Ever Happy!* The text of Spier's books receives varied critical response. Reviewers praise *Of Dikes and Windmills* for its technical clarity and its engaging narrative, while they criticize *Bored—Nothing to Do* for its overdependence on conversation to advance the story line. Critics additionally note Spier's use of sex-role stereotyping in this book and in *People*, which receives complaints for its perpetuation of white, male supremacy and its use of stereotypic costumes. Nevertheless, there is almost universal praise for *People*'s message of respect and tolerance for the variety of the world's population.

Spier strives to entertain his readers by capturing their interest and sparking their intellectual curiosity. He believes that a good book should be "childlike," but never childish. His consistent success among both critics and the picture book audience demonstrates the achievement of his aims. Among Spier's numerous awards are the 1962 Caldecott Honor Book Award for *The Fox Went Out on a Chilly Night*, the 1967 *Boston Globe-Horn Book* Award for *London Bridge Is Falling Down!*, and the 1970 Christopher Award for *The Erie Canal*. *Noah's Ark* received the Caldecott Award in 1978, the Lewis Carroll Shelf Award, the Christopher Award, and the New York Times Choice of Best Illustrated Children's Books of the Year Award in 1977, the International Board on Books for Young People (IBBY) Honor List Award in 1980, and the American Book Award in 1982.

Courtesy of Peter E. Spier

(See also *Contemporary Authors*, Vols. 5-8, rev. ed. and *Something about the Author*, Vol. 4.)

AUTHOR'S COMMENTARY

[A] mistake I try to avoid is depending on second-hand research. Whenever possible, I go to the setting of each book to make preliminary pictures. If I didn't do my homework, my Wisconsin farm would probably look like one in North Holland (where I grew up); my cows would always be Frisian. There is no substitute for an artist seeing and absorbing the feel of a place; you can't just take it easy, stay home and work from picture postcards.

The pleasantest compliments I receive are from teachers telling me they use one of my picture books in social studies classes because of their accurate details—when someone says, "I'm from New England and I know just where you stood when you drew page 19 in 'The Fox Went Out on a Chilly Night!'"

But aiming for authenticity can be another trap. Doing fieldwork for "The Erie Canal," I was sketching a stately old gingerbread house standing beside the overgrown towpath and an old canal lock. "Used to be the Canal Hotel," remarked an old fellow watching the drawing. "Grand place . . . chandeliers . . . a long bar . . . lots of lovely girls. . . ." Only half listening, I kept working on the picture, which took half a day to perfect. When I showed it to the Erie Canal museum curator, he cried, "You can't use that! Canal *Hotel?* Ha! It was a whorehouse!"

Sidestepping such bloopers, trying to give a children's book a long and happy life by not dating it with illustrations showing trendy mini- or maxiskirts, autos sporting fins and other ephemera—these are tricky enough gambits at home, but nothing to what I encounter abroad. Since most of my books are published in foreign countries, I travel to meet publishing professionals, wherever and whenever I can, in sessions that are illuminating but sometimes dismaying.

"Only the very wealthy live in a home like this one—and they would never paint it themselves," declared the German publisher when he saw the perfectly ordinary, middle-class house pictured in **"Oh, Were They Ever Happy!"**

In another book, a frog appeared in a pet store. "*Mais non, Monsieur Spier*," insisted the French publisher. "*Impossible!* The frog belongs in the food market." (p. 93)

A picture book, when you come down to it, is a tall order. But I wouldn't want to spend my life working at anything else. The rewards are splendid, even if they don't impress many people outside one's field. (p. 94)

> *"The Frog Belongs in the Food Market and Other Perils of an Illustrator,"* in Publishers Weekly *(reprinted from the July 25, 1980 issue of* Publishers Weekly, *published by R. R. Bowker Company, a Xerox company; copyright © 1980 by Xerox Corporation), Vol. 218, No. 4, July 25, 1980, pp. 93-4.*

GENERAL COMMENTARY

Blessings on thee, Peter Spier! And on the first two books in your Mother Goose Library! Children will bless you for the instant delight both books will give them—delight that will instantly transform your versions of **"To Market! To Market!"** and **"London Bridge Is Falling Down"** into beloved classics, to join your [**"The Fox Went out on a Chilly Night"**]. Parents and grandparents who will be begged for just one more look before bedtime will bless you for your illustrations that have the vigor of Hogarth and are so pleasantly crowded with people and places that it will be many bedtimes before the reader and his young companion will have seen everything. Then both will want to start all over again!

> *A review of "To Market! To Market!" and "London Bridge Is Falling Down,"* in Publishers Weekly *(reprinted from the September 11, 1967 issue of* Publishers Weekly, *published by R. R. Bowker Company; copyright © 1967 by R. R. Bowker Company), Vol. 192, No. 11, September 11, 1967, p. 68.*

More conventional [than Beni Montresor's *I Saw a Ship A-Sailing*], though no less engaging, are the two new Peter Spier offerings: *London Bridge Is Falling Down!* and *To Market! To Market!* They are both studies in visual minutiae, in which each cobblestone, each window-frame, each blade of grass is lovingly and faithfully recorded. And yet Spier's special gift is his capacity for making a virtue out of an obsessive love for detail. His all-inclusive landscape of things and events will keep any child involved and engrossed, page after page. *London Bridge Is Falling Down!* is a real *tour de force.* Spier erects, demolishes, re-erects and re-demolishes that old bridge until one just prays that nothing else of a calamitous nature will befall it. And he sets down everything accurately, having stud-

ied (and included in the book) the historical facts concerning London Bridge. Stylistically, it seems that Spier has drawn inspiration from Hogarth's marvelously effulgent drawings.

While *London Bridge Is Falling Down!* dwells on this single nursery rhyme, *To Market! To Market!* uses a variety of verses, all concerned with early American bucolic or market-place themes. Once again, historical facts have been studied and included, producing a book of winning period drawings that continually ring true. (pp. 2-3)

> *John Gruen, "Wild, Crazy, Mixed-Up Mother Goose," in* Book World—The Washington Post *(© 1967 Postrib Corp.; reprinted by permission of* Chicago Tribune *and* The Washington Post*), Part II, November 5, 1967, pp. 2-3.*

Peter Spier . . . has created two more intensely satisfying picture books [**"London Bridge Is Falling Down"** and **"To Market! To Market!"**]. One is always regretting that his output in this field is so small, but on looking at the two books under review, the reason becomes immediately apparent: the creation of such meticulous and witty detail in pen and ink and colour wash is no seven-day labour.

"London Bridge Is Falling Down" depicts verse by verse an absorbing series of vivid scenes of early eighteenth-century London life. From the picture of consternation in the architect's office . . .—do we recognize Sir C. Wren?—to the hilarious scenes of disasters, the delightful incidental scenes such as the tobacco shop . . . , every page is a visual feast. (pp. 313-14)

The beautiful, hilarious illustrations [for **"To Market! To Market!"**] are set in early nineteenth-century Delaware, America, the market scenes taking place in New Castle, named in the late seventeenth century after Newcastle-upon-Tyne. There is a historical postscript which, however, is not essential for full enjoyment of the pictures. The dew-fresh countryside will be readily recognized as home territory by English children.

A four-year-old who looked at them with me said "I *want* those books". No further recommendation needed! (p. 314)

> *G. V. Barton, in her review of "London Bridge Is Falling Down" and "To Market! To Market!" in* Children's Book News *(copyright © 1968 by Baker Book Services Ltd.), Vol. 3, No. 6, November-December, 1968, pp. 313-14.*

The new Mother Goose library is a joy and I hope instalments will reach us quickly from America. . . . [Spier's] fine, finicky, detailed pictures have a touch of Caldecott in their delight in rustic happening and their apt comical interpretation of traditional rhyme. Like the Caldecott picture-books, these two [*To Market! To Market!* and *London Bridge is Falling Down*] deserve to last far beyond the present generation.

> *Margery Fisher, in her review of "To Market! To Market!" and "London Bridge Is Falling Down," in her* Growing Point, *Vol. 7, No. 6, December, 1968, p. 1244.*

We already know Peter Spier in this country, as the master of an unfashionably precise style. While most book-artists today make their impression with lovely great dollops of paint, he fills his pictures with carefully observed detail, drawn in line and then coloured delicately. His work has in consequence a "period" flavour which is precisely suited to his new Mother Goose Library. These are new interpretations of old traditional rhymes. Their appeal is on several levels. Small children will enjoy the little jokes in the subsidiary action which is going on in every picture. Something is happening all over the place. Older children and grown-ups will be absorbed by the fine and accurate architectural drawing and by the artist's sense of period. Teachers may be tempted to turn each picture into a lesson, an entertaining one, but not quite such fun as the unadulterated book. Mr. Spier may not be sufficiently with-it to be a Caldecott winner, but these books [*London Bridge is Falling Down* and *To Market! To Market!*] belong on the shelf with Caldecott's own.

A review of "London Bridge Is Falling Down" and "To Market! To Market!" in The Junior Bookshelf, *Vol. 33, No. 1, February, 1969, p. 21.*

And So My Garden Grows, the title of a recent book by Peter Spier, might also describe his burgeoning career and the charming books he has designed and illustrated. Spier's "garden" is prospering, and grows more beautiful every day as he carefully tends and nurtures it. (p. 49)

[In] 1960, Peter Spier conceived the idea of illustrating the old folk song, *The Fox Went Out On A Chilly Night.* . . . The illustrations in line, both in black-and-white and color, are charming and humorous, with much authentic detail. Spier chose New England as the background for the simple story. What is unique is Spier's concern for historical and pictorial accuracy. We find no anachronisms in his illustrations. Background details of towns, farms, farm implements, even old graveyards are the result of careful on-the-spot research by the artist. Spier made several trips to New England to sketch appropriate background material for his book. An examination of his extensive files reveals notations of place, date, and other data of interest on all his sketches. Spier must know the background firsthand; he is not satisfied with photographs or magazine pictures. Before taking off on such a trip, he makes a careful dummy of his proposed book. He has a general idea of what kind of an illustration will go on each page, and therefore knows what to look for on his travels. He may want a typical barnyard in which the fox forages; he knows he wants to draw a town "green," and so he searches for just the right place. The final illustrations in the book are not just literal sketches of actual places. Often Spier will take details from different sketches he has made on-the-spot and combine them for the most effective illustration. Elements and details may be arranged in new, imaginative combinations. If Spier draws a plough or a bedwarmer or a church steeple, he has documented drawings to support his illustration. As he sketches the scenes, he makes complete color notes for his later work on the final illustrations in his studio. Each illustration in *The Fox Went Out On A Chilly Night* is filled with a wealth of authentic detail that will delight children *and* adults. (pp. 55, 82)

In 1967, Peter Spier conceived the idea of a series of books for Doubleday titled The Mother Goose Library. It was his plan to choose well-known nursery and folk rhymes and give them a fresh and original presentation. . . . In the preparation of the illustrations for [*To Market! To Market!*] Peter Spier traveled to the New Castle of today, gathering source material from still extant public buildings and stone houses, and sketching the surrounding countryside. He makes careful notes to himself, written in a Spier-kind of shorthand—part Dutch, part English, on these detailed drawings. On his sketching trips, Spier also notes unusual place names, and other bits of local color which strike his fancy. . . . Features of Spier's work are the consummate skill and accurate detail of his drawing; his clean, clear, precise line; the charm and humor of his view-

point; and his scholarly approach to the presentation of his subject matter. Spier, however, is no musty-dusty pedant—rather his aim is to delight and to teach his audience, to pique their interest, and arouse their intellectual curiosity while entertaining them. Although these books are categorized by the publisher as suitable for children "up to eight" years of age, an adult can enjoy them as much as a teen-ager or an elementary-school child. The more often you look at Peter Spier's illustrations, the more you see to savor and enjoy. (pp. 82-3)

One of the interesting features which Spier always includes in his books is an author's note explaining his approach to the subject matter and giving the historical background of his illustrations. (p. 83)

Spier's actual working procedure on book assignments is interesting. He prepares a complete dummy, the exact size of his proposed book with detailed pencil drawings, and a paste-up of the blocks of type. It is a "working model" of the book to come. Spier knows beforehand what illustrations he will put on each page: *e.g.* he wants a church here; a town square there, and so on. He travels to the area he is going to depict to sketch from actual places—towns, buildings, people. He is always "looking for some new angle," for he says, "no one's imagination is sufficient to make up all the details." He leaves nothing to chance; his research is thorough. Anything that is unusual catches his eye; a unique fence; a strange old tree; an amusing café. These he sees and records in his sketchbook, making notes on color and detail. Since his travel time is limited, Spier works hard sketching every day in order to capture the essence of an area. In the field he uses pen and ink, but no color, trusting to his sharp memory and color notations for later use. He rarely relies on photographs, except in poor weather when he cannot find suitable shelter for on-the-spot sketching. Returning to his studio from these trips, Spier sets out on a period of long hours of hard work at his drawing table. He makes detailed sketches in pencil in his dummy, exactly as they will appear in the final book. Then, using a 192 mapping pen, Spier makes his final drawings in ink. The printer pulls a non-photo blue proof of this drawing. Then Spier sets about applying his color to these "blues." As he paints, he uses an acetate overlay on which is printed his line drawing in order to check the register of the line drawing to the color. Work on the "blues" (which are very faint) is tedious and requires great care and patience, as well as a creative eye for color application. The reward of such a procedure, according to Spier, is the assurance of retaining a clear, clean black line. After painting, the "blues," now in full color, and the acetate overlay are returned to the printer. Finally the artist sees four-color proofs of his work.

Spier firmly believes in the importance of drawing and the necessity of drawing from life. He says that once an artist "masters" forms and shapes, they "belong to him for life." However, he must continue to renew and refresh this mastery through continued drawing. (pp. 84-5)

Peter Spier sets high standards for himself, demanding his best. He is exact and thorough in his research. His work is careful, detailed, and precise, yet has spontaneity, humor, and charm. His fine illustrations possess a joyous quality; they delight as well as teach. (pp. 85-6)

Joan Hess Michel, "The Illustrations of Peter Spier," in American Artist *(copyright © 1969 by Billboard Publications, Inc.), Vol. 33, No. 9, October, 1969, pp. 49-55, 82-86.*

Following earlier books in the Mother Goose Library, the author has collected rhymes relevant to two new themes—the maiden voyage of a sailing ship in **Hurrah, We're Outward Bound** and the effect of enclosure in garden, estate or orchard in **And So My Garden Grows**. . . . The loving, odd and humorous details of these pages, the incomparable use of color, mass, and line, commend these books to a personal and permanent collection.

> *Margery Fisher, in her review of "Hurrah, We're Outward Bound" and "And So My Garden Grows," in her* Growing Point, *Vol. 8, No. 4, October, 1969, p. 1402.*

[Peter Spier's] illustrations are to most juvenile scenery what a Tiepolo ceiling is to a hand-decorated pup tent. Too many children's books present lumpily massive, poster-hued semi-primitive drawings that intrigue for only one or two cheerful skim-throughs. Spier, by contrast, spends months accumulating visual research and folios of tiny sketches for his subjects. When he shows the 19th century harbor of Honfleur (in **Hurrah We're Outward Bound!**) or the 18th century Thameside (in **London Bridge Is Falling Down!**), he knows as much about the shops and ships, the rigs and ragamuffins as a sharp eye and a keen mind can acquire. The result encourages young (and old) to brood upon details and be delighted by the beauty of black ink and watercolor washes that blend a Delacroix-like delicacy with the liveliness of Thomas Rowlandson.

> *"For the Young: Dreams and Memories," in* Time *(copyright 1970 Time Inc.; all rights reserved; reprinted by permission from* Time), *Vol. 96, No. 25, December 21, 1970, p. 68.**

[Spier's] children say he writes "nice books." While they are realistic, as witness **Noah's Ark**, there is no murder, mayhem or blood and guts. They're happy books. . . .

Peter Spier's illustrations are warm and human, his stories are easily understood, and children of all ages (early primary to adult) can enjoy. (p. 20)

> *"Peter Spier, Author/Illustrator, and How He Lived Happily Ever After," in* Early Years *(© copyright 1981 by Alan Raymond Inc.; reprinted with permission of the publisher, Darien, CT 06820), Vol. 12, No. 2, October, 1981, pp. 20-21, 53.*

Peter Spier uses watercolors to compose meticulously detailed and aesthetically pleasing scenes with a touch of nostalgia. The exuberant pages of **Noah's Ark** exemplify his art. Careful attention to the hundreds of small details Spier puts into his work will reward readers with the fullest delight. (p. 117)

> *Bernice E. Cullinan, with Mary K. Karrer and Arlene M. Pillar, "Picture Books: The Art in Picture Books," in their* Literature and the Child *(© Harcourt Brace Jovanovich, Inc.; reprinted by permission of the publisher), Harcourt Brace Jovanovich, Inc., 1981, pp. 116-18.*

THE FOX WENT OUT ON A CHILLY NIGHT: AN OLD SONG (1961)

A folk song about a fox stealing a goose from a farmyard illustrated with lovely pictures of the New England countryside done in muted colors with a soft sky blue predominating. It is an unusually beautiful picture book, but the song it is based on doesn't seem worthy of the fine illustrations.

> *A review of "The Fox Went Out on a Chilly Night," in* Publishers Weekly *(reprinted from the July 17, 1961 issue of* Publishers Weekly, *published by R. R. Bowker Company; copyright © 1961 by R. R. Bowker Company), Vol. 180, No. 3, July 17, 1961, p. 70.*

That fox made a very long trip, . . . and as many times as I've looked through the book, I still hold my breath at the beauty of the countryside on that cold autumn night: the sprawling, ramshackle barns and settling stone walls, the thick, bristling growth that covers the rolling land, the farm equipment rusting and crumbling in the fields, the fiery maples, the old, untended graveyards, and the sleeping trees, the ripe disorder of the barnyards, and moonlight, pumpkins, and squash left about wherever they happen to fall.

> *Emily Maxwell, in her review of "The Fox Went Out on a Chilly Night," in* The New Yorker *(© 1961 by The New Yorker Magazine, Inc.), Vol. XXXVIII, No. 40, November 18, 1961, p. 231.*

A true picture book in the Caldecott-Brooke tradition. Fine drawing, lovely colors, and pictures so full of amusing details that young viewers will make fresh discoveries every time they scrutinize (as they surely will) these beautiful, action-filled pages. Before making this book, Mr. Spier . . . made an extensive tour of New England, sketching every detail of farm and village life. The keenness of his observation and his delight in what he saw are reflected on every page. Truly one of the most beautiful and childlike books in many years.

> *Margaret Warren Brown, in her review of "The Fox Went Out on a Chilly Night," in* The Horn Book Magazine *(copyright, 1961, by the Horn Book, Inc., Boston), Vol. XXXVII, No. 6, December, 1961, p. 548.*

New England in the fall is the background for a series of pictures by the modern artist, Peter Spier, who follows the Caldecott tradition. . . . [They] form a perfectly delightful pictorial narrative to accompany the words of an old song. . . . Here is the fox leaving his den on a "chilly night" to go to the town-o to steal some geese to "grease" his chin. Over covered bridges, through churchyards, and across fields he speeds, regardless of danger, gets his geese and races back through the village, past tobacco barns until he reaches his burrow (nicely furnished like a New England house) and his ten little ones. . . . As lively and attractive a rendering of the traditional New England landscape as we have seen to divert the young.

> *Margaret Sherwood Libby, in her review of "The Fox Went Out on a Chilly Night," in* New York Herald Tribune *(© I.H.T. Corporation; reprinted by permission), February 25, 1962, p. 11.*

LONDON BRIDGE IS FALLING DOWN! (1967)

[Ed Emberley's "London Bridge Is Falling Down"] has had the misfortune to appear in the same season as an enormously robust **"London Bridge Is Falling Down!"** . . . by Peter Spier. This one, inaugurating a Mother Goose Library series, shows an 18th-century London surging with life and movement: all types of craft ply the Thames by night and day; slopbuckets are emptied from overhead; merchants offer their wares (including tobacco leaves from the colonies). Music and a sub-

"A couple of you will grease my chin   before I leave this town-o, town-o, town-o.

From The Fox Went Out on a Chilly Night: An Old Song, *illustrated by Peter Spier.*

stantial history are included, but are likely to be missed amid all the splendid details of Spier's illustrations.

> *George A. Woods, "A Gaggle of Goose and Grimm,"*
> *in* The New York Times Book Review *(© 1967 by*
> *The New York Times Company; reprinted by per-*
> *mission), October 29, 1967, p. 42.**

For the child who enjoys big pictures filled with small details, this version of the familiar verses should be a small treasure. Each illustration is a double-page spread teeming with action. The colors are subdued save for a bright red-orange, and the pages are crowded with scenes containing authentic details (in costume, architecture, signs, etc.) as well as amusing caricatures.

> *Zena Sutherland, in her review of "London Bridge*
> *Is Falling Down," in* Saturday Review *(© 1967 Sat-*
> *urday Review Magazine Co.; reprinted by permis-*
> *sion), Vol. L, No. 45, November 11, 1967, p. 41.*

[Eighteen traditional verses describe] a succession of conditions for building up the famous broken bridge. . . . The wonderfully detailed color pictures . . . bursting with activity and the faithful architectural and engineering minutiae make this something of a social document as well as a highly entertaining picture book. (p. 744)

> *Virginia Haviland, in her review of "London Bridge*
> *Is Falling Down," in* The Horn Book Magazine
> *(copyright © 1967, by The Horn Book, Inc., Boston),*
> *Vol. XLII, No. 6, December, 1967, pp. 743-44.*

TO MARKET! TO MARKET! (1967)

Nineteen traditional rhymes and proverbs have been woven into a charming tapestry of 19th century American rural life. Countless small details engage the imagination in pictures of water wheels, town squares, smithies, and barnyards, with historical and geographical background provided in a closing section. Most of the rhymes date back to English sources, but they seem quite at home in the New England setting. (pp. 165-66)

> *Della Thomas, in her review of "To Market! To*
> *Market!" in* School Library Journal, *an appendix to*
> Library Journal *(reprinted from the October, 1967*
> *issue of* School Library Journal, *published by R. R.*
> *Bowker Co./A Xerox Corporation; copyright © 1967),*
> *Vol. 14, No. 2, October, 1967, pp. 165-66.*

[The] artist draws New Castle, Delaware, as a vivid background for an American family's trip to market in "let us say 1828." The jolly verses have inspired sprightly scenes of pigs, geese, cows, farming activities, Georgian houses, and an old church with box pews; the people, animals, and domesticity are interpreted with great humor as well as with meticulous attention to authentic backgrounds. An appendix adds information about this old seaside community so carefully preserved and restored as a picturesque market town "of the new nation." (p. 744)

> *Virginia Haviland, in her review of "To Market! To*
> *Market!" in* The Horn Book Magazine *(copyright ©*
> *1967, by The Horn Book, Inc., Boston), Vol. XLIII,*
> *No. 6, December, 1967, pp. 743-44.*

To open this volume is to enter the world of the perfect. On every page there are scenes of village life, complete in every detail, depicting the spectrum of country life in all its most ideal aspects—the farmyard, the blacksmith's forge, the small country town with its market place, the church, complete with the inscriptions on the memorial plaques. Each illustration is balanced by a short traditional verse and the whole volume seems to breathe the very atmosphere of pastoral life. . . . Here the summers are always filled with sunshine, all the pigs retain their pristine pinkness, and even all the eggs are large and brown.

A book such as this will provide adults with a pang of nostalgia, and their children with hours of escapism.

> *Gabrielle Maunder, in her review of "To Market!*
> *To Market!" in* The School Librarian, *Vol. 17, No.*
> *1, September, 1969, p. 334.*

HURRAH, WE'RE OUTWARD BOUND! (1968)

Artist Peter Spier sets the course of the 19th-century three-master, La Jeune Française, on her maiden voyage, for New York and home again. Sailors reef and furl, heave and haul to the words of the text—traditional sea chanteys, rhymes and proverbs that sing of the weather, work, of good brandy and "nasty beef," of girls left behind, "the wild delight of the sailor homeward bound." A special chant of praise for Spier's colorfully illustrated panoramas of sea and port which carry the romance of the age of sail in every authentic detail from bowsprit to stern, from ship to shore.

> George A. Woods, in his review of "Hurrah, We're Outward Bound!" in The New York Times Book Review (© 1968 by The New York Times Company; reprinted by permission), June 9, 1968, p. 28.

And hurrah for another Peter Spier-Mother Goose Library book! ... And if any small-mouthed "it wasn't June 11th, it was June 12th" type objects because the chanteys and rhymes are held together by a slender thread, tell him, "Peter Spier wove that slender thread, which makes it a magic thread." Then hit him over the head with a belaying pin.

> A review of "Hurrah, We're Outward Bound," in Publishers Weekly (reprinted from the June 24, 1968, issue of Publishers Weekly, published by R. R. Bowker Company, a Xerox company; copyright © 1968 by Xerox Corporation), Vol. 193, No. 26, June 24, 1968, p. 68.

[In **Hurrah, We're Outward Bound!**] the artist presents nineteenth-century scenes of ships, sea and shore, accompanied by the jaunty verses of traditional chanteys and rhymes. (At least one, however, "Little Drops of Water," is an unacknowledged poem—by Julia A. F. Carney.) ... Once again the artist combines his zeal for historical accuracy and minute detail with his natural joyousness, to make panoramic pictures in warm, muted color, brimming with bustle, energy, and movement.

> Ethel L. Heins, in her review of "Hurrah, We're Outward Bound!" in The Horn Book Magazine (copyright ©1968 by The Horn Book, Inc., Boston), Vol. XLIV, No. 5, October, 1968, p. 555.

AND SO MY GARDEN GROWS (1969)

"Peter Spier's Italian sketchbook" is accompanied by an assortment of nursery rhymes having to do with flowers, birds, fountains, barnyard animals—all the accoutrements of a cultivated landscape. However, the pictures have very little to do with the text (or vice versa): Mistress Mary's garden doesn't grow silver bells or cockleshells or anything approximating them. ... The rhymes that are really maxims make the least sense of all: "A hedge between keeps friendship green" shows two children in a formal garden filled with hedges—and between them the chief impediment (which they look as if they'd like to leap) is a pool of water. The terminal notes identify the scenes quite precisely. ... If the notes accompanied the pictures, Peter Spier's Italian sketchbook would be a sparkling memento of old Tuscany.

> A review of "And So My Garden Grows," in Kirkus Reviews (copyright © 1969 The Kirkus Service, Inc.), Vol. XXXVII, No. 6, March 15, 1969, p. 301.

Peter Spier's warm, pleasantly busy Italian landscapes are twice the unfortunate victims of poor judgment. They are joined with generally unrelated, very un-Italian sounding nursery rhymes in what appears to be an effort to make the book part of the Mother Goose Library Series. The notes ... at the back about the actual scenes depicted would have been a much more interesting, suitable accompaniment for the pictures. In fact, it is only from this back section and the jacket flap that readers of any age can find out what is actually happening in the book—that the whole thing "is the daydream of two 19th-century children." And, in this forced, incongruous picture-text combination, the illustrations suffer from the distracting, cluttered format on marginless pages that are temporarily joined by the flimsy binding.

> Marilyn R. Singer, in her review of "And So My Garden Grows," in School Library Journal, an appendix to Library Journal (reprinted from the September, 1969 issue of School Library Journal, published by R. R. Bowker Co./A Xerox Corporation; copyright © 1969), Vol. 16, No. 1, September, 1969, p. 106.

[For **And So My Garden Grows**], Spier traveled to Italy to collect source material for his illustrations. He visited many famous gardens there, among them Bernard Berenson's villa, I Tatti (circa 1020), ... The Villa Della Petraia (fourteenth century) in Fiesole, San Gimignano (fourteenth century), and the water garden of Villa Gamberaia in Settignano. Each of these gardens is recreated in exact detail, but general scenes of the Italian countryside are drawn from many different places and recreated anew by the artist. Like the other books in this series, **And So My Garden Grows** is more than just an ordinary picture book. Through his careful attention to detail and historical accuracy as well as his lovely drawings in delicate colors, Spier captures and recreates the mood of Italy in summer. The book becomes a teaching medium as well as a diversion. Spier's lively, lovely drawings full of charm and the humor of unexpected details make *each* of his books a special prize. (p. 84)

> Joan Hess Michel, "The Illustrations of Peter Spier," in American Artist (copyright © 1969 by Billboard Publications, Inc.), Vol. 33, No. 9, October, 1969, pp. 49-55, 82-86.

It is hard to imagine quite how Peter Spier could still improve upon some of his past productions for "The Mother Goose Library", but his latest book, **And So My Garden Grows**, is certainly the most colorful so far. ... As children pore over the extraordinary depth of these pictures, as they surely will, they may even feel that they already have half a foot in this magical land, so brilliantly has it been brought to life in these pages.

> "Gardens and Verses," in The Times Literary Supplement (© Times Newspapers Ltd. (London) 1969; reproduced from The Times Literary Supplement by permission), No. 3529, October 16, 1969, p. 1193.*

OF DIKES AND WINDMILLS (1969)

It is especially pleasing when an artist in one genre proves to be adept in another, and the many admirers of Peter Spier's picture-book illustrations will doubtless be gratified to find that he has the easy humor of the raconteur, and the ability to balance long views and small details that mark the best informational writers. A fascinating study of Holland's centuries-old battle against the sea, *Of Dikes and Windmills* combines historical background with facts about hydraulic engineering and robust and affectionate anecdotes. The precise and charming illustrations are as useful as they are attractive, and the maps and diagrams are lucid. (p. 75)

> *Zena Sutherland, in her review of "Of Dikes and Windmills," in* Saturday Review *(© 1970 Saturday Review Magazine Co.; reprinted by permission), Vol. LIII, No. 4, January 24, 1970, pp. 37, 75.*

Peter Spier is well known as an award-winning illustrator, and the pictures which lavishly embellish his text—deft two-color line drawings and vibrant watercolors, together with maps, diagrams and construction drawings—are among the best he has ever done. But he is also a master storyteller. His themes—puny man pitted against mighty nature, little Holland against large and expanding Spain and England—are the stuff of which epics are made; yet Mr. Spier is never portentous, sustaining a light, informal style as he recounts, with humor and affection, the astonishing deeds (and, on occasion, misdeeds) of his redoubtable countrymen.

Long before the reader finishes **"Of Dikes and Windmills"**—knowing that he will one day want to go back to it—he will have learned that it is a true labor of love by a master craftsman. A pity it is being marketed as a juvenile for it deserves a much wider audience.

> *Ormonde De Kay, Jr., in his review of "Of Dikes and Windmills," in* The New York Times Book Review *(©1970 by The New York Times Company; reprinted by permission), February 1, 1970, p. 30.*

A lively account of the Dutch and their building of Holland by dyke, windmill, and polder. Some political history is included—the siege of Leyden, for example—but emphasis is on the war against the steadily rising seas. Detailed charts illustrate the evolution of different types of windmills, canals, and polders; there are many maps, and the decorative watercolor illustrations, largely in green, are informatively captioned. Though technical, the book is written in an easy, conversational style reminiscent of Hendrik van Loon's *The Story of Mankind* (Liveright, or Tudor, 1951). Not an introduction to the study of the country, this is an additional reference tool which points up particularly well the courage, resiliency, and ingenuity of the Dutch, and which will be especially appreciated by mechanically-minded youngsters and travelers to Holland. It can supplement such titles as Barnouw's *The Land and People of Holland* (Lippincott, 1961) or van De Groot's *The Netherlands* (Fideler, 1969). . . .

> *Margaret N. Coughlan, in her review of "Of Dikes and Windmills," in* School Library Journal, *an appendix to* Library Journal *(reprinted from the April, 1970 issue of* School Library Journal, *published by R. R. Bowker Co./A Xerox Corporation; copyright © 1970), Vol. 16, No. 8, April, 1970, p. 137.*

THE ERIE CANAL (1970)

Don't be misled by its title: this is no "upper New York State bookseller please note" regional book. Not when it's Peter Spier who welcomes you aboard for a trip along the Erie Canal as it was in the 1800s, through the locks, past the old towns, past the barges, from Albany to Buffalo, with the rollicking words of the "Erie Canal" folk song ringing in your ears. Don't miss the boat, not *Peter Spier's* boat.

> *A review of "The Erie Canal," in* Publishers Weekly *(reprinted from the September 7, 1970 issue of* Publishers Weekly, *published by R. R. Bowker Company, a Xerox company; copyright © 1970 by Xerox Corporation), Vol. 198, No. 10, September 7, 1970, p. 61.*

It is the rhythm and the heartiness of ballad subjects that give special advantage to **"The Erie Canal"**. . . . The artist's evocation of the bustling life along the Erie Canal in the last century is so alive and incisively detailed, you can almost smell the docks and hear the cries of the bargemen. . . .

And in the verses of this well-known work song . . . , the twanging banjos are never far away. The book contains the music for the song. . . . [It] also has a chatty and useful history of the Erie Canal in the back.

> *Lisa Hammel, in her review of "The Erie Canal," in* The New York Times Book Review *(© 1970 by The New York Times Company; reprinted by permission), September 20, 1970, p. 46.*

The artist, a master of the panoramic picture book, has created another piece of scenographic Americana. . . . Mr. Spier records detail with the meticulous accuracy of the historian and the appreciative eye of the artist. His characteristic full-color pictures—many of them doublespreads—are full of boats, buildings, animals, and people, all involved in the bustling activity on and along the banks of the canal.

> *Ethel L. Heins, in her review of "The Erie Canal," in* The Horn Book Magazine *(copyright © 1970 by The Horn Book, Inc., Boston), Vol. XLVI, No. 5, October, 1970, p. 472.*

We all know Peter Spier's style now. He is the master in our day of the crowded picture, packing it full of rich and lively detail without spoiling its design. . . . These are pictures for children—and adults—to read. Something interesting and relevant is happening in every corner. The book has been carefully researched, but Mr. Spier carries his scholarship gaily, finding fun in a byway of the industrial past. A lovely book. (p. 297)

> *A review of "The Erie Canal," in* The Junior Bookshelf, *Vol. 35, No. 5, October, 1971, pp. 296-97.*

From the moment when the mules are led from their stables to the last peaceful drift through a wooded gorge, the *Small Hope's* voyage from Albany to Buffalo is pure delight for anyone prepared to take enough time to notice the entrancing detail of the pictures, the costume of the 1850's, the amusing incidents at canal side, under and over bridges, in small town and lonely field. Peter Spier's crowded scenes in delicate watercolour have never been better than in this happy interpretation of a popular song of sixty years ago.

> *Margery Fisher, in her review of "The Erie Canal," in her* Growing Point, *Vol. 10, No. 6, December, 1971, p. 1855.*

GOBBLE, GROWL, GRUNT (1971)

It's not hard to believe the jacket blurb's claim that over 600 animals are portrayed in this buzzing succession of double-page spreads, each crowded with a jumble of creatures and Spier's orthographic interpretation of the noises they make. There's the predictable community of barnyard fowl with its clucks and gobbles and honks, a more ingenious water scene with hippos (RRUMMPF), flamingos (ONGK), crocodiles (silent) . . . and many many more in all sorts of poses and juxtapositions. To an adult it's distractingly busy, but you probably won't be allowed to turn a page until every last bee has been buzZEEEEEEEEingly vocalized.

> *A review of "Gobble, Growl, Grunt," in* Kirkus Reviews *(copyright © 1971 The Kirkus Service, Inc.), Vol. XXXIX, No. 19, October 1, 1971, p. 1068.*

Some 600 animals, all drawn with care, humor and visual clarity, fly, leap and graze in the pages of this book. . . . The pictures are arranged with good zoological sense. One page takes you to the African veld, another to the deep sea, a third to the night woods, and so on; it is biogeography (or ecology, in the fashionable phrasing). The animals too are far from being stiff and static; the baby elephant showers in its mother's trunk fountain, the seal quite unexpectedly balances an ostrich egg on its nose. It is zoology that is neither trite nor overexotic; the familiar house mouse is here, a clown-hero throughout the book, along with the oryx and the cassowary.

This bestiary is enough to make a first-class book in itself, but it does not account for the essence of the most original and satisfying young children's science book of the year. The animals are noisy; next to each one is some apt phonetic rendering of the sounds it makes. These representations are conventional where that sounds right, as in the bullfrog's *jug o' rum more rum;* unexpected, as in the two-page chorus of 71 drab, gregarious starlings murmuring *fee-you* and *sweet, twee* and *weet,* or absolutely novel, as the *arrrf-arf* of the colorful toucan. The broad deck of the snorting Indian rhinoceros rocks by as a squadron of oxpeckers aboard chirp *key, key, key.* There is a hushed page too: the snail, the mute swan, the moth and the condor. These are not idle inventions; they sum up many a zoo visit and many an interview with zoological travelers. The distant future and the little apprentice reader of today have here a wonderful guide to English sounds as they are spelled. No other book this year combines as much observation, helpful pedagogy and sheer fun.

> *Philip Morrison and Phylis Morrison, in their review of "Gobble, Growl, Grunt," in* Scientific American *(copyright © 1971 by Scientific American, Inc.; all rights reserved), Vol. 225, No. 6, December, 1971, p. 107.*

Just from the title **"Gobble Growl Grunt"** . . . , one knows Peter Spier's book is going to be about sounds. . . . But each creature's often amusing, and a surprisingly accurate contribution to the symphony of the zoological garden is only a part of it. For this is also a beginner's guide to the fauna of water, earth and air. But not any old guide: While the animals are meticulously drawn, identified and grouped on each page according to family or habit or habitat, they are also exuberantly alive. It is not just about sound, but a book about life. If you're going to get a child one book about animals, this might be it.

> *Lisa Hammel, "A Sound Way of Learning," in* The New York Times Book Review *(© 1972 by The New York Times Company; reprinted by permission), January 23, 1972, p. 8.**

Peter Spier may not be quite in the world's Top Ten for sheer artistic ability, but he is well up in the list of the most lovable of picture book makers. He has always been a master of meaningful detail; every corner of his designs has some delectable fragment inviting close study. In his new offering he gives us

not words but animal noises. Across page after page sprawl creatures great and small, each howling or squeaking his characteristic sound. . . . At last after all these piercing, terrifying, deafening noises to the last-page silent comfort of starfish, worm and ladybird. In the drawing Mr. Spier achieves high humour with no sacrifice of zoological fidelity. A joyous book. One for all ages, including the oldest.

> *A review of "Gobble, Growl, Grunt," in* The Junior Bookshelf, *Vol. 36, No. 5, October, 1972, p. 308.*

Peter Spier can not only draw animals of every kind superbly well, but can also give them expressions which seem to be exactly typical of their characters. . . . All are coloured in delicate shades which, whilst in some cases not being true to life, nevertheless make a very attractive picture book. The title presents the main idea of the book, which is not only to illustrate each animal, but also to show, in pronounceable word form, the kind of noise each one makes. What a difficult task this must have been and how well Peter Spier has succeeded. The book would not be out of place in a natural history section, although it would require what I consider to be the only omission—but an important one—an alphabetical name index, as the animals are not in any planned sequence and the pages are not numbered. Ages three to six. (It could be useful in infants' schools for teaching sounds related to visual sources.)

> *Edward Hudson, in his review of "Gobble, Growl, Grunt," in* Children's Book Review *(© 1973 Five Owls Press Ltd.; all rights reserved), Vol. II, No. 6, December, 1972, p. 181.*

CRASH! BANG! BOOM! (1972)

Ringing a change on his successful *Gobble, Growl, Grunt* . . . , Spier offers as many orthographic interpretations, in the same busy format, of the sounds of inanimate objects—vehicles, domestic appliances, power tools, natural phenomena, and inevitably musical instruments. Reactions to the specific items are bound to vary: to one reader words like SMACK for a kiss and RRRING-RRRING for a phone and too many others were totally unoriginal while others like DENGA-DENGA-DENGA for a sidewalk drill and FFFFOOOO for a sniffle seemed wildly and arbitrarily inapt—but all of these were perhaps redeemed by the FRRRRIT of a paper tear, MIRRA-MIRRA-MIRRA of a room air conditioner and FUDDA-FUDDA-FUDDA-FUDDA of a film projector. In any case Spier has introduced a game with endless possibilities, and if some of the pages (especially of kitchen, laundry and bathroom devices) are visually unexciting others (of athletes, orchestras, construction work) combine the charm and accuracy for which he is noted with enough miniature likenesses of cacophonous action to make the SKRRR-ITs of turning pages few and far between.

> *A review of "Crash! Bang! Boom!" in* Kirkus Reviews *(copyright © 1972 The Kirkus Service, Inc.), Vol. XL, No. 12, June 15, 1972, p. 671.*

In a colorful cacophony of precise sound, the illustrator . . . sets out to capture visually the audible quality of inanimate objects. . . . Clean white pages are filled with detailed, bright-colored pictures of objects grouped according to use, relationship, or activity: the YOU-YOU-YOU-YOU-YOU-YOU of a police siren pursues the AR-ROOOOM! of two middle-aged manic motorcyclists; the WHIRRRRRRRR's, GLUB-GLUB-GLUB-GLUB's, and SPLITTER SPLATTER's commonly heard in a kitchen. Something is always happening in this new-style audio-visual delight, and full kudos must be given to anyone who can characterize the sound of an eraser at work: UFFA-UFFA-UFFA. In the final analysis, *CRASH! BANG! BOOM!* is simply a lot of fun. For preschool-age children. (pp. 458-59)

> *Sheryl B. Andrews, in her review of "Crash! Bang! Boom!" in* The Horn Book Magazine *(copyright © 1972 by The Horn Book, Inc., Boston), Vol. XLVIII, No. 5, October, 1972, pp. 458-59.*

The sounds of a child's world—from the "CLANG CLANG" of a train signal to the "KISSSH-KISSSSSH" of a breaking wave—are the only text in this excellent concept book. Peter Spier's high-spirited, detailed watercolor illustrations identify each sound source. Different categories fill each double page: sounds of the schoolroom, of sporting events, of holiday celebrations, etc. Such common household sounds as that of a light switch, brushing hair, and gargling will be recognized by the smallest listeners. The book is well suited for reading aloud, and kindergarten and primary grade children are sure to enjoy increasing their noise repertoire.

> *Patricia Berglund, in her review of "Crash! Bang! Boom!" in* School Library Journal, *an appendix to* Library Journal *(reprinted from the October, 1972 issue of* School Library Journal, *published by R. R. Bowker Co./A Xerox Corporation; copyright © 1972), Vol. 19, No. 2, October, 1972, p. 107.*

FAST-SLOW, HIGH-LOW: A BOOK OF OPPOSITES (1972)

The difference between night and day is in Peter Spier's **"Fast-Slow, High-Low"** . . .—and between 28 other pairs of opposites such as deep-shallow, wet-dry, heavy-light, hard-soft. His is a book of conceptual exercises highlighting contrasting differences in size, speed, time, space, etc. Sounds intimidating? Hardly. Not the way Mr. Spier presents it, lightly, amusingly and always clearly in over 500 illustrations. "Straight" for instance, are strands of spaghetti right out of the package, while "crooked" has them on the plate after they've been cooked. The pair loud-quiet is illustrated by a monk praying, a baby bawling, a broom sweeping, a vacuum whirring. Easy. Yet not always; sometimes the child will have to stretch his mind and think. That's always to the good.

> *George A. Woods, "Three Picture Books," in* The New York Times Book Review *(© 1973 by The New York Times Company; reprinted by permission), February 18, 1973, p. 8.*

Mr. Spier's illustrations of the different pairs he chooses are funny, helpful and stimulating. The innumerable pictures are small, delicate and colourful, and the two-year-old will have as much fun identifying them as the four-year-old will find in discovering what they are trying to tell him.

> *A review of "Fast-Slow, High-Low," in* The Times Literary Supplement *(© Times Newspapers Ltd. (London) 1973; reproduced from* The Times Literary Supplement *by permission), No. 3734, September 28, 1973, p. 1126.*

There are few books for the youngest child which exhibit the wit and purpose of Peter Spier's latest book. . . . The pages are crowded with humorous and ingenious examples to stimulate the reader into discovering which pairs go together. It is both instructive and delightfully frivolous. For example, a very long snake goes with a very short fish, snub-nosed pigs press against long-trunked elephants.

Warmly recommended to parents and teachers seeking new ideas to arouse their young children's imaginations.

> *Gabrielle Maunder, in her review of "Fast-Slow, High-Low," in* Children's Book Review *(© 1973 Five Owls Press Ltd.; all rights reserved), Vol. III, No. 5, October, 1973, p. 140.*

As a method of learning about relationships, this crowded gallery of neat, recognisable and often amusing pictures has every chance of being effective. The detail of the illustrations will ensure a flood of questions from young children. . . . Full marks to Peter Spier for a simple idea most efficiently and pleasantly executed.

> *A review of "Fast-Slow, High-Low," in* The Junior Bookshelf, *Vol. 38, No. 1, February, 1974, p. 17.*

THE STAR-SPANGLED BANNER (1973)

Peter Spier, do you know what might be said by some as a result of this book? That you're a flag-waving superpatriot, man, you're way out—of step. Maybe they'll say: If you want to make the scene you've got to have a healthy contempt for patriotism, pull down the statues and the pedestals, too. "Land of the free and home of the brave"? Rubbish! Burn the flag! Come on, you know we've denuded our forests, gouged scars in the earth, defrauded the poor, lacerated the land and left neon sores of Finger Lickin' Good, Dine & Dance, Dew Drop Inn. . . .

And yet strange things happen when "The Star-Spangled Banner" is played: a lump in the throat, a shiver passes up and down the spine, the eyes mist. There's a strange chemistry at work, a principle, a belief, a sentiment, an ideal for which many did indeed sacrifice lives, fortunes and honor. So I'll go along with you, Peter Spier, because you've put romance back into the love affair, reminded us in stirring, sweeping scenes of the action and the dream. Admittedly the job's not done. Ideals are forever. Here you've restored the vision.

What has America today got to do with Francis Scott Key and Fort McHenry, the bombardment in 1814? Everything. There is a continuum to history; the present is rooted in the past. We're looking again as we once did for something o'er the ramparts in the dawn's early light, that which we proudly hailed at the twilight's last gleaming. You show us that past, Peter Spier, the orange morning sky, the rocket's red glare, make us feel the earth trembling through that awesome, deafening cannonade, make us hear the creak of the rigging, look up and see sails furled in the mist-shrouded blue-gray sky. You make us walk oaken decks, past pulleys and capstans and gunports. . . .

You've not gloried in war but in perseverance of the pursuit of an ideal. Illustrating three verses of the anthem you've reminded us once more of our former, child-like simplicity and belief, restored them. We may not get many more chances. Important, too, is that you've shown us our diversity—Quaker, Catholic, Protestant, Jew, Amish, Mormon and more—pointed out the tasks ahead, the wars to be won in housing and food, in the laboratory and outer space.

Good for you, Peter Spier, good for kids today and unborn, and good for America.

George A. Woods, in his review of "The Star Spangled Banner," in The New York Times Book Review *(© 1973 by The New York Times Company; reprinted by permission), October 21, 1973, p. 8.*

[Spier] has given a new kind of life to the American National Anthem. Not only has he magnificently portrayed the British bombardment of Fort McHenry during the War of 1812, but he has expanded the meaning of the text of the first two verses and of the last verse of Francis Scott Key's poem. Boston, Philadelphia, Washington, D.C., and New York are represented in present-day vignettes of places associated with the history of "The land of the free and the home of the brave." Industry and agriculture, urban development and moon walking, and many different kinds of houses of religious worship round out the presentation of the positive aspects of the American experience. At the beginning of the book, the mood is set by the detailed line drawings of sailing vessels and by the panoramic doublespreads vigorous with the flight of rockets. The pastel watercolor tones are never mawkish or sentimental but convey the dramatic feeling for space made possible by the sizable dimensions of the book. At the end of the volume there are four pages of historical notes and reproductions, as well as a copy of the music and of all four verses of the National Anthem. (pp. 40-1)

Paul Heins, in his review of "The Star-Spangled Banner," in The Horn Book Magazine *(copyright © 1974 by The Horn Book, Inc., Boston), Vol. L, No. 1, February, 1974, pp. 40-1.*

Peter Spier illustrates the lyrics of our national anthem in lovely watercolor paintings. . . . Included is a readable and accurate history of the War of 1812 with an explanation of how Francis Scott Key, a Georgetown lawyer, came to watch the fierce and decisive battle; what happened to the original poem; and why it became our national anthem. The music, in an easy-to-play rendition, and the lyrics to all four verses appear at the end. Spier has also designed unusual end papers which show each of the flags of the Revolution and the United States and the dates they were in use, as well as 65 flags of the government and the Armed Forces. An outstanding and beautiful book, this provides valuable information on flags and on the war that prompted our national anthem.

Phyllis Galt, in her review of "The Star-Spangled Banner," in School Library Journal, *an appendix to* Library Journal *(reprinted from the February, 1974 issue of* School Library Journal, *published by R. R. Bowker Co./A Xerox Corporation; copyright © 1974), Vol. 20, No. 6, February, 1974, p. 564.*

The poem . . . has an ideal illustrator in Peter Spier, who has a superb technique, a keen sense of history and of irony, and whose pictures blend actuality and fine composition. The big double-spreads are atmospheric as well as detailed, and the artist moves them gently out of the turmoil of 1814 to modern New York and the surface of the moon.

A review of "The Star-Spangled Banner," in The Junior Bookshelf, *Vol. 40, No. 3, June, 1976, p. 146.*

TIN LIZZIE   (1975)

The last two pages of the book are for the mechanically-minded— meticulous diagrams labeling the individual parts of a Model

From The Star-Spangled Banner, *illustrated by Peter Spier.*

T. It's perfect for those who want to know a crankcase draincock from a steering knuckle.

The rest of us, though, are just along for the ride. Spier's drawings are invariably pleasing, detailed-filled panoramas that capture the changing face of changing times; the full-color paintings are suffused with the rumpled comfort of an unstarched cotton shirt. What might, in different hands, have made us carsick becomes, under Spier's direction, an enjoyable piece of Americana.

Stephen Krensky, in his review of "Tin Lizzie," in The New York Times Book Review *(© 1975 by The New York Times Company; reprinted by permission), November 16, 1975, p. 46.*

The artist's sensitivity to American scenery has always been present in his work; the book, executed in his characteristic, delicate watercolors, depicts fifty years of American history— as seen and lived by ordinary citizens. The result is page after page of fascinating, detailed scenes. And the final endpapers, showing all of the car's parts, give added evidence that Peter Spier never forgets his audience.

Anita Silvey, in her review of "Tin Lizzie," in The Horn Book Magazine *(copyright © 1976 by the Horn Book, Inc., Boston), Vol. LII, No. 1, February, 1976, p. 43.*

A tribute to the Model T Ford of 1909. The author-artist follows one model to a Wisconsin small-town where after startling horses and people for several years the car is accepted; sold to a young couple, it travels widely and later returns to the Mid-

West to become vehicle-of-all-work on a farm; left to rot in the field at last, it is bought and restored as a vintage car. A social history in itself, this book, for Peter Spier, as always generous with detail, has shown Tin Lizzie in the company of penny-farthings and container trucks, carrying folk in every kind of costume past every kind of building over sixty years. An exhilarating and well-documented sequence of pleasing water-colour pictures.

> *Margery Fisher, in her review of "Tin Lizzie," in her* Growing Point, *Vol. 15, No. 7, January, 1977, p. 3051.*

NOAH'S ARK   (1977; British edition as *The Great Flood*)

AUTHOR'S COMMENTARY

One of the questions I am often asked is: "Why did you decide to do *Noah's Ark*?" The answer is simple: Because I have wanted to retell the story for years. The final catalyst was the seventeenth-century Dutch poem by Jacob Revius, which has the faith and, above all, the childlike simplicity which I found moving and inspiring. It was obviously not an original idea, and I went to our library to look at Bowker's *Books in Print* to find out precisely how unoriginal it actually was. There were over twenty *Noah*'s in print. The library owned seven different versions, and when I tried to have a look at them, I found that they were nearly always taken out on loan. So I bought all the versions I could get hold of to see what other artists had done with Noah. Some were good, others were less so. But I found that virtually all the books had the same slant; the Flood was invariably depicted as a joyous, sun-filled Caribbean cruise: happy flood, happy Noah (wearing a sailor's cap), happy beasts. No drownings, nothing to indicate God's wrath. It was difficult even to recognize the Bible text in any of those books, and it was not what I had in mind at all. A few books were a bit more sombre and followed the Bible closely, without adding any unexpected sidelights or intimate glimpses. None of them showed Noah shoveling manure or even hinted at the stench and the mess inside. It was then that I knew that there was room for one more *Noah's Ark*.

When working on the layout of the book, not in sketches yet but with written notes, I had the ark floating away and the waters rising higher and higher, the animals that remained behind standing knee-deep, then waist-deep, in the water—as I later showed in the book. The next page showed hundreds of drowned animals awash in the waves, some with their heads down, others with their legs sticking up in the air, with small creatures and birds having saved themselves on the floating carcasses. It was certainly dramatic. But it was to be a book for small children, and I decided that it went too far in its grisliness and left that part out.

I always find it difficult to determine where that invisible line, the border between good taste and bad, runs. Between the believable and the unbelievable. Between the acceptable and the unacceptable. Between the grim and the gruesome. Between the necessary and the superfluous. But the pieces fell slowly into their proper places, and today it seems to me as if the book created itself and I was the ever-present and interested observer.

Whenever I finish a new book, I show it to my children to hear their reaction. In *Noah*'s case it was encouraging. They said, "It's all right." That was the highest praise I could expect. This is not always the case. When I showed them my newest book *Oh, Were They Ever Happy* . . . , they told me that it was "kidstuff" (which of course it is supposed to be!) and, adding insult to injury, asked if it was really necessary to put *our* name on the cover? (pp. 375-76)

I have, very frankly, always had my doubts about the basis on which book prizes are awarded. I do not for a single moment believe that my *Noah's Ark* is the most distinguished picture book of the year. I believe, with a few memorable exceptions, that such a book does not exist. There are almost always a handful of books worthy of the distinction. Besides, if that book really existed and could be identified on an infallible basis, it would win every prize given that year. Yet that never seems to happen. (p. 377)

Although I know it is the fate of some award-winning picture books to languish on library shelves, it is my hope, and the end to which my efforts are really directed, to produce a book that not only pleases me but also will be popular with children. (pp. 377-78)

> *Peter Spier, "Caldecott Award Acceptance" (reprinted by permission of the author), in* The Horn Book Magazine, *Vol. LIV, No. 4, August, 1978, pp. 372-78.*

A seventeenth-century Dutch poem . . . opens the otherwise almost wordless book. Skillfully translated by the artist and set in a readable, appropriately archaic type, the artlessly reverent verses add an unexpected dimension to the full-color pictures. Peter Spier's characteristic panoramas are marvels of minute detail, activity, vitality, and humor; a few of the scenes are quiescent and serenely beautiful. The artwork is presented on single pages and in double-page spreads as well as in small vertical and horizontal panels, and even the handsome endpapers, title page, and half-title page add to the dramatic narrative. Another outstanding work by an artist whose picture books are notable for their aesthetic quality, integrity, and engaging wholesomeness. (pp. 525-26)

> *Ethel L. Heins, in her review of "Noah's Ark," in* The Horn Book Magazine *(copyright © 1977 by the Horn Book, Inc., Boston), Vol. LIII, No. 5, October, 1977, pp. 525-26.*

Highly detailed pen-and-ink and watercolor illustrations lavishly depict the Old Testament ark story with a heavy emphasis on the animals. Thousands of these watching creatures are seen calmly awaiting their fate as the waters rise and the ark floats away—a gentle yet strong portrayal of the death of those left behind. Although some may be "jarred" by the anachronism of Noah having glass jars in which to save the insect world and by the slighting that Noah's wife gets, Spier's is nevertheless a warmly original interpretation of the ancient disaster with welcome touches of humor and poignancy. (p. 104)

> *Craighton Hippenhammer, in his review of "Noah's Ark," in* School Library Journal *(reprinted from the October, 1977 issue of* School Library Journal, *published by R. R. Bowker Co./A Xerox Corporation; copyright © 1977), Vol. 24, No. 2, October, 1977, pp. 103-04.*

The picture book of the season has to be *Noah's Ark*. . . . [It contains] marvelously detailed and delicately colored drawings of Noah, the ark, the rains, and, above all, the animals. Funny, too.

> *William Cole, in his review of "Noah's Ark," in* Saturday Review *(© 1977 Saturday Review Maga-*

From Noah's Ark, *illustrated by Peter Spier*

zine Co.; reprinted by permission), Vol. 5, No. 5, November 26, 1977, p. 41.

"Wide and stark, / Was the ark. . . . / Creatures all, / Large and small, . . . / Fierce and tame, / In they came, / Pair by pair, / Gross and fair." So for 30 couplets runs the beat of the . . . poem given us in strong rhyme by Peter Spier. Then, with not another word, this artist shows us how the voyage was, the old myth made luminous by a powerful imagination and a brush marvelously devoted to the truth. The meticulous and colorful ink and wash drawings lead us the entire way to the new world.

> *Philip Morrison and Phylis Morrison, in their review of "Noah's Ark," in* Scientific American *(copyright © 1977 by Scientific American, Inc.; all rights reserved), Vol. 237, No. 6, December, 1977, p. 36.*

The 1977 Caldecott Medal winner is a most remarkable book. Apart from two biblical phrases at beginning and end, and [a poem about the flood], the story is told entirely in pictures teeming with imaginatively conceived detail. Peter Spier gives a marvellous sense of the weight of Noah's task in building the ark, and splendid double-page vistas of it resisting the rising waters, storms and tempests, with strange solitary seascapes. The bare bones of *Genesis* are filled out by practical considerations of which, one feels, one ought to have been aware: the other animals watch the closed ark as the waters rise; it is a heavy task to feed and clean out so many different varieties of animal, who need so many different types of accommodation, including of course a large pool; Noah has great anxieties, a sense of responsibility, and also of pride in 'his' animals, particularly those who manage to multiply *before* going forth. Most dramatic of all, perhaps, is the desolate scene inside the ark after all the animals rush out, leaving the cats in triumphant possession of the deserted kitchen quarters. By contrast, the fertile landscape cultivated by Noah beneath the rainbow is shown in beautifully glowing colours. Others than young readers will see the story hereafter in a new light.

> *A review of "The Great Flood," in* The Junior Bookshelf, *Vol. 43, No. 1, February, 1979, p. 22.*

The poem on the first page, . . . printed in elegant old type, a pleasure to the senses, tells the story of the Flood. The rest of the book tells the story again in pictures, beautifully detailed and realistic right down to the natural increase of the mice and the cats, the superior exuberance of the whales and fishes in their element under the flood, the barnacles on the bottom of the Ark when it is stranded on Ararat, and the dreadful mess left after the animals have disembarked. Teeming pages contrast with empty ones: a great clear page of flood under the rain with a tiny Ark at the edge, a white dove flying over a whole page of waves. This book deserved its Caldecott medal.

> *Dorothy Nimmo, in her review of "The Great Flood," in* The School Librarian, *Vol. 27, No. 3, September, 1979, p. 240.*

OH, WERE THEY EVER HAPPY! (1978; British edition as *Nothing Like a Fresh Coat of Paint*)

A delicious contemporary tale—and extended joke—in jellybean colors. Three children, whose babysitter fails to show while their parents are out buying paint to do the outside of their large, white colonial house, decide to surprise them and do it themselves. Marshalling left-over paint cans from garage and basement, ladders, brushes, and their own talents, they paint everything in sight in a magnificent rainbow of tints. What a grand mess! (The bathroom clean-up is a gem.) As the neighbors stare in amazement at the red dog, the striped fence, and the plaid facade, the kids are pleased as can be—"Won't they be happy when they come home?" they crow in anticipation of adult approval. The title is the sarcastic answer. Although much of the detail that makes Spier's books such continuing favorites will be lost on story-hour audiences, the idea will strike them as enormously funny and the spare text is simple enough for newly independent readers.

> *Marjorie Lewis, in her review of "Oh, Were They Ever Happy!" in* School Library Journal *(reprinted from the April, 1978 issue of* School Library Journal, *published by R. R. Bowker Co./A Xerox Corporation; copyright © 1978), Vol. 24, No. 8, April, 1978, p. 78.*

I am an ardent fan of the affectionate detail and color-washed charm of the artist Peter Spier's Mother Goose Library. . . . The place in this new picture book looks like an expensive suburban house. After the parents drive off for the day in their station wagon, the children paint the house. . . .

The finished job made my blood run cold. Have I scraped too many clapboards and puttied too many windows to see the humor in the appalling clean-up job the parents have in store? I think it's not just that. One just can't quite believe the tall tale because the setting is so real: behold the wonderful miscellany in the garage—the kitty litter, the acetylene torches, the rotary mower! This particular disaster couldn't happen here. Rabbit children might swab their little bungalow in the woods with all the colors of the rainbow, but not these normal, intelligent children in a suburban house with a television antenna on the chimney and a sprinkler on the lawn.

> *Jane Langton, in her review of "Oh, Were They Ever Happy!" in* The New York Times Book Review *(© 1979 by The New York Times Company; reprinted by permission), February 18, 1979, p. 20.*

Peter Spier has long been a favourite of mine. **Nothing like a fresh coat of paint** does not have the rich detail that is so absorbing a feature of many of his books, but it has his lively freshness, here put to the service of a slapstick humour that really opens the generation gap. . . . A minimal text, following [the children's] absorption in the work and their pleasure in contemplating their parents' delight, accompanies pictures showing the growth of the most appalling mess you have ever seen. Half the joke is that they are such good children, so eager to help, so careful to clean up (that cat should not be allowed to lick her technicolour coat) remembering even to put the cans ready for the dustman—in a colossal oozing pyramid on the lawn.

> *Joy Chant, in her review of "Nothing Like a Fresh Coat of Paint," in* The Times Literary Supplement *(© Times Newspapers Ltd. (London) 1981; reproduced from* The Times Literary Supplement *by permission), No. 4069, March 27, 1981, p. 342.*

BORED—NOTHING TO DO! (1978)

Spier's detailed, action-filled watercolor illustrations show two boys scavenging through a house and yard to find parts to build an airplane (that's airplane, *not* model airplane) and succeeding. After all, their mother had told them to find something to do because she was never bored at their age. Kids will definitely enjoy this book for it abounds in adventure and tongue-in-cheek humor. Regrettably, the story is also full of sex-role stereotyping. Mother always wears an apron (unless she's knitting). She faints into her husband's arms when she sees her sons in the air. When it is time to punish the boys, Father gives the spanking while Mother gives a nurturing kiss. Spier's expressive illustrations overpower the weak, choppy text ("Hard work! 'Need wire?' That is easy. How about that?") which reads like a collection of captions. The book would have worked far better as a story-without-words.

> *Gemma DeVinney, in her review of "Bored—Nothing to Do!" in* School Library Journal *(reprinted from the December, 1978 issue of* School Library Journal, *published by R. R. Bowker Co./A Xerox Corporation; copyright © 1978), Vol. 25, No. 4, December, 1978, p. 47.*

The text of this lively cautionary tale for parents consists mainly of snatches of conversation—'To make it run, turn the key', 'Where are my sheets?', 'I think they are angry'—which add

piquancy for young readers to the story-in-pictures. . . . Sharp colour and innumerable small, amusing details make the pictures as readable as they are skilful.

> *Margery Fisher, in her review of "Bored—Nothing to Do!" in her* Growing Point, *Vol. 18, No. 4, November, 1979, p. 3608.*

Peter Spier has [whatever it is that makes a picture book work] in a most original form. His latest—**Bored—Nothing to Do** . . . is a winner. [It contains] a minimal bold text and wonderfully detailed pictures. . . . The book ends with a two-page spread with details of a Piper Super Cub, as an extra bonus.

> *Virginia Makins, "A Laugh a Minute," in* The Times Educational Supplement *(© Times Newspapers Ltd. (London) 1979; reproduced from* The Times Educational Supplement *by permission), No. 3311, November 23, 1979, p. 30.*

Here is one of the most individual of artists at his best. . . . Mr. Spier's familiar line and wash drawings are packed with detail, all of it exact and practical. . . . A book for the whole family but specially for handy teenagers who must not be put off by the picture book format. This is not kid's stuff.

> *A review of "Bored—Nothing to Do!" in* The Junior Bookshelf, *Vol. 44, No. 3, June, 1980, p. 122.*

THE LEGEND OF NEW AMSTERDAM (1979)

In his well-known panoramic yet highly detailed style the artist lovingly pictures New Amsterdam in 1660 as a Dutch city with brick houses, elaborately gabled roofs, and windmills; and in his texts and multicolored drawings he describes the activities and sights that might have appealed to the children of the colony: the grist mill, the fort, the shipyard, glass blowing, and Peter Stuyvesant himself. What the children liked best of all, however, was to tease Annetje Jans Bogardus, who had lost her mind when her husband was killed by the Indians. According to the author-illustrator, she was called Crazy Annie and would constantly point to the sky and say, "'Look! Can't you see? People and stones!'" The author-artist rounds out his account by showing how New Amsterdam turned into nineteenth-century New York; and—like Arnold Lobel in *On the Day Peter Stuyvesant Sailed into Town* (Harper)—he designed a two-page spread revealing the skyline of the modern city, as if to demonstrate that Annie's words had been prophetic. The last page of the book supplies a description of and a key to the residential street plan of New Amsterdam, which is limned on the final endpaper.

> *Paul Heins, in his review of "The Legend of New Amsterdam," in* The Horn Book Magazine *(copyright © 1979 by The Horn Book, Inc., Boston), Vol. LV, No. 5, October, 1979, p. 527.*

I've long admired the lively pen and watercolor precision of Peter Spier, particularly his books set in 18th- and 19th-century America ("The Fox Went Out on a Chilly Night," "The Erie Canal") and England ("London Bridge Is Falling Down"). So I eagerly opened his latest, "The Legend of New Amsterdam" . . . , and to my delight discovered furiously detailed renderings of life in the 17th-century Dutch colony. But as I read the text and turned the pages, my affections waned: Instead of doing a straight historical survey (or a day in the life of a New Amsterdam boy and girl) the book turns into an awkward tale of a dotty old New Amsterdam widow (Crazy Annie) who used to look up at the sky and yell, "People and stone, people and stone" and be teased for it by the children (instructive detail, that)—all of which serves as a kind of psychic tease for Mr. Spier's last picture: towering skyscrapers in New York City today. No trouble with the art, just the ill-conceived and boring story, which sinks the book into New York harbor. (pp. 51, 66)

> Harold C.K. Rice, "The Book with the Pictures," in The New York Times Book Review (© 1979 by The New York Times Company; reprinted by permission), November 11, 1979, pp. 51, 66.

In *The Legend of New Amsterdam* Peter Spier offers readers from six to ten years of age a marvelous array of facts. . . . Full color impressionistic paintings detail and extend the informative text. Children will enjoy the bits of humor sprinkled throughout this fine factual picture book.

> A review of "The Legend of New Amsterdam" (copyright 1980 by the International Reading Association, Inc.; reprinted with permission of the International Reading Association), in The Reading Teacher, Vol. 33, No. 8, May, 1980, p. 972.

PEOPLE (1980)

Illustrating [the theme of the diversity and uniqueness of the world's people] are a plethora of examples from the shapes of noses, to the games people play, to individual inclinations (for solitude or company), to gradations of wealth. . . . The national variations tend to be overplayed (the English domiciles pictured are a castle and a Kate Greenaway cottage, the Scandinavian a log compound not seen outside museums), giving kids a "picturesque" impression of what the world is like that resurrects some very old-fashioned stereotypes (Russian eating habits are represented, for goodness sakes, by Cossacks carrying flaming skewers). And one might ask whether this hodge-podge is really the place to tell kids that "Most people are decent, honest, friendly, and well meaning, but some are none of these"—as exemplified by prisoners behind barred windows. But taken un-seriously, it's nothing worse than a waste of time—especially in a world whose authentic differences kids can see every day on TV.

> A review of "People," in Kirkus Reviews (copyright © 1980 The Kirkus Service, Inc.), Vol. XLVIII, No. 19, October 1, 1980, p. 1296.

This noted illustrator's latest book takes an oversize format . . . to encompass the whole earth, seen glimmering in space on the endpapers. The world's people crowd the jacket and title page in colorful profusion of national dress. Fascinatingly detailed small-color sketches examine the diverse forms our common humanity takes. Myriad physiques and features (including a half page of eyes), games, pets, foods, holidays and hierarchies receive dynamic spot treatment in light but thought-provoking ways, interspersed with facts and figures. Several pages on communication illustrate the hand alphabet and samples of 40 world scripts, including Oriental vertical scripts and their variants. A street scene of dreary sameness is contrasted with one of bustling variety. Birth, death, and ways some individuals are remembered (Mr. du Trampolin for the trampoline, JFK for Kennedy airport) are mentioned. The tone of the simple, direct text is sometimes overenthusiastic; many sentences end in unnecessary exclamation points. . . . A wonderful introduction to a global view that will answer and arouse

curiosity in the young and act as an absorbing reminder for any age.

> Ruth M. McConnell, in her review of "People," in School Library Journal (reprinted from the November, 1980 issue of School Library Journal, published by R. R. Bowker Co./A Xerox Corporation; copyright © 1980), Vol. 27, No. 3, November, 1980, p. 67.

[It] will probably take you more than an hour to peruse [this] largely pictorial presentation of the uniqueness of individuals. Mr. Spier shows the differences among peoples, for instance, in dress, domicile, occupation, religion and communication. . . . He also points out the differences in people's tastes in pets, foods, recreation as well as in their physical distinctions: Half a page is devoted to 54 different nose configurations.

Peter Spier is one of our most popular American artists and has been honored with the Caldecott Medal in 1978 for **"Noah's Ark."** His illustrations for **"The Fox Went Out on a Chilly Night"** in 1962 were even better. Mr. Spier is not a "fine" artist in the classic sense but his work possesses a charming, colorful "lookability" to which children as well as adults respond. This almost encyclopedic oversized volume with its message of respect and tolerance will be no exception.

> George A. Woods, in his review of "People," in The New York Times Book Review (© 1980 by The New York Times Company; reprinted by permission), December 7, 1980, p. 41.

People is a book that no doubt was created with the best of intentions. Nonetheless, it perpetuates grossly biased images. If the book were only words, one would welcome its author's attempt to help children recognize and appreciate human diversity. But a picture's worth a thousand words and Spier's illustrations, which often intrigue and fascinate with their detail, all too often destroy that which the words intend to create.

A panorama of the garden of Eden, on the opening pages, depicts a white Adam and Eve walking alone in a world ultimately to be populated in large part by people of color. On subsequent pages, one finds grotesquely drawn faces of all colors, but people of color seem most hideous. Slits and slants suffice for eyes for Asians. Feathers and tipis identify American Indians. Stereotypic costumes predominate for Third World people. A number of Third World women—but no white women—are shown with bare breasts. Whites, usually shown in modern clothing, predominate in depictions of contempo-

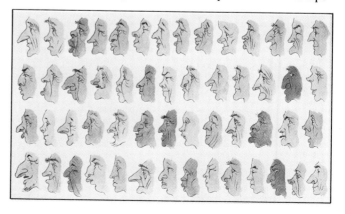

From People, *written and illustrated by Peter Spier.*

rary, technological settings, while Third World people appear more frequently in "primitive" settings.

Of the 40 or so examples of the "few of us . . . remembered long, long after we're gone" for a range of achievements, all are white except for Cheops and Mohandas Gandhi, and almost all are male. Males also predominate in depictions of occupations, and women predominate among those who cry and hold babies.

The book's final message is that "each and every one of us is unlike any other." Unfortunately, the differences depicted by Spier too frequently rely on stereotypic and demeaning imagery. Indeed, the book as a whole would be more likely to perpetuate white and male chauvinism than it would be to break them down.

> *Robert Moore, in his review of "People," in* Interracial Books for Children *(reprinted by permission of* Interracial Books for Children Bulletin, *1841 Broadway, New York, N.Y. 10023), Vol. 12, No. 1, 1981, p. 14.*

Here is a picture book for everyone in the family and each one of us will find it intriguing. . . . By the end of the book we realise how insular our attitudes are and why we must consider other points of view. The book contains much information and even young children will learn a lot from it. While ostensibly a picture book, it would not be out of place in any of the primary classes at school or as a present to anyone up to about 10 or 11 years of age. It is a thought-provoking book, subtle, clever, entertaining and informative and it is most certainly an excellent book to have in the house or school library.

> *Margaret Walker, in her review of "People," in* Book Window *(© 1981 S.C.B.A. and contributors), Vol. 8, No. 3, Summer, 1981, p. 23.*

BILL'S SERVICE STATION, THE FIREHOUSE, THE FOOD MARKET, MY SCHOOL, THE PET STORE, THE TOY SHOP (VILLAGE BOOKS) (1981; British edition as *Bill's Garage, The Fire Station*)

Peter Spier's board books are cut attractively into the different shapes of the village buildings they describe: the *Fire Station,* the *Food Market,* the *Pet Shop,* the *Toy Shop, Bill's Garage* and *My School.* The artist has devoted as much energy to these board books as he does to his other picture books. In the shops there is an enormous variety of fruit, veg, toys and pets (to say nothing of the flea collar, rawhide bone and cat scratching post). Readers can learn to recognize every item of a fireman's equipment and will no doubt find it useful to know about socket-spanners, ratchet wrenches and feeler gauges. Peter Spier's style of clipped text can be difficult to read but is suited to this sort of book in which there is little or no story. The flavour is American but, apart from the selection of names and a fire hydrant, there is little to puzzle an English reader.

> *Lucy Micklethwait, "Second Helpings," in* The Times Literary Supplement *(© Times Newspapers Ltd. (London) 1981; reproduced from* The Times Literary Supplement *by permission), No. 4094, September 18, 1981, p. 1066.**

Stand these board-books on the floor and they become a village around which quick-witted infants will soon devise games and mini-dramas. Open each book, to find a sensible text firmly outlining one aspect of everyday life. Look at the pictures, in

Peter Spier's most lively and persuasive manner, and the child can see innumerable details and enlarge his vocabulary with the proper terms, while attendant adults can enjoy the dry, alert humour in word and picture. A marvellously economical source of enjoyment and pleasurable, unconscious learning, with a piquant flavour of the American way of life.

> *Margery Fisher, in her review of "Bill's Garage," "The Fire Station," "The Toy Shop," "My School," "The Pet Shop," "The Food Market," in her* Growing Point, *Vol. 20, No. 4, November, 1981, p. 3984.*

The subjects of these books are certainly of interest, but the appeal to [one to three year olds] is uneven, with thin story lines supported by cozily cluttered illustrations. In the least useful of the series, *My School,* one teacher is referred to as "fat" while another is "the skinny one." A double-page spread illustrates and names the children in the school (several with names parents will stumble over; and the names, in general, should be of little interest to children). *Fire House* will pique curiosity, but adults will wonder why "fireman" is used in preference to "firefighter," particularly when the fire chief's children (two girls and a boy) are pictured with the comment, "Maybe they will be firemen some day." *The Pet Store* follows two children around the store where we see pet supplies, fish, birds and small rodents. Varieties of birds and fish are identified, but for no clear reason mice and their relations are given a paragraph of encyclopedic information. *Bill's Service Station* is the scene of much activity. "'Boy oh boy,' says Bill, 'it's a madhouse today!'" (This is repeated throughout.) The dialogue is not in the King's English, but much of it is the kind of substandard usage likely to be heard at a gas station, and the pictures and diagrams will hold the attention of incipient auto enthusiasts. Given the price of each title, it would be wise to weigh the need for board books against the average quality of the series. (pp. 82-3)

> *Brenda Durrin Maloney, in her review of "Bill's Service Station," "Firehouse," "The Food Market," "My School," "The Pet Store," "The Toy Shop," in* School Library Journal *(reprinted from the November, 1981 issue of* School Library Journal, *published by R. R. Bowker Co./A Xerox Corporation; copyright © 1981), Vol. 28, No. 3, November, 1981, pp. 82-3.*

Younger children can also latch onto real-estate mania. Peter Spier has written and illustrated six durable little books. . . . The books are colorful and realistic, though the vocabulary at times seems unnecessarily difficult. (Try out "hydraulic floor jack" on your 3-year-old.)

> *Susan Bolotin, in her review of "Food Market," "Firehouse," "The Toy Shop," "The Pet Store," "Bill's Service Station," and "My School," in* The New York Times Book Review *(© 1982 by The New York Times Company; reprinted by permission), January 3, 1982, p. 14.*

RAIN (1982)

In the opening picture in Peter Spier's **"Rain"** . . . a girl and her younger brother, a dog and a cat play in a backyard garden, and a cloud appears as a gray smudge in the corner. On the next page raindrops fall, and the cat is the first to take cover. The youngsters, in rain gear, go on a watercolored adventure through their town. . . . No words are needed in this book; Mr. Spier's brush gives us rain black and silver, bent flowers, leaves afloat in gutter maelstroms, the spongy shimmer of wet footprints on a path and that homey childhood backyard, so subtly transformed after the rain that you can gaze for hours at the colors in the before and after versions. His 84 pictures conjure up rain you can almost feel and hear, in a book that begins and ends with warm splashes of color in the summer world.

> *"Cats and Dogs," in* The New York Times Book Review *(© 1982 by The New York Times Company; reprinted by permission), April 25, 1982, p. 35.*

This text without words is exquisitely suited to the task of showing children the many moods of a downpour. It is rich in detail and has a boy and girl with whom the young reader may identify. Teachers may use it to extend the language experiences of their students. The "after the storm" endpaper is particularly bright and exciting. Everything about this book says "quality" and "beauty."

> *Barbara S. Worth, in her review of "Rain," in* Children's Book Review Service *(copyright © 1982 Children's Book Review Service Inc.), Vol. 10, No. 11, June, 1982, p. 103.*

Although lacking the spacious feeling of *Noah's Ark* . . . , [*Rain*] is similar in format with numerous vignettes arranged on most of the pages. An occasional full-page painting or double-page spread effectively varies the design and displays the artist's skillful creation of sloshy, wet scenes. . . . At first glance the pages appear crowded; but the eye moves easily from one vibrant watercolor to the next, and the book's appeal lies in the abundant detail that invites repeated exploration. (pp. 395-96)

> *Kate M. Flanagan, in her review of "Rain," in* The Horn Book Magazine *(copyright © 1982 by The Horn Book, Inc., Boston), Vol. LVIII, No. 4, August, 1982, pp. 395-96.*

Rain recounts exactly what the title suggests: an out-from-under-the-umbrella view of two kids on the loose in a summer downpour. No words are required to create this loose-jointed rainy-day romp: filling an upturned umbrella from an overflowing downspout, slipping in a puddle, picking water-logged flowers before racing home to a hot bath, supper, sleep and, finally, a radiant new day. Small vignettes set in white alternate with full-(and double-) page watercolors, all imbued not only with a lively sense of doing, but with the wonder of seeing as well; a spiderweb hung with droplets, water whooshing down a storm drain, a cat sheltering beneath a car. If this is not Spier at his award-winning best, it is nevertheless a refreshing look at a common phenomenon—one which children will recognize and grown-ups remember—sure to wash the cynical grit from even the most city-bleary eye.

> *Kristi L. Thomas, in her review of "Rain," in* School Library Journal, *(reprinted from the August, 1982 issue of* School Library Journal, *published by R. R. Bowker Co./A Xerox Corporation; copyright © 1982), Vol. 28, No. 10, August, 1982, p. 107.*

Patti Stren

1949-

Canadian author/illustrator of fiction.

Stren combines humorous stories with simple, cartoon-style line drawings to create her picture books, which critics consider among the funniest of recent publications. By using lovable animal characters, works such as *Hug Me* and *Sloan & Philamina* explore universal themes such as the need for love and understanding. Some reviewers feel adults might appreciate Stren's books even more than children, since her wit may be too sophisticated for young readers to comprehend. Her first novel, *There's a Rainbow in My Closet*, received mixed reviews. Critics find Emma and her non-stereotyped grandmother appealing, but are unconvinced by the dialogue. They agree, however, that Stren's illustrations, presented as the work of the nine-year-old protagonist, are realistic and engaging.

After studying to be a Montessori teacher and working with autistic children in Israel, Stren pursued art studies under cartoonist R. O. Blechman and author/illustrator Maurice Sendak. Her first hardcover book, *Hug Me*, was produced in school and became a children's best-seller with a college cult following. Throughout her life, Stren agonized over her inability to draw realistically. Today she says, "If there's one kid out there who has secret drawings, she should know it doesn't have to be realistic, doesn't have to be perfect. I didn't look up 'Anteater' . . . to see what they were like when I drew Sloan. My creatures are as I imagine them to be." With her urban Jewish wit, her expert cartoons, and her sensitive characterizations, Stren is a significant Canadian author for children.

GENERAL COMMENTARY

Stren is blithely unconcerned with the conventional—like the quirky creatures in her books: Elliot Kravitz, the porcupine who needs a hug, and Sloan, the anteater who falls in love with an ant. . . .

[Stren has said of herself,] "I spend a lot of time with my head in the oven." Still, for an angst-ridden author, Stren is producing some of the funniest kids' books in years. Her charmed combination of tender schlock and urban wit has made her the Fran Lebowitz of the short-pants set.

> Ann Johnston, "Kids' Lit's Own Fran Lebowitz,"
> *in* Maclean's Magazine (© 1979 by Maclean's Magazine; *reprinted by permission), Vol. 92, No. 51, December 17, 1979, p. 47.*

HUG ME (1977)

A porcupine who wants to be hugged has more possibilities than a bunny who wants to be snuggled, and perhaps Stren's ending—Elliot meets a girl porcupine with the same wish and they gratify each other, "very gently"—is an inevitable as it is predictable. Meanwhile there are spots of wit in Elliot's displaced yearnings and in the other animals' reactions to his attempts to ingratiate himself; and Stren's light, short-cut sketches

have a distinctive if derivative look. But the fact that Elliot doesn't look much like a porcupine is indicative of the sensibility at work: only Elliot's problem and its built-in solution gear this for children; the rest partakes of a more sophisticated sort of cuteness.

> *A review of "Hug Me," in* Kirkus Reviews (*copyright © 1977 The Kirkus Service, Inc.), Vol. XLV, No. 15, August 1, 1977, p. 783.*

Stren's little book bids fair to become a lasting favorite, not only with little kids but with older folk. It's the kind of bright picture book that finds its way into college bookstores and is offered as a love token by yearning swains. . . . The author-illustrator provides a tender but surprising finale to this little tale which owes a lot of its attraction to her expert cartoons and more to her sly wit.

> *A review of "Hug Me," in* Publishers Weekly (*reprinted from the August 22, 1977 issue of* Publishers Weekly, *published by R. R. Bowker Company, a Xerox company; copyright © 1977 by Xerox Corporation), Vol. 212, No. 8, August 22, 1977, p. 66.*

Trivia question: Name your favorite literary porcupine. (Name *any* literary porcupine.) Answer: Elliot Kravitz. He is the prickly, thus intrinsically unhuggable, hero of this picture story about the search for love. Since children are less sentimental than grown-ups, they may not all be entranced by Stren's wispy line drawings and happy ending, but try the book on the nearest angst-ridden adult.

> *Georgess McHargue, in her review of "Hug Me,"* in The New York Times Book Review *(© 1977 by The New York Times Company; reprinted by permission), October 16, 1977, p. 47.*

Although the plot boils down to porcupine wants hug—porcupine gets hug, there's enough humor in style and situation to amuse the lap audience; the line drawings are repetitive, but they have a Thurberish flair. . . . [The story has] a predictable and therefore slightly downbeat ending.

> *Zena Sutherland, in her review of "Hug Me," in* Bulletin of the Center for Children's Books *(reprinted by permission of The University of Chicago Press; © 1978 by The University of Chicago), Vol. 31, No. 6, February, 1978, p. 102.*

[*Hug Me*] is a simple, unpretentious but thoroughly delightful little book. . . . This story achieves its success for three reasons: it presents a simple but universal message—our need to love and be loved. Moreover, it is simply told; Patti Stren's prose is clear and concise, never belaboring or over expanding on points. But most importantly, the pen and ink sketches, although simple to the point of plainness, capture Elliot's inner feelings. They make limited use of color—yellow—to give variety. And they also give some dialogue. For example, as Elliot embraces a telephone pole, ten little birds, colored yellow, perch on the wires, one of them announcing, "If he tries to hug me, I'll slug him."

> *Jon C. Stott, in his review of "Hug Me," in* The World of Children's Books *(© 1978 Jon C. Stott), Vol. III, No. 1, Spring, 1978, p. 32.*

Universality of theme most often produces those books which can be appreciated on a number of levels. This title, dealing as it does, with the need for someone to love—to hug, will be enjoyed by the sophisticated reader on one level, while at the same time a younger child will delight in the perplexities posed by the situation. (p. 80)

The happy ending to Elliot's trials may be predictable, but it is also satisfying, for everyone can realize the necessity for at least one person to love.

The sophisticated line drawings, which at first glance seem careless, expand the text, adding humour and subtlety. Illustrations and text combine in a satisfying unity.

The story line is fun, but the theme makes this a good choice for older children too, and could well be used as an antidote to the never-ending spate of superficial identity crisis novels. (p. 81)

> *Alixe E. Hambleton, in her review of "Hug Me," in* In Review: Canadian Books for Children, *Vol. 12, No. 3, Summer, 1978, pp. 80-1.*

BO THE CONSTRICTOR THAT COULDN'T   (1978)

The story concerns an unusual snake, a boa constrictor who was spoiling the reputation of all his kind because he liked to

From Hug Me, *written and illustrated by Patti Stren.*

wrap himself around other animals and kiss them instead of squeezing and swallowing them. He tries planting a vegetable garden, but boas are not supposed to eat vegetables. So his friends undertake to teach him his duty and this also fails. Finally, they reach a compromise. Bo learns to make scary faces so that the boa constrictors can go back to being feared and, when no one is looking, he still kisses the animals.

Stren's idea is an excellent one for a picture book. However, I feel that the execution leaves something to be desired. The introduction is too detailed and too long. (The first paragraph contains seven sentences of which the first three are perhaps superfluous to the action). One needs a short, snappy beginning to catch a preschooler's immediate interest. The other pages stick to a couple of sentences per illustration. There are also a few places in which Stren repeats the same concept to no discernible purpose. This interrupts the narrative flow and causes some distraction. I would have preferred another reason for Bo giving up his vegetables than the fact that it's not done, but the resolution is good. (I did wonder, though, what Bo was going to eat!)

I feel that the colourful, attractive picture book could still be used to advantage in a preschool storyhour. The illustrations are large and simple with few details to confuse and would carry well to large groups. The children to whom I read the story were not totally attentive, hence my stated reservations, but they seemed to enjoy the fact that the hero was a boa constrictor.

> *Nancy Ward, in her review of "Bo the Constrictor That Couldn't," in* In Review: Canadian Books for Children, *Vol. 12, No. 4, Autumn, 1978, p. 79.*

SLOAN & PHILAMINA: OR HOW TO MAKE FRIENDS WITH YOUR LUNCH   (1979)

Stren's ink lines, with splashes of blue-green, suggest the influence of *New Yorker* cartoonist Edward Koren but she adds a dash of her own piquant humor to the sketches, reflections of her jokey tale. Sloan the anteater agrees to become a pal of Philamina, his intended snack, when she proves she knows endless elephant jokes and that they are otherwise compatible. The two are happily inseparable until the anteater colony becomes aware of the scandal and warns Sloan to eat Philamina, "or else." Just when all seems lost, he gets the bright idea of throwing a party for all the local ants and anteaters. They have such a good time that they all make a firm pact to live and let live. The doings strike one as a trifle too complicated and protracted, but little humans will undoubtedly chuckle through the pages.

A review of "Sloan & Philamina: Or How to Make Friends with Your Lunch," in Publishers Weekly *(reprinted from the May 14, 1979 issue of* Publishers Weekly, *published by R. R. Bowker Company, a Xerox company; copyright © 1979 by Xerox Corporation), Vol. 215, No. 20, May 14, 1979, p. 210.*

While kids enjoy the elephant jokes grownups might or might not be amused by Stren's throw-away allusions to ERA, Grossingers, Henry Higgins, and Philamina's Cousin Ramona who has a Ph.D. in philosophy but drives a taxi in New York. As in *Hug Me* . . . , Stren is still into being cute for grownups at the expense of getting in touch with children—but her offbeat doodles and quips can be funny. The publishers give this the usual picture-book-age designation, but we'd tend to try it out on hip readers-alone who can scan all the little asides and pick up on some of the references. (For Canadians like the author, Philamina's Aunti Gnish should go over.)

A review of "Sloan & Philamina: Or How to Make Friends with Your Lunch," in Kirkus Reviews *(copyright © 1979 The Kirkus Service, Inc.), Vol. XLVII, No. 10, May 15, 1979, p. 574.*

The picture book crowd is not likely to join in the merriment. The story is uninvolving and overlong, the squiggly line drawings difficult to decode. Parents, perhaps, will enjoy the ballooned asides, e.g., two dancing ants: "Ever since ERA, you never let me lead."

Janet French, in her review of "Sloan & Philamina: Or How to Make Friends with Your Lunch," in School Library Journal *(reprinted from the September, 1979 issue of* School Library Journal, *published by R. R. Bowker Co./A Xerox Corporation; copyright © 1979), Vol. 26, No. 1, September, 1979, p. 122.*

I have always been a Patti Stren fan! (p. 57)

I like *Sloan & Philamina*! I like the sense of humour, which is a delightful combination of childish corn (the elephant jokes), Jewish comic lines (Philamina's Uncle Lou spent the last years as a stand-up comic on the Borscht Belt) and references picked up only by the adult reader (Sloan waltzes Philamina around the room singing, "I've got it. By George. I've got it.") I even think that the whole story can be seen as an adult tale of love between two people of totally different backgrounds.

I like Patti's illustrations, the fragile sketches, the tiny ants riding motorcycles across the end papers. I like poring over the conversations which appear in cartoon style balloons. I delight in the page where a single line of text says, "Philamina sat in the middle of the letter and cried harder," and the illustration shows a forlorn and tearful ant sitting in the middle of a hate letter written to Sloan by the anteaters.

My children and Patti's books seem to be growing up together. The five year olds who brought stuffed animals to the *Hug Me* party became the six year olds who talked with Patti and *Bo*, and are now the seven year olds who remembered Patti's visit and were delighted to see *Sloan & Philamina* in print. I can only hope that they will meet Mountain Rose the lady wrestler (another character in Patti's head) next year!

In a recent interview in the Toronto Star, Patti said, "I write my books for me, but they are marketable to children." This philosophy seems particularly plain in *Sloan & Philamina*. From my point of view, I can only applaud that philosophy and talent which gives me such delight in reading the stories aloud and at the same time entertains and entrances the children. (pp. 57-8)

Marjorie Kelley, in her review of "Sloan & Philamina: Or How to Make Friends with Your Lunch," in In Review: Canadian Books for Children, *Vol. 13, No. 5, October, 1979, pp. 57-8.*

Scrabbly, lively, broken-line drawings illustrate a story about the friendship between an ant (Philamina) and an anteater (Sloan) who, in the drawings, looks more like a crocodile. . . . Blithe and bouncy, the book can gently infuse some positive thoughts on prejudging, and it's fun. The question is, for whom is it fun? Designated by the publisher as a read-aloud book, the story may be amusing for that group, but only independent readers can fully appreciate the sophisticated jokes or read the many comments in the comic strip style balloons.

Zena Sutherland, in her review of "Sloan & Philamina: Or How to Make Friends with Your Lunch," in Bulletin of the Center for Children's Books *(reprinted by permission of The University of Chicago Press; © 1979 by The University of Chicago), Vol. 33, No. 3, November, 1979, p. 59.*

Once again Patti Stren champions the nonconformist in *Sloan and Philamina*. . . . Stren's attention to detail—animals in sneakers and blue polyester leisure suits—and her tender-hearted humor make this book a wonderful encore to her best-selling *Hug Me*.

Ann Johnston, in her review of "Sloan & Philamina: Or How to Make Friends with Your Lunch," in Maclean's Magazine *(© 1979 by* Maclean's Magazine; *reprinted by permission), Vol. 92, No. 51, December 17, 1979, p. 49.*

THERE'S A RAINBOW IN MY CLOSET (1979)

Emma is a fourth grader who loves to draw and paint. When her mother goes to Europe on business, Emma's largely unknown grandmother comes to stay with her and her father. Emma gradually warms to the woman who is so much like herself. Gramma loves art and music, Gramma projects a rainbow into Emma's closet with the help of eyeglasses and a mirror, Gramma not only likes to fish but doesn't mind baiting hooks. Above all, Gramma is someone who appreciates Emma's creativity and urges her to trust her own feelings. Feelings are really the focus of this story in which there is much affect and little action. That could be a fine thing if there were less simplification ("You see, Emma. It's like this. There are two kinds of people in the world . . . ") or more authenticity in the dialogue, which seems especially forced when Emma talks with her friend Edgar ("Worms! You give me worms! Some best friend you are! What are you trying to do—shock me into forgetting my problems?''). Even so, libraries that have a need for reassuringly soft stories à la Rod McKuen may want to add this unabashedly sentimental book.

Mary B. Nickerson, in her review of "There's a Rainbow in My Closet," in School Library Journal *(reprinted from the September, 1979 issue of* School Library Journal, *published by R. R. Bowker Co./A Xerox Corporation; copyright © 1979), Vol. 26, No. 1, September, 1979, p. 149.*

The characters in the book are appealing, the story is gentle, sometimes amusing, sometimes touching, but nothing much happens. Stren's porcupines and anteaters have more to offer than her pre-adolescents. (p. 21)

Mary Ainslie Smith, "In the Beginning," in Books in Canada, *Vol. 9, No. 2, February, 1980, pp. 21-3.**

In **There's A Rainbow in My Closet**, Patti Stren once again explores the child's need for love and acceptance despite individual differences, a theme she depicted with wit and originality in **Sloan and Philamina**. In this novel for younger children (8-11), however, the treatment becomes maudlin and self-indulgent. . . .

The novel is loosely episodic if not repetitious with much time spent getting the heroine up, dressed, fed, and back to bed. The dialogue, especially between Emma and her friend Edgar is unconvincing; they sound like five year olds at one moment and adolescents the next. The message that was intuited amid laughter in **Sloan and Philamina** is here spelled out by adults: by Emma's father and grandmother, and by her teacher.

Most young readers will enjoy grandmother's original Surprise Test; some may relate to the sensitive Emma. I found her a bit of a pain.

Jacquie Hunt, in her review of "There's a Rainbow in My Closet," in Quill and Quire *(reprinted by permission of* Quill and Quire), *Vol. 46, No. 2, February, 1980, p. 44.*

This is a novel about individuality. Stren's drawings, which are Emma's drawings, reinforce the theme. The Emmas who read the book will love meeting a character so like themselves. The non-Emmas may get some appreciation of the importance of the particular uniqueness of each of us.

I have no doubt that this is an autobiographical novel. Emma and Patti Stren are too much alike for it to be otherwise. Writing a novel based on your own childhood, your memories, and, I suspect, your family's childhood memories, and placing it in the present time does cause problems. This novel is set in 1979—the teacher is Ms. Pickett; the kids trade Reggie Jackson baseball cards and make ribit jokes; grandmothers live in condominiums in Florida. But that same Ms. Pickett is a teacher of the past with her sarcasm, her surprise tests, and her ever present red pencil which even attacks the children's drawings. Also, Ms. Pickett announces at 1:30 that school will dismiss an hour early because of a teachers' meeting. What! In today's world all changes in regular school hours must be announced well in advance so that crossing guards can be rescheduled, working mothers can plan their children's care, etc. On that day when Emma gets out of school at 2 p.m. she pays a surprise visit to her father's clock shop, and he closes up the shop and

spends the rest of the afternoon with her. Nostalgia for a bygone era?

More serious, however, is what time does to Gramma. She tells Emma that she came to Canada to marry, and could never go back to Russia because the Revolution occurred. That means that she was married before 1917. Even a child bride would be nearly 80 by now, enjoying her great-grandchildren, not babysitting a nine year old grandchild. Patti Stren's Gramma it could be; Emma's, no.

Lest I be accused of attacking minor details which the child reader will not notice, I point them out because I believe that this lack of continuity in time weakens the total structure and takes away from the believability of the novel.

There are in addition three further assaults on believability. First of all, Emma is in Grade 4, therefore about nine years old. She finally learns to ride her two-wheeler. My Grade 4 students tell me they learned to ride two-wheelers at ages five and six.

Secondly, why doesn't Emma know her Gramma? We are told that "She lives in Florida because in cold weather her joints hurt," and that Emma hasn't seen her since she was really little and doesn't remember anything about her. Yet this woman drops everything and comes on less than a week's notice to look after this unknown grandchild for two months. Then after Emma and Gramma have become such good friends, Emma doesn't want Gramma to leave when her mother comes home. Father simply says that he'll ask Gramma to stay, that she'll have to go back to Florida for the winter, but that Emma can visit her there during winter vacations. Such a simple way to maintain a relationship. Why did so many years go by before they thought of it?

Finally, the novel has made such a fine statement about individuality that even Ms. Pickett seems to have come to a realization of its importance. And then Stren has her make the statement to her class, "Maybe next time you all can try and write poems with pictures like Emma's." If I were Emma, I'd want to go back to the days of hiding my work!

I think Stren's novel will find some appreciative readers. I am sorry that she didn't pay more attention to details of time and character which would have given it more credibility. (pp. 56-7)

Marjorie Kelley, in her review of "There's a Rainbow in My Closet," in In Review: Canadian Books for Children, *Vol. 14, No. 2, April, 1980, pp. 56-7.*

There's a Rainbow in My Closet combats ageist stereotypes with verve. . . . [Gramma] sparkles. More than this, she is perceptive, understanding and loving.

My only reservation about this book has to do with Emma's mother. For one thing, it is hard to believe that she can be Gramma's daughter; she seems to have been impervious to Gramma's influence. Besides, the mother's coldness, her devotion only to her career and her failure even to send letters worth mentioning in the book suggest that working women are failures as mothers. However, the overall message of the book is not only anti-ageist but anti-sexist as well. Gramma and Emma are powerful females, and Edgar and Emma's father are sensitive, supportive males. (p. 17)

Anne G. Toensmeier, in her review of "There's a Rainbow in My Closet," in Interracial Books for

Children Bulletin *(reprinted by permission of* Interracial Books for Children Bulletin, *1841 Broadway, New York, N.Y. 10023), Vol. 11, No. 5, 1980, pp. 16-17.*

Patti Stren's first novel *there's a rainbow in my closet* presents us with an engaging heroine, creative and lively, shy and noisy, strong-minded yet vulnerable, never sweet yet wholly endearing. The book resembles its main character in more ways than one.

It too, is occasionally awkward and unsure, now and then exasperating, and yet, in spite of these momentary lapses, entertaining, sensitive and memorable. There is also a refreshing intimacy and honesty in the way Patti Stren writes of childhood. Here is a new voice and a welcome one. (p. 68)

The adults in this novel, while definitely alive, are not wholly convincing. For two people who appear to understand each other, Emma's parents seem to have communicated no more than superficially about their daughter. Gramma is practically perfect. It is true that she only has to keep up her absorption with Emma after school hours and for the duration of a visit. Nevertheless she lives in Florida because of her arthritis and it must be severe to have kept her living that far from Emma's family. Surely fatigue and pain would shorten her temper now and then and limit her enthusiasm. She sets an implausibly high standard for grandmothers called in to cope with children during family crises. True as this may be, the reader is not concerned about it for this is Emma's story, not Gramma's, and Emma is entirely real.

Particularly interesting and moving is the way Patti Stren lets us experience, through Emma, the excitement and total involvement of the artist during the act of creating. This is described beautifully and with loving detail. To take time to do this in a child's book shows courage and skill for the author cannot hold the reader captive with lively dialogue or fast-paced action. Creating is a solitary business and cannot be hurried or easily dramatized. Patti Stren has caught the essence of this absorbed and concentrated time and has shown the tremendous internal suspense within the artist. Will the creation come close to the dream? Emma's does, but it is also made clear that this comes about as the result of authentic vision, brooding, trying and failing and trying again until it is right at last. Emma's tools of the trade are described with fond attention and will enthrall children who hunger for specificity. Just as dozens of children have kept notebooks after reading *Harriet the Spy*, so many will now experiment with painting like Emma.

Adults, be they parents, teachers, grammas, or interested bystanders, should get some help with how to encourage and enjoy children like Emma (and most children are like Emma *some* of the time.) Gramma's Surprise Test is inspired. So is her way of helping Emma see Ms. Pickett's point of view. While Emma sees Gramma's sadness as she remembers her home and family lost to her in the Russian Revolution and asks her about it, Gramma shares her sorrow with the child honestly. She does not dwell on this grief, burdening Emma with too great a pain for her to bear, but neither does she brush the child's question aside or make light of her own loss. Emma is distressed but she grows as she seeks to comfort her grandmother. The reader will share in this deepening of sympathy.

Patti Stren does not fall into the error of making Emma wise beyond her years and so putting her out of the reader's reach. She considers trying to solace Gramma with an elephant joke.

While this book is insightful and tender, it is also really funny and down-to-earth. It speaks in today's idiom without depending too much on slang that would soon date it.

The illustrations are gentle and puckish. Just as one cannot mistake Maurice Sendak's pictures for those of anyone else, so Patti Stren's are unmistakable. Emma's pictures show Stren's influence but still belong to Emma.

Emma's feelings on the day she makes her speech are not just described vividly but are entered into and lived through by every reader. The fact that Emma is, on the whole, happy and outgoing makes this an especially appealing experience. Here is one of the greatest charms of this book. It demonstrates the contradictions in each of us and lets children know their moments of panic are not unique to them but are familiar to all of us. And for the rare child with a true creative gift, a compulsion to realize some inner vision, for the child such as Patti Stren herself must have been, *there's a rainbow in my closet* is of intense significance. It says it is exciting and deeply satisfying to make your own thing and that, when you can bear to risk sharing what you have made, somewhere there is an audience eager to see it. What Mom may see as just another picture to tack up and forget, what Ms. Pickett may criticize and mark wrong, Gramma will recognize as important. Just as Emma keeps painting in spite of her mother and Ms. Pickett, others will be encouraged to have faith in themselves, knowing that someday a gramma may come.

A funny book, a tender, wistful story, a tough, lively, endearing novel full of shifts in tone and mood, full of colour—especially purple. A book as surprising and delightful as a rainbow in your closet. (pp. 69-71)

Jean Little, *"A Rainbow for Emma," in* Canadian Children's Literature: A Journal of Criticism and Review *(Box 335, Guelph, Ontario, Canada N1H6K5), No. 22, 1981, pp. 68-71.*

MOUNTAIN ROSE (1982)

This is a wonderfully silly tale accompanied by drawings which are no less wonderfully silly, depicting faithfully the main events in the text and also providing humorous and satirical asides.

Amy Rolnick, *in her review of "Mountain Rose," in* School Library Journal *(reprinted from the March, 1982 issue of* School Library Journal, *published by R. R. Bowker Co./A Xerox Corporation; copyright ©1982), Vol. 28, No. 7, March, 1982, p. 140.*

A shaggy non-sequitur in deadpan style, hand lettering, and quick, quirky doodles. . . . This flat, ingenuous life story maintains a share of what-happens-next interest, but the interest is let down in the end by the sheer irrelevance of what does happen.

A review of *"Mountain Rose," in* Kirkus Reviews *(copyright © 1982 The Kirkus Service, Inc.), Vol. L, No. 5, March 1, 1982, p. 272.*

At the age of six, Rose is orphaned and separated from her twin brother. She is also unusually big—so big "that she needed her own zip code." The side remarks and hilarious illustrations that fill every page will delight readers as they follow Rose from a disastrous beginning as an outcast in elementary school to the day she becomes Mountain Rose, Champion Wrestler of the World. The ferocious opponent who challenges her for the championship turns out to be none other than her long-lost twin. This is one of the funniest books I've read in a long time.

Arlene Stolzer Sandner, in her review of "Mountain Rose," in Children's Book Review Service *(copyright © 1982 Children's Book Review Service Inc.), Vol. 10, No. 10, May, 1982, p. 95.*

Stren's drawings, black and white overlaid with red, are very funny, fitting the tenor of the story she tells. It is earthy if not downright vulgar but not offensive and kids will love following the fortunes of Rose. . . . [The] plot doesn't matter; it's the ludicrous setup on each page that will tickle kids.

A review of "Mountain Rose," in Publishers Weekly *(reprinted from the May 7, 1982 issue of* Publishers Weekly, *published by R. R. Bowker Company, a Xerox company; copyright © 1982 by Xerox Corporation), Vol. 221, No. 19, May 7, 1982, p. 79.*

Mountain Rose can be read on two levels. On one level, it is about an extraordinarily big girl, who hates being different and gradually learns to "feel good about herself". It is a book which will be welcomed by those who appreciate non-sexist literature for children.

The story is also about Mountain Rose's trials and adventures as a woman wrestler. . . . The suspense [of her match with

Gardenia Gus] holds the readers' attention and the resolution of the plot is surprising and effective.

The story is told in a style that is replete with humour and verve. The illustrations are skillful and full of wit. After having read **Hug Me** and **Sloan & Philamina,** one has high expectations of Patti Stren, and they are not disappointed by **Mountain Rose.**

A review of "Mountain Rose," in Children's Book News *(reprinted by permission of The Children's Book Centre, Toronto, Canada), Vol. 5, No. 1, June, 1982.*

I'M ONLY AFRAID OF THE DARK (AT NIGHT!) (1982)

How an Arctic owl named Harold Tribune—a typical Stren touch—deals with his fear of the dark. . . . [Harold and Gert's] solution may not be available to everyone, but Stren's gentle ridicule might elicit some response. Her drawings, as usual, give a loose, free look to a stiffer story that needs the lift.

A review of "I'm Only Afraid of the Dark (At Night!)," in Kirkus Reviews *(copyright © 1982 The Kirkus Service, Inc.), Vol. L, No. 13, July 1, 1982, p. 731.*

What makes this book so thoroughly satisfying? "It's silly . . . but in a neat kind of way. There's this owl, Harold, who's afraid of the dark. And his best friend, Gert, makes him do all these weird things to stop being afraid only, the thing is,

From Mountain Rose, *written and illustrated by Patti Stren.*

Gert's afraid of the dark, too. In the end, Harold and Gert help each other. There're lots of jokes, too. And the art is like in a comic book, only better. Everybody talks to each other in the pictures, only it's different stuff from the typed story. Like a whole other book. I liked the part about the slugs the best. Slug-hunting, slug-slugging, slug-sandwiches. UGH! Owls like to eat slugs as much as me and my friends like peanut-butter and jam.'' That is what the child inside me says and perhaps that is the secret of Stren's success, her gift to reach the authentic heart and spirit of the child. She does so in a charming, vulnerable, original style. Brava!

> *Leigh Dean, in her review of "I'm Only Afraid of the Dark (At Night!)," in* Children's Book Review Service *(copyright © 1982 Children's Book Review Service Inc.), Vol. 11, No. 1, September, 1982, p. 5.*

Chris Van Allsburg

1949-

American author/illustrator of fiction.

An accomplished artist and sculptor whose works are displayed in major art museums, Van Allsburg became intrigued with the challenge of bringing his style and vision to the field of children's book illustration. He inspires much critical acclaim by using dramatic perspectives in his three-dimensional black-and-white drawings; reviewers also praise his use of dark and light to give balance and show form. His picture books explore the theme of reality-versus-illusion in the everyday world, and they show the anxiety that occurs when fantasy enters real life without warning. Van Allsburg often uses touches of humor to relieve the tension of his text and illustrations.

While regarding Van Allsburg as a major talent, some critics see his stories as merely a framework for his artistic virtuosity. They feel that adult knowledge and experience are needed to fully comprehend and appreciate his books. With *Ben's Dream,* for instance, they comment that few children would know such world landmarks as the Parthenon and St. Basil's in Moscow, much less recognize them half-submerged as Van Allsburg depicts them. Reviewers are unanimous, however, in applauding Van Allsburg's extraordinary artistry, noting the haunting, magical traits of his pencil drawings in *The Garden of Abdul Gasazi* and the startling, mysterious quality of his *Jumanji* illustrations. Rarely, if ever, has a newcomer to children's book illustration been so quickly and widely recognized. *The Garden of Abdul Gasazi* was a Caldecott Honor Book, an A.L.A. Notable Book, and received the *Boston Globe-Horn Book* Award for Illustration in 1980. It was placed on the *New York Times* Choice of Best Illustrated Children's Books of the Year list in 1979 and the International Board on Books for Young People (IBBY) Honor List in 1982. *Jumanji* won the Caldecott Medal in 1981 and was a *New York Times* Best Illustrated Book of the Year. It was designated an A.L.A. Notable Book and a *Boston Globe-Horn Book* Award Honor Book in 1982.

AUTHOR'S COMMENTARY

[Fever] may be a misleading description of my own rather deliberate approach, but there is a constant urge to create. I am fascinated by the act of making something real that at one point is only an idea. It is challenging and beguiling to sense something inside, put it on paper (or carve it in stone), and then step back and see how much has got lost in the process. The inevitability of losing some of the idea in trying to bring it to life is what keeps me working. I am always certain that next time, I'll lose less.

Ideas themselves have varied origins. In writing and illustrating *Jumanji,* the inspiration was my recollection of vague disappointment in playing board games as a child. Even when I owned Park Place with three hotels, I never felt truly rich, and not being able to interrogate Colonel Mustard personally was always a letdown. Another motivating element for *Jumanji* was a fascination I have with seeing things where they don't belong. The pictures in newspapers of cars that have run amok and crashed into people's living rooms always get my attention. There's the room, almost normal: sofa, TV, amused home-

owner, end tables, and the front half of an Oldsmobile. It occurred to me that if an Oldsmobile in the living room looked that good, a herd of rhinoceros could have real possibilities.

I am surprised now that my fairly recent discovery of the illustrated book as a way of expressing ideas did not happen earlier. It is a unique medium that allows an artist-author to deal with the passage of time, the unfolding of events, in the same way film does. The opportunity to create a small world between two pieces of cardboard, where time exists yet stands still, where people talk and I tell them what to say, is exciting and rewarding. (p. 382)

> Chris Van Allsburg, "Caldecott Medal Acceptance" (originally a speech given at the American Library Association convention on July 12, 1982; copyright © 1982 by Chris Van Allsburg), in The Horn Book Magazine, *Vol. LVIII, No. 4, August, 1982, pp. 380-83.*

GENERAL COMMENTARY

Looking back over *The Garden of Abdul Gasazi, Jumanji,* and *Ben's Dream . . . ,* I think it is clear that houses big and small have been the main sets around and inside of which Chris's dramas unfold. (pp. 384-85)

The standards he sets for his students [Van Allsburg teaches illustration at the Rhode Island School of Design] are high—but not as high as those he sets for himself. If Chris has a competitive streak, it is evident only in his determination to make each of his drawings better than the one that preceded it. It is perhaps his abhorrence of mediocrity that stands out above all his other virtues and quirks. His refusal to accept anything of inferior quality or of tainted integrity is as evident in his work as it is in all other aspects of his life. . . . For Chris no detail is insignificant, no technical problem insurmountable, no challenge to the imagination too great. (p. 387)

> *David Macaulay, "Chris Van Allsburg," in* The Horn Book Magazine *(copyright © 1982 by The Horn Book, Inc., Boston), Vol. LVIII, No. 4, August, 1982, pp. 384-87.*

THE GARDEN OF ABDUL GASAZI (1979)

["**The Garden of Abdul Gasazi**" contains] ultra-sophisticated black-and-white drawings. . . . This is Mr. Van Allsburg's first children's book, and it certainly marks an important debut. . . .

It must be said that the text is a little stiff, forced, even slightly condescending, and the plot seems too arbitrary—it's not as haunting and magical as it tries to be. But the illustrations are extraordinarily haunting and magical. Every leaf and beam of sunlight has a slightly ominous, surreal glow that uses nostalgia and our memories of Orson Welles's "The Magnificent Ambersons" and E. L. Doctorow's "Ragtime" to fine effect. This is without question one of the best—and most original—picture books in years. (p. 51)

> *Harold C. K. Rice, "The Books with the Pictures," in* The New York Times Book Review *(©1979 by The New York Times Company; reprinted by permission), November 11, 1979, pp. 51, 66-7.**

With only a carbon pencil, Van Allsburg creates a garden that is imaginative in its conception and wondrous in its graphic fulfillment. Illusions of light and shadow, rendered through the meticulously shaded, intricate drawings, provide an underlying quality of hushed surrealism, seemingly poised at the brink of expectancy. The artist tempers this tone with realistic touches of humor, human emotion, and action, bringing the pictures more solidly into the realm of the child. Many of the large, full-page illustrations are unusually executed with strong central focus: a particularly intriguing example depicts the boy, Alan, running through a leaf-covered stone gate and down a tree-lined tunnel to a distant place beyond. This visual enchantment is ably matched by a subtle, surprise-ending tale in which Alan, following the dog Fritz, meets the retired magician Abdul Gasazi in a forbidden garden filled with gigantic topiary figures and has an eerie experience that magically overlaps into his everyday world.

> *Barbara Elleman, in her review of "The Garden of Abdul Gasazi," in* Booklist *(reprinted by permission of the American Library Association; copyright © 1979 by the American Library Association), Vol. 76, No. 6, November 15, 1979, p. 510.*

Van Allsburg's technique is impressive; and beyond these technical considerations he has also succeeded in evoking a surreal, slightly sinister, and decidedly mysterious world that invites long, uneasy looks. The story is less compelling. A boy charged with minding a dog loses Fritz in a magician's garden, is told

From The Garden of Abdul Gasazi, *written and illustrated by Chris Van Allsburg.*

by the magician that Fritz has been changed into a duck, but finds on his return that Fritz (as a dog) has beat him home. The obligatory teaser at the end (Fritz turns up with the boy's cap, which was last seen flying off in the duck's beak) doesn't give the story any of the pictures' hypnotic power; and the book's oversized format (9 x 12) establishes it as essentially a showcase for the illustrations—a dubious reason for "creating" a picture book.

> *A review of "The Garden of Abdul Gasazi," in* Kirkus Reviews *(copyright © 1979 The Kirkus Service, Inc.), Vol. XLVII, No. 23, December 1, 1979, p. 1373.*

Few black-and-white drawings have caught [the incongruous logic of dreams] as well as **The Garden of Abdul Gasazi**. . . . Long after the spell ends, an eerie residue remains, like a dream that persists in the waking world. Chris Van Allsburg's narrative leans too hard on pictures of topiary animals and foreboding dwellings, but his brilliant illustrations resemble snapshots taken by the brain of Poe. (p. 99)

> *Stefan Kanfer, "A Child's Portion of Good Reading," in* Time *(copyright 1979 Time Inc.; all rights reserved; reprinted by permission from* Time*), Vol. 114, No. 23, December 3, 1979, pp. 98-100.**

The story, which goes on to a tantalizing conclusion, serves essentially as an ambitious libretto for a series of carefully composed, technically expert pictures. Stippled tones of gray and precisely outlined figures generate three-dimensional sculptured and architectural forms. Monumental human beings as well as stylized structures are bathed in light and shade, and all of the illustrations suggest in effect the pointillism of Seurat. Consequently, boy and dog, magician and duck are singularly static, while the pictures are filled with a mystical kind of immobility. Decidedly not a picture book for young children but a large virtuoso production—mannered and bordering on the occult. (p. 50)

> *Paul Heins, in his review of "The Garden of Abdul Gasazi," in* The Horn Book Magazine *(copyright ©*

1980 by The Horn Book, Inc., Boston), Vol. LVI, No. 1, February, 1980, pp. 49-50.

[In *The Garden of Abdul Gasazi*] the illustrations take precedence over the text. The story . . . is nicely conceived but rather hesitantly put together. Sometimes it gives the impression of a resumé of a longer story (frequently resorting to phrases such as "some distance beyond", "after a long search" or "an hour later"). On the other hand the black and white illustrations are executed with a very sure hand: there is some wonderfully expressive play of light and shade, great lurking shadows, and skies luminously clouded or starry, all fitting in with the slightly sinister mood of the story.

Kicki Moxon Browne, "To Amuse and Entertain," in The Times Literary Supplement (© Times Newspapers Ltd. (London) 1981; reproduced from The Times Literary Supplement by permission), No. 4094, September 18, 1981, p. 1067.*

JUMANJI (1981)

The "**Jumanji**" story line is developed out of a joke any child of boardgame age can catch: What if that last instruction on board games ("It will not be over until . . . ") were somehow serious, as one's parents' instructions ("Be good!") are supposed to be? What if disobedience had consequences? The moralizing potential in the joke (reminiscent of Dr. Seuss's "The Cat in the Hat") comes through with pleasantly ironic light-heartedness. Peter and Judy's parents have gone off to the opera, leaving instructions that the children keep the house neat, because after the opera the parents will be bringing friends by. The children tear up the house before they find and play the Jumanji game, but when the game is over and the parents return, everything is tidy. One muses, "How much of the havoc was caused by the wild animals, how much by . . . ?"

Here as in "**The Garden of Abdul Gasazi**," what keeps one returning to the book is the pictures. Mr. Van Allsburg's illustrations have a beautiful simplicity of design, balance, texture and a subtle intelligence beyond the call of illustration. In the first picture, after the parents have left and before the children have found the game, we see Peter up in an armchair, kneeling, looking down toward the darkness under the chair as if something might lurk there, and Judy looking thoughtfully into her dollhouse. What is under the chair is a dark train, and beside the chair is a ball, both hinting at motion and distance. The same hint is carried by the picture's perspective, with its vanishing point somewhere inside or behind Judy. The picture is very still—frozen time, potential outrush.

In the second illustration, the rush has begun—the two children run off the end of a sidewalk onto grass and into light. In the foreground is a dark evergreen whose top points, as if incidentally, toward "out there," and beside the tree is a dark equestrian statue, two of its feet lifted as if to gallop after the children; above the horse are white pigeons with extended wings. Many pictures in the book have such hints, such secrets—in the foreground of the picture in which the children start their game are the dark, sternly lined-up books and pipe of the absent father; on the piano in the picture in which Peter sees the lion is sheet music with a readable, weirdly musing E-minor tune.

The writing in "**Jumanji**" is more ordinary. The plot has nothing much to ponder, no rare sparkle, and the style is, though serviceable, undistinguished. (Mr. Van Allsburg is

needlessly self-conscious about verbal repetition, shifting from "Peter" to "the boy" and from "the lion" to "the big cat"; and his wit sometimes flags, as when he gives a piano the brand name "Baldway.") But the weaknesses do no great harm. The story exists as an excuse for the art work, and it serves well enough. (pp. 49, 64)

John Gardner, "Fun and Games and Dark Imaginings," in The New York Times Book Review (© 1981 by The New York Times Company; reprinted by permission), April 26, 1981, pp. 49, 64-5.*

[The magic in Van Allsburg's world] is always waiting to leak into the everyday. . . . As in *The Garden of Abdul Gasazi* . . . , which *Jumanji* outdoes in story terms, real and unreal rub shoulders in three-dimensional drawings extraordinary for the multiplicity of gray tones the artist achieves and the startling contrasts with brilliant white. The eye-fooling angles, looming shadows and shifting perspectives are worthy of Hitchcock, yet all these "special effects" are supplied with only a pencil.

Pamela D. Pollack, in her review of "Jumanji," in School Library Journal (reprinted from the May, 1981 issue of School Library Journal, published by R. R. Bowker Co./A Xerox Corporation; copyright © 1981), Vol. 27, No. 9, May, 1981, p. 60.

Van Allsburg's consummate draftsmanship creates stunning, velvet-flat, black-and-white scenes that are endlessly fascinating. Vistas of a familiar household world gone amok are seen from startling floor or ceiling perspectives that heighten the story's sense of slightly sinister suspense. The tone of the text lightens the sense of danger in a fantasy come true, but this remains a potent vision that lingers on and on.

Denise M. Wilms, in her review of "Jumanji," in Booklist (reprinted by permission of the American Library Association; copyright © 1981 by the American Library Association), Vol. 77, No. 18, May 15, 1981, p. 1258.

The first thing that needs to be said about this book is that, as in Chris Van Allsburg's first book, *The Garden of Abdul Gasazi,* its pictures are astonishing. With each new page you find yourself exclaiming over their polish, their superbly accomplished rendering, and if, like me, you know a little about the medium—Conté—you wonder how in the world Van Allsburg has managed to keep it so clean and precise, right down to the high glaze on vases and lamp bases. And then, after that, you are struck with the great fun he has had with what can best be called "camera angles"—you imagine him setting up scaffolding, climbing all over it to find the most surprising point of view, and then bringing the audience up—or down—with him to see rooms and furniture and people in a whole new way.

He is not concerned consistently with textures. A lion's hide, a rhinoceros' skin, walls, floors, even the upholstery of chairs are the same, all densely smooth—which makes a page of hairy monkeys or his glossy vases conspicuous. Light, however, is important throughout, as it must be in black-and-white pictures, and contrasts are everywhere strong and effective. But it is not a cheery sunlight; it is cold and soft, like the light before a snowstorm, and not because of its black-and-whiteness, or the Conté pencil. This coldness must be assumed to be deliberate, and is in fact a feature, in a curious way, of the story itself.

Versions have been told often before, most familiarly in Seuss' *The Cat in the Hat:* something, or someone, comes into the life of a child or two left alone by adults for a few hours, and causes unbelievable havoc, all of which miraculously vanishes before the adults return. . . .

There is a lot of anxiety in *Jumanji* that is not present in the same way in *The Cat in the Hat* or its cousins, and everything in the book contributes to that mood: the cold light of the environment, the very smoothness of the textures, the odd angles, and, for me, a curious sense of silence. . . . [There] is no sound, and this makes the story eerie and dreamlike—even, perhaps, nightmarish. Would a child find it so? That's an unanswerable question, since no one knows the anonymous "child" for whom children's books are presumably created. . . . Some children will love *Jumanji,* some will be frightened by it. But most, I expect, will be dazzled by Van Allsburg's skill as an artist.

He is not particularly a writer. The story is told a little stiffly, and the game of Jumanji is impossible to play: of the 10 throws of the dice, only two allow progress. Of the eight remaining, four are "lose-a-turn," and four are retreats of one, two, or three spaces. So it is hard to see how Judy manages to win at it. The story was, as so many picture books are, created as a vehicle for the illustrations instead of the other way around. I wish we would stop doing that. For all of the highly visual nature of their universe, modern children *of all ages* still demand—or at least deserve—a strong story well told.

Adults mustn't allow themselves to be "blown away," as the current jargon has it, by beautiful pictures alone. Still, *Jumanji* has a stronger, more engrossing story than many in its category, in part because of the tension it creates. Read it—don't just look at it—before you buy it. That's the only way to find out whether the child or children in your life will find it satisfying.

> Natalie Babbitt, 'Volcano Erupts, Go Back Three Spaces,'' in *Book World—The Washington Post (© 1981, The Washington Post), July 12, 1981, p. 6.*

Substance or shadow, real or imagined, the bizarre and mythical world of Jumanji exists because of its own logic and the luminous precision of the full-page, black-and-white illustrations. Through the masterly use of light and shadow, the interplay of design elements, and audacious changes in perspective and composition, the artist conveys an impression of color without losing the dramatic contrast of black and white. As in *The Garden of Abdul Gasazi* . . . , he successfully explores the semimagical country of the mind in which reality and illusion exist as conjoined yet distinct entities. (p. 417)

> Mary M. Burns, in her review of "Jumanji," in *The Horn Book Magazine (copyright © 1981 by The Horn Book, Inc., Boston), Vol. LVII, No. 4, August, 1981, pp. 416-17.*

In an epoch when colorful volumes crowd each other out in bookshops, the black-and-white *Jumanji* . . . is more than refreshing; it is a revelation. With his second book . . . , Chris Van Allsburg has become a master of Conté crayon and diabolical narrative. . . . Every hair, every blade of grass is meticulously recorded, and incongruities like a rhino charging a telephone are presented with haunting deadpan accuracy. (p. 79)

> Stefan Kanfer, "A World Charged with Miracles," in *Time (copyright 1981 Time Inc.; all rights reserved; reprinted by permission from Time), Vol. 118, No. 26, December 21, 1981, pp. 76, 79.**

From Jumanji, *written and illustrated by Chris Van Allsburg.*

BEN'S DREAM (1982)

[The] extraordinarily inventive author-illustrator presents a third splendid entry. . . . The story idea, so economically carried out in the text, is illustrated in the artist's meticulous drawings, marvels of symbolism, reality, imagination and perspective.

> A review of "Ben's Dream," in *Publishers Weekly (reprinted from the April 9, 1982 issue of* Publishers Weekly, *published by R. R. Bowker Company, a Xerox company; copyright © 1982 by Xerox Corporation), Vol. 221, No. 15, April 9, 1982, p. 50.*

Do kids still (did they ever) bone up on "great landmarks of the world?" Well, Ben's teacher is going to give Ben and Margaret's class a test on same—but when Ben sits down to study, it begins to rain, he falls asleep . . . and dreams that his house floats past the "great landmarks," now half-submerged, and, passing the Sphinx, he sees Margaret at the window of her floating house too. Then they find out they had the same dream. The notion allows for some of Van Allsburg's characteristic dramatic perspectives—except that, in this instance, they have no dramatic function—as we see the campanile of St. Mark's and Ben's house from the air, or the house floating through the ironwork of the Eiffel Tower, approaching the columns of the Parthenon, passing among the onion domes of St. Basil's in Moscow. None, as it happens, is anywhere identified, and some of the best-known might elude adults in this partial depiction (e.g., the understructure of the Eiffel Tower without a sign of Paris). Two bits are slightly humorous: the house barely clearing the Great Wall of China and, at the close, Mount Rushmore's George Washington saying, "Ben, wake up." It turns out to be Margaret, at the window. For pictorial effects and visual imagination, Van Allsburg can't touch Mitsumasa Anno—and to pretend that these essentially banal pictures have deep meanings is flimflam (unless you really want to take Margaret and Ben and the water and the towers seriously). But some kids might enjoy the watery tour of the sights as such. (pp. 487-88)

> A review of "Ben's Dream," in *Kirkus Reviews (copyright © 1982 The Kirkus Service, Inc.), Vol. L, No. 8, April 15, 1982, pp. 487-88.*

It is a brave step for an artist who has had great and immediate success with a style to change it. Chris Van Allsburg does just that in his third picture book, **"Ben's Dream."** Abandoning the richly penciled, magic realism that brought him acclaim . . . , he has picked up a pen. A superb technician, he uses it to imitate wood engravings, along lines similar to those worked by Rockwell Kent. While this is a new visual approach for Van Allsburg, the theme of the book has intrigued him before. . . .

Displayed on 11 wordless double pages, [the great landmarks Ben sees in his dream] are portraits of Big Ben, the Statue of Liberty, the Leaning Tower of Pisa and so on each one partially submerged, looking as if it were engraved from a surreal photograph. At the end Ben awakens from his dream . . . or was he really sleeping?

This framework for fantasy has been well used in children's literature as varied as "Alice's Adventures in Wonderland," "Little Nemo" and "Where the Wild Things Are." Here it seems more a device to hang some handsome pictures on than a new means of exploring illusion and reality. Van Allsburg is an artist of unusual ability, but even the most exceptional illustrations require the armature of a strong story or wordless drama. Without it, the resulting work is a picture exhibition rather than that wedding of art and narrative thought, a complete picture book. The former may win prizes; the latter wins the child. (p. 46)

Karla Kuskin, "The Complete Illustrator," in The New York Times Book Review *(© 1982 by The New York Times Company; reprinted by permission), April 25, 1982, pp. 31, 46.**

At first glance this latest Van Allsburg . . . looks like the work of David Macaulay. . . . Unlike the sensuous velvet blacks he seduced us with in his first two books, we are treated here to a multitude of linear patterns, suggestive of engravers' marks, with almost a total lack of solid black shapes. In the extremely simple and brief text (three pages to start and two to finish), Van Allsburg sets the stage for something spooky in spite of the matter-of-fact dialogue. . . . Each [monument] is partially submerged and seen only as a fragment, sometimes from a part of Ben's house, sometimes with the house floating nearby, always from unusual perspectives. There is a striking view of the Eiffel Tower that suggests a giant piece of a ferris wheel; onion domes of Moscow's St. Basil, floating like fish, bob on the flood waters. One need not know the monuments in order to sense their distinction. Indeed, seeing them thus might well move readers to search out more about each one. . . . Are we to speculate, as in *Jumanji*, about the nature of reality? The text may stimulate such thoughts. The pictures . . . sometimes provide humor but consistently provide mystery and the majesty of the monuments. There is a rightness to this view of our world, inviting readers to join the cruise. (pp. 66-7)

Kenneth Marantz, in his review of "Ben's Dream," in School Library Journal *(reprinted from the May, 1982 issue of* School Library Journal, *published by R. R. Bowker Co./A Xerox Corporation; copyright © 1982), Vol. 28, No. 9, May, 1982, pp. 66-7.*

The solidity and the perspective of Van Allsburg's fine-lined drawings are impressive, the text a vehicle for an idea rather than a story. The question is, who is the audience for this? What text there is reads as though it were designed for a read-aloud audience, but appreciation and recognition of the landmarks may require older readers, especially in such drawings as the one of the Eiffel Tower, which shows the intricate structural supports at an unusual angle, rather than the whole structure.

Zena Sutherland, in her review of "Ben's Dream," in Bulletin of the Center for Children's Books *(re-*

From Ben's Dream, *written and illustrated by Chris Van Allsburg.*

printed by permission of The University of Chicago Press; © 1982 by The University of Chicago), Vol. 35, No. 11, July-August, 1982, p. 217.

Of course there is no such thing as magic. Or is there? Once again, the creator of **The Garden of Abdul Gasazi** and **Jumanji** . . . leaves us in some doubt. . . . In a marvelous series of double-page black-and-white pictures meticulously textured with hatching, one shares Ben's voyage past such sights as the Statue of Liberty, the Sphinx, and the Mount Rushmore presidents, all with flood waters lapping about their respective chins and waists. Dramatic angles, close-ups from above and below, and careful architectural details which recall the work of David Macaulay dazzle the eye and the imagination. . . . A visual tour de force.

*Ethel R. Twichell, in her review of "Ben's Dream,"
in* The Horn Book Magazine *(copyright © 1982 by The Horn Book, Inc., Boston), Vol. LVIII, No. 4, August, 1982, p. 396.*

Nancy Willard

1936-

American author of poetry, fiction, and nonfiction.

Willard has recently become one of the most prominent contemporary writers for children. She has stated that a good children's book, like a classic folktale and the works of such authors as Lewis Carroll and William Blake, increases in meaning and becomes more valuable as the child matures; many of Willard's books reflect this belief. Critics praise the ageless quality of her work, and applaud her creative use of langauge, her fanciful imagination, and the dreamlike quality of her stories and poems. Willard's prose for children includes short story collections on the fantastic adventures of Anatole, picture books in a folklore style, and a semi-autobiographical story for older chldren, *The Highest Hit*. Her first poetry collection for children, *A Visit to William Blake's Inn*, is also the first book of verse to win the Newbery Medal since its establishment in 1922.

Willard began her career as a writer in elementary school, and had several poems and stories published in literary magazines and college publications before she earned her doctorate in modern literature. She is also an artist and illustrates children's books for other writers. Her themes, settings, and characters are inspired by her sculptures, dreams, and childhood memories. Combined with her literary interests and talents, these sources bring forth imaginative and lyrical books for children. *Sailing to Cythera, and Other Anatole Stories* and its sequel *Island of the Grass King: The Further Adventures of Anatole* are praised for their natural blend of reality and fantasy. Critics are particularly pleased with the tale in which the main character—named after Willard's son, James Anatole—enters Cythera through his bedroom wallpaper. The island in her sequel was inspired by *The Tempest* and includes names and character types from Shakespeare and the Brothers Grimm. While some critics say that her use of these characters is purposeless and sometimes confusing in a book for children, others state that these references add to the timeless appeal of Willard's works.

Willard's original fairy tales *Simple Pictures, Strangers' Bread*, and *The Marzipan Moon* all vary stylistically. Although reviewers dislike her abstraction and inconsistency and the religious moral in *Strangers' Bread*, most of them approve of her utilization of the simplicity, repetition, and rhythm of the classics. *Simple Pictures* is especially noted for these qualities and for its flowing, humorous story. *The Highest Hit* is Willard's only work of realistic fiction. While often discredited for its lack of plot and inclusion of too much incidental action, it is also praised for Willard's prose style and unobtrusive moral.

A Visit to William Blake's Inn has its roots in Willard's childhood. She discovered Blake's poetry at the age of seven, and as a young girl was impressed with her mother's definition of an inn as "[A] resting place for travelers, like a hotel, only friendlier . . . A great many interesting people stayed there." She decided that "inn" was synonymous with the comfort and

openness of her own home, which was frequently shared with fascinating relatives and friends. Willard created a large wood model of her conception of Blake's inn, complete with his engravings and a variety of self-made figures. Many of the characters appearing in *A Visit to William Blake's Inn* represent the inhabitants of her model. Concerning this method of making sculptures prior to many of her books Willard has said, "I like to have these characters around me for a while before I set them down. They help me to create the story because they become so real to me." While some critics object to Willard's irreverent association with Blake—stating that her mythical settings and humor resemble the work of Edward Lear and Carroll—most of them are highly pleased with her use of language, her wit and perception, and her fresh images. Through her unique approach to children's literature, Willard has produced books which follow the traditions of the classics. As well as the 1982 Newbery Award, Willard received the Golden Kite Honor Book selection in 1981 for *A Visit to William Blake's Inn;* the Lewis Carroll Shelf Award in 1974 for *Sailing to Cythera, and Other Anatole Stories* and in 1979 for *Island of the Grass King: The Further Adventures of Anatole*. She has also received many awards for her adult poetry, essays, and short stories.

(See also *Contemporary Literary Criticism*, Vol. 7 and *Contemporary Authors*, Vols. 89-92.)

AUTHOR'S COMMENTARY

There are two ways of hiding something in writing. You leave it out, or you disguise it. What is left out is lost. What is disguised is saved but only for those who can see through the disguise. Nevertheless, disguises themselves can be very attractive. Parables, allegories, satires, and a good many fairy tales are disguises, for they contain ideas more complicated than the surface story which hides them.

When you hide something, you often return to find more than you hid. I learned this not from literature but from my favorite all-purpose hiding place in the house where I grew up, my parents' closet. (p. 556)

[The] only things my mother consciously hid in the closet were Christmas presents. My sister and I found them one year, to our great dismay. The next year I hid my presents there, and my sister, without anyone else's knowledge, hid hers there as well. So when my mother went to the closet to fetch the presents she'd hidden for us, she found they had multiplied, in a sort of reversal of the parable of the talents. That is often the way with hiding places. What you hide suffers a sea-change. What you find is not exactly what you hid.

I felt very much as my mother must have felt, when I finished my last book for children, *The Island of the Grass King*. . . . It tells of a child who travels to an enchanted island and rescues a king whose kingdom is an earthly paradise, the Garden of Eden before the Fall. Because an imaginary garden must be real before you can write about it, I took for my model the most enchanted island I knew: the island on which Shakespeare set *The Tempest*. Here magic and nature are inseparable—a natural abode of witches and magicians.

So I read Shakespeare and the sources he might have used to invent his island before I tried to invent mine. I wondered if my editor would ask me, why hide literary allusions in a story for children, who probably won't recognize them? She did not ask. But if she had, I would have answered that reading Shakespeare helped me to shape my own story and that the snatches of Shakespeare's songs and speeches are part of the story I want to tell. And although the child reading my book won't recognize them, I hope they will be obvious to a well-read adult reader. Children's books should be big enough for children to grow into. When I grew up, I did not put my favorite children's books away with other childish things. I enjoyed them on a different level. But in spite of the allusions I hid in my book, my purpose in writing was to entertain. I was writing an adventure story, not an allegory. Or so I thought when I sent it off to my editor.

She wrote back an enthusiastic letter, which included the various interpretations of the book given by her staff. One reader claimed that the trip to the island was a hallucination. The Grass King, of course, was marijuana. Another saw it as an allegory about the political conditions in Cuba. Nobody noticed Shakespeare. I was amazed. How did Cuba and marijuana get into my book? Because someone had found them, were they really there? How much came from craft, how much from inspiration, and how much from pure accident? And how consciously can a writer use symbols without becoming self-conscious and pedantic?

The first books that made me ask these questions were *Alice's Adventures in Wonderland* and *Through the Looking-Glass*. Lewis Carroll is a hider after my own heart. The house where he grew up had a loose floorboard in the nursery, under which later occupants found the treasures he hid there: a child's white glove, a thimble, a left shoe, a fragment of a poem scrawled on a piece of wood. Glove, thimble, left shoe, poems—all these things turn up years later in the *Alice* books, where the author himself hides behind a pseudonym. (pp. 556-57)

Some critics have read the *Alice* books as satire; others have called them allegories. The truth is, Dodgson set out to write neither one. He did, however, write stories in which he hid ideas, people, and events familiar to him, though he did not do so in a systematic way. He also took his time writing down his stories, and time seems to have a great deal to do with how successfully a writer changes the parochial into the universal.

I learned the hard way how awful a story can be if you have not waited until it is ready to be written. Let me go back to my book, *The Island of the Grass King*. Four years ago I tried to write that book. It was meant to be a sequel to a collection of stories, *Sailing to Cythera* . . . about the adventures of a boy named Anatole. In *The Island of the Grass King* one of the characters is a pirate. To help me create that character, I read an enormous number of books on pirates. One of the scenes takes place in the sky. To help me describe the sky, I read a vast number of books on astronomy.

I read too much. I had the trappings of characters but not the characters themselves. I had the details of a setting but not the story to give it significance. (p. 559)

[My editors informed me that the] writing was abysmal. All the reports of the readers agreed. How, asked one, could anyone capable of writing *Sailing to Cythera* have written so badly?

The next morning I took up a copy of *Sailing to Cythera* and asked myself, what did I do so effortlessly in this book that I failed to do in the second? Effortlessly—that was the secret. I had not written *Sailing to Cythera* out of months of research. I had written out of the memories of my own childhood. When I was a child, I greatly admired the wallpaper in a restaurant to which I was sometimes taken as a reward for memorizing a difficult piano piece. It showed shepherds and shepherdesses dancing under willow trees, courting under rose arbors, and piping to one another across flocks of immaculate white sheep. Whenever I saw that idyllic country, I wanted to walk on that grass and hear the birds, rare as nightingales and twice as beautiful. Perhaps all fairy tales are really ways of making impossible wishes come true. As I could not go into the wallpaper myself, I sent my character into it, where he learned a little about magic and a lot about love.

Years after the restaurant had been converted into a pizza parlor, I was a student at the University of Michigan; I was dozing in an art history lecture when there flashed across the screen the very country which the wallpaper had imitated so badly. The painting was *The Embarkation for Cythera* by the eighteenth-century French painter Antoine Watteau. It showed a party of aristocrats preparing to set sail for the island of Cythera, from which the goddess of love, Venus, received the name Cytherea. The art history instructor called these people pilgrims, and he drew our attention to the autumnal light, the sunny distances, and a great many other things which I have now forgotten. How long ago I first saw that painting, and how little I thought of it afterward! But when I wanted to describe what things looked like on the other side of the wallpaper, the painting came back to me.

Remembering this, I looked again at my disastrous fifty pages. They had come into the world trailing clouds of research; they were born of other people's books, not my own experience. So I put *The Island of the Grass King* away and wrote, instead, a book about a girl who plays baseball, and to the best of my knowledge there isn't a symbol in it. Not a trace of satire, not a smidgen of allegory. I forgot about the book I'd wanted to write and couldn't. But the wonderful thing about failures in writing is, although you forget them, they do not forget you. Left alone, they assume their proper shape. Like children who survive all their parents' plans for them, they grow up in their own way. They return, not when you call them but when some trivial episode wakes them.

The story I had wanted to write in *The Island of the Grass King* returned two years later when I was polishing my mother's silver, those forks and teapots so often lost in odd corners of our house. I was polishing a coffeepot whose handle was a griffin with a tail that twined around the spout and somewhere along the way burst into leaves. Half the pot was bright with my diligence. The other half was dark, and I could not make out the design at all. It was as if one side were awake, and the other side asleep, and so it is with us, I thought; we spend half our lives doing things and the other half dreaming about them. Outside the rain began to fall, though the sun was shining, and my mother said, "Rain and sun together! The devil is beating his wife."

And I remembered, suddenly, the wise woman of my childhood whom I believed caused both weather and seasons: Mother Holle. I first met her in one of Grimm's fairy tales, and I did not know that her name means hell in German. I only knew that she lived under the earth and that she sometimes hired mortal girls to help her with her housework. Their chief duty was to shake out her feather beds, for this shaking of feathers below the earth caused snow to fall on the surface of the earth. From this memory sprang the three wise women who run the world in *The Island of the Grass King*. The first is the Maker; she makes all the creatures, and as the old ones wear out, she makes new ones. The second is the Mender; she keeps everything in repair, and she heals the torn and broken. The third is the Breaker, who destroys whatever the Mender cannot save.

So out of that odd recollection grew the finished version of my book. My reading on pirates and astronomy was there, but it had got so mixed up with my own memories that what came forth was quite different from either. With children's books, as with adult books, writing is a matter of words and silence, of pounding the material into submission and letting go of it, of trying to finish so many pages a day while telling yourself that you have all the time in the world. It's important to keep in mind the story you want to write. But it is even more important to forget it. Kafka understood this when he told a friend why an artist's material "must be worked on by the spirit." The writer not only gathers experience, he masters what is experienced.

I believe that for most writers there are three kinds of stories. The first is the story which you choose to write and which you believe you understand. The second is the story which chooses you, and where it comes from you don't know, for the material seems to have been worked on out of your sight and hearing. The third is the story that starts out as the first kind and ends up as the second. What you know is changed into more than you know. When the author of *Alice's Adventures in Wonderland* was asked to explain a poem he had written, he excused himself with the remark, "Words mean more than we mean to express when we use them; so a whole book ought to mean a great deal more than the writer meant." (pp. 559-62)

It's no surprise that many writers of stories for children heard fairy stories long before they ever heard the word *symbol*. So did many of us, and so it will always be, as long as there are grownups to tell stories and children to ask for them. Of all the writers for children whose imaginations were fed on fairy tales, Hans Christian Andersen was surely one of the most fortunate. The place where he heard fairy tales has long since vanished from our world, yet for centuries it was one of the great storehouses of folk literature. This was the spinning room, where women sat spinning at their wheels and worked together during the long winter. To make the time pass more pleasantly, they told each other stories. (p. 563)

Andersen knew, as the greatest writers for children always know, that fairy tales are not only for children. One evening he was leaving the theater after a play, and he overheard someone say that the play ought not to be taken seriously, as it was only a fairy tale. "I was indignant," exclaimed Andersen. "In the whole realm of poetry no domain is so boundless as that of the fairy tale. It reaches from the blood-drenched graves of antiquity to the pious legends of a child's picture-book."

Isn't it odd that so simple a story can carry our deepest fears and desires in so small a space? Is that why I like stories that hide ideas—so that I can find them again, like a ring lost in the house, all the more precious when I find it because I had forgotten it? . . . Is it for the pleasure of discovering what we already know that we hide familiar things in fantastic stories where straw turns into gold, words into spells, and ourselves into heroes? (pp. 563-64)

Nancy Willard, "The Spinning Room: Symbols and Storytellers" (a revision of a lecture delivered at the Bread Loaf Writer's Conference, Middlebury, Vermont, August, 1979; reprinted by permission of the author), in The Horn Book Magazine *(copyright © 1980 by The Horn Book, Inc., Boston), Vol. LVI, No. 5, October, 1980, pp. 555-64.*

SAILING TO CYTHERA, AND OTHER ANATOLE STORIES (1974)

[*Sailing to Cythera, and Other Anatole Stories*] is a collection of short tales, all fantasies and all believable. Magic is the necessary ingredient, a gift which the little boy hero, Anatole, uses wisely in all his exploits. Few children will be able to resist the book as a whole; most will probably settle on "**The Wise Soldier of Sellebak**" as their favorite.

A review of "Sailing to Cythera," in Publishers Weekly *(reprinted from the September 9, 1974 issue of* Publishers Weekly, *published by R. R. Bowker Company, a Xerox company; copyright © 1974 by Xerox Corporation), Vol. 206, No. 11, September 9, 1974, p. 68.*

The three stories in "**Sailing to Cythera**" have no upper [age limit]. These timeless, American-yet-placeless fantasies . . . [are] full of the kind of echoes that will reverberate round a child's imagination for decades, or for life. Imagine: a tiny speck in the sky flies nearer, seems first a bird, then a fairy-tale angel, and then—"It was a man in a suit as white as snow and as bright as water, and he was riding a book, and when he saw Anatole, he sang out, 'Who called the west wind?'. . . ."

Try it on any book-loving child of seven or up. He or she may remember you for it for a very long time.

Susan Cooper, in her review of "Sailing to Cythera," in The Christian Science Monitor (reprinted by permission from The Christian Science Monitor; © 1974 The Christian Science Publishing Society; all rights reserved), November 6, 1974, p. 11.*

There is a key to the writing of fantasy and though there are many ways to describe it, I know that its essence has to do with logic. Let one logical brick slip out of the story and Alice may not get to Wonderland. . . .

It is this premise that causes me to gaze at **"Sailing to Cythera"** with a doubting eye. For here are three tales which seem to have been spun out from moment to moment. It is almost as if the author were writing down anything that came to mind, using a large umbrella of fantasy as a rationale. And it is rather too bad, for she writes beautifully and has a vivid imagination.

In the first tale, her young hero Anatole takes a long journey with his cat to visit the cat's aunt, Pitterpat. And that is all I can tell you. I do not know why they have taken this journey, or why the story is called **"Gospel Train,"** or why they come home. We are told, unconvincingly, that Aunt Pitterpat is giving a christening party for her "ninth skin"—but anyone past the age of 5 knows that cats do not get new skins and that the number nine refers to lives. And in the second story we meet an amnesiac soldier who is trying to recover 30 lost years. With Anatole's help, he rises into the air, flies like a bird over the ocean and arrives back in his home town, a mythical place called Sellebak. And from there on, I am lost.

The third tale, however, hangs together very well and has a definite charm. Perhaps this is because it is the simplest. . . . The entrances and exits to fantasy-land are here excellently done, and one only wishes that the whole book had had this quality. Nancy Willard is so talented a writer that she must learn to go more slowly and discover the Why of things. The Wherefores will then take care of themselves.

Barbara Wersba, in her review of "Sailing to Cythera, and Other Anatole Stories," in The New York Times Book Review (© 1974 by The New York Times Company; reprinted by permission), December 8, 1974, p. 8.

When Anatole finally gets to see the Sun's mother (get it?) he produces for her amusement a Van Houten's cocoa advertisement that unfolds into a magnificent, fairy-tale tea party setting for forty. This sort of breathtaking triumph is managed now and again in the course of three short fantasy voyages that are, for the most part, disturbingly vague. . . . Only the third Anatole adventure really makes sense. . . . This third chapter alone may make Anatole a worthwhile acquaintance—but parents who lack the imagination to fill all the gaps Willard leaves open might just think he's more trouble than he's worth. (pp. 19-20)

A review of "Sailing to Cythera: And Other Anatole Stories," in Kirkus Reviews (copyright © 1975 The Kirkus Service, Inc.), Vol. XLIII, No. 1, January 1, 1975, pp. 19-20.

These three magical but cozy stories . . . rankle at first because of their adult consciousness; yet they grow on the reader and leave a fresh, satisfying memory. . . . The mode of fantasy is highly eclectic, borrowing from oral and written traditions and liberally sprinkled with original ideas. Although at times the author seems to wander idly among remembrances of childhood fantasies, she soon returns to well-paced, more clearly focused writing.

A review of "Sailing to Cythera, and Other Anatole Stories," in The Booklist (reprinted by permission of the American Library Association; copyright © 1975 by the American Library Association), Vol. 71, No. 11, February 1, 1975, p. 573.

Reading Willard, one is reminded both of Lewis Carroll and C. S. Lewis: the mythic settings and themes evoke Lewis, but the lucidly labyrinthine dream-plots move with the magic of Alice. Nevertheless, Willard has her own personal vision, a stunning blend of myth and reality. . . . Death and mutability are the principal themes in these stories. A cat dies and a grandfather is paralyzed, but Anatole is gently led—along with the reader—down a path of reconciliation and wisdom, so that beneath the surfaces of Anatole's little visions the lines of spiritual allegory begin to emerge; and the effect is as wholesome as it is delightful. The writing itself leaves little to be desired, as Willard's sentences move with the lucid and inevitable rhythms that one expects in a fine children's story. (p. 290)

William H. Green, "Six Fantasies: Theme and Style," in Children's Literature: Annual of The Modern Language Association Seminar on Children's Literature and The Children's Literature Association, Volume 5, edited by Francelia Butler (© 1976 by Francelia Butler; all rights reserved), Temple University Press, 1976, pp. 288-93.*

THE WELL-MANNERED BALLOON   (1976)

"A very well-mannered balloon," James' parents say about this big new blue one with the pirate's face. . . . But after James' parents go to bed, the balloon goes on an ill-mannered rampage. . . . James at last destroys the balloon by feeding it a pin cushion, whereupon it bursts and everything it has eaten tumbles out and back into place—before James' fantasy has really had a chance to cut loose. . . . Perhaps the author is too well-mannered. . . . [Her] story is a little too much like a psych book example. . . .

A review of "The Well-Mannered Balloon," in Kirkus Reviews (copyright © 1976 The Kirkus Service, Inc.), Vol. XLIV, No. 8, April 15, 1976, p. 466.

James's parents are impressed with his new balloon. It does not ask for water before bed or want to do jumpies as James does. However, with lights out, the balloon's true demanding nature surfaces. . . . Children may enjoy some of the nonsense, but the story does not rest on a firm enough base of character and feeling to be believable.

Alice Low, in her review of "The Well-Mannered Balloon," in Children's Book Review Service (copyright © 1976 Children's Book Review Service Inc.), Vol. 4, No. 13, July, 1976, p. 108.

There is dry humor in the author's treatment of parent-child relationships, and a nice use of patterned repetition in the fantasy sequence, but the fantasy and its realistic matrix don't quite mesh.

Zena Sutherland, in her review of "The Well-Mannered Balloon," in Bulletin of the Center for Children's Books (reprinted by permission of The Uni-

versity of Chicago Press; © 1976 by The University of Chicago), Vol. 30, No. 2, October, 1976, p. 35.

Children approve of the way James handles the problem and enjoy the humor as they anticipate the satisfying conclusion. Younger readers like this story when read aloud.

> *Donna Harsh, Joyce Boone and Eva Culver, in their review of "The Well-Mannered Balloon" (copyright 1977 by the International Reading Association, Inc.; reprinted with permission of the International Reading Association and), in* The Reading Teacher, *Vol. 31, No. 1, October, 1977, p. 18.*

SIMPLE PICTURES ARE BEST   (1977)

The combination of Willard's whimsical imagination and [Tomie] De Paola's jaunty, affectionate pictures makes their book a special treat. When a rotund shoemaker and his wife have their photograph taken, they cram all their worldly goods into camera range. The exasperated photographer keeps reminding the couple that simple pictures are best but they pay no attention. Readers will squirm with anticipation as each bizarre item adds suspense and humor. The ending piles on more surprises, with a final one proving that the photographer's maxim is well founded.

> *A review of "Simple Pictures Are Best," in* Publishers Weekly *(reprinted from the February 21, 1977 issue of* Publishers Weekly, *published by R. R. Bowker Company, a Xerox company; copyright © 1977 by Xerox Corporation), Vol. 211, No. 8, February 21, 1977, p. 78.*

Children will enjoy chiming in with the photographer's refrain, "Simple pictures are best," each time the shoemaker or his wife rush off to include something dear to them in their already crowded anniversary snapshot. . . . The smooth flowing cumulative story, simple and direct but rich in pithy descriptions and similes, is certain to be a story time hit.

> *Judith S. Kronick, in her review of "Simple Pictures Are Best," in* School Library Journal *(reprinted from the March, 1977 issue of* School Library Journal, *published by R. R. Bowker Co./A Xerox Corporation; copyright © 1977), Vol. 23, No. 7, March, 1977, p. 139.*

There's some nonsense, humor, . . . and the appeals of cumulation and repetition, but the ending is flat and the couple's amusement at a potentially dangerous and certainly frightening situation is a dubious element in the story.

> *Zena Sutherland, in her review of "Simple Pictures Are Best," in* Bulletin of the Center for Children's Books *(reprinted by permission of The University of Chicago Press; © 1977 by The University of Chicago), Vol. 30, No. 11, July/August, 1977, p. 184.*

Sharing folktales in the classroom is an ideal way to stimulate creative dramatics, for the plots of these stories are simple, short, and action-packed, involving a small number of characters. Some of the picture books written in folktale style can add variety by providing fresh plots and new twists.

Simple Pictures Are Best by Nancy Willard . . . is an appropriate choice. . . .

The story is one which children can enjoy acting out just as they remember it, preparing simple props and performing spontaneously. It is especially adaptable to pantomime, in which individual children show what they think James, the helper, might have done to make the couple laugh. It can be used well for the "fractured story" approach, also, with children acting out the taking of pictures with favorite items from their own classroom.

> *Ruth M. Noyce, in her review of "Simple Pictures Are Best" (copyright 1979 by the International Reading Association, Inc.; reprinted with permission of the International Reading Association and Ruth M. Noyce), in* The Reading Teacher, *Vol. 32, No. 4, January, 1979, p. 445.*

STRANGERS' BREAD   (1977)

[Anatole is] back in a new, endearing adventure. . . . Anatole is delivering a loaf of Russian pumpernickel to his friend, elderly Mrs. Chiba. . . . But this errand is jinxed. A fox, a rabbit and other animals join the boy and all beg for a slice of bread. He can't refuse the hungry creatures. But what is he to tell Mrs. Chiba when he arrives at her house with an empty bag? The answer is a deft and lovely surprise.

> *A review of "Strangers' Bread," in* Publishers Weekly *(reprinted from the July 25, 1977 issue of* Publishers Weekly, *published by R. R. Bowker Company, a Xerox company; copyright © 19 by Xerox Corporation), Vol. 212, No. 4, July 25, 1977, p. 71.*

This is a good-natured little story full of mostly unimportant inconsistencies. . . . [The strangers] sit a little uneasily for me in a story that opens with mention of such literal things as Nabisco saltines, but it is all meant to be taken literally, apparently, since—unlike Dr. Seuss's "Mulberry Street" adventure—there is no evidence that what happened en route was a figment of the hero's imagination.

> *Natalie Babbitt, in her review of "Strangers' Bread," in* The New York Times Book Review *(© 1977 by The New York Times Company; reprinted by permission), September, 1977, p. 36.*

Willard's modern day parable about sharing may be too abstract for young readers as well as too parochial for placement on public school and library shelves. . . . The pen-and-ink sketches [by David McPhail] are delightful but fail to save the story from preachy perdition.

> *Barbara S. Worth, in her review of "Strangers' Bread," in* Children's Book Review Service *(copyright © 1977 Children's Book Review Service Inc.), Vol. 6, No. 4, December, 1977, p. 33.*

A cumulative style, imaginative sly animals, and a satisfactory ending will delight children and adults. A bucolic tale bound to be read again and again. Who could resist a foxy starving poet who ". . . plays such splendid music, that the flowers and trees along the road bent forward to listen."

> *Ruth M. Stein, in her review of "Strangers' Bread" (copyright © 1978 by the National Council of Teachers of English; reprinted by permission of the publisher and the author), in* Language Arts, *Vol. 55, No. 5, May, 1978, p. 625.*

THE HIGHEST HIT (1978)

Kate Schmidt has a lot of irons in the fire. . . . She proceeds with all [her] projects in a unique, yet everyday way. The first-person narrative is episodic, even incidental, with nothing rounded out; one ludicrous situation follows another with very casual development and little attention to transition or time sequence. But the scenes are linked by an imaginative style, funny exchanges, and true-to-life details that children will enjoy.

> *Betsy Hearne, in her review of "The Highest Hit," in* Booklist *(reprinted by permission of the American Library Association: copyright © 1978 by the American Library Association), Vol. 74, No. 17, May 1, 1978, p. 1440.*

Readers who demand lots of sensational action will stay away from **"The Highest Hit,"** and bad cess to them. Those who respond to human warmth, a loving precision of language and the lives of real, individual children will treasure it, and they will be the gainers.

Nancy Willard is a poet, and she tells her story in prose as natural and unpretentious as grass. Kate's mother learns to play baseball; Kate's friend has a crush on an Episcopal priest. . . . Somebody wears Frankenstein fangs to communion; somebody else wins a prize for the smallest pet in the show by submitting a germ. (Faith being, as the author forbears from reminding us, the evidence of things not seen.) Though this is very far from being that dreary thing, a novel with a theological message, it does seem to inspire me to biblical paraphrase: those who have ears to hear, let them hear.

> *Georgess McHargue, in her review of "The Highest Hit," in* The New York Times Book Review *(© 1978 by The New York Times Company; reprinted by permission), May 21, 1978, p. 26.*

Willard comes very close to commiting a humorist's worst sin—trying too hard. Her main character and narrator, Kate, is a child to whom things never cease to happen. . . . None of Kate's family or acquaintances are without their idiosyncrasies, their droll remarks, or colorful habits. The story moves along at the pace of a television sitcom, with as much action and as little substance. Children whose taste in entertainment has been formed watching "Eight Is Enough" or "The Brady Bunch" will find this funny, but not even its tacked-on lesson—"A hit is a triumph of right over wrong, joy over grief. . . . We're all in this together, Kate"—can elevate it above the trivial.

> *Linda Silver, in her review of "The Highest Hit," in* School Library Journal *(reprinted from the September, 1978 issue of* School Library Journal, *published by R. R. Bowker Co./A Xerox Corporation; copyright © 1978), Vol. 25, No. 1, September, 1978, p. 152.*

There's no real storyline, but the writing has a light, yeasty quality and Kate's antics are diverse and amusing. Not a substantial book, but lively, wholesome, and entertaining.

> *Zena Sutherland, in her review of "The Highest Hit," in* Bulletin of the Center for Children's Books *(reprinted by permission of The University of Chicago Press; © 1978 by The University of Chicago), Vol. 32, No. 3, November, 1978, p. 56.*

The Highest Hit found its way into publication with anticipated applause. It was a witty, warm novel in which the protagonist Kate, among other things, developed a deep friendship with an elderly neighbor. This relationship and her family's concern for a mentally ill relative are treated with gentle sensitivity, humor, and genuine love—long before such subjects became popular. (p. 376)

> *Barbara Lucas, "Nancy Willard," in* The Horn Book Magazine *(copyrighted, 1982, by The Horn Book, Inc., Boston), Vol. LVIII, No. 4, August, 1982, pp. 374-79.*

THE ISLAND OF THE GRASS KING: THE FURTHER ADVENTURES OF ANATOLE (1979)

The best way to describe Anatole's new adventure—one long story rather than a group of three as in **"Sailing to Cythera"**—might be to call **"The Island of the Grass King"** an exquisite, undisciplined flight of fancy. . . .

What saves Nancy Willard's tale from becoming a jumble of highly imaginative but arbitrary dream images are the beauty of its language and its palpable warmth. Her affection for her little hero and the unpredictable island he visits is highly contagious. But there is no single thread or source or point of view to tie events and characters together. The tale lacks both the underlying simplicity of a true fairy tale and the upside-down logic of a true dream fantasy. References to other works crop up unexpectedly: The island is called Sycorax, the mother of Shakespeare's Caliban; Plumpet, the cat, refers to "The Book of Names" (for cats), which strongly recalls T. S. Eliot, and a fragment of Tennyson's "Crossing the Bar" is quoted by the large green rabbit, Captain Lark. But none of these is credited anywhere, and one wonders how many more such examples one may have overlooked. There is a suspicion that Miss Willard has put into her story whatever came into her mind, both of hark-backs *and* fanciful flights.

It would be extremely unfair to say that because of these things, the book does not work. It is fresh, loving and gentle, its images and characters largely new and all attractive, and though it has plenty of dangers and suspense, it is ideal for bedtime reading-aloud. You seldom find the language so lovingly and creatively used these days.

> *Natalie Babbitt, in her review of "The Island of the Grass King," in* The New York Times Book Review *(© 1979 by The New York Times Company; reprinted by permission), May 27, 1979, p. 25.*

Anatole, the little hero of *Sailing to Cythera* . . . , now rides a winged horse to the island of Sycorax, seeking fennel from the crown of the King of the Grass to treat his grandmother's asthma. The quest turns into a rather arbitrary treasure hunt, as Anatole is aided by the Keeper of the Roads, imprisoned in the Kingdom of the Dogs, directed to Mother Weather-sky's garden, and then, before he gets there, sent instead and in turn to the Four Winds and The Mender and the wild boar who can read the book of invisible spells. . . . Willard conjures up some effective images: a field full of ships' figureheads standing in the sand with their eyes raised to heaven; the Mender herself, a young woman in a robe of dried leaves who sorts and stitches claws, horns, birds' wings, and skins to the light of candles held by snakes. But her wonders are mere fanciful imaginings, fine decorations that fit no scheme, and thus grow tiresome.

A review of "The Island of the Grass King," in Kirkus Reviews (copyright © 1979 The Kirkus Service, Inc.), Vol. XLVII, No. 12, June 15, 1979, p. 686.

[Make-believe] and reality blend joyfully [in *The Island of the Grass King: The Further Adventures of Anatole*] . . . The only works comparable in pure romance and humor to the Anatole stories are the inventions of Lewis Carroll.

A review of "The Island of the Grass King: The Further Adventures of Anatole," in Publishers Weekly (reprinted from the June 18, 1979 issue of Publishers Weekly, published by R. R. Bowker Company, a Xerox company; copyright © 1979 by Xerox Corporation), Vol. 215, No. 25, June 18, 1979, p. 93.

Magic and fantasy are mingled inextricably with the marvelous workings of nature. Domesticity (a cat and a coffee pot for companions, interest in food, fear of the dark) meshes seamlessly with cosmology (the Four Winds, a vegetation-figure, the attic where night is stored each day, the house of creation at the top of the rainbow). This is a book for those who revel in the unexpected, in wonderful invention, in powerful and vivid and even mystical fancy. It is fluent, graceful, full of details that surprise yet rub together comfortably with a kind of kaleidoscopic consistency. There are snatches and echoes of poetry, unobtrusive allusions (to *The Tempest*, especially), flashes of humor and of insight into children, and no sentimentality (the pet cat talks, but also likes a little mole for supper). (pp. 150-51)

Patricia Dooley, in her review of "The Island of the Grass King: The Further Adventures of Anatole," in School Library Journal (reprinted from the September, 1979 issue of School Library Journal, published by R. R. Bowker Co./A Xerox Corporation; copyright © 1979), Vol. 26, No. 1, September, 1979, pp. 150-51.

THE MARZIPAN MOON (1981)

Willard's version of the homily that humble objects are best concerns a poor priest whose birthday brings no gifts of food from his parishioners. Holding the cracked clay pot he did receive from one, the priest idly wishes that he could have a new marzipan moon every morning. From that day on he has; and though the pot grants no further wishes, he's happy enough with that—until the Bishop visits and insists on spying on the pot. The main chance for author and artist [Marcia Sewall] comes here, and both make something of it, but what? Willard has two almonds emerge from the pot and, from them, two creatures made of gargoyle heads, firewood arms, flour sack bodies, and muffler legs. These odd creatures produce the marzipan with a "God bless [everyone]" chant . . .—but their peculiar, insect-like appearance is less benign. What happens then is unsurprising: the Bishop, who wants the marzipan, discards the clay pot and has a splendid gold-and-silver casket made for the almonds and placed on the main altar of the cathedral. Needless to say, that's the end of the marzipan. Willard tells the story fluently. . . . However, even if marzipan on the altar can be seen as amusingly incongruous instead of just farfetched, the almond creatures are representative of the whole: the parts, though suggestive and sometimes striking, don't cohere with the unconscious necessity of a seasoned folk tale.

A review of "The Marzipan Moon," in Kirkus Reviews (copyright © 1981 The Kirkus Service, Inc.), Vol. XLIX, No. 7, April 1, 1981, p. 428.

More than what happened to dinosaurs, I wondered as a child what ever happened to the days of "Once upon a time;" when wishes came true and fairy godmothers materialized at the drop of a heroine's tear. Had Nancy Willard been writing when I was young, I would have found the answer I longed to hear: Once-upon-a-time is still alive and well, right here and now.

"The Marzipan Moon" is a modest tour de force, a contemporary fairytale absolutely convincing in its real-world evocation of a wistful old priest and his "church so poor that even the mice stayed away." Because we believe unreservedly in the hero and his handful of woebegone parishioners, we also believe in the present he receives—a cracked clay crock that can grant just one wish. As any mortal unmindful of the power of his gift might do, the cleric idly wishes for "a marzipan moon on my kitchen table every morning." All of the characters, from down-at-heel congregants to the sententious bishop who covets his colleague's good fortune, ring wonderously true. . . . At the wry denouement, the bishop intones, "The Lord giveth and the Lord taketh away." Happily, the born storyteller giveth and the sweet aftertaste—like that of marzipan—lingers long.

Selma G. Lanes, in her review of "The Marzipan Moon," in The New York Times Book Review (© 1981 by The New York Times Company; reprinted by permission), July 12, 1981, p. 30.

The story is not without interest and creativity, but the image of the greedy bishop is Chaucerian and medieval, amiss in today's ecumenical climate. The placement of the rich casket on the altar is distasteful as is the old priest's abandonment of his former spare life for the warmth and ease of the cathedral, where the bishop has brought him. Older children and adults could find fruit for discussion here; the book's more probable younger readers do not have the maturity to see the clerics as symbols; to them, appearance is reality.

Mary I. Purucker, in her review of "The Marzipan Moon," in School Library Journal (reprinted from the August, 1981 issue of School Library Journal, published by R. R. Bowker Co./A Xerox Corporation; copyright © 1981), Vol. 27, No. 10, August, 1981, p. 72.

This is a rather strange book. The length (48 pages) and copious illustrations suggest a picture book, but the publishers' blurb, the symbolism, and the moral of the story suggest an older audience. The story is very much like a modern fairy tale, a "Once upon a time . . . " and the wish-come-true story. But it does not have a happy ending; instead, a lesson is taught. Yet the lesson blatantly stated at the end is not the same lesson that is subtly given elsewhere. These comments notwithstanding, the book has a lovely charm. . . . It might be worth acquiring one copy. A final quibble: would children know what marzipan is?

Maureen O'Connor, in her review of "The Marzipan Moon," in Children's Book Review Service (copyright © 1981 Children's Book Review Service Inc.), Vol. 10, No. 2, October, 1981, p. 16.

A VISIT TO WILLIAM BLAKE'S INN: POEMS FOR INNOCENT AND EXPERIENCED TRAVELERS (1981)

Inventive nonsense is fortunately frequent in children's poetry, and it sells, too; witness Shel Silverstein. But good lyrical verse is not frequent and does not sell. . . . Willard's book contains both inventive nonsense and lyrical poetry, light humor and profound points. . . .

The poetry itself is, in keeping with Blake's own, mystical, with that occasional piercing quality of a child's perceptions. It does not matter in the least whether children know or care who William Blake is. He could be the Man in the Moon—an apt identity in this case. Just say he's a writer who had some far-out ideas in the old days. There are levels here that children will enjoy, and levels that will elude them. There are, in fact, some intriguing parallels with Blake's own poetry, but they belong to a longer-winded study. Suffice it to say that Willard has caught her balance between the simplicity and complexity of things in a tone similar to that of Blake's cycle of poems, *Songs of Innocence and Experience*. Better than a description is a taste of the actual creation. One of the most lilting pieces is **"Blake Leads a Walk on the Milky Way."** . . .

There isn't space to examine this book page by page, detail by detail, but perhaps children will have the chance to. Certainly any librarian with the money to buy poetry and the heart to share it will try to. The conception, images, and nuances make one dust off that old worn word, *interesting,* an adjective even more to be cherished—when it is earned—than *award-winning.*

> *Betsy Hearne, in her review of "A Visit to William Blake's Inn: Poems for Innocent and Experienced Travelers," in* Booklist *(reprinted by permission of the American Library Association; copyright © 1981 by the American Library Assocation), Vol. 78, No. 1, September 1, 1981, p. 41.*

It is about time that Nancy Willard . . . composed a book of verses for children, and *A Visit to William Blake's Inn: Poems for Innocent and Experienced Travelers* . . . is all one would expect from this distinguished poet. . . . These elegant, crisp and clean rhymes describe an enchanted wayside inn where dragons bake the morning bread and a man in a marmalade hat leads the Tyger and the King of the Cats in a dance. Surely Edward Lear and Lewis Carroll could not have asked for a better place to spend a pleasant night than here.

> *Michael Patrick Hearn, "Poets, Players, Pirates and Pictures," in* Book World—The Washington Post *(©1981, The Washington Post), November 8, 1981, p. 20.**

Nancy Willard has written a magical and original collection of metrical verses. . . . The poems are rich verbally, seldom labored and happily loony at times. The spell is momentarily broken by the Father William tone of "'I'm terribly cold,' said the rabbit. / 'My paws are becoming quite blue.'" But overall, Willard's conception and execution are inspired. She is that rarest jewel among children's verse writers—a poet never cloying, never cute.

> *Peter Neumeyer, in his review of "A Visit to William Blake's Inn: Poems for Innocent and Experienced Travelers," in* School Library Journal *(reprinted from the December, 1981 issue of* School Library Journal, *published by R. R. Bowker Co./A Xerox Corporation; copyright © 1981), Vol. 28, No. 4, December, 1981, p. 69.*

In spite of the assertion in the title (and the sub-title, 'Poems for Innocent and Experienced Travellers'), Blake is at some distance from this verse picture-book. . . . If there is any giant behind the jaunty travelogue it is possibly Edward Lear ('The man in the marmalade hat arrived in the middle of March') or Carroll (the Wise Cow sleeps on a cloud 'and in the morning ate it raw on freshly buttered bread'). Because the author acknowledges a devotion to Blake starting at the age of seven, one has to bear this claim in mind and to conclude that the influence has been considerably modified by less important personal associations, for in the sparkling images and implied metaphysics of the poems there is little of Blake's plangently wise simplicity. . . . [The verses are] whimsical and occasionally facetious, crammed with enigmatic, profuse, riddlingly tangential associations.

> *Margery Fisher, in her review of "A Visit to William Blake's Inn," in her* Growing Point, *Vol. 21, No. 1, May, 1982, p. 3909.*

[*A Visit to William Blake's Inn*] will irritate those who know Blake and puzzle those who do not. One might describe the verse as by Emily Dickinson out of *Practical Cats*, with touches of Carroll and Lear, but pleasant and imaginative though it is, it is light-years away from the burning missionary zeal and mystical depth of the *Songs of Innocence and Experience* to which Nancy Willard deliberately and insistently relates her work. The brief extract from "Tyger, tyger, burning bright" in the introduction, contrasted with her travesty of that and other poems, particularly "Ah sunflower, weary of time," amply demonstrates the point. It would be a pity if, at an impressionable age such as that at which Mrs. Willard herself first met Blake, young readers should be left with such an off-beat image of him.

> *A review of "A Visit to William Blake's Inn," in* The Junior Bookshelf, *Vol. 46, No. 3, June, 1982, p. 95.*

[*A Visit to William Blake's Inn*], even if it is the most eccentric of children's books, is a sincere and wholehearted tribute to a uniquely great man. . . . (pp. 138, 141)

Altogether a book as odd as it is delightful. [Willard's] wise in not attempting to match [her style] with Blake's own. . . . I don't know what young readers will make of it. Introduced on the side lines during an introduction to Blake, or to the history of the Regency, it might have a stimulating effect. Those, young or old, who savour the way-out may well take warmly to its gentle charms. (p. 141)

> *Marcus Crouch, in his review of "A Visit to William Blake's Inn," in* The School Librarian, *Vol. 30, No. 2, June, 1982, pp. 138, 141.*

APPENDIX

THE EXCERPTS IN CLR, VOLUME 5, WERE REPRINTED FROM THE FOLLOWING PERIODICALS:

The Academy
American Artist
Appraisal: Science Books for Young People
The Athenaeum
The Atlantic Monthly
Best Sellers
Book Week—New York Herald Tribune
Book Week—The Sunday Herald Tribune
Book Week—The Washington Post
Book Window
Book World—Chicago Tribune
Book World—Washington Post
Book World—The Washington Post
Bookbird
Booklist
The Booklist
The Booklist and Subscription Books
   Bulletin
The Bookman, London
The Bookman, New York
Books
Books for Your Children
Books in Canada
Bulletin of the Center for Children's Books
Canadian Children's Literature: A Journal of
   Criticism and Review
Catholic Library World
Childhood Education
Children's Book News
Children's Book Review
Children's Book Review Service
Children's Literature: Annual of The
   Modern Language Association Seminar
   on Children's Literature and The
   Children's Literature Association

Children's Literature Association Quarterly
Children's literature in education
The Christian Science Monitor
Commonweal
Dance Magazine
Early Years
The Economist
Elementary English
The Fortnightly Review
Forum
Growing Point
The Horn Book Magazine
In Review
Interracial Books for Children Bulletin
The Journal of Negro Education
Journal of Reading
The Junior Bookshelf
Junior Libraries
Kirkus Reviews
Kirkus Service
Language Arts
Library Journal
The Lion and the Unicorn
The Listener
The London Mercury
Maclean's Magazine
The National Observer
New Catholic World
New Statesman
New York Herald Tribune
New York Herald Tribune Book Review
New York Herald Tribune Books
New York Herald Tribune Weekly Book
   Review
The New York Times

The New York Times Book Review
The New York Times Saturday Review
The New York Times Saturday Review of
   Books
The New Yorker
Newsweek
Publishers Weekly
Punch
Quill and Quire
The Reading Teacher
Saturday Review
The Saturday Review
The School Librarian
The School Librarian and School Library
   Review
School Library Journal
School Media Quarterly
Science and Children
Science Books
Science Books & Films
Scientific American
Signal
The Spectator
Time
The Times Educational Supplement
The Times Literary Supplement
Top of the News
Vanity Fair
The Village Voice
Virginia Kirkus' Bookshop Service
Virginia Kirkus' Service
Voice of Youth Advocates
Wilson Library Bulletin
The World of Children's Books
Young Readers Review

THE EXCERPTS IN CLR, VOLUME 5, WERE REPRINTED FROM THE FOLLOWING BOOKS:

Attebery, Brian. The Fantasy Tradition in American Literature: From Irving to Le Guin. *Indiana University Press, 1980.*

Avery, Gillian. Childhood's Pattern: A Study of the Heroes and Heroines of Childhood's Fiction, 1770-1950. *Hodder and Stoughton, 1975.*

Bader, Barbara. American Picturebooks from Noah's Ark to the Beast Within. *Macmillan, 1976.*

Bader, Barbara; Binns, Betty; and Eisenman, Alvin, eds. Children's Book Showcase 1977. *Children's Book Council, 1977.*

Baskin, Barbara H., and Harris, Karen H. Notes from a Different Drummer: A Guide to Juvenile Fiction Portraying the Handicapped. *Bowker, 1977.*

Baskin, Barbara H., and Harris, Karen H. Books for the Gifted Child. *Bowker, 1980.*

Bennett, Arnold. Books and Persons: Being Comments on a Past Epoch, 1908-1911. *Doran, 1917.*

Blount, Margaret. Animal Land: The Creatures of Children's Fiction. *Morrow, 1975.*

Books for Children: 1960-65. *American Library Association, 1966.*

Cameron, Eleanor. The Green and Burning Tree: On the Writing and Enjoyment of Children's Books. *Atlantic-Little, Brown, 1969.*

Chalmers, Patrick R. Kenneth Grahame: Life, Letters and Unpublished Work. *Methuen Co. Ltd., 1933.*

Cullinan, Bernice E.; Karrer, Mary K.; and Pillar, Arlene M. Literature and the Child. *Harcourt Brace Jovanovich, 1981.*

Dreyer, Sharon Spredemann. The Bookfinder: A Guide to Children's Literature about the Needs and Problems of Youth Aged 2-15. *American Guidance Service, Inc., 1977.*

Egoff, Sheila. Thursday's Child: Trends and Patterns in Contemporary Children's Literature. *American Library Association, 1981.*

Egoff, Sheila; Stubbs, G. T.; and Ashley, L. F., eds. Only Connect: Readings on Children's Literature. *Oxford University Press, 1969.*

Essays Presented to Charles Williams. *Oxford University Press, 1947.*

Fisher, Margery. Intent Upon Reading: A Critical Appraisal of Modern Fiction for Children. *Hodder & Stoughton Children's Books, 1961.*

Fisher, Margery. Matters of Fact: Aspects of Non-Fiction for Children. *Thomas Y. Crowell Co., Inc., 1972.*

Fisher, Margery. Who's Who in Children's Books: A Treasury of the Familiar Characters of Childhood. *Holt, Rinehart and Winston, Weidenfeld & Nicolson, 1975.*

Graham, Eleanor. Kenneth Grahame. *Henry Z. Walck, Incorporated, 1963.*

Green, Peter. Kenneth Grahame 1859-1932: A Study of His Life, Work and Times. *John Murray, 1959.*

Hazard, Paul. Books, Children and Men. *4th ed. Translated by Marguerite Mitchell. Horn Book, 1960.*

Hoffman, Miriam, and Samuels, Eva, eds. Authors and Illustrators of Children's Books: Writings on Their Lives and Works. *R. R. Bowker Company, 1972.*

Hürlimann, Bettina. Three Centuries of Children's Books in Europe. *Edited and translated by Brian W. Alderson. Oxford University Press, 1967.*

Issues in Children's Book Selection: A School Library Journal/Library Journal Anthology. *Bowker, 1973.*

Kingman, Lee, ed. Newbery and Caldecott Medal Books 1966-1975. *Horn Book, 1975.*

Kingman, Lee; Hogarth, Grace Allen; and Quimby, Harriet, eds. Illustrators of Children's Books 1967-1976. *Horn Book, 1978.*

Lanes, Selma G. Down the Rabbit Hole: Adventures and Misadventures in the Realm of Children's Literature. *Atheneum, 1972.*

Lonsdale, Bernard J., and Mackintosh, Helen K. Children Experience Literature. *Random House, 1973.*

Lukens, Rebecca J. A Critical Handbook of Children's Literature. *Scott, Foresman, 1976.*

MacCann, Donnarae, and Richard, Olga. The Child's First Books: A Critical Study of Pictures and Texts. *Wilson, 1973.*

Mead, Margaret. Foreword to Sweet Pea: A Black Girl Growing Up in the Rural South, *by Jill Krementz. Harcourt Brace Jovanovich, 1969.*

Meek, Margaret; Warlow, Aidan; and Barton, Griselda. The Cool Web: The Pattern of Children's Reading. *The Bodley Head, 1977.*

Meigs, Cornelia; Eaton, Anne Thaxter; Nesbitt, Elizabeth; and Viguers, Ruth Hill. A Critical History of Children's Literature. *Rev. ed. Edited by Cornelia Meigs. Macmillan, 1969.*

Milne, A. A. Not That It Matters. *8th ed. Methuen & Co. Ltd., 1927.*

Parker, W. M. Modern Scottish Writers. *W. Hodge & Co., 1917, Books for Libraries Press, 1968.*

Rudman, Masha Kabakow. Children's Literature: An Issues Approach. *D.C. Heath and Company, 1976.*

Sadker, Myra Pollack, and Sadker, David Miller. Now Upon a Time: A Contemporary View of Children's Literature. *Harper & Row, 1977.*

Sale, Roger. Fairy Tales and After: From Snow White to E. B. White. *Harvard University Press, 1978.*

Sebesta, Sam Leaton, and Iverson, William J. Literature for Thursday's Child. *Science Research Associates, 1975.*

Smith, Lillian H. The Unreluctant Years: A Critical Approach to Children's Literature. *American Library Association, 1953.*

Spirt, Diana L. Introducing More Books: A Guide for the Middle Grades. *R. R. Bowker Company, 1978.*

Sutherland, Zena; Monson, Dianne L.; and Arbuthnot, May Hill. Children and Books. *6th ed. Scott, Foresman, 1981.*

Sutherland, Zena, ed. The Best in Children's Books: The University of Chicago Guide to Children's Literature, 1966-1972. *University of Chicago Press, 1973.*

Swinnerton, Frank. Tokefield Papers: Old and New. *Rev. ed. Hamish Hamilton, 1949.*

Thwaite, Mary F. From Primer to Pleasure in Reading: An Introduction to the History of Children's Books in England from the Invention of Printing to 1914 with an Outline of Some Developments in Other Countries. *2nd ed. The Horn Book, Inc., 1972.*

Tymn, Marshall B.; Zahorski, Kenneth J.; and Boyer, Robert H. Fantasy Literature: A Core Collection and Reference Guide. *Bowker, 1979.*

CUMULATIVE INDEX TO AUTHORS

Aiken, Joan 1
Alcott, Louisa May 1
Alexander, Lloyd 1, 5
Anglund, Joan Walsh 1
Anno, Mitsumasa 2
Ardizzone, Edward 3
Armstrong, William H. 1
Aruego, Ariane and Jose
    Aruego 5
Aruego, Jose 5
Ashley, Bernard 4
Babbitt, Natalie 2
Bacon, Martha 3
Bawden, Nina 2
Baylor, Byrd 3
Bendick, Candy, Robert Bendick,
    Jr., and Jeanne Bendick 5
Bendick, Jeanne 5
Bendick, Robert and Jeanne
    Bendick 5
Bendick, Robert, Jr., Candy
    Bendick, and Jeanne
    Bendick 5
Berk, Barbara and Jeanne
    Bendick 5
Bethancourt, T(homas)
    Ernesto 3
Bland, Edith
    See Nesbit, E. 3
Bleeker, Sonia and Herbert
    S(pencer) Zim 2
Blume, Judy 2
Bond, (Thomas) Michael 1
Boston, L(ucy) M(aria) 3
Bova, Ben(jamin) 3
Brunhoff, Jean de 4
Brunhoff, Jean de and Laurent de
    Brunhoff 4
Brunhoff, Laurent de 4

Brunhoff, Laurent de and Jean de
    Brunhoff 4
Burnford, Sheila 2
Burton, Hester 1
Byars, Betsy 1
Cameron, Eleanor 1
Carroll, Lewis 2
Charles, Nicholas J.
    See Kuskin, Karla 4
Christopher, John 2
Cleary, Beverly 2
Clifton, Lucille 5
Coatsworth, Elizabeth 2
Cobb, Vicki 2
Cole, Joanna 5
Collier, Christopher and James
    Lincoln Collier 3
Collier, James Lincoln 3
Collier, James Lincoln and
    Christopher Collier 3
Collodi, Carlo 5
Conley, Robert L.
    See O'Brien, Robert C. 2
Cooper, Susan 4
Corbett, Scott 1
Crossley-Holland, Kevin and Jill
    Paton Walsh 2
Dahl, Roald 1
de Angeli, Marguerite 1
DeJong, Meindert 1
de Paola, Tomie 4
de Paola, Thomas Anthony
    See de Paola, Tomie 4
Dewey, Ariane and Jose
    Aruego 5
Dodgson, Charles Lutwidge
    See Carroll, Lewis 2
Donovan, John 3

du Bois, William (Sherman)
    Pène 1
du Bois, William (Sherman) Pène
    and Lee Po 1
Edmondson, Madeleine and
    Joanna Cole 5
Edmund, Sean
    See Pringle, Laurence 4
Emberley, Barbara 5
Emberley, Barbara and Ed
    Emberley 5
Emberley, Ed 5
Emberley, Ed and Barbara
    Emberley 5
Engdahl, Sylvia Louise 2
Enright, Elizabeth 4
Estes, Eleanor 2
Feelings, Muriel L. 5
Feelings, Muriel L. and Tom
    Feelings 5
Feelings, Tom 5
Feelings, Tom and Muriel L.
    Feelings 5
Fitzgerald, John D. 1
Fitzhardinge, Joan Margaret
    See Joan Phipson 5
Fitzhugh, Louise 1
Fitzhugh, Louise and Sandra
    Scoppettone 1
Fleischman, (Albert) Sid(ney) 1
Fox, Paula 1
Fritz, Jean 2
Gág, Wanda 4
Gahr, David and Julius Lester 2
Geisel, Theodor Seuss 1
George, Jean Craighead 1
Glubok, Shirley 1
Goffstein, M(arilyn) B(rooke) 3
Grahame, Kenneth 5

Greene, Bette 2
Greenfield, Eloise 4
Greenfield, Eloise and Lessie
    Jones Little 4
Gripe, Maria 5
Hamilton, Virginia 1
Haskins, James 3
Henry, Marguerite 4
Hentoff, Nat 1
Hinton, S(usan) E(loise) 3
Hoban, Russell 3
Hogrogian, Nonny 2
Houston, James 3
Hughes, Ted 3
Hunt, Irene 1
Hunt, Joyce and Millicent E(llis)
    Selsam 1
Hunter, Kristin 3
Huston, Anne and Jane Yolen 4
Iwamatsu, Jun Atsushi
    See Yashima, Taro 4
Jansson, Tove 2
Kark, Nina Mary Mabey
    See Bawden, Nina 2
Kästner, Erich 4
Keats, Ezra Jack 1
Klein, Norma 2
Konigsburg, E(laine) L(obl) 1
Korinetz, Yuri 2
Krahn, Fernando 3
Krahn, Fernando and Maria de la
    Luz Krahn 3
Krahn, Maria de la Luz and
    Fernando Krahn 3
Krantz, Lucretia and Herbert
    S(pencer) Zim 2
Krementz, Jill 5
Kurelek, William 2
Kuskin, Karla 4

Langstaff, Carol and John
   Langstaff 3
Langstaff, John 3
Langstaff, John and Carol
   Langstaff 3
Langstaff, John and Nancy
   Langstaff 3
Langstaff, Nancy and John
   Langstaff 3
Lawson, Robert 2
Lear, Edward 1
Lee, Dennis 3
Lee Po and William (Sherman)
   Pène du Bois 1
Le Guin, Ursula K(roeber) 3
L'Engle, Madeleine 1
Lester, Julius 2
Lester, Julius and David Gahr 2
Levin, Marcia and Jeanne
   Bendick 5
Lewis, C(live) S(taples) 3
Lewis, Gogo and Seon
   Manley 3
Lindgren, Astrid 1
Little, Jean 4
Little, Lessie Jones and Eloise
   Greenfield 4
Lobel, Arnold 5
Lorenzini, Carlo
   See Collodi, Carlo 5
Macaulay, David 3
Manley, Seon 3
Manley, Seon and Gogo
   Lewis 3
Mathis, Sharon Bell 3
McHargue, Georgess 2
Milne, A(lan) A(lexander) 1
Mitsumasa Anno
   See Anno, Mitsumasa 2
Monjo, F(erdinand) N. 2

Morrow, Betty and Millicent
   E(llis) Selsam 1
Myers, Walter Dean 4
Nesbit, E(dith) 3
Oakeshott, Ewart and Henry
   Treece 2
O'Brien, Robert C. 2
O'Connor, Patrick
   See Wibberley, Leonard 3
O'Dell, Scott 1
Paisley, Tom
   See Bethancourt, T. Ernesto 3
Peyton, K. M. 3
Phipson, Joan 5
Pinkwater, D(aniel) Manus 4
Pinkwater, D(aniel) Manus and
   Jill Pinkwater 4
Pinkwater, Jill and D(aniel)
   Manus Pinkwater 4
Po Lee
   See Lee Po 1
Potter, Beatrix 1
Pringle, Laurence 4
Quarles, Benjamin and Dorothy
   Sterling 1
Raskin, Ellen 1
Rey, H(ans) A(ugusto) 5
Rey, H(ans) A(ugusto) and
   Margret Rey 5
Rey, Margret 5
Rey, Margret and H(ans)
   A(ugusto) 5
Sachs, Marilyn 2
Sasek, Miroslav 4
Scarry, Richard 3
Schwartz, Alvin 3
Schweitzer, Byrd Baylor
   See Baylor, Byrd 3
Scoppettone, Sandra and Louise
   Fitzhugh 1

Selsam, Millicent E(llis) 1
Selsam, Millicent E(llis) and
   Joyce Hunt 1
Selsam, Millicent E(llis) and
   Betty Morrow 1
Sendak, Maurice 1
Serraillier, Ian 2
Seuss, Dr.
   See Geisel, Theodor Seuss 1
Shulevitz, Uri 5
Silverstein, Shel 5
Simon, Leonard and Jeanne
   Bendick 5
Singer, Isaac Bashevis 1
Skelly, James R. and Herbert
   S(pencer) Zim 2
Slote, Alfred 4
Sneve, Virginia Driving Hawk 2
Southall, Ivan 2
Spier, Peter 5
Steig, William 2
Steptoe, John 2
Sterling, Dorothy 1
Sterling, Dorothy and Benjamin
   Quarles 1
Stren, Patti 5
Suhl, Yuri 2
Sutcliff, Rosemary 1
Tobias, Tobi 4
Townsend, John Rowe 2
Travers, P(amela) L(yndon) 2
Treece, Henry 2
Treece, Henry and Ewart
   Oakeshott 2
Tunis, Edwin 2
Uncle Gus
   See Rey, H(ans) A(ugusto) 5
Uncle Shelby
   See Silverstein, Shel 5
Ungerer, Tomi 3

Van Allsburg, Chris 5
Viorst, Judith 3
Walsh, Jill Paton 3
Walsh, Jill Paton and Kevin
   Crossley-Holland 3
Warren, Marian and Jeanne
   Bendick 5
Watson, Clyde 3
Weiss, Harvey 4
Wersba, Barbara 3
White, E(lwyn) B(rooks) 1
White, Robb 3
Wibberley, Leonard 3
Wilder, Laura Ingalls 2
Wildsmith, Brian 2
Willard, Barbara 2
Willard, Nancy 5
Williams, Kit 4
Wojciechowska, Maia 1
Wrightson, Patricia 4
Yashima, Mitsu and Taro
   Yashima 4
Yashima, Taro 4
Yashima, Taro and Mitsu
   Yashima 4
Yep, Laurence 3
Yolen, Jane 4
Yolen, Jane and Anne Huston 4
Zim, Herbert S(pencer) 2
Zim, Herbert S(pencer) and Sonia
   Bleeker 2
Zim, Herbert S(pencer) and
   Lucretia Krantz 2
Zim, Herbert S(pencer) and
   James R. Skelly 2
Zimnik, Reiner 3
Zindel, Paul 3
Zolotow, Charlotte (Shapiro) 2

CUMULATIVE INDEX TO TITLES

A & THE; or, William T. C.
Baumgarten Comes to Town
(Raskin) **1**:155
A Is for Always (Anglund) **1**:19
ABC (Lear) **1**:126
The ABC Bunny (Gág) **4**:90
ABCDEFGHIJKLMNOP-
QRSTUVWXYZ
(Kuskin) **4**:138
About the B'nai Bagels
(Konigsburg) **1**:119
About the Sleeping Beauty
(Travers) **2**:176
The Acorn Quest (Yolen) **4**:268
Across Five Aprils (Hunt) **1**:109
Across the Sea (Goffstein) **3**:57
Adam Clayton Powell: Portrait of
a Marching Black
(Haskins) **3**:63
Adventures in Making: The
Romance of Crafts Around the
World (Manley) **3**:145
The Adventures of Pinocchio
(Collodi) **5**:69
Africa Dream (Greenfield) **4**:100
The Age of Giant Mammals
(Cohen) **3**:37
Air in Fact and Fancy
(Slote) **4**:199
Akavak: An Eskimo Journey
(Houston) **3**:84
Alan Mendelsohn, the Boy from
Mars (Pinkwater) **4**:169
Album of Dogs (Henry) **4**:112
Album of Horses (Henry) **4**:112
Alexander and the Terrible,
Horrible, No Good, Very Bad
Day (Viorst) **3**:207

Alexander Soames: His Poems
(Kuskin) **4**:137
Alice's Adventures in Wonderland
(Carroll) **2**:31
All about Horses (Henry) **4**:114
All Around You (Bendick) **5**:36
All in the Woodland Early
(Yolen) **4**:265
All My Men (Ashley) **4**:15
All Sizes of Noises
(Kuskin) **4**:137
All Upon a Stone (George) **1**:89
All Us Come Cross the Water
(Clifton) **5**:54
The Alley (Estes) **2**:73
The Alligator Case (du
Bois) **1**:62
Alligator Pie (Lee) **3**:115
Alligators All Around
(Sendak) **1**:167
Alligators and Crocodiles
(Zim) **2**:225
All-of-a-Sudden Susan
(Coatsworth) **2**:53
Allumette: A Fable, with Due
Respect to Hans Christian
Andersen, the Grimm Brothers,
and the Honorable Ambrose
Bierce (Ungerer) **3**:199
The Almost All-White Rabbity Cat
(DeJong) **1**:55
Alone in the Wild Forest
(Singer) **1**:173
Along Came a Dog
(DeJong) **1**:56
Altogether, One at a Time
(Konigsburg) **1**:119
Always Reddy (Henry) **4**:110

Amanda, Dreaming
(Wersba) **3**:215
The Amazing Laser (Bova) **3**:31
Amifika (Clifton) **5**:58
Amos and Boris (Steig) **2**:158
Amy and Laura (Sachs) **2**:131
Amy Moves In (Sachs) **2**:131
Ancient Monuments and How
They Were Built (Cohen) **3**:37
The Ancient Visitors
(Cohen) **3**:38
And It Rained (Raskin) **1**:155
And So My Garden Grows
(Spier) **5**:219
And Then What Happened, Paul
Revere? (Fritz) **2**:79
And to Think That I Saw It on
Mulberry Street (Geisel) **1**:84
Andy (That's My Name) (de
Paola) **4**:55
Angie's First Case
(Sobol) **4**:212
Animal Territories (Cohen) **3**:38
The Animals and the Ark
(Kuskin) **4**:135
Animals and Their Niches: How
Species Share Resources
(Pringle) **4**:183
Animals as Parents
(Selsam) **1**:159
The Animals' Conference
(Kästner) **4**:125
Annaluise and Anton
(Kästner) **4**:123
Anno's Alphabet: An Adventure in
Imagination (Anno) **2**:1
Any Me I Want to Be: Poems
(Kuskin) **4**:140

The Apple and Other Fruits
(Selsam) **1**:160
Apples (Hogrogian) **2**:87
April Fools (Krahn) **3**:103
Apt. 3 (Keats) **1**:113
Arabel's Raven (Aiken) **1**:2
Archimedes and the Door of
Science (Bendick) **5**:40
Are You There God? It's Me,
Margaret. (Blume) **2**:15
The Arm of the Starfish
(L'Engle) **1**:129
Armitage, Armitage, Fly Away
Home (Aiken) **1**:2
Armored Animals (Zim) **2**:225
The Armourer's House
(Sutcliff) **1**:183
Around Fred's Bed
(Pinkwater) **4**:165
Art and Archaeology
(Glubok) **1**:95
The Art of America from Jackson
to Lincoln (Glubok) **1**:95
The Art of America in the Gilded
Age (Glubok) **1**:95
The Art of Ancient Mexico
(Glubok) **1**:96
The Art of Ancient Peru
(Glubok) **1**:96
The Art of China (Glubok) **1**:97
The Art of India (Glubok) **1**:97
The Art of Japan (Glubok) **1**:97
The Art of Lands in the Bible
(Glubok) **1**:98
The Art of the Etruscans
(Glubok) **1**:98
The Art of the New American
Nation (Glubok) **1**:99

The Art of the North American Indian (Glubok) 1:99
The Art of the Northwest Coast Indians (Glubok) 1:99
The Art of the Spanish in the United States and Puerto Rico (Glubok) 1:100
Arthur Mitchell (Tobias) 4:215
Arts and Crafts You Can Eat (Cobb) 2:64
Ash Road (Southall) 2:147
At the Beach (Tobias) 4:217
Attar of the Ice Valley (Wibberley) 3:224
Auno and Tauno: A Story of Finland (Henry) 4:109
Babar and Father Christmas (Brunhoff) 4:32
Babar and His Children (Brunhoff) 4:32
Babar and the Old Lady (Brunhoff) 4:37
Babar and the Professor (Brunhoff) 4:34
Babar and the Wully-Wully (Brunhoff) 4:39
Babar at Home (Brunhoff) 4:32
Babar at the Seashore (Brunhoff) 4:38
Babar at the Seaside (Brunhoff) 4:38
Babar Comes to America (Brunhoff) 4:36
Babar Goes on a Picnic (Brunhoff) 4:38
Babar Goes Skiing (Brunhoff) 4:38
Babar in the Snow (Brunhoff) 4:38
Babar Loses His Crown (Brunhoff) 4:37
Babar the Gardener (Brunhoff) 4:38
Babar the King (Brunhoff) 4:31
Babar Visits Another Planet (Brunhoff) 4:38
Babar's Birthday Surprise (Brunhoff) 4:38
Babar's Castle (Brunhoff) 4:35
Babar's Childhood (Brunhoff) 4:37
Babar's Coronation (Brunhoff) 4:37
Babar's Cousin: That Rascal Arthur (Brunhoff) 4:33
Babar's Day Out (Brunhoff) 4:38
Babar's Fair (Brunhoff) 4:34
Babar's French Lessons (Brunhoff) 4:35
Babar's Mystery (Brunhoff) 4:39
Babar's Picnic (Brunhoff) 4:34
Babar's Trunk (Brunhoff) 4:38
Babar's Visit to Bird Island (Brunhoff) 4:34
A Baby Sister for Frances (Hoban) 3:75
The Bad Island (Steig) 2:158
The Bad Speller (Steig) 2:159
The Baker and the Basilisk (McHargue) 2:117

The Ballad of St. Simeon (Serraillier) 2:135
The Ballad of the Pilgrim Cat (Wibberley) 3:224
Bang Bang You're Dead (Fitzhugh and Scoppettone) 1:71
Barefoot in the Grass (Armstrong) 1:22
A Bargain for Frances (Hoban) 3:75
The Baseball Trick (Corbett) 1:42
Bass and Billy Martin (Phipson) 5:182
The Bastable Children (Nesbit) 3:161
Battleground: The United States Army in World War II (Collier) 3:44
The Bear and the People (Zimnik) 3:242
A Bear Called Paddington (Bond) 1:27
Bear Circus (du Bois) 1:62
The Bear Who Saw the Spring (Kuskin) 4:136
The Bear's House (Sachs) 2:131
The Bears of the Air (Lobel) 5:164
Bear's Picture (Pinkwater) 4:162
The Beast of Monsieur Racine (Ungerer) 3:200
The Beast with the Magical Horn (Cameron) 1:39
The Beasts of Never (McHargue) 2:117
Bedtime for Frances (Hoban) 3:75
The Beethoven Medal (Peyton) 3:171
Beezus and Ramona (Cleary) 2:45
Before You Came This Way (Baylor) 3:13
Benjamin West and His Cat Grimalkin (Henry) 4:110
Ben's Dream (Van Allsburg) 5:240
Benson Boy (Southall) 2:148
Beowulf (Sutcliff) 1:183
Beowulf the Warrior (Serraillier) 2:135
Bertie's Escapade (Grahame) 5:135
Bess and the Sphinx (Coatsworth) 2:53
Best Word Book Ever (Scarry) 3:182
Betrayed (Sneve) 2:143
Beyond the Burning Lands (Christopher) 2:37
Beyond the Tomorrow Mountains (Engdahl) 2:69
Beyond the Weir Bridge (Burton) 1:30
Big Anthony and the Magic Ring (de Paola) 4:62
The Big Cleanup (Weiss) 4:224
The Big Joke Game (Corbett) 1:43

The Big Orange Splot (Pinkwater) 4:166
Bill and Pete (de Paola) 4:61
Bill Bergson and the White Rose Rescue (Lindgren) 1:135
Bill Bergson Lives Dangerously (Lindgren) 1:135
Bill Bergson, Master Detective (Lindgren) 1:135
Bill's Garage (Spier) 5:228
Bill's Service Station (Spier) 5:228
Billy Goat and His Well-Fed Friends (Hogrogian) 2:87
Billy's Balloon Ride (Zimnik) 3:242
Billy's Picture (Rey) 5:196
Binary Numbers (Watson) 3:211
The Bird Smugglers (Phipson) 5:184
Birds at Home (Henry) 4:109
Birkin (Phipson) 5:180
Birth of a Forest (Selsam) 1:160
Birth of an Island (Selsam) 1:160
Birthday (Steptoe) 2:162
A Birthday Wish (Emberley) 5:100
The Bishop and the Devil (Serraillier) 2:136
The Black BC's (Clifton) 5:53
The Black Cauldron (Alexander) 1:11; 5:18
The Black Death, 1347-1351 (Cohen) 3:39
Black Folktales (Lester) 2:112
Black Gold (Henry) 4:113
Black Hearts in Battersea (Aiken) 1:2
The Black Pearl (O'Dell) 1:145
Black Pilgrimage (Feelings) 5:106
The Blonk from Beneath the Sea (Bendick) 5:38
Blood (Zim) 2:225
The Bloody Country (Collier and Collier) 3:44
Blowfish Live in the Sea (Fox) 1:76
Blubber (Blume) 2:16
Blue Moose (Pinkwater) 4:163
The Blue Thing (Pinkwater) 4:166
Blue Trees, Red Sky (Klein) 2:97
Bo the Constrictor That Couldn't (Stren) 5:231
The Body Snatchers (Cohen) 3:39
Bones (Zim) 2:226
Bonhomme and the Huge Beast (Brunhoff) 4:39
The Book of Dragons (Nesbit) 3:162
The Book of Nursery and Mother Goose Rhymes (de Angeli) 1:52
The Book of Three (Alexander) 1:12; 5:18
Border Hawk: August Bondi (Alexander) 5:17
Bored—Nothing to Do! (Spier) 5:226

Born to Trot (Henry) 4:111
Boss Cat (Hunter) 3:97
The Boundary Riders (Phipson) 5:178
A Boy Had a Mother Who Bought Him a Hat (Kuskin) 4:141
The Boy Who Didn't Believe in Spring (Clifton) 5:54
The Boy Who Spoke Chimp (Yolen) 4:268
Brady (Fritz) 2:79
Brainstorm (Myers) 4:157
Brave Buffalo Fighter (Waditaka Tatanka Kisisohitika) (Fitzgerald) 1:69
The Brave Cowboy (Anglund) 1:19
Bread and Honey (Southall) 2:149
Bread and Jam for Frances (Hoban) 3:76
Break in the Sun (Ashley) 4:17
Brian Wildsmith's ABC (Wildsmith) 2:208
Brian Wildsmith's Birds (Wildsmith) 2:208
Brian Wildsmith's Circus (Wildsmith) 2:209
Brian Wildsmith's Fishes (Wildsmith) 2:210
Brian Wildsmith's Mother Goose: A Collection of Nursery Rhymes (Wildsmith) 2:210
Brian Wildsmith's 1, 2, 3's (Wildsmith) 2:211
Brian Wildsmith's Puzzles (Wildsmith) 2:211
Brian Wildsmith's The Twelve Days of Christmas (Wildsmith) 2:212
Brian Wildsmith's Wild Animals (Wildsmith) 2:212
Brighty of the Grand Canyon (Henry) 4:112
Brother Dusty-Feet (Sutcliff) 1:184
Brothers of the Wind (Yolen) 4:268
Bubbles (Greenfield) 4:96
The Bug That Laid the Golden Eggs (Selsam) 1:160
Bulbs, Corms, and Such (Selsam) 1:161
The Burning of Njal (Treece) 2:182
Busiest People Ever (Scarry) 3:183
By the Great Horn Spoon! (Fleischman) 1:73
By the Shores of Silver Lake (Wilder) 2:205
A Calf Is Born (Cole) 5:64
Call Me Bandicoot (du Bois) 1:63
Camilla (L'Engle) 1:129
Candy (White) 3:220
The Capricorn Bracelet (Sutcliff) 1:184
Captain Kidd's Cat (Lawson) 2:109
Captain of the Planter: The Story of Robert Smalls (Sterling) 1:177

Cargo Ships (Zim and
  Skelly) **2**:226
Carrie's War (Bawden) **2**:10
The Case of the Gone Goose
  (Corbett) **1**:43
The Case of the Silver Skull
  (Corbett) **1**:43
The Castle of Llyr
  (Alexander) **1**:12; **5**:19
The Castle of Yew (Boston) **3**:26
Castors Away (Burton) **1**:30
The Cat and the Captain
  (Coatsworth) **2**:54
The Cat in the Hat (Geisel) **1**:84
The Cat Who Went to Heaven
  (Coatsworth) **2**:54
*The Cat Who Wished to Be a
  Man* (Alexander) **1**:12; **5**:22
Caterpillars (Sterling) **1**:178
*Cathedral: The Story of Its
  Construction*
  (Macaulay) **3**:140
The Cats (Phipson) **5**:184
A Cat's Body (Cole) **5**:68
The Cave above Delphi
  (Corbett) **1**:43
CDB! (Steig) **2**:159
Cecily G. and the Nine Monkeys
  (Rey) **5**:192
Cells: The Basic Structure of Life
  (Cobb) **2**:64
*Central City/Spread City: The
  Metropolitan Regions Where
  More and More of Us Spend
  Our Lives* (Schwartz) **3**:188
The Centurion (Treece) **2**:183
Ceramics: From Clay to Kiln
  (Weiss) **4**:223
*Chains, Webs, and Pyramids:
  The Flow of Energy in Nature*
  (Pringle) **4**:179
*The Challenge of the Green
  Knight* (Serraillier) **2**:136
Chancy and the Grand Rascal
  (Fleischman) **1**:73
The Changing Earth
  (Viorst) **3**:207
Charity at Home
  (Willard) **2**:216
*Charlie and the Chocolate
  Factory* (Dahl) **1**:49
*Charlie and the Great Glass
  Elevator* (Dahl) **1**:50
"Charlie Needs a Cloak" (de
  Paola) **4**:55
Charlotte's Web (White) **1**:193
Chasing the Goblins Away
  (Tobias) **4**:216
Chaucer and His World
  (Serraillier) **2**:137
The Chichi Hoohoo Bogeyman
  (Sneve) **3**:144
A Chick Hatches (Cole) **5**:64
Chicken Soup with Rice
  (Sendak) **1**:167
Child of the Owl (Yep) **3**:235
The Children Come Running
  (Coatsworth) **2**:54
The Children of Green Knowe
  (Boston) **3**:26
The Children of Noisy Village
  (Lindgren) **1**:135

*Childtimes: A Three-Generation
  Memoir* (Greenfield and
  Little) **4**:101
Chinaman's Reef Is Ours
  (Southall) **2**:149
Chipmunks on the Doorstep
  (Tunis) **2**:191
Christmas in Noisy Village
  (Lindgren) **1**:136
Christmas in the Stable
  (Lindgren) **1**:136
Christmas Is a Time of Giving
  (Anglund) **1**:19
Christmas Manger (Rey) **5**:194
The Chronicles of Narnia
  (Lewis) **3**:126
Cinnabar, the One O'Clock Fox
  (Henry) **4**:113
*City: A Story of Roman Planning
  and Construction*
  (Macaulay) **3**:142
*City and Suburb: Exploring an
  Ecosystem* (Pringle) **4**:180
City of Darkness (Bova) **3**:32
The City of Gold and Lead
  (Christopher) **2**:38
*The Clashing Rocks: The Story of
  Jason* (Serraillier) **2**:137
*Clay, Wood, and Wire: A How-
  To-Do-It Book of Sculpture*
  (Weiss) **4**:220
*The Cloud Book: Words and
  Pictures* (de Paola) **4**:57
The Clown of God: An Old Story
  (de Paola) **4**:61
The Coat-Hanger Christmas Tree
  (Estes) **2**:73
Cockroaches (Cole) **5**:61
*Cockroaches: Here, There, and
  Everywhere* (Pringle) **4**:176
*C.O.L.A.R.: A Tale of Outer
  Space* (Slote) **4**:203
A Cold Wind Blowing
  (Willard) **2**:216
Coll and His White Pig
  (Alexander) **1**:13; **5**:19
Collage and Construction
  (Weiss) **4**:225
*Colonial Craftsmen and the
  Beginnings of American
  Industry* (Tunis) **2**:192
Colonial Living (Tunis) **2**:192
Comet in Moominland
  (Jansson) **2**:93
Commercial Fishing (Zim and
  Krantz) **2**:226
The Complete Book of Dragons
  (Nesbit) **3**:162
Confessions of an Only Child
  (Klein) **2**:97
*The Controversial Coyote:
  Predation, Politics, and
  Ecology* (Pringle) **4**:182
Corals (Zim) **2**:226
The Country of the Heart
  (Wersba) **3**:215
The Court of the Stone Children
  (Cameron) **1**:39
The Courtship of Animals
  (Selsam) **1**:161
Cowboy and His Friend
  (Anglund) **1**:19

The Cowboy's Christmas
  (Anglund) **1**:20
Cowboy's Secret Life
  (Anglund) **1**:20
Coyote Cry (Baylor) **3**:14
Coyote in Manhattan
  (George) **1**:89
Crabs (Zim and Krantz) **2**:227
The Crane (Zimnik) **3**:242
Crash! Bang! Boom!
  (Spier) **5**:221
*The Creoles of Color of New
  Orleans* (Haskins) **3**:63
*A Crocodile's Tale: A Philippine
  Folk Tale* (Aruego and
  Aruego) **5**:30
The Crooked Snake
  (Wrightson) **4**:240
*Cross Your Fingers, Spit in Your
  Hat: Superstitions and Other
  Beliefs* (Schwartz) **3**:188
Crow Boy (Yashima) **4**:251
The Cruise of the Arctic Star
  (O'Dell) **1**:145
The Cuckoo Tree (Aiken) **1**:3
Curious George (Rey) **5**:193
Curious George Flies a Kite
  (Rey) **5**:198
Curious George Gets a Medal
  (Rey) **5**:198
*Curious George Goes to the
  Hospital* (Rey) **5**:199
*Curious George Learns the
  Alphabet* (Rey) **5**:199
Curious George Rides a Bike
  (Rey) **5**:196
Curious George Takes a Job
  (Rey) **5**:196
The Curse of Cain
  (Southall) **2**:150
Cutlass Island (Corbett) **1**:44
Daisy (Coatsworth) **2**:54
Daisy Summerfield's Style
  (Goffstein) **3**:58
Dance in the Desert
  (L'Engle) **1**:130
The Dancing Camel
  (Byars) **1**:35
*Danger Point: The Wreck of the
  Birkenhead* (Corbett) **1**:44
Danny Goes to the Hospital
  (Collier) **3**:44
The Dark Bright Water
  (Wrightson) **4**:246
The Dark Canoe (O'Dell) **1**:146
The Dark Is Rising
  (Cooper) **4**:44
Darlene (Greenfield) **4**:103
Dawn (Shulevitz) **5**:206
*A Dawn in the Trees: Thomas
  Jefferson, the Years 1776 to
  1789* (Wibberley) **3**:224
Dawn of Fear (Cooper) **4**:43
Dawn Wind (Sutcliff) **1**:184
*A Day of Pleasure: Stories of a
  Boy Growing Up in Warsaw*
  (Singer) **1**:173
*The Day the Numbers
  Disappeared* (Bendick and
  Simon) **5**:40
Daydreamers (Greenfield) **4**:103
Days with Frog and Toad
  (Lobel) **5**:173

Dead Man's Light
  (Corbett) **1**:44
Deadmen's Cave
  (Wibberley) **3**:225
Dear Readers and Riders
  (Henry) **4**:115
Death Is Natural (Pringle) **4**:181
Deathwatch (White) **3**:221
Deenie (Blume) **2**:16
Desert Dan (Coatsworth) **2**:55
The Desert Is Theirs
  (Baylor) **3**:14
*The Devil Rides with Me and
  Other Fantastic Stories*
  (Slote) **4**:203
The Devil's Storybook
  (Babbit) **2**:5
Dick Foote and the Shark
  (Babbitt) **2**:5
*Did I Ever Tell You How Lucky
  You Are?* (Geisel) **1**:85
Died on a Rainy Sunday
  (Aiken) **1**:3
Dinner Ladies Don't Count
  (Ashley) **4**:18
Dinosaur Story (Cole) **5**:63
Dinosaurs (Zim) **2**:227
*Dinosaurs and People: Fossils,
  Facts, and Fantasies*
  (Pringle) **4**:184
Dinosaurs and Their World
  (Pringle) **4**:174
The Disappearing Dog Trick
  (Corbett) **1**:44
Disaster (Sobol) **4**:211
*Discovering the Royal Tombs at
  Ur* (Glubok) **1**:100
Do Tigers Ever Bite Kings?
  (Wersba) **3**:216
A Dog and a Half
  (Willard) **2**:217
The Dog Days of Arthur Cane
  (Bethancourt) **3**:18
*Dogs and Dragons, Trees and
  Dreams: A Collection of Poems*
  (Kuskin) **4**:144
The Dolphin Crossing
  (Walsh) **2**:197
Dom and Va (Christopher) **2**:39
Dominic (Steig) **2**:159
*The Dong with the Luminous
  Nose* (Lear) **1**:127
*"Don't Play Dead Before You
  Have To"*
  (Wojciechowska) **1**:196
Don't You Remember?
  (Clifton) **5**:55
The Door in the Wall (de
  Angeli) **1**:53
Door to the North
  (Coatsworth) **2**:55
Dorrie's Book (Sachs) **2**:132
The Double Quest (Sobol) **4**:206
Down Half the World
  (Coatsworth) **2**:55
Down to Earth
  (Wrightson) **4**:242
*Dr. Anno's Magical Midnight
  Circus* (Anno) **2**:2
Dr. Merlin's Magic Shop
  (Corbett) **1**:45

Dr. Seuss's ABC (Geisel)   **1**:85

Dr. Seuss's Sleep Book (Geisel)   **1**:85

Dragon Night and Other Lullabies (Yolen)   **4**:266

The Dragon Takes a Wife (Myers)   **4**:156

Dragonwings (Yep)   **3**:236

Dream Days (Grahame)   **5**:128

The Dream Time (Treece)   **2**:183

The Dream Watcher (Wersba)   **3**:216

Dream Weaver (Yolen)   **4**:265

Dreams (Keats)   **1**:114

Dreams, Visions & Drugs: A Search for Other Realities (Cohen)   **3**:39

The Drinking Gourd (Monjo)   **2**:120

Drummer Hoff (Emberley)   **5**:94

Duck on a Pond (Willard)   **2**:217

The Dueling Machine (Bova)   **3**:32

Eagle Mask: A West Coast Indian Tale (Houston)   **3**:85

The Eagle of the Ninth (Sutcliff)   **1**:185

Early Thunder (Fritz)   **2**:80

The Earthsea Trilogy (Le Guin)   **3**:118

The Easter Cat (DeJong)   **1**:56

Ecology (Bendick)   **5**:48

Ecology: Science of Survival (Pringle)   **4**:175

Ed Emberley's A B C (Emberley)   **5**:100

Ed Emberley's Amazing Look Through Book (Emberley)   **5**:101

Ed Emberley's Big Green Drawing Book (Emberley)   **5**:102

Ed Emberley's Big Orange Drawing Book (Emberley)   **5**:102

Ed Emberley's Big Purple Drawing Book (Emberley)   **5**:103

Ed Emberley's Crazy Mixed-Up Face Game (Emberley)   **5**:103

Ed Emberley's Drawing Book: Make a World (Emberley)   **5**:98

Ed Emberley's Drawing Book of Animals (Emberley)   **5**:97

Ed Emberley's Drawing Book of Faces (Emberley)   **5**:99

Ed Emberley's Great Thumbprint Drawing Book (Emberley)   **5**:100

The Edge of the Cloud (Peyton)   **3**:172

Egg Thoughts, and Other Frances Songs (Hoban)   **3**:76

Egg to Chick (Selsam)   **1**:161

Eight for a Secret (Willard)   **2**:217

The Eighteenth Emergency (Byars)   **1**:35

Electronics for Boys and Girls (Bendick)   **5**:34

Elidor and the Golden Ball (McHargue)   **2**:117

Elijah the Slave (Singer)   **1**:174

Elisabeth the Cow Ghost (du Bois)   **1**:63

Elizabite: The Adventures of a Carnivorous Plant (Rey)   **5**:194

Ellen Dellen (Gripe)   **5**:148

Ellen Tebbits (Cleary)   **2**:45

Eloquent Crusader: Ernestine Rose (Suhl)   **2**:165

Elvis! Elvis! (Gripe)   **5**:148

Elvis and His Friends (Gripe)   **5**:148

Elvis and His Secret (Gripe)   **5**:148

Elvis Karlsson (Gripe)   **5**:148

The Emergency Book (Bendick)   **5**:41

Emil and Piggy Beast (Lindgren)   **1**:136

Emil and the Detectives (Kästner)   **4**:121

Emil's Pranks (Lindgren)   **1**:136

Emily's Runaway Imagination (Cleary)   **2**:45

Emmet Otter's Jug-Band Christmas (Hoban)   **3**:76

The Emperor and the Kite (Yolen)   **4**:257

The Emperor's Winding Sheet (Walsh)   **2**:197

The Enchanted: An Incredible Tale (Coatsworth)   **2**:56

The Enchanted Castle (Nesbit)   **3**:162

The Enchanted Island: Stories from Shakespeare (Serraillier)   **2**:137

Enchantress from the Stars (Engdahl)   **2**:69

Encounter Near Venus (Wibberley)   **3**:225

Encyclopedia Brown and the Case of the Dead Eagles (Sobol)   **4**:210

Encyclopedia Brown and the Case of the Midnight Visitor (Sobol)   **4**:211

Encyclopedia Brown and the Case of the Secret Pitch (Sobol)   **4**:207

Encyclopedia Brown, Boy Detective (Sobol)   **4**:207

Encyclopedia Brown Carries On (Sobol)   **4**:212

Encyclopedia Brown Finds the Clues (Sobol)   **4**:208

Encyclopedia Brown Gets His Man (Sobol)   **4**:208

Encyclopedia Brown Lends a Hand (Sobol)   **4**:210

Encyclopedia Brown Saves the Day (Sobol)   **4**:209

Encyclopedia Brown Shows the Way (Sobol)   **4**:209

Encyclopedia Brown Solves Them All (Sobol)   **4**:208

Encyclopedia Brown Takes the Case (Sobol)   **4**:209

Encyclopedia Brown's Record Book of Weird and Wonderful Facts (Sobol)   **4**:211

End of Exile (Bova)   **3**:32

An Enemy at Green Knowe (Boston)   **3**:27

Energy: Power for People (Pringle)   **4**:179

The Epics of Everest (Wibberley)   **3**:226

The Erie Canal (Spier)   **5**:220

Estuaries: Where Rivers Meet the Sea (Pringle)   **4**:178

Ever Ride a Dinosaur? (Corbett)   **1**:45

Everett Anderson's Christmas Coming (Clifton)   **5**:54

Everett Anderson's Friend (Clifton)   **5**:57

Everett Anderson's Nine Month Long (Clifton)   **5**:59

Everett Anderson's 1-2-3 (Clifton)   **5**:58

Everett Anderson's Year (Clifton)   **5**:55

Everybody Needs a Rock (Baylor)   **3**:15

Exiled from Earth (Bova)   **3**:33

The Expeditions of Willis Partridge (Weiss)   **4**:222

The Exploits of Moominpappa (Jansson)   **2**:93

Fables (Lobel)   **5**:174

Facts, Frauds, and Phantasms: A Survey of the Spiritualist Movement (McHargue)   **2**:118

A Fall from the Sky: The Story of Daedalus (Serraillier)   **2**:138

Fall Is Here! (Sterling)   **1**:178

Family (Donovan)   **3**:51

The Family Christmas Tree Book (de Paola)   **4**:65

The Family Conspiracy (Phipson)   **5**:179

The Family Tower (Willard)   **2**:217

Fantastic Mr. Fox (Dahl)   **1**:51

Far Out the Long Canal (DeJong)   **1**:57

The Far Side of Evil (Engdahl)   **2**:70

Farmer Palmer's Wagon Ride (Steig)   **2**:160

The Farthest Shore (Le Guin)   **3**:123

Fast Sam, Cool Clyde, and Stuff (Myers)   **4**:156

Fast-Slow, High-Low: A Book of Opposites (Spier)   **5**:222

Fat Elliot and the Gorilla (Pinkwater)   **4**:162

Fat Men from Space (Pinkwater)   **4**:168

Father Fox's Pennyrhymes (Watson)   **3**:211

A Father Like That (Zolotow)   **2**:233

The Fearsome Inn (Singer)   **1**:174

The Feather Star (Wrightson)   **4**:241

Fiddlestrings (de Angeli)   **1**:53

Fifteen (Cleary)   **2**:46

Fighting Men: How Men Have Fought through the Ages (Treece and Oakeshott)   **2**:184

Fighting Shirley Chisholm (Haskins)   **3**:64

Fin M'Coul: The Giant of Knockmany Hill (de Paola)   **4**:66

Find the Constellations (Rey)   **5**:196

Find the Hidden Insect (Cole)   **5**:66

Finding Out about Jobs: TV Reporting (Bendick and Bendick)   **5**:48

Finn Family Moomintroll (Jansson)   **2**:93

Finn's Folly (Southall)   **2**:150

The Fire Station (Spier)   **5**:228

The Firehouse (Spier)   **5**:228

Fireweed (Walsh)   **2**:198

The First ABC (Lear)   **1**:127

First Adventure (Coatsworth)   **2**:56

The First Book of Airplanes (Bendick)   **5**:37

The First Book of Fishes (Bendick)   **5**:41

The First Book of How to Fix It (Bendick and Berk)   **5**:39

The First Book of Medieval Man (Sobol)   **4**:206

The First Book of Ships (Bendick)   **5**:38

The First Book of Space Travel (Bendick)   **5**:37

The First Book of Supermarkets (Bendick)   **5**:37

The First Book of Time (Bendick)   **5**:40

The First Four Years (Wilder)   **2**:205

A First Look at Birds (Selsam and Hunt)   **1**:162

A First Look at Leaves (Selsam)   **1**:162

A First Look at Mammals (Selsam and Hunt)   **1**:162

The First Peko-Neko Bird (Krahn and Krahn)   **3**:103

First Pink Light (Greenfield)   **4**:99

The First Two Lives of Lukas-Kasha (Alexander)   **5**:24

Fish for Supper (Goffstein)   **3**:58

A Fish Hatches (Cole)   **5**:65

Fish Head (Fritz)   **2**:80

Five Children and It (Nesbit)   **3**:163

Flambards (Peyton)   **3**:172

Flambards in Summer (Peyton)   **3**:173

The Flambards Trilogy (Peyton)   **3**:173

Fleas (Cole)   **5**:62

Flicks (de Paola)   **4**:63

Flight of Exiles (Bova)   **3**:33

Flight to the Forest (Willard)   **2**:218

Flint's Island (Wibberley)   **3**:226

Flocks of Birds (Zolotow)   **2**:234

The Flood at Reedsmere (Burton)   **1**:31

Fly into Danger (Phipson)   **5**:184

Fly-By-Night (Peyton)   **3**:176

A Flying Saucer Full of Spaghetti (Krahn)   3:104
Follow a Fisher (Pringle)   4:178
The Food Market (Spier)   5:228
The Fools of Chelm and Their History (Singer)   1:174
Forest of the Night (Townsend)   2:169
Forever (Blume)   2:17
Forever Free: The Story of the Emancipation Proclamation (Sterling)   1:178
The Foundling and Other Tales of Prydain (Alexander)   1:13; 5:22
The Four Donkeys (Alexander)   1:14
Four Stories for Four Seasons (de Paola)   4:59
The Four-Story Mistake (Enright)   4:74
The Fox Friend (Coatsworth)   2:57
The Fox Hole (Southall)   2:151
Fox in Socks (Geisel)   1:85
The Fox Went Out on a Chilly Night: An Old Song (Spier)   5:217
Franklin Stein (Raskin)   1:155
Freedom Train: The Story of Harriet Tubman (Sterling)   1:179
A Friend Is Someone Who Likes You (Anglund)   1:20
Friend Monkey (Travers)   2:177
Friend: The Story of George Fox and the Quakers (Yolen)   4:259
Frog and Toad All Year (Lobel)   5:170
Frog and Toad Are Friends (Lobel)   5:165
Frog and Toad Together (Lobel)   5:167
Frog Went A-Courtin' (Langstaff)   3:109
The Frogmen (White)   3:221
A Frog's Body (Cole)   5:66
From Anna (Little)   4:151
From Lew Alcindor to Kareem Abdul Jabbar (Haskins)   3:64
From Pond to Prairie: The Changing World of a Pond and Its Life (Pringle)   4:176
From the Mixed-Up Files of Mrs. Basil E. Frankweiler (Konigsburg)   1:120
Frontier Living (Tunis)   2:192
Funniest Storybook Ever (Scarry)   3:183
Funny Bananas (McHargue)   2:118
The Funny Thing (Gág)   4:89
The Further Adventures of Robinson Crusoe (Treece)   2:184
The Gadget Book (Weiss)   4:226
The Gales of Spring: Thomas Jefferson, the Years 1789-1801 (Wibberley)   3:226
Games and Puzzles You Can Make Yourself (Weiss)   4:228

The Garden of Abdul Gasazi (Van Allsburg)   5:238
Gases (Cobb)   2:65
The Gats! (Goffstein)   3:59
Gaudenzia, Pride of the Palio (Henry)   4:113
The Gentle Desert: Exploring an Ecosystem (Pringle)   4:183
(George) (Konigsburg)   1:120
George and Red (Coatsworth)   2:57
George Washington's Breakfast (Fritz)   2:81
Ghost in a Four-Room Apartment (Raskin)   1:156
The Ghost in the Noonday Sun (Fleischman)   1:74
Ghost Paddle: A Northwest Coast Indian Tale (Houston)   3:85
The Giant (du Bois)   1:63
The Giant Golden Book of Cat Stories (Coatsworth)   2:57
Giant John (Lobel)   5:163
The Giants' Farm (Yolen)   4:263
The Giants Go Camping (Yolen)   4:265
The Gift of Sarah Barker (Yolen)   4:267
Ginger Pye (Estes)   2:73
A Giraffe and a Half (Silverstein)   5:209
The Girl Who Cried Flowers, and Other Tales (Yolen)   4:260
The Girl Who Loved the Wind (Yolen)   4:260
Girls Can Be Anything (Klein)   2:98
Give Dad My Best (Collier)   3:45
The Giving Tree (Silverstein)   5:209
Glasblasarns Barn (Gripe)   5:144
The Glassblower's Children (Gripe)   5:144
Glimpses of Louisa (Alcott)   1:9
Go and Hush the Baby (Byars)   1:35
Gobble, Growl, Grunt (Spier)   5:220
Goggles! (Keats)   1:114
Gold: The Fascinating Story of the Noble Metal through the Ages (Cohen)   3:40
The Golden Age (Grahame)   5:126
The Golden One (Treece)   2:185
The Golden Serpent (Myers)   4:160
Goldengrove (Walsh)   2:199
Goldie, the Dollmaker (Goffstein)   3:59
Golly Gump Swallowed a Fly (Cole)   5:68
A Gondola for Fun (Weiss)   4:220
Gone Is Gone; or, The Story of a Man Who Wanted to Do Housework (Gág)   4:90
Gone-Away Lake (Enright)   4:75
Good Ethan (Fox)   1:77
The Good Knight Ghost (Bendick)   5:38

Good Luck Duck (DeJong)   1:57
Good Luck to the Rider (Phipson)   5:177
Good News (Greenfield)   4:96
Good Night, Prof, Dear (Townsend)   2:170
Good Old James (Donovan)   3:51
Good, Says Jerome (Clifton)   5:55
Good-bye to the Jungle (Townsend)   2:171
Goodnight (Hoban)   3:77
Goody Hall (Babbitt)   2:6
The Gorgon's Head: The Story of Perseus (Serraillier)   2:138
Grand Papa and Ellen Aroon (Monjo)   2:121
Grandmother Cat and the Hermit (Coatsworth)   2:58
Grasshopper on the Road (Lobel)   5:172
The Great Blueness and Other Predicaments (Lobel)   5:165
The Great Brain (Fitzgerald)   1:69
The Great Brain at the Academy (Fitzgerald)   1:69
The Great Brain Reforms (Fitzgerald)   1:69
The Great Flood (Spier)   5:224
The Great Wheel (Lawson)   2:109
The Green Coat (Gripe)   5:148
Green Eggs and Ham (Geisel)   1:86
The Green Flash and Other Tales of Horror, Suspense, and Fantasy (Aiken)   1:4
Green Says Go (Emberley)   5:96
Greenwitch (Cooper)   4:45
Gregory Griggs and Other Nursery Rhyme People (Lobel)   5:172
Greta the Strong (Sobol)   4:209
The Grey King (Cooper)   4:47
Greyling: A Picture Story from the Islands of Shetland (Yolen)   4:257
The Groober (Byars)   1:36
The Grove of Green Holly (Willard)   5:218
Growing Pains: Diaries and Drawings for the Years 1908-1917 (Gág)   4:91
The Guardians (Christopher)   2:39
Guarneri: Story of a Genius (Wibberley)   3:227
Guests in the Promised Land (Hunter)   3:98
Gull Number 737 (George)   1:89
Hadassah: Esther the Orphan Queen (Armstrong)   1:22
The Hand of Apollo (Coatsworth)   2:58
A Handful of Thieves (Bawden)   2:11
Hang Tough, Paul Mather (Slote)   4:200
Happy Times in Noisy Village (Lindgren)   1:137

The Hard Life of the Teenager (Collier)   3:45
The Hare and the Tortoise (Wildsmith)   2:212
The Hare and the Tortoise & the Tortoise and the Hare/La Liebre y la Tortuga y la Tortuga y la Liebre (du Bois and Lee Po)   1:63
Harriet the Spy (Fitzhugh)   1:71
The Hat (Ungerer)   3:200
The Hating Book (Zolotow)   2:234
Have a Happy Measle, a Merry Mumps, and a Cheery Chickenpox (Bendick, Bendick, and Bendick)   5:38
Havelok the Dane (Serraillier)   2:139
Hawk, I'm Your Brother (Baylor)   3:15
Head in the Clouds (Southall)   2:152
Heat (Cobb)   2:65
Heat and Temperature (Bendick)   5:47
Heather, Oak, and Olive: Three Stories (Sutcliff)   1:185
Hector Protector and As I Went over the Water (Sendak)   1:167
Helga's Dowry: A Troll Love Story (de Paola)   4:59
Hell's Edge (Townsend)   2:172
Helping Horse (Phipson)   5:183
The Henchmans at Home (Burton)   1:31
Hengest's Tale (Walsh)   2:200
Henry and Ribsy (Cleary)   2:46
Henry and the Paper Route (Cleary)   2:47
Henry Huggins (Cleary)   2:47
Heracles the Strong (Serraillier)   2:139
Herbert Hated Being Small (Kuskin)   4:143
Here Comes Thursday! (Bond)   1:27
Here I Stay (Coatsworth)   2:58
Heritage of the Star (Engdahl)   2:70
Herman the Loser (Hoban)   3:77
The Hermit and Harry and Me (Hogrogian)   2:88
Heroes and History (Sutcliff)   1:186
Hetty (Willard)   2:218
"Hey, What's Wrong with This One?" (Wojciechowska)   1:196
Hi, Cat! (Keats)   1:114
Hi! Ho! The Rattlin' Bog: And Other Folk Songs for Group Singing (Langstaff)   3:109
Hickory Stick Rag (Watson)   3:212
The Hidden World: Life under a Rock (Pringle)   4:181
Hide and Seek (Coatsworth)   2:59
Higglety Pigglety Pop! or, There Must Be More to Life (Sendak)   1:168

The High Deeds of Finn MacCool (Sutcliff) **1**:186

High Elk's Treasure (Sneve) **2**:144

The High King (Alexander) **1**:14; **5**:21

The Highest Hit (Willard) **5**:248

Hildegarde and Maximilian (Krahn) **3**:104

Hills End (Southall) **2**:152

Hobo Toad and the Motorcycle Gang (Yolen) **4**:259

The Hoboken Chicken Emergency (Pinkwater) **4**:167

Hoists, Cranes, and Derricks (Zim) **2**:227

Hold Zero! (George) **1**:90

The Hollywood Kid (Wojciechowska) **1**:197

Home from Far (Little) **4**:147

The Home Run Trick (Corbett) **1**:45

Hop on Pop (Geisel) **1**:86

Horned Helmet (Treece) **2**:185

The Horse and His Boy (Lewis) **3**:134

A Horse Came Running (DeJong) **1**:57

The Horse in the Camel Suit (du Bois) **1**:64

Horse with Eight Hands (Phipson) **5**:183

A Horse's Body (Cole) **5**:66

Horton Hears a Who! (Geisel) **1**:86

The Hotshot (Slote) **4**:202

The Hound of Ulster (Sutcliff) **1**:186

The House of Dies Drear (Hamilton) **1**:103

The House of Secrets (Bawden) **2**:12

The House of Sixty Fathers (DeJong) **1**:58

The House of Wings (Byars) **1**:36

The House with Roots (Willard) **2**:218

How Animals Behave (Bendick) **5**:48

How Animals Live Together (Selsam) **1**:162

How Animals Tell Time (Selsam) **1**:163

How Beastly! (Yolen) **4**:266

How Heredity Works: Why Living Things Are As They Are (Bendick) **5**:47

How It Feels When a Parent Dies (Krementz) **5**:155

How Many Miles to Babylon? (Fox) **1**:77

How Much and How Many: The Story of Weights and Measures (Bendick) **5**:35

How Puppies Grow (Selsam) **1**:163

How Santa Claus Had a Long and Difficult Journey Delivering His Presents (Krahn) **3**:104

How the Doctor Knows You're Fine (Cobb) **2**:65

How the Grinch Stole Christmas (Geisel) **1**:86

How the Whale Became (Hughes) **3**:92

How to Be a Hero (Weiss) **4**:225

How to Be an Inventor (Weiss) **4**:230

How to Make a Cloud (Bendick) **5**:44

How to Make Your Own Books (Weiss) **4**:227

How to Make Your Own Movies: An Introduction to Filmmaking (Weiss) **4**:227

How to Run a Railroad: Everything You Need to Know about Model Trains (Weiss) **4**:228

How Tom Beat Captain Najork and His Hired Sportsmen (Hoban) **3**:78

How We Got Our First Cat (Tobias) **4**:218

How Your Mother and Father Met, and What Happened After (Tobias) **4**:217

Hug Me (Stren) **5**:230

Hugo (Gripe) **5**:142

Hugo and Josephine (Gripe) **5**:143

Hugo och Josefin (Gripe) **5**:143

The Hullabaloo ABC (Cleary) **2**:47

Human Nature-Animal Nature: The Biology of Human Behavior (Cohen) **3**:40

The Hundred Penny Box (Mathis) **3**:149

The Hundredth Dove and Other Tales (Yolen) **4**:264

The Hunting of the Snark: An Agony in Eight Fits (Carroll) **2**:34

Hurrah, We're Outward Bound! (Spier) **5**:219

Hurry Home, Candy (DeJong) **1**:58

I, Adam (Fritz) **2**:81

I Am Papa Snap and These Are My Favorite No Such Stories (Ungerer) **3**:201

I Go by Sea, I Go by Land (Travers) **2**:178

I Klockornas Tid (Gripe) **5**:145

I Love My Mother (Zindel) **3**:248

I Never Loved Your Mind (Zindel) **3**:248

I Own the Racecourse! (Wrightson) **4**:242

I Wish That I Had Duck Feet (Geisel) **1**:87

The Ice Is Coming (Wrightson) **4**:245

If All the Swords in England (Willard) **2**:219

If I Had My Way (Klein) **2**:98

If I Ran the Circus (Geisel) **1**:87

If I Ran the Zoo (Geisel) **1**:87

If It Weren't for You (Zolotow) **2**:234

Iggie's House (Blume) **2**:17

I'll Get There. It Better Be Worth the Trip. (Donovan) **3**:52

The Illustrated Marguerite Henry (Henry) **4**:116

I'm Only Afraid of the Dark (At Night!) (Stren) **5**:235

I'm Really Dragged but Nothing Gets Me Down (Hentoff) **1**:107

I'm Trying to Tell You (Ashley) **4**:18

The Impossible People: A History Natural and Unnatural of Beings Terrible and Wonderful (McHargue) **2**:118

In a Beaver Valley: How Beavers Change the Land (Pringle) **4**:175

In My Garden (Zolotow) **2**:235

In Search of Ghosts (Cohen) **3**:40

In Spite of All Terror (Burton) **1**:32

In the Company of Clowns: A Commedia (Bacon) **3**:11

In the Country of Ourselves (Hentoff) **1**:108

In the Flaky Frosty Morning (Kuskin) **4**:140

In the Middle of the Trees (Kuskin) **4**:135

In the Middle of the World (Korinetz) **4**:130

In the Night Kitchen (Sendak) **1**:168

In the Time of the Bells (Gripe) **5**:145

The Incredible Journey (Burnford) **2**:19

Indian Encounters: An Anthology of Stories and Poems (Coatsworth) **2**:59

Indian Mound Farm (Coatsworth) **2**:59

Indian Summer (Monjo) **2**:121

Indians (Tunis) **2**:193

Inside Jazz (Collier) **3**:45

Intelligence: What Is It? (Cohen) **3**:41

Into the Woods: Exploring the Forest Ecosystem (Pringle) **4**:178

The Intruder (Townsend) **2**:172

The Invaders: Three Stories (Treece) **2**:185

The Inway Investigators; or, The Mystery at McCracken's Place (Yolen) **4**:258

The Iron Giant: A Story in Five Nights (Hughes) **3**:92

The Iron Lily (Willard) **2**:220

Is This a Baby Dinosaur? (Selsam) **1**:163

Isabel's Noel (Yolen) **4**:257

Isamu Noguchi: The Life of a Sculptor (Tobias) **4**:214

Island of the Blue Dolphins (O'Dell) **1**:146

The Island of the Grass King: The Further Adventures of Anatole (Willard) **5**:248

It Ain't All for Nothin' (Myers) **4**:158

It Happened One Summer (Phipson) **5**:178

It's Not the End of the World (Blume) **2**:17

It's Not What You Expect (Klein) **2**:98

Jake (Slote) **4**:199

Jambo Means Hello: Swahili Alphabet Book (Feelings) **5**:107

James and the Giant Peach (Dahl) **1**:51

James and the Rain (Kuskin) **4**:134

Jane, Wishing (Tobias) **4**:216

Janey (Zolotow) **2**:235

Jazz Country (Hentoff) **1**:108

Jean and Johnny (Cleary) **2**:48

Jennie's Hat (Keats) **1**:115

Jennifer, Hecate, Macbeth, William McKinley, and Me, Elizabeth (Konigsburg) **1**:121

Jethro and the Jumbie (Cooper) **4**:49

The Jezebel Wolf (Monjo) **2**:122

Jim Along, Josie: A Collection of Folk Songs and Singing Games for Young Children (Langstaff and Langstaff) **3**:110

Jimmy Yellow Hawk (Sneve) **2**:145

Jingo Django (Fleischman) **1**:74

Jock's Island (Coatsworth) **2**:59

Joe and the Snow (de Paola) **4**:54

John Henry: An American Legend (Keats) **1**:115

Johnny the Clockmaker (Ardizzone) **3**:4

Jokes from Black Folks (Haskins) **3**:65

Jonah, the Fisherman (Zimnik) **3**:243

Josefin (Gripe) **5**:142

Josephine (Gripe) **5**:142

Josh (Southall) **2**:153

Journey Behind the Wind (Wrightson) **4**:247

Journey between Worlds (Engdahl) **2**:70

Journey from Peppermint Street (DeJong) **1**:58

Journey to Jericho (O'Dell) **1**:147

Journey to Untor (Wibberley) **3**:228

The Journey with Jonah (L'Engle) **1**:130

Journeys of Sebastian (Krahn) **3**:105

Juan and the Asuangs (Aruego) **5**:28

Julia's House (Gripe) **5**:147

Julias Hus och Nattpappan (Gripe) **5**:147

Julie of the Wolves (George) **1**:90

Jumanji (Van Allsburg) **5**:239

June Anne June Spoon and Her Very Adventurous Search for the Moon (Kuskin) **4**:139

The Juniper Tree, and Other Tales from Grimm (Sendak) 1:169
Just Like Everyone Else (Kuskin) 4:135
Justin Morgan Had a Horse (Henry) 4:109
Kate (Little) 4:150
Kate Rider (Burton) 1:32
Keep Calm (Phipson) 5:185
Kenny's Window (Sendak) 1:170
The Kestrel (Alexander) 5:25
The Kids' Cat Book (de Paola) 4:63
A Kind of Wild Justice (Ashley) 4:16
The King and His Friends (Aruego) 5:27
King George's Head Was Made of Lead (Monjo) 2:122
King Grisly-Beard (Sendak) 1:171
King of the Wind (Henry) 4:111
The Kingdom and the Cave (Aiken) 1:4
A Kingdom in a Horse (Wojciechowska) 1:197
The King's Beard (Wibberley) 3:228
The King's Falcon (Fox) 1:78
The King's Fifth (O'Dell) 1:148
The King's Fountain (Alexander) 1:15; 5:22
Kintu: A Congo Adventure (Enright) 4:71
Kiviok's Magic Journey: An Eskimo Legend (Houston) 3:86
Klippity Klop (Emberley) 5:98
The Knee-High Man, and Other Tales (Lester) 2:112
Kneeknock Rise (Babbitt) 2:6
The Knight and the Dragon (de Paola) 4:64
Knight's Fee (Sutcliff) 1:187
Knights in Armor (Glubok) 1:100
Ladies of the Gothics: Tales of Romance and Terror by the Gentle Sex (Manley and Lewis) 3:145
The Lady of Guadalupe (de Paola) 4:63
Lafcadio, the Lion Who Shot Back (Silverstein) 5:208
The Land Beyond (Gripe) 5:145
The Land of Forgotten Beasts (Wersba) 3:217
Landet Utanfor (Gripe) 5:145
The Lantern Bearers (Sutcliff) 1:187
The Lark and the Laurel (Willard) 2:220
The Last Battle (Lewis) 3:135
The Last Battle (Wibberley) 3:228
The Last Guru (Pinkwater) 4:168
The Last Little Cat (DeJong) 1:59
The Last Viking (Treece) 2:186
Laura's Luck (Sachs) 2:132

The Lazy Bear (Wildsmith) 2:213
Lazy Tommy Pumpkinhead (du Bois) 1:64
The Legend of New Amsterdam (Spier) 5:226
The Legend of Old Befana: An Italian Christmas Story (de Paola) 4:65
The Lemonade Trick (Corbett) 1:46
Lens and Shutter: An Introduction to Photography (Weiss) 4:226
Leopard's Prey (Wibberley) 3:229
Let Me Fall Before I Fly (Wersba) 3:218
Let the Balloon Go (Southall) 2:153
A Letter to Amy (Keats) 1:115
Letters to Horseface: Being the Story of Wolfgang Amadeus Mozart's Journey to Italy, 1769-1770, When He Was a Boy of Fourteen (Monjo) 2:123
Life and Death (Zim and Bleeker) 2:228
The Life and Death of a Brave Bull (Wojciechowska) 1:198
The Life and Death of Martin Luther King, Jr. (Haskins) 3:65
The Life of Winston Churchill (Wibberley) 3:229
Lift Every Voice (Sterling and Quarles) 1:179
A Light in the Attic (Silverstein) 5:212
Lighthouse Island (Coatsworth) 2:60
Lightning (Bendick) 5:39
Lightning and Thunder (Zim) 2:228
A Likely Place (Fox) 1:78
Limericks by Lear (Lear) 1:127
Lines Scribbled on an Envelope and Other Poems (L'Engle) 1:131
The Lion, the Witch and the Wardrobe (Lewis) 3:135
Lisa and Lottie (Kästner) 4:124
Listen for the Fig Tree (Mathis) 3:149
Listen for the Singing (Little) 4:152
Listen to the Crows (Pringle) 4:180
Little Babar Books (Brunhoff) 4:37, 38
The Little Brute Family (Hoban) 3:78
The Little Cow and the Turtle (DeJong) 1:59
The Little Drummer Boy (Keats) 1:116
Little House in the Big Woods (Wilder) 2:205
Little House on the Prairie (Wilder) 2:206
The Little Man (Kästner) 4:127
The Little Man and the Big Thief (Kästner) 4:127

The Little Man and the Little Miss (Kästner) 4:127
A Little Oven (Estes) 2:74
The Little Roaring Tiger (Zimnik) 3:243
A Little Schubert (Goffstein) 3:59
The Little Spotted Fish (Yolen) 4:261
Little Tim and the Brave Sea Captain (Ardizzone) 3:5
Little Town on the Prairie (Wilder) 2:206
Little Women (Alcott) 1:10
The Little Wood Duck (Wildsmith) 2:213
Lives at Stake: The Science and Politics of Environmental Health (Pringle) 4:185
Living Things (Bendick) 5:42
Lizard Music (Pinkwater) 4:164
Lock, Stock, and Barrel (Sobol) 4:207
The Lollipop Princess: A Play for Paper Dolls in One Act (Estes) 2:74
London Bridge Is Falling Down (Emberley) 5:96
London Bridge Is Falling Down! (Spier) 5:217
Long Ago When I Was Young (Nesbit) 3:164
The Long and Short of Measurement (Cobb) 2:66
Long Journey Home: Stories from Black History (Lester) 2:113
The Long Secret (Fitzhugh) 1:72
The Long Winter (Wilder) 2:206
Look through My Window (Little) 4:149
Look What I Can Do (Aruego) 5:29
The Lorax (Geisel) 1:87
The Lost Dispatch: A Story of Antietam (Sobol) 4:206
Lotta on Troublemaker Street (Lindgren) 1:137
Lottie and Lisa (Kästner) 4:124
The Lotus Caves (Christopher) 2:40
Love and Tennis (Slote) 4:202
Love Is a Special Way of Feeling (Anglund) 1:20
The Luckiest Girl (Cleary) 2:48
The Lucky Stone (Clifton) 5:59
Lucretia Mott, Gentle Warrior (Sterling) 1:179
Lucy Brown and Mr. Grimes (Ardizzone) 3:5
Lumberjack (Kurelek) 2:101
M. C. Higgins, The Great (Hamilton) 1:104
Machine Tools (Zim and Skelly) 2:229
The MacLeod Place (Armstrong) 1:22
Magic Camera (Pinkwater) 4:162
The Magic City (Nesbit) 3:164
The Magic Finger (Dahl) 1:52
The Magic Moscow (Pinkwater) 4:171
The Magician (Shulevitz) 5:205

The Magician's Nephew (Lewis) 3:135
Making Music for Money (Collier) 3:46
The Making of an Afro-American: Martin Robison Delaney, 1812-1885 (Sterling) 1:180
The Making of Man: The Story of Our Ancient Ancestors (Collier) 3:46
Making Sense of Money (Cobb) 3:66
Making the Movies (Bendick) 5:34
Man Changes the Weather (Bova) 3:34
The Man Who Played Accordion Music (Tobias) 4:218
The Man Who Talked to a Tree (Baylor) 3:15
The Man Who Took the Indoors Out (Lobel) 5:168
Man with a Sword (Treece) 2:186
The Man with the Purple Eyes (Zolotow) 2:235
The Maplin Bird (Peyton) 3:177
Maria Tallchief (Tobias) 4:213
Marian Anderson (Tobias) 4:213
The Mark of the Horse Lord (Sutcliff) 1:188
Marra's World (Coatsworth) 2:60
Martha, the Movie Mouse (Lobel) 5:164
The Marvelous Misadventures of Sebastian (Alexander) 1:16; 5:21
Marvin K. Mooney Will You Please Go Now (Geisel) 1:88
Mary Jane (Sterling) 1:180
Mary McLeod Bethune (Greenfield) 4:99
Mary Poppins (Travers) 2:178
Mary Poppins from A to Z (Travers) 2:179
Mary Poppins in the Park (Travers) 2:179
The Marzipan Moon (Willard) 5:249
Masquerade (Williams) 4:231
Matt and Jo (Southall) 2:155
Matt Gargan's Boy (Slote) 4:201
Maurice's Room (Fox) 1:79
Mazel and Shlimazel; or, The Milk of the Lioness (Singer) 1:175
McBroom Tells the Truth (Fleischman) 1:75
McBroom's Ghost (Fleischman) 1:75
McBroom's Zoo (Fleischman) 1:75
Me and My Captain (Goffstein) 3:60
Me and My Little Brain (Fleischman) 1:70
Me and Neesie (Greenfield) 4:99
Me and Willie and Pa: The Story of Abraham Lincoln and His Son Tad (Monjo) 2:124
Measuring (Bendick) 5:45
Medicine (Zim) 2:229

Meet My Folks! (Hughes)   3:93
Meet the Austins
   (L'Engle)   1:131
The Mellops' Go Spelunking
   (Ungerer)   3:202
Men of the Hills (Treece)   2:187
The Mermaid and the Whale
   (McHargue)   2:119
The Merrymaker (Suhl)   2:165
Michael Bird-Boy (de
   Paola)   4:57
Microbes at Work
   (Selsam)   1:163
The Middle Moffat (Estes)   2:74
The Midnight Fox (Byars)   1:36
Midnight Is a Place (Aiken)   1:4
The Mighty Ones (DeJong)   1:59
Milkweed (Selsam)   1:164
*The Milky Way Galaxy: Man's
   Exploration of the Stars*
   (Bova)   3:34
Millions of Cats (Gág)   4:87
The Mills of God
   (Armstrong)   1:23
Mine for Keeps (Little)   4:147
Ming Lo Moves the Mountain
   (Lobel)   5:176
*The Minnow Family—Chubs,
   Dace, Minnows, and Shiners*
   (Pringle)   4:180
The Minstrel and the Mountain
   (Yolen)   4:257
Miranda the Great (Estes)   2:74
The Missing Piece
   (Silverstein)   5:211
*The Missing Piece Meets the Big
   O* (Silverstein)   5:212
*Mistresses of Mystery: Two
   Centuries of Suspense Stories
   by the Gentle Sex* (Manley and
   Lewis)   3:145
Misty of Chincoteague
   (Henry)   4:110
Mitch and Amy (Cleary)   2:48
*Model Buildings and How to
   Make Them* (Weiss)   4:229
*Model Cars and Trucks and How
   to Build Them* (Weiss)   4:227
*Moe Q. McGlutch, He Smoked
   Too Much* (Raskin)   1:156
The Moffats (Estes)   2:75
*Moja Means One: Swahili
   Counting Book*
   (Feelings)   5:105
Mojo and the Russians
   (Myers)   4:157
Mom, the Wolf Man, and Me
   (Klein)   2:99
Momo's Kitten (Yashima and
   Yashima)   4:253
Monkeys (Zim)   2:229
The Monsters' Ball (de
   Paola)   4:54
Moominpappa at Sea
   (Jansson)   2:94
Moominsummer Madness
   (Jansson)   2:94
Moominvalley in November
   (Jansson)   2:94
The Moon by Night
   (L'Engle)   1:132
The Moon in Fact and Fancy
   (Slote)   4:198

Moon Man (Ungerer)   3:202
*The Moon Ribbon: And Other
   Tales* (Yolen)   4:262
The Mooncusser's Daughter
   (Aiken)   1:5
*Moon-Whales and Other Moon
   Poems* (Hughes)   3:93
*More Adventures of the Great
   Brain* (Fitzgerald)   1:70
More Tales from Grimm
   (Gág)   4:94
Morning Is a Little Child
   (Anglund)   1:21
The Mortal Instruments
   (Bethancourt)   3:18
Motion and Gravity
   (Bendick)   5:45
*Motors and Engines and How
   They Work* (Weiss)   4:225
Mountain Rose (Stren)   5:234
The Mouse and His Child
   (Hoban)   3:78
The Mouse and the Motorcycle
   (Cleary)   2:48
Mouse Soup (Lobel)   5:171
Mouse Tales (Lobel)   5:168
Moving Day (Tobias)   4:215
Mr. Bass' Planetoid
   (Cameron)   1:40
Mr. Mysterious & Company
   (Fleischman)   1:75
Mr. Noah and the Second Flood
   (Burnford)   2:20
Mr. Revere and I
   (Lawson)   2:110
*Mrs. Frisby and the Rats of
   NIMH* (O'Brien)   2:127
Muley-Ears, Nobody's Dog
   (Henry)   4:113
Mummies (McHargue)   2:119
*Museum: The Story of America's
   Treasure Houses*
   (Schwartz)   3:189
Mustang, Wild Spirit of the West
   (Henry)   4:115
My Brother Fine with Me
   (Clifton)   5:56
My Brother Sam Is Dead (Collier
   and Collier)   3:47
My Crazy Sister
   (Goffstein)   3:60
My Darling, My Hamburger
   (Zindel)   3:249
My Father, the Coach
   (Slote)   4:200
My Friend Jacob (Clifton)   5:60
My Friend John
   (Zolotow)   3:236
My Heart's in Greenwich Village
   (Manley)   3:146
My Heart's in the Heather
   (Manley)   3:146
*My Mama Says There Aren't Any
   Zombies, Ghosts, Vampires,
   Creatures, Demons, Monsters,
   Fiends, Goblins, or Things*
   (Viorst)   3:208
My Puppy Is Born (Cole)   5:63
My Robot Buddy (Slote)   4:201
My School (Spier)   5:228
My Side of the Mountain
   (George)   1:91

My Special Best Words
   (Steptoe)   2:163
My Trip to Alpha I (Slote)   4:202
*The Mysterious Disappearance of
   Leon (I Mean Noel)*
   (Raskin)   1:156
*The Mystery of the Giant
   Footsteps* (Krahn)   3:105
*The Mystery of the Loch Ness
   Monster* (Bendick)   5:49
Names, Sets, and Numbers
   (Bendick)   5:43
*Nana Upstairs and Nana
   Downstairs* (de Paola)   4:54
Naomi in the Middle
   (Klein)   2:100
The Nargun and the Stars
   (Wrightson)   4:244
*Nathaniel Hawthorne: Captain of
   the Imagination*
   (Manley)   3:147
Nattpappan (Gripe)   5:146
*Natural Fire: Its Ecology in
   Forests* (Pringle)   4:184
*Near the Window Tree: Poems
   and Notes* (Kuskin)   4:142
A Near Thing for Captain Najork
   (Hoban)   3:81
A Necklace of Raindrops
   (Aiken)   1:6
Nessie the Monster
   (Hughes)   3:94
*New York City Too Far from
   Tampa Blues*
   (Bethancourt)   3:19
*Nicholas and the Fast Moving
   Diesel* (Ardizzone)   3:6
Nicholas Knock and Other People
   (Lee)   3:116
Nicky Goes to the Doctor
   (Scarry)   3:184
Night Again (Kuskin)   4:144
Night Birds on Nantucket
   (Aiken)   1:6
The Night Daddy (Gripe)   5:146
Night Fall (Aiken)   1:6
Night's Nice (Emberley)   5:92
Nine Lives (Alexander)   5:18
No Bath Tonight (Yolen)   4:265
No Beat of Drum (Burton)   1:32
No Kiss for Mother
   (Ungerer)   3:202
No Promises in the Wind
   (Hunt)   1:109
Noah's Ark (Spier)   5:224
The Noble Doll
   (Coatsworth)   2:60
Nobody Plays with a Cabbage
   (DeJong)   1:60
*Nobody's Family Is Going to
   Change* (Fitzhugh)   1:73
Nonsense Book (Lear)   1:127
Not What You Expected
   (Aiken)   1:7
Notes to a Science Fiction Writer
   (Bova)   3:35
Nothing at All (Gág)   4:92
*Nothing Ever Happens on My
   Block* (Raskin)   1:157
*Nothing Like a Fresh Coat of
   Paint* (Spier)   5:225
Now One Foot, Now the Other
   (de Paola)   4:65

*Nuclear Power: From Physics to
   Politics* (Pringle)   4:185
The Nursery "Alice"
   (Carroll)   2:35
Nutshell Library (Sendak)   1:171
Observation (Bendick)   5:45
*Odyssey of Courage: The Story of
   Alvar Nunez Cabeza de Vaca*
   (Wojciechowska)   1:198
Of Course Polly Can Ride a Bike
   (Lindgren)   1:137
Of Dikes and Windmills
   (Spier)   5:219
Oh, A-Hunting We Will Go
   (Langstaff)   3:110
Oh, Were They Ever Happy!
   (Spier)   5:225
Oh What a Noise!
   (Shulevitz)   5:204
Ol' Dan Tucker
   (Langstaff)   3:110
The Old Testament (de
   Angeli)   1:53
An Older Kind of Magic
   (Wrightson)   4:244
An Old-Fashioned Thanksgiving
   (Alcott)   1:11
Oliver Button Is a Sissy (de
   Paola)   4:62
On Beyond Zebra (Geisel)   1:88
*On Christmas Day in the
   Morning!* (Langstaff)   3:110
*On the Day Peter Stuyvesant
   Sailed into Town*
   (Lobel)   5:166
On the Other Side of the Gate
   (Suhl)   2:165
On the Way home
   (Wilder)   2:206
Once On a Time (Milne)   1:142
The One Bad Thing about Father
   (Monjo)   2:124
One by Sea (Corbett)   1:46
*One Earth, Many People: The
   Challenge of Human
   Population Growth*
   (Pringle)   4:175
One Fine Day (Hogrogian)   2:88
*One Fish, Two Fish, Red Fish,
   Blue Fish* (Geisel)   1:88
*One I Love, Two I Love: And
   Other Loving Mother Goose
   Rhymes* (Hogrogian)   2:88
One Monday Morning
   (Shulevitz)   5:202
The One Pig with Horns
   (Brunhoff)   4:40
One Small Blue Bead
   (Baylor)   3:16
One to Grow On (Little)   4:149
*One Was Johnny: A Counting
   Book* (Sendak)   1:172
One Wide River to Cross
   (Emberley)   5:93
The Only Earth We Have
   (Pringle)   4:174
Orlando, the Brave Vulture
   (Ungerer)   3:203
*Otherwise Known as Sheila the
   Great* (Blume)   2:17
Otto and the Magic Potatoes (du
   Bois)   1:64
Otto at Sea (du Bois)   1:65

Otto in Texas (du Bois) 1:65
Our Hungry Earth: The World Food Crisis (Pringle) 4:181
Outcast (Sutcliff) 1:189
The Outsiders (Hinton) 3:70
Over Sea, Under Stone (Cooper) 4:42
The Owl and the Pussycat (Lear) 1:127
The Owl and the Woodpecker (Wildsmith) 2:213
Owl at Home (Lobel) 5:169
Paddington Abroad (Bond) 1:28
Paddington at Large (Bond) 1:28
Paddington at Work (Bond) 1:28
Paddington Bear (Bond) 1:28
Paddington Helps Out (Bond) 1:29
Paddington Marches On (Bond) 1:29
Paddington Takes the Air (Bond) 1:29
Paint, Brush, and Palette (Weiss) 4:223
Pancakes for Breakfast (de Paola) 4:60
Paper, Ink, and Roller: Print-Making for Beginners (Weiss) 4:220
Pappa Pellerin's Daughter (Gripe) 5:143
Pappa Pellerins Dotter (Gripe) 5:143
The Parade Book (Emberley) 5:91
Pardon Me, You're Stepping on My Eyeball! (Zindel) 3:250
Parker Pig, Esquire (de Paola) 4:54
Parrakeets (Zim) 2:229
A Pattern of Roses (Peyton) 3:177
Paul Robeson (Greenfield) 4:98
Paul Robeson: The Life and Times of a Free Black Man (Hamilton) 1:104
Paul's Horse, Herman (Weiss) 4:221
The Peaceable Kingdom (Coatsworth) 2:60
The Pedaling Man, and Other Poems (Hoban) 3:81
Pencil, Pen, and Brush Drawing for Beginners (Weiss) 4:222
Pennington's Heir (Peyton) 3:178
Pennington's Last Term (Peyton) 3:178
People (Spier) 5:227
The People's Choice: The Story of Candidates, Campaigns, and Elections (Schwartz) 3:190
The Peppermint Pig (Bawden) 2:12
Perilous Pilgrimage (Treece) 2:187
Pet Show! (Keats) 1:116
The Pet Store (Spier) 5:228
Peter and Butch (Phipson) 5:181
Peter and Veronica (Sachs) 2:132

Peter Graves (du Bois) 1:65
Peter Treegate's War (Wibberley) 3:229
Peter's Chair (Keats) 1:116
Petey (Tobias) 4:217
Philip Hall Likes Me. I Reckon Maybe (Greene) 2:85
Phoebe's Revolt (Babbitt) 2:6
Pickle Creature (Pinkwater) 4:169
Picnic at Babar's (Brunhoff) 4:34
A Piece of the Power: Four Black Mayors (Haskins) 3:65
Pierre: A Cautionary Tale (Sendak) 1:172
The Pigman (Zindel) 3:251
The Pig-Tale (Carroll) 2:35
Pilyo the Piranha (Aruego) 5:29
Pinky Pye (Estes) 2:75
Pipes and Plumbing Systems (Zim and Skelly) 2:230
Pippa Passes (Corbett) 1:46
Pippi Goes on Board (Lindgren) 1:138
Pippi in the South Sea (Lindgren) 1:138
Pippi Longstocking (Lindgren) 1:138
Pirate's Island (Townsend) 2:173
The Place (Coatsworth) 2:61
A Place to Live (Bendick) 5:43
The Plan for Birdsmarsh (Peyton) 3:180
The Planet of Junior Brown (Hamilton) 1:104
The Planet-Girded Suns: Man's View of Other Solar Systems (Engdahl) 2:71
Plants in Winter (Cole) 5:63
Plenty of Fish (Selsam) 1:164
Plink, Plink, Plink (Baylor) 3:16
A Pocket Full of Seeds (Sachs) 2:133
The Pocket Mouse (Willard) 2:221
Poems of Lewis Carroll (Carroll) 2:35
Poetry Is (Hughes) 3:94
Polly's Tiger (Phipson) 5:183
The Pooh Story Book (Milne) 1:142
The Pool of Fire (Christopher) 2:41
Poor Richard in France (Monjo) 2:129
The Popcorn Book (de Paola) 4:60
Porko Von Popbutton (du Bois) 1:65
Portfolio of Horse Paintings (Henry) 4:112
Portfolio of Horses (Henry) 4:112
Portrait of Ivan (Fox) 1:79
Practical Music Theory: How Music Is Put Together from Bach to Rock (Collier) 3:48
A Prairie Boy's Summer (Kurelek) 2:103
A Prairie Boy's Winter (Kurelek) 2:103

Pretty Pretty Peggy Moffitt (du Bois) 1:66
Pretzel (Rey) 5:195
Pretzel and the Puppies (Rey) 5:195
Prince Bertram the Bad (Lobel) 5:163
Prince Caspian: The Return to Narnia (Lewis) 3:136
The Prince in Waiting (Christopher) 2:41
The Prince of the Dolomites: An Old Italian Tale (de Paola) 4:64
Prince Rabbit and the Princess Who Could Not Laugh (Milne) 1:143
Profiles in Black Power (Haskins) 3:66
The Proud Circus Horse (Zimnik) 3:244
A Proud Taste for Scarlet and Miniver (Konigsburg) 1:122
The Prydain Chronicles (Alexander) 1:16
Psst! Doggie— (Keats) 1:117
Punch and Judy (Emberley) 5:92
Puppy Summer (DeJong) 1:60
Putting the Sun to Work (Bendick) 5:49
Pyramid (Macaulay) 3:143
Python's Party (Wildsmith) 2:214
The Quangle Wangle's Hat (Lear) 1:127
The Quarreling Book (Zolotow) 2:236
The Queen Elizabeth Story (Sutcliff) 1:189
The Quest of Captain Cook (Selsam) 1:164
Questions and Answers about Ants (Selsam) 1:165
Questions and Answers about Horses (Selsam) 1:165
The Quicksand Book (de Paola) 4:59
Quips & Quirks (Watson) 3:213
The Quitting Deal (Tobias) 4:215
Rabbit Hill (Lawson) 2:110
A Racecourse for Andy (Wrightson) 4:242
Raffy and the Nine Monkeys (Rey) 5:192
The Railway Children (Nesbit) 3:164
Rain (Spier) 5:228
Rain Rain Rivers (Shulevitz) 5:203
Ralph Bunche: A Most Reluctant Hero (Haskins) 3:66
Ramona the Brave (Cleary) 2:49
Ramona the Pest (Cleary) 2:49
Rasmus and the Vagabond (Lindgren) 1:139
Ray Charles (Mathis) 3:151
The Real Hole (Cleary) 2:50
The Real Thief (Steig) 3:160
The Rebel (Burton) 1:33
Recycling Resources (Pringle) 4:179

Red Pawns (Wibberley) 3:229
The Red Room Riddle (Corbett) 1:46
Religions (Haskins) 3:66
The Reluctant Dragon (Grahame) 5:135
Remove Protective Coating a Little at a Time (Donovan) 3:53
The Renowned History of Little Red Riding-Hood (Hogrogian) 2:89
The Return of the Great Brain (Fitzgerald) 1:70
Return of the Moose (Pinkwater) 4:169
Return to Gone-Away (Enright) 4:76
Revolutionaries: Agents of Change (Haskins) 3:67
Ribsy (Cleary) 2:50
Rich and Famous: The Future Adventures of George Stable (Collier) 3:48
Richard Scarry's Animal Nursery Tales (Scarry) 3:185
Richard Scarry's Color Book (Scarry) 3:185
Richard Scarry's Great Big Air Book (Scarry) 3:185
The Richleighs of Tantamount (Cleary) 3:221
Ride into Danger (Treece) 2:188
Riders of the Storm (Burton) 1:34
Ring Out! A Book of Bells (Yolen) 4:261
The River and the Forest (Korinetz) 4:131
River Winding (Zolotow) 2:236
The Road to Miklagard (Treece) 2:188
Roar and More (Kuskin) 4:134
Robert Fulton, Boy Craftsman (Henry) 4:109
Robin and His Merry Men (Serraillier) 2:139
Robin in the Greenwood: Ballads of Robin Hood (Serraillier) 2:140
The Robot and Rebecca and the Missing Owser (Yolen) 4:268
The Robot and Rebecca: The Mystery of the Code-Carrying Kids (Yolen) 4:266
Rock Star (Collier) 3:48
The Rocks of Honey (Wrightson) 4:241
Roland the Minstrel Pig (Steig) 2:161
A Room Made of Windows (Cameron) 1:40
Rooster Brother (Hogrogian) 2:89
Rosa Parks (Greenfield) 4:97
The Rose on My Cake (Kuskin) 4:138
Rosebud (Emberley) 5:93
Rosie and Michael (Viorst) 3:208
The Rotten Years (Wojciechowska) 1:198

Rudi and the Distelfink
  (Monjo)   2:125
Rudyard Kipling: Creative
  Adventurer (Manley)   3:147
Rufus M. (Estes)   2:75
Rumble Fish (Hinton)   3:71
Run for the Money
  (Corbett)   1:47
Run Softly, Go Fast
  (Wersba)   3:218
Saber-Toothed Tiger and Other
  Ice Age Mammals (Cole)   5:65
The Sailing Hatrack
  (Coatsworth)   2:61
Sailing Small Boats
  (Weiss)   4:224
Sailing to Cythera, and Other
  Anatole Stories
  (Willard)   5:245
Saint George and the Dragon: A
  Mummer's Play
  (Langstaff)   3:111
San Domingo: The Medicine Hat
  Stallion (Henry)   4:116
San Francisco (Fritz)   2:81
Sand and Snow (Kuskin)   4:139
The Saturdays (Enright)   4:73
Science Experiments You Can Eat
  (Cobb)   2:66
The Sea Egg (Boston)   3:28
The Sea Is All Around
  (Enright)   4:72
Sea So Big, Ship So Small
  (Bendick)   5:40
Sea Star, Orphan of
  Chincoteague (Henry)   4:111
The Sea-Beggar's Son
  (Monjo)   2:125
Seacrow Island
  (Lindgren)   1:139
The Search for Delicious
  (Babbitt)   2:7
Seashore Story (Yashima)   4:254
Season Songs (Hughes)   3:95
The Seasons for Singing:
  American Christmas Songs and
  Carols (Langstaff)   3:111
The Sea-Thing Child
  (Hoban)   3:82
The Secret (Coatsworth)   2:61
Secret Agents Four
  (Sobol)   4:208
The Secret Box (Cole)   5:61
Secret of the Hawk
  (Wibberley)   3:230
The Secret of the Sachem's Tree
  (Monjo)   2:125
Secret Sea (White)   3:222
See the Circus (Rey)   5:198
See through the Sea (Selsam and
  Morrow)   1:165
The Seeing Stick (Yolen)   4:264
The Self-Made Snowman
  (Krahn)   3:105
Sense of Direction: Up and Down
  and All Around (Cobb)   2:67
Serafina the Giraffe
  (Brunhoff)   4:35
Seventeen Seconds
  (Southall)   2:155
The Seventh Mandarin
  (Yolen)   4:259

Shadow of a Bull
  (Wojciechowska)   1:199
Shadrach (DeJong)   1:60
Shaka, King of the Zulus: A
  Biography (Cohen)   3:42
Shapes (Bendick)   5:42
Sharks (Zim)   2:230
Shaw's Fortune: The Picture
  Story of a Colonial Plantation
  (Tunis)   2:194
She Come Bringing Me That
  Little Baby Girl
  (Greenfield)   4:97
The Shield Ring (Sutcliff)   1:189
Shimmy Shimmy Coke-Ca-Pop! A
  Collection of City Children's
  Street Games and Rhymes
  (Langstaff and
  Langstaff)   3:112
Ship Models and How to Build
  Them (Weiss)   4:227
Shirlick Holmes and the Case of
  the Wandering Wardrobe
  (Yolen)   4:267
Sia Lives on Kilimanjaro
  (Lindgren)   1:140
Sidewalk Story (Mathis)   3:151
Silent Ship, Silent Sea
  (White)   3:222
Silky: An Incredible Tale
  (Coatsworth)   2:61
The Silver Branch
  (Sutcliff)   1:190
The Silver Chair (Lewis)   3:136
The Silver Crown
  (O'Brien)   2:128
Silver on the Tree (Cooper)   4:47
The Silver Sword
  (Serraillier)   2:141
Simon (Sutcliff)   1:190
Simon Boom Gives a Wedding
  (Suhl)   2:166
Simon's Song (Emberley)   5:97
Simple Gifts: The Story of the
  Shakers (Yolen)   4:263
Simple Pictures Are Best
  (Willard)   5:247
The Simple Prince
  (Yolen)   4:264
Sing Down the Moon
  (O'Dell)   1:148
The Singing Hill (DeJong)   1:61
A Single Light
  (Wojciechowska)   1:199
Sister (Greenfield)   4:97
Six and Silver (Phipson)   5:178
Skates! (Keats)   1:117
The Sky Was Blue
  (Zolotow)   2:236
Slater's Mill (Monjo)   2:126
The Slave Dancer (Fox)   1:79
Sleepy People (Goffstein)   3:61
Sloan & Philamina: Or, How to
  Make Friends with Your Lunch
  (Stren)   5:231
The Sly Old Cat (Potter)   1:153
Small Pig (Lobel)   5:164
Smeller Martin (Lawson)   2:111
Smoke from Cromwell's Time
  (Aiken)   1:7
Snail, Where Are You?
  (Ungerer)   3:203
Snails (Zim and Krantz)   2:230

A Snake's Body (Cole)   5:67
Snippy and Snappy (Gág)   4:89
Snow Tracks (George)   1:92
The Snowy Day (Keats)   1:117
Social Welfare (Myers)   4:157
Socks (Cleary)   2:51
Soldier and Tsar in the Forest: A
  Russian Tale
  (Shulevitz)   5:205
Soldier, Soldier, Won't You
  Marry Me? (Langstaff)   3:112
Solids, Liquids, and Gases
  (Bendick)   5:47
Some of the Days of Everett
  Anderson (Clifton)   5:53
The Something (Babbitt)   2:8
Sometimes I Dance Mountains
  (Baylor)   3:16
The Song in My Drum
  (Hoban)   3:82
Songs of the Dream People:
  Chants and Images from the
  Indians and Eskimos of North
  America (Houston)   3:86
Songs of the Fog Maiden (de
  Paola)   4:62
Sonora Beautiful (Clifton)   5:60
Sophia Scrooby Preserved
  (Bacon)   3:11
The Sorely Trying Day
  (Hoban)   3:82
The Soul Brothers and Sister Lou
  (Hunter)   3:99
Sounder (Armstrong)   1:23
Sour Land (Armstrong)   1:24
South Swell (Wibberley)   3:230
Space and Time (Bendick)   5:42
A Space Story (Kuskin)   4:143
The Sparrow Bush
  (Coatsworth)   2:62
Speak Out in Thunder Tones:
  Letters and Other Writings by
  Black Northerners, 1787-1865
  (Sterling)   1:181
A Spell Is Cast (Cameron)   1:41
Spiderweb for Two: A Melendy
  Maze (Enright)   4:75
The Spirit of the Lord: Revivalism
  in America (Cohen)   3:42
The Splintered Sword
  (Serraillier)   2:188
Spotty (Rey)   5:195
The Sprig of Broom
  (Willard)   2:222
Spring Begins in March
  (Little)   4:148
Spring Comes to the Ocean
  (George)   1:92
Spring Is a New Beginning
  (Anglund)   1:21
Spring Is Here! (Sterling)   1:181
Square As A House
  (Kuskin)   4:136
Squib (Bawden)   2:13
Squirrels (Wildsmith)   2:214
Stand in the Wind (Little)   4:151
The Star-Spangled Banner
  (Spier)   5:222
Stevie (Steptoe)   2:163
Sticks, Spools, and Feathers
  (Weiss)   4:223
The Stone Doll of Sister Brute
  (Hoban)   3:83

The Stone-Faced Boy (Fox)   1:81
Stoneflight (McHargue)   2:120
The Stones of Green Knowe
  (Boston)   3:28
Storm from the West
  (Willard)   2:222
Stormy, Misty's Foal
  (Henry)   4:114
The Story of a Puppet
  (Collodi)   5:69
The Story of Babar, the Little
  Elephant (Brunhoff)   4:30
The Story of Paul Bunyan
  (Emberley)   5:92
The Story of Stevie Wonder
  (Haskins)   3:67
The Story of the Amulet
  (Nesbit)   3:165
Storybook Dictionary
  (Scarry)   3:186
A Storybook from Tomi Ungerer
  (Ungerer)   3:203
The Stowaway to the Mushroom
  Planet (Cameron)   1:41
A Stranger at Green Knowe
  (Boston)   3:29
Stranger on the Ball Club
  (Slote)   4:199
Strangers' Bread
  (Willard)   5:247
Street Gangs: Yesterday and
  Today (Haskins)   3:68
Strega Nona: An Old Tale (de
  Paola)   4:57
Stuart Little (White)   1:195
The Sultan's Perfect Tree
  (Yolen)   4:263
The Summer Book
  (Jansson)   2:95
The Summer Night
  (Zolotow)   2:237
Summer of My German Soldier
  (Greene)   2:86
The Summer of the Falcon
  (George)   1:93
The Summer of the Swans
  (Byars)   1:37
The Summer People
  (Townsend)   2:174
The Summer with Spike
  (Willard)   2:223
The Sun (Zim)   2:231
Sunday Morning (Viorst)   3:209
Super People: Who Will They Be?
  (Bendick)   5:50
Superpuppy: How to Choose,
  Raise, and Train the Best
  Possible Dog for You
  (Pinkwater and
  Pinkwater)   4:167
Supersuits (Cobb)   2:67
Suppose You Met a Witch
  (Serraillier)   2:142
Surrender (White)   3:222
The Survivor (White)   3:223
The Survivors (Hunter)   3:101
Sweet Pea: A Black Girl Growing
  Up in the Rural South
  (Krementz)   5:150
Sweetwater (Yep)   3:238
The Sword of Esau
  (Southall)   2:156

The Sword of the Spirits
(Christopher)   **2**:42
Sword of the Wilderness
(Coatsworth)   **2**:62
Swords from the North
(Treece)   **2**:189
Sylvester and the Magic Pebble
(Steig)   **2**:161
Sylvie and Bruno (Carroll)   **2**:36
*Symbiosis: A Book of Unusual
Friendships* (Aruego)   **5**:28
The Tailor of Gloucester
(Potter)   **1**:153
Take a Number (Bendick and
Levin)   **5**:39
Take Wing (Little)   **4**:148
Taking Sides (Klein)   **2**:100
The Tale of the Faithful Dove
(Potter)   **1**:153
The Tale of Three Landlubbers
(Serraillier)   **2**:143
The Tale of Tuppenny
(Potter)   **1**:154
Tales from Grimm (Gág)   **4**:91
Tales of a Fourth Grade Nothing
(Blume)   **2**:18
The Tales of Olga da Polga
(Bond)   **1**:29
Talk about a Family
(Greenfield)   **4**:101
Talking with the Animals
(Cohen)   **3**:42
Tamar's Wager
(Coatsworth)   **2**:62
Taran Wanderer
(Alexander)   **1**:17; **5**:20
Tatsinda (Enright)   **4**:76
The Tavern at the Ferry
(Tunis)   **2**:194
Teacup Full of Roses
(Mathis)   **3**:151
Tear Down the Walls!
(Sterling)   **1**:181
***The Teddy Bear Habit: or, How I
Became a Winner***
(Collier)   **3**:49
*Teen-Age Treasury of Good
Humor* (Manley)   **3**:148
*Teen-Age Treasury of Our
Science World* (Manley and
Lewis)   **3**:148
Teen-Age Treasury of the Arts
(Manley and Lewis)   **3**:148
Telephone Systems (Zim and
Skelly)   **2**:231
Television Works Like This
(Bendick and Bendick)   **5**:36
*The Tenth Good Thing about
Barney* (Viorst)   **3**:209
The Terrible Churnadryne
(Cameron)   **1**:41
The Terrible Roar
(Pinkwater)   **4**:161
Terry and the Caterpillars
(Selsam)   **1**:166
Terry on the Fence
(Ashley)   **4**:15
That Was Then, This Is Now
(Hinton)   **3**:72
Then Again, Maybe I Won't
(Blume)   **2**:18
Then There Were Five
(Enright)   **4**:75

There, Far Beyond the River
(Korinetz)   **4**:129
There's a Rainbow in My Closet
(Stren)   **5**:232
These Happy Golden Years
(Wilder)   **2**:207
They Put on Masks
(Baylor)   **3**:17
They Walk in the Night
(Coatsworth)   **2**:63
Thimble Summer (Enright)   **4**:71
*Things to Make and Do for
Valentine's Day* (de
Paola)   **4**:58
The Third Road (Bacon)   **3**:12
The Thirteen Days of Yule
(Hogrogian)   **2**:89
The Thirteen Moons
(George)   **1**:93
*The 35th of May; or, Conrad's
Ride to the South Seas*
(Kästner)   **4**:123
*This Is a River: Exploring an
Ecosystem* (Pringle)   **4**:176
This Is Australia (Sasek)   **4**:196
This Is Cape Kennedy
(Sasek)   **4**:193
This Is Edinburgh
(Sasek)   **4**:190
This Is Greece (Sasek)   **4**:194
This Is Historic Britain
(Sasek)   **4**:196
This Is Hong Kong
(Sasek)   **4**:194
This Is Ireland (Sasek)   **4**:193
This Is Israel (Sasek)   **4**:192
This Is London (Sasek)   **4**:188
This Is Munich (Sasek)   **4**:191
This Is New York (Sasek)   **4**:189
This Is Paris (Sasek)   **4**:187
This Is Rome (Sasek)   **4**:189
This Is San Francisco
(Sasek)   **4**:192
This Is Texas (Sasek)   **4**:194
This Is the United Nations
(Sasek)   **4**:195
This Is Venice (Sasek)   **4**:192
This Is Washington, D.C.
(Sasek)   **4**:195
This Star Shall Abide
(Engdahl)   **2**:71
Threat to the Barkers
(Phipson)   **5**:179
Three and One to Carry
(Willard)   **2**:223
Three Big Hogs
(Pinkwater)   **4**:164
Three Gay Tales from Grimm
(Gág)   **4**:93
Three on the Run
(Bawden)   **2**:14
The Three Robbers
(Ungerer)   **3**:204
Three Wishes (Clifton)   **5**:58
*Through the Broken Mirror with
Alice* (Wojciechowska)   **1**:200
*Through the Eyes of Wonder:
Science Fiction and Science*
(Bova)   **3**:35
*Through the Looking Glass and
What Alice Found There*
(Carroll)   **2**:36

Thunder in the Sky
(Peyton)   **3**:180
A Tide Flowing (Phipson)   **5**:186
A Tiger Called Thomas
(Zolotow)   **2**:237
*The Tiger's Bones, and Other
Plays for Children*
(Hughes)   **3**:96
Tikta' liktak: An Eskimo Legend
(Houston)   **3**:86
Till the Break of Day
(Wojciechowska)   **1**:200
Tim All Alone (Ardizzone)   **3**:6
Tim and Charlotte
(Ardizzone)   **3**:6
Tim and Ginger (Ardizzone)   **3**:7
Tim in Danger (Ardizzone)   **3**:7
Tim to the Lighthouse
(Ardizzone)   **3**:7
Tim to the Rescue
(Ardizzone)   **3**:8
*Time and Mr. Bass: A Mushroom
Planet Book* (Cameron)   **1**:42
*Time Cat: The Remarkable
Journey of Jason and Gareth*
(Alexander)   **5**:18
*Time of the Harvest: Thomas
Jefferson, the Years 1801-1826*
(Wibberley)   **3**:230
Time of Trial (Burton)   **1**:34
*Time-Ago Lost: More Tales of
Jahdu* (Hamilton)   **1**:105
Time-Ago Tales of Jahdu
(Hamilton)   **1**:106
The Times They Used to Be
(Clifton)   **5**:56
Tim's Last Voyage
(Ardizzone)   **3**:8
Tin Lizzie (Spier)   **5**:223
To Be a Slave (Lester)   **2**:114
To Market! To Market!
(Spier)   **5**:218
To the Wild Sky (Southall)   **2**:156
Toad of Toad Hall
(Milne)   **1**:143
Tom and the Two Handles
(Hoban)   **3**:83
Tom Fox and the Apple Pie
(Watson)   **3**:213
The Tombs of Atuan (Le
Guin)   **3**:123
*Tomfoolery: Trickery and Foolery
with Words* (Schwartz)   **3**:190
Tommy Helps, Too (Rey)   **5**:194
Toolmaker (Walsh)   **2**:201
Tony and Me (Slote)   **4**:200
Tooth-Gnasher Superflash
(Pinkwater)   **4**:171
The Toppling Towers
(Willard)   **2**:223
*Topsy-Turvies: Pictures to Stretch
the Imagination* (Anno)   **2**:2
*The Topsy-Turvy Emperor of
China* (Singer)   **1**:175
The Tough Winter
(Lawson)   **2**:111
The Town Cats and Other Tales
(Alexander)   **5**:23
The Toy Shop (Spier)   **5**:228
Tractors (Zim and Skelly)   **2**:231
Trail of Apple Blossoms
(Hunt)   **1**:110
Train Ride (Steptoe)   **2**:164

The Transfigured Hart
(Yolen)   **4**:261
The Travels of Babar
(Brunhoff)   **4**:31
The Treasure (Shulevitz)   **5**:206
The Treasure of Topo-El-Bampo
(O'Dell)   **1**:148
Tree House Island
(Corbett)   **1**:47
A Treeful of Pigs (Lobel)   **5**:173
Treegate's Raiders
(Wibberley)   **3**:231
The Treegate Series
(Wibberley)   **3**:231
Tristan and Iseult
(Sutcliff)   **1**:190
Trouble in the Jungle
(Townsend)   **2**:175
The Trouble with Donovan Croft
(Ashley)   **4**:14
Trucks (Zim and Skelly)   **2**:232
True Sea Adventures
(Sobol)   **4**:210
The Trumpet of the Swan
(White)   **1**:195
Trust a City Kid (Yolen and
Huston)   **4**:256
The Truth about Mary Rose
(Sachs)   **2**:133
The Truthful Harp
(Alexander)   **1**:18; **5**:20
*Try It Again, Sam: Safety When
You Walk* (Viorst)   **3**:210
Tuck Everlasting (Babbitt)   **2**:8
Tuned Out
(Wojciechowska)   **1**:200
Tunes for a Small Harmonica
(Wersba)   **3**:220
The Tunnel of Hugsy Goode
(Estes)   **2**:75
Turkey for Christmas (de
Angeli)   **1**:54
The Turnabout Trick
(Corbett)   **1**:47
Twenty-Four and Stanley
(Weiss)   **4**:219
*The Twenty-Four Days Before
Christmas* (L'Engle)   **1**:132
The Twenty-One Balloons (du
Bois)   **1**:66
*Twins: The Story of Multiple
Births* (Cole and
Edmondson)   **5**:62
*Twist, Wiggle, and Squirm: A
Book about Earthworms*
(Pringle)   **4**:177
*A Twister of Twists, a Tangler of
Tongues* (Schwartz)   **3**:190
Two Laughable Lyrics
(Lear)   **1**:128
Two Love Stories (Lester)   **2**:115
The Two Old Bachelors
(Lear)   **1**:128
Two Piano Tuners
(Goffstein)   **3**:61
Umbrella (Yashima)   **4**:253
Uncle Elephant (Lobel)   **5**:175
Uncle Lemon's Spring
(Yolen)   **4**:267
Uncle Misha's Partisans
(Suhl)   **2**:166
Under the Green Willow
(Coatsworth)   **2**:63

Title Index

Underground (Macaulay)   3:144
The Underside of the Leaf (Goffstein)   3:61
The Unfriendly Book (Zolotow)   2:237
The Universe (Zim)   2:232
University: The Students, Faculty, and Campus Life at One University (Schwartz)   3:191
Up a Road Slowly (Hunt)   1:110
Up Periscope (White)   3:223
Upside-Downers: More Pictures to Stretch the Imagination (Anno)   2:2
Uptown (Steptoe)   2:164
The Uses of Space (Bova)   3:36
Vaccination and You (Cohen)   3:43
Vegetables from Stems and Leaves (Selsam)   1:166
Veronica Ganz (Sachs)   2:134
Very Far Away from Anywhere Else (Le Guin)   3:123
A Very Young Circus Flyer (Krementz)   5:154
A Very Young Dancer (Krementz)   5:151
A Very Young Gymnast (Krementz)   5:153
A Very Young Rider (Krementz)   5:152
A Very Young Skater (Krementz)   5:154
The Vicksburg Veteran (Monjo)   2:126
Viking's Dawn (Treece)   2:189
Viking's Sunset (Treece)   2:189
Village Books (Spier)   5:228
The Village Tree (Yashima)   4:250
A Visit to William Blake's Inn: Poems for Innocent and Experienced Travelers (Willard)   5:250
The Voyage of the Dawn Treader (Lewis)   3:137
Wagging Tails: An Album of Dogs (Henry)   4:112
Wake Up and Goodnight (Zolotow)   2:237
Walk a Mile and Get Nowhere (Southall)   2:157
Wall Street: The Story of the Stock Exchange (Sterling)   1:182
The Wanderers (Coatsworth)   2:63
The War and the Protest: Viet Nam (Haskins)   3:68
War Dog (Treece)   2:190
Warrior Scarlet (Sutcliff)   1:191
Watch Out for the Chicken Feet in Your Soup (de Paola)   4:56
The Watcher in the Garden (Phipson)   5:186
Watchers in the Wild: The New Science of Ethology (Cohen)   3:43
Water Plants (Pringle)   4:179
Watson, the Smartest Dog in the U.S.A. (Kuskin)   4:139
Waves (Zim)   2:232
The Way Home (Phipson)   5:182

The Way of Danger: The Story of Theseus (Serraillier)   2:143
We Hide, You Seek (Aruego and Dewey)   5:30
The Weather Changes Man (Bova)   3:36
W.E.B. DuBois: A Biography (Hamilton)   1:106
The Well-Mannered Balloon (Willard)   5:246
Westmark (Alexander)   5:24
Westward to Vinland (Treece)   2:190
What Color Is Love? (Anglund)   1:21
What Did You Bring Me? (Kuskin)   4:141
What Do People Do All Day? (Scarry)   3:186
What Do You Think? An Introduction to Public Opinion: How It Forms, Functions, and Affects Our Lives (Schwartz)   3:191
What Does It Do and How Does It Work? (Hoban)   3:83
What Holds It Together (Weiss)   4:228
What Is a Man? (Krahn)   3:106
What It's All About (Klein)   2:101
What Made You You? (Bendick)   5:44
What Makes a Boat Float? (Corbett)   1:47
What Makes a Light Go On? (Corbett)   1:48
What Makes a Plane Fly? (Corbett)   1:48
What Shall We Do with the Land? (Pringle)   4:186
What to Do: Everyday Guides for Everyone (Bendick and Warren)   5:41
The Wheel on the School (DeJong)   1:61
Wheels: A Pictorial History (Tunis)   2:194
When Clay Sings (Baylor)   3:17
When Everyone Was Fast Asleep (de Paola)   4:57
When I Have a Little Girl (Zolotow)   2:238
When I Have a Son (Zolotow)   2:238
When I Was a Boy (Kästner)   4:126
When I Was a Little Boy (Kästner)   4:126
When Shlemiel Went to Warsaw and Other Stories (Singer)   1:176
When the City Stopped (Phipson)   5:185
When the Pie Was Opened (Little)   4:148
When the Wind Stops (Zolotow)   2:238
When Thunders Spoke (Sneve)   2:145
Where Does the Day Go? (Myers)   4:155

Where the Sidewalk Ends (Silverstein)   5:210
Where the Wild Things Are (Sendak)   1:172
Where Was Patrick Henry on the 29th of May? (Fritz)   2:81
Where's My Baby? (Rey)   5:195
Which Horse Is William? (Kuskin)   4:136
The Whispering Mountain (Aiken)   1:8
Whistle for Willie (Keats)   1:118
The White Archer: An Eskimo Legend (Houston)   3:87
The White Horse Gang (Bawden)   2:14
The White Marble (Zolotow)   2:239
The White Mountains (Christopher)   2:43
The White Mountains Trilogy (Christopher)   2:43
The White Room (Coatsworth)   2:64
White Stallion of Lipizza (Henry)   4:114
Whizz! (Lear)   1:128
Who I Am (Lester)   2:115
Who Really Killed Cock Robin? (George)   1:94
Who, Said Sue, Said Whoo? (Raskin)   1:157
Who Will Comfort Toffle? (Jansson)   2:95
Whoppers: Tall Tales and Other Lies (Schwartz)   3:192
Who's Seen the Scissors? (Krahn)   3:106
Who's That Stepping on Plymouth Rock (Fritz)   2:82
Why Can't I? (Bendick)   5:43
Why Don't You Get a Horse, Sam Adams? (Fritz)   2:82
Why Noah Chose the Dove (Singer)   1:176
Why Things Change: The Story of Evolution (Bendick)   5:46
The Wicked City (Singer)   1:176
Wiggle to the Laundromat (Lee)   3:116
Wild Foods: A Beginner's Guide to Identifying, Harvesting, and Cooking Safe and Tasty Plants from the Outdoors (Pringle)   4:183
Wild in the World (Donovan)   3:54
Wild Jack (Christopher)   2:43
The Wildest Horse Race in the World (Henry)   4:113
William's Doll (Zolotow)   2:239
A Wind in the Door (L'Engle)   1:132
The Wind in the Willows (Grahame)   5:128
The Windswept City: A Novel of the Trojan War (Treece)   2:191
The Wing on a Flea: A Book about Shapes (Emberley)   5:90
The Winged Colt of Casa Mia (Byars)   1:37
Wingman (Pinkwater)   4:163

Winter Tales from Poland (Wojciechowska)   1:200
Winterthing (Aiken)   1:8
The Witch Family (Estes)   2:76
The Witch Who Wasn't (Yolen)   4:256
Witchcraft, Mysticism and Magic in the Black World (Haskins)   3:69
The Witch's Brat (Sutcliff)   1:191
The Witch's Daughter (Bawden)   2:15
Witcracks: Jokes and Jests from American Folklore (Schwartz)   3:192
Wizard Crystal (Pinkwater)   4:162
The Wizard in the Tree (Alexander)   1:18; 5:23
The Wizard Islands (Yolen)   4:260
A Wizard of Earthsea (Le Guin)   3:124
The Wizard of Op (Emberley)   5:99
The Wizard of Washington Square (Yolen)   4:258
Wolf Run: A Caribou Eskimo Tale (Houston)   3:88
The Wolves of Willoughby Chase (Aiken)   1:8
The Wonderful Dragon of Timlin (de Paola)   4:53
The Wonderful Flight to the Mushroom Planet (Cameron)   1:42
Wordhoard: Anglo-Saxon Stories (Walsh and Crossley-Holland)   2:201
Working with Cardboard and Paper (Weiss)   4:229
The World of Christopher Robin (Milne)   1:143
The World of Pooh (Milne)   1:143
World on a String: The Story of Kites (Yolen)   4:258
The World's Greatest Freak Show (Raskin)   1:157
The Worms of Kukumlina (Pinkwater)   4:171
A Wrinkle in Time (L'Engle)   1:133
The Wuggie Norple Story (Pinkwater)   4:170
Yertle the Turtle and Other Stories (Geisel)   1:88
Yobgorgle: Mystery Monster of Lake Ontario (Pinkwater)   4:170
The Young Ardizzone: An Autobiographical Fragment (Ardizzone)   3:8
The Young Landlords (Myers)   4:159
Young Man from the Piedmont: The Youth of Thomas Jefferson (Wibberley)   3:232
The Young Unicorns (L'Engle)   1:134
The Young United States: 1783 to 1830 (Tunis)   2:195

Your Brain and How It Works (Zim)   **2**:232

Your Heart and How It Works (Zim)   **2**:233

Your Stomach and Digestive Tract (Zim)   **2**:233

Z for Zachariah (O'Brien)   **2**:129

Zamani Goes to Market (Feelings)   **5**:105

Zebulon Pike, Soldier and Explorer (Wibberley)   **3**:233

Zeee (Enright)   **4**:77

Zeely (Hamilton)   **1**:106

Zeralda's Ogre (Ungerer)   **3**:204

Zlateh the Goat, and Other Stories (Singer)   **1**:177

A Zoo for Mister Muster (Lobel)   **5**:163

Zozo (Rey)   **5**:193

Zozo Flies a Kite (Rey)   **5**:198

Zozo Gets a Medal (Rey)   **5**:198

Zozo Goes to the Hospital (Rey)   **5**:199

Zozo Learns the Alphabet (Rey)   **5**:199

Zozo Rides a Bike (Rey)   **5**:196

Zozo Takes a Job (Rey)   **5**:196

Title Index

CUMULATIVE INDEX TO CRITICS

Abdal-Haqq, Ismat
Lucille Clifton 5:60

Abrahamson, Richard F.
Tomie de Paola 4:53

Abramson, Jane
Natalie Babbitt 2:5
Nina Bawden 2:12
Judy Blume 2:16
Beverly Cleary 2:49
Muriel L. Feelings and Tom
Feelings 5:107
S. E. Hinton 3:71
Sharon Bell Mathis 3:150
D. Manus Pinkwater 4:162
Ellen Raskin 1:156

Adam, Beatrice M.
Beverly Cleary 2:49
James Houston 3:87

Adams, John
Ted Hughes 3:90

Adkins, Alice
Marilyn Sachs 2:133

Adkins, Laurence
Ted Hughes 3:92

Aers, Lesley
E. Nesbit 3:165

Alderson, Brian W.
Joan Aiken 1:3, 4
Paula Fox 1:77
Theodor Seuss Geisel 1:87
Jean Craighead George 1:91
Russell Hoban 3:77, 82
Nonny Hogrogian 2:88
Fernando Krahn 3:104
John Langstaff 3:113
Arnold Lobel 5:167, 169

Maurice Sendak 1:169
Ian Serraillier 2:136, 140
Isaac Bashevis Singer 1:176
William Steig 2:161
Rosemary Sutcliff 1:184
Tomi Ungerer 3:200, 201
Judith Viorst 3:209
Clyde Watson 3:212
Reiner Zimnik 3:243
Paul Zindel 3:254

Alderson, S. William
Susan Cooper 4:45, 46

Alderson, Valerie
Yuri Suhl 2:167
Tomi Ungerer 3:203
Brian Wildsmith 2:208, 211
Paul Zindel 3:250

Aldridge, Judith
Betsy Byars 1:36
Elizabeth Coatsworth 2:62, 63
Robert C. O'Brien 2:128
K. M. Peyton 3:177
Barbara Willard 2:216, 220,
222

Alexander, Daryl
Louise Fitzhugh and Sandra
Scoppettone 1:71

Alexander, Lloyd
Lloyd Alexander 5:13

Alexander, Rae
William H. Armstrong 1:24

Alexander, Sue
D. Manus Pinkwater 4:167

Allen, John
E. L. Konigsburg 1:120

Allen, Merritt P.
Leonard Wibberley 3:230

Allen, Patricia H.
Joan Walsh Anglund 1:21
Ed Emberley and Barbara
Emberley 5:93
Elizabeth Enright 4:77
Louise Fitzhugh 1:72
Irene Hunt 1:109

Alpern, Joyce
Jean Fritz 2:79
Norma Klein 2:98
F. N. Monjo 2:125
Leonard Wibberley 3:230

Altemus, Evelyn Goss
Ellen Raskin 1:157

Alterman, Loraine
James Lincoln Collier 3:46

Amis, Martin
S. E. Hinton 3:72

Amory, Judith M.
L. M. Boston 3:29

Anable, David
Lucille Clifton 5:58
Eloise Greenfield 4:99

Andersenn, Erik
Henry Treece 2:188

Anderson, A. J.
Alvin Schwartz 3:191

Anderson, Mary Jane
Tobi Tobias 4:215

Anderson, Merrilee
Jill Krementz 5:151

Andreae, Christopher
Shirley Glubok 1:98

Andrejevic, Helen
Ed Emberley and Barbara
Emberley 5:98

Andrews, Peter
Daniel Cohen 3:39
Leonard Wibberley 3:228

Andrews, Sheryl B.
Mitsumasa Anno 2:2
John Christopher 2:38, 42
Sylvia Louise Engdahl 2:70
Sid Fleischman 1:74
Virginia Hamilton 1:106
S. E. Hinton 3:72
Russell Hoban 3:75
Ursula K. Le Guin 3:123
K. M. Peyton 3:179
Joan Phipson 5:178
Millicent E. Selsam 1:161
Peter Spier 5:221
Rosemary Sutcliff 1:185
John Rowe Townsend 2:174
Judith Viorst 3:209
Barbara Wersba 3:219
Leonard Wibberley 3:226
Charlotte Zolotow 2:236

Andrews, Siri M.
Beverly Cleary 2:45, 47
William Pène du Bois 1:64
Eleanor Estes 2:74
Theodor Seuss Geisel 1:87
Erich Kästner 4:124
Robert Lawson 2:111
Astrid Lindgren 1:139
Rosemary Sutcliff 1:189

Andrus, Gertrude
H. A. Rey and Margret Rey
5:195

Anson, Brooke
John Donovan 3:56
S. E. Hinton 3:73
Julius Lester 2:114
Georgess McHargue 2:119

Appel, Dr. Ida J.
Jose Aruego 5:27

Arbuthnot, May Hill
Joan Aiken 1:1
Louisa May Alcott 1:11
Lloyd Alexander 1:16; 5:17
Edward Ardizzone 3:5
Byrd Baylor 3:16
Jeanne Bendick 5:34
Sheila Burnford 2:19
John Christopher 2:43
Beverly Cleary 2:45
Elizabeth Coatsworth 2:53
Carlo Collodi 5:83
Susan Cooper 4:42
Roald Dahl 1:49
Marguerite de Angeli 1:52, 53
Meindert DeJong 1:55
William Pène du Bois 1:66
Eleanor Estes 2:72, 73
Muriel L. Feelings and Tom
    Feelings 5:107
Louise Fitzhugh 1:72
Paula Fox 1:76
Theodor Seuss Geisel 1:84
Shirley Glubok 1:94
Maria Gripe 5:141
Marguerite Henry 4:108, 108,
    112
Nat Hentoff 1:108
Russell Hoban 3:76
Kristin Hunter 3:101
E. L. Konigsburg 1:121
Robert Lawson 2:111, 111
Edward Lear 1:126
Madeleine L'Engle 1:134
Arnold Lobel 5:162
A. A. Milne 1:141
Walter Dean Myers 4:155
Scott O'Dell 1:147
Beatrix Potter 1:152
Laurence Pringle 4:173
M. Sasek 1:190
Millicent E. Selsam 1:159
Maurice Sendak 1:171, 172
Alfred Slote 4:199
Dorothy Sterling 1:178, 181
Rosemary Sutcliff 1:183
Tobi Tobias 4:213
John Rowe Townsend 2:173
Henry Treece 2:182
Edwin Tunis 2:193
Harvey Weiss 4:219
Leonard Wibberley 3:232
Laura Ingalls Wilder 2:203
Brian Wildsmith 2:207, 208,
    211
Maia Wojciechowska 1:196
Herbert S. Zim 2:227
Charlotte Zolotow 2:233

Ardizzone, Edward
Edward Ardizzone 3:1

Armstrong, Helen
Irene Hunt 1:110

Armstrong, Louise
John Donovan 3:52

Ashley, Bernard
Bernard Ashley 4:13

Asimov, Isaac
Ben Bova 3:35
Millicent E. Selsam 1:163

Aspey, Wayne P.
Jeanne Bendick 5:48

Attebery, Brian
Lloyd Alexander 5:17

Atwater, Judith
Joan Aiken 1:7
Daniel Cohen 3:40

Atwood, Hayden
Fernando Krahn 3:107
Tobi Tobias 4:217

Auden, W. H.
Lewis Carroll 2:23

Auerbach, Nina
Lewis Carroll 2:27

Avery, Gillian
Lewis Carroll 2:32
Kenneth Grahame 5:121

Avila, Sister
Nina Bawden 2:11
Paula Fox 1:81
Jill Paton Walsh 2:199

Babbitt, Natalie
Jose Aruego 5:28
Elizabeth Coatsworth 2:63
Susan Cooper 4:47
Tomie de Paola 4:66
Arnold Lobel 5:176
Ian Serraillier 2:142
Ivan Southall 2:153
Chris Van Allsburg 5:239
Judith Viorst 3:208
Barbara Wersba 3:215
Nancy Willard 5:247, 248
Jane Yolen 4:264
Reiner Zimnik 3:242

Bach, Alice
Lewis Carroll 2:35
Norma Klein 2:101
Judith Viorst 3:208

Bacon, Betty
Tomie de Paola 4:53

Bacon, Martha
L. M. Boston 3:28
Carlo Collodi 5:72
John Donovan 3:52
Nat Hentoff 1:107
Madeleine L'Engle 1:130, 134
Beatrix Potter 1:153

Bader, Barbara
Jeanne Bendick 5:36
Joanna Cole 5:65
Russell Hoban 3:74, 77
Fernando Krahn 3:103
Karla Kuskin 4:134
H. A. Rey and Margret Rey
    5:192
Tomi Ungerer 3:197
Taro Yashima 4:249

Bagg, Susan
Laura Ingalls Wilder 2:204

Bagshaw, Marguerite
Scott Corbett 1:46
A. A. Milne 1:143

Baker, Augusta
Dorothy Sterling 1:179

Baker, Barbara
Bernard Ashley 4:17
Jane Yolen 4:267

Baker, Nina Brown
Elizabeth Coatsworth 2:55

Balducci, Carolyn
Norma Klein 2:98

Baldwin, Michael
John Rowe Townsend 2:173

Ballou, Mary E.
Reiner Zimnik 3:243

Bandler, Michael J.
Uri Shulevitz 5:204, 205
William Steig 2:158
Judith Viorst 3:207
Brian Wildsmith 2:211
Charlotte Zolotow 2:234

Banfield, Beryle
Eloise Greenfield 4:101

Banks, James A.
Kristin Hunter 3:101

Bannon, Barbara A.
A. A. Milne 1:142

Barker, June
Byrd Baylor 3:16

Barker, Robert
Arnold Lobel 5:168
Joan Phipson 5:183

Barkis, Cecilia
Joan Phipson 5:185

Barlow, Ruth C.
Erich Kästner 4:125

Barnes, Clive
Jill Kremenz 5:152

Barnes, Pat
Vicki Cobb 2:65

Barr, Donald
A. A. Milne 1:141

Barton, Mrs. G. V.
Edward Ardizzone 3:7
K. M. Peyton 3:176
Peter Spier 5:215

Baskin, Barbara H.
Lloyd Alexander 5:24
Maria Gripe 5:145
Joan Phipson 5:181

Bassett, Lydia
Sharon Bell Mathis 3:149

Bauman, Margaret M.
Elizabeth Coatsworth 2:54

Baumholtz, Joyce
K. M. Peyton 3:177

Bazarov, Konstantin
Yuri Korinetz 4:129

Beard, Patricia D.
Madeleine L'Engle 1:134

Bearden, Joe
Jean Fritz 2:82
F. N. Monjo 2:121, 123

Beasley, Lee
Tomie de Paola 4:62

Beatley, Beryl B.
Jeanne Bendick 5:49
Joanna Cole 5:63

Beatty, Elaine E.
Marguerite Henry 4:112

Beatty, Jerome, Jr.
Michael Bond 1:29
James Lincoln Collier 3:49
William Pène du Bois 1:64
Fernando Krahn and Maria de
    la Luz Krahn 3:103
Jane Yolen 4:257, 266
Charlotte Zolotow 2:234

Bechtel, Louise Seaman
Jeanne Bendick 5:37
Elizabeth Coatsworth 2:51
Elizabeth Enright 4:75
Kenneth Grahame 5:135
Marguerite Henry 4:111, 111,
    112
Erich Kästner 4:124, 125
Taro Yashima 4:251

Beck, John
Madeleine L'Engle 1:134

Becker, May Lamberton
Jeanne Bendick 5:34, 35
Jean de Brunhoff and Laurent
    de Brunhoff 4:30, 31, 32, 33
Elizabeth Enright 4:71, 72, 74,
    75
Wanda Gág 4:91, 92
Marguerite Henry 4:109, 110,
    110
H. A. Rey and Margret Rey
    5:193, 194, 196

Beer, Patricia
L. M. Boston 3:29

Belcher, R. Gregory
Jeanne Bendick 5:48
Laurence Pringle 4:178, 181,
    184, 185

Belden, Shirley C.
Rosemary Sutcliff 1:188

Bell, Anthea
Erich Kästner 4:127
E. Nesbit 3:154, 162, 165
H. A. Rey and Margret Rey
    5:200
Brian Wildsmith 2:210

Bell, Arthur
Maurice Sendak 1:168

Bell, Mabel B.
Ezra Jack Keats 1:118

Bell, Robert
Bernard Ashley 4:15, 16
John Donovan 3:53
S. E. Hinton 3:73
Kristin Hunter 3:101
Joan Phipson 5:183

Bellows, Silence Buck
Joan Aiken 1:8
Elizabeth Coatsworth 2:55
Scott Corbett 1:47
Eleanor Estes 2:77
Karla Kuskin 4:135, 137

Bender, Rose S.
Marguerite Henry 4:116

Bendick, Jeanne
Jeanne Bendick 5:33

Benét, Rosemary Carr
Jean de Brunhoff and Laurent
de Brunhoff 4:32

Benét, William Rose
Jean de Brunhoff and Laurent
de Brunhoff 4:31

Bennett, Arnold
Kenneth Grahame 5:130

Berge, Jody
James Lincoln Collier 3:45

Bergenheim, Robert C.
Jeanne Bendick 5:40

Berglund, Patricia
Peter Spier 5:222

Berkowitz, Nancy
Joan Aiken 1:8
Hester Burton 1:34
K. M. Peyton 3:173
Barbara Willard 2:216, 220

Berkvist, Margaret
Shirley Glubok 1:95
Donald J. Sobol 4:207
Barbara Willard 2:218

Berkvist, Robert
Ben Bova 3:32
Scott Corbett 1:44
S. E. Hinton 3:71
James Houston 3:87
M. Sasek 4:196
Alfred Slote 4:198
Ivan Southall 2:157
Henry Treece 2:183, 189

Bermel, Joyce
James Lincoln Collier 3:45

Bernard, Annabelle R.
Millicent E. Selsam 1:162

Bernard, Jacqueline
Martha Bacon 3:12

Berner, Elsa
Harvey Weiss 4:220

Bernstein, Arlene
Laurence Pringle 4:184

Bernstein, Joanne E.
Nonny Hogrogian 2:88

Berry, Mabel
Nina Bawden 2:15

Bettelheim, Bruno
Maurice Sendak 1:172

Bettersworth, John K.
Irene Hunt 1:109

Bird, Francis
Jean de Brunhoff and Laurent
de Brunhoff 4:33

Birmingham, Mary Louise
Jane Yolen and Anne Huston
4:256
Charlotte Zolotow 2:239

Bishop, Claire Huchet
Edward Ardizzone 3:5
Taro Yashima 4:250

Bisset, Donald J.
Virginia Hamilton 1:104
David Macaulay 3:144

Bitterman, Suzanne
Laurence Pringle 4:177

Black, Irma Simonton
Joan Walsh Anglund 1:20
Marguerite Henry 4:114
Russell Hoban 3:83

Blackstock, Charity
Jean Craighead George 1:91
Leonard Wibberley 3:226

Blaine, Marge
Tobi Tobias 4:215

Blank, Annette C.
Tomie de Paola 4:63

Blaustein, Elliot H.
Jeanne Bendick 5:49
Joanna Cole 5:66

Blishen, Edward
Susan Cooper 4:46
Russell Hoban 3:82
E. Nesbit 3:164
Joan Phipson 5:182
Maurice Sendak 1:170

Bloh, Joseph C.
Leonard Wibberley 3:231

Blos, Joan W.
Lucille Clifton 5:59
Karla Kuskin 4:134, 145

Blount, Margaret
Jean de Brunhoff and Laurent
de Brunhoff 4:27
Kenneth Grahame 5:135
Russell Hoban 3:80
Erich Kästner 4:125
C. S. Lewis 3:134
E. Nesbit 3:162, 164

Blue, Margaret
James Haskins 3:65
Alvin Schwartz 3:189, 191,
192

Blythe, Ronald
Ted Hughes 3:95

Boatwright, Taliaferro
Hester Burton 1:32
Scott Corbett 1:46
K. M. Peyton 3:180
Robb White 3:223

Bodger, Joan H.
L. M. Boston 3:26, 27

Bogart, Gary
Kristin Hunter 3:101

Bogle, Helen
Ezra Jack Keats 1:115

Boisse, Josette A.
Jeanne Bendick 5:43

Bolotin, Susan
Peter Spier 5:228

Bond, Nancy
Jeanne Bendick 5:43

Boone, Joyce
Nancy Willard 5:247

Boston, Howard
Henry Treece 2:188

Boston, Lucy
L. M. Boston 3:20, 28

Bouchard, Lois Kalb
Roald Dahl 1:49

Boudreau, Ingeborg
Tomie de Paola 4:54
Arnold Lobel 5:167
Marilyn Sachs 2:132

Bova, Ben
Ben Bova 3:29

Bowker, Alan
Jeanne Bendick 5:37

Bowker, E.
M. Sasek 4:195

Boye, Inger
Scott Corbett 1:43
Astrid Lindgren 1:138

Boyer, Robert H.
Lloyd Alexander 5:16

Boyle, Helen
Betsy Byars 1:35

Boylston, Helen Dore
Jeanne Bendick 5:35

Bradley, Lynn
Norma Klein 2:97
Karla Kuskin 4:143

Bradshaw, V. A.
Arnold Lobel 5:163

Brady, Charles A.
C. S. Lewis 3:135

Braybrooke, Neville
Kenneth Grahame 5:112

Bregman, Alice Miller
Jean Craighead George 1:90
M. B. Goffstein 3:62
E. L. Konigsburg 1:122
Brian Wildsmith 2:212

Brenner, Barbara
Laurence Pringle 4:183

Brewer, Joan Scherer
Tobi Tobias 4:217

Brien, Alan
Jean de Brunhoff and Laurent
de Brunhoff 4:24

Britton, Barbara
Joan Phipson 5:183

Broderick, Dorothy M.
William H. Armstrong 1:24
Judy Blume 2:16, 19
Michael Bond 1:28
Meindert DeJong 1:60
Sid Fleischman 1:73, 75
Paula Fox 1:76, 81
Jean Fritz 2:80
Virginia Hamilton 1:106
Irene Hunt 1:110
E. L. Konigsburg 1:119

Brody, Julia Jussim
Meindert DeJong 1:56

Brogan, Helen M.
Meindert DeJong 1:60
Astrid Lindgren 1:135
Reiner Zimnik 3:243

Brophy, Brigid
Louisa May Alcott 1:10

Brotman, Sonia
Ben Bova 3:32, 35

Broughton, Glenda
Tomie de Paola 4:63

Brown, Dee
James Houston 3:86

Brown, Karen
Byrd Baylor 3:17
John Steptoe 2:163

Brown, Margaret Warren
Jeanne Bendick and Barbara
Berk 5:39
Eleanor Cameron 1:40
Scott Corbett 1:44
Theodor Seuss Geisel 1:85
Edward Lear 1:127
Astrid Lindgren 1:138
Millicent E. Selsam 1:164, 166
Peter Spier 5:217
Dorothy Sterling 1:178
Tomi Ungerer 3:202
Harvey Weiss 4:223
Barbara Willard 2:217

Brown, Patricia Mahoney
John Langstaff 3:112

Brown, Ralph Adams
Walter Dean Myers 4:157

Browne, Kicki Moxon
Chris Van Allsburg 5:239

Buck, Ruth Moss
Karla Kuskin 4:136, 137

Buckmaster, Henrietta
Ian Serraillier 2:138

Budd, Susan M.
Ivan Southall 2:150, 151

Buell, Ellen Lewis
Lloyd Alexander 5:18
Joan Walsh Anglund 1:19, 21
Edward Ardizzone 3:6, 8
Jeanne Bendick 5:36, 37, 38
Michael Bond 1:29
Jean de Brunhoff and Laurent
de Brunhoff 4:34
Beverly Cleary 2:45, 46, 47,
48
Elizabeth Coatsworth 2:57, 60
Meindert DeJong 1:61
Elizabeth Enright 4:75, 76
Eleanor Estes 2:73
Wanda Gág 4:94
Theodor Seuss Geisel 1:88
Shirley Glubok 1:98
Kenneth Grahame 5:135
Virginia Hamilton 1:103
Marguerite Henry 4:109, 110,
113, 113
Erich Kästner 4:124
Karla Kuskin 4:137
John Langstaff 3:109
Robert Lawson 2:109
Madeleine L'Engle 1:132, 133
Seon Manley 3:145, 148
Scott O'Dell 1:147
H. A. Rey and Margret Rey
5:194, 195, 196, 196, 196,
197, 198, 198
M. Sasek 4:188, 189
Dorothy Sterling 1:179
Rosemary Sutcliff 1:186
P. L. Travers 2:179
Edwin Tunis 2:192
Tomi Ungerer 3:203, 204
Jill Paton Walsh 2:199, 201
Harvey Weiss 4:219, 222

Leonard Wibberley 3:224
Laura Ingalls Wilder 2:206
Maia Wojciechowska 1:197

Bull, Ruth P.
Jeanne Bendick and Marian
Warren 5:41

Bulman, Learned T.
Edwin Tunis 2:192

Burch, Robert
Ivan Southall 2:154

Burger, Marjorie
Elizabeth Coatsworth 2:58
Eleanor Estes 2:73

Burger, Nash K.
Jean Fritz 2:82
David Macaulay 3:141
Edwin Tunis 2:195

Burns, Mary M.
Joan Aiken 1:7
Lloyd Alexander 1:18
Bernard Ashley 4:16
Nina Bawden 2:10
Byrd Baylor 3:14
Judy Blume 2:18
Michael Bond 1:28
Hester Burton 1:33
Eleanor Cameron 1:40
Lucille Clifton 5:54
Susan Cooper 4:47
Scott Corbett 1:45
Tomie de Paola 4:58, 63
Sylvia Louise Engdahl 2:70
John D. Fitzgerald 1:69, 70
Sid Fleischman 1:75
Shirley Glubok 1:99
M. B. Goffstein 3:60
Bette Greene 2:86
Eloise Greenfield and Lessie
Jones Little 4:101
Maria Gripe 5:142
Yuri Korinetz 4:130
Jill Krementz 5:155
Robert Lawson 2:107, 108
Arnold Lobel 5:171, 172, 173,
176
David Macaulay 3:144
Sharon Bell Mathis 3:152
Georgess McHargue 2:119
F. N. Monjo 2:122, 124, 126
Robert C. O'Brien 2:127
Joan Phipson 5:185
D. Manus Pinkwater 4:166
Laurence Pringle 4:180
Marilyn Sachs 2:134
Alvin Schwartz 3:192, 193
Ian Serraillier 2:139
Uri Shulevitz 5:207
Donald J. Sobol 4:210
Ivan Southall 2:155
William Steig 2:160
Dorothy Sterling 1:181
Tobi Tobias 4:215
Chris Van Allsburg 5:240
Jill Paton Walsh 2:201
Clyde Watson 3:212
Harvey Weiss 4:228, 229
Leonard Wibberley 3:228, 229
Charlotte Zolotow 2:235

Burns, Paul C.
Marguerite de Angeli 1:52

Burr, Elizabeth
Donald J. Sobol 4:206

Burroughs, Polly
Paula Fox 1:79

Burrows, Alvena Treut
Karla Kuskin 4:137

Burton, Charlotte
Michael Bond 1:30

Burton, Gabrielle
Norma Klein 2:97

Burtt, Kent Garland
Ed Emberley and Barbara
Emberley 5:93
Arnold Lobel 5:165

Bush, Margaret
Daniel Cohen 3:43
Joanna Cole 5:63, 66, 66
Laurence Pringle 4:184
Herbert S. Zim and Lucretia
Krantz 2:231
Charlotte Zolotow 2:236

Bush, Susan
Jeanne Bendick 5:39

Butler, Thomas A.
Harvey Weiss 4:226

Butts, Dennis
K. M. Peyton 3:173

Byars, Betsy
Lloyd Alexander 5:24
Bette Greene 2:85

Byars, Pat
William Steig 2:162

Byler, Mary Gloyne
F. N. Monjo 2:122

Byrd, C. Maxine
Eloise Greenfield 4:99

Camarata, Corinne
Jean de Brunhoff and Laurent
de Brunhoff 4:39
Tobi Tobias 4:216

Cambon, Glauco
Carlo Collodi 5:73

Cameron, Eleanor
Lloyd Alexander 5:15, 20
Susan Cooper 4:45
Roald Dahl 1:49, 50
Elizabeth Enright 4:69, 77
Eleanor Estes 2:77
Louise Fitzhugh 1:71
Wanda Gág 4:85
Nat Hentoff 1:107
Ursula K. Le Guin 3:124
Sharon Bell Mathis 3:152
E. Nesbit 3:166
Beatrix Potter 1:152
John Rowe Townsend 2:172
E. B. White 1:194
Laura Ingalls Wilder 2:203,
205

Campbell, Peter
Edward Ardizzone 3:8

Camper, Shirley
Jean Fritz 2:80

Canavan, Roberta Nolan
Marguerite de Angeli 1:53
Yuri Suhl 2:165

Canham, Patience M.
Eleanor Cameron 1:39
Sylvia Louise Engdahl 2:71
Paula Fox 1:77
Barbara Willard 2:222

Canoles, Marian
Scott Corbett 1:43

Canzler, Lillian
M. B. Goffstein 3:60

Cape, William
Laurence Pringle 4:181

Carlsen, G. Robert
Sharon Bell Mathis 3:152

Carlson, Dudley Brown
Susan Cooper 4:43

Carr, Marion
Lloyd Alexander 1:16
Maria Gripe 5:148

Carson, Dale
Sharon Bell Mathis 3:150

Cart, Michael
Daniel Cohen 3:41
Virginia Hamilton 1:105
S. E. Hinton 3:72
Georgess McHargue 2:118

Carter, Ann
Ivan Southall 2:155

Castor, Gladys Crofoot
Marguerite Henry 4:111

Catania, Susan
Vicki Cobb 2:65

Cathon, Laura E.
Joan Walsh Anglund 1:20
Scott Corbett 1:46
Theodor Seuss Geisel 1:88
Maurice Sendak 1:170
Rosemary Sutcliff 1:190
Edwin Tunis 2:193

Catton, William B.
Leonard Wibberley 3:227

Causley, Charles
Jeanne Bendick 5:38

Caviston, John F.
T. Ernesto Bethancourt 3:19
James Haskins 3:64, 69

Caywood, Carolyn
Alfred Slote 4:203

Cech, John
Tomie de Paola 4:62
D. Manus Pinkwater 4:170

Cecil, Laura
Joan Phipson 5:184

Chalmers, Patrick R.
Kenneth Grahame 5:131

Chamberlain, Ellen
Roald Dahl 1:50

Chambers, Aidan
Nina Bawden 2:11
L. M. Boston 3:26
S. E. Hinton 3:71
Reiner Zimnik 3:243

Chant, Joy
Peter Spier 5:226

Chatfield, Carol
Scott Corbett 1:45
Theodor Seuss Geisel 1:85

Nonny Hogrogian 2:87
Arnold Lobel 5:168
F. N. Monjo 2:124, 125
Tobi Tobias 4:217

Chatham, Margaret L.
Joanna Cole 5:68
Karla Kuskin 4:143
Alfred Slote 4:202, 203

Cheney, Frances Nell
Richard Scarry 3:186

Cheuse, Alan
Byrd Baylor 3:18
Virginia Driving Hawk Sneve
2:145

Chin, Frank
Laurence Yep 3:238

Cianciolo, Patricia Jean
Meindert DeJong 1:54

Cimino, Maria
William Pène du Bois 1:63
Robert Lawson 2:109
Taro Yashima 4:251, 253

Claibourne, Louis
K. M. Peyton 3:172

Clark, Bonnie
Jean Little 4:151

Clark, Linda Lawson
Jean Craighead George 1:94
M. B. Goffstein 3:59
Marguerite Henry 4:109

Clark, Maie Wall
Jean Fritz 2:82

Clark, Palmer Price
Beverly Cleary 2:46

Clark, Pat
Taro Yashima 4:250

Clarke, Loretta
Paul Zindel 3:252

Clayton, Walter
Kenneth Grahame 5:130

Cleaver, Pamela T.
Natalie Babbitt 2:7
K. M. Peyton 3:178

Clements, Bruce
John Rowe Townsend 2:174

Clemons, Walter
Maurice Sendak 1:169

Clifton, Fred
Muriel L. Feelings and Tom
Feelings 5:106

Clifton, Lucille
Muriel L. Feelings and Tom
Feelings 5:106

Coatsworth, Elizabeth
Wanda Gág 4:87

Cobb, Jane
Jeanne Bendick 5:35
Elizabeth Coatsworth 2:56
Elizabeth Enright 4:77

Cohen, Merrie Lou
Ted Hughes 3:96

Cohen, Morton N.
Seon Manley 3:148

Cohen, Phyllis
Lloyd Alexander 5:20
Karla Kuskin 4:139

Colbath, Mary Lou
Lloyd Alexander 5:15

Colberg, Donald A.
Daniel Cohen 3:39
James Lincoln Collier 3:48

Cole, Sheila R.
Judith Viorst 3:209

Cole, William
Jose Aruego and Ariane Dewey
5:31
Elizabeth Coatsworth 2:60
Tomie de Paola 4:63
William Pène du Bois 1:62
Ted Hughes 3:93
Dennis Lee 3:116
Alvin Schwartz 3:190, 192
Shel Silverstein 5:209, 210
Peter Spier 5:224
Tomi Ungerer 3:200

Coleman, Jean
Laurence Pringle 4:175

Coleman, John
Edward Ardizzone 3:6
Erich Kästner 4:126
Brian Wildsmith 2:210

Coles, Robert
Nat Hentoff 1:108

Colum, Padraic
Erich Kästner 4:122
Rosemary Sutcliff 1:187

Colverson, S. G.
Harvey Weiss 4:227

Colvin, Marilyn
Tomie de Paola 4:53

Colwell, Eileen H.
Rosemary Sutcliff 1:182
Laura Ingalls Wilder 2:202

Conklin, Gladys
Dorothy Sterling 1:178
Herbert S. Zim 2:227

Conner, John W.
John Donovan 3:55
M. B. Goffstein 3:62
James Haskins 3:64
Ted Hughes 3:94
Jean Little 4:150
K. M. Peyton 3:172, 179
Jill Paton Walsh 2:199
Barbara Wersba 3:219
Robb White 3:221
Maia Wojciechowska 1:196
Paul Zindel 3:249, 250

Connole, John M.
Scott Corbett 1:46
Robb White 3:223

Cooper, B. W.
Beverley Cleary 2:46

Cooper, Ilene
Lucille Clifton 5:60

Cooper, Susan
Bette Greene 2:85
Yuri Korinetz 4:130
Uri Shulevitz 5:206
Leonard Wibberley 3:228

Nancy Willard 5:245

Cooper, Sylvia R.
Georgess McHargue 2:120

Copeland, Hazel
James Haskins 3:64
Sharon Bell Mathis 3:149

Corke, Hilary
Kit Williams 4:231

Cortez, Rochelle
Sharon Bell Mathis 3:150, 152

Cosgrave, Mary Silva
Hester Burton 1:33
Seon Manley 3:146
Donald J. Sobol 4:207
Barbara Wersba 3:216
Barbara Willard 2:222

Coté, Catherine A.
Ed Emberley and Barbara
Emberley 5:99

Cott, Jonathan
P. L. Travers 2:176
Maia Wojciechowska 1:198

Coughlan, Margaret N.
Joan Aiken 1:7
James Houston 3:88
Peter Spier 5:220

Coutard, Vera L.
Shirley Glubok 1:96

Cowen, Robert C.
Millicent E. Selsam 1:160

Cox, Richard W.
Wanda Gág 4:86

Coyle, Cathy S.
Elizabeth Coatsworth 2:53
Norma Klein 2:101

Crago, Hugh
John Christopher 2:37, 38, 40,
41, 42, 43
Patricia Wrightson 4:237

Crago, Maureen
John Christopher 2:37, 40, 43
Patricia Wrightson 4:237

Craig, Patricia
Bernard Ashley 4:15

Craven, Thomas
Wanda Gág 4:91

Crawshaw, Helen B.
Lewis Carroll 2:35
John D. Fitzgerald 1:69
James Houston 3:87
Millicent E. Selsam 1:164
Isaac Bashevis Singer 1:177
Ivan Southall 2:148
Henry Treece 2:183, 186, 189
Brian Wildsmith 2:211

Croome, Lesley
Maria Gripe 5:145

Crossley, Winnifred Moffett
L. M. Boston 3:28

Crossley-Holland, Kevin
E. Nesbit 3:162
Tomi Ungerer 3:200, 205

Crossley-Holland, Ruth
Russell Hoban 3:76

Crouch, Marcus S.
Joan Aiken 1:1
Lloyd Alexander 1:16
Edward Ardizzone 3:2, 5
Nina Bawden 2:12
Michael Bond 1:27
L. M. Boston 3:21
Hester Burton 1:31, 32
John Christopher 2:40
Meindert DeJong 1:62
William Pène du Bois 1:66
Elizabeth Enright 4:72
Wanda Gág 4:83
Maria Gripe 5:145, 146
Russell Hoban 3:81, 82
Tove Jansson 2:91, 92, 93
Madeleine L'Engle 1:134
C. S. Lewis 3:134
Astrid Lindgren 1:135
Arnold Lobel 5:173
David Macaulay 3:141
E. Nesbit 3:155, 165
K. M. Peyton 3:170, 172, 173,
176, 179
Beatrix Potter 1:151
H. A. Rey and Margret Rey
5:190
Ian Serraillier 2:141, 142
Rosemary Sutcliff 1:183, 188,
189
John Rowe Townsend 2:173
P. L. Travers 2:176
Henry Treece 2:182, 183
Leonard Wibberley 3:225
Nancy Willard 5:250
Charlotte Zolotow 2:236

Croxson, Mary
E. Nesbit 3:158

Cullen, Elinor S.
Natalie Babbitt 2:5
Michael Bond 1:27
Betsy Byars 1:36
John D. Fitzgerald 1:69
E. L. Konigsburg 1:119, 121
Madeleine L'Engle 1:130
John Rowe Townsend 2:171
Tomi Ungerer 3:202
Judith Viorst 3:209
Barbara Willard 2:218

Cullinan, Bernice E.
Muriel L. Feelings and Tom
Feelings 5:108
Arnold Lobel 5:162
Shel Silverstein 5:211
Peter Spier 5:217

Culver, Eva
Nancy Willard 5:247

Cummins, Julie
Vicki Cobb 2:64

Cunliffe, John A.
Nonny Hogrogian 2:89
Ezra Jack Keats 1:115
Tomi Ungerer 3:205

Cunningham, Bronnie
Russell Hoban 3:78

Cunningham, Julia
Barbara Wersba 3:218

Cunningham, Richard B.
C. S. Lewis 3:134

Currah, Ann
Tomie de Paola 4:53
Richard Scarry 3:186

Cuts, Patricia M.
William Kurelek 2:103
Astrid Lindgren 1:137

Daane, Jeanette
Judy Blume 2:16

Dahl, Patricia
Nina Bawden 2:15
Henry Treece 2:189

Dalgliesh, Alice
Joan Walsh Anglund 1:19
Nina Bawden 2:14
Jean de Brunhoff and Laurent
de Brunhoff 4:30
Beverly Cleary 2:46, 49
Elizabeth Coatsworth 2:60
Scott Corbett 1:46
Roald Dahl 1:52
William Pène du Bois 1:62
Elizabeth Enright 4:76, 77
Eleanor Estes 2:73
Wanda Gág 4:90
Shirley Glubok 1:95, 98
Marguerite Henry 4:114, 114
Ezra Jack Keats 1:115, 118
Edward Lear 1:128
Seon Manley 3:147
Joan Phipson 5:179
Ellen Raskin 1:157
M. Sasek 4:191, 192, 193
Maurice Sendak 1:171
Donald J. Sobol 4:207
Dorothy Sterling 1:178
P. L. Travers 2:179
Edwin Tunis 2:192
Brian Wildsmith 2:208, 209,
210
Herbert S. Zim 2:232

Dalphin, Marcia
Erich Kästner 4:122

Daltry, Patience M.
Nina Bawden 2:11
Michael Bond 1:29
John Christopher 2:43
Beverly Cleary 2:48, 50
Ed Emberley and Barbara
Emberley 5:96
Eleanor Estes 2:73
Paula Fox 1:79
Irene Hunt 1:109
Ezra Jack Keats 1:117
Marilyn Sachs 2:131, 135
Maurice Sendak 1:168, 173
Donald J. Sobol 4:208, 208
William Steig 2:161
Brian Wildsmith 2:211
Charlotte Zolotow 2:238

Daly, Maureen
M. Sasek 4:192

Dame, Lena
Fernando Krahn 3:105

Daniels, Lee A.
Lucille Clifton 5:56

Danischewsky, Nina
Lloyd Alexander 5:19
Hester Burton 1:33
Elizabeth Coatsworth 2:58

Darch, Marilyn
Ursula K. Le Guin 3:123

Darling, Frances C.
H. A. Rey and Margret Rey
5:195

Darton, F. J. Harvey
Lewis Carroll 2:23

Davidson, Ellen M.
Ed Emberley and Barbara
Emberley 5:99

Davie, Susan
Georgess McHargue 2:120

Davis, Christopher
James Haskins 3:69
Alvin Schwartz 3:189

Davis, Irene
Elizabeth Coatsworth 2:61
Russell Hoban 3:82

Davis, Lavinia R.
Marguerite Henry 4:112, 113
Astrid Lindgren 1:138, 139
Henry Treece 2:188

Davis, Mary Gould
Astrid Lindgren 1:135
E. B. White 1:195

Davis, Thurston N.
Alvin Schwartz 3:191

Dawson, Dorotha
Jeanne Bendick 5:34

Day, Nancy Jane
Dorothy Sterling 1:182

Dean, Leigh
Shel Silverstein 5:212, 212
Patti Stren 5:235

Deg, Margaret
F. N. Monjo 2:121

De Jong, Susan
Laurence Pringle 4:184

De Kay, Ormonde, Jr.
Peter Spier 5:220

De la Mare, Walter
Lewis Carroll 2:22

Deland, Leah
Jean Fritz 2:83

DeLuca, Geraldine
Arnold Lobel 5:157

DeMott, Benjamin
Russell Hoban 3:74

Denis, Sr. M.
Maria Gripe 5:143

De Paola, Tomie
Tomie de Paola 4:50

Dermos, Lavinia C.
Joanna Cole 5:67

DeVinney, Gemma
Ed Emberley and Barbara
Emberley 5:101
Peter Spier 5:226

DeWaard, Cheryl
Ben Bova 3:32

De Wit, Dorothy
Virginia Hamilton 1:105

Dhus, Madge M.
Jill Krementz 5:154

Didzun, V'Anne
David Macaulay 3:141

Diercks, Eileen K.
Patricia Wrightson 4:244

Dietz, Charles R.
Henry Treece 2:190

Digilio, Alice
Shel Silverstein 5:212

Dill, Barbara
Byrd Baylor 3:15
Michael Bond 1:28
Lucille Clifton 5:55, 58
Joanna Cole 5:64
David Macaulay 3:144
Ian Serraillier 2:142

Doak, Elizabeth
Theodor Seuss Geisel 1:88
Taro Yashima 4:253

Dobbins, Elsie T.
Jeanne Bendick 5:37
Eleanor Cameron 1:41
Elizabeth Coatsworth 2:57
H. A. Rey and Margret Rey
5:195
Dorothy Sterling 1:181
Brian Wildsmith 2:210

Dobbins, Janet
Tomie de Paola 4:55

Dodd, Wayne
Laurence Yep 3:238

Dodson, Marguerite A.
Arnold Lobel 5:163
Ian Serraillier 2:143

Dohm, J. H.
Lewis Carroll 2:32

Dohm, Janice H.
Reiner Zimnik 3:243

Domowitz, Janet
Laurence Pringle 4:183

Donelson, Kenneth L.
Paul Zindel 3:244

Donovan, John
Arnold Lobel 5:169

Dooley, Patricia
Arnold Lobel 5:175, 176
Nancy Willard 5:249

Dorsey, Margaret A.
Lloyd Alexander 5:21
William H. Armstrong 1:23
Judy Blume 2:18
Hester Burton 1:31
Betsy Byars 1:36
John Christopher 2:39
Meindert DeJong 1:55
Sylvia Louise Engdahl 2:69
Shirley Glubok 1:97
Nonny Hogrogian 2:90
Ted Hughes 3:93
Tove Jansson 2:95
Ezra Jack Keats 1:116
Madeleine L'Engle 1:132
Marilyn Sachs 2:132, 134
Uri Shulevitz 5:206
Isaac Bashevis Singer 1:174
Ivan Southall 2:153, 156
William Steig 2:160, 161
John Rowe Townsend 2:170

E. B. White 1:196

Doubleday, Richard
Erich Kästner 4:127

Draper, Charlotte W.
Walter Dean Myers 4:158

Dreyer, Sharon Spredemann
Lucille Clifton 5:55
Joanna Cole 5:62
Joan Phipson 5:179

Drummon, A. H., Jr.
Laurence Pringle 4:180

Drysdale, Susan
Scott Corbett 1:45

Dubivsky, Barbara
M. Sasek 4:196

Dudley, Laurie
Joan Walsh Anglund 1:21
Jean de Brunhoff and Laurent
de Brunhoff 4:35
Maurice Sendak 1:171

Duff, Annis
P. L. Travers 2:176
Laura Ingalls Wilder 2:202

Dukler, Margot
H. A. Rey and Margret Rey
5:190

Dunbar, Ernest
Muriel L. Feelings and Tom
Feelings 5:106

Dunn, Dennis
Ted Hughes 3:96

Dunning, D. Covalt
D. Manus Pinkwater and Jill
Pinkwater 4:168

Dunning, Jennifer
Tomie de Paola 4:59, 59
Jane Yolen 4:263

Dunning, Stephen A.
Madeleine L'Engle 1:130

Eager, Edward
E. Nesbit 3:153

Eakin, Mary K.
Edward Ardizzone 3:6

Eaton, Anne Thaxter
Louisa May Alcott 1:9
Jean de Brunhoff and Laurent
de Brunhoff 4:32
Lewis Carroll 2:26
Elizabeth Coatsworth 2:54
Elizabeth Enright 4:71
Wanda Gág 4:89, 90, 90, 91,
93, 93
Erich Kästner 4:123
Edward Lear 1:126
H. A. Rey and Margret Rey
5:192, 193, 194, 194
Laura Ingalls Wilder 2:202

Eaton, Gale
Joan Phipson 5:187

Eaton, Joan M.
Tomie de Paola 4:54

Eble, Mary
Walter Dean Myers 4:155

Edelman, Elaine
Tomie de Paola 4:66

Edmonds, May H.
Alvin Schwartz 3:192

Edwards, Lynn
Lucille Clifton 5:58
Eloise Greenfield 4:99

Egoff, Sheila A.
Sheila Burnford 2:19
Carlo Collodi 5:83
Louise Fitzhugh 1:71
Maria Gripe 5:142
James Houston 3:83, 86
Dennis Lee 3:115
Jean Little 4:146

Ehlert, Alice D.
Tomie de Paola 4:54
Sid Fleischman 1:75
Arnold Lobel 5:171

Eichenberg, Fritz
Wanda Gág 4:93
Arnold Lobel 5:163
H. A. Rey and Margret Rey
5:189

Eifler, Deborah
Jane Yolen 4:257

Eiseman, Alberta
Karla Kuskin 4:138
Madeleine L'Engle 1:131
Astrid Lindgren 1:135

Eisenman, Alvin
Karla Kuskin 4:141
David Macaulay 3:144

Elleman, Barbara
Ed Emberley and Barbara
Emberley 5:100
Norma Klein 2:97
Donald J. Sobol 4:212
Chris Van Allsburg 5:238
Jane Yolen 4:268, 268

Ellison, Shirley
Joan Aiken 1:6
Hester Burton 1:33
Jean Little 4:149

Elman, Richard M.
Isaac Bashevis Singer 1:173

Elmer, Cathleen Burns
Virginia Driving Hawk Sneve
2:144

Elswit, Sharon
Eloise Greenfield 4:101

Emberley, Ed
Ed Emberley and Barbara
Emberley 5:94

Emerson, Sally
Susan Cooper 4:45

Emmens, Carol A.
Alvin Schwartz 3:190, 193

Engel, Marian
Joan Aiken 1:4

English, Betsy
Dennis Lee 3:116

Engstrom, Norman A.
Laurence Pringle 4:182

Enright, Elizabeth
Joan Aiken 1:7
Nina Bawden 2:15

Elizabeth Enright **4**:67
Eleanor Estes **2**:73
Joan Phipson **5**:179, 180

Epstein, Jason
Edwin Tunis **2**:193

Erhard, Sallie Hope
Jeanne Bendick **5**:48

Erisman, Fred
Elizabeth Enright **4**:74

Espinosa, Michael
Tomie de Paola **4**:64

Ethelreda, Sister M., R.S.M.
Alvin Schwartz **3**:191

Evans, Ann
Maria Gripe **5**:148

Evans, Ernestine
Wanda Gág **4**:80, 87
Erich Kästner **4**:123, 125

Exell, Pat
Jean Little **4**:148

Eyre, Frank
L. M. Boston **3**:25
K. M. Peyton **3**:171
John Rowe Townsend **2**:169
P. L. Travers **2**:176
Henry Treece **2**:182

Fabri, Ralph
Harvey Weiss **4**:227

Fadiman, Clifton
Theodor Seuss Geisel **1**:83
Kenneth Grahame **5**:133

Fagan, Esther
Karla Kuskin **4**:143

Fairbanks, A. Harris
Shel Silverstein **5**:210

Fanning, Peter
Bernard Ashley **4**:18
Tomie de Paola **4**:61

Fantastes
Ursula K. Le Guin **3**:119

Farjeon, Eleanor
Edward Ardizzone **3**:7

Farmer, Penelope
Susan Cooper **4**:48
Maria Gripe **5**:144
Russell Hoban **3**:80
E. L. Konigsburg **1**:122
Reiner Zimnik **3**:243

Farquhar, Margaret C.
Millicent E. Selsam **1**:164

Farr, Pamela C.
Jeanne Bendick **5**:34

Farrar, Nancy
Ian Serraillier **2**:140

Farrell, Diane
Joan Aiken **1**:8
Lloyd Alexander **1**:15
Martha Bacon **3**:11
Hester Burton **1**:30
Betsy Byars **1**:37
M. B. Goffstein **3**:59
Virginia Hamilton **1**:106
Erich Kästner **4**:128
Ezra Jack Keats **1**:114
Jean Little **4**:149
K. M. Peyton **3**:177

Isaac Bashevis Singer **1**:176
Rosemary Sutcliff **1**:191
Paul Zindel **3**:250

Fast, Howard
Jean Fritz **2**:80

Fehlig, Teresa Anne
Ed Emberley and Barbara
Emberley **5**:92

Feiffer, Jules
Ellen Raskin **1**:157

Feld, Norma Malina
Tomie de Paola **4**:57

Feldman, Irving
Isaac Bashevis Singer **1**:177

Fenner, Phyllis
Meindert DeJong **1**:59
Robert Lawson **2**:109

Fenton, Edward
Maia Wojciechowska **1**:199

Ferris, Helen
Wanda Gág **4**:89

Fesler, Elma
Jose Aruego **5**:27

Fiant, Elena
Beverly Cleary **2**:48

Field, Carolyn W.
Donald J. Sobol **4**:207
Rosemary Sutcliff **1**:189

Field, Colin
L. M. Boston **3**:28

Field, Rachel
Wanda Gág **4**:89, 89

Figueroa, Carmen D.
T. Ernesto Bethancourt **3**:20

Fischer, Marjorie
Elizabeth Enright **4**:76
Erich Kästner **4**:125
Robert Lawson **2**:110
Robb White **3**:220

Fish, Alphoretta
Millicent E. Selsam **1**:163
Herbert S. Zim **2**:230

Fish, Mary Ann
Jose Aruego and Ariane
Aruego **5**:30

Fisher, Margery
Lloyd Alexander **5**:16, 18, 19,
19
Edward Ardizzone **3**:6
Bernard Ashley **4**:15, 16, 17
Natalie Babbitt **2**:7
Nina Bawden **2**:11, 13
Jeanne Bendick **5**:41, 42, 42
Jean de Brunhoff and Laurent
de Brunhoff **4**:27, 31, 35,
35, 39
Lewis Carroll **2**:31, 36
John Christopher **2**:44
Beverly Cleary **2**:46, 47, 49,
50
Vicki Cobb **2**:67
Carlo Collodi **5**:80
Susan Cooper **4**:42, 46, 47, 48
Tomie de Paola **4**:57
Elizabeth Enright **4**:68, 70
Eleanor Estes **2**:73, 75, 77
Wanda Gág **4**:89

Kenneth Grahame **5**:132
Maria Gripe **5**:143, 144, 147,
147, 148
Marguerite Henry **4**:114
S. E. Hinton **3**:72
Russell Hoban **3**:81
Nonny Hogrogian **2**:89
James Houston **3**:87
Ted Hughes **3**:92, 93
Tove Jansson **2**:91, 92
Erich Kästner **4**:122
Norma Klein **2**:100
Yuri Korinetz **4**:130, 131
Robert Lawson **2**:109, 111
Ursula K. Le Guin **3**:123
C. S. Lewis **3**:135, 136, 137
Arnold Lobel **5**:162, 164, 165,
167, 168, 170, 173, 174
David Macaulay **3**:142
E. Nesbit **3**:165
Robert C. O'Brien **2**:128
K. M. Peyton **3**:173, 178
Joan Phipson **5**:182, 183, 184,
185, 185
H. A. Rey and Margret Rey
5:191
Ian Serraillier **2**:142
Shel Silverstein **5**:210, 211
Ivan Southall **2**:153, 155
Peter Spier **5**:215, 217, 220,
223, 226, 228
William Steig **2**:162
Yuri Suhl **2**:166
John Rowe Townsend **2**:173,
175
P. L. Travers **2**:175, 178
Henry Treece **2**:180, 184, 187
Tomi Ungerer **3**:200, 204
Laura Ingalls Wilder **2**:204
Barbara Willard **2**:214, 216,
217, 218, 219, 220, 221,
222, 223
Nancy Willard **5**:250
Kit Williams **4**:232
Patricia Wrightson **4**:236, 241,
242, 243, 245, 245, 247
Taro Yashima **4**:253
Jane Yolen **4**:261

Flaherty, Joe
Tomi Ungerer **3**:201

Flanagan, Kate M.
Walter Dean Myers **4**:159
Peter Spier **5**:229

Fleeson, William
Herbert S. Zim **2**:229

Fleming, Alice
E. L. Konigsburg **1**:120

Fleming, Frances
Leonard Wibberley **3**:231

Fleming, Thomas
S. E. Hinton **3**:70

Flowers, Ann A.
Lloyd Alexander **5**:23
T. Ernesto Bethancourt **3**:19
Joanna Cole **5**:175
Susan Cooper **4**:48
Tomie de Paola **4**:65
Arnold Lobel **5**:175
Joan Phipson **5**:186
Patricia Wrightson **4**:246

Flynn, Anne M.
Kit Williams **4**:233

Folcarelli, Ralph J.
Ben Bova **3**:34

Foley, F. W.
John Christopher **2**:41

Foner, Eric
Julius Lester **2**:113

Foote, Timothy
Ed Emberley and Barbara
Emberley **5**:98
William Kurelek **2**:102
P. L. Travers **2**:178

Foreman, Stephen Howard
Ted Hughes **3**:96

Forman, Jack
John Christopher **2**:44
James Lincoln Collier **3**:48
James Haskins **3**:68
Nat Hentoff **1**:108

Forman, James
Scott O'Dell **1**:148

Forman, William M.
Dorothy Sterling **1**:180

Fortier, Ovide V.
Sylvia Louise Engdahl **2**:71

Foster, Frances
Nina Bawden **2**:14

Foster, Thomas
Millicent E. Selsam **1**:159

Fox, Geoffrey
Ivan Southall **2**:145, 149, 151,
152, 154

Fox, Martin
Tomi Ungerer **3**:195

Franklin, K. L.
Ben Bova **3**:36
Alfred Slote **4**:198

Freeman, Donald
Theodor Seuss Geisel **1**:84

Freeman, Ruth S.
Theodor Seuss Geisel **1**:83
Edward Lear **1**:126
Beatrix Potter **1**:152

Fremont-Smith, Eliot
William Kurelek **2**:102
Arnold Lobel **5**:171
David Macaulay **3**:141
Richard Scarry **3**:186
Isaac Bashevis Singer **1**:175
William Steig **2**:160
Tomi Ungerer **3**:200

French, Janet D.
Meindert DeJong **1**:56
Tomie de Paola **4**:65
John D. Fitzgerald **1**:70
Ellen Raskin **1**:157
Alfred Slote **4**:198
Patti Stren **5**:232
Barbara Wersba **3**:218
Charlotte Zolotow **2**:237

Fretz, Sada
Joan Walsh Anglund **1**:21
Jean Craighead George **1**:91
Nonny Hogrogian **2**:89
Ursula K. Le Guin **3**:123

Isaac Bashevis Singer 1:174

Friesem, Rebecca Ricky
Isaac Bashevis Singer 1:173
Yuri Suhl 2:166

Fritz, Jean
Lloyd Alexander 1:13, 15, 16,
17; 5:23, 24
Natalie Babbitt 2:6
Nina Bawden 2:12
Betsy Byars 1:36
Meindert DeJong 1:55, 58
Eleanor Estes 2:76
Scott O'Dell 1:148
Marilyn Sachs 2:134
Maia Wojciechowska 1:198,
200

Fry, Donald K.
Elizabeth Coatsworth 2:63
Jane Yolen 4:269

Fuerst, Julia B.
Jean Little 4:152

Fuller, Edmund
Elizabeth Coatsworth 2:61
Donald J. Sobol 4:206

Fuller, Helen
Joan Walsh Anglund 1:20

Fuller, Hoyt W.
Lucille Clifton 5:53

Fuller, John
Russell Hoban 3:76
Yuri Korinetz 4:130
P. L. Travers 2:178
Tomi Ungerer 3:205

Gág, Wanda
Wanda Gág 4:79

Gagné, Sarah
Joanna Cole 5:66, 67
Laurence Pringle 4:181, 182,
185

Gallant, Charlotte A.
Henry Treece and Ewart
Oakeshott 2:184

Gallivan, Marion F. Van Orsdale
Herbert S. Zim 2:233

Galt, Phyllis
Jean Fritz 2:79
F. N. Monjo 2:124
Peter Spier 5:223

Gannon, Susan R.
Carlo Collodi 5:80, 81

Garden, Nancy
Virginia Hamilton 1:105
Jean Little 4:150

Gardin, Martha L.
Ian Serraillier 2:141

Gardner, Jane E.
Daniel Cohen 3:42
Laurence Yep 3:238

Gardner, John
Chris Van Allsburg 5:239

Gardner, Marilyn
Irene Hunt 1:111
Barbara Willard 2:216
Jane Yolen 4:259

Gardner, Martin
Lewis Carroll 2:24

Gardner, Richard A.
James Lincoln Collier 3:45

Garey, Dorothy
Astrid Lindgren 1:138

Garfield, Leon
David Macaulay 3:141
K. M. Peyton 3:173
John Rowe Townsend 2:170

Garraty, John A.
Leonard Wibberley 3:233

Garrett, Pat
Brian Wildsmith 2:208, 211

Garside, Edward B.
Shirley Glubok 1:100

Gaugh, Patricia Lee
Walter Dean Myers 4:159

Geller, Evelyn
William H. Armstrong 1:24
M. B. Goffstein 3:59, 61
Julius Lester 2:114

Gellert, Roger
Bernard Ashley 4:15

Geniesse, Jane
D. Manus Pinkwater 4:163

Gentleman, David
Tomi Ungerer 3:201

Georgiou, Constantine
Louisa May Alcott 1:11
Lloyd Alexander 1:12
Sheila Burnford 2:20
Lewis Carroll 2:27
Beverly Cleary 2:47, 48
Elizabeth Coatsworth 2:54, 58
Roald Dahl 1:50, 52
Marguerite de Angeli 1:53
Elizabeth Enright 4:72
Louise Fitzhugh 1:72
Jean Fritz 2:80
James Houston 3:87
Irene Hunt 1:111
John Langstaff 3:110
Robert Lawson 2:110
Madeleine L'Engle 1:134
A. A. Milne 1:141
Scott O'Dell 1:147
Beatrix Potter 1:153
Maurice Sendak 1:168, 172
Rosemary Sutcliff 1:191
E. B. White 1:194
Laura Ingalls Wilder 2:203
Brian Wildsmith 2:208

Gerhardt, Lillian N.
Joan Aiken 1:2
Lloyd Alexander 1:15; 5:20,
20, 21, 22
Mitsumasa Anno 2:1
Beverly Cleary 2:51
James Lincoln Collier 3:49
Meindert DeJong 1:58
Eleanor Estes 2:75
Maria Gripe 5:144
S. E. Hinton 3:70
Irene Hunt 1:109
Ezra Jack Keats 1:114, 117
Fernando Krahn 3:106
Richard Scarry 3:187
Ian Serraillier 2:142
Uri Shulevitz 5:202
Brian Wildsmith 2:213

Geringer, Laura
Jill Krementz 5:154

Gersoni-Edelman, Diane
Lloyd Alexander 1:15
William H. Armstrong 1:23, 24
Jeanne Bendick 5:45
Lucille Clifton 5:54, 54
Nat Hentoff 1:107, 108
Russell Hoban 3:76, 82
Nonny Hogrogian 2:87
Norma Klein 2:98
Julius Lester 2:113
Ellen Raskin 1:157
William Steig 2:159
John Steptoe 2:164
John Rowe Townsend 2:174
Tomi Ungerer 3:203
Judith Viorst 3:207
Barbara Wersba 3:217

Gersoni-Stavn, Diane
See Gersoni-Edelman, Diane

Gibbons, Stella
C. S. Lewis 3:127

Gibson, Barbara
Daniel Cohen 3:37
Brian Wildsmith 2:210

Gibson, Walker
Elizabeth Coatsworth 2:62
Russell Hoban 3:82
Ian Serraillier 2:136

Gilderdale, Betty
Patricia Wrightson 4:239

Gilfond, Henry
Shirley Glubok 1:95
Jane Yolen 4:258

Gilkerson, Tally
John Langstaff 3:113

Giller, Pamela R.
Joanna Cole 5:64

Gilles, Susanne
Hester Burton 1:32
Charlotte Zolotow 2:235

Gillespie, John T.
Joan Aiken 1:9
Lloyd Alexander 1:15
Sheila Burnford 2:19
Beverly Cleary 2:46
Scott Corbett 1:46
Roald Dahl 1:49
Meindert DeJong 1:58
William Pène du Bois 1:66
Eleanor Estes 2:74
Louise Fitzhugh 1:71
Paula Fox 1:78
Jean Craighead George 1:92
Virginia Hamilton 1:107
Irene Hunt 1:109
E. L. Konigsburg 1:120
Robert Lawson 2:111
Madeleine L'Engle 1:132, 134
Astrid Lindgren 1:138
Seon Manley 3:148
Scott O'Dell 1:147
Ivan Southall 2:154
John Rowe Townsend 2:174
P. L. Travers 2:178
Henry Treece 2:183
E. B. White 1:194, 195
Laura Ingalls Wilder 2:207

Maia Wojciechowska 1:199

Gillis, Elizabeth
Joanna Cole and Madeleine
Edmondson 5:62
Tomie de Paola 4:59

Girson, Rochelle
Theodor Seuss Geisel 1:87

Glaser, Eleanor
Lewis Carroll 2:34
Arnold Lobel 5:166
Laurence Pringle 4:175
Judith Viorst 3:210
Brian Wildsmith 2:213

Glastonbury, Marion
Yuri Korinetz 4:130, 131
E. B. White 1:193, 195
Jane Yolen 4:264

Glazer, Suzanne M.
Theodor Seuss Geisel 1:85

Gleason, George
Laurence Pringle 4:178, 183,
184
Millicent E. Selsam 1:160
Edwin Tunis 2:194

Glixon, David M.
Richard Scarry 3:186

Glueck, Grace H.
Lewis Carroll 2:34
M. Sasek 4:192

Goddard, Donald
Ben Bova 3:34

Goddard, Rosalind K.
Lucille Clifton 5:56
Bette Greene 2:85
Julius Lester 2:113

Godley, Eveline C.
E. Nesbit 3:161

Goldberg, Lazar
Tomie de Paola 4:60

Goldberger, Judith
Tobi Tobias 4:218

Goodman, Ellen
Beverly Cleary 2:50
Scott Corbett 1:43
Donald J. Sobol 4:208

Goodwin, June
Lloyd Alexander 1:13; 5:22
Isaac Bashevis Singer 1:176

Goodwin, Polly
Edward Ardizzone 3:6
Byrd Baylor 3:16
Eleanor Cameron 1:40
Elizabeth Coatsworth 2:54
Meindert DeJong 1:59
William Pène du Bois 1:64, 66
Ed Emberley and Barbara
Emberley 5:96
John D. Fitzgerald 1:69
Paula Fox 1:81
Jean Fritz 2:80
Jean Craighead George 1:34
Shirley Glubok 1:99, 101
M. B. Goffstein 3:58
Marguerite Henry 4:113, 113
Ted Hughes 3:93
Kristin Hunter 3:101
E. L. Konigsburg 1:120

Karla Kuskin 4:136
John Langstaff 3:111
Madeleine L'Engle 1:130
Astrid Lindgren 1:136
Jean Little 4:149
Seon Manley 3:145, 146
F. N. Monjo 2:121, 122
Scott O'Dell 1:145
M. Sasek 4:189, 192, 194
Isaac Bashevis Singer 1:174, 175
William Steig 2:161
John Steptoe 2:164
Tomi Ungerer 3:201
Harvey Weiss 4:222, 224
Barbara Wersba 3:216
Brian Wildsmith 2:209, 212
Maia Wojciechowska 1:197, 199
Jane Yolen 4:258

Goonan, Thomas
Jeanne Bendick and Marcia Levin 5:39

Gordon, Anitra
Daniel Cohen 3:42
Shirley Glubok 1:101
James Haskins 3:66

Gordon, Cecilia
John Rowe Townsend 2:169

Gottlieb, Annie
Sharon Bell Mathis 3:149

Gottlieb, Gerald
Elizabeth Coatsworth 2:58
Robb White 3:222

Gottlieb, Robin
Nina Bawden 2:12
Jean Craighead George 1:89
Irene Hunt 1:110
Marilyn Sachs 2:134

Gougeon, Gail
Jill KKrementz 5:153

Gough, John
C. S. Lewis 3:133

Graff, Henry F.
Leonard Wibberley 3:227, 231

Graham, Beryl
Eloise Greenfield 4:100

Graham, Eleanor
Jean de Brunhoff and Laurent de Brunhoff 4:20
Kenneth Grahame 5:120
C. S. Lewis 3:135

Graham, Tricia
Laurence Pringle 4:179

Grave, Elizabeth F.
Millicent E. Selsam 1:160
Barbara Willard 2:217

Graves, Elizabeth Minot
Edward Ardizzone 3:9
Eleanor Cameron 1:39
Elizabeth Coatsworth 2:60
James Houston 3:86
Kristin Hunter 3:99
Sharon Bell Mathis 3:151
Uri Shulevitz 5:204
Charlotte Zolotow 2:237

Gray, Dorothy
Eleanor Cameron 1:42

Gray, Hildagarde
Bernard Ashley 4:15
Maria Gripe 5:149

Gray, Mrs. John G.
Joan Aiken 1:3
Eleanor Cameron 1:41
Daniel Cohen 3:42, 43
Paula Fox 1:76
Jean Craighead George 1:91
James Haskins 3:63, 66, 68
Kristin Hunter 3:99
Madeleine L'Engle 1:132
Walter Dean Myers 4:156
Dorothy Sterling 1:180
Barbara Wersba 3:216
Robb White 3:222

Green, Candida Lycett
Ed Emberley and Barbara Emberley 5:96

Green, Peter
Kenneth Grahame 5:114, 135
A. A. Milne 1:142

Green, Rayna
John Langstaff and Carol Langstaff 3:112
Alvin Schwartz 3:193

Green, Roger Lancelyn
Lewis Carroll 2:26, 34
Kenneth Grahame 5:113
Edward Lear 1:125
C. S. Lewis 3:128
A. A. Milne 1:141
E. Nesbit 3:157
Rosemary Sutcliff 1:188
P. L. Travers 2:176

Green, William H.
Seon Manley and Gogo Lewis 3:145
Nancy Willard 5:246
Laurence Yep 3:239

Greene, Graham
Beatrix Potter 1:151

Greenfield, Eloise
Eloise Greenfield 4:95
Sharon Bell Mathis 3:152

Greenfield, Josh
Paul Zindel 3:249

Greenlaw, M. Jean
Lloyd Alexander 5:25

Greenspun, Roger
Sid Fleischman 1:74

Greenwood, Anne
Ed Emberley and Barbara Emberley 5:97

Gregory, Helen
Bernard Ashley 4:18
Susan Cooper 4:49
Tomie de Paola 4:63
Ed Emberley and Barbara Emberley 5:98
Tobi Tobias 4:215

Gremillion, Virginia
Tomie de Paola 4:65

Griffin, John Howard
Julius Lester 2:114

Griffin, Nancy
Walter Dean Myers 4:156
Ellen Raskin 1:157

Marilyn Sachs 2:133, 135
Ivan Southall 2:151

Grimes, Nikki
T. Ernesto Bethancourt 3:19
Lucille Clifton 5:58
James Haskins 3:65

Gripe, Maria
Maria Gripe 5:137

Grnya, Marge
James Houston 3:86

Gruen, John
Ed Emberley and Barbara Emberley 5:96
Peter Spier 5:215
Tomi Ungerer 3:195

Gualtieri, Devlin M.
H. A. Rey and Margret Rey 5:197

Guiney, Elizabeth M.
Henry Treece 2:188

Gunzenhauser, Dorothy
Karla Kuskin 4:140

Haakonsen, Harry O.
Jeanne Bendick 5:45

Haas, Diane
James Lincoln Collier 3:46
James Haskins 3:68

Hagliden, Stein
Astrid Lindgren 1:138

Hakadan, Elizabeth
Jane Yolen 4:257

Halbreich, Susan T.
William Pène du Bois 1:65

Haley, Beverly A.
Paul Zindel 3:244

Hall, Elizabeth
Judy Blume 2:17
Jill Paton Walsh 2:198

Hall, Elvajean
Astrid Lindgren 1:140

Hall, Joan Joffe
Seon Manley and Gogo Lewis 3:146

Hall, Lynn
William H. Armstrong 1:23

Haman, A. C.
Jose Aruego 5:28
Joanna Cole and Madeleine Edmondson 5:62
Laurence Pringle 4:177

Hambleton, Alixe E.
Patti Stren 5:231

Hamilton, Clayton
Kenneth Grahame 5:110

Hamilton, Virginia
Alfred Slote 4:203

Hamley, Dennis
Yuri Korinetz 4:131

Hamlin, Marjorie D.
Lloyd Alexander 1:15; 5:21

Hammel, Lisa
Byrd Baylor 3:16
John Christopher 2:40
Peter Spier 5:220, 221

Hammond, Kristin E.
Norma Klein 2:98

Hanely, Karen Stang
Jane Yolen 4:268

Hanley, Wayne
Jeanne Bendick 5:46, 50
Daniel Cohen 3:38
Laurence Pringle 4:184

Hannabuss, C. Stuart
Meindert DeJong 1:56
Sylvia Louise Engdahl 2:70
Paula Fox 1:81
Bette Green 2:86
Russell Hoban 3:82
Ursula K. Le Guin 3:123, 125
Ian Serraillier 2:139
Jill Paton Walsh 2:198, 200
Patricia Wrightson 4:244

Hannam, Charles
David Macaulay 3:144

Hanratty, Jerome
Elizabeth Enright 4:72

Harada, Violet H.
Jane Yolen 4:265

Hardcastle, Barbara
F. N. Monjo 2:122

Hardee, Ethel R.
Byrd Baylor 3:17

Hardendorff, Jeanne B.
Sid Fleischman 1:75

Hardy, Melody E.
Kristin Hunter 3:102

Harmon, Elva
Ted Hughes 3:93
E. L. Konigsburg 1:120
Arnold Lobel 5:164

Harrington, Pat
Joanna Cole 5:66

Harrington, Patricia G.
Millicent E. Selsam 1:165

Harris, Janet
Sharon Bell Mathis 3:151

Harris, Karen H.
Lloyd Alexander 5:24
Tomie de Paola 4:66
Maria Gripe 5:145
Joan Phipson 5:181
H. A. Rey and Margret Rey 5:194
Barbara Wersba 3:216

Harsh, Donna
Nancy Willard 5:247

Haskell, Ann S.
D. Manus Pinkwater 4:161

Haskins, James S.
Walter Dean Myers 4:159

Hautzig, Esther
Meindert DeJong 1:60

Haviland, Virginia
Joan Aiken 1:2, 3, 6
Lloyd Alexander 1:14
Joan Walsh Anglund 1:20
Mitsumasa Anno 2:2
Edward Ardizzone 3:7
Natalie Babbitt 2:6, 7
Nina Bawden 2:15

Critic Index

Byrd Baylor 3:14
Jeanne Bendick 5:38
Michael Bond 1:27, 29, 30
L. M. Boston 3:29
Hester Burton 1:31
Betsy Byars 1:38
Eleanor Cameron 1:41, 42
John Christopher 2:38
Elizabeth Coatsworth 2:62, 63, 64
James Lincoln Collier and Christopher Collier 3:47
Susan Cooper 4:45
Scott Corbett 1:44, 45, 46, 47
Roald Dahl 1:52
Meindert DeJong 1:55, 57, 59, 60
John Donovan 3:51
William Pène du Bois 1:62, 65
Ed Emberley and Barbara Emberley 5:92, 95, 96, 96
Muriel L. Feelings and Tom Feelings 5:105
Sid Fleischman 1:74
Paula Fox 1:76, 79
Jean Fritz 2:79
Jean Craighead George 1:90, 92
Shirley Glubok 1:98, 99, 100
Eloise Greenfield 4:99
Virginia Hamilton 1:103, 107
Russell Hoban 3:76
Nonny Hogrogian 2:89
James Houston 3:86, 87
Ted Hughes 3:93
Tove Jansson 2:94
Ezra Jack Keats 1:116, 118
E. L. Konigsburg 1:119
Karla Kuskin 4:135, 138
John Langstaff 3:109, 110
Robert Lawson 2:110
Julius Lester 2:113
C. S. Lewis 3:137
Astrid Lindgren 1:136,137
Jean Little 4:150, 150, 151
Arnold Lobel 5:165, 168
Georgess McHargue 2:120
F. N. Monjo 2:121, 123
Scott O'Dell 1:146
K. M. Peyton 3:173
Ellen Raskin 1:156
H. A. Rey and Margret Rey 5:199
Marilyn Sachs 2:133
M. Sasek 4:189, 192, 192
Millicent E. Selsam 1:160
Maurice Sendak 1:167, 170, 172
Ian Serraillier 2:135
Uri Shulevitz 5:206
Donald J. Sobol 4:206
Ivan Southall 2:157
Peter Spier 5:218, 218
William Steig 2:158
Dorothy Sterling 1:178, 179
Dorothy Sterling and Benjamin Quarles 1:179
Yuri Suhl 2:166
Rosemary Sutcliff 1:184, 189, 190, 191
John Rowe Townsend 2:174
P. L. Travers 2:179

Edwin Tunis 2:191, 192, 193, 194
Clyde Watson 3:213
Harvey Weiss 4:221, 229
Barbara Wersba 3:217
Leonard Wibberley 3:224, 225, 226, 228, 230
Laura Ingalls Wilder 2:205, 206
Brian Wildsmith 2:210, 212
Barbara Willard 2:217, 223
Patricia Wrightson 4:241, 244
Taro Yashima 4:251, 254
Jane Yolen 4:259
Jane Yolen and Anne Huston 4:256
Herbert S. Zim 2:225, 227, 230, 231
Reiner Zimnik 3:242
Charlotte Zolotow 2:235

Hayes, Sarah
Madeleine L'Engle 1:133

Haynes, Elizabeth
Betsy Byars 1:37
John Christopher 2:38, 42
Sylvia Louise Engdahl 2:69, 70, 71

Haynes, John
Ivan Southall 2:154
Patricia Wrightson 4:243

Hazard, Paul
Lewis Carroll 2:31
Carlo Collodi 5:70

Hearn, Michael Patrick
Nancy Willard 5:250

Hearne, Betsy
Natalie Babbitt 2:8
Lucille Clifton 5:55, 57
Elizabeth Coatsworth 2:60
Norma Klein 2:101
Jill Krementz 5:156
Nancy Willard 5:248, 250
Patricia Wrightson 4:247

Hector, Mary Louise
Madeleine L'Engle 1:130
Astrid Lindgren 1:137
Ian Serraillier 2:138, 143

Heffernan, Tom
Ivan Southall 2:148

Heide, Florence
John Steptoe 2:165
Rosemary Sutcliff 1:183

Heifman, Sally
Ed Emberley and Barbara Emberley 5:96

Heilbrun, Carolyn
Louise Fitzhugh 1:72
Nat Hentoff 1:108

Heins, Ethel L.
Joan Aiken 1:2, 4, 8
Lloyd Alexander 1:13, 18; 5:25
Mitsumasa Anno 2:1, 2
Edward Ardizzone 3:6
William H. Armstrong 1:23
Nina Bawden 2:8, 13
Byrd Baylor 3:16
L. M. Boston 3:28
Hester Burton 1:31
Betsy Byars 1:36, 37

Eleanor Cameron 1:40
Beverly Cleary 2:48, 49, 50
Lucille Clifton 5:58
Elizabeth Coatsworth 2:54
Scott Corbett 1:43, 47
Meindert DeJong 1:56
Tomie de Paola 4:61
William Pène du Bois 1:62, 64
Ed Emberley and Barbara Emberley 5:101
Eleanor Estes 2:73, 74
Louise Fitzhugh 1:73
Sid Fleischman 1:73
Paula Fox 1:77, 79
Jean Fritz 2:79, 82
Jean Craighead George 1:89
M. B. Goffstein 3:59
Bette Greene 2:85
Eloise Greenfield 4:97, 103
Virginia Hamilton 1:104
Marguerite Henry 4:114
Nonny Hogrogian 2:89
James Houston 3:85, 86
Ezra Jack Keats 1:113, 116
Norma Klein 2:99
E. L. Konigsburg 1:119
Fernando Krahn 3:106
William Kurelek 2:103
Karla Kuskin 4:138, 141
John Langstaff 3:110
John Langstaff and Nancy Langstaff 3:110
Dennis Lee 3:115
Ursula K. Le Guin 3:124
Arnold Lobel 5:172, 174
David Macaulay 3:140
Sharon Bell Mathis 3:149, 151
A. A. Milne 1:143
F. N. Monjo 2:125
Walter Dean Myers 4:157
Scott O'Dell 1:147
Joan Phipson 5:186
Beatrix Potter 1:153
Ellen Raskin 1:155, 156
Marilyn Sachs 2:133
Maurice Sendak 1:168
Peter Spier 5:219, 220, 224
William Steig 2:160, 162
John Steptoe 2:164
Henry Treece 2:185
Tomi Ungerer 3:203
Jill Paton Walsh 2:197, 199
Clyde Watson 3:213
Barbara Wersba 3:218
Brian Wildsmith 2:212
Patricia Wrightson 4:244
Jane Yolen 4:266

Heins, Paul
Joan Aiken 1:4, 5
Lloyd Alexander 1:15, 16; 5:26
Edward Ardizzone 3:8
William H. Armstrong 1:25
Natalie Babbitt 2:5
Martha Bacon 3:11
T. Ernesto Bethancourt 3:18
Ben Bova 3:32, 35
Hester Burton 1:32
John Christopher 2:39, 41
Elizabeth Coatsworth 2:57
Carlo Collodi 5:83
Roald Dahl 1:51
Meindert DeJong 1:57

John Donovan 3:54, 55
William Pène du Bois and Lee Po 1:63
Sylvia Louise Engdahl 2:69, 72
Muriel L. Feelings and Tom Feelings 5:107
Paula Fox 1:77, 78, 81
Shirley Glubok 1:97, 100
M. B. Goffstein 3:60
Maria Gripe 5:144, 146, 149
Virginia Hamilton 1:105
Ted Hughes 3:95, 97
Kristin Hunter 3:98
E. L. Konigsburg 1:121, 122
William Kurelek 2:102
John Langstaff 3:111
Dennis Lee 3:116
Ursula K. Le Guin 3:123
Madeleine L'Engle 1:131
Julius Lester 2:114
Arnold Lobel 5:168, 174
David Macaulay 3:143
Georgess McHargue 2:120
Walter Dean Myers 4:156, 160
E. Nesbit 3:162
Robert C. O'Brien 2:129
Scott O'Dell 1:148, 149
Joan Phipson 5:184, 186
Beatrix Potter 1:154
Ellen Raskin 1:155
M. Sasek 4:196
Maurice Sendak 1:168, 170
Ian Serraillier 2:136, 137, 140
Ivan Southall 2:148, 150, 151, 153, 155, 156
Peter Spier 5:223, 226
Dorothy Sterling 1:180
Yuri Suhl 2:166
Rosemary Sutcliff 1:186, 187, 190
John Rowe Townsend 2:170, 171, 173
P. L. Travers 2:177
Henry Treece 2:183, 186, 190, 191
Chris Van Allsburg 5:238
Jill Paton Walsh 2:197, 201
Jill Paton Walsh and Kevin Crossley-Holland 2:201
Harvey Weiss 4:228, 230
Barbara Wersba 3:218
E. B. White 1:196
Robb White 3:221
Patricia Wrightson 4:245
Laurence Yep 3:238
Paul Zindel 3:250

Heisig, James W.
Carlo Collodi 5:77

Hellerich, Janet
Hester Burton 1:31
Charlotte Zolotow 2:238

Hemenway, Leone R.
F. N. Monjo 2:122
Laurence Pringle 4:178
Harvey Weiss 4:225

Henke, James T.
Paul Zindel 3:245

Henniker-Heaton, Peter J.
John Christopher 2:39, 43

Henninge, Rose
Laurence Pringle 4:174

Henry, Marguerite
Marguerite Henry 4:104

Hentoff, Margot
Paula Fox 1:77
Paul Zindel 3:249

Hentoff, Nat
Paula Fox 1:77
S. E. Hinton 3:70
Maurice Sendak 1:167

Herman, Gertrude B.
Joan Walsh Anglund 1:20
Julius Lester 2:112
Jean Little 4:148
M. Sasek 4:187
John Rowe Townsend 2:174
Maia Wojciechowska 1:200
Charlotte Zolotow 2:234

Herr, Marian A.
Beverly Cleary 2:47
Elizabeth Coatsworth 2:59
Marguerite Henry 4:114

Hess, John L.
Vicki Cobb 2:64
Astrid Lindgren 1:139

Heylman, Katherine M.
Jeanne Bendick 5:38
Michael Bond 1:28
Roald Dahl 1:51
Russell Hoban 3:75
Beatrix Potter 1:153
Donald J. Sobol 4:209, 210

Hibberd, Dominic
K. M. Peyton 3:174

Hiesberger, Jean Marie
Shel Silverstein 5:209, 212

Higgins, James E.
C. S. Lewis 3:129

Higgins, Judith
Edward Ardizzone 3:5
Eleanor Cameron 1:41
John D. Fitzgerald 1:69
E. Nesbit 3:165
E. B. White 1:196

Hinckle, Warren
Lewis Carroll 2:34

Hines, Ruth
Marguerite de Angeli 1:52

Hines, Theodore C.
Jeanne Bendick 5:40
Seon Manley and Gogo Lewis
3:148

Hinton, Susan
S. E. Hinton 3:69

Hippenhammer, Craighton
Peter Spier 5:224

Hirsch, Felix E.
Erich Kästner 4:127

Hoag, David G.
Laurence Pringle 4:185

Hoare, Geoffrey
David Macaulay 3:140

Hoban, Russell
Russell Hoban 3:73, 78

Hoberman, Judith Sloane
Robert Lawson 2:110
Julius Lester 2:115

Hodapp, Patricia G.
Ellen Raskin 1:156

Hodgdon, Renarick
Laurence Pringle 4:181

Hodges, Elizabeth
Rosemary Sutcliff 1:188
Henry Treece 2:185, 186
E. B. White 1:195

Hodges, Elizabeth D.
Jean Little 4:147

Hodges, Margaret
Isaac Bashevis Singer 1:177

Hoff, Syd
Betsy Byars 1:35

Hoffman, Lyla
Jane Yolen 4:264

Hofrichter, Ruth J.
Erich Kästner 4:122

Holbrook, David
C. S. Lewis 3:131

Hollindale, Peter
C. S. Lewis 3:132

Hollowood, Jane
John Christopher 2:41

Holtze, Sally Holmes
Maria Gripe 5:145
Jill Krementz 5:152

Holzheimer, Diane
Joanna Cole 5:66, 66
Tomie de Paola 4:57
Laurence Pringle 4:179, 180

Homer, Patricia
Ed Emberley and Barbara
Emberley 5:103

Hood, Eric
Henry Treece 2:187

Hood, Robert
Jean Craighead George 1:92
Madeleine L'Engle 1:129
Scott O'Dell 1:146
Ivan Southall 2:152
Robb White 3:221

Hood, Stuart
John Donovan 3:53

Hooper, Walter
C. S. Lewis 3:129

Hopper, B. J.
Jeanne Bendick 5:37

Horchler, Richard
Jane Yolen 4:260

Hormel, Olive Deane
Ian Serraillier 2:142

Hotelling, Carole
Mitsumasa Anno 2:2

Hough, Carolyn A.
Russell Hoban 3:83

Hough, Marianne
Eleanor Cameron 1:41
Scott Corbett 1:45

Houston, James
Jean Craighead George 1:90

Howard, Richard
Elizabeth Coatsworth 2:62
Karla Kuskin 4:139

Howley, Edith C.
Seon Manley 3:146

Hoyle, Bertrand Gary
Jeanne Bendick 5:50

Hoyt, Olga
Reiner Zimnik 3:243, 244

Hubbard, Henry W.
Jeanne Bendick 5:40
Herbert S. Zim 2:232

Huck, Charlotte S.
Marguerite Henry 4:108
M. Sasek 4:188
Taro Yashima 4:248, 252

Huddleston, Marsha E.
Jeanne Bendick and Robert
Bendick 5:48

Huddy, Mrs. D.
Leonard Wibberley 3:230

Hudson, E.
Jean de Brunhoff and Laurent
de Brunhoff 4:38

Hudson, Edward
Jose Aruego 5:29
Ezra Jack Keats 1:113, 114,
116
Peter Spier 5:221

Hudson, Eric
Michael Bond 1:29
Roald Dahl 1:51

Huff, Stuart
Madeleine L'Engle 1:129

Hugh, Sister Mary
Rosemary Sutcliff 1:187

Hughes, Shirley
Edward Ardizzone 3:9

Hughes, Ted
Ted Hughes 3:89, 90

Hulton, Clara
Georgess McHargue 2:117

Humes, Linda
Eloise Greenfield 4:99

Hungerford, Edward B.
Ian Serraillier 2:137

Hunt, Jacquie
Patti Stren 5:233

Hunter, Charlayne
Jill Krementz 5:150

Hunter, Kristin
Kristin Hunter 3:97, 99

Hunter, Lynn S.
Ed Emberley and Barbara
Emberley 5:100, 102, 103
Harvey Weiss 4:229, 229

Hurley, Beatrice Davis
Herbert S. Zim 2:231

Hurley, Beatrice J.
Wanda Gág 4:82

Hürlimann, Bettina
Jean de Brunhoff and Laurent
de Brunhoff 4:25
Lewis Carroll 2:34
Carlo Collodi 5:71
Tove Jansson 2:92
Erich Kästner 4:117
Maurice Sendak 1:167

P. L. Travers 2:176
Reiner Zimnik 3:241

Hurwitz, Johanna
Nina Bawden 2:14
Elizabeth Coatsworth 2:62

Hyatt, Pat
Uri Shulevitz 5:206

Infantino, Cynthia Percak
Tomie de Paola 4:58

Inglis, Fred
Ted Hughes 3:93

Ingmanson, Dale E.
Laurence Pringle 4:183

Ingram, Phyllis
Tomie de Paola 4:58
Jane Yolen 4:263

Irvine, S.
Arnold Lobel 5:164

Israel, Callie
Jean Little 4:148

Iverson, William J.
Lloyd Alexander 5:22

Izard, Anne
Beverly Cleary 2:50
Meindert DeJong 1:57
Ed Emberley and Barbara
Emberley 5:90
Theodor Seuss Geisel 1:86
Ezra Jack Keats 1:115
Jean Little 4:147
Arnold Lobel 5:165
Marilyn Sachs 2:132
Brian Wildsmith 2:210, 211
Charlotte Zolotow 2:236

Jackel, Susan
Jean Little 4:153

Jackson, Charlotte
Joan Walsh Anglund 1:19, 20
Beverly Cleary 2:46, 51
Scott Corbett 1:44
Jean Craighead George 1:93
P. L. Travers 2:179
Leonard Wibberley 3:227
Brian Wildsmith 2:211

Jackson, Jeff
Jean de Brunhoff and Laurent
de Brunhoff 4:38
Ezra Jack Keats 1:114

Jackson, Shirley
Theodor Seuss Geisel 1:83

Jacobs, William Jay
Madeleine L'Engle 1:134

Jaffee, Cyrisse
M. B. Goffstein 3:58

Jago, Wendy
Ursula K. Le Guin 3:125

James, David L.
Susan Cooper 4:44

James, Miriam
Jean Craighead George 1:93

Jan, Isabelle
Erich Kästner 4:125
Edward Lear 1:126
Laura Ingalls Wilder 2:203

Janeczko, Paul
Barbara Wersba 3:214

Janeway, Elizabeth
Louisa May Alcott 1:9, 10

Jaquith, F. Luree
Joanna Cole 5:65

Jaspersohn, William
Jill Krementz 5:153
Uri Shulevitz 5:207

Jellinek, Roger
M. Sasek 4:194
Ian Serraillier 2:138

Jenkins, Betty Lanier
Eloise Greenfield 4:97
Sharon Bell Mathis 3:151

Jenkins, Miss J. S.
Leonard Wibberley 3:224

Jenkins, Marie M.
Joanna Cole 5:64
Laurence Pringle 4:181

Jennings, Vivien
Maria Gripe 5:147

John, Morley
Barbara Willard 2:223

Johnson, Alexandra
Jane Yolen 4:263

Johnson, Carolyn
Maria Gripe 5:148
Jean Little 4:151

Johnson, Elizabeth
Eleanor Cameron 1:42
Marguerite Henry 4:109
Astrid Lindgren 1:135
Rosemary Sutcliff 1:184

Johnson, Linda
Judy Blume 2:18

Johnson, Marjorie
Eloise Greenfield 4:98

Johnson, Siddie Joe
H. A. Rey and Margret Rey
5:195

Johnston, Ann
Patti Stren 5:230, 232

Johnston, Denis
M. Sasek 4:193

Johnston, Margaret E.
Dennis Lee 3:115

Jonas, Gerald
Ben Bova 3:33
Alfred Slote 4:202

Jones, Darwin
Herbert S. Zim and Lucretia
Krantz 2:226

Jones, Dorothy S.
Leonard Wibberley 3:226

Jones, Helen L.
Robert Lawson 2:108

Jones, Loretta B.
James Lincoln Collier 3:48
Jill Paton Walsh 2:198

Jones, Raymond E.
Tomie de Paola 4:59
Jane Yolen 4:263

Jones, Sarah
Rosemary Sutcliff 1:190

Jones, Trevelyn
Russell Hoban 3:75
Jean Little 4:149
F. N. Monjo 2:121, 124

Jordan, Alice M.
Jean de Brunhoff and Laurent
de Brunhoff 4:33
Elizabeth Coatsworth 2:55
Meindert DeJong 1:57
Marguerite Henry 4:110, 110
H. A. Rey and Margret Rey
5:193, 196

Jordan, Fellis L.
Tomie de Paola 4:66
Donald J. Sobol 4:212

Jordan, June Meyer
William H. Armstrong 1:23
Lucille Clifton 5:54, 55, 55
John Donovan 3:54

Jordan, René
Herbert S. Zim 2:232

Julian, Janet
Walter Dean Myers 4:157

Jussim, Julia
Lloyd Alexander 5:18

K., Marjorie Zaum
Uri Shulevitz 5:202

Kain, Fritz
Jeanne Bendick and Marcia
Levin 5:40
Jeanne Bendick and Leonard
Simon 5:40

Kane, Alice E.
James Houston 3:84

Kane, Henry B.
Jean Craighead George 1:93

Kane, Martha T.
Laurence Pringle 4:182

Kanfer, Stefan
Karla Kuskin 4:143, 144
David Macaulay 3:144
Chris Van Allsburg 5:238, 240

Kanon, Joseph
Lewis Carroll 2:36

Kappas, Katharine H.
Beverly Cleary 2:46

Karesh, Deborah S.
Ed Emberley and Barbara
Emberley 5:99

Karlin, Barbara
T. Ernesto Bethancourt 3:18
David Macaulay 3:144
Richard Scarry 3:183
Donald J. Sobol 4:211
Barbara Wersba 3:220

Karrer, Mary K.
Muriel L. Feelings and Tom
Feelings 5:108
Arnold Lobel 5:162
Shel Silverstein 5:211
Peter Spier 5:217

Katz, William Loren
Julius Lester 2:113

Kaye, Marilyn
Karla Kuskin 4:143
Yuri Suhl 2:165

Keiser, Richard K.
Joanna Cole 5:65

Kelley, Marjorie
Patti Stren 5:232, 233

Kellman, Amy
Lloyd Alexander 1:13, 14, 16
Byrd Baylor 3:15
Betsy Byars 1:37
James Lincoln Collier and
Christopher Collier 3:47
Roald Dahl 1:51
Sid Fleischman 1:73
Virginia Hamilton 1:106
E. L. Konigsburg 1:120, 121
Maurice Sendak 1:169
Alfred Slote 4:200

Kelly, Audrey J.
Jeanne Bendick 5:35

Kelly, Mary Ann
Elizabeth Coatsworth 2:57

Kelly, Therese C.
Dorothy Sterling 1:182
Rosemary Sutcliff 1:190
Leonard Wibberley 3:227

Kemball-Cook, Jessica
John Christopher 2:39, 44
William Pène du Bois 1:65
Sylvia Louise Engdahl 2:70
Robert C. O'Brien 2:129
Paul Zindel 3:251

Kemp, Gene
Robert C. O'Brien 2:127

Kemper, Anne Weaver
Shirley Glubok 1:97

Kennedy, J. P.
Joanna Cole 5:67

Kennedy, Mopsy Strange
Richard Scarry 3:183

Kennedy, X. J.
Shel Silverstein 5:213
Jane Yolen 4:266

Kennerly, Sarah Law
Joan Aiken 1:4
Natalie Babbitt 2:6
Nina Bawden 2:14
Eleanor Cameron 1:40
Scott Corbett 1:43, 47
Sid Fleischman 1:74
Georgess McHargue 2:118
Donald J. Sobol 4:210

Kent, Heddie
Jeanne Bendick 5:46, 47, 49
James Lincoln Collier 3:46
Laurence Pringle 4:178
Harvey Weiss 4:229

Kent, Patt Parsells
Jane Yolen 4:267

Kibel, Alvin C.
Lewis Carroll 2:29, 36

Kieran, Margaret Ford
John Langstaff 3:109

Kilby, Clyde S.
C. S. Lewis 3:126

Kilpatrick, Clayton E.
Hester Burton 1:30
Maia Wojciechowska 1:199

Kimmel, Eric A.
E. L. Konigsburg 1:119
Isaac Bashevis Singer 1:173

Kinchen, Robert
James Lincoln Collier 3:44

King, Cynthia
Jane Yolen 4:262

King, Dorothy M.
Charlotte Zolotow 2:237

King, Martha Bennett
Lloyd Alexander 5:20
Louise Fitzhugh 1:71
Donald J. Sobol 4:209

Kingston, Carolyn T.
Jean Little 4:148

Kingston, Maxine Hong
Laurence Yep 3:235

Kinkead, Katherine T.
H. A. Rey and Margret Rey
5:196

Kinsey, Helen E.
Maurice Sendak 1:169

Kirby, Emma H.
Rosemary Sutcliff 1:186

Kirkland, Frances
Wanda Gág 4:79

Kirkland, Winifred
Wanda Gág 4:79

Klein, Nancy
Beatrix Potter 1:154

Klemin, Diana
Tomi Ungerer 3:204

Kley, Ronald J.
Jeanne Bendick 5:49
Joanna Cole 5:63, 65
James Lincoln Collier 3:46
Laurence Pringle 4:174

Klockner, Karen M.
Jill Krementz 5:153

Kluger, Richard
Arnold Lobel 5:164
Barbara Wersba 3:216
Charlotte Zolotow 2:238

Kolb, Muriel
Elizabeth Coatsworth 2:59

Komaiko, Deborah
Tomie de Paola 4:55

Korn, Barbara
Harvey Weiss 4:225

Kouzel, Daisy
Lewis Carroll 2:35
William Pène du Bois and Lee
Po 1:164
Karla Kuskin 4:141

Krarup, Agnes
Meindert DeJong 1:56

Krensky, Stephen
Peter Spier 5:223

Kronick, Judith S.
Tomie de Paola 4:57
Ezra Jack Keats 1:117
Arnold Lobel 5:168
Judith Viorst 3:209
Nancy Willard 5:247

Kuhn, Doris Young
Elizabeth Coatsworth 2:51
Marguerite Henry 4:108
Taro Yashima 4:252

Kunitz, Isadora
Vicki Cobb 2:66
Daniel Cohen 3:42, 43
James Lincoln Collier 3:45
Herbert S. Zim 2:229
Herbert S. Zim and Sonia
Bleeker 2:228

Kurtz, Nan Pavey
Judy Blume 2:18

Kuskin, Karla
Mitsumasa Anno 2:1
Jose Aruego and Ariane
Aruego 5:30
Byrd Baylor 3:18
Jean de Brunhoff and Laurent
de Brunhoff 4:38
Tomie de Paola 4:55
Ed Emberley and Barbara
Emberley 5:99
M. B. Goffstein 3:59
Norma Klein 2:98
William Kurelek 2:102
Karla Kuskin 4:132
Arnold Lobel 5:176
David Macaulay 3:141
Georgess McHargue 2:120
Uri Shulevitz 5:206
Alfred Slote 4:202
William Steig 2:160, 160
Tomi Ungerer 3:200
Chris Van Allsburg 5:241
Brian Wildsmith 2:213
Jane Yolen 4:263

La Farge, Oliver
Edwin Tunis 2:193

Lampert, Eileen
Ed Emberley and Barbara
Emberley 5:92

Lancaster, Lesley
D. Manus Pinkwater 4:164

Lanes, Selma G.
Lloyd Alexander 1:14, 16
Joan Walsh Anglund 1:18
Natalie Babbitt 2:6
Betsy Byars 1:35
Ed Emberley and Barbara
Emberley 5:90, 100
Theodor Seuss Geisel 1:84
M. B. Goffstein 3:57, 61, 62
Nonny Hogrogian 2:88, 89
Ezra Jack Keats 1:113
William Kurelek 2:104
Arnold Lobel 5:166
Beatrix Potter 1:152
Richard Scarry 3:181, 184
Maurice Sendak 1:167
Uri Shulevitz 5:205
William Steig 2:159
John Steptoe 2:162, 163, 164
Tomi Ungerer 3:196, 200
Clyde Watson 3:212
E. B. White 1:195
Nancy Willard 5:249
Jane Yolen 4:257, 265
Charlotte Zolotow 2:238

Langley, Gene
Ed Emberley and Barbara
Emberley 5:100
D. Manus Pinkwater 4:166

Langton, Jane
Betsy Byars 1:38
Eloise Greenfield 4:97
Virginia Hamilton 1:104
Norma Klein 2:97
Peter Spier 5:225
Patricia Wrightson 4:245
Jane Yolen 4:264

Lantz, Fran
D. Manus Pinkwater 4:169

La Rocque, Geraldine E.
S. E. Hinton 3:71
Madeleine L'Engle 1:131

Larrick, Nancy
Arnold Lobel 5:172
Tobi Tobias 4:216

Lask, Thomas
Ted Hughes 3:94, 95
Edward Lear 1:127
Seon Manley and Gogo Lewis
3:148
A. A. Milne 1:143
Ian Serraillier 2:137

Laski, Audrey
Bernard Ashley 4:15
Maria Gripe 5:139

Last, R. W.
Erich Kästner 4:118

Lathrop, Dorothy P.
Beatrix Potter 1:151

Laurence, Margaret
Jean Little 4:151

Lavender, Carolyn H.
Charlotte Zolotow 2:236

Lavender, Ralph
Jane Yolen 4:264

Lawson, John
Natalie Babbitt 2:7

Lazarus, Keo Felker
Michael Bond 1:30

Lazer, Ellen Abby
Barbara Wersba 3:220

Leach, Edmund
Jean de Brunhoff and Laurent
de Brunhoff 4:22

Learmont, Lavinia Marina
Roald Dahl 1:51
Tove Jansson 2:94
K. M. Peyton 3:177

Lederer, Norman
Dorothy Sterling 1:181

Lee, Dennis
Dennis Lee 3:113

Le Guin, Ursula K.
Sylvia Louise Engdahl 2:69
Ursula K. Le Guin 3:117

Lehmann-Haupt, Christopher
Lucille Clifton 5:58

Lembeck, Carolyn S.
Jill Krementz 5:155

Lembo, Diana
Joan Aiken 1:9
Lloyd Alexander 1:15
Sheila Burnford 2:19
Beverly Cleary 2:46
Scott Corbett 1:46
Roald Dahl 1:49
Meindert DeJong 1:58
William Pène du Bois 1:66
Eleanor Estes 2:74
Louise Fitzhugh 1:71
Paula Fox 1:78
Jean Craighead George 1:92
Virginia Hamilton 1:107
Irene Hunt 1:109
E. L. Konigsburg 1:120
Robert Lawson 2:111
Madeleine L'Engle 1:132, 134
Astrid Lindgren 1:138
Scott O'Dell 1:147
Ivan Southall 2:154
John Rowe Townsend 2:174
P. L. Travers 2:178
E. B. White 1:194, 195
Laura Ingalls Wilder 2:207
Maia Wojciechowska 1:199

L'Engle, Madeleine
K. M. Peyton 3:173
Barbara Wersba 3:218

Lent, Henry B.
Robb White 3:223

Leonberger, Janet
Kristin Hunter 3:102

Leone, Arthur T.
Jill Paton Walsh 2:200

Le Pelley, Guernsey
Theodor Seuss Geisel 1:85
Scott O'Dell 1:146
D. Manus Pinkwater 4:167
Tomi Ungerer 3:200

Lerman, Leo
Elizabeth Enright 4:74

Lester, Julius
Paula Fox 1:80
Eloise Greenfield 4:98
John Steptoe 2:163

Levin, Harry
Lewis Carroll 2:24

Levine, Bernice
Jean Fritz 2:80
Maia Wojciechowska 1:199

Levitas, Gloria
Byrd Baylor 3:13
Georgess McHargue 2:118

Levy, Charlotte C.
John Rowe Townsend 2:170

Levy, Willa M.
Eleanor Estes 2:76

Levy, William Turner
Jean Fritz 2:81

Lewis, C. S.
Kenneth Grahame 5:131
C. S. Lewis 3:125, 135
E. Nesbit 3:161

Lewis, Claudia
William Pène du Bois 1:65

Lewis, Marjorie
Lloyd Alexander 5:23
Lucille Clifton 5:53, 59
Elizabeth Coatsworth 2:53
Tomie de Paola 4:62
John Donovan 3:51
Ed Emberley and Barbara
Emberley 5:96
M. B. Goffstein 3:58
Eloise Greenfield 4:100
Maria Gripe 5:147
D. Manus Pinkwater 4:164
Shel Silverstein 5:213
Peter Spier 5:225
Tobi Tobias 4:216
Tomi Ungerer 3:200, 204
Clyde Watson 5:212
Brian Wildsmith 2:211, 214
Laurence Yep 3:235

Lewis, Naomi
Paula Fox 1:81
Erich Kästner 4:126
Julius Lester 2:113
K. M. Peyton 3:172, 173

Libby, Margaret Sherwood
Joan Aiken 1:2, 9
Lloyd Alexander 1:13, 16; 5:19
Joan Walsh Anglund 1:20
Jeanne Bendick 5:38, 40
Jeanne Bendick, Candy
Bendick, and Robert
Bendick, Jr. 5:38
Michael Bond 1:28
Jean de Brunhoff and Laurent
de Brunhoff 4:34, 34, 35
Hester Burton 1:34
Eleanor Cameron 1:39
Beverly Cleary 2:49
Meindert DeJong 1:57
William Pène du Bois 1:63
Elizabeth Enright 4:75
Sid Fleischman 1:73
Theodor Seuss Geisel 1:85
Jean Craighead George 1:90
Marguerite Henry 4:114
Ted Hughes 3:92
Ezra Jack Keats 1:115
Karla Kuskin 4:135, 135, 137,
138
Astrid Lindgren 1:135
Arnold Lobel 5:163, 163
H. A. Rey and Margret Rey
5:198, 198
M. Sasek 4:193
Maurice Sendak 1:173
Ian Serraillier 2:138, 143
Ivan Southall 2:153, 157
Peter Spier 5:217
Rosemary Sutcliff 1:186, 189
P. L. Travers 2:178, 179
Henry Treece 2:185
Edwin Tunis 2:192, 193
Harvey Weiss 4:222, 223
Barbara Wersba 3:218
Leonard Wibberley 3:231
Brian Wildsmith 2:208
Maia Wojciechowska 1:199
Taro Yashima and Mitsu
Yashima 4:253
Jane Yolen 4:256
Charlotte Zolotow 2:236, 237

Lichtenberg, Linda H.
Alvin Schwartz 3:189

Lichtenberg, Margaret Klee
Arnold Lobel 5:172

Lieb, Jean B.
Alvin Schwartz 3:190
Leonard Wibberley 3:231

Light, Dorothy
Madeleine L'Engle 1:134

Lindquist, Jennie D.
L. M. Boston 3:27
Beverly Cleary 2:45, 47
Meindert DeJong 1:56, 58, 59, 61
William Pène du Bois 1:63, 64
Eleanor Estes 2:74
Jean Fritz 2:81
Theodor Seuss Geisel 1:87
Marguerite Henry 4:111
Erich Kästner 4:124
Robert Lawson 2:112
C. S. Lewis 3:135
Astrid Lindgren 1:135, 139
H. A. Rey and Margret Rey 5:197, 198
Rosemary Sutcliff 1:183, 189, 189, 190
Edwin Tunis 2:195
Harvey Weiss 4:220
E. B. White 1:193
Leonard Wibberley 3:228
Taro Yashima 4:251
Herbert S. Zim 2:229
Reiner Zimnik 3:244

Lindskoog, Kathryn Ann
C. S. Lewis 3:134

Linfield, Eric
Jeanne Bendick 5:41

Lingeman, Richard R.
Shel Silverstein 5:208

Lipkind, William
Edward Lear 1:127
Madeleine L'Engle 1:133

Lipson, Eden Ross
Jill Krementz 5:153

Lipsyte, Robert
Walter Dean Myers 4:156

Litsinger, Kathryn A.
Scott O'Dell 1:146

Little, Jean
Patti Stren 5:234

Lively, Penelope
C. S. Lewis 3:128

Livingston, Myra Cohn
Scott O'Dell 1:146

Long, Joanna R.
Millicent E. Selsam 1:164

Long, Norwood
Jeanne Bendick and Robert Bendick 5:36

Long, Sidney D.
Lloyd Alexander 1:12
Byrd Baylor 3:14
John Christopher 2:40
Eleanor Estes 2:75
Muriel L. Feelings and Tom Feelings 5:105

Shirley Glubok 1:95
M. B. Goffstein 3:58, 61
Virginia Hamilton 1:105
Nonny Hogrogian 2:88
James Houston 3:85
Arnold Lobel 5:164, 166
Georgess McHargue 2:119
Joan Phipson 5:182
Ellen Raskin 1:157
Alvin Schwartz 3:192
Maurice Sendak 1:171
Isaac Bashevis Singer 1:173
William Steig 2:161
John Steptoe 2:162
Edwin Tunis 2:194, 195
Harvey Weiss 4:227
Brian Wildsmith 2:212
Jane Yolen 4:260

Long, William H.
Tomie de Paola 4:57

Longsworth, Polly
Rosemary Sutcliff 1:186

Lonsdale, Bernard J.
Wanda Gág 4:90
H. A. Rey and Margret Rey 5:191

Lorraine, Walter
Arnold Lobel 5:162

Losinski, Julia
Scott Corbett 1:44
Madeleine L'Engle 1:129, 130, 130
Rosemary Sutcliff 1:189

Low, Alice
Eleanor Cameron 1:42
Jean Craighead George 1:89
Russell Hoban 3:82
Arnold Lobel 5:172
Harvey Weiss 4:221
Nancy Willard 5:246

Lucas, Barbara
Nancy Willard 5:248

Luckey, Eleanore Braun
John Donovan 3:54

Lukens, Rebecca J.
Jeanne Bendick 5:43
Ben Bova 3:33
Maria Gripe 5:149
E. Nesbit 3:163
Patricia Wrightson 4:246

Lundbergh, Holger
Harvey Weiss 4:225

Lurie, Alison
Jean de Brunhoff and Laurent de Brunhoff 4:36
Russell Hoban 3:83
Tove Jansson 2:94
Erich Kästner 4:127
Jill Paton Walsh 2:200

Luzer, Richard
Jill Krementz 5:153
Alfred Slote 4:203

Lyhne, Nancy D.
Tomie de Paola 4:65

Macaulay, David
Chris Van Allsburg 5:237

MacBean, Margaret
Rosemary Sutcliff 1:185

MacCann, Donnarae
Jean de Brunhoff and Laurent de Brunhoff 4:27
Wanda Gág 4:88
Karla Kuskin 4:134
H. A. Rey and Margret Rey 5:191
Tomi Ungerer 3:203
Taro Yashima 4:248
Reiner Zimnik 3:241

MacCleod, Anne S.
Russell Hoban 3:81

MacDonald, Ruth K.
Lucille Clifton 5:59

MacDuffie, Bruce L.
John Donovan 3:53
Scott O'Dell 1:146
Isaac Bashevis Singer 1:174
Jill Paton Walsh 2:202

Mackintosh, Helen K.
Wanda Gág 4:90
H. A. Rey and Margret Rey 5:191

Maddocks, Melvin
Madeleine L'Engle 1:131
Arnold Lobel 5:163

Madsen, Alan L.
John Christopher 2:43

Magid, Nora L.
Louisa May Alcott 1:11
Edward Lear 1:128
Beatrix Potter 1:153
Millicent E. Selsam 1:161
William Steig 2:159

Mahon, Margaret
Scott Corbett 1:47
Donald J. Sobol 4:206

Maier, Pauline
James Lincoln Collier and Christopher Collier 3:47

Mailloux, Heloise P.
Beverly Cleary 2:45
Theodor Seuss Geisel 1:85
C. S. Lewis 3:135
Dorothy Sterling 1:182
Rosemary Sutcliff 1:185
Robb White 3:224
Leonard Wibberley 3:229

Makins, Virginia
Susan Cooper 4:49
Arnold Lobel 5:164, 172
Peter Spier 5:226

Malcolm, Janet
John Rowe Townsend 2:171
Tomi Ungerer 3:205
Charlotte Zolotow 2:234

Malone, Elizabeth
Rosemary Sutcliff 1:190

Maloney, Brenda Durrin
Peter Spier 5:228

Manes, Esther
Lewis Carroll 2:35

Manlove, Colin N.
E. Nesbit 3:159

Manning, Patricia
Lloyd Alexander 5:24
Walter Dean Myers 4:157

D. Manus Pinkwater 4:170

Mano, D. Keith
Susan Cooper 4:44
Isaac Bashevis Singer 1:173

Manthorne, Jane
Hester Burton 1:31
John Rowe Townsend 2:171, 172, 173
Henry Treece 2:189
Robb White 3:223
Maia Wojciechowska 1:200

Maples, Houston L.
Lloyd Alexander 1:16; 5:21, 22
Louise Fitzhugh 1:72
Madeleine L'Engle 1:130
Astrid Lindgren 1:137
Joan Phipson 5:181
Dorothy Sterling 1:179
Henry Treece 2:189
Robb White 3:222
Leonard Wibberley 3:225, 226
Barbara Willard 2:218
Maia Wojciechowska 1:197

Marantz, Kenneth
Tomie de Paola 4:53
Chris Van Allsburg 5:241

Marcus, Ed Celina
Muriel L. Feelings and Tom Feelings 5:107

Markowsky, Juliet Kellogg
Joanna Cole 5:64
E. B. White 1:194
Herbert S. Zim and Lucretia Krantz 2:227

Marris, Ruth
Edward Ardizzone 3:8

Marsden, Alan L.
Leonard Wibberley 3:226

Marsh, Allan T.
Alvin Schwartz 3:190
Harvey Weiss 4:223

Marsh, Pamela
Joan Walsh Anglund 1:20, 21
Jeanne Bendick and Marcia Levin 5:39
Michael Bond 1:27
Betsy Byars 1:37
Meindert DeJong 1:60
Ed Emberley and Barbara Emberley 5:90, 92, 98
Elizabeth Enright 4:76
Theodor Seuss Geisel 1:83
Shirley Glubok 1:98
Irene Hunt 1:110
Tove Jansson 2:94
Ezra Jack Keats 1:116
Astrid Lindgren 1:135, 137, 139
Joan Phipson 5:180
Uri Shulevitz 5:204
Donald J. Sobol 4:208
William Steig 2:159
John Steptoe 2:165
Dorothy Sterling 1:180
Jill Paton Walsh 2:198
Harvey Weiss 4:223
Barbara Willard 2:217, 219, 221
Maia Wojciechowska 1:200

Taro Yashima **4**:253
Martin, Allie Beth
A. A. Milne **1**:142
Ivan Southall **2**:148
Dorothy Sterling and Benjamin
Quarles **1**:179
Taro Yashima and Mitsu
Yashima **4**:253
Martin, B. J.
Jill Krementz **5**:152
Martin, Constance
Maurice Sendak **1**:172
Martin, Rosemary S.
Jose Aruego **5**:29
Martinez, Elizabeth
Byrd Baylor **3**:15
Marx, Marion
Betsy Byars **1**:35
Brian Wildsmith **2**:209
Mason, Mary B.
Elizabeth Coatsworth **2**:55
Ivan Southall **2**:157
Charlotte Zolotow **2**:237
Masten, Helen Adams
Theodor Seuss Geisel **1**:84
Mathes, Miriam S.
Lloyd Alexander **5**:18
Jean Fritz **2**:80
Scott O'Dell **1**:147
Mathews, Virginia H.
H. A. Rey and Margret Rey
5:196
Mathorne, Jane
Donald J. Sobol **4**:208
Matthews, Anne E.
Jeanne Bendick **5**:49
Joanna Cole **5**:62
Laurence Pringle **4**:175
Matthews, Steven
Walter Dean Myers **4**:158
Maunder, Gabrielle
Meindert DeJong **1**:57
Russell Hoban **3**:77
Peter Spier **5**:218, 222
William Steig **2**:160
Clyde Watson **3**:213
Brian Wildsmith **2**:213
Maxwell, Emily
M. Sasek **4**:187
Peter Spier **5**:217
Maxwell, Margaret
P. L. Travers **2**:177
Charlotte Zolotow **2**:237, 239
May, Derwent
Edward Ardizzone **3**:6, 8
Russell Hoban **3**:78
Maurice Sendak **1**:169
Tomi Ungerer **3**:201
May, Jill P.
Richard Scarry **3**:185
May, Julian
Daniel Cohen **3**:43
Jean Craighead George **1**:89
McAdam, Sister Agnes
Nonny Hogrogian **2**:87

McBeth, Marilynn
M. Sasek **4**:194
McCarthy, Colman
James Haskins **3**:68
McCauley, Barbara S.
Ezra Jack Keats **1**:118
Jean Little **4**:148
McCloskey, Margaret
James Houston **3**:87
McConnell, Ruth M.
Byrd Baylor **3**:14
Maria Gripe **5**:146
William Kurelek **2**:102, 103
Edward Lear **1**:128
Georgess McHargue **2**:119
Peter Spier **5**:227
Barbara Wersba **3**:215
McCoy, Barbara R.
T. Ernesto Bethancourt **3**:18
McCullough, David W.
Arnold Lobel **5**:173
McCullough, Marilyn
James Houston **3**:88
McDaniel, Jessica
Beverly Cleary **2**:50
McDonald, Elaine T.
Sid Fleischman **1**:75
McDonnell, Christine
Lucille Clifton **5**:60
Eloise Greenfield **4**:101
Patricia Wrightson **4**:243
McDonough, Irma
William Kurelek **2**:104
McDowell, Myles
Paul Zindel **3**:244
McElderry, Margaret K.
Susan Cooper **4**:42
McEvoy, Ruth M.
Rosemary Sutcliff **1**:185
McGarvey, Jack
Richard Scarry **3**:186
McGrady, Hope H.
Ed Emberley and Barbara
Emberley **5**:92
Theodor Seuss Geisel **1**:86
H. A. Rey and Margret Rey
5:199
McGrath, Joan
D. Manus Pinkwater **4**:170
McGregor, Della
L. M. Boston **3**:27
Eleanor Cameron **1**:40
Theodor Seuss Geisel **1**:86, 88
McGrew, Mary Lou
Lloyd Alexander **1**:14
McGuire, Alice Brooks
Eleanor Cameron **1**:42
H. A. Rey and Margret Rey
5:197
McHargue, Georgess
Joan Aiken **1**:3
Lloyd Alexander **5**:25
Byrd Baylor **3**:17
Daniel Cohen **3**:40
Susan Cooper **4**:46
Tomie de Paola **4**:60, 63, 63

E. L. Konigsburg **1**:119, 122
D. Manus Pinkwater **4**:168
Virginia Driving Hawk Sneve
2:144
Patti Stren **5**:230
Barbara Wersba **3**:216
Nancy Willard **5**:248
Laurence Yep **3**:236
McKeithen-Boes, Anne
Jane Yolen **4**:265
McKenzie, Patricia Alice
Scott Corbett **1**:47
McKown, Robin
Hester Burton **1**:33
McLaughlin, Pat
Shel Silverstein **5**:209, 212
McLellan, Joseph
Norma Klein **2**:99
Ivan Southall **2**:152
McLeod, Alex
K. M. Peyton **3**:179
McWhinney, Michael
Dorothy Sterling **1**:178
McWilliams, Robert
Jeanne Bendick **5**:49
Mead, Margaret
Jill Krementz **5**:151
Medway, J.
Bernard Ashley **4**:14
Meek, Margaret
Nina Bawden **2**:10
John Christopher **2**:42
K. M. Peyton **3**:172, 173, 177,
178
Brian Wildsmith **2**:211, 213
Meigs, Cornelia
Louisa May Alcott **1**:9, 10
Melesh, Rosemarie
Lucille Clifton **5**:60
Meltzer, Milton
Jean Little **4**:152
Melville, Robert
Tomi Ungerer **3**:200
**Melvin, Sister M. Constance,
I.H.M.**
Martha Bacon **3**:11
James Lincoln Collier **3**:46
John Donovan **3**:53
Robb White **3**:221
Mendelsohn, Leonard R.
James Houston **3**:85
William Kurelek **2**:104
Menke, Edward W.
Donald J. Sobol **4**:211
Meras, Phyllis
James Houston **3**:85
Mercer, Joan Bodger
Brian Wildsmith **2**:211
Mercier, Jean F.
Byrd Baylor **3**:17
T. Ernesto Bethancourt **3**:19
James Lincoln Collier **3**:45
John Donovan **3**:51
M. B. Goffstein **3**:58
Ted Hughes **3**:95

Fernando Krahn **3**:103, 105,
106
Jill Krementz **5**:151
Judith Viorst **3**:208
Merriam, Eve
Natalie Babbitt **2**:5
Carlo Collodi **5**:71
Ed Emberley and Barbara
Emberley **5**:95
Ted Hughes **3**:95
Tomi Ungerer **3**:203, 205
Brian Wildsmith **2**:207
Taro Yashima **4**:254
Merrick, Anne
Roald Dahl **1**:50
Merrill, Vicki
Muriel L. Feelings and Tom
Feelings **5**:105
Meyer, Sandra
Meindert DeJong **1**:58
Ian Serraillier **2**:139
Meyers, Susan
Joan Phipson **5**:184
Michalik, Ann P.
Paula Fox **1**:76
Laurence Pringle **4**:175
Michel, Joan Hess
Peter Spier **5**:216, 219
Tomi Ungerer **3**:195
Mickish, Verle
Shirley Glubok **1**:98
Micklethwait, Lucy
Peter Spier **5**:228
Middleton, Richard
Kenneth Grahame **5**:129
Mignosi, Pietro
Carlo Collodi **5**:70
Millar, Neil
Joan Walsh Anglund **1**:21
Lucille Clifton **5**:53
Maria Gripe **5**:142, 142
Madeleine L'Engle **1**:131
Jean Little **4**:149
Georgess McHargue **2**:117
John Rowe Townsend **2**:172
Charlotte Zolotow **2**:236
Miller, Alice
Byrd Baylor **3**:17
Miller, Barbara S.
Lucille Clifton **5**:53
John Steptoe **2**:164
Harvey Weiss **4**:225
Miller, Bertha Mahoney
C. S. Lewis **3**:136
Miller, Beverly B.
Shirley Glubok **1**:95
Miller, Elizabeth L.
Richard Scarry **3**:185
Miller, Jonathan
Edward Ardizzone **3**:6
Miller, Judith K.
Jean Craighead George **1**:89
Miller, Karl
Jean de Brunhoff and Laurent
de Brunhoff **4**:35
M. Sasek **4**:190, 191

Miller, M. H.
Nina Bawden 2:11
John Rowe Townsend 2:172, 175

Miller, Sara
Lloyd Alexander 5:23
D. Manus Pinkwater 4:168

Millington, Valerie
Charlotte Zolotow 2:238

Mills, Joyce White
Eloise Greenfield 4:98

Milne, A. A.
Jean de Brunhoff and Laurent de Brunhoff 4:31
Kenneth Grahame 5:130

Milne, Lorus
Millicent E. Selsam 1:161

Milne, Margery
Millicent E. Selsam 1:161

Milton, Joyce
Tomie de Paola 4:59
Maria Gripe 5:149
Arnold Lobel 5:172
Shel Silverstein 5:212

Minudri, Regina
Judy Blume 2:17

Mitchell, Elizabeth
John Langstaff 3:109
Rosemary Sutcliff 1:183

Mitchell, Penelope M.
Ben Bova 3:32

Mogg, Sylvia
Elizabeth Coatsworth 2:53
Maria Gripe 5:139
Reiner Zimnik 3:242

Mohr, Nelda
Bernard Ashley 4:16
D. Manus Pinkwater 4:171

Moline, Ruth E.
Virginia Hamilton 1:104
David Macaulay 3:144

Molson, Francis
Jean Little 4:150

Monette, Elizabeth
Tomie de Paola 4:64
Eloise Greenfield 4:103

Monheit, Albert
Eleanor Cameron 1:40

Monson, Dianne L.
Lloyd Alexander 5:17
Jeanne Bendick 5:34
Carlo Collodi 5:83
Susan Cooper 4:42
Muriel L. Feelings and Tom Feelings 5:107
Maria Gripe 5:141
Arnold Lobel 5:162
Walter Dean Myers 4:155
Laurence Pringle 4:173
M. Sasek 4:190
Tobi Tobias 4:213
Harvey Weiss 4:219

Montgomery, John W.
C. S. Lewis 3:134

Montgomery, Margot
Dennis Lee 3:116

Moody, Barbara S.
Barbara Wersba 3:218

Moore, Anne Carroll
Elizabeth Coatsworth 2:55, 56
Elizabeth Enright 4:76
Eleanor Estes 2:74
Wanda Gág 4:79, 87, 91, 92, 93, 94
Theodor Seuss Geisel 1:87
Erich Kästner 4:121
Robert Lawson 2:110, 111
Beatrix Potter 1:151
P. L. Travers 2:179
E. B. White 1:193

Moore, Doris Langley
E. Nesbit 3:157, 163, 164, 165

Moore, Emily R.
Lucille Clifton 5:56

Moore, Robert
Peter Spier 5:227

Moore, Rosa Ann
Laura Ingalls Wilder 2:204

Mordvinoff, Nicholas
Taro Yashima 4:251

Morrison, Allan
Ivan Southall 2:146, 151, 154

Morrison, Frances L.
Jeanne Bendick 5:35
Jeanne Bendick and Robert Bendick 5:36

Morrison, Harriet
Millicent E. Selsam 1:163

Morrison, J. Allan
Ivan Southall 2:152
Barbara Wersba 3:217

Morrison, Philip
Mitsumasa Anno 2:2, 3
Byrd Baylor 3:17
Daniel Cohen 3:38
John Langstaff and Carol Langstaff 3:112
Laurence Pringle 4:179
Peter Spier 5:221, 225
Edwin Tunis 2:191
Harvey Weiss 4:226

Morrison, Phylis
Mitsumasa Anno 2:2, 3
Byrd Baylor 3:17
Daniel Cohen 3:38
John Langstaff and Carol Langstaff 3:112
Laurence Pringle 4:179
Peter Spier 5:221, 225
Edwin Tunis 2:191
Harvey Weiss 4:226

Morrison, Toni
Sharon Bell Mathis 3:151
Dorothy Sterling 1:180

Morrissey, Thomas J.
Carlo Collodi 5:84, 86

Morse, Brian
Ted Hughes 3:91

Morse, Jane C.
Arnold Lobel 5:163

Mortimer, Penelope
E. Nesbit 3:164

Mosel, Arlene
Lloyd Alexander 1:13
William Pène du Bois 1:63
Russell Hoban 3:77

Moss, Elaine
Martha Bacon 3:12
Jean de Brunhoff and Laurent de Brunhoff 4:36
Arnold Lobel 5:170
David Macaulay 3:141
Richard Scarry 3:181

Moulton, Priscilla L.
Ed Emberley and Barbara Emberley 5:93
Ezra Jack Keats 1:118
Edward Lear 1:126
Marilyn Sachs 2:131
Millicent E. Selsam 1:161
Dorothy Sterling 1:179, 181
Henry Treece 2:186
Harvey Weiss 4:223
Leonard Wibberley 3:225, 231
Barbara Willard 2:216
Charlotte Zolotow 2:234

Moxom, Priscilla
William H. Armstrong 1:22
Shirley Glubok 1:96
Seon Manley 3:147

Muirhead, Gail E.
Norma Klein 2:100

Mullan, Eunice G.
H. A. Rey and Margret Rey 5:194

Mumford, Olive
Russell Hoban 3:83

Munch, Theodore
Jeanne Bendick 5:49, 50

Munro, Mary
Marguerite Henry 4:115

Murphy, Aileen O'Brien
Betsy Byars 1:35
Lewis Carroll 2:35
Theodor Seuss Geisel 1:87
Nonny Hogrogian 2:89
Dorothy Sterling 1:181
Rosemary Sutcliff 1:191

Murphy, Joan
Russell Hoban 3:81
Paul Zindel 3:252

Murray, Marguerite M.
Donald J. Sobol 4:208

Murray, Michele
Madeleine L'Engle 1:132
Marilyn Sachs 2:134
Ivan Southall 2:153
Jill Paton Walsh 2:199

Myers, Andrew B.
Ian Serraillier 2:139

Myers, Terry
Elizabeth Coatsworth 2:56

Nash, Donald J.
Jeanne Bendick 5:48

Nash, Mary
Joan Aiken 1:7
Joan Phipson 5:180

Natov, Roni
Arnold Lobel 5:157

Naughton, John
Kit Williams 4:232

Nelson, Alix
Norma Klein 2:101

Nerney, Jeraline N.
Hester Burton 1:34
Betsy Byars 1:37

Nesbitt, Elizabeth
Eleanor Cameron 1:41
Carlo Collodi 5:72
Beatrix Potter 1:152
Laura Ingalls Wilder 2:202

Neufeld, John
Susan Cooper 4:43

Neumeyer, Peter
Nancy Willard 5:250

Nevett, Micki
Ed Emberley and Barbara Emberley 5:100

Neville, Emily
Louisa May Alcott 1:9

Newburg, Victor
Hester Burton 1:32

Newfield, Marcia
Richard Scarry 3:184

Newland, Mary Reed
James Lincoln Collier 3:45
John Langstaff 3:110

Newlands, Evelyn F.
Herbert S. Zim and James R. Skelly 2:232

Newton, David E.
Jeanne Bendick 5:47, 47

Nichols, Lois K.
Joanna Cole 5:68

Nichols, Margaret M.
D. Manus Pinkwater 4:170

Nickerson, Mary B.
Shel Silverstein 5:212
Patti Stren 5:232

Nilsen, Aileen Pace
Ursula K. Le Guin 3:124
Walter Dean Myers 4:156
Barbara Wersba 3:219
Taro Yashima 4:254

Nimmo, Dorothy
S. E. Hinton 3:72
Peter Spier 5:225

Nissenson, Hugh
Isaac Bashevis Singer 1:174, 177

Nixon, Peter
Ursula K. Le Guin 3:123

Noah, Carolyn
Joanna Cole 5:65

Noble, Doris
Isaac Bashevis Singer 1:175

Noonan, Eileen
Daniel Cohen 3:42

Nordell, Roderick
Ezra Jack Keats 1:117
Karla Kuskin 4:136
Edward Lear 1:127
A. A. Milne 1:143

H. A. Rey and Margret Rey
5:198, 198, 199

Nordstrom, Ursula
Eleanor Estes 2:74
Jean Fritz 2:80
Charlotte Zolotow 2:238

Norsworthy, James A., Jr.
John Donovan 3:52
David Macaulay 3:143

Novak, Barbara
Jose Aruego 5:29
John Steptoe 2:163
Tomi Ungerer 3:201
Charlotte Zolotow 2:234

Novinger, Margaret
Beverly Cleary 2:44

Noyce, Ruth M.
Nancy Willard 5:247

Noyes, Judy
Sheila Burnford 2:20

Nye, Robert
William H. Armstrong 1:23
Betsy Byars 1:38
Ursula K. Le Guin 3:118

Nykiel, Joanne
John Christopher 2:42

O'Connell, Margaret F.
Jose Aruego 5:28
William Pène du Bois 1:66
Elizabeth Enright 4:77
Ivan Southall 2:147
Harvey Weiss 4:224

O'Connor, Maureen
Nancy Willard 5:249

O'Dell, Scott
Edwin Tunis 2:193

Odland, Norine
Marguerite Henry 4:108

O'Doherty, Barbara Novak
Lloyd Alexander 1:13
Elizabeth Coatsworth 2:61
Ed Emberley and Barbara
Emberley 5:93
Ellen Raskin 1:157

O'Doherty, Brian
Shirley Glubok 1:99
Maurice Sendak 1:166

O'Donnell, Sister Marie, S.J.
Fernando Krahn 3:105

Offerman, Sister Mary Columba
Sharon Bell Mathis 3:150

Offit, Sidney
K. M. Peyton 3:179
John Rowe Townsend 2:171

Offord, Lenore Glen
Scott Corbett 1:44

Oglesby, Leora
Dorothy Sterling 1:181
Robb White 3:223

O'Gorman, Ned
M. B. Goffstein 3:59

O'Neal, Susan
Kristin Hunter 3:100

Oppenheim, Shulamith
P. L. Travers 2:178

O'Reilly, Jane
Lucille Clifton 5:54
Russell Hoban 3:77

Orgel, Doris
Eleanor Cameron 1:40
Ivan Southall 2:148
Barbara Wersba 3:218
Jane Yolen 4:262

Orr, Nancy Young
Eleanor Estes 2:74
Taro Yashima 4:254

Orvig, Mary
Maria Gripe 5:140
Tove Jansson 2:92
Astrid Lindgren 1:138

Ostermann, Robert
Lloyd Alexander 5:21

Paaswell, Robert E.
Herbert S. Zim and James R.
Skelly 2:230

Pace, Rose Mary
Elizabeth Coatsworth 2:58

Padalino, John J.
Laurence Pringle 4:181

Paige, Nancy F.
H. A. Rey and Margret Rey
5:200

Palmer, Nancy
Joanna Cole 5:68
Arnold Lobel 5:176

Pancella, John R.
Laurence Pringle 4:176, 180

Paperny, Myra
Jean Little 4:153

Pappas, Robin
Arnold Lobel 5:174

Parker, W. M.
Kenneth Grahame 5:110

Parrott, F. P.
L. M. Boston 3:26

Parsons, Gordon
K. M. Peyton 3:177, 180
Joan Phipson 5:182
Leonard Wibberley 3:224

Pastorello, Lea Rae
Marguerite Henry 4:112, 115
Herbert S. Zim 2:225

Patterson, Janice P.
Tomie de Paola 4:65
Reiner Zimnik 3:242
Jane Yolen 4:266

Payne, Katharine C.
Tomie de Paola 4:60

Payne, Margaret
Patricia Wrightson 4:240

Pearce, Philippa
Natalie Babbitt 2:8

Peck, Richard
William Kurelek 2:103
David Macaulay 3:142, 143

Peck, Robert Newton
William Kurelek 2:102

Peel, Marie
Jill Paton Walsh 2:198

Peet, Creighton
Jeanne Bendick 5:35
Jeanne Bendick and Robert
Bendick 5:36

Pegau, Ruth M.
Georgess McHargue 2:117
Leonard Wibberley 3:229

Pelmas, Ruth H.
Laurence Yep 3:238

Pennington, Ashley Jane
Walter Dean Myers 4:158, 159

Perkins, Flossie
Jane Yolen 4:257

Perkins, Huel D.
Kristin Hunter 3:98

Perry, Frank
Joan Phipson 5:186

Perry, Katherine
Ellen Raskin 1:156

Perry, Marcia L.
Joan Aiken 1:8
Martha Bacon 3:11

Perry, Thelma D.
Eloise Greenfield 4:100

Petrini, Enzo
Carlo Collodi 5:80

Petts, Margot
William H. Armstrong 1:24
Martha Bacon 3:12
Nina Bawden 2:14
Hester Burton 1:34
Eleanor Cameron 1:41
E. L. Konigsburg 1:120
Robert C. O'Brien 2:127
K. M. Peyton 3:171

Pettyjohn, Leila Davenport
Eloise Greenfield 4:103

Peyton, K. M.
K. M. Peyton 3:169

Pfau, Donald F.
Russell Hoban 3:82
John Langstaff and Carol
Langstaff 3:112

Phelps, Robert
Jean de Brunhoff and Laurent
de Brunhoff 4:36

Phillips, Althea L.
Joanna Cole 5:67

Phillips, David
Elizabeth Coatsworth 2:64

Phillpot, Clive
Russell Hoban 3:78

Phipps, Mildred R.
Maurice Sendak 1:171

Phy, Allene Stuart
Jane Yolen 4:264

Pickles, Susan L.
Scott Corbett 1:47
F. N. Monjo 2:126

Piehl, Kathy
Bernard Ashley 4:16

Pierce, Robert J.
Tobi Tobias 4:214

Pillar, Arlene M.
Muriel L. Feelings and Tom
Feelings 5:108
Arnold Lobel 5:162
Shel Silverstein 5:211
Peter Spier 5:217

Pinder, Sheila
Charlotte Zolotow 2:235

Pinizzotto, Dana Whitney
Ed Emberley and Barbara
Emberley 5:103

Piper, John
Jean de Brunhoff and Laurent
de Brunhoff 4:20, 33

Pippett, Aileen
Joan Aiken 1:6, 8
William Pène du Bois 1:62
Paula Fox 1:78
A. A. Milne 1:142
Ian Serraillier 2:138

Plommer, W. H.
David Macaulay 3:142

Plumb, Robert
Ben Bova 3:34

Poarch, Margaret
Ezra Jack Keats 1:115
Arnold Lobel 5:164
Ivan Southall 2:154

Pogrebin, Letty Cottin
Norma Klein 2:99

Polacheck, Janet G.
James Haskins 3:66, 67
Walter Dean Myers 4:157
Jane Yolen 4:259

Poll, Bernard
James Haskins 3:67

Pollack, Pamela D.
Lucille Clifton 5:55
Tomie de Paola 4:61
Russell Hoban 3:81
Norma Klein 2:98
Fernando Krahn 3:106
John Langstaff 3:111
Robert C. O'Brien 2:130
D. Manus Pinkwater 4:169
Tomi Ungerer 3:201
Chris Van Allsburg 5:239
Judith Viorst 3:210
Maia Wojciechowska 1:198

Poltarnees, Welleran
Edward Ardizzone 3:4
Tomi Ungerer 3:205

Porter, Diane
Hester Burton 1:30

Portteus, Elnora M.
F. N. Monjo 2:126
Edwin Tunis 2:192
Leonard Wibberley 3:225, 233

Postell, Frances
Daniel Cohen 3:43
Robert C. O'Brien 2:128

Potter, Marjorie F.
Kenneth Grahame 5:135

Powell, Jane
S. E. Hinton 3:72

Prescott, Peter S.
Lewis Carroll 2:36

Pretorius, Jean
    William Pène du Bois **1**:64
Prezzolini, Giuseppe
    Carlo Collodi **5**:70
Pringle, Laurence
    Laurence Pringle **4**:172
Pryce-Jones, Alan
    Kenneth Grahame **5**:111
Purnell, Idella
    Jean de Brunhoff and Laurent
        de Brunhoff **4**:31
Purtill, Richard
    C. S. Lewis **3**:134
Purton, Rowland
    Harvey Weiss **4**:227
Purucker, Mary I.
    Jean Craighead George **1**:94
    James Houston **3**:86
    Laurence Pringle **4**:176
    Virginia Driving Hawk Sneve
        2:144
    Nancy Willard **5**:249
Queen, Renee
    Jane Yolen **4**:266, 268
Quigley, Isabel
    Betsy Byars **1**:38
    Russell Hoban **3**:79
    Barbara Willard **2**:215
Quimby, Harriet B.
    Karla Kuskin **4**:138
    Edward Lear **1**:126
Rackin, Donald
    Lewis Carroll **2**:34
Raley, Lucile W.
    Jean Craighead George **1**:92
Rand, Laurie
    Edward Lear **1**:127
Ransome, Arthur
    Kenneth Grahame **5**:129
Raskin, Ellen
    D. Manus Pinkwater **4**:162
Rathbun, Norma
    Theodor Seuss Geisel **1**:87
Rausen, Ruth
    Lloyd Alexander **1**:12
Rawson, Sheila M.
    Brian Wildsmith **2**:208
Ray, Colin
    K. M. Peyton **3**:176
Ray, Sheila
    S. E. Hinton **3**:73
Read, Esther H.
    Jeanne Bendick **5**:48
Reamer, Joan
    Jean de Brunhoff and Laurent
        de Brunhoff **4**:39
Reamer, Lynn B.
    Kristin Hunter **3**:98
Reeder, Kik
    Astrid Lindgren **1**:138
Rees, David L.
    John Donovan **3**:53
    John D. Fitzgerald **1**:70
    S. E. Hinton **3**:72, 73

    Julius Lester **2**:115
    K. M. Peyton **3**:178
    Joan Phipson **5**:183
    Leonard Wibberley **3**:226
Reese, Virginia
    Byrd Baylor **3**:15
    Jeanne Bendick **5**:47
    Ben Bova **3**:36
Reid, D. M.
    James Houston **3**:85
Reiss, Johanna
    Marilyn Sachs **2**:133
Remnitz, Virginia Yeaman
    Kenneth Grahame **5**:126
Rennert, Maggie
    Elizabeth Coatsworth **2**:61
    Meindert DeJong **1**:60
Rey, H. A.
    H. A. Rey and Margret Rey
        5:189
Rey, Margret
    H. A. Rey and Margret Rey
        5:189
Reynolds, Donald B., Jr.
    Michael Bond **1**:30
Reynolds, Jean
    Ed Emberley and Barbara
        Emberley **5**:89
Rholes, Julia
    Laurence Pringle **4**:186
Rhys, Aneurin
    John Donovan **3**:53
    Paul Zindel **3**:249
Ribalow, Harold V.
    Lloyd Alexander **5**:17
Ribner, Sue
    Norma Klein **2**:100
Rice, Harold C. K.
    Jean de Brunhoff and Laurent
        de Brunhoff **4**:40
    Tomie de Paola **4**:61, 62, 62,
        64
    Karla Kuskin **4**:144
    Arnold Lobel **5**:173
    D. Manus Pinkwater **4**:170
    Uri Shulevitz **5**:207
    Peter Spier **5**:226
    Chris Van Allsburg **5**:238
Richard, Ethel
    Julius Lester **2**:112
    Herbert S. Zim **2**:232
Richard, Olga
    Jean de Brunhoff and Laurent
        de Brunhoff **4**:27
    Wanda Gág **4**:88
    Karla Kuskin **4**:134
    H. A. Rey and Margret Rey
        5:191
    Tomi Ungerer **3**:203
    Taro Yashima **4**:248
    Reiner Zimnik **3**:241
Richardson, Joanna
    Edward Lear **1**:125
Richardson, Judy
    Lucille Clifton **5**:55
    Eloise Greenfield **4**:97

Richardson, Patrick
    Jean de Brunhoff and Laurent
        de Brunhoff **4**:23
Ridley, Clifford A.
    Ed Emberley and Barbara
        Emberley **5**:97
Ridolfino, Carole
    Laurence Pringle **4**:180
Ritter, Karen
    Jill Kremente **5**:155
Rizzolo, Clare D.
    Kristin Hunter **3**:97
Robbins, Sidney
    L. M. Boston **3**:29
Robinson, Beryl
    Lloyd Alexander **1**:14
    Louisa May Alcott **1**:11
    Byrd Baylor **3**:18
    Ben Bova **3**:33
    Hester Burton **1**:31, 34
    Betsy Byars **1**:35
    Lucille Clifton **5**:55
    Scott Corbett **1**:46
    Jean Craighead George **1**:94
    Virginia Hamilton **1**:104
    Nonny Hogrogian **2**:87
    James Houston **3**:88
    Ezra Jack Keats **1**:114
    Edward Lear **1**:128
    Astrid Lindgren **1**:136
    Arnold Lobel **5**:169
    David Macaulay **3**:143
    K. M. Peyton **3**:178
    Marilyn Sachs **2**:132
    Uri Shulevitz **5**:205
    Isaac Bashevis Singer **1**:177
    Virginia Driving Hawk Sneve
        2:145
    Harvey Weiss **4**:226
    Leonard Wibberley **3**:230
    Brian Wildsmith **2**:213
    Barbara Willard **2**:216, 220,
        222
Robinson, Debbie
    Daniel Cohen **3**:39
    Joanna Cole **5**:63
Robinson, Ruth
    Ben Bova **3**:33
    E. L. Konigsburg **1**:120
    K. M. Peyton **3**:178
    Rosemary Sutcliff **1**:184
    Leonard Wibberley **3**:230
Rochman, Hazel
    Lloyd Alexander **5**:25
Rock, Sister Mary E.
    Jeanne Bendick **5**:43
Rodway, Stella
    Barbara Wersba **3**:218
Roedder, Kathleen
    James Haskins **3**:68
Rogers, Timothy
    Ted Hughes **3**:93
    Tomi Ungerer **3**:202
Rogge, Whitney
    Jill Kremente **5**:152
Rogow, Roberta
    James Lincoln Collier and
        Christopher Collier **3**:47

    Virginia Driving Hawk Sneve
        2:144, 145
Roiphe, Anne
    Shel Silverstein **5**:211
Rolnick, Amy
    Patti Stren **5**:234
Rose, Jasper
    L. M. Boston **3**:21
Rose, Karel
    Lucille Clifton **5**:57
Rosenfeld, Judith
    Sharon Bell Mathis **3**:152
Rosenthal, Lenore
    Donald J. Sobol **4**:211
Ross, Catherine
    Jane Yolen **4**:257
Ross, Eulalie Steinmetz
    C. S. Lewis **3**:136
    Millicent E. Selsam and Betty
        Morrow **1**:165
Rowe, Susan
    Judy Blume **2**:17
Roxburgh, Stephen D.
    Jane Yolen **4**:264
Royds, Pamela
    Ted Hughes **3**:93
    K. M. Peyton **3**:173
Rudin, Ellen
    Tomie de Paola **4**:64
Rudman, Masha Kabakow
    Maria Gripe **5**:147
    Jill Kremente **5**:151
Rue, Eloise
    Eleanor Cameron **1**:39
    Arnold Lobel **5**:163
Ruffin, Carolyn F.
    Tove Jansson **2**:93
Rupnik, Sara K.
    F. N. Monjo **2**:125
Russ, Lavinia
    Joan Aiken **1**:7, 10
    Louisa May Alcott **1**:10
    Byrd Baylor **3**:16
    Ben Bova **3**:32
    James Lincoln Collier **3**:49
    John Donovan **3**:52
    Roald Dahl **1**:52
    Sid Fleischman **1**:75
    M. B. Goffstein **3**:57, 59
    James Houston **3**:87
    Kristin Hunter **3**:100
    Fernando Krahn **3**:104, 105
    John Langstaff **3**:109
    A. A. Milne **1**:143
    F. N. Monjo **2**:121, 124
    Scott O'Dell **1**:148
    K. M. Peyton **3**:180
    Richard Scarry **3**:186
    Isaac Bashevis Singer **1**:177
    Judith Viorst **3**:207
    Clyde Watson **3**:212
    Barbara Wersba **3**:216
    Maia Wojciechowska **1**:197
    Paul Zindel **3**:248, 250, 251
Ruthenberg, Arlene
    John Rowe Townsend **2**:173

Ryan, Stephen P.
　Seon Manley 3:147

Rybicki, Steve
　Russell Hoban 3:81

Ryder, Betty L.
　James Houston 3:85

Rydin, Lena
　Maria Gripe 5:140

Sadker, David Miller
　H. A. Rey and Margret Rey
　　5:192

Sadker, Myra Pollack
　H. A. Rey and Margret Rey
　　5:192

Sagar, Keith
　Ted Hughes 3:92

Sale, Roger
　Jean de Brunhoff and Laurent
　　de Brunhoff 4:27
　Carlo Collodi 5:81
　Kenneth Grahame 5:121

Salway, Lance
　E. Nesbit 3:164
　Leonard Wibberley 3:227
　Paul Zindel 3:251

Sanborn, Everett C.
　Herbert S. Zim 2:233

Sanders, Jacqueline
　Louise Fitzhugh 1:71

Sandner, Arlene Stolzer
　Patti Stren 5:234

Sandrof, Ivan
　Leonard Wibberley 3:224

Sanhuber, Holly
　Jane Yolen 4:267

Sarton, Mary
　Elizabeth Coatsworth 2:56

Sayers, Frances Clarke
　Eleanor Estes 2:72

Scanlon, Laura Polla
　Martha Bacon 3:12
　John Donovan 3:53
　William Pène du Bois 1:66
　E. L. Konigsburg 1:119
　Barbara Wersba 3:217
　Maia Wojciechowska 1:197

Scarf, Maggie
　William H. Armstrong 1:22

Scheer, George F.
　Edwin Tunis 2:194

Scherf, Walter
　Reiner Zimnik 3:242

Schickel, Richard
　Betsy Byars 1:35

Schmidt, Donald J.
　Herbert S. Zim and James R.
　　Skelly 2:229

Schmidt, Sandra
　Betsy Byars 1:35

Schneider, Judith
　John Langstaff and Carol
　　Langstaff 3:112

Schoenfeld, Madalynne
　Seon Manley 3:146

Scholes, Robert
　Ursula K. Le Guin 3:118, 120

Schonberg, Harold C.
　F. N. Monjo 2:123

Schram, Barbara A.
　Richard Scarry 3:182
　Shel Silverstein 5:209

Schroeder, Melinda
　Edward Ardizzone 3:5
　T. Ernesto Bethancourt 3:18
　Judy Blume 2:17
　Tomie de Paola 4:54
　Ezra Jack Keats 1:113
　D. Manus Pinkwater 4:165
　Uri Shulevitz 5:204
　John Steptoe 2:163
　Tobi Tobias 4:215
　Charlotte Zolotow 2:239

Schumacher, Dorothy
　Ben Bova 3:35

Schwartz, Albert V.
　William H. Armstrong 1:24
　Paula Fox 1:80
　P. L. Travers 2:178

Schwartz, Alvin
　Alvin Schwartz 3:187

Schwartz, Sanford
　Maurice Sendak 1:171

Schweibish, Ann D.
　D. Manus Pinkwater 4:161
　Millicent E. Selsam 1:164, 165
　William Steig 2:158
　Edwin Tunis 2:191
　Harvey Weiss 4:227
　Brian Wildsmith 2:209

Schweinitz, Eleanor von
　See von Schweinitz, Eleanor

Scoggin, Margaret C.
　Jeanne Bendick 5:35
　Elizabeth Coatsworth 2:61
　Nat Hentoff 1:109

Scott, Lael
　Judy Blume 2:18

Scott, Marian Herr
　Jill Paton Walsh 2:197

Seacord, Laura F.
　Elizabeth Coatsworth 2:58

Sebesta, Sam Leaton
　Lloyd Alexander 5:22

Segal, Jonathan
　John Christopher 2:39

Selsam, Millicent E.
　Jean Craighead George 1:92,
　　93

Seltzer, Hara L.
　Ed Emberley and Barbara
　　Emberley 5:101

Semrad, Alberita R.
　Marguerite Henry 4:112

Sendak, Maurice
　Jean de Brunhoff and Laurent
　　de Brunhoff 4:28
　Brian Wildsmith 2:210

Serata, Gertrude
　William H. Armstrong 1:22
　Yuri Suhl 2:166

Seybolt, Cynthia T.
　D. Manus Pinkwater 4:163

Shaffer, Blanche Weber
　Meindert DeJong 1:60
　William Pène du Bois 1:65

Shaffer, Dallas Y.
　Elizabeth Coatsworth 2:60

Shannon, George
　Tomie de Paola 4:64
　Patricia Wrightson 4:247

Shapiro, Leila C.
　Norma Klein 2:101

Shaw, Spencer G.
　Dorothy Sterling 1:178

Sheehan, Ethna
　Byrd Baylor 3:16
　Eleanor Cameron 1:40
　Paula Fox 1:77
　E. L. Konigsburg 1:123
　Karla Kuskin 4:143
　Paul Zindel 3:248

Sheehan, Susan
　P. L. Travers 2:177

Shepard, Mary Ellen
　Eloise Greenfield 4:98

Shepard, Paul
　Arnold Lobel 5:166

Shepard, Ray Anthony
　James Haskins 3:63

Shepard, Richard F.
　William Pène du Bois 1:65

Sherrard-Smith, Barbara
　Bernard Ashley 4:14

Shippey, T. A.
　Ursula K. Le Guin 3:120

Showers, Paul
　Jeanne Bendick 5:44
　Edwin Tunis 2:192
　Herbert S. Zim and Sonia
　　Bleeker 2:228
　Herbert S. Zim and James R.
　　Skelly 2:228

Showstack, Margo
　Tomie de Paola 4:65

Shulevitz, Uri
　Uri Shulevitz 5:201

Shumberger, Phyllis
　Beatrix Potter 1:154
　Ian Serraillier 2:135

Shupe, Frank L.
　Harvey Weiss 4:220

Siegel, R. A.
　Tomi Ungerer 3:198

Silver, Linda R.
　Lloyd Alexander 5:22
　Russell Hoban 3:76
　Nancy Willard 5:248

Silvey, Anita
　Lewis Carroll 2:36
　John Christopher 2:43
　Lucille Clifton 5:54, 56
　Vicki Cobb 2:64
　Tomie de Paola 4:55, 57
　Muriel L. Feelings and Tom
　　Feelings 5:107
　Jean Fritz 2:82

Shirley Glubok 1:97
　M. B. Goffstein 3:60
　S. E. Hinton 3:71
　John Langstaff 3:110
　Madeleine L'Engle 1:133
　Seon Manley and Gogo Lewis
　　3:145
　Sharon Bell Mathis 3:151
　Georgess McHargue 2:118
　F. N. Monjo 2:125
　Alvin Schwartz 3:188, 190
　Millicent E. Selsam 1:161
　Isaac Bashevis Singer 1:175
　Peter Spier 5:223
　Tomi Ungerer 3:203
　Brian Wildsmith 2:214
　Charlotte Zolotow 2:239

Sima, Judith
　Jeanne Bendick 5:44

Simon, Seymour
　Joanna Cole 5:65

Simons, Mary
　Jeanne Bendick and Marian
　　Warren 5:41

Sims, Rudine
　Lucille Clifton 5:51

Singer, Marilyn R.
　Mitsumasa Anno 2:2
　Tomie de Paola 4:62
　Paula Fox 1:79
　Eloise Greenfield and Lessie
　　Jones Little 4:102
　Norma Klein 2:99
　Fernando Krahn 3:104
　Karla Kuskin 4:141
　Georgess McHargue 2:118
　Isaac Bashevis Singer 1:175
　Peter Spier 5:219
　Tobi Tobias 4:218
　Jane Yolen 4:260
　Paul Zindel 3:250

Sive, Mary R.
　Alvin Schwartz 3:190

Skahill, Helen
　Tomi Ungerer 3:204

Sloan, Florence Bethune
　Elizabeth Enright 4:73, 73
　H. A. Rey and Margret Rey
　　5:193

Slung, Michele
　Lucille Clifton 5:59
　Arnold Lobel 5:175
　Walter Dean Myers 4:160
　D. Manus Pinkwater 4:169

Smaridge, Norah
　Richard Scarry 3:181

Smeltzer, Sister Mary Ethelreda
　John Langstaff 3:110

Smith, Alice
　Karla Kuskin 4:143

Smith, Alice G.
　James Lincoln Collier 3:45

Smith, C.E.J.
　Elizabeth Coatsworth 2:61
　Susan Cooper 4:43
　John D. Fitzgerald 1:70
　S. E. Hinton 3:71
　Yuri Korinetz 4:130

Critic Index

Scott O'Dell **1**:148
Joan Phipson **5**:182
Ivan Southall **2**:155
John Rowe Townsend **2**:169
Laura Ingalls Wilder **2**:205

Smith, Daryl D.
Herbert S. Zim **2**:226

Smith, Ethanne
Jeanne Bendick **5**:47

Smith, Francis
Marguerite Henry **4**:110

Smith, Irene
Robert Lawson **2**:111
Rosemary Sutcliff **1**:183

Smith, James Steel
Louisa May Alcott **1**:9
Elizabeth Enright **4**:73
Theodor Seuss Geisel **1**:83
E. B. White **1**:194
Taro Yashima **4**:252

Smith, Janet Adam
Lloyd Alexander **1**:12
Martha Bacon **3**:13
Nina Bawden **2**:14
Jean de Brunhoff and Laurent
  de Brunhoff **4**:34
Ted Hughes **3**:92

Smith, Janie M.
Marguerite Henry **4**:111

Smith, Jennifer Farley
Betsy Byars **1**:35
Muriel L. Feelings and Tom
  Feelings **5**:105
Virginia Hamilton **1**:106
E. L. Konigsburg **1**:122
John Langstaff **3**:111
Julius Lester **2**:113
Arnold Lobel **5**:167
Georgess McHargue **2**:119
Beatrix Potter **1**:154
Marilyn Sachs **2**:133

Smith, Kathryn A.
Kenneth Grahame **5**:121, 135

Smith, Lillian H.
Edward Ardizzone **3**:5
Jean de Brunhoff and Laurent
  de Brunhoff **4**:30
Lewis Carroll **2**:31
E. Nesbit **3**:161
H. A. Rey and Margret Rey
  5:190

Smith, Mary Ainslie
Patti Stren **5**:233

Smith, Norman F.
Harvey Weiss **4**:229

Smith, Sherwin D.
Shel Silverstein **5**:210

Smith, Shirley A.
Jeanne Bendick **5**:45
Vicki Cobb **2**:65, 67
Daniel Cohen **3**:40
Joanna Cole **5**:62
Harvey Weiss **4**:226
Herbert S. Zim and James R.
  Skelly **2**:230, 231

Smith, Stevie
Lloyd Alexander **5**:18

Smith, William Jay
Edward Lear **1**:127

Smothers, Joyce W.
Maria Gripe **5**:145

Smyth, Frances
Wanda Gág **4**:92

Sobol, Donald J.
Donald J. Sobol **4**:205

Solomon, Doris
Natalie Babbitt **2**:7

Sorenson, Marian
Scott Corbett **1**:45
Sid Fleischman **1**:73
Jean Craighead George **1**:93
Astrid Lindgren **1**:137, 140
Joan Phipson **5**:179
Millicent E. Selsam **1**:160

Sourian, Peter
Bette Greene **2**:86

Spain, Frances Lander
John Langstaff **3**:109

Speer, Eunice H.
Leonard Wibberley **3**:233

Spence, Patricia
James Haskins **3**:63

Sperber, Ann
Karla Kuskin **4**:142
Ellen Raskin **1**:157

Spier, Peter
Jean Fritz **2**:79
Peter Spier **5**:224

Spirt, Diana L.
Jill Krementz **5**:153
D. Manus Pinkwater **4**:165

Sprague, Susan
Laurence Pringle **4**:181

Stableford, Brian
Laurence Yep **3**:238

Stackpole, John D.
Jeanne Bendick **5**:44
Tomie de Paola **4**:57

Stafford, I. Elizabeth
Scott Corbett **1**:44
Rosemary Sutcliff **1**:185

Stafford, Jean
Lloyd Alexander **1**:13
Natalie Babbitt **2**:6
Vicki Cobb **2**:67
E. Nesbit **3**:162
William Steig **2**:158, 160
Jill Paton Walsh **2**:200
Brian Wildsmith **2**:212
Jane Yolen **4**:262
Paul Zindel **3**:249

Standard, Elinore
Roald Dahl **1**:52
Virginia Hamilton **1**:106

Stanton, Lorraine
Maria Gripe **5**:140

Stanton, Susan
Maria Gripe **5**:139, 143
Fernando Krahn **3**:104
Tobi Tobias **4**:213

Stavn, Diane Gersoni
See **Gersoni-Edelman, Diane**

Stein, Robert J.
Joanna Cole **5**:66
Joanna Cole and Madeleine
  Edmondson **5**:62

Stein, Ruth M.
Lloyd Alexander **5**:25
Lucille Clifton **5**:58
James Lincoln Collier and
  Christopher Collier **3**:44
John Donovan **3**:51
Joan Phipson **5**:186
Shel Silverstein **5**:212
Nancy Willard **5**:247

Steinberg, Sybil
T. Ernesto Bethancourt **3**:18

Steinmetz, Eulalie
Elizabeth Enright **4**:75

Stenson, Leah Deland
Tomie de Paola **4**:56
David Macaulay **3**:143
Marilyn Sachs **2**:132

Stephenson, Marjorie
Shirley Glubok **1**:95

Sterck, Kenneth
Kenneth Grahame **5**:133

Sterling, Dorothy
Virginia Hamilton **1**:103

Stevenson, Drew
Jean de Brunhoff and Laurent
  de Brunhoff **4**:39

Stewart, Evelyn
Karla Kuskin **4**:140
Arnold Lobel **5**:167

Stewart, Lynne
Muriel L. Feelings and Tom
  Feelings **5**:105
Virginia Hamilton **1**:106

Stimpfle, Nedra
Kristin Hunter **3**:101

Stitt, Martita U.
Jeanne Bendick **5**:45

Stoer, Marion West
Jean Fritz **2**:81
Rosemary Sutcliff **1**:185
Henry Treece **2**:185
Maia Wojciechowska **1**:197

Stolz, Mary
Hester Burton **1**:34
Madeleine L'Engle **1**:130

Stone, Helen
Edward Ardizzone **3**:8

Storr, Catherine
Nina Bawden **2**:14
John Christopher **2**:42
Tove Jansson **2**:95
K. M. Peyton **3**:176

Stott, Jon C.
Tomie de Paola **4**:59
Ed Emberley and Barbara
  Emberley **5**:90
Patti Stren **5**:231

Stowe, Peter
Joanna Cole **5**:67

Strang, Mary
Meindert DeJong **1**:61

Streatfeild, Noël
E. Nesbit **3**:153

Strothman, Janet
Jose Aruego **5**:29

Stubbs, Harry C.
Ben Bova **3**:35
Vicki Cobb **2**:65, 66, 67
Daniel Cohen **3**:40
Sylvia Louise Engdahl **2**:71
Laurence Pringle **4**:184
Clyde Watson **3**:211
Herbert S. Zim **2**:226
Herbert S. Zim and Sonia
  Bleeker **2**:228
Herbert S. Zim and Lucretia
  Krantz **2**:227

Sturdivant, Nan
Jill Paton Walsh **2**:201

Styron, Rose
Karla Kuskin **4**:144

Sullivan, Peggy
Ed Emberley and Barbara
  Emberley **5**:91
Elizabeth Enright **4**:76
Marilyn Sachs **2**:131, 134

Sully, J.
Kenneth Grahame **5**:127

Supree, Burt
Ed Emberley and Barbara
  Emberley **5**:101
Arnold Lobel **5**:172

Sustare, B. Dennis
Laurence Pringle **4**:182

Sutherland, Zena
Joan Aiken **1**:1, 2, 3, 4, 5, 6,
  7, 8, 9
Louisa May Alcott **1**:10, 11, 11
Lloyd Alexander **1**:12, 13, 14,
  15, 16, 16, 17, 18; **5**:17, 20,
  22, 25, 26
Joan Walsh Anglund **1**:19, 20,
  21, 22
Mitsumasa Anno **2**:1, 2
Edward Ardizzone **3**:5, 6
William H. Armstrong **1**:22,
  23, 24, 25
Jose Aruego **5**:30
Jose Aruego and Ariane
  Aruego **5**:30
Jose Aruego and Ariane Dewey
  5:31
Bernard Ashley **4**:18
Natalie Babbitt **2**:5, 6, 7, 8
Martha Bacon **3**:11, 12
Nina Bawden **2**:11, 12, 14
Byrd Baylor **3**:13, 14, 15, 16,
  17
Jeanne Bendick **5**:34, 41, 43,
  45, 50
T. Ernesto Bethancourt **3**:19
Judy Blume **2**:16, 17, 18, 19
Michael Bond **1**:27, 28, 29, 30
Ben Bova **3**:32, 33, 34, 36
Sheila Burnford **2**:19, 19, 20
Hester Burton **1**:30, 31, 32, 33,
  34
Betsy Byars **1**:35, 36, 37, 38
Eleanor Cameron **1**:39, 40, 41,
  42
Lewis Carroll **2**:36
John Christopher **2**:37, 39, 40,
  41, 42, 43, 44

Beverly Cleary **2**:45, 45, 47, 48, 49, 50, 51
Lucille Clifton **5**:54, 55, 56, 56, 59, 60
Elizabeth Coatsworth **2**:53, 53, 54, 55, 57, 58, 59, 60, 61, 63, 64
Vicki Cobb **2**:66, 67
Joanna Cole **5**:63, 64, 67
James Lincoln Collier **3**:44, 46
James Lincoln Collier and Christopher Collier **3**:47
Carlo Collodi **5**:83
Susan Cooper **4**:42, 49
Scott Corbett **1**:43, 44, 45, 46, 47, 48
Roald Dahl **1**:49, 49, 51, 52
Marguerite de Angeli **1**:52, 53, 53, 54
Meindert DeJong **1**:55, 55, 56, 57, 58, 59, 60, 61
Tomie de Paola **4**:54, 55, 57, 60, 64, 64, 65, 65
John Donovan **3**:51, 56
William Pène du Bois **1**:62, 63, 64, 65, 66, 66
Ed Emberley and Barbara Emberley **5**:92, 98, 99, 101
Sylvia Louise Engdahl **2**:69, 71, 72
Eleanor Estes **2**:73, 73, 74, 75, 76, 77
Muriel L. Feelings and Tom Feelings **5**:105, 106, 107, 107
John D. Fitzgerald **1**:69, 70
Louise Fitzhugh **1**:71, 72
Sid Fleischman **1**:73, 74, 75
Paula Fox **1**:76, 76, 77, 78, 79, 81
Jean Fritz **2**:79, 81, 82, 83
Theodor Seuss Geisel **1**:84, 85, 86, 87
Jean Craighead George **1**:89, 90, 91, 92, 94
Shirley Glubok **1**:94, 95, 96, 97, 98, 99, 100, 101
M. B. Goffstein **3**:58, 59, 60, 61, 62
Bette Greene **2**:85
Eloise Greenfield **4**:96, 97, 97, 98, 99, 99, 100, 101
Maria Gripe **5**:141, 143, 143, 147, 148, 149
Virginia Hamilton **1**:103, 104, 105, 106, 107
James Haskins **3**:63, 64, 65, 66, 67, 68
Marguerite Henry **4**:108, 112, 115, 115, 116
Nat Hentoff **1**:108, 108
Russell Hoban **3**:76, 77, 81, 82
Nonny Hogrogian **2**:87, 88, 89, 90
James Houston **3**:85, 86, 87, 88
Ted Hughes **3**:93, 95
Irene Hunt **1**:109, 110, 111
Kristin Hunter **3**:98, 99, 100, 101
Tove Jansson **2**:93, 94, 95
Ezra Jack Keats **1**:114, 115, 116, 117, 118

Norma Klein **2**:98, 99, 100, 101
E. L. Konigsburg **1**:119, 120, 121, 121, 122
Fernando Krahn **3**:106
Jill Krementz **5**:151, 153, 154
William Kurelek **2**:103
Karla Kuskin **4**:139, 140, 144
John Langstaff and Carol Langstaff **3**:112
Robert Lawson **2**:111
Edward Lear **1**:126, 126, 127, 128
Dennis Lee **3**:116
Madeleine L'Engle **1**:129, 130, 131, 132, 133, 134, 134
Julius Lester **2**:112, 113, 114
Astrid Lindgren **1**:136, 137, 139
Jean Little **4**:147, 147, 148, 150, 151, 152
Arnold Lobel **5**:162, 165, 166, 169, 171, 173, 175
David Macaulay **3**:141, 143
Seon Manley **3**:146, 148
Sharon Bell Mathis **3**:149, 151
Georgess McHargue **2**:119, 120
A. A. Milne **1**:141
F. N. Monjo **2**:121, 122, 123, 124, 125, 126
Walter Dean Myers **4**:155, 156, 157, 157, 158, 159
E. Nesbit **3**:164
Robert C. O'Brien **2**:127, 128, 129
Scott O'Dell **1**:145, 146, 147, 147, 148
K. M. Peyton **3**:172, 177
Joan Phipson **5**:181, 183, 183, 185, 186
D. Manus Pinkwater **4**:164, 165, 169, 169, 170, 171
Beatrix Potter **1**:152, 153, 154
Laurence Pringle **4**:173, 178, 179, 183, 185
Ellen Raskin **1**:155, 156, 157
Marilyn Sachs **2**:131, 132, 133, 134, 135
M. Sasek **4**:190, 194, 194, 196, 197
Richard Scarry **3**:184, 187
Alvin Schwartz **3**:189, 191, 192
Millicent E. Selsam **1**:159, 159, 160, 161, 162, 163, 164, 165, 166
Millicent E. Selsam and Joyce Hunt **1**:162
Maurice Sendak **1**:167, 168, 169, 170, 171, 171, 172, 172
Ian Serraillier **2**:135, 137, 138, 142, 143
Uri Shulevitz **5**:203, 205, 206
Shel Silverstein **5**:208, 213
Isaac Bashevis Singer **1**:173, 174, 175, 176, 177
Alfred Slote **4**:199, 199, 200, 200, 201, 201, 202, 202, 202, 203, 204
Virginia Driving Hawk Sneve **2**:144, 145

Donald J. Sobol **4**:209, 211, 212
Ivan Southall **2**:148, 150, 152, 153, 154, 156
Peter Spier **5**:218, 219
William Steig **2**:158, 159, 160, 161, 162
John Steptoe **2**:163, 164, 165
Dorothy Sterling **1**:178, 178, 180, 181, 181, 182
Dorothy Sterling and Benjamin Quarles **1**:179
Patti Stren **5**:231, 232
Yuri Suhl **2**:166, 167
Rosemary Sutcliff **1**:183, 184, 185, 186, 187, 188, 189, 190, 191
Tobi Tobias **4**:213, 214, 214, 215, 216, 217, 217, 217
John Rowe Townsend **2**:170, 171, 172, 173, 173, 174, 175
P. L. Travers **2**:178, 179
Henry Treece **2**:183, 184, 185, 186, 187, 188, 189, 190, 191
Edwin Tunis **2**:192, 193, 193, 194, 195
Tomi Ungerer **3**:200, 202, 203
Chris Van Allsburg **5**:241
Judith Viorst **3**:207, 208
Jill Paton Walsh **2**:197, 198, 199, 200, 201
Harvey Weiss **4**:219, 223, 225, 227, 228
Barbara Wersba **3**:216, 217, 219, 220
E. B. White **1**:195, 196
Leonard Wibberley **3**:225, 228, 229, 231, 232
Laura Ingalls Wilder **2**:205
Brian Wildsmith **2**:207, 208, 209, 210, 211, 211, 212, 213, 214
Barbara Willard **2**:216, 217, 218, 219, 220, 221, 223, 224
Nancy Willard **5**:246, 247, 248
Maia Wojciechowska **1**:196, 196, 197, 198, 199, 200, 201
Patricia Wrightson **4**:242, 244, 247
Taro Yashima **4**:254
Laurence Yep **3**:236
Jane Yolen **4**:257, 257, 258, 258, 260, 261, 265
Herbert S. Zim **2**:226, 227, 232, 233
Herbert S. Zim and Sonia Bleeker **2**:228
Herbert S. Zim and James R. Skelly **2**:232
Paul Zindel **3**:248, 251
Charlotte Zolotow **2**:233, 234, 235, 236, 237, 238, 239

Swan, Annalyn
Arnold Lobel **5**:162
Uri Shulevitz **5**:207

Swanton, Averil
Maurice Sendak **1**:169, 170

Swift, Esther M.
Sid Fleischman **1**:73

Swinnerton, Frank
Kenneth Grahame **5**:131

Sykes, Christopher
Lewis Carroll **2**:29

Sykes, Margaret P.
Jane Yolen **4**:259

Symons, Julian
Ted Hughes **3**:95

Tabari, Alice
Vicki Cobb **2**:66

Tandy, Lynette
Jane Yolen **4**:268

Tate, Binnie
Paula Fox **1**:78, 80
Virginia Hamilton **1**:103
John Steptoe **2**:164

Taylor, Jason R.
Harvey Weiss **4**:229

Taylor, Mark
Lloyd Alexander **1**:14
Eleanor Cameron **1**:40

Taylor, Mary Agnes
Lucille Clifton **5**:57
Wanda Gág **4**:90

Taylor, Millicent
Millicent E. Selsam **1**:159, 162
Dorothy Sterling **1**:178

Taylor, Nora E.
Hester Burton **1**:35

Teltsch, Kathleen
M. Sasek **4**:195

Teres, Michael
Byrd Baylor **3**:17

Teres, Rosemary
Byrd Baylor **3**:17

Terris, Susan
Robert C. O'Brien **2**:129

Terry, Ann
Ed Emberley and Barbara Emberley **5**:100

Tetrault, Yvette
Karla Kuskin **4**:143

Thiele, Barbara
Dennis Lee **3**:116

Thomas, Della
Joan Walsh Anglund **1**:19
Jeanne Bendick **5**:43
Scott O'Dell **1**:145
Ian Serraillier **2**:138
Peter Spier **5**:218
Barbara Wersba **3**:216
Brian Wildsmith **2**:211

Thomas, H. M.
Laurence Pringle **4**:175

Thomas, Kristi L.
Jose Aruego and Ariane Dewey **5**:30
Peter Spier **5**:229
Jane Yolen **4**:266

Thompson, Judith
Kristin Hunter **3**:100
John Steptoe **2**:164

Critic Index

Thomson, Jean C.
Natalie Babbitt 2:6, 8
Nina Bawden 2:12
Judy Blume 2:17
John Christopher 2:38, 41
James Lincoln Collier 3:49
Paula Fox 1:81
Seon Manley 3:146
Robert C. O'Brien 2:129
William Steig 2:161
Barbara Wersba 3:219
Leonard Wibberley 3:224

Thrash, Sarah M.
Judy Blume 2:19
John D. Fitzgerald 1:70

Thwaite, Ann
Bernard Ashley 4:15, 16, 17
Nina Bawden 2:11
Russell Hoban 3:79
Kristin Hunter 3:101
Joan Phipson 5:185

Thwaite, Mary F.
Lewis Carroll 2:27
Carlo Collodi 5:76

Timberlake, Pat
Byrd Baylor 3:18

Tindall, Gillian
Susan Cooper 4:43

Toensmeier, Anne G.
Patti Stren 5:233

Tolman, Bonnie
Joanna Cole 5:63

Toney, Joyce
Eloise Greenfield 4:99

Tonkin, Patricia
Alvin Schwartz 3:191

Tornquist, Elizabeth
Jane Yolen and Anne Huston
4:256

Toulson, Shirley
Ursula K. Le Guin 3:123

Toups, Polly A.
Joanna Cole 5:64

Townsend, John Rowe
Joan Aiken 1:1, 6
Louisa May Alcott 1:11
Lloyd Alexander 1:17
William H. Armstrong 1:24
Nina Bawden 2:11
Judy Blume 2:16
L. M. Boston 3:25
Betsy Byars 1:37
Lewis Carroll 2:31
John Christopher 2:37, 40, 43
Elizabeth Coatsworth 2:54
Meindert DeJong 1:54, 55
John Donovan 3:53
Louise Fitzhugh 1:72
Sid Fleischman 1:73
Paula Fox 1:76, 76
Virginia Hamilton 1:104, 105,
107
S. E. Hinton 3:71
Russell Hoban 3:80, 82
Ted Hughes 3:93
Ezra Jack Keats 1:113, 117,
118
Robert Lawson 2:109

Edward Lear 1:126
Madeleine L'Engle 1:129
A. A. Milne 1:142
Robert C. O'Brien 2:128
Scott O'Dell 1:145, 147
K. M. Peyton 3:171
Beatrix Potter 1:152
Maurice Sendak 1:167, 169,
173
Ian Serraillier 2:142
Ivan Southall 2:147, 150, 153,
157
William Steig 2:162
Rosemary Sutcliff 1:182, 183
P. L. Travers 2:178
Henry Treece 2:184
Jill Paton Walsh 2:199, 200
Barbara Wersba 3:219
E. B. White 1:194, 195, 196
Laura Ingalls Wilder 2:206
Brian Wildsmith 2:207
Patricia Wrightson 4:239, 241,
241, 241
Paul Zindel 3:250

Travers, P. L.
L. M. Boston 3:24

Trease, Geoffrey
K. M. Peyton 3:173

Tremper, Ellen
Lucille Clifton 5:57

Tucker, Nicholas
Edward Ardizzone 3:3
Nina Bawden 2:10
Kenneth Grahame 5:132
Virginia Hamilton 1:104
Ezra Jack Keats 1:115
K. M. Peyton 3:178
Marilyn Sachs 2:134

Tunis, John R.
Maia Wojciechowska 1:199

Turkish, Dr. Marion P.
Jose Aruego 5:27

Turnbaugh, Douglas Blair
Jill Krementz 5:152

Twichell, Ethel R.
Chris Van Allsburg 5:242

Tymn, Marshall B.
Lloyd Alexander 5:16

Ullom, Judith C.
Elizabeth Coatsworth 2:56

Unickel, Martha
Nina Bawden 2:12
Beverly Cleary 2:49

Unsworth, Robert
Walter Dean Myers 4:157
Laurence Pringle 4:185

Updike, John
E. B. White 1:195

Urban, Kathleen
Barbara Willard 2:223

Ury, Claude
Alvin Schwartz 3:191

Van Allsburg, Chris
Chris Van Allsburg 5:237

Van den Haag, Ernest
John Donovan 3:52

Vanderbilt, Gloria
Ted Hughes 3:92

Van Norman, C. Elta
Robert Lawson 2:111

Van Schaick, George
John Christopher 2:39
Barbara Willard 2:220

Vaughn, Alden T.
Maia Wojciechowska 1:198

Vervoort, Patricia
Richard Scarry 3:186
Charlotte Zolotow 2:234

Vidal, Gore
E. Nesbit 3:155

Viguers, Ruth Hill
Joan Aiken 1:1
Lloyd Alexander 1:13, 15, 17;
5:18, 18, 19, 19
Joan Walsh Anglund 1:20, 21
Edward Ardizzone 3:5
Natalie Babbitt 2:7
Nina Bawden 2:14
Sheila Burnford 2:19
Hester Burton 1:35
Eleanor Cameron 1:41, 42
Beverly Cleary 2:45
Elizabeth Coatsworth 2:52, 53,
56, 59, 60, 61
Marguerite de Angeli 1:53
Meindert DeJong 1:54
William Pène du Bois 1:62, 63
Ed Emberley and Barbara
Emberley 5:92, 93
Sylvia Louise Engdahl 2:70
Elizabeth Enright 4:76, 77
Eleanor Estes 2:72, 75, 76
Sid Fleischman 1:75
Paula Fox 1:77
Jean Fritz 2:80
Wanda Gág 4:88
Jean Craighead George 1:72
Irene Hunt 1:109, 110, 111
Erich Kästner 4:122, 126
Ezra Jack Keats 1:117
E. L. Konigsburg 1:118, 120,
121
Robert Lawson 2:111
Edward Lear 1:128
Madeleine L'Engle 1:129, 130,
131, 133, 134
Astrid Lindgren 1:136, 139
Jean Little 4:147, 148
A. A. Milne 1:141
Robert C. O'Brien 2:129
Scott O'Dell 1:145, 147, 148
K. M. Peyton 3:177, 180
Joan Phipson 5:179, 179, 181
Maurice Sendak 1:168
Uri Shulevitz 5:203
Isaac Bashevis Singer 1:174,
175
Donald J. Sobol 4:207
Dorothy Sterling 1:180
Rosemary Sutcliff 1:184, 187
John Rowe Townsend 2:171
E. B. White 1:194
Leonard Wibberley 3:224, 229,
232
Laura Ingalls Wilder 2:203
Barbara Willard 2:218, 219
Maia Wojciechowska 1:199

Patricia Wrightson 4:242
Reiner Zimnik 3:243
Charlotte Zolotow 2:235

Vinton, Iris
Jeanne Bendick 5:37
John Langstaff and Carol
Langstaff 3:112
Edwin Tunis 2:194

Viorst, Judith
Tomi Ungerer 3:202

Von Schweinitz, Eleanor
Edward Ardizzone 3:8
K. M. Peyton 3:172, 173
Tomi Ungerer 3:200
Brian Wildsmith 2:213
Jane Yolen 4:259, 260

Vorwerk, Mary E.
Isaac Bashevis Singer 1:176

Wagner, Diane
Nina Bawden 2:15

Wagner, Jerome
Laurence Pringle 4:176

Walbridge, Earl F.
C. S. Lewis 3:135

Walker, Alice
William H. Armstrong 1:25

Walker, Barbara
Lucille Clifton 5:56
Julius Lester and David Gahr
2:115
Sharon Bell Mathis 3:151

Walker, Helen E.
Theodor Seuss Geisel 1:85

Walker, Margaret
Peter Spier 5:228

Walker, Marilyn
Herbert S. Zim and James R.
Skelly 2:232

Walker, Paul
Millicent E. Selsam 1:161, 165

Wallace, Willard M.
James Lincoln Collier and
Christopher Collier 3:44

Walsh, Chad
Jean Craighead George 1:89
Madeleine L'Engle 1:131
C. S. Lewis 3:134, 135, 136
Henry Treece 2:189, 190
Barbara Willard 2:219

Walsh, Jill Paton
Hester Burton 1:32
Susan Cooper 4:47, 47
Henry Treece 2:185

Ward, Lynd
Wanda Gág 4:81, 89, 89

Ward, Nancy
Patti Stren 5:231

Warlow, Aidan
Kit Williams 4:233

Watson, Emily Strauss
Eloise Greenfield 4:103

Watt, Lois Belfield
Muriel L. Feelings and Tom
Feelings 5:105
Edward Lear 1:129
Sharon Bell Mathis 3:152

Waugh, Dorothy
Ed Emberley and Barbara
Emberley 5:89

Wayland, Shirley
Byrd Baylor 3:16

Weales, Gerald
E. B. White 1:194

Weaver, Anne C.
Kristin Hunter 3:98

Weber, Diane I.
Jill Paton Walsh 2:198

Weekley, Jill S.
Joan Aiken 1:5

Weeks, Brigitte
L. M. Boston 3:29
James Haskins 3:65
Arnold Lobel 5:172
D. Manus Pinkwater 4:165,
167, 167
Shel Silverstein 5:211

Weeks, Ramona
Joan Walsh Anglund 1:18

Weiler, A. H.
Maia Wojciechowska 1:197

Weinstein, Shirley
Maia Wojciechowska 1:200

Weir, Sandra
Vicki Cobb 2:66

Weisberger, Bernard A.
Ivan Southall 2:156

Weitzman, Lenore J.
Jane Yolen 4:257

Weller, Joan
Donald J. Sobol 4:210

Wells, Leota
Jean Fritz 2:81

Welsh, Mary
Barbara Willard 2:219

Welty, Eudora
Natalie Babbitt 2:6
Erich Kästner 4:128

Wennerblad, Sonja
Jeanne Bendick 5:38
Marguerite Henry 4:113
Leonard Wibberley 3:229

Wentroth, Mary Ann
Byrd Baylor 3:14, 18
Ivan Southall 2:150
Jane Yolen 4:258

Wersba, Barbara
Lloyd Alexander 1:18; 5:22, 24
Nina Bawden 2:10, 14
L. M. Boston 3:28
Eleanor Cameron 1:39
John Donovan 3:55
Ed Emberley and Barbara
Emberley 5:92
M. B. Goffstein 3:59, 62
Maria Gripe 5:146
Russell Hoban 3:79
Tove Jansson 2:92
Erich Kästner 4:127
Georgess McHargue 2:117, 119
Jill Paton Walsh 2:199
Nancy Willard 5:246
Reiner Zimnik 3:243

Werstein, Irving
F. N. Monjo 2:126
Barbara Wersba 3:217
Paul Zindel 3:251

Weston, Annette
Robert Lawson 2:107

Weston, John
John Donovan 3:52
Nat Hentoff 1:107

Whedon, Julia
Betsy Byars 1:36
Roald Dahl 1:51
Meindert DeJong 1:55
F. N. Monjo 2:126

White, Alison
Edward Lear 1:125

White, E. B.
Laura Ingalls Wilder 2:204

White, Mrs. J.
Richard Scarry 3:187

Whitman, Digby B.
John Christopher 2:39
James Houston 3:85, 87
Tove Jansson 2:93
Scott O'Dell 1:146
John Rowe Townsend 2:172,
173

Whittaker, Jane
James Haskins 3:68

Wibberley, Leonard
Leonard Wibberley 3:231

Wignes, Lyle H.
Hester Burton 1:33

Willard, Nancy
Karla Kuskin 4:142
Nancy Willard 5:244

Willett, Holly
Jill Krementz 5:156

Williams, Deborah H.
Julius Lester and David Gahr
2:115

Williams, Gladys
Ivan Southall 2:153
P. L. Travers 2:178
Brian Wildsmith 2:214
Barbara Willard 2:222

Williams, Jay
Kenneth Grahame 5:133

Williams, John A.
Julius Lester 2:112

Williams, Judith
Georgess McHargue 2:119

Williams, Shirley
Charlotte Zolotow 2:239

Williams, Timothy C.
Joanna Cole 5:67

Williamson, Laura B.
Laurence Pringle 4:180

Willison, Marilyn
Judith Viorst 3:207

Wilms, Denise M.
Lucille Clifton 5:59
Ed Emberley and Barbara
Emberley 5:101, 102, 103
Eloise Greenfield 4:103

Marguerite Henry 4:116
Jill Krementz 5:154
Arnold Lobel 5:176
Laurence Pringle 4:183, 186
Marilyn Sachs 2:132
Virginia Driving Hawk Sneve
2:144
Donald J. Sobol 4:211, 212
Tobi Tobias 4:217, 217
Chris Van Allsburg 5:239
Jane Yolen 4:267, 269

Wilson, Edmund
Lewis Carroll 2:22

Wilson, Euple L.
Byrd Baylor 3:13

Wilson, Geraldine L.
Eloise Greenfield and Lessie
Jones Little 4:102

Wilt, Miriam E.
Marguerite Henry 4:106

Wilton, Shirley M.
Daniel Cohen 3:39
Susan Cooper 4:47, 48
David Macaulay 3:142
Tobi Tobias 4:214
Jill Paton Walsh 2:201

Winch, Dorothy
Millicent E. Selsam 1:166

Winder, David
Nonny Hogrogian 2:88

Winebrenner, D. Kenneth
Harvey Weiss 4:220

Winters, Kay
Shel Silverstein 5:210

Wintrob, Ralph J.
Jean Little 4:149

Woggon, Michele
Tomie de Paola 4:59

Wohl, Lauren L.
M. B. Goffstein 3:58

Wohlsen, Grace
Maia Wojciechowska 1:198

Wojciechowska, Maia
Madeleine L'Engle 1:134

Wolitzer, Hilma
Jill Krementz 5:155

Wong, Howard W.
Jeanne Bendick 5:45

Wood, Anne
Bernard Ashley 4:17
Susan Cooper 4:41
Julius Lester 2:115
Brian Wildsmith 2:209

Wood, James Playsted
Louisa May Alcott 1:10
Scott Corbett 1:45
Henry Treece 2:191

Woodard, Gloria
Kristin Hunter 3:100
John Steptoe 2:164

Woods, Beverly
Walter Dean Myers 4:160

Woods, George A.
Joan Walsh Anglund 1:19
Natalie Babbitt 2:8
Elizabeth Coatsworth 2:63

Roald Dahl 1:52
Ed Emberley and Barbara
Emberley 5:91, 96, 97
Theodor Seuss Geisel 1:85
Shirley Glubok 1:101
M. B. Goffstein 3:57, 60, 61
Nonny Hogrogian 2:90
Ezra Jack Keats 1:115, 116,
118
Karla Kuskin 4:134, 135, 136,
136
Arnold Lobel 5:164
D. Manus Pinkwater 4:162
H. A. Rey and Margret Rey
5:198, 199, 199
M. Sasek 4:189, 194
Uri Shulevitz 5:203, 203
Peter Spier 5:217, 219, 222,
222, 227
William Steig 2:158, 159, 161
Tobi Tobias 4:216
Tomi Ungerer 3:202
Clyde Watson 3:211, 212, 213
Leonard Wibberley 3:233
Taro Yashima 4:253
Jane Yolen 4:257
Charlotte Zolotow 2:236, 237

Woods, Katherine
Wanda Gág 4:92

Woodward, Nancy Hyden
Jane Yolen 4:259

Worden, Linda
D. Manus Pinkwater 4:171

Worth, Barbara S.
Jean de Brunhoff and Laurent
de Brunhoff 4:40
Peter Spier 5:229
Nancy Willard 5:247

Worthing, Sarita M.
Barbara Willard 2:223

Wortis, Avi
Beatrix Potter 1:154

Wright, Helen
Tobi Tobias 4:213

Wright, Oscar
Harvey Weiss 4:224

Wrightson, Patricia
Patricia Wrightson 4:234

Wunderlich, Richard
Carlo Collodi 5:84

Wundheiler, Luitgard
Millicent E. Selsam 1:159

Wylie, Jane
Edward Ardizzone 3:5
Beverly Cleary 2:51
Elizabeth Coatsworth 2:60
Scott Corbett 1:44

Yep, Laurence
Laurence Yep 3:236

Yolen, Jane
Mitsumasa Anno 2:2
Jose Aruego 5:29
Sid Fleischman 1:74
Russell Hoban 3:75
Norma Klein 2:100
Fernando Krahn 3:104
Robert C. O'Brien 2:128
Scott O'Dell 1:147

Ellen Raskin 1:156
Jane Yolen 4:255

Young, Christina Carr
Kristin Hunter 3:99
Sharon Bell Mathis 3:149
Alvin Schwartz 3:192

Young, Doris A.
M. Sasek 4:188
Taro Yashima 4:248

Young, Nancy
Leonard Wibberley 3:232

Young, Robert F., S.J.
James Lincoln Collier 3:48

Yucht, Alice H.
Judith Viorst 3:208

Yuill, Phyllis
Ellen Raskin 1:155

Zahorski, Kenneth J.
Lloyd Alexander 5:16

Zarookian, Cherie
Roald Dahl 1:51
M. B. Goffstein 3:60

Ian Serraillier 2:143
Alfred Slote 4:201
Donald J. Sobol 4:209
Barbara Willard 2:217

Zemach, Harve
Lucille Clifton 5:53

Zemach, Margot
Lucille Clifton 5:53

Ziner, Feenie
Ivan Southall 2:149
Rosemary Sutcliff 1:184

Zola, Meguido
Jean Little 4:146

Zvirin, Stephanie
Laurence Pringle 4:185
Jane Yolen 4:267